Telecommunications, Mass Media, and Democracy

Telecommunications, Mass Media, and Democracy

The Battle for the Control of U.S. Broadcasting, 1928–1935

ROBERT W. McCHESNEY

New York   Oxford
Oxford University Press
1993

Oxford University Press

Oxford   New York   Toronto
Delhi   Bombay   Calcutta   Madras   Karachi
Kuala Lumpur   Singapore   Hong Kong   Tokyo
Nairobi   Dar es Salaam   Cape Town
Melbourne   Auckland   Madrid
and associated companies in
Berlin   Ibadan

Copyright © 1993 by Robert W. McChesney

Published by Oxford University Press, Inc.,
200 Madison Avenue, New York, New York 10016

Oxford is a registered trademark of Oxford University Press

Library of Congress Cataloging-in-Publication Data
McChesney, Robert Waterman, 1952–
Telecommunications, mass media, and democracy :
the battle for the control of U.S. broadcasting,
1928–1935 / Robert W. McChesney.
p. cm.   Includes bibliographical references (p.   ) and index.
ISBN 0-19-507174-3
1. Radio broadcasting policy—United States—History.
I. Title.
HE8698.M34   1993   384.54'0973–dc20
92–15440

3   5   7   9   8   6   4

Printed in the United States of America
on acid-free paper

For Inger

Acknowledgments

Many people have helped me with this book, although only I am responsible for its failings. This project began in 1986 with graduate seminar papers at the University of Washington for Roger Simpson and Don Pember. I would like to thank Roger and Don and the following faculty and staff at Washington for their support and encouragement: Tony Giffard, Lance Bennett, Jerry Baldasty, Jack Berryman, and Pat Dinning. The late Bill Ames was my Ph.D. supervisor until his death in 1989 and his influence will always mark my work. At least I hope so.

My colleagues at Wisconsin–Madison have been very supportive, in particular Steve Vaughn, Sharon Dunwoody, Jack McLeod, and Jim Baughman. Jim has read the manuscript, along with all my earlier work, and has provided me with tough and insightful criticism. Whatever rigor is in the pages that follow is due in part to Jim's input. It would be impossible for a colleague to be more helpful than he has been to me. Cindy Schkirkie has provided me considerable assistance with my numerous photocopying and mailing requests.

This book is based in large part upon archival work. I would like to thank the staffs of the Library of Congress, the National Archives in both Washington, D.C., and Suitland, MD, the State Historical Society of Wisconsin, Princeton University Library, the AT&T Archives, the Chicago Historical Society, the New York Public Library, the Herbert Hoover Presidential Library, the Franklin D. Roosevelt Presidential Library, the Western Reserve Historical Society, the Rare Books and Manuscripts and Oral History offices in Butler Library at Columbia University, and the Owen D. Young Library at St. Lawrence University for their unfailing assistance.

I also want to thank the following scholars who read portions of the manuscript or earlier papers and have helped me with their comments and/

or encouragement: Edward S. Herman, Thomas Ferguson, Jay Blumler, Dallas Smythe, Marsha Siefert, William S. Solomon, Richard Du Boff, Christopher Simpson, James Curran, Ben Bagdikian, George Gerbner, Chuck Whitney, Ellis Hawley, William Boddy, Patricia Aufderheide, Herbert I. Schiller, James Carey, Bruce Cumings, Tom Streeter, Ellen Wartella, Paul Sweezy, Eric Rothenbuhler, Joel Bleifuss, Jeff Cohen, and Martin Lee. I also required my graduate seminar in broadcasting history to read a draft of the book; their comments were helpful and revealed a commitment to ruthless criticism for which I was not entirely prepared. Special thanks go to Erik Barnouw and John C. Nerone who took time from their schedules to read the entire manuscript and provide me with several helpful criticisms.

I have also received very useful instruction on specific points that appear in the book from Gwenyth Jackaway, Richard M. Schmidt, Nathan Godfried, Robert Britt Horwitz, Susan Douglas, Robert Burke, Jean Toll, Richard Rorty, Ward Quaal, Tom Lewis, Steve Classen, Sally Bedell Smith, Lizabeth Cohen, Garth Jowett, Ian Jarvie, and Louise Benjamin. Andrew Feldman and Inger L. Stole have provided me with research help on numerous occasions, often times of a very demanding nature. It will be difficult to repay them. My general political and intellectual analysis has been sharpened by regular discussions with Vivek Chibber and John Bellamy "Duke" Foster. Interactions with Bruce Need, David Ross, and Greg Feise have kept my spirits high when loneliness threatened to set me off course.

At Oxford University Press David Roll and Wendy Driscoll have done a grand job with a project they inherited. Thanks to Rachel Toor for the confidence she showed in my research from the very beginning. Ellen Fuchs and Steve Bedney have gone out of their way to address the angst of a novice author. That this book is being published by Oxford is due mostly to Dan Schiller. Perhaps the best part of the entire experience has been getting to know Dan and making a close friend for life. I only hope this work begins to justify the enormous amount of work Dan has done on its behalf.

Finally, throughout this project I have received the unconditional love and support of my parents, Meg and Parker McChesney. My wife, Inger L. Stole, understands fully the needs of a scholar, providing me with incalculable assistance while inspiring me with a work ethic that makes my own pale by comparison. Our exuberant daughter, Amy, has kept me from taking myself or much else too seriously, all the while reminding me why it is so important to make the good fight. I dedicate this book to my best friend, my most demanding critic and my true love. Without her, this volume would not exist.

Contents

Contents

Abbreviations

FREC	Federal Radio Education Committee
GE	General Electric
ICC	Interstate Commerce Commission
INS	International News Service
NAB	National Association of Broadcasters
NACRE	National Advisory Council on Radio in Education
NANA	North America Newspaper Alliance
NASU	National Association of State Universities
NBC	National Broadcasting Company
NCEB	National Conference on Education Broadcasting
NCER	National Committee on Education by Radio
NCPT	National Congress of Parents and Teachers
NEA	National Education Association
NREA	National Radio Editors Association
NUEA	National University Education Association
PWBF	Pacific-Western Broadcasting Federation
RCA	Radio Corporation of America
SCIC	Senate Committee on Interstate Commerce
TVA	Tennessee Valley Authority
UPA	United Press Association

Principal Characters

Alexander, Gross W.	PWBF director
Aylesworth, Merlin H.	NBC president
Baldwin, Roger N.	ACLU director
Bellows, Henry A.	original FRC member; CBS executive; NAB lobbyist
Bliven, Bruce	editor, *The New Republic*; broadcast reformer
Bolton, Frances Payne	Payne Fund president & principle donor
Brown, Thad	FRC and FCC member
Caldwell, Louis G.	first FRC General Counsel; ABA communications committee chair; leading commercial broadcasting attorney
Caldwell, Orestes H.	FRC member; radio trade publication editor
Codel, Martin	journalist; founder of trade publication *Broadcasting*
Coltrane, Eugene J.	NCER field worker and lobbyist
Cooper, William John	commissioner of education in Hoover administration; helped organize NCER
Couzens, James	senator (R-Mich.); ranking Republican on SCIC
Crandall, Ella Phillips	Payne Fund secretary
Crane, Arthur	University of Wyoming president; NCER activist

Daniels, Josephus	FDR's ambassador to Mexico and long-time confidant
Davis, Ewin L.	representative (D-Tenn.); sponsored 1928 Davis amendment
Davis, H. O.	*Ventura Free Press* publisher; Payne Fund officer
Davis, Jerome	Yale University professor; broadcast reform advocate
Dill, Clarence C.	senator (D-Wash.); co-author and primary Senate sponsor of Radio Act of 1927 and Communications Act of 1934
Dunlap, Orrin, Jr.	*New York Times* radio editor
Eckstein, Henry	ACLU Radio Committee member
Ernst, Morris	ACLU Radio Committee member
Evans, S. Howard	Payne Fund operative and lobbyist
Fess, Simeon	senator (R-Ohio); sponsored NCER fixed-percentage legislation in 1931 and 1932
Green, William	AFL president; member of NBC Advisory Council and the NACRE
Hale, Florence	NEA official; cooperated with NBC on educational programming
Hanley, James	FRC member; supported Wagner–Hatfield amendment
Harney, Father John B.	director of Paulist Fathers, owners of station WLWL
Hatfield, Henry	senator (R-WV); sponsor of broadcast reform measures
Hettinger, Herman	University of Pennsylvania economist; chief NAB researcher
Hooper, Stanford C.	director of navy radio; dissident member of Roper Committee
Howe, Louis McHenry	FDR's secretary and adviser
Kaltenborn, Hans V.	CBS commentator
Keith, Alice	director of CBS educational radio; went on to become broadcast reformer
Keppel, Frederick	Carnegie Corporation president; led formation of the NACRE

Lafount, Harold	FRC member
Morgan, Joy Elmer	NCER chairman; NEA journal editor
Nockels, Edward	director of WCFL, Chicago Federation of Labor station
Orton, William A.	Smith College professor; broadcast reform proponent
Paley, William S.	CBS president
Perry, Armstrong	Payne Fund adviser; NCER official
Pickard, Sam	1928–1929 FRC member; became CBS executive
Rayburn, Sam	representative (D-Tex.); House sponsor of Communications Act of 1934
Randall, Harris K.	broadcast reformer; founder of ARAL and CCBB
Reith, Sir John C. W.	BBC managing director
Robinson, Ira E.	FRC member who opposed General Order 40
Roper, Daniel C.	FDR's Secretary of Commerce
Rorty, James	former advertising copywriter; radical opponent of commercial broadcasting
Russell, Frank M.	NBC's chief Washington, D.C., lobbyist
Saltzman, Charles McKinley	FRC member during Hoover administration; served as de facto chair of Roper Committee
Sarnoff, David	RCA executive
Sykes, Eugene O.	FRC and FCC member
Taishoff, Sol	journalist; editor of trade publication *Broadcasting*
Thomas, Norman	ACLU Radio Committee member
Tyler, Tracy F.	NCER official
Tyson, Levering	NACRE director
Wagner, Robert F.	senator (D-NY); sponsor of Wagner–Hatfield amendment

Webster, Bethuel M., Jr. second FRC general counsel; ACLU Radio Committee member

White, Wallace representative and senator (R-Maine); co-sponsor of Radio Act of 1927

Wilbur, Ray Lyman Hoover administration secretary of the interior; established Wilbur Committee to study crisis in educational radio

Woehlke, Walter journalist; active in *Ventura Free Press* radio campaign

Young, Owen D. GE president; founder of RCA

Telecommunications, Mass Media, and Democracy

CHAPTER 1

Introduction

Radio broadcasting emerged dramatically between 1920 and 1922 in the United States, capturing the popular imagination in a manner that was rare, if not unprecedented. By the end of the decade the modern network-dominated, advertising-supported system of radio broadcasting had come into existence. By 1935 the system was entrenched economically, politically, and ideologically, and it would provide the basis for the eventual development of television in the 1940s and 1950s. Between 1928 and 1935, however, some elements of American society actively opposed the emerging commercial set-up and attempted to have a significant portion of the ether set aside for noncommercial and nonprofit utilization. Elements of education, labor, religion, the press, civic groups, and the intelligentsia created the opposition and reflected a general social dissatisfaction with the contours of the emerging commercial system. This opposition coalesced, more or less, into a broadcast reform movement that generated a significant critique of the limitations of network-dominated, advertising-supported broadcasting for the communication requirements of a democratic society. It also struggled to rouse public opinion to support federal legislation that would markedly recast U.S. broadcasting. The passage of the Communications Act of 1934, which still remains the reigning statute for radio and television, effectively ended whatever opportunity for legitimate opposition to commercial broadcasting had existed during these years.

This episode is immediately remarkable in two respects. First, it arguably constitutes the sole instance in which the structure and control of a major mass medium were subject to anything close to legitimate political debate in U.S. history. Since the middle 1930s, the topic has been decidedly ''off-limits'' in public discourse.[1] This subsequent lack of public debate is especially striking in light of the considerable body of evidence that suggests

3

that the oligopolistic and commercial basis of the U.S. mass media has had a tremendous and distinct impact upon the nature of the messages communicated to the citizenry.[2] Moreover, the subject of how best to organize and support the mass media has been and is a legitimate issue, in varying degrees, in most other nations on earth. In this sense, this is a clear case of American exceptionalism.

Second, it has been neglected or trivialized in virtually all broadcasting history. To some extent this is explained by the unquestioned rule over broadcasting historiography for decades, beginning with Gleason L. Archer's *Big Business and Radio* in 1938, by works sponsored by or affiliated with the commercial broadcasting industry.[3] It was typified by scholars like Walter B. Emery, whose work routinely extolled U.S. broadcasting as being the sole logical system for a society dedicated to democracy and freedom.[4] In such apologia, the notion of opposition to commercial broadcasting on principled grounds was inconceivable; therefore it was never even broached. Erik Barnouw's massive three-volume *A History of Broadcasting in the United States* in the late 1960s broke this industry stranglehold and provided the entre for future critical explorations into radio and television history. Given the scope of his project, however, Barnouw made only passing reference to the battle over broadcasting policy in the early 1930s; his overriding research interests lay elsewhere.[5]

Since Barnouw, a new generation of historians has removed the rose-tinted glasses and taken a hard look at the origins of U.S. radio broadcasting, one that does not presuppose the superiority of the U.S. commercial broadcasting set-up over all imaginable alternatives. Much of this work has been exemplary. Nonetheless, the entire corpus of this critical research provides the same deterministic explanation as the earlier school, replacing the earlier platitudes about democracy with a vision of all-powerful communication corporations and a dominating ideology of capitalism as leading to the "unavoidable" adoption of the status quo.[6] In this new, critical interpretation of the origins of the U.S. broadcasting set-up, the public is passive, ignorant, and mostly nonexistent before the corporate juggernaut that dominates public policy. Moreover, the matter is settled and removed from the political playing field long before commercial broadcasting has even come into existence. As perhaps the most accomplished critical history has concluded, the American broadcasting system was in place "technologically, economically, legislatively, and ideologically" by 1922. There would be "no major break in this ideological frame" that private corporations should dominate broadcasting thereafter, to be supported by commercial advertising.[7]

In all of these approaches, almost without exception, the Radio Act of 1927 is regarded as the final chapter, if not the piece de resistance, in the development of the status quo. As one recent scholar has stated, it "settled once and for all any lingering doubts about private leadership in the internal development of the American radio industry."[8] The Communications Act of 1934, to the extent it is discussed at all, is dismissed as the sequel legislation to the 1927 Radio Act since the 1934 act "essentially reproduced" the 1927 act verbatim.[9] Accordingly, scholars have directed their attention to the period preceding 1927 in the belief that this is the period in which any real debate regarding broadcast policy must have taken place. Indeed, armed with this presupposition, the deterministic explanation is quite plausible, even inescapable, when evaluating the period prior to 1927. There is no question that there was no organized and coherent public opposition to commercial broadcasting because the system did not yet exist. It is striking, however, that there has been almost no systematic research on the development of U.S. broadcasting policy in the years between 1927 and 1934. Furthermore, the little work on this period that has been done has been either cursory or ignored.[10]

This study attempts to correct this oversight and present a comprehensive picture of the debate that transpired between 1928 and 1935 over how best to structure and control American radio broadcasting. Since the Radio Act of 1927 had established radio regulation only on a temporary basis, Congress considered legislation for the permanent regulation of broadcasting in every session until the passage of the Communications Act. After seven years, is it reasonable to assume that Congress casually rubber stamped the Radio Act of 1927 when it drafted and passed the Communications Act? If anything, broadcast legislation proved to be a "hot potato" for Congress throughout this period with few in Congress expressing unbridled support for the status quo. Moreover, it was only in 1928 and 1929 that the modern network-dominated, advertising-supported broadcasting system came into existence and, therefore, only then that significant elements of the American population had a chance to experience commercial broadcasting and formulate a response. Several elements of U.S. society responded to commercial broadcasting in the most negative manner imaginable and strove to radically reconstruct U.S. broadcasting. This broadcast reform movement was the sworn enemy of the commercial broadcasting industry, which concurrently sought to establish monopoly control over the ether, eliminate any organized opposition to their modus operandi, and consolidate the industry economically, legislatively, and ideologically. This consolidation, accomplished at the expense of the reformers, was completed by the mid 1930s.

This study provides a revisionist interpretation of American broadcasting history, one that regards the emerging status quo as the product of an intense and multifaceted political fight with obvious winners and losers, not as the "natural" American system or as the product of consensus. Moreover, I call into question the deterministic position that, while quite critical of the commercial broadcasting, nonetheless posits the status quo as in place by the mid 1920s with minimal public concern or input. While the reformers of the early 1930s failed in their efforts to recast U.S. broadcasting, they were not without historical impact. At the very least, their activities were largely responsible for postponing the complete legislative and ideological consolidation of the status quo from 1930 or 1931 to 1935 and beyond. In addition, the nature and quality of the broadcast reform movement's criticism of the status quo has been almost entirely overlooked before now. Indeed, the broadcast reformers and the many intellectuals sympathetic to their cause generated a critique of the limitations of a capitalist media system for a democratic society that anticipates much of the most trenchant recent media criticism.

Two provisos need be offered for what follows. First, not only is this study centered around the activities of the broadcast reformers in the early 1930s, but it also proceeds with a good deal of sympathy for their cause. On one hand, I find the reform movement's critique of commercial broadcasting compelling along with its argument that a democratic society is best-served if, at the very least, a significant portion of its broadcasting is not subject to the capital accumulation process.[11] More important, I regard the immediate aim of the broadcast reform movement, that of establishing a public debate over how best to organize media services in a self-governing society, to be commendable in principle. The nature of the control and structure of the mass media is an explicitly political issue that should be the subject of public discussion. To the extent that it is not fair game for open inquiry, U.S. society is less democratic than it should be.

Having admitted to these leanings, I should add that I do not hold the commercial broadcasters morally negligent for their failure to adhere to some higher social ethos than the business instinct that they, quite rationally, displayed in full-force. It is the broadcast reform movement that receives the brunt of my pointed criticism. Yet while I have made every effort to present the position of the industry as accurately as possible, my treatment may sometimes seem one-dimensional, especially in comparison to the multilayered examination of the reformers. This is primarily because those that controlled the commercial broadcasting interests marched in lockstep on the issues discussed in this study. While there were great debates on many aspects of the business of broadcasting, all major commercial broadcasters opposed the aims of the broadcast reform movement without hesitation. In addition, the broadcasters engaged in this struggle from a commanding position, without incentive to open the debate up to a full-fledged public study and debate. Thus, the industry's arguments often appear as much as public relations exercises meant to obfuscate the issues, rather than sincere attempts to educate the public and draw it into the discussion. The motivation of the reformers, as outsiders dependent upon popular support if they were to have any hope for success, was exactly the opposite.

Second, although this study will analyze the process by which Congress adopted permanent communications legislation in greater detail than any previous work has attempted, I will not provide a comprehensive account of all the important factors that influenced the Communications Act of 1934. The rudder for what follows is the effort of the broadcast reform movement to exact reform legislation, and the development and passage of the Communications Act will be presented in this context. By no means does this suggest that the quest for broadcast reform was the sole or even primary fight regarding radio broadcasting in the early 1930s. Although the commercial broadcasting industry was deeply, almost obsessively, concerned with the activities of the reformers, it, like Congress, had several other pressing issues to address.

Three of these issues deserve mention, as they were also important factors in the process by which permanent legislation was generated and passed. First, the drive to pass legislation for the permanent regulation of broadcasting was an aspect of the broader move to establish permanent regulation of communications and a corresponding national communications policy. Although the commercial broadcasters tended to lobby autonomously and to regard their legislative needs as distinct, this was the acknowledged backdrop against which they operated. Second, the government's antitrust suit against the Radio Corporation of America (RCA) in the early 1930s influenced how Congress and the public regarded both communications and broadcasting legislation. Third, the need to develop a U.S. position for the international conferences to allocate the world's airwaves put distinct pressures on Congress and government officials. I will strive not to exaggerate the importance of the broadcast reform fight, while bringing these related issues into the discussion whenever their inclusion is necessary.[12] Their absence elsewhere does not signify their unimportance.

Chapter 2 examines the nature of U.S. broadcasting before 1927, the passage of the Radio Act of 1927, and the Federal Radio Commission's General Order 40, which effectively ordained the network-dominated, advertising-supported basis of U.S. broadcasting in the autumn of 1928. Chapter 2 will also chronicle the nature of the emerging commercial order, the demise of nonprofit and noncommercial broadcasting, and identify the first stirrings of opposition in 1929 and 1930. Chapters 3 and 4 profile the various elements of American society that comprised the broadcast reform movement. Chapter 3 discusses the two campaigns subsidized by Payne Fund: the National Committee on Education by Radio (NCER) and the *Ventura Free Press* radio campaign. The NCER was an umbrella group of nine major national educational groups formed late in 1930 to organize educators and the public in support of the radical reform of broadcasting. The *Free Press* radio campaign, on the other hand, both lobbied for reform legislation with the NCER and attempted to generate favorable coverage of the reform movement in the nation's newspapers, as well as to organize support for reform among newspaper publishers.

In Chapter 4 I profile the balance of the broadcast reform movement, which included elements of organized labor and the Radio Committee of the American Civil Liberties Union (ACLU). The emergence of broadcasting brought to the fore the traditional and important concern about the relationship of the government to the media (a complex issue for any type of broadcasting system, as the experience of the British Broadcasting Corporation (BBC) makes clear). Because broadcasters were licensed by the state, they were especially cognizant of how they handled politically sensitive issues. This was true in the early 1930s when Congress was actively considering how best to provide for the permanent regulation of broadcasting. At this time, however, those most actively concerned with issues of free speech, including labor organizations and the ACLU, were unwilling to accept commercial networks and advertisers as legitimate stewards of the airwaves. In their minds, the central question was more fundamental: how could the public best promote free speech through the democratic allocation of the limited number of broadcast frequencies? The ACLU's conviction that commercial broadcasting was inherently incapable of presenting controversial programming and innately undemocratic, even if there was no government censorship, led to the formation of its Radio Committee in 1933. The ACLU's hostility to commercial broadcasting also reflected the mostly negative response of U.S. intellectuals to the status quo. Chapter 4 concludes by profiling this position.

Chapter 5 summarizes the major themes in the broadcast reform movement's critique of commercial broadcasting. It also discusses the various alternatives that the reformers suggested. The chapter will address the prominent role played by both the BBC and Canada, which in 1932 resolved for a nonprofit and noncommercial broadcasting system after lengthy study and debate. Chapter 5 will then turn its attention to an assessment of the commercial broadcasting industry, its powerful political lobby, its arguments on behalf of the status quo, and its activities to undermine the reform movement and to legitimate the status quo. Both sides of the struggle for the control of U.S. broadcasting linked their cause to visions of the role of radio and the mass media in a democratic society, and the appropriate role for the marketplace and for public policy in such a democracy. Accordingly, this debate has great currency for contemporary examinations of the meaning of democracy.

The battle for the control of U.S. broadcasting unfolds chronologically in chapters 6–9. Chapter 6 addresses the first great wave of reform activity on Capitol Hill between 1930 and 1932, when public dissatisfaction with the commercial basis of U.S. broadcasting was at its greatest and when the reform movement found the most support in Congress. Chapter 6 will also discuss the role of the Standing Committee on Communications of the American Bar Association (ABA) in squashing the reform movement. This chapter of U.S. legal history, neglected heretofore, suggests a high level of cooperation between a committee of the ABA and the commercial broadcasting industry to direct public policy in a manner that benefited the legal community's burgeoning commercial broadcasting practices more directly than any particular public interest. With the assistance of the ABA and a handful of important members of Congress opposed to reform, the commercial broadcasting industry successfully repelled the reform efforts by the summer of 1932.

Chapter 7 reviews the eighteen-month period between June 1932 and January 1934 when Congress was inactive regarding communication legislation. During this year and one-half the broadcast reform movement devoted most of its resources and attention to generating publicity for the issue and public support for broadcast reform. The central battleground in this fight for public opinion was the newspaper industry, which the reformers regarded as their natural ally. The commercial broadcasters not only defused this threat, but they even counted the newspaper industry as their informal ally by the end of 1933. Indeed, by viewing press–radio relations in the context of the battle for broadcast reform, the much noted "press–radio war" of the early 1930s will come into clearer perspective than has been the case heretofore.[13] The other battle in 1933 was for the allegiance of newly inaugurated President Franklin D. Roosevelt. In this contest the reformers attempted to link broadcast reform to the panoply of reform issues associated with the New Deal while the commercial broadcasters asserted their importance to Roosevelt as a mass medium. Despite considerable support for broadcast reform in the Roosevelt administration, the president elected to support tacitly the legislative agenda of the commercial broadcasters.

Chapter 8 provides a detailed picture of the process by which the Communications Act of 1934 was drafted, debated, passed by Congress, and signed into law in June 1934. Although seemingly battered into oblivion by the end of 1933, the broadcast reform movement regenerated with new sources of support in the spring of 1934. By April it appeared that the Wagner–Hatfield amendment, which would have required that 25 percent of the broadcast channels be reserved for nonprofit groups, would pass the U.S. Senate. The Wagner–Hatfield amendment was eventually defeated after a particularly intense lobbying campaign by the commercial broadcasters. The reformers lost primarily because congressional proponents of the status quo inserted a clause in the Communications Act requiring the new Federal Communications Commission (FCC) to hold hearings on the Wagner–Hatfield proposal and report back to Congress in 1935 if it found the principle worthwhile. These FCC hearings, which took place in the fall of 1934, were the sole instance in the history of U.S. broadcasting in which a public body directly addressed fundamental structural concerns. To nobody's surprise, the FCC recommended no changes in the status quo as a result of the hearings. The status quo was entrenched both economically and legislatively.

Chapter 9 chronicles the disintegration of the broadcast reform movement as it became clear that the status quo was beyond political challenge. With the collapse of organized opposition to commercial broadcasting, the industry was in a position to accomplish ideological closure: Commercial broadcasting was inherently American and democratic, and to even consider alternatives was not only ludicrous but dangerous. Soon thereafter this process was complete. Liberal thinkers, who at the outset of the decade had regarded commercial broadcasting as an affront to democratic principles, came to accept the status quo as the appropriate broadcast system for American democracy. Moreover, the late 1930s witnessed the emergence of the first great campaign to "deregulate" U.S. broadcasting, effectively giving commercial broadcasters property rights in the ether. Like the press–radio war, this episode will appear as a far less-principled exercise than might otherwise be the case in the context of the battle for the control of U.S. broadcasting described herein.[14]

The conclusion in Chapter 10 consists of two sections. The chapter first discusses how a recognition of the battle to control U.S. broadcasting demands that several fundamental revisions be made in the received wisdom concerning the origins of the status quo. In essence, the scholarship and contemporary debate regarding U.S. broadcasting rest on a somewhat erroneous foundation. This chapter suggests many of the ways U.S. broadcasting history needs to be reformulated. The balance of Chapter 10 will turn to a discussion of why the reform movement failed in its campaign to recast U.S. broadcasting. This discussion first focuses upon short-term factors, such as the role of the 1930s economic depression and the political incompetence of the reform movement. It then addresses some broader long-run factors, such as the inability to criticize capitalism in U.S. political culture and the immense ideological and political power of the media industries, which not only derailed the reform movement of the early 1930s, but also assisted in effectively circumventing any possibility of broaching debate regarding media structure in the public sphere to the present day.

Some clarification of terminology is in order at the outset. I use the term *commercial broadcasting*, even though it might be more accurate to say *capitalist broadcasting*, which refers to private, for-profit control of broadcasting where revenues are generated exclusively by selling time to commercial advertisers. In economic terms, commercial broadcasting has two components: private, for-profit control, and advertising, which need not necessarily be linked. For example, nonprofit broadcasters often sold advertising, while many for-profit broadcasters commenced operation years before commercial advertising even existed in the modern sense. The term *status quo* was used routinely by all observers in the early 1930s to refer to the U.S. system of network-dominated, advertising-supported broadcasting, and I use the term in that sense. Likewise, in the early 1930s many people referred to the electromagnetic spectrum as the *ether*. Although we have since learned that this term is scientifically inaccurate, I employ the term *ether* to maintain consistency with the works I cite from the period.

What follows is a discussion of a unique period in American history, a period in which it was possible to address fundamental questions of the structure and control of a basic mass medium. But radio broadcasting was not the sole prize of this contest. To varying degrees, all the players in the early 1930s recognized that the battle for control of radio broadcasting would probably determine the manner in which television would be developed, as its arrival was on the horizon. This was also a period of grand aspirations, dramatic visions, and flamboyent rhetoric in which a revolutionary new technology was seen as having the capacity to either liberate or imprison the populace, depending upon how society elected to employ it. This study is dedicated to uncovering and examining precisely what occurred during those tumultuous years with the aim not only of making sense of the past, but also to provide the capacity to better recognize the central issues of the present, so society may act upon them wisely in the future.

CHAPTER 2

General Order 40
and the Emergence
of Commercial Broadcasting,
1925–1930

The roots of the battle for the control of U.S. broadcasting lay in the 1920s. This chapter reviews the major developments of this decade, first looking at the nature of U.S. broadcasting as it emerged in the years 1920–1927, and then discussing the deliberations surrounding the passage of the Radio Act of 1927. The chapter concludes by evaluating the important general reallocation of the airwaves instituted by the Federal Radio Commission (FRC) in 1928, which effectively laid the foundation for the future of U.S. AM radio broadcasting. The general reallocation also provided the spark to the movement that arose to do battle with commercial broadcasting in the United States in the early 1930s.

American Broadcasting Through the Passage
of the Radio Act of 1927

Most histories of U.S. broadcasting in the 1920s agree on a few basic points. First, almost all research emphasizes the manner in which radio communication was dominated by a handful of enormous corporations, most notably RCA, which was established in 1919 under the auspices of the U.S. government. RCA was partially owned by General Electric (GE) and Westinghouse. By the early 1920s the radio industry—indeed, the entire communications industry—had been carefully divided through patent agreements among the large firms. RCA and Westinghouse each launched a handful of radio broadcasting stations in the early and mid-1920s, although the scholarship tends to emphasize the American Telephone & Telegraph (AT&T) Company's WEAF of New York because it was the first station to regularly sell airtime to commercial interests as a means of making itself self-sufficient.

This "toll" broadcasting, as it was called, is usually considered the first step on the path to an advertising-based radio broadcasting system.[1]

Second, most scholarship highlights the role played by Secretary of Commerce Herbert Hoover, who assumed the regulation of broadcasting under the Radio Act of 1912, which had been passed to coordinate point-to-point communication and did not anticipate the emergence of broadcasting. Hoover issued broadcast licenses and assigned frequency wavelengths until the passage of the Radio Act of 1927, thus establishing himself as a figure of paramount importance in the development of the industry. Adamant in his belief in the superiority of having broadcasting "in the hands of private enterprise," Hoover believed that "those directly engaged in radio, particularly in broadcasting, should be able, to a very large extent, to regulate and govern themselves." Hoover accordingly convened four radio conferences between 1922 and 1925, mostly of broadcasters and radio manufacturers, to provide him direction as he regulated the burgeoning industry. These conferences were also intended to provide the broadcasters with an opportunity to develop self-regulation, which Hoover argued would quite properly minimize the role of government radio regulation. In 1925 RCA's chief engineer wrote to Hoover:

> It is a duty as well as a pleasure, to work with a division of government which shows so complete an understanding of the needs of the radio industry and so strong a determination to assist in guiding the industry to intelligent solutions of its various problems.[2]

Third, the scholarship emphasizes that the general public, to the extent it considered the policy issues surrounding this new technology, was generally in concert with the preceding developments, and certainly was not opposed in principle to what was transpiring. Radio broadcasting, Hoover noted, provided "one of the few instances that I know of when the whole industry and country is praying for more regulation."[3] Moreover, research acknowledges how the development of broadcasting as a capitalist industry was effectively unavoidable in view of the historically unprecedented high esteem accorded private enterprise in U.S. political culture in the 1920s. In sum, the scholarship emphasizes how the loosely regulated, private, for-profit, network-dominated, advertising-supported basis of U.S. broadcasting was implicit to the system from its beginning, with public support if not outright enthusiasm. The passage of the Radio Act of 1927, which established the FRC, effectively codified these developments and removed the issues from public and congressional contemplation thereafter.

There is an element of truth to each of the preceding statements. Left alone, however, they present a distorted picture of U.S. broadcasting in the 1920s, one that makes it almost impossible to comprehend the events between

1928 and 1935. It was true, for example, that there was agreement that broadcasting should not be owned or controlled by the government in virtually all public discussions of broadcasting; this matter was seemingly closed, to the extent it was ever open, with Secretary of the Navy Josephus Daniels's failed attempt in 1918 and 1919 to have the radio communications industry nationalized.[4] There was little sense prior to 1927, however, that private control meant broadcasting should be dominated by networks, guided solely by the profit motive, and supported by advertising revenues.[5] Indeed, in several important respects, the nature of U.S. broadcasting prior to 1927 was markedly different from the system that would emerge by the end of the decade. A more accurate picture may result from examining these differences in addition to emphasizing the similarities.

For example, although RCA, GE, AT&T, Westinghouse, and a few other corporations effectively dominated most aspects of the radio industry, broadcasting eluded the corporate net for much of the decade. The first national network, the National Broadcasting Company (NBC), was established in late 1926 by RCA when it purchased AT&T's broadcasting properties. The other major network, the Columbia Broadcasting System (CBS), was not created until 1927. In retrospect, it is clear that when launched the two networks and their affiliated stations were the dynamic component of U.S. broadcasting. Prior to the late 1920s, however, network broadcasting was rudimentary at best, consisting of a small portion of U.S. radio stations and was barely commented upon.

So what was the nature of U.S. broadcasting in the mid–1920s? A significant percentage of the stations were operated by nonprofit organizations like religious groups, civic organizations, labor unions, and, in particular, colleges and universities. One hundred seventy-six broadcast licenses were issued to colleges and universities between 1921 and 1925; in 1925 there were 128 active college broadcasting stations. Almost as many broadcasters were affiliated with the other types of nonprofit organizations. Nonprofit broadcasters played a distinct and notable role in U.S. broadcasting throughout the 1920s; one scholar has gone so far as to term them the ''true pioneers'' of American broadcasting.[6] ''It is too often overlooked,'' commented C. M. Jansky, Jr., one of the leading radio engineers of the period, that ''in the general scheme of broadcasting in the United States our educational institutions were at the start of things distinctly in on the ground floor.''[7]

Even those private broadcasters that were operated by for-profit enterprises were not ''professional'' broadcasters in the modern sense. Newspapers, department stores, power companies, automobile dealerships, and other private concerns owned and operated most of these stations. Their raison d'être was to generate favorable publicity for the owner's primary enterprise, not to generate profits in their own right. There was little sense that broadcasting could be profitable throughout the 1920s. As the American Bar Association

(ABA) observed regarding broadcasting in the mid-1920s: "The conception of broadcasting as a business, with sale of time as its economic basis, was held by only a few."[8] The unprofitable status of broadcasting was emphasized by the FRC and the networks themselves as late as 1928 and 1929.[9] An AT&T survey of U.S. broadcasting in 1926 determined that approximately one-half of U.S stations were operated to generate publicity for the owner's primary enterprise, while one-third were operated by nonprofit groups for eleemosynary purposes. Only 4.3 percent of U.S. stations were characterized as being "commercial broadcasters," while a mere one-quarter of U.S. stations permitted the public to purchase airtime for its own use.[10]

In fact, the economic instability of radio broadcasting was its overriding feature in the mid-1920s. For example, the number of stations affiliated with colleges and universities fell from 128 to 95 between 1925 and 1927, due almost entirely to a lack of funds.[11] Throughout these years, discussion centered on how to make radio broadcasting self-sufficient. On more than one occasion, RCA executive David Sarnoff called for broadcasting to be conducted by a national nonprofit and noncommercial network, to be subsidized by "those who derive profits" from radio set manufacturing and related industries.[12] A contest conducted by trade publication *Radio Broadcast* in 1925 to determine how best to support broadcasting awarded first prize to a plan to have the federal government administer a fund collected from an annual radio set fee, à la Britain, to subsidize noncommercial broadcasting.[13] Even AT&T was unconvinced that its "toll" program was workable; in 1924, it briefly attempted to support its activities by having WEAF solicit listeners for direct donations to subsidize the programming.[14] As one observer noted in 1925, "the broadcasters and the manufacturers are as much at sea as anybody else as to the future."[15]

It is striking how infrequently direct advertising is mentioned as an acceptable source for revenues. Indeed, commercial advertising in the modern sense of the term was almost nonexistent prior to 1928. In 1925 the advertising representative of General Mills called upon twenty large broadcasters and was unable to purchase time from any of them. In 1927 the American Newspaper Publishers Association (ANPA) even assured its members, "Fortunately, direct advertising by radio is well-nigh an impossibility."[16] The toll broadcasting of AT&T restricted the firms that purchased airtime "to giving their name and the name of their product." AT&T's ability to sell its airtime was undermined by the willingness of the other stations, including those owned by RCA and Westinghouse, to give time away for free.[17] The basis upon which AT&T attempted to make toll broadcasting attractive was not that it would directly stimulate sales, but rather that it would bring "good will publicity" to the sponsor and "humanize" their relations with their customers. This "indirect" notion of radio advertising was held by all observers until 1927 or 1928.[18] Moreover, there was widespread antipathy to the very notion of permitting commercial advertisers access to the airwaves; even the relatively less intrusive indirect form of the early and mid-1920s met with controversy. As late as 1929, NBC presented itself first and foremost as a public service corporation that would only sell that amount of advertising necessary to subsidize first-rate noncommercial programming, "the finer things which are not sponsored commercially," as NBC President Merlin Aylesworth phrased it.[19]

Finally, during his reign as secretary of commerce (1921–1929), Hoover did not set out exclusively or even primarily to enhance the capitalist development of the ether, although when the hegemony of the networks was challenged during his presidency (1929–1933) he resolutely avoided antagonizing the commercial broadcasters.

As emphatic as he was concerning the need for private ownership, Hoover equally stressed the duty of the government to regulate this "great public service" in the interests of the listener. He insisted that radio broadcasters had a public service obligation beyond that of maximizing profits and he opposed having the ether become dominated by a handful of corporations. He also repeatedly criticized the large role of "amusement" in radio programming to the exclusion of public affairs and educational fare.[20] Although a staunch advocate of advertising per se, Hoover argued that broadcasters should minimize its role on the air since a radio listener, unlike a reader, could not "ignore advertising in which he is not interested." Otherwise, he argued, "there lies within it the possibility of great harm and even vital danger to the entire broadcasting structure." Hoover also commended college radio stations as "a step toward the realization of the true mission of radio." With little recognition of, or taste for, the eventual role assumed by advertising, Hoover pondered how broadcasting could become economically viable. In 1924 he solicited major foundations to subsidize educational programming. In the same year Hoover also called for a 2 percent tax on radio set sales to "pay for daily programs of the best skill and talent."[21]

This was the context of U.S. broadcasting in the mid-1920s. After the Fourth National Radio Conference in 1925, Hoover argued permanent legislation regulating broadcasting was now necessary for the industry to break through its impasse. Seven different bills to provide permanent regulation had been introduced since 1923, but none of them could gather enough support. A major stumbling block was partisan concerns about whether broadcast regulation should be housed in an independent administrative agency or remain in the Department of Commerce.[22] When Congress failed to pass legislation in 1926, Hoover requested that the attorney general give him an opinion whether the existing licensing of stations by the Department of Commerce was constitutional. The attorney general replied that it was not, and a test case also ruled the existing regulation unconstitutional since the Radio Act of 1912 had provided no criteria for licensing. Hoover then discontinued all regulation, thus ushering in what came to be termed the "break-down of the law" period; within six months more than 200 new broadcasters began to operate, increasing the total wattage from 378,000 to 647,000, and many did not respect the frequencies being used by others.[23] The ether had become chaotic. Congress then moved quickly, as Hoover imagined it would, to pass the Radio Act of 1927.

The committee deliberations concerning the Radio Act of 1927 and the overall debate in Congress were what one might expect for emergency legislation. The NAB and the commercial broadcasters were instrumental in getting the legislation passed; educators and nonprofit broadcasters, on the other hand, played almost no role in its drafting. There was certainly no general sense of alarm that the bill was being passed against the interests of nonprofit broadcasting. Educational and nonprofit broadcasters who would eventually oppose commercial broadcasting contacted members of Congress to urge the Radio Act's passage in order to bring stability to the ether. To many, the purpose of the legislation was to preserve the ether as a public domain and to prevent "a monopoly in the air" by RCA and the other major radio corporations. This was, in fact, the progressive spirit in which the legislation was presented by Senator C. C. Dill (D-Wash.), its primary sponsor, as well as Secretary Hoover.[24]

The committee hearings were dominated by concerns over the short-term business problems of the broadcasters, while the entire congressional debate over the Radio Act of 1927 ignored any discussion of fundamental broadcasting policy. One scholar concluded his exhaustive research on the debate over the Radio Act of 1927 by stating: "The 1927 radio debates stimulated only limited speculation as to the future of commercial broadcasting." Erik Barnouw has noted that while it had become clear by the early 1930s that U.S. broadcasting was a network-dominated and commercially supported system: "This system had never been formally adopted. There had never been a moment when Congress confronted the question: Shall we have a nationwide broadcasting system financed by advertising?" Moreover, few members of Congress had any sense of the issues involved at the time; the legislation was the product of but a few members of Congress, most notably Senator Dill.[25]

At the time, however, this lack of discussion was understandable; the Radio Act of 1927, which passed Congress in February, was to provide temporary regulation to correct the immediate problem. As a compromise between those who wanted an independent agency and those who wanted to keep regulation in the Commerce Department, the Radio Act established the five-member FRC on an interim, one-year basis to assign broadcast license and bring order to the air. Certain non–policy-related functions were kept in the Commerce Department. As Secretary Hoover remarked upon the Radio Act's passage, it was now "possible to eventually clear up the chaos of interference and howls in radio reception.''[26] There was a general consensus that the FRC would have to reduce the total number of broadcasters so that the remaining stations would be able to broadcast effectively. The FRC would be renewed annually until 1929, when it was extended indefinitely, but the matter was not considered settled by anyone at the time. Indeed, the permanent regulation of broadcasting was an issue before congressional committees in every session until the passage of the Communications Act of 1934.

The Radio Act of 1927 did not provide specific guidelines for the FRC to use in evaluating the contending applicants for the limited number of frequencies. Rather, the legislation called for the FRC to allocate licenses on the basis of which prospective broadcaster best served the "public interest, convenience, or necessity," a phrase adopted from public utilities law. Although the phrase may well have had a distinct meaning with regard to articulating the nature of the relationship between the government and industry, Congress clearly had no particular notion as to how the term should be applied to the thorny problems of broadcasting. If nothing else, the inclusion of this phrase was thought necessary to render the FRC's licensing powers constitutional.[27] Senator Dill made it clear that he thought it best to grant the FRC broad powers and tremendous leeway in dealing with the difficult and controversial issue of license allocation and regulation: "Congress would find it extremely difficult, if not impossible, to legislate on all the situations and conditions that develop from time to time. For this reason, the radio law granted the Federal Radio Commission, which it established, extremely broad powers." For the regulatory body to successfully fulfill this function, Dill argued, it would require "men of big ability and big vision."[28]

The FRC and the Reallocation of the Airwaves

The new FRC proceeded expeditiously to fulfill its mandate. On March 17, FRC member Eugene O. Sykes spoke to the nation over the radio to "acquaint" the public with the FRC and "its general plan of work." Sykes stated that the FRC would act as "traffic cops" in bringing order to the spectrum:

> Our hope is to interfere with the legitimate traffic as little as we can, and still eliminate the danger of accident. We are counting on the drivers, which means the broadcasters, to help us, because it is they who in the long run are the worst sufferers from the accidents.

In short, the FRC planned to continue along the lines followed by Hoover. It would allow the industry to determine the nature of broadcast regulation as much as possible, regarding it as an ally. Almost immediately, some nonprofit broadcasters sensed that the FRC's definition of "broadcaster" referred solely to large commercial broadcasters, rendering their existence marginal. If this is the sentiment of the new FRC, one university station radio engineer wrote, "then the broadcasting stations of the educational institutions may as well close up."[29]

Following the Hoover precedent, the FRC convened four days of hearings between March 29 and April 1 to hear how broadcasters believed the FRC could best regulate broadcasting. All but a few of the fifty or so witnesses were representatives of commercial broadcasters, radio manufacturers, or some other commercial enterprise. The agenda for the hearings was structured around engineering concerns and the sessions were dominated by the testimony of corporate-affiliated radio engineers. The tenor of the conclave was congenial and industry-oriented, with the FRC seemingly regarding the profit-orientation of the industry as a given. As one newspaper account noted, the large broadcasters revealed a "smug confidence" toward the hearings, "content for the most part to sit silent" as the FRC was regarded as working in their interests. There was little indication that the FRC regarded itself as responsible for major policy decisions regarding the future of U.S. broadcasting. The sole "policy"-type opinion that was presented with little criticism was the opinion of one Department of Commerce official that "the success of radio broadcasting lay in doing away with small and unimportant stations."[30]

The few noncommercial voices that appeared at the hearings took exception to this sentiment and urged the FRC to consider whether its seeming acceptance of the domination of the profit motive fulfilled the "public interest" charter of the Radio Act. Edward Nockels, a representative of the Chicago Federation of Labor (CFL), who managed the CFL's radio station WCFL, stated that radio should not be "left open to exploitation for profit," and that stations should be operated on a nonprofit basis with the direct support of their listeners. Morris Ernst of the American Civil Liberties Union (ACLU) noted that the power vested in the FRC "is the greatest power ever vested in the history of mankind by legislative act in any group of citizens." After acknowledging that his opinion would "not be popular with the gentlemen in the room," he argued that radio as a "public utility is not entirely consistent with a motive of profitmaking." Ernst called for the FRC to give preference to nonprofit broadcasters in its assignment of frequencies in order to protect the diversity of opinion necessary for democracy. Both Ernst and Nockels were received politely, although after Nockels's presentation one FRC member noted that his topic "was not in accordance with our program."[31]

In any case, the FRC did not accomplish its mandate in its first year, which scholars have termed "a nightmare for all concerned." Two of the five prospective FRC commissioners, who had been handpicked by Hoover, failed to gain Senate approval because they were caught in the partisan political crossfire between Hoover's allies and congressional leaders, and between Republicans and Democrats. Then, coincidentally, two of the three that did get approved died almost immediately thereafter. In addition, Congress failed to approve the FRC's budget, leaving the active members without salary and encouraging one of them, Henry A. Bellows, to resign in November to accept a position as a vice-president at CBS. The FRC abandoned the initial program adopted at its April 29, 1927, meeting to develop a plan to completely reallocate the airwaves and sharply reduce the number of broadcasters.[32] Instead, the FRC simply attempted to accommodate all the existing 733 stations through the sharing of the ninety frequencies. In addition, the FRC made limited efforts to set aside *clear channels,* frequencies that would have only one broadcaster operating at very high power on a nationwide basis. During the FRC's first year, the beneficiaries of the ad hoc allocation process were the largest stations, generally affiliated with the networks, while the smaller and nonprofit broadcasters continued to struggle to survive.[33]

Congress was far from satisfied with either the FRC's performance during this first year or with the emerging contours of U.S. broadcasting. During the hearings before congressional committees to extend the FRC's tenure an additional year in January and February 1928, members of the FRC were repeatedly questioned about the unchecked and stunningly rapid emergence of "chain" broadcasting to its position of near dominance as well as the sharp decline in the role of nonprofit broadcasting. "A lot of the colleges are not satisfied with the places they have" on the broadcast spectrum, acknowledged the FRC's Sykes to the House Committee on the Merchant Marine and Fisheries in January 1928. "We are trying now and working to give a lot of the colleges a more satisfactory place on the broadcast spectrum."[34]

Of the first twenty-five stations set aside for clear channels by the FRC, twenty-three had been licensed to broadcasters affiliated with NBC. This generated considerable alarm for Congress, particularly as large portions of the country were receiving the same chain program simultaneously on most of the stations available to any given area. "I am receiving letters every day from all over the country protesting bitterly," stated Representative Ewin Davis (D-Tenn.) in his interrogation of FRC member Orestes H. Caldwell. "Was that action taken because the commission believed the people of this country wanted all of the choice stations given to the chain stations?" Caldwell acknowledged that this was clearly not the intent of Congress nor of the Radio Act of 1927, but he defended the FRC's actions as being made in the best interest of the listeners.[35]

In similar questioning by Representative Clay Briggs (D-Tex.), Sykes, like Caldwell, defended the FRC's actions and stated that the FRC, unlike

Congress, had received more letters in favor of the chains than opposed to them. Nonetheless, he acknowledged that to "fulfill our duty" to provide listeners with "as much diversity as we can" it would be imperative for the FRC to permit nonprofit broadcasters access to some of the high-power cleared channels. FRC member Harold Lafount assured a hostile Senator Dill in hearings before the Senate Committee on Interstate Commerce in February 1928 that "I am against chain broadcasting in the sense that they might occupy all of the cleared channels."[36] "It seems the chains are being the object of attack," the president of the NAB despondently wrote to the FRC's Lafount in January 1928, "by all of Congress."[37]

In January and February 1928, key figures in the Senate, including Dill, threatened to block the extension of the FRC for an additional year unless Congress also passed complementary legislation that would require the FRC to break up the emerging "chain dominance," to reduce the maximum power allowances so less capitalized stations could compete, and to turn over more of the prime clear channels to independent and educational broadcasters. Working assiduously, the radio lobby and the FRC members were able to remove much of the "sting" from these proposals, but not all.[38] Congress ultimately voted to maintain the FRC for another year, but instead of allowing the FRC complete discretion to determine its own plan of action, it passed the Davis Amendment, so-called after its sponsor Rep. Davis, in March 1928. This required the FRC to make a complete reallocation of the airwaves in order to equalize the number of stations among five geographic "zones." This measure had considerable support among southerners and westerners who felt, with justification, that the broadcast spectrum was dominated by stations from the eastern seaboard and the industrial Midwest. In spirit, the Davis Amendment was also meant as an attack on chain domination, which explains why the networks and their allies were so opposed to it. With its passage, the FRC was forced to generate a permanent and general reallocation plan that would necessitate a complete reshuffling of stations and frequency assignments. The NAB and the networks reacted with alarm and began lobbying the FRC to permit the "natural evolution" of U.S. broadcasting with a minimum of "disturbance in present broadcasting . . . rather than radical sweeping changes."[39]

Any concerns that the reallocation would threaten the emerging contours of commercial broadcasting would prove unfounded. Immediately after the passage of the Davis Amendment, the FRC created an allocating committee of Commissioners Caldwell and Sam Pickard to "consult with experts" and work out a general "reallocation which will comply with the legislation just passed by Congress." Lafount met with the allocating committee and served as an informal member throughout the spring and summer of 1928.[40] Prior to joining the FRC, Lafount had served as a director for several radio manufacturing firms and had been in the process of opening his own commercial radio station. Upon leaving the FRC in the early 1930s, Lafount embarked upon a twenty-year career as a commercial broadcasting executive.[41]

Caldwell, a trained electrical engineer, had served as an editor for McGraw-Hill and had edited such trade publications as *Electrical World, Electrical Merchandising,* and *Radio Retailing.* He viewed his tenure at the FRC as a temporary "loan" of his services to the government by his employer, and he returned to his post at McGraw-Hill in 1929. NBC President Aylesworth had been a leading sponsor of Caldwell's appointment to the FRC, and the trade publication editor brought a genuine enthusiasm for commercial broadcasting to Washington, D.C. In a speech to the NAB annual convention in September 1927, he implored his "broadcasting friends" to "extend the number of radio listeners until we put a set in every home." Caldwell promised the assistance of the FRC to "put radio where it really belongs." As the only trained engineer on the FRC, Caldwell played a particularly large role in the development of the reallocation in 1928. "Mr. Caldwell," Lafount noted in 1931, is "wholly responsible for the present system of broadcasting in this country."[42] Pickard, too, had a short tenure on the FRC. He would leave the FRC in 1929 to become a vice-president at CBS, where he was in charge of expanding the CBS network from some forty-seven affiliated stations in February 1929 to seventy-six stations in 1931 and ninety-one affiliates in 1933.[43]

Although the initial confidential memorandum on the reallocation acknowledged that the FRC would determine "which stations or group of stations shall have the assignments" and which would not, the allocating committee explicitly regarded reallocation as strictly an "engineering" problem. The allocating committee accordingly met several times with a group of radio engineers to establish reallocation criteria because the FRC did not have its own staff engineer until the autumn of 1928, when the reallocation was put into effect. These experts were selected by the chief radio engineer for AT&T, and all of the engineers were employed by the government, radio manufacturers, or commercial broadcasters. The press and members of Congress were invited to one open meeting, but the balance of the sessions were closed and unpublicized. Given the emphasis on engineering and technical criteria for making the reallocation, and the secrecy of the meetings, the process was devoid of controversy.[44]

The tentative report of this group of engineers was presented to the FRC on April 11 and stated that the one fundamental change that was necessary was the creation of a "considerable number" of high-powered clear channels "upon which only one station operates" nationally. Developing a large number of these "clear channel" stations was also a high priority for the networks and the large commercial broadcasters; they were the broadcasters best equipped with the capital and resources necessary to broadcast on such a basis. The confusion regarding the appropriate course for U.S. broadcasting that had engulfed even the largest broadcasters as recently as 1926 had disappeared by 1928, at least in their private communications. One NBC executive wrote to the FRC's Caldwell in January 1928 that "the only plan" for successful radio broadcasting that "holds promise of any degree of success is the development of network systems for national advertising purposes." Nevertheless, in presenting the report, the AT&T engineer stated that there was no self-interest behind the engineers' recommendations: "The reason for this is a purely physical fact."[45]

This is not to suggest any "conspiracy" by these engineers on behalf of their present or potential future employers. The FRC had specifically instructed the engineers to regard the reallocation as an engineering—not a policy—problem. In addition, the eventual opponents of the reallocation were largely oblivious to the existence of these proceedings in the spring of 1928, and they seemed to be ignorant of their general significance. There was little controversy in the air. Most important, radio engineers were arguably more dependent upon the dominant radio corporations than were their colleagues in other branches of engineering. In the first two decades of the century they had responded to the oligopolization of the radio industry by abandoning efforts to be independent "out of frustration and survival instinct." As David Noble observes, they "flocked to corporate employment in exchange for security."[46] The 1920s were halcyon days for corporate radio engineers. In June 1928 RCA's chief engineer informed the Institute of Radio Engineers, of which he also served as president, that the cooperative relationship between the radio industry and radio engineers filled "a fundamental need" and was "a provider of rich rewards both in public esteem and commercial success." The radio engineers could have thoroughly internalized the commercial basis of broadcasting as being synonymous with the highest possible "service of radio to the public." Engineering plans that turned over the best slots to the best capitalized stations appeared as common sense, and efforts to interfere with commercial domination were routinely dismissed as a violation of sound engineering principles in radio regulation.[47]

At the same time, it would be difficult to exaggerate the harmonious and extensive relationship that had developed between the FRC on the one hand and NBC, CBS, and the NAB on the other hand. This relationship is all the more striking given the near total lack of contact the FRC had with nonprofit broadcasters, public interest groups that might have an interest in broadcast policy, and even members of Congress. The allocating committee was in constant touch with commercial broadcasting executives, and CBS Vice-President (and former FRC member) Bellows assisted the FRC throughout 1928 as it put together the reallocation plan. The FRC granted the NAB and the networks as well as the radio manufacturers a chance to respond to the report of the radio engineer's committee in a special hearing two weeks after it had been released.[48] The FRC's attitude toward the commercial networks was evident in a May 1928 letter from Caldwell to Aylesworth in which he saluted NBC for its "wonderful public service." Caldwell concluded that "the fact that demagogues have a chance to attack you is due solely to lack of understanding on the part of the public of the full measure of your great contributions."[49] When Caldwell was attacked by members of Congress for being overly friendly to the "radio trust," he responded that radio had become a "football for politicians" who provided "sophistries" on the topic to win votes, but who would be best to stay away from broadcasting policy as they were uninformed on the topic.[50] Any notion that the FRC saw its role as that of protecting the "public interest" from the selfish aims of the commercial broadcasters is almost entirely absent from the records; if anything, the exact opposite was the case.

Accordingly, the FRC's reallocation clearly had the look of one that would be sensitive to the needs of the fledgling commercial broadcasting industry. In short, it would recognize, crystallize, and further encourage the dominant trends within broadcasting over the previous two or three years and make no effort to counteract these developments through public policy.

By early summer a consensus on the FRC and in the broadcasting industry emerged in favor of establishing a large number of clear channels for high-powered broadcasting in addition to having a number of regional channels that several broadcasters could use simultaneously at lower power, much like the engineers' committee had recommended in April. The engineers and commercial broadcasters favored a sharp reduction in the total number of broadcasters and, if that was not politically feasible, it was recommended that several broadcasters might share the same channel but each be assigned different times of day to broadcast. During the summer the FRC debated specific proposals to implement the reallocation and attempted to "sell" the idea behind the reallocation among the broadcasters. In addition, before the final decisions were made about which stations to favor and which to disfavor in the reallocation, the allocating committee contacted a handful of major radio editors to receive their input regarding which were the most popular stations in their communities.[51]

The final measure the FRC took before implementing the reallocation was to hire Louis G. Caldwell as its first general counsel in the summer of 1928. The need for a general counsel became evident when the FRC's attempt to remove 164 marginal broadcasters through General Order 32 in May 1928 had been ineffectual and had proven a procedural disaster.[52] Caldwell, no relation to FRC member Orestes H. Caldwell, was by all accounts a brilliant and visionary commercial broadcasting attorney. He had worked for Colonel Robert McCormick's *Chicago Tribune* and the *Tribune*'s radio station, WGN, in Chicago. Caldwell had been sent to Washington specifically to protect the *Tribune*'s radio interests and to assist in the development of broadcast leg-

24

islation and regulation. Louis Caldwell was also the chairman of the Standing Committee on Communications of the American Bar Association, which was producing extensive semi-official annual reports on broadcasting policy during this period. He was a proponent of the commercial and chain development of the ether. Louis Caldwell was selected for the position of general counsel, among other reasons, because he had written a forty-two-page reallocation plan that incorporated most of the ideas of the radio engineers and commercial broadcasters. Within a few weeks as FRC counsel, Caldwell had effectively taken over the implementation of the reallocation and was making policy decisions that he acknowledged were "not strictly within the scope of the duties of the general counsel." Shortly after the implementation of the reallocation, in February 1929, Caldwell resigned as general counsel and returned to his practice as a commercial broadcasting attorney.[53]

The FRC announced its reallocation plan in August 1928. Called General Order 40, it went into effect in November. In addition to forty clear channels and thirty-four regional channels, the plan called for the remaining frequencies to be low-power local channels that would accommodate thirty broadcasters in each zone. A full 94 percent of the broadcasters had their frequency assignments altered by the reallocation. (The 6 percent that were unaffected were chain owned or affiliated stations on clear channels.) Louis Caldwell's former employer, WGN, received a clear channel license to broadcast at the maximum 50,000 watts. The FRC's newly appointed chief engineer defended the reallocation plan as "the only reasonable solution of this dilemma."[54] In its statement accompanying the announcement of General Order 40, the FRC acknowledged that Congress had given it no indication as how to determine the meaning of public interest, convenience, or necessity. The statement asserted that the FRC had interpreted the phrase as meaning that the FRC should strive "to bring about the best possible broadcasting reception conditions throughout the United States," and thus favor those broadcasters with the best technical equipment. The FRC statement also noted that "broadcasting stations are not given these great privileges by the United States government for the primary benefit of advertisers," adding that "advertising is usually offensive to the listening public."[55]

To lower the number of stations, the FRC utilized its process whereby anybody could challenge an existing broadcaster for its frequency assignment at the end of the three-month term accorded each license. In general, the FRC would have the various applicants for a particular frequency ultimately share its usage (unless there was a successful commercial broadcaster already in place, in which case its status was effectively unchallengable) and allocate the majority of the hours to the station it deemed most worthy. In the long run, the station accorded the fewest hours on a shared channel often found it very difficult to stay on the air. Needless to say, this direct head-to-head competition for the scarce broadcast channels created great antipathy between the contending applicants, particularly, as was often the case, when commercial broadcasters successfully challenged nonprofit broadcasters for the use of their frequencies. Indeed, in one case, hearings between nonprofit WEVD and commercial WFOX of New York had to end prematurely because the attorneys for the two sides began to engage in a fistfight. In any case, without having to actually turn down the license renewal applications of very many broadcasters, there were 100 fewer stations on the air within a year of the implementation of General Order 40.[56]

In this context, the precise criteria by which the FRC elected to interpret the term public interest, convenience, or necessity would go a long way toward determining which of the various broadcasters would be favored in the general reallocation and which would be under constant pressure simply to maintain their licenses or their totals of assigned broadcast hours in the cases of shared frequencies. The FRC had to spell out its interpretation of this term in the numerous hearings, appeals, and court challenges that followed in the wake of the reallocation; it published its interpretation of public interest, convenience, or necessity in the FRC's *Third Annual Report,* which was published in 1929. The sketchy criteria touched on in the August 1928 FRC statement that accompanied the announcement of General Order 40 did not provide a strong enough fortress from which to defend the licensing decisions made in the reallocation.

Indeed, the 1929 FRC stated position regarding the meaning of public interest, convenience or necessity maintained little of the tenor of the comments regarding the meaning of the term that had been expressed in the FRC's 1928 statement. For example, the FRC only made brief mention of the need to favor stations with the best capitalization and the highest quality transmitting equipment in its legal defense of the reallocation. This explanation of the reallocation would again be offered commonly before Congress and in public forums by members of the FRC and advocates of commercial broadcasting in the years that followed, and it had a certain unimpeachable, if circular, logic. Having created forty national clear channel slots and many more relatively high-power regional assignments, the FRC argued that it was obviously in the public interest to assign these channels to broadcasters who had the equipment to take advantage of these slots. In the immediate aftermath of General Order 40, however, this defense was of partial value as some of the disfavored nonprofit broadcasters had more sizable capital investments and operations than the upstart capitalist broadcasters who were vying for the use of their broadcast channels. Hence the need to justify the policy on other grounds. Similarly, the 1929 legal defense of General Order 40 dropped the acknowledgment of the public antipathy toward advertising, as its emergence was the most immediately recognizable consequence of the reallocation.

The FRC opinion in this matter was written by Louis Caldwell and it mirrors his comments on the subject in the ABA Standing Committee on Communications 1929 report.[57] Based upon the testimony of FRC members to Congressional committees in 1929, it seems apparent that none of them had developed their positions on this matter to the extent of Caldwell. As this interpretation of the public interest, convenience, or necessity has played such a pivotal role in U.S. broadcast policy, it merits some elaboration.

First, the FRC stated that broadcasting was not a common carrier in the sense of the other public utilities (i.e., that each station would be required to permit anybody who so desired access to their facilities if they were willing to pay a fair price). Rather, the FRC argued that broadcasters were not licensed to serve *users,* but rather to serve *listeners.* Therefore, the criteria public interest, convenience, or necessity meant that the FRC would favor broadcasters who seemed the most inclined toward serving the public and who were the least inclined toward promoting their own "private or selfish interests." The only exception to this criteria was commercial advertising, which the FRC conceded was conducted for selfish interests, "because advertising furnishes the economic support for the service and thus makes it possible." Although the excesses of advertising needed to be regulated, the FRC made it clear that it had no interest in inhibiting the financial support it brought to the industry. "Without advertising, broadcasting would not exist," the FRC stated, with apparent disregard for the several score noncommercial stations still in operation.[58]

Second, the FRC determined that the stations that best served the public interest were those that attempted to serve the "entire listening public within the listening area of the station." To do this the broadcaster needed to provide "a well-rounded program" of entertainment as well as cultural programming. The FRC was not particularly interested in delineating the specifics of what constituted "well-rounded" programming. Rather, the marketplace would serve as the arbiter: "The commission has great confidence in the sound judgment of the listening public . . . as to what type of programs are in its own best interest." The FRC termed these broadcasters *general public service* stations.

The type of stations that earned the FRC's disfavor, in contrast to the general public service stations, were termed *propaganda* stations. It emphasized that the term was not meant derogatorily but, rather, to stress that these broadcasters were more interested in spreading their particular viewpoint than in reaching the broadest possible audience with whatever programming was most attractive. It observed, "There is not room in the broadcast band for every school of thought, religious, political, social, and economic, each to have its separate broadcasting station, its mouthpiece in the ether."[59] Consequently, since every group could not have its own "mouthpiece," then, according to the FRC, *no* such group should be entitled to have the privilege of a broadcast license. Hence, ownership by any group not primarily motivated by profit automatically earmarked a station to the FRC as one with propaganda inclinations. Moreover, by the FRC's interpretation, commercial advertising is deemed the *only* legitimate form of financial support for a broadcaster, as by definition any other form of support had propaganda strings attached.

This interpretation of the public interest, convenience, or necessity was a clear endorsement of the private commercial development of the airwaves. The FRC's *Third Annual Report* stated baldly that a general public service broadcaster has "a claim of preference over a propaganda station," when they contended for access to the same channel. Even if propaganda stations attempted to "accompany their messages with entertainment and other program features of interest to the public," the FRC asserted they did not merit the same treatment as general public service stations that did the same things since, among other things, the propaganda stations would be "constantly subject to the very human temptation not to be fair to opposing schools of thought."[60]

Numerous nonprofit stations would fall victim to this logic and see their hours reduced and the time turned over to capitalist broadcasters, often affiliated with one of the two networks. As the FRC informed WCFL, the nonprofit "Voice of Labor" affiliated with the CFL, when it lost its hearing for more hours to the *Chicago Tribune*'s WGN: "There are numerous groups of the general public that might similarly demand the exclusive use of a frequency for their benefit. There are nearly five million Masons in the United States and about as many Odd Fellows."[61] By the FRC's logic, if the public desired the type of programming offered by the propaganda stations, it would make this interest known through the marketplace and the general public service broadcasters would find it in their interest to provide such programming. Hence, it would be best for educators and other nonprofit broadcasters to learn to work through the facilities of the general public service stations, rather than to attempt to develop and maintain their own facilities.

In the *Third Annual Report,* the FRC argued that its interpretation of the public interest, convenience, or necessity would best serve the interests of free speech and the desire for a balanced presentation of political views. None of the propaganda stations could be expected to bring balance so their reduction or elimination only boded well for the discussion of public issues. Furthermore, the general public service broadcasters, according to the FRC, since they had no selfish propaganda aims, tacitly recognized their "broader duty" to open and balanced debate. Indeed, the FRC proclaimed that the "great majority" of the broadcasters were going far beyond the letter of the law in their presentation of differing viewpoints on social issues.[62]

Nevertheless, the FRC concluded its interpretation of the public interest, convenience, or necessity by addressing the concern that its policies would leave the listening public "at the mercy of the broadcaster." It argued that this was an unfounded fear for two reasons. First, the listener could shift away from stations he or she did not like and the market would act as a corrective on recalcitrant broadcasters. Second, the FRC stated that the efforts of the networks to establish "advisory boards" of prominent citizens to monitor their public affairs programming seemed to be very effective. Thus the marketplace and self-regulation rendered extensive government intervention in the public interest unnecessary.

The Emerging Status Quo and the Reaction of the Immediate Parties

Following the implementation of General Order 40, U.S. broadcasting rapidly crystallized as a system dominated by two nationwide chains supported by commercial advertising. Whereas NBC had twenty-eight affiliates and CBS had sixteen for a combined 6.4 percent of the broadcast stations in 1927, they combined to account for 30 percent of the stations within four years. This, alone, understates their emergence, as all but three of the forty clear channels were soon owned or affiliated with one of the two networks and approximately one-half of the remaining 70 percent of the stations were low-power independent broadcasters operating with limited hours on shared frequencies. Within two years the average independent station had a power of 566 watts, while one of NBC's seventy-four stations averaged over 10,000 watts. By 1935 only four of the sixty-two stations that broadcast at 5,000 or more watts did not have a network affiliation. When hours on the air and the level of power are factored into the equation, NBC and CBS accounted for nearly 70 percent of American broadcasting by 1931. One study estimated that by the mid–1930s some 97 percent of total nighttime broadcasting, when smaller stations were often not licensed to broadcast, was conducted by NBC, CBS, or their affiliates. NBC was the larger of the two, operating two distinct national networks, the red network and the blue network.[63]

Network expansion was accompanied by the dramatic emergence of direct commercial advertising to a position of prominence in U.S. broadcasting. GE's Owen D. Young, founder of RCA and a guiding force behind the creation of NBC, blamed the degeneration of NBC from its "public service" origins to becoming a conduit for commercialism upon the greed of national advertisers. They came "posthaste," Young's biographers noted, "with fistfuls of money, to buy air time."[64] The evidence suggests that it was more the networks and the NAB who actively promoted the use of radio for direct advertising. (Accordingly, when radio advertising came under severe attack in the early 1930s, it was the broadcasters and not the advertising community that rallied to its defense.) For example, the NAB established a commercial committee in 1928 that was responsible for working with the American

Association of Advertising Agencies (AAAA) to establish a coherent set of guidelines and to promote the use of radio. NBC hired long-time advertising executive Frank Arnold specifically to promote radio before the advertising community and to corporate executives. Arnold noted that, with only a few exceptions, "the door of every advertising agency was closed to solicitors for radio" when he began his work in 1927. Such was not the case for long; by the end of the decade most major New York agencies had radio departments. Perhaps most important, NBC President Merlin Aylesworth personally called on many major national accounts to sell airtime on the new network. With a tremendous gift for sales, Aylesworth accomplished his mission, as one aide recalls, "with tremendous rapidity."[65]

Radio advertising, therefore, which was a marginal phenomenon in 1927 with barely any national component whatsoever, accounted for $100 million in 1930 alone. By 1934 annual national advertising expenditures alone approached $75 million, and that was during an economic depression no less. CBS had a sixfold increase in advertising sales in fiscal 1929 alone and unabashedly proclaimed broadcasting was "the greatest media development in the history of advertising" in its 1929–1930 promotional literature.[66] One study conducted by the trade publication *Radio Retailing* in 1931 determined that, on average, fifteen minutes of every hour were turned over to explicit sales messages. The *Christian Science Monitor* estimated explicit sales talks at twelve minutes per hour. The networks shortly abandoned much of the task of producing programming to advertising agencies, which provided the shows that surrounded their clients's sales messages, thus rendering the distinction between advertising and nonadvertising time of limited value. The growth of the networks and the emergence of advertising, though distinct, were mutually reinforcing. One study has found that 80 percent of radio advertising revenue in 1929 went to 20 percent of the stations, all network-owned or affiliated.[67]

Philip Rosen hardly exaggerates when he describes the period between 1928 and 1933 as one of "prosperous, almost triumphant expansion" for commercial broadcasters. Erik Barnouw has noted that in the brief period between 1928 and 1933, "almost all forms of enterprise that would dominate radio and television in decades to come had taken shape." Nor is this an assessment that requires hindsight. In reviewing the growth of the two networks, one observer concluded in 1930 that "nothing in American history has paralleled this mushroom growth."[68]

The other side of the same coin, however, was reflected in the equally dramatic decline in the role played by nonprofit broadcasters in the U.S. The number of broadcasting stations affiliated with colleges and universities declined from ninety-five in 1927 to less than half that figure in 1930. The number of overall nonprofit broadcasters would decline from over 200 in 1927 to some sixty-five in 1934, almost all of which were marginal in terms of power and impact. By 1934 nonprofit broadcasting accounted for only 2 percent of total U.S. broadcast time.[69] For most Americans, it effectively did not exist.

Most nonprofit broadcasters, who had been hard-pressed to raise funds to subsidize their efforts before General Order 40, found themselves in a "vicious cycle" where the FRC lowered their hours and power to the benefit of well-capitalized or soon-to-be well-capitalized capitalist broadcasters, and thus made it all that much more difficult for the nonprofit broadcasters to generate the funds from their governing bodies necessary to be successful. This was the scenario for most of the educational and nonprofit stations that went off the air in the late 1920s and early 1930s. The director of the soon-to-be extinct University of Arkansas station wrote:

> Now the Federal Radio Commission has come along and taken away all of the hours that are worth anything and has left us with hours that are absolutely no good either for commercial programs or for educational programs. The Commission may boast that it has never cut an educational station off the air. It merely cuts off our head, our arms, and our legs, and then allows us to die a natural death.

Even the most established of the university stations, the University of Wisconsin's WHA, found itself in a struggle before the FRC to keep its hours and power.[70]

Adding to the crisis facing nonprofit broadcasters was that much of what money they could raise had to be applied to pay for expenses to defend their licenses every three months before the FRC in Washington, D.C. "Ever since the new broadcast structure was put in effect in the fall of 1928," the director of the University of Illinois radio station wrote to a congressman in 1930, "we practically wasted all of the money that the university has put into our broadcasting efforts" defending the station license before the FRC, so that "it has been impossible for the people of the state, who own the University and consequently this station, to benefit from the educational features which we have attempted to give them." Another educator criticized the FRC for letting "the commercial stations compel the college stations to spend their scanty funds in sending representatives to Washington" in seemingly endless license hearings. In short, there was considerable outrage among many of the nonprofit broadcasters expressed toward the FRC during this period. One prominent educational broadcaster wrote that the FRC was giving the educational broadcasters "a very raw deal," and termed the FRC as "belonging heart and soul to the big commercial interests."[71]

To many educators and nonprofit broadcasters, the problem with the FRC stemmed from its strictly commercial interpretation of public interest, convenience, or necessity. As one observed,

Under that philosophy the educational station is being tolerated rather than accepted and encouraged by the regulatory body of the government. That philosophy is a purely commercial one which compels all stations to operate according to commercial standards. If such a basis of operation were to be applied to education generally the colleges and universities of the United States could not justify their existence.

"It is unfair," one college president complained, "to leave educators in a position where they have to compete against clowns." "The Federal Radio Commission," one college station manager complained, seems to believe that an "educational station ought to die" if it could not compete with capitalist broadcasters, "just as a kitten that is thrown under the feet of an elephant ought to die, if it cannot avoid being trampled to death."[72]

Even those not connected with nonprofit broadcasting were not especially impressed by the FRC as a policymaking and regulatory body. The tenor of the congressional hearings to renew the FRC in early 1929 was as antagonistic as they had been prior to the passage of the Davis amendment. "The great feeling about radio in this country," stated Senator Dill, "is that it will be monopolized by the few wealthy interests." Moreover, the concern was not simply with network domination, but with the striking emergence of advertising. After hearing Orestes Caldwell defend advertising as the only conceivable method of financing the clear channel stations, "because the expense of operating such a station is very large," one congressman, Charles Gifford (D-Mass.), reacted angrily and asked Caldwell some fundamental questions. Do you "approve of giving over the radio to the advertisers' whims in operating these stations?" he asked. "Do you not think the principle of radio is tremendously broader than that?" Caldwell defended advertising, stating "there seems to be no other way to finance these wonderful programs," and added that the topic of advertising was "one of the broader problems Congress should take up." "The broader problems," Gifford responded, "are what I think we made a commission for."[73]

The FRC's second general counsel had similar disdain for the commission. Bethuel M. Webster, Jr., replaced Louis Caldwell as general counsel for the FRC early in 1929 and then quit in disgust before the end of the year. Webster was unimpressed with the reallocation; in his view the FRC "gave away valuable public channels without getting anything in return." Webster regarded the major radio corporations as having undue influence over the FRC. By the early 1930s, he would become active in the ACLU's efforts to establish a coherent U.S. broadcasting policy. Webster characterized the FRC as an institution of "unparalleled mediocrity and ineptitude" whose members "knew little or nothing about radio or the law." To Webster, the FRC was comprised of "semi-retired sailors, soldiers or lawyers, men lacking the vision or energy to undertake departures from established notions and routine." Hence, the "tendency, if not the deliberate policy, of the licensing authority has been to crystallize the status quo.''[74] Few observers at the time characterized the body as anything remotely close to the ''philosopher kings'' that Senator Dill had envisioned. Except for the appreciation displayed by the commercial broadcasting industry, the FRC was a largely unpopular body throughout its seven-year history.

As much as the nonprofit broadcasters were hostile toward the FRC, they were every bit as hostile toward the networks and the commercial broadcasting industry. The format whereby capitalist broadcasters applied directly for frequencies occupied by nonprofit broadcasters and attempted to establish to the FRC their superiority at serving the ''public interest'' certainly did not lay the groundwork for cordial relations. To many educators, it seemed that commercial broadcasters would not be satisfied until all the educational broadcasters had been driven from the air. ''On all fronts the commercial radio interests advanced their lines,'' observed the NCER, the leading educational radio organization, as it reviewed the developments between 1928 and 1930. ''The two powerful chains, NBC and CBS, trained their heaviest artillery, ruthlessly ignoring protestations of smaller stations, crushing educational stations under a broad heel, spiked with hobnails of commerce.''[75]

Most nonprofit broadcasters had approved of the passage of the Radio Act of 1927, albeit without any great enthusiasm, and had regarded the FRC, at least initially, as a step toward stabilizing U.S. broadcasting, nonprofit and otherwise. In its earlier versions, the legislation that became the Radio Act of 1927 had included wording that would have required the FRC to *favor* nonprofit broadcasters in the allocation of broadcast licenses, but this wording was withdrawn in committee because, it was argued, such a mandate was already implicit in the term public interest, convenience, or necessity.[76] The Congress followed the leadership of Senator Dill, whose belief in giving the FRC free reign was cited earlier. Louis Caldwell had likewise approved of Congress granting the FRC carte blanche to interpret public interest, convenience, or necessity as it saw fit without any additional congressional ''encroachment.'' ''While this phrase may seem broad and vague,'' he wrote, ''any more specific test would have been dangerous.'' Given this sort of almost arbitrary authority, some proponents of nonprofit broadcasting had hoped and even expected the new FRC to enact, as one proponent noted, ''radical changes in the radio structure by way of correcting mistakes which had developed in its haphazard growth.''[77]

Any hopes along these lines were dashed with the implementation of General Order 40. ''The battle was begun in earnest,'' wrote the NCER, ''in the summer of 1928 soon after the enactment of the Commission's General Order 40.'' WCFL's Nockels termed General Order 40 ''infamous'' and noted that with its implementation, ''the radio air has been monopolized so that the Big Power interests, Big Business, and the Big Newspaper interests have gotten all the cleared radio channels and nobody else has a 'peep-in.' ''

Nor was the importance of the reallocation lost on the commercial broadcasters or the FRC. "The allocation of 1928 was of fundamental importance in this field," observed the NAB's chief researcher in 1934, and as a result "Radio began to flourish as an advertising medium" and "Network structures were extended." In 1931, the FRC's Lafount characterized General Order 40 as providing "the structure or very foundation upon which broadcasting has been built, and upon which the success or failure of every branch of the radio industry must depend."[78] As a leading radio engineer informed the NAB annual convention in October 1928, General Order 40 was "Radio's Emancipation Proclamation."[79]

It is curious that when the FRC implemented General Order 40 and it became clear that educational and nonprofit broadcasters were at best being treated on equal terms with the commercial broadcasters, members of the FRC had a markedly different interpretation of the meaning of the Radio Act of 1927 than that of Dill and Louis Caldwell, as the exchange between Orestes Caldwell and Representative Gifford cited earlier suggests. FRC Chairman Charles McKinley Saltzman explained to educators in 1931 that: "The Commission wishes to help the cause of education and the plans of educators, but it can only do so in accordance with the provisions of the law that prescribes its powers." Saltzman's interpretation of the Radio Act of 1927 was not that it was the vague yet powerful instrument that Senator Dill and Louis Caldwell claimed it to be, but, rather, that in it the FRC's "powers, limitations, and functions" were "prescribed in considerable detail." FRC member Lafount would inform another conference of educational broadcasters in 1931 that "under existing law the Commission cannot favor an educational institution. It must be treated like any citizen, any other group, any other applicant. I see nothing in the law that would justify the Commission's doing otherwise, regardless of our interest in education."[80]

This stance taken by the FRC upset the educators to no end. Armstrong Perry, who was one of the leading proponents of educational broadcasting, observed:

> The Federal Radio Commission . . . take[s] the attitude that the radio laws compel them to consider all stations as being on the same basis, whether they are operated for private profit or as public institutions. This does not accord with the point of view of the men in Congress who made the law. It related rather to other phases of the strategy of the dominant radio group.[81]

Despite this claim to be neutrally administering a tightly worded statute, FRC members revealed considerable enthusiasm for network and commercial broadcasting when not addressing groups of educators. The most vociferous in this regard was arguably Lafount. "Commercialism is the heart of the broadcasting industry in the United States," he wrote in 1931. "What has education contributed to radio? Not one thing. What has commercialism contributed? Everything—the lifeblood of the industry." Lafount termed radio "this wonderful instrument of commerce." To Lafount, the purpose of regulation was clear. "To make possible the presenting of the best possible programs," he informed the Senate Committee on Interstate Commerce in February 1929, the FRC was essentially obliged to make the operation of a broadcast station profitable and do nothing that would "endanger the revenues" of a station.[82] After a field trip to visit Western stations in the summer of 1929, Lafount was delighted to report that "practically all commercial broadcasting stations are now operating at a profit," and that "the west is highly appreciative of the wonderful programs broadcast by the two eastern chain broadcasting companies." "Experts everywhere now agree," Lafount noted in 1931, that the U.S. broadcasting system "is as perfect as it could be made."[83]

The only exception to the near unanimous praise for the emerging status quo elicited by an FRC member was provided by Judge Ira E. Robinson. While serving as the acting chairman of the FRC in 1928, Robinson was the only member to oppose the reallocation. He was not swayed by the "expert" opinion of the radio engineers which recommended the establishment of high-power, clear channel stations. He wrote:

> True, radio engineers have testified that high power is the thing. But those who have so testified are naturally by their employment "big business minded." These engineers have, however, been so commendably loyal to those with whom they are associated, as to at no time refer to the real reason for the demand for high power.[84]

After voting against General Order 40, Robinson wrote a memo to Louis Caldwell stating that "I want to go on record that I shall ever oppose the use of the air, undoubtedly belonging to all the public, being 'grabbed' by private interests." Moreover, Robinson refused to participate in any of the hearings stemming from General Order 40, deeming it "unethical and improper" to participate, "based on his opposition to the whole reallocation." Robinson described himself as "an advocate of educational broadcasting. It should not be depressed for commercial purposes."[85]

If Robinson did not participate in the countless hearings that resulted from General Order 40, he did use his position to denounce the FRC policy. He went before the House Committee on the Merchant Marine and Fisheries in January 1929 and announced his opposition to General Order 40 on the grounds that it was weighted in favor of the chains and against independent and educational broadcasters. The status of radio for listeners was "better under the old allocation." Robinson had no shortage of enemies; one radio trade publication commended the "progressive members" of the FRC for overruling "Robinson's obstructive tactics" and putting through the allocation. In October 1929 an informal meeting was arranged in Washington,

D.C., between Robinson and NBC executives to clear the air. It quickly degenerated into a heated and bitter exchange between Robinson and Aylesworth on the merits of commercial broadcasting.[86] The commercial broadcasters organized a stiff opposition to his reappointment to the FRC in 1929, but elements of the industry backed off when it became apparent that if Robinson was not reappointed, it would draw unfavorable publicity to the FRC and its relationship to the industry. As former FRC member and CBS executive Sam Pickard confidentially telegraphed the White House, disposing of Robinson "would cause political stir and much bad feeling generally seriously handicapping future effort" by the FRC. Robinson was reappointed after congressional leaders went to the White House and informed President Hoover that unless Robinson was included among the nominees, the Senate would hold up the entire schedule of five appointments.[87]

Although critical of the reallocation, Robinson was not opposed to the private and commercial development of the ether; rather, he was opposed to the monopolistic tendencies of network control and the lack of interest in regulating the amount of advertising exhibited by the balance of the FRC's members. Robinson did not accept the notion that the FRC was forced by the Radio Act of 1927 to favor a commercial network system in its licensing practices. "Time after time I have said I do not see why it is that the educational stations have the limited assignments given them," he told a conference of educators in 1930 in what would be a seminal speech for the movement that arose to oppose the status quo. "The present allocation is all wrong." Robinson, however, was skeptical about the ability of the FRC to reform the situation. When asked what steps educators should take to preserve and expand the role of nonprofit broadcasting, Robinson responded emphatically: "This is the only way you can do it. I know your situation." He added, "get the whole body of educators to come down to Congress as these other lobbyists do and hang around and demand."[88] This marked a critical turning point; henceforth, efforts at reform would be addressed to Congress and the public-at-large. The FRC was dismissed as hopelessly bankrupt.

By the end of the decade, the contours of the modern U.S. network-dominated, advertising-supported broadcasting system were in place. In only a few short years U.S. broadcast policy had been developed and set in place with a minimum of informed public debate or participation. At best even Congress had played a minor role, and, to the extent that it actually deliberated on the nature of U.S. broadcasting, it was not necessarily in concert with the path that the FRC pursued. Similarly, only a year after the implementation of General Order 40, the battle lines had been drawn. On one side were the two emerging networks, national advertisers, the commercial broadcasting industry, and, to no small extent, the FRC. On the other side were the displaced and disadvantaged nonprofit broadcasters, soon to be joined by several civic groups, numerous intellectuals, and organizations like the

ACLU, which were appalled by the implications of a commercially supported, network broadcasting system for U.S. politics and culture. The battle would be short and one-sided, but it provides the sole instance in modern U.S. history in which the structure and control of an established mass medium would be a legitimate issue for public debate.

CHAPTER 3

The Broadcast Reform Movement I: The Payne Fund and Ferment Among the Educators

In the aftermath of General Order 40, the contours of the network-dominated, advertising-supported broadcasting system fell into place with astonishing speed. Almost as quickly, a coherent and organized opposition to commercial broadcasting emerged in the United States. This chapter and the next will profile the elements of the broadcast reform movement that dotted the political landscape between 1930 and 1935, focusing on clarifying the origins, structures, and programs of the various groups that came to oppose commercial broadcasting. This chapter will concentrate upon those activities subsidized by the Payne Fund: The NCER and the *Ventura Free Press*. Through the NCER the Payne Fund hoped to capitalize upon educators' dissatisfaction with commercial broadcasting and to mobilize momentum for broadcast reform. Similarly, through the campaign directed under the aegis of the *Ventura Free Press,* the Payne Fund attempted to enlist newspaper publishers and the general public to the cause of broadcast reform.

The Payne Fund and Radio Broadcasting, 1927–1930

The Payne Fund was formally established in 1927, with its origin in the Committee for the Study of Juvenile Reading, which had been founded in 1925. The Payne Fund's founder and primary benefactor was Frances Payne Bolton, whose grandfather had accumulated a vast fortune through his involvement with Standard Oil in its early years. Without a capital endowment or trust fund, almost all of the Payne Fund's donations were provided in grants earmarked for specific projects by Bolton, her brother, William Bingham II, and her sister, Elizabeth Blossom. The identities of Bingham and Blossom were kept in the strictest confidence by the fund and Payne Fund recipients knew only that their grants came from anonymous donors. Created with the aim of supporting projects that would promote citizenship, social welfare, and education, the Payne Fund quickly took an interest in mass communication and sponsored a series of studies of the effects of motion pictures in the late 1920s and early 1930s. These trailblazing studies are world famous and have earned the Payne Fund considerable prestige within mass communication research circles. The Payne Fund saw its mission as temporary; it expected to fade out of existence as the experiments and projects it launched were subsequently adopted and supported by other private or public philanthropies. The Payne Fund eschewed self-promotion for its activities, although only rarely, as in the case of the *Ventura Free Press,* did it actually subsidize an activity surreptitiously.[1]

The Payne Fund was based in New York City and, at its outset, had a two-person administrative staff of H. M. Clymer, its president, and Ella Phillips Crandall, its secretary. Bolton assumed the role of president by 1931 when Clymer's health failed. Bolton was a staunch Republican from the progressive wing of the party whose husband, Chester, was a Republican member of the U.S. House of Representatives. As Chester Bolton was concerned that being linked with Payne Fund activities might damage his political career, he played almost no role in the Fund's activities. Moreover, his sensitivity only underscored the goal of the Payne Fund to operate with as little fanfare as possible. Although the Payne Fund had both a Board of Directors and an Executive Committee, it was a small and intimate operation where no major decisions were made without Bolton's approval. Bolton, in turn, relied heavily upon the judgment of Crandall, who maintained direct and regular contact with each of the Payne Fund projects.[2]

The Payne Fund took an immediate interest in the educational potential of radio. In 1926 Clymer inspected the educational broadcasting activities of the BBC and was impressed with what he saw. In 1927 the Payne Fund financed a survey that was conducted with the cooperation of the National Education Association (NEA) and which addressed the best potential uses of radio in the classroom. The survey concluded that "any curriculum for a school of the air which is intended to be an effective factor in education must be prepared by educators" and "unhampered by the necessity of carrying propaganda for any commercial"[3] group. The report of the survey was submitted to the NEA at its 1928 convention with the request that the NEA formally resolve "to provide educational leadership for school broadcasting" and oversee the establishment of a national "School of the Air" to be broadcast over commercial stations. The NEA rejected the measure in a close vote, recommending instead that "the whole matter of radio broadcasting be reserved for further investigation and study."[4]

From the beginning the radio counsel for the Payne Fund was Armstrong

Perry, a freelance journalist. As an executive with the Boy Scouts of America, Perry developed a strong interest in radio. He testified for the Boy Scouts before the First National Radio Conference in 1922, imploring the government to operate several broadcast stations at public expense. Upon leaving the Boy Scouts, Perry became an active correspondent on broadcasting matters, and his work was held in high regard by Clymer and the Payne Fund. By 1927 he was effectively working full time for the Payne Fund, conducting radio education research, which included the study prepared for the 1928 NEA convention.[5] The major study that resulted from his research in 1927–1929, *Radio in Education,* was published by the Payne Fund in 1929 to much acclaim. Even the NAB, the trade association of the commercial broadcasters, characterized it as a "splendid collection of information," and it was the first book on the subject in the Library of Congress.[6] Perry's judgment would guide Payne Fund activities regarding radio broadcasting for the next several years.

Following the rejection of the Payne Fund proposal by the NEA convention in 1928, Perry pursued the Payne Fund goal of establishing a School of the Air on two fronts. First, he sought and received written commitments from both of the national chains, NBC and CBS, to offer the necessary air time and facilities "without charge," for a national school of the air to be "supervised by educational authorities."[7] Second, believing the NEA or some national educational body needed to manage a national school of the air, Perry attempted to rouse enthusiasm for the project within the educational community. "I see no evidence," he concluded in 1929, "that any educational organization will do so on a national basis." A key stumbling block for getting support from educators was finding philanthropists willing to put up the money so the educators could take advantage of the time being offered by the networks. For example, in early 1929 CBS informed Perry that it would take $500,000 to pay the expenses for a school of the air on their network and advised Perry that unless he or the NEA raised the money, it would present its own scaled down educational programming. Perry spent months soliciting donations for the project in vain.[8]

By April 1929 a flustered Perry concluded that the educational programming of the chains would not be conducted under the direction of educators, leaving a situation where "schools will be flooded" with "radio programs prepared for advertising purposes rather than educational value." Clymer wrote the NEA that unless fast action was taken "the schools may well become the victims of misdirected effort carried on without educational ideals." At the Payne Fund's urging, the Department of Superintendence of the NEA passed a resolution in May calling for Secretary of the Interior Ray Lyman Wilbur—whose department housed the Office of Education—to convene a committee to address the crisis afflicting education in U.S. radio broadcasting. The Payne Fund volunteered to put up $5000 to pay for the activities of this committee.[9]

Wilbur obliged and the meeting was called for May 24, 1929, in Washington, D.C. Wilbur had served as president of Stanford University prior to accepting his cabinet post and he had been a strong proponent of educational broadcasting. Much to Wilbur's dismay, Stanford's radio station had discontinued operations due to lack of funds. He was on record as being opposed to letting radio "come entirely under the control of those who can find some greater profit in some other field than that of education."[10] The May 24 meeting included representatives of NBC and CBS who assured the secretary that they were more than willing to work with educators and to provide air time for educational broadcasting and that there was no reason for alarm. Wilbur nevertheless appointed an Advisory Committee on Education by Radio under Commissioner of Education William John Cooper on June 6 to make a "thorough fact-finding study of the situation." Dubbed the "Wilbur Committee," Cooper then appointed a subcommittee on fact-finding to conduct field research and propose solutions to the problem. Funding for this fact-finding subcommittee was provided by the Carnegie Corporation and the Penney Fund in addition to the Payne Fund.[11]

The fact-finding subcommittee included Presidents Merlin H. Aylesworth of NBC and William S. Paley of CBS and other representatives of commercial broadcasting. It had no representatives from the college and nonprofit broadcasting stations, much to the dismay of college broadcasters, although it did include some educators.[12] The Payne Fund formally "lent" the services of Armstrong Perry to the fact-finding subcommittee for the balance of 1929, as Cooper wanted the report of the fact-finding subcommittee on his desk by the end of the year. The fact-finding subcommittee was chaired by H. Robinson Shiperd, an adult educator and a member of the NEA's radio committee. Perry and the Payne Fund were unimpressed by Shiperd and the manner in which he ran the subcommittee. Perry even wrote to Shiperd's past employers to see if he had actually had the experience in higher education that he claimed. Crandall wrote to Perry that "we are having frequent evidence of extraordinary confusion, contradictions, and delays in the work of his office, and of serious cross-purposes between him and Dr. Cooper." Perry elected to conduct his research for the fact-finding subcommittee independent of Shiperd's oversight and to submit a separate report to Cooper. He spent much of the latter half of 1929 touring the United States, particularly the Midwest, interviewing educators and educational broadcasters regarding the situation.[13]

It was during his research in the summer and autumn of 1929 that Perry's stance toward U.S. broadcasting underwent two fundamental transformations. First, Perry became increasingly skeptical about the commitment of the commercial broadcasters to provide free air time for educational broadcasting to be directed by independent, nonprofit educational organizations like the NEA. "Broadcasting stations have discovered that it gives them better standing with the public to have educational programs," he wrote in October, "but as they all need to cover expenses at least and many of them are looking for profits, their educational programs take on more and more of a commercial aspect." In August he commented to Crandall that "the study of the commercialization of school radio programs alone may keep one man busy."[14] Moreover, 1929 witnessed the first great wave of commercial advertising over the air and this had ignominious implications for educational programs, as "the tendency is to crowd these into unsalable hours." Perry noted that educational broadcasting was in an unstable situation where it was "subject to being deprived of the privilege" to broadcast by the commercial station when advertisers emerged willing to pay cash for the air time. He concluded that there was the "possibility" that "all the time available on stations covering any considerable territory will be sold for advertising purposes."[15]

Second, in his travels Perry finally located a group of educators that seemed to grasp the importance of radio for education and who were willing and eager to do what was necessary to accomplish their goals: the college and university broadcasting stations. "It seems to me," he wrote to Crandall in October, "that educational programs prepared by educators and broadcast from stations over which educators have a measure of control might become ideal."[16] Perry was appalled that the FRC seemingly favored the commercial broadcasters over the college stations in the license hearings. He found the college stations were "unprotected" by the FRC as they were "attacked constantly by commercial broadcasters." By November Perry had resolved that working through the auspices of commercial broadcasters was a bankrupt strategy for educators and that the immediate solution to the problem was to preserve and develop "state and college broadcasting stations for educational purposes." Perry urged both the NEA and the Payne Fund to adopt this position.[17]

The forty-seven-page report of the fact-finding subcommittee, when presented to the Wilbur Committee as a whole on December 30, echoed many of Perry's sentiments. The report dismissed the concern of commercial broadcasters for educational programming as "they are under the necessity of selling their time" and "they appear to believe that a very little education is plenty for their audiences." The report went on to note that "it is clear that the basic purposes of the two groups [broadcasters and educators] are widely divergent" and that the commercial interests seemed intent on occupying all the frequencies: "Apparently, the only thing that could prevent this would be an early and united effort on the part of the educational forces of the country to have radio channels permanently reserved for the use of educational stations." Despite this rhetoric, the report backed off from any sweeping proposals. Immediately after observing that the "difficulty of a partnership so radical . . . is very great," the report called for the two sides to "compromise" and "work together." The report concluded that "both groups must actively and whole-heartedly put their skills at each other's service." Although these recommendations were far from threatening to the commercial broadcasters, both networks filed "minority reports" that challenged the report's attacks on the willingness of commercial broadcasters to broadcast educational programs.[18]

Perry submitted his twenty-three-page report later in the day. His report combined much of the fact-finding subcommittee's report analysis with more radical solutions. "The control of radio channels is the most important question," he informed the Wilbur Committee during his presentation, while calling for the reservation of channels for education. Perry emphasized the need for quick action to protect the remaining educational stations: "The choice evidently must be made in the immediate future and followed by prompt action. With radio channels valued at $1,000,000 or more, there would appear to be little chance of educators recovering any that now pass out of their control." Immediately after Perry spoke, network representatives challenged his analysis and dismissed his proposal as unnecessary, emphasizing that "broadcasting companies are willing to give ample time for educational programs and would exercise no censorship whatsoever."[19]

The seven-page final report, submitted to Wilbur by Cooper on February 18, 1930, accepted the commercial broadcasters' declarations of interest in educational broadcasting at face value. Cooper, though sympathetic to the plight of educational broadcasters, elected not to attack the commercial broadcasters, whose influence on the final report was unmistakable. The report recommended that a permanent radio section be established within the Office of Education to conduct research on education by radio and to "attempt to prevent conflicts between various broadcasting interests." In short, this new section would coordinate the usage of commercial facilities by educational interests; there was no mention in the report of the need to reserve channels for the control of educators.[20] To the networks, the report of the Wilbur Committee settled the matter for all time. It was now only necessary for the government to assist the educators to develop quality educational programs to be carried over the commercial stations. To Perry and the educational broadcasters, on the other hand, the Wilbur Committee report simply ignored the crisis that had brought about the creation of the committee in the first place.

Wilbur approved of Cooper establishing a radio section in the Office of Education but noted that there could be no funding until as late as June 1931. The Payne Fund then offered to "lend" Perry to Commissioner Cooper on a part-time basis to serve as the first specialist in radio education for the

Office of Education until Congress authorized a budget for the radio section. Cooper respected Perry from their dealings on the Wilbur Committee and instructed him to take charge of all of the radio correspondence and activities of the Office of Education and to keep him "up to date on radio." "This places me in a very satisfactory position," Perry wrote to Crandall. "It apparently means that we can go right on with the investigations that The Payne Fund would like to make independently if they were not made under the auspices of the Office of Education."[21] Perry used his position to co-ordinate the educational broadcasters and to promote their cause before Cooper and Wilbur. At his urging, in May 1930 Wilbur demanded that FRC Chairman Saltzman explain what the FRC could do to protect the educational broadcasters from extinction. Saltzman replied that the FRC was powerless to alter the situation under the law and that, in any case, the "best results" would be obtained by the educational interests "working out some plan" with the "existing facilities."[22]

To Perry, Saltzman's response only confirmed that "it is extremely difficult for a publicly owned station, or one owned by an educational institution, to secure anything from the Commission." If anything, the crisis for educational broadcasting had worsened in 1930; between January and the end of July, twenty-three of the remaining seventy-seven educational broadcasters had discontinued operations. Having given up on the FRC and the executive branch to enact the necessary broadcast reform, Perry spent the summer attempting to convince educators, the Payne Fund, and Cooper and Wilbur that the most pressing concern for education was to organize a group to lobby Congress to pass legislation to protect the educational stations.[23] When Judge Ira Robinson made his attack on commercial broadcasting and his call for the educators to organize a group to lobby Congress for broadcast reform in June [see p. 36], Perry convinced Cooper to have copies of the speech sent to hundreds of politicians and educators nationwide. Robinson's address contained "enough good ammunition to blow up the whole commercial radio works," Perry wrote to Crandall. "He laid bare the whole broadcasting situation and told educators what to do about it."[24]

Perry found an increasingly sympathetic audience among the educators. "The efforts of the Fund to arouse the interest of educators has succeeded tremendously," he noted. "There is a growing demand for the reservation of radio channels for education." In July, the Association of College and University Broadcast Stations (ACUBS) passed a resolution calling for Congress to pass legislation to reserve some broadcast channels for noncommercial and educational use. Perry was extending his inroads in the NEA and establishing contacts with the Association of Land Grant Colleges and Universities (ALGCU) and the National Association of State Universities (NASU).[25]

Perry found himself in a more sensitive position as he attempted to convince the Payne Fund of the need to finance an organization of educators that would challenge commercial broadcasters and seek to enact legislation to protect educational broadcasting. After all, the Payne Fund was established to be a nonpartisan philanthropy that would fund educational research, not political lobbying efforts. By July, however, Crandall wrote to Perry to tell him that there was "no opposition within the Executive Committee of the Fund" to the direction his work was taking and she urged him to formally "lay out a new plan of action more valuable than the original project." Perry met with Crandall and proposed that the Payne Fund allocate money for an educator activist group. Crandall agreed that it was within the Payne Fund's mission "to see facilities and time reserved for educational purposes free from all other considerations." Moreover, she said that such a campaign would "be a direct blow against the monopolistic intentions and efforts of commercial broadcasters and other vast industrial combinations." Crandall gave Perry's proposal an unconditional endorsement.[26]

In September one of the three Payne Fund donors made a $200,000 grant for a five-year program in educational radio along the lines proposed by Perry. The donor specified only that the money should be used to protect college and university broadcasting stations and to prevent the domination of the ether by "stations operated for profit." One Payne Fund adviser argued that this committee should be made up of "go-getters, fighters, people who were sore out of their own experiences." Crandall, Bolton, and Perry met in Washington, D.C., on September 25 to decide how to go about establishing the new group. Although the Payne Fund grant was not public knowledge, Perry was authorized to discuss it with Cooper and select leaders of educational groups to solicit their input.[27]

By this time Cooper was firmly committed to broadcast reform legislation; the effect of Perry's influence over the course of 1930 was evident. By late summer Perry had convinced Cooper of the need to convene a meeting of educational broadcasters to form an educational group. Perry kept Cooper fully apprised of his fund-raising efforts with the Payne Fund. He also organized the conference that was set for October 13 and served as the conference secretary: Cooper sent invitations to fifty-three persons, mostly representing educational groups or educational broadcasters. Perry selected these people because they "were disgruntled or not satisfied or thought that there might be something to gain by coming to an organizational meeting."[28] Representatives of the networks and the FRC were also invited and appeared, but they were in the distinct minority. Unlike the Wilbur Committee, this gathering had no interest in discussing how to improve relations between the commercial broadcasters and educators. As Commissioner Cooper stated in his opening address, the conference was called to deal with "the fear that before education knows what it wants to do commercial stations will have practically monopolized the channels open for radio broadcasting."[29]

With little suspense, the conference passed two resolutions. The first resolution called for Congress to pass a law requiring the at least 15 percent of the broadcast facilities be reserved for educational and nonprofit groups. The second resolution called for the "immediate organization" of a committee comprised of several leading educational organizations to protect and promote educational broadcasting. The resolution called for Commissioner Cooper to appoint this new committee and stated that, as the committee's first order of business, it should promote legislation to set aside 15 percent of the channels for the use of educators. In late October Cooper appointed Joy Elmer Morgan, editor of the *Journal of the National Education Association* to be chairman of the new group along with representatives from each of these nine groups: the NEA, the ACUBS, the National University Extension Association (NUEA), the NASU, the Jesuit Education Association, the ALGCU, the National Catholic Education Association, the National Council of State Superintendents, and the American Council on Education. The group represented a cross-section of U.S. higher education organizations and took the name the National Committee on Education by Radio (NCER). Thereafter, Cooper would have nothing formal to do with the NCER, stating it would be inappropriate for a government official to be a member of a group chartered to lobby Congress on a specific issue.[30]

Preliminary discussions about the Payne Fund's role in supporting the new group had taken place between the fund, Cooper and representatives of the NEA, and other educators in early October. They centered around the roles that the various existing education groups, particularly the NEA, would play in the new group. Although it was clear that the Payne Fund would support the new group, nothing was formally settled. These talks were highly confidential; for example, Joy Elmer Morgan was oblivious to the Payne Fund's involvement in the October conference and had no idea that there was such a large block of money already set aside for the new group. Negotiations to formally establish the Payne Fund as the sponsor of the NCER commenced in earnest in November and December.[31] The Payne Fund insisted that the NCER be a legitimate organization managed by the nine educational groups designated by Cooper in October, and that it not be a front group for the fund. As Crandall put it, the Payne Fund wanted to avoid "the untenable position of undertaking to do for educators what educators are now prepared to do for themselves with financial assistance from the Payne Fund."[32] For the duration of the NCER's existence the role of the Payne Fund as benefactor would be accorded very little publicity, although there was no attempt to keep it secret. At its first meeting on December 30, 1930, the NCER formally resolved to ask the Payne Fund for a five-year $200,000 grant. The Payne Fund's Executive Committee approved the request on January 20, 1931.[33]

This was not lost on the commercial broadcasters. Throughout the spring and summer, NBC and CBS had attempted to impress Cooper with their plans for educational broadcasting. Perry attended these sessions and his skepticism toward the commercial broadcasters convinced Cooper that these measures would not suffice. In November the NAB's annual convention formally resolved against the proposed legislation to set aside 15 percent of the channels for nonprofit broadcasters. Concurrently, CBS vice-president and NAB lobbyist Henry A. Bellows wrote presidential aide Walter H. Newton to protest the "movement" for the 15 percent legislation "apparently on foot, sponsored chiefly by a certain Armstrong Perry of the Interior Department." Newton queried Wilbur regarding Perry's activities, who in turn queried Cooper. Cooper came to Perry's defense. "The radio matter is an exceedingly complicated one. It must be kept in mind that all other countries," Cooper informed Wilbur on December 8, "have retained broadcasting as a government monopoly." The Radio Act of 1927, despite progressive aims, "is working to the advantage of the commercial broadcasters and to the disadvantage of the small educational station." Cooper concluded that he "should like to see the whole subject debated before Congress with a view of ascertaining whether or not the present basis is the best basis for promoting the public interest."[34]

In the opinion of the Payne Fund's Executive Committee, the establishment of the NCER constituted "the fulfillment of the Payne Fund's objectives and efforts over a period of approximately three and one half years." One prominent educator wrote to Clymer congratulating him for "the splendid step forward" the Payne Fund had taken in financing the NCER, stating it "will go down in history as one of the milestones of educational achievement."[35] Perry could not help but see the irony in the Payne Fund's turn to sponsoring the NCER from an original program that intended to promote a national School of the Air over the commercial chains. In a letter sent in early March 1931 to executives at CBS, Perry noted:

> I certainly am aware that your company holds a very vigorous opinion against the setting aside of certain channels for educational broadcasting. This opinion has helped to turn hundreds of thousands of dollars of philanthropic money, which was appropriated for the purpose of developing public interest in your educational programs and those of other companies into other channels where it is developing a nationwide reaction against commercial broadcasting.[36]

The National Committee on Education by Radio

The NCER was formally chartered so that the nine constituent groups would each assign a representative to the group. These representatives would meet four to six times annually with each of the nine representatives having one vote in basic policy decisions. Joy Elmer Morgan was the NEA representative and was formally elected as the NCER's Chairman. The full-time staff was comprised of Tracy Tyler, although the Payne Fund "lent" the services of Armstrong Perry to the NCER for most of the group's first five years. The NCER regarded itself as far more than a body representing the interests of existing educational broadcasters; after all, member group ACUBS, which would be rechristened as the National Association of Educational Broadcasters in 1934, was already in existence for that purpose. To Arthur Crane, NCER representative from the NASU and president of the University of Wyoming, the NCER had the "large function" of arousing "a healthy sentiment towards the improvement of radio broadcasting as a great means of public communication." This task was made all the more important and difficult due to the "opposition" of the "entrenched commercial interests."[37] The very idea of cooperation between educators and commercial broadcasters was dismissed as "not possible." "That practice has been tried for nearly a decade and has proved unworkable," Morgan stated in 1931. "It is no longer open to discussion."[38]

It was Morgan who gave the NCER its public identity. He brought to the NCER a missionary zeal for reforming U.S. broadcasting. A devotee of nineteenth century educator Horace Mann and strongly influenced by the Midwest populist tradition, Morgan had been active in the public utilities movement in addition to serving as editor of the *Journal of the National Education Association* since 1920. Perry was enthusiastic when Morgan agreed to serve as chairman of the committee, informing Crandall that "Morgan has been restless for a long time to do something for education by radio."[39] Morgan had worked with Perry in his capacity with the NEA. In 1928 Morgan spoke before the NAB convention to urge the commercial broadcasters to assist in an ambitious program to provide an hour of daily instruction by radio for the nation's public schools. Like Perry, Morgan soon became disillusioned with the commitment of the commercial broadcasters to the cause of education.[40] Morgan's biographer noted that for the next four years Morgan "studied, planned, wrote, spoke, ate, and slept radio." Morgan could be stirringly eloquent in his advocacy of educational broadcasting. "When we speak of education's rights on the air," he noted, in contrast to the FRC's notion that any broadcasting not pursued for profit was selfish "propaganda," "we are not talking about the needs and wishes of some special group. We are talking about the needs of the people themselves."[41]

Morgan shifted the fight for broadcast reform to a broader political plane and cast the ensuing battle with commercial broadcasters in almost apocalyptic terms:

> As a result of radio broadcasting, there will probably develop during the twentieth century either chaos or a world-order of civilization. Whether it shall be one or the other will depend largely upon whether broadcasting be used as a tool of education or as an instrument of selfish greed. So far, our American radio interests have thrown their major influence on the side of greed. . . . There

has never been in the entire history of the United States an example of mis-management and lack of vision so colossal and far-reaching in its consequences as our turning of the radio channels almost exclusively into commercial hands.

To Morgan, commercial control of the ether had significance far beyond the immediate impact upon college broadcasters; it implied a private self-serving dictatorship over a vital public resource that threatened the foundations of a democratic society.[42] "I believe we are dealing here," he informed the 1932 convention of the NUEA, "with one of the most crucial issues that was ever presented to civilization at any time in its entire history." In the very depths of the Great Depression, Morgan would write that America cannot "solve any of its major political problems without first solving the radio problem."[43]

Morgan threw himself into the radio fight even before the NCER had been officially established, sending thousands of letters to state secretaries, state commissioners, state superintendents, educators, and politicians attacking commercial broadcasting and promoting the importance of broadcast reform in October and November 1930. Over the next five years, Morgan, Tyler, and Perry would make hundreds of public addresses and write scores of articles along these lines. In early January 1931 Morgan drafted the text of a bill that would require the FRC to set aside 15 percent of the channels for nonprofit, educational broadcasting and he convinced Senator Simeon Fess (R-Ohio) to introduce the measure. Morgan was never especially enthusiastic about what would be termed the "Fess bill," characterizing it as "an emergency and not a final measure."[44] He was on record as being in favor in principle of establishing a public, noncommercial network along the lines of the BBC, perhaps even as a monopoly as in Britain, although he recognized that this was not NCER policy and acted accordingly.[45]

Relations between the NCER and the commercial broadcasters were antagonistic from the outset. As Tyler put it, "the commercial broadcasters thru [sic] the chains and the National Association of Broadcasters, their trade organization, are doing all that they can to wreck the educational stations." The NAB formally resolved against the 15 percent measure at its November 1930 convention, even before the measure had been introduced in Congress.[46] The commercial broadcasting trade publication *Broadcasting* routinely characterized the NCER as "a group of misguided pedagogues" who were "professional reformers" with "silly demands." In one editorial, *Broadcasting* described the NCER as "childish" and as "a racket by which a few zealots want to justify the jobs they are holding." At no point is there any sense that the commercial broadcasters took the concerns of the NCER seriously. "Interests that have stood passively by and were unwilling to bear the trials of pioneering," [sic] the NAB newsletter *Broadcasters' News Bulletin* stated concerning the NCER, "are now endeavoring to invade the broadcast band at the expense of the existing stations." Morgan, given his flamboyant rhetoric, was a particular target of commercial broadcasters' derision. *Broadcasting* dismissed him as "coming from the ranks of primary school men," who "had to be fighting something all the time" with an "unreasoning sort of crusading."[47]

The day-to-day administration of the NCER was left to Research Director and Secretary Tyler, who earned a Ph.D. in education at Columbia University in 1931. His dissertation on the use of radio by land-grant institutions brought him to the NCER's attention. Tyler had many functions at the NCER, including that of coordinating research on radio education. The Payne Fund was insistent that the NCER consider this part of its mandate, and research was included in the NCER budget beginning in 1932. Tyler responded with several research projects. He also established an informal network of all the educational broadcasters and coordinated the sharing of programs between them. This was a popular function and Tyler arranged to have scores of programs distributed; in general, he coordinated the distribution of series of programs produced at the larger college stations like Wisconsin, Illinois, and Ohio State to the smaller college stations at no charge.[48]

Tyler's most pressing function at the NCER, however, was to edit its weekly bulletin, *Education by Radio,* which commenced operations in February 1931 with a press run of 2,090. The purpose of *Education by Radio* was to provide "reliable information" on "the many aspects of the radio problem." Morgan argued that the publication was necessary because "misinformation has been spread so deliberately by selfish and greedy interests that even public officials have found it difficult to get the facts." The publication, always sent free to a controlled mailing list of educators, broadcasters, and politicians, had a circulation of 7,000 in 1932 and reached its peak of 10,085 in 1934, by which time it was issued twice monthly. *Education by Radio* was four pages long and offered original articles along with reprints of speeches and articles from other publications.[49]

Perry had two important functions with the NCER. First, he became the NCER's recognized authority on international broadcasting and foreign broadcasting systems. He regarded the commercial broadcasters as "lying outrageously about the nature and results of foreign systems," almost all of which were nonprofit and noncommercial.[50] Perry spent three months in Europe in the autumn of 1931 conducting a survey of European broadcasting systems and establishing ties with foreign broadcasting officials. He became especially close with officials at the BBC. "There is no indication that the 'American Plan' is wanted in any other country, either by governments, companies, or listeners," Perry concluded, and "the world is having a quiet laugh at our expense."[51] He also represented the NCER at the International Radio Telegraphic Conference in Madrid in 1932 and at the North American Radio Conference in Mexico City in 1933, hoping to provide a voice on behalf of noncommercial broadcasting to the network-dominated U.S. delegations.[52]

Second, Perry left his post in the Office of Education in 1931 to become director of the NCER's Service Bureau, the purpose of which was to represent educational stations in hearings before the FRC. The Service Bureau kept offices in the National Press Building, within walking distance of the FRC headquarters, whereas the balance of the NCER's activities were conducted out of offices in the NEA Building. For example, between February 1, 1932, and September 26, 1934, there were 1,426 applications by commercial interests before the FRC for the use of frequencies occupied at least partially by educational broadcasters. In any given month, as many as one-half of the educational broadcasters would face a commercial challenge before the FRC. In these cases Perry would notify the stations of the impending hearings and acquaint them with the issues involved.[53] At Perry's insistence, the NCER hired Horace Lohnes in 1932 on a part-time basis to act as the Service Bureau's counsel and to represent college stations at no charge in FRC hearings. In his first six months on the job, Lohnes handled fourteen cases before the FRC and advised many other stations; he would remain on the NCER payroll until 1935. The Service Bureau was credited with helping to stabilize the number of college broadcasting stations by the end of 1932.[54]

Perry also served as the liaison between the NCER and the Payne Fund offices in New York. Perry filed regular confidential reports on the NCER to Crandall, who would also meet with Morgan a few times each year to assess the NCER's performance. Bolton would also meet with Morgan once or twice each year; she would admit to Morgan she and the fund had a deep interest in the NCER's work. "We are not like other groups, we of the Payne Fund. We are keenly interested in every possible angle of the activities which we sponsor and we like to be known for our ideas as well as our money." Nevertheless, Bolton was adamant that the Payne Fund "emphatically" disavowed "the least intention or desire to influence the policies of your Committee even when our judgments may be at variance."[55] The Payne Fund kept its word in this respect. When Perry made it clear by 1933 that there was considerable "dissatisfaction within the Committee itself regarding" Morgan's performance as chairman, Crandall and Bolton remained in the background, deeming it inappropriate to intervene in NCER internal affairs. At most, Crandall reaffirmed to Morgan that the NCER would not receive any additional Payne Fund money after the initial five-year grant was exhausted, as had been the stated plan from the outset.[56]

To some extent the discontent within the NCER and also the dissatisfaction the Payne Fund increasingly felt with the NCER's performance was due to the NCER's inability to organize the educational community solidly in its camp. It was true that virtually all major educational organizations routinely passed resolutions in support of the NCER; indeed, some of these groups, like the National Congress of Parents and Teachers, passed resolutions calling for the complete nationalization of radio broadcasting. It was also true that a 1933 NCER survey of 631 college administrators found that only 4.4 percent expressed themselves as "being satisfied with the system of radio now in use."[57] Nevertheless, some elements of the educational community continued to work with commercial broadcasters and disliked the NCER's approach because it "would precipitate a long and bitter fight and would alienate the friendship of the commercial stations." Others, like ACUBS Director R. C. Higgy, thought educators should eschew the "aggressive demands for the rights of College and University broadcasters, as exemplified by the articles of Perry, Morgan, Tyler," as "we can get more by being friendly to the big commercial broadcasters." Still other educators, perhaps a majority, remained seemingly disinterested in the debate.[58]

National Advisory Council on Radio in Education

Part of the NCER's difficulty in unifying the educational community on behalf of broadcast reform stemmed from the fact that it was not the only national organization concerned with education on radio. In 1930 the National Advisory Council on Radio in Education (NACRE) was established by the American Association for Adult Education (AAAE), which itself had been established by the Carnegie Corporation in 1926. President Frederick Keppel of the Carnegie Corporation worked closely with Owen D. Young and NBC executives as plans for the group were developed. The NACRE was established to provide a "liaison between education and the industry" and, unlike the NCER, it favored cooperation between educators and commercial broadcasters. The NUEA radio committee noted that the NCER and the NACRE "presumably represent the same faction, and yet the two are quite far apart in so far as any cooperation is concerned."[59] There existed among the public and educators what Erik Barnouw has termed a "glorious confusion" about what each of them stood for. Even some of the scholarship on this period has failed to differentiate between the two groups.[60]

The Carnegie Corporation and the AAAE were unabashed proponents of commercial broadcasting, without any interest in nonprofit broadcasting stations. The Carnegie Corporation envisioned a bold plan whereby it would provide the networks with educational programming, which was a distinct contrast to the Payne Fund position that educational broadcasting had to be under the unconditional control of legitimate educational organizations.[61] The 1929 AAAE convention praised the NBC and CBS for their "generous" offers of airtime for educational purposes and concluded that "evidence abounds that both the educational and industry groups are one in the principle objectives of encouraging the broadcasting of educational material of high grade and proven worth." In early 1929 the AAAE and the Carnegie Corporation reached a tentative agreement with NBC to establish a group that would provide the network with high-grade educational broadcasts. The Carnegie Corporation contributed $15,000 to the AAAE to conduct a six-month study of the broadcasting industry to see if there was general support for the idea. The study was canceled when Secretary Wilbur established his committee to study educational broadcasting; the AAAE contacted Commissioner Cooper shortly thereafter and offered its time and money to assist in the Wilbur Committee study. Cooper agreed to have the AAAE take responsibility for all research concerning adult education.[62]

Once the Wilbur Committee had completed its work, in early 1930, the NACRE was formally established with funding by the Carnegie Corporation and John D. Rockefeller, Jr., and a prestigious board of directors that included Robert M. Hutchins, president of the University of Chicago, Owen Young, Robert Millikan, president of the California Institute of Technology, and Walter Dill Scott, president of Northwestern University. The NACRE saw its mission as that of providing the broadcasting industry with a "representative organization to which it can turn for advice and counsel in educational matters."[63] The director of the NACRE was Levering Tyson, an adult educator from Columbia University who had coordinated Columbia's educational broadcasts over WEAF between 1925 and 1928. Ironically, Tyson acknowledged that the Columbia–WEAF program collapsed because "changes in the policy of the station after the commercial side of broadcasting became so highly developed, resulted in a complete abandonment of the whole educational experiment idea which we had." This "great disappointment" had little effect on Tyson's outlook; the primary work of the NACRE would be to provide the networks, primarily NBC, with educational programs in the early 1930s.[64] NBC even regarded the NACRE informally as its educational "branch." Merlin Aylesworth praised the NACRE's work as being "of the greatest importance in the educational field."[65]

To Tyson, the final recommendations of the Wilbur Committee provided a virtual mandate for the NACRE's establishment. Hence, when Cooper called for the Chicago conference in October 1930, Tyson considered the move an "inexplicable stab in the back" that only undercut the NACRE's efforts to create cooperation between educators and commercial broadcasters. Tyson was invited to Chicago as the NACRE's representative only to be subjected to considerable criticism for his "cooperative" approach to the commercial broadcasters. Cooper's memo to Wilbur regarding the conference emphasized that there were "several expressions of distrust" toward the NACRE during the deliberations. Tyson acknowledged that "many of those present" at the Chicago conference believed the NACRE had been created by the radio trust "as a smokescreen for its monopolistic tendencies."[66] One participant insisted that the NACRE be forbidden to participate in the new NCER because its approach would "injure the whole movement." Tyson, however, had no interest in getting involved with a group like the NCER. The NACRE was formally committed to "absolute neutrality" on policy issues, especially the "controversial question of facilities."[67]

Tyson rigorously presented the NACRE as being "determined not to enter" the controversy rampant in radio. Rather, the NACRE would "maintain a neutral position," reveal "a lot of courage," and "sit on the fence and be shot at from both sides."[68] There is little evidence, however, that Tyson and the NACRE were ever "shot at" by the commercial broadcasters, at least in any public pronouncements. The commercial broadcasting trade press routinely praised the NACRE for being "impartial and cooperative" with "its object being pure research rather than blind antagonism." On occasion, attacks on the NCER were accompanied by praise for the NACRE as the "able" and legitimate representative of U.S. higher education.[69] "The way the magazine 'Radio Digest' and some of the other organs of the commercial industry keep 'playing up' the Council," the NCER's Tyler wrote Tyson in December 1931, "makes those who have the best interests of educational stations at heart feel that there must be some reason back of this support."[70] The commercial broadcasters and the trade press also provided considerable and favorable attention to the NACRE's activities and its lavish annual conventions, which, as Tyler commented, were "pretty well 'packed' with commercial people." In short, to the commercial broadcasters, the NACRE was the solution to the problem of education on radio.[71]

Moreover, Tyson generally exonerated the commercial broadcasters for the crisis surrounding educational broadcasting; he accepted the commercial broadcasters' argument that the core problem with education on radio was that educators had little idea how to produce effective programs. Tyson was less charitable toward those critical of commercial broadcasting and, particularly, the NCER, which he claimed "wasted time in a fruitless and unwarranted disagreement . . . in a destructive attack upon the American broadcasting system." Tyson would go before the NAB convention in 1931 and accuse the critics of broadcasting of "a lot of nauseating loose talk and a lot of uninformed writing." He stated that "the time has come for educators and critics to quit telling the broadcasters how rotten they are."[72] In the NACRE's private communications, Tyson was even less sparing. The NCER, he wrote to Keppel, was "a belligerent and propagandistic organization which has allied itself with every disgruntled element appearing in the field." To Tyson, the NCER's "executives have attempted in every way to throw sand into our machinery."[73] In Tyson's view, the commercial system was entrenched and the wise move for educators would be to recognize the situation and act accordingly.

The NCER revealed similar contempt for the NACRE, although it, too, maintained a mostly cordial veneer to its relations in public. Perry expressed the sentiments of all regarding Tyson's constant proclamations of "neutrality" on the topic of broadcast reform: "We know how far from neutral he is!" Many educators affiliated with the NCER nonetheless regarded Tyson as honorable. Tyler, on the other hand, termed him "a pretty slippery individual."[74] One Payne Fund adviser called the NACRE "a smokescreen to further the efforts of the radio monopolies in gobbling up broadcasting." Most of the educators associated with the NCER, however, admitted that the NACRE had a genuine interest in providing educational programs on radio. The educators associated with the NACRE were the "unwitting patsies" of the commercial broadcasters, as one educator put it, who "just couldn't turn down all the good money" made available to them to work within the existing system.[75] Perry and Morgan conceded that the NACRE put many "very good" educational programs on the air.[76]

More broadly, the tension between the NCER and the NACRE reflected the conflict between the Carnegie Corporation and the Payne Fund over which organization, and which approach, would prove dominant in determining the course of education by radio. Bolton had studied the Carnegie Corporation's activities in 1930 when determining whether there was a need for a group like the one Perry was proposing. She concluded that the NACRE "is not particularly popular with the educators of this country."[77] As Morgan put it, the NACRE was a "privately appointed" group with no formal ties to the educational community, "founded by Carnegie and Rockefeller funds." *Education by Radio* characterized the Carnegie Corporation as the "enemy of free democratic education."[78] Both sides recognized that by sponsoring the NCER, the Payne Fund was effectively repudiating the NACRE's co-operative approach toward the commercial broadcasters. "If Payne Fund money was not available this whole agitation," a distraught Tyson wrote to Keppel, "would die from lack of nourishment." Accordingly, Tyson spent considerable effort attempting to "shut off this source of Payne Fund money" by continually attempting "the possibility of bringing Mrs. Bolton into our camp."[79] Bolton spurned Tyson's overtures to serve on the NACRE's board of directors.[80]

If anything, Bolton and the Payne Fund were increasingly repulsed by the NACRE's approach throughout the early 1930s, their occasional dissatisfaction with the NCER's ineffectuality notwithstanding. The Payne Fund was angry at what it regarded as the NACRE's (and Carnegie Corporation's) stated ambition to become "the mouthpiece of all education" with regard to radio, leaving the Payne Fund no apparent role. "Tyson's pandering to the commercial interests" is blatant, Crandall wrote to Bolton in 1932, "and his intellectual dishonesty toward the educational cause" is "clear."[81] The Payne Fund regarded the NACRE as an unequivocal ally of the commercial broadcasters, especially NBC. "Anything told to Dr. Tyson," one Payne

Fund memo noted in 1930, "went promptly to" the executives at NBC. "The tie-up there seems close and getting closer." Indeed, Tyson had confidential correspondence with NBC in the early 1930s in which he would share this analysis of various educators' stances toward the commercial networks and toward the broadcast reform movement.[82]

To leave the discussion of Tyson and the NACRE at this point, however, would be doing both an injustice. Tyson certainly did not view his role at that of being a "bagman" for the commercial broadcasters. In correspondence with Keppel, Tyson was candid in his appraisal of the status quo. "Because of the inane advertising," he wrote in 1933, "there are few countries in which so many poor programs are broadcast."[83] His correspondence with NBC executives reveals a man who, having accepted the status quo as unalterable if not necessarily the best possible system, was willing to confer public relations benefits upon the network in return for having educational programming broadcast. This was the explicit quid pro quo that both sides recognized from the outset. Tyson acknowledged that NBC and CBS "are not interested" in the NACRE "from any educational motive." As Keppel concluded, NBC "will be useful to the NACRE just so long as the NACRE is useful to it."[84] Tyson attempted to form strategic alliances within NBC with those considered more sympathetic to education, although even network employees conceded that "those favoring education are in the minority." He refused to back down from his stance that educational programming should have no commercial sponsorship. Tyson was also willing to fight the network executives whenever, as was occasionally the case, NACRE programs were canceled or switched to less desirable times because advertisers purchased the time slots that had been assigned to the NACRE.[85]

As such, Tyson and the NACRE were regarded with disdain in NBC's internal correspondence. After spelling out the attributes of good radio programs, one NBC executive noted that "none of these are to be found generally in NACRE programs." In a letter defending the level of educational broadcasting in the United States, Aylesworth confided to the BBC's managing director, Sir John Reith, that NACRE programs were "dull and poorly prepared."[86] Tyson's commitment to commercial broadcasting was continually questioned by NBC executives, and internal memos were invariably exchanged following any public utterance by Tyson that could be construed as being even mildly critical of the existing order. One executive even termed him a "red," much to Tyson's own amusement.[87] The most bitter internal exchange followed a speech by Tyson in 1934 when he rather uncharacteristically asserted that the "profit motive" in broadcasting was "generally inconsistent with the public welfare." Aylesworth finally had to instruct his executives to keep the issue in perspective: "Mr. Tyson is a good fellow and his motives are not to be questioned."[88]

The *Ventura Free Press* Radio Campaign

The Payne Fund's sponsorship of broadcast reform did not end with its grant to the NCER. It would also spend nearly $50,000 between July 1931 and the summer of 1933 for an anticommercial broadcasting campaign conducted under the auspices of the *Ventura Free Press,* a small daily newspaper in Ventura, California, just north of Los Angeles.[89] Just as Armstrong Perry had counseled Bolton, Crandall, and the Payne Fund of the need to support a group like the NCER, H. O. Davis pushed the Payne Fund to subsidize this campaign.

Davis was a successful business executive and entrepreneur with experience in the automobile industry and in managing several motion picture studios, including the Universal Film Company and the Mack Sennett Film Company, between 1915 and 1920. His forte was reorganizing stagnant enterprises. Davis served as editor of the *Ladies Home Journal* beginning in 1920, and as an executive for the Curtis Publishing Company and the Hearst newspaper chain until his retirement at the age of 48 in 1925. Davis was civic-minded as well. He directed the San Diego Exposition of 1915 and was chairman of the Building Committee for the 1932 Los Angeles Summer Olympics. Davis was brought to the attention of the Payne Fund by William H. Short, who had the same relationship to the fund for its film activities as Perry did for its radio activities.[90]

Early in 1930 Davis proposed that the Payne Fund provide seed money for a magazine to be intended for working-class young women. This magazine would consist primarily of fiction, but would "gradually and inconspicuously" integrate "literary, educational, and cultural features" once a readership had been established. Davis said the aim was to publish "the *Saturday Evening Post* for young women." The Payne Fund approved his proposal in principle and it authorized Davis to study the matter further and attempt to locate additional financial support. More important, Crandall and Bolton were so impressed by their dealings with Davis that he was elected to the Payne Fund's board of directors for a three-year term in July 1930. Davis's plans for the women's magazine, however, were indefinitely postponed in early 1931 due to the "general business depression."[91]

As a Payne Fund board member, however, Davis was becoming aware of its heavy involvement in radio, which Crandall informed him was "the most impressive example" of what the Payne Fund could accomplish. In May 1931 Davis conceived of a plan to have the Payne Fund subsidize a campaign, distinct from that of the NCER, to lobby on behalf of broadcast reform before Congress and to generate popular opposition to the status quo. Davis also recommended that the campaign be conducted through a newspaper he had just purchased, the *Ventura Free Press.* He added that the campaign seek to enlist the support of newspaper publishers because they should be sympathetic to a campaign for "the removal of advertising from the air." The Payne Fund approved the proposal in June, liking the idea of marshaling additional resources to the fight for broadcast reform. It regarded the *Free Press* radio campaign as a whirlwind effort that could accomplish its aims within six months. Davis hired two journalists, Walter Woehlke, former editor of *Sunset Magazine* and Harold Carew, former editorial writer for the *Boston Globe* and the *Christian Science Monitor,* to work full-time on the campaign out of the *Ventura Free Press* offices.[92]

The Payne Fund made two revisions to Davis's proposal. First, it provided Davis and the *Ventura Free Press* campaign with the services of S. Howard Evans, who "would handle the political side of the radio fight." Evans had come to the Payne Fund as an assistant to President Clymer in 1930 after working in various administrative positions following his 1926 graduation from Syracuse University. Like Davis and Carew, Evans was a "Bull Moose" Republican, which certainly did not upset his chances of success with Bolton and Crandall, who held his judgment in high regard.[93] "We are all constantly and increasingly impressed with his political wisdom," Crandall wrote to Davis in 1931, "and with his calm assurance and his deliberate action." Evans would serve as Davis's lobbyist in Washington, D.C., and as his primary activist among the newspaper publishers. Evans would acknowledge "confidentially" his belief that "radio should be and ultimately must be taken over by the Government," although this was not the formal *Ventura Free Press* position.[94]

Second, the Payne Fund insisted that its support for the *Ventura Free Press* radio campaign be kept strictly confidential, stating only that it might be embarrassing for Bolton's congressman husband as well as the Payne Fund were it public knowledge that the group was funding such a controversy-laden enterprise. This secret was kept rigorously; Representative Bolton and even the NCER, aside from Perry, were unaware of the Payne Fund role in the *Ventura Free Press* campaign. Evans moved out of the Payne Fund offices and worked out of his home in Garden City, Long Island, for the next two years. To the public, Evans was no longer an employee of the Payne Fund; rather, he was the special editorial representative of the *Ventura Free Press*. In truth, however, he remained on the Payne Fund payroll.[95]

The *Ventura Free Press* radio campaign was launched in July 1931. "The objective of the campaign, as I understand it," Woehlke wrote in a memo, "is the complete overthrow of the present system." This campaign was seen as taking place on three fronts: in Congress, among newspaper publishers, and in the general public.[96] "For ten years the public has been taught by the commercial broadcasters, with the whole-hearted assistance of all American newspapers, to believe that the system of broadcasting supported entirely by paid advertising, is the very best system in the universe and cannot be improved upon," a Woehlke memo noted. "This opinion is wide-spread and tenacious." The fundamental aim of the *Ventura Free Press* radio campaign was to change this "wide-spread opinion," provide the "leadership" to direct the burgeoning "rebellion" against the status quo, and thereby make it possible for "radical improvements in broadcasting" to take place. Davis was unequivocal about the goal of the campaign in his first general mailing. The campaign was a "national attack on the radio combine" with the goal of the "removal of advertising from the air," along with the elimination of the overall "exploitation" of radio broadcasting for "private profit."[97]

The *Ventura Free Press* campaign had many components. Evans guided the lobbying efforts with Congress and newspaper publishers, staying in almost daily contact with Woehlke. Woehlke and Carew wrote monthly "anticommercialism radio bulletins," which were signed by Davis and sent to a mailing list of 1,950 daily newspaper publishers and another 1,000 people connected with the newspaper industry. Woehlke and Carew also provided a free news service to between 300 and 700 newspapers between 1931 and 1933; the columns generally covered broadcasting. Consequently, the *Ventura Free Press* dubbed itself the "most widely quoted newspaper west of the Rockies." On average, the radio campaign sent out nearly 9,000 pieces of circular mail and 250 personal letters each month in the first fourteen months of the campaign.[98] The crowning achievement of the campaign may have been the publication of *The Empire of the Air* in January 1932 by the *Free Press*. This was a 200-page critique of commercial broadcasting that was also distributed in sixty-one installments to newspapers nationwide. According to Davis, some 400 of them published the series in its entirety. Davis called *The Empire of the Air* the "textbook" of the broadcast reform movement. In 1933, the *Ventura Free Press* would publish and distribute a study based on a one-day survey of the programming of 206 commercial stations nationwide. It found "an astonishing amount of duplication" and "monotonous mediocrity." Bolton wrote to Davis that the *Ventura Free Press* radio campaign "gives such evidence of activity that I am breathless!"[99]

This activity did not escape the attention of the commercial broadcasters. *Broadcasting* termed one "anticommercialism radio bulletin," which provided a sixteen-point program for newspaper publishers to coordinate and stimulate anticommercial broadcasting activity in their communities, as "probably the most vicious campaign ever leveled against American radio."[100] *Broadcasting* termed Davis the "self-appointed crusader against radio broadcasting" from "that unimportant suburban Los Angeles newspaper" and assumed he was launching the campaign merely to "shake down" one of the networks for a lucrative station affiliation for his newspaper. "Mr. Davis can save himself much time, effort and money by acting on the matter of a radio affiliation—if anyone will affiliate with him—right now."[101]

David Sarnoff wrote a confidential memo to Aylesworth on the *Ventura*

Free Press campaign, commenting "I think it merits your serious attention." NBC would go to great lengths to undercut the *Free Press* campaign among newspaper publishers, as will be discussed in Chapter 6.[102] Through six newspaper publishers who also owned NBC-affiliated radio stations, Aylesworth and NBC executives surreptitiously monitored the *Free Press* campaign. One publisher even solicited a friend to do some "detective work" and determine Davis's "real motive" for launching the fight against commercial broadcasting. This undercover approach proved unsuccessful.[103] Aylesworth, like *Broadcasting,* exhibited contempt for Davis and his enterprise, stating that "the boys at Ventura" had simply "worked up" a "racketeering scheme" so they could get in on the broadcasting riches. "It is a low game as you know," he wrote to one newspaper publisher.[104]

Two problems plagued the *Ventura Free Press* radio campaign from the outset. First, many important newspaper publishers demanded that the *Free Press* provide an alternative model for broadcasting and not merely criticize the existing system. This was a sticky issue, perhaps constituting the Achilles' heel of the broadcast reform movement as a whole throughout the early 1930s. Davis, like Evans, was sympathetic to establishing a BBC-type system in the United States, and he considered government ownership of all of broadcasting as "distinctly preferable to a private monopoly." Deeming government ownership not in "favor with a majority of the people," however, Davis and the *Ventura Free Press* simply proposed a variety of schemes to sharply reduce the amount of direct advertising and to reserve channels for nonprofit broadcasters. As such, Davis was unable to determine a system that would provide adequate resources to nonprofit, nonadvertising-supported broadcasting facilities.[105]

Second, many publishers regarded the *Ventura Free Press* radio campaign with suspicion, thinking "that anyone endeavoring to solve the radio problem without asking them to cough up, must have some ulterior motive." One publisher told Evans that he "could not understand how any west-coast publisher," let alone the *Ventura Free Press,* "could afford an eastern representative." When Woehlke traveled to Oklahoma to talk to newspaper publishers, he was asked four times in one day, "Where does Davis get the money?"[106] The *Free Press* editor attempted to explain Davis's sponsorship of a national radio campaign at the 1931 American Newspaper Publishers Association convention as a means to enhance the "prestige" of his admittedly nondescript newspaper; similarly, Davis would provide this explanation in his correspondence with NBC's mole newspaper publishers. This explanation, however, was simply not accepted. The California Editorial Association refused even to consider a *Ventura Free Press* resolution for broadcast reform at its annual meeting in 1931 until it found out "who was supporting" the *Free Press* campaign and what they "wanted out of it."[107] By September 1931, Davis was imploring Bolton and Crandall to let him say "frankly" that the *Free Press* had a "grant from the Payne Fund to assist it in clarifying the radio situation." Bolton and Crandall refused to budge. Finally, Evans worked out a compromise. In confidential memoranda to selected persistent newspaper publishers, the Payne Fund would "admit" that Evans was on the Payne Fund payroll. Otherwise, however, all sides would insist that the *Ventura Free Press* radio campaign was being directed and paid for by Davis without any connection to the fund.[108]

The secret relationship of the Payne Fund to the *Ventura Free Press* radio campaign did not make it any easier for the *Free Press* to coordinate its activities with the NCER. As it developed, these two groups had strained relations from the outset. Davis wrote to Bolton that he wanted Morgan and the NCER to "openly endorse the Free Press campaign and aggressively work with it."[109] Unfortunately for Davis, relations soured even before the *Free Press* radio campaign was launched. "It soon became evident," Crandall wrote to Perry regarding a meeting between Davis and Morgan in June 1931, "that there was no possibility of a meeting of the minds between him [Morgan] on the one hand and Mr. Davis and Mr. Evans on the other." Whereas the press campaign was "an immediate emergency program," Morgan argued that "conservative bodies of educators cannot be forced to act in any such way." Instead, Morgan envisioned a "three to five year project of slow, steady infiltration of ideas and plans."[110]

Thereafter, Davis, Woehlke, and Evans maintained a fairly distant working relationship with the NCER, but their internal correspondence was littered with disparaging comments about the educators, whom they regarded as having no political savvy or aggressiveness whatsoever. "I really doubt if you can expect much of him," Evans wrote to Woehlke regarding Morgan, "because after all he is only a Ph.D. He simply has no news sense." "We are getting neither cooperation nor support from Mr. Joy Morgan," Davis wrote to Crandall. "He is not of much help."[111] "The whole educational crowd," a frustrated Woehlke wrote to Evans after Tyler failed to mail him a report as he had promised, "is a bunch of theorists with no idea how to run a publicity campaign. Tell them to jump off the North end of a ferry boat going South."[112]

In the squabble between the NCER and the *Ventura Free Press*, the Payne Fund's sympathies tended toward the *Free Press;* some of its ultimate dissatisfaction with Morgan and the NCER may well be traceable to this episode. Bolton followed the *Free Press* campaign with a singular devotion, reading copies of all the correspondence exchanged between Crandall and Evans and Woehlke, and clipping all the *Ventura Free Press* editorials for a scrapbook. She was not, however, uncritical toward the *Free Press* itself. In her enthusiasm at Woehlke's and Carew's editorials, she requested that copies of the entire newspaper be mailed to her. Bolton was "quite shocked at the character of the paper itself." She was "surprised and disappointed" to find what was "decidedly," in her opinion, "a sensational sheet with what seemed" a "quite unnecessary emphasis on crime." Moreover, Davis had hired his daughter to write a column for the *Free Press,* which "distressed" Bolton. It expressed "provincial, flippant, and even destructive criticisms on the most weighty issues of the day."[113] Perhaps the tenor of the *Free Press* influenced some of Woehlke's and Carew's editorials; the Payne Fund attorney warned them to tone down their rhetoric regarding the "radio trust" for fear of potential libel suits. It became standard procedure to have the Payne Fund attorney review any potentially controversial *Free Press* radio writings.[114]

As it would develop, neither the NCER nor the *Ventura Free Press* radio campaign would prove successful, although both groups had a discernible effect upon the debate over broadcasting in the early 1930s. The Payne Fund devoted over $250,000 to the cause of broadcast reform during this period, with the lofty aim of mobilizing educator, newspaper, and public dissatisfaction with commercial broadcasting into a coherent movement to reconstruct the U.S. broadcasting system. In terms of money grants alone, the Payne Fund subsidies to the NCER and the *Ventura Free Press* dwarfed all other expenditures for broadcast reform combined. As such, one could marshal an argument that without the Payne Fund, there would not have been much of a broadcast reform movement, if there would have been one at all. At the very least, any broadcast reform movement without the Payne Fund's vision, direction, and money would have been but a shadow of what came into place in the early 1930s.

The Broadcast Reform Movement II: Nonprofit Broadcasters, Civic Organizations, and Intellectuals

While the activities sponsored by the Payne Fund, the NCER, and the *Ventura Free Press* radio campaign would play a paramount role in the broadcast reform movement of the early 1930s, they were by no means alone. The broadcast reform movement enjoyed the participation of three other displaced and harassed nonprofit broadcasters: the Chicago Federation of Labor's WCFL, which was the official station of the American Federation of Labor (AFL), the New York–based Paulist Fathers' WLWL, and the Pacific-Western Broadcasting Federation of Pasadena, California. Each of these three stations began in the 1920s with lofty ambitions for public service, only to face in short order the same financial and political crises that decimated the ranks of the university broadcasting stations.

The opposition to commercial broadcasting was not limited to nonprofit broadcasters. The ACLU established a Radio Committee in 1933 to address what it regarded as fundamental flaws in the commercial broadcasting setup for free expression and democracy. This chapter will examine the activities of these groups in the reform movement and then discuss the broader response of U.S. intellectuals to the emerging contours of commercial broadcasting in the early 1930s. As will be seen, the trajectory of this response was decidedly negative and the intellectual community, accordingly, helped the broadcast reformers. Finally, moving from the sublime to the ridiculous, the chapter will profile Harris K. Randall and his assorted efforts at broadcast reform that, although fruitless, were energetic and may have tarnished the public image of the broadcast reform movement.

Edward Nockels, WCFL, and Organized Labor

Unlike colleges and universities, labor unions did not embrace radio broadcasting with widespread enthusiasm. The AFL first considered the idea of owning and operating its own broadcasting station in 1922 and discussed the matter periodically for the next three years before formally rejecting it at its 1925 convention. The AFL acknowledged that broadcasting was quite significant for the labor movement but determined that local trade unions could purchase time on existing radio stations. This followed from the generally conciliatory attitude toward private, for-profit broadcasters of AFL president William Green, who would note in 1928 that "ownership of a station is not necessary in order to have time allocated for discussion of the problems of workers."[1] This attitude was not universally held in the ranks of organized labor, but only the AFL-member CFL would actively pursue the establishment of a labor radio broadcasting station.

Like the AFL, the CFL, which was established in 1896, was primarily composed of traditional craft unions. However, after the election of reformer John Fitzpatrick to the post of CFL president in 1905 and the appointment of his "teammate" Edward Nockels to the post of CFL secretary at about the same time, the fortunes of the CFL took a decided left turn. Fitzpatrick and Nockels were regarded by some as "radical fabians," and they were close friends with radical labor organizer Mother Jones.[2] After cleaning up the corruption they inherited in the CFL, Fitzpatrick and Nockels turned their attention to expanding the union's power base. Specifically, following the First World War, Fitzpatrick and Nockels launched a major trade union organizing drive in the steel industry with the assistance of William Z. Foster, who would go on to become a leading U.S. communist. This was a bold national move, in the spirit of Eugene Debs, to establish an alternative to the "Gomperism" of the AFL and unify the working class for political action. In addition, the CFL formed a Labor Party, out of its disgust with the existing political parties, and ran Fitzpatrick as its candidate for mayor of Chicago in 1919. Fitzpatrick garnered only 8 percent of the vote and the Labor Party collapsed. Similarly, the steel organizing drive fizzled and was officially terminated in January 1920, heralding a decade of retrenchment for organized labor. As Nockels would later comment, this "bitter experience" taught that a movement had to "be built from the bottom up, rather than from the top down."[3]

One legacy of the CFL's postwar attempt to expand the power of organized labor that survived was the CFL's *New Majority* weekly newspaper, which began operations in 1919. The CFL also launched a labor news service that survived into the 1920s. Fitzpatrick commented that the commercial press was aimed at "making a profit and establishing conservative thought-control" and could not, therefore, be relied upon by labor for an accurate portrayal of their movement. By the mid-1920s Fitzpatrick came under increasing pressure from the AFL hierarchy to tone down the CFL's more radical rhetoric and positions. Fitzpatrick finally acquiesced and the CFL's newspaper changed its name from the *New Majority* to the *Federation News* in 1924.

Editorial policy shifted to the right, albeit still noticeably to the left of the AFL executive council.[4]

It was this aggressive spirit and antimainstream media stance that fueled the CFL's approach to radio broadcasting. In 1924 the CFL Executive Board gave the CFL full power to pursue the establishment of a broadcasting station. The CFL regarded the AFL's official 1925 policy of simply working through existing broadcasters as "unsatisfactory" and proceeded with its plans to establish a labor station. As one union local representative observed at a regular CFL meeting, radio was "being used by the enemies of organized labor for the spreading of anti-union propaganda." The person primarily responsible for getting WCFL on the air in July 1926 was Nockels, who served as the CFL's secretary until his death in 1937. Nockels was a self-educated gas-fitter born in Dubuque, Iowa, in 1870; by the 1890s he had already made his mark in the Chicago labor movement as a feisty and uncompromising progressive. "He was a bluff, gruff, and outspoken man," one observer has noted, "who believed in saying what he felt in as few words as possible." It was Nockels who kept the radio project alive in 1925 and 1926 when, as Fitzpatrick admitted, "the CFL executive board was not at all enthused to the radio project and I practically deserted the secretary." Nockels, considered "more radical" than Fitzpatrick, served as WCFL's managing director until his death and his commitment to the "Voice of Labor," as the station was immediately dubbed, was in the more radical tradition of the CFL of the immediate postwar years.[5]

Nockels envisioned WCFL as a nonprofit station supported by contributions from workers that would be at the forefront of the progressive political movement. Formally, the station was chartered to "influence or educate the public mind upon the meaning and objects of Trade Unions and of the Federation of Labor, correct wrong impressions by broadcasting the truth, and advance progressive economic ideas which when put into operation will benefit the masses of the nation." More to the point, Nockels stated that the purpose of WCFL was to help "awaken the slumbering giant of labor." In 1928 WCFL entered into agreement with the Farmer's Educational and Co-operative Movement of America to provide broadcast service to farmers. For a brief period, WCFL even tagged itself as the "Voice of Farmer-Labor." In 1927 WCFL launched the quarterly *WCFL Radio Magazine* to complement its broadcast programming and to generate much needed revenue for the station. The magazine had a circulation of between 70,000 and 100,000 in the late 1920s.[6]

WCFL was one of the last of the nonprofit stations to go on the air during this period, and it was the only labor-affiliated station. In 1925 the CFL hired radio expert William J. H. Strong, who had advised the Republican National Committee on political broadcasting to conduct a study on the feasibility of an independent labor station. Strong's November 1925 report urged the CFL to act quickly as broadcasting "is rapidly become restricted" and "those who would get 'on the air' have no time to lose." Nockels attempted unsuccessfully to purchase the license and facilities of an existing Chicago station. He was convinced that antilabor interests had pressured the stations with which he was negotiating not to sell to the CFL. There were grounds for this sentiment. In March 1926 one Midwest employers bulletin speculated about the implications of a labor radio station:

> Think of the speeches that may go forth. Wild and radical speeches listened to by hundreds of thousands. These wild men in their wild talks regardless of consequences, may reach the ear, possibly inadvertently, of your influential and trusted employee, who may be detracted from paths favorable to his employer's success.

Nockels abandoned his efforts to purchase an existing station and used labor's contacts in Washington, D.C., to get a new license, moving with such dispatch that WCFL was on the air by July 1926. Its launching was regarded as little short of "a miracle."[7]

WCFL's relations with the FRC were similar to those of the college broadcasters. In May 1927 WCFL was shifted by the FRC from the 610 to the 620 frequency and was told to share the hours with WLTS, a station operated by Lane Technical High School of Chicago. Not yet suspicious of the FRC, Nockels blamed the move on the "Capital-owned stations" that "are now seeking to monopolize the air" and are "urging" the FRC to reduce the "power and latitude of Labor's one station, WCFL."[8] In September 1928 the FRC assigned several other stations to 620 and reduced WCFL's power to 1,000 watts. WCFL immediately protested to the FRC and made plans with commercial station WJJD to share a clear channel station at either the 620 or the 820 frequency. These plans were tentatively approved by Sam Pickard, the FRC commissioner for the zone covering Chicago.

With the implementation of General Order 40, however, WCFL was assigned to the 970 frequency, which it was to share with NBC Seattle affiliate KJR. Moreover, WCFL was reduced to 1,000 watts power and was not permitted to broadcast after daylight hours, so that it would not interfere with KJR's signal. "WCFL, at present deprived of the most desirable time to broadcast—after 8 P.M.—cannot, accordingly, function as an educational publicity agency when the majority have the time and opportunity to listen it," the CFL's *Federation News* editorialized in 1929. "Instead the public will hear the other side of the story." For the next several years WCFL would have several expensive and time-consuming hearings in its effort to earn a clear channel with 50,000 watts power, all of which it would invariably lose. Indeed, the FRC had singled out WCFL in its *Third Annual Report* as precisely the type of "propaganda" station that did not merit a broadcast license since there were not enough channels to satisfy all the potential purveyors of propaganda.[9]

WCFL also quickly encountered the same financial problems that faced the other nonprofit broadcasters. Nockels' original idea was for every CFL member to donate $1.00 each year to support the station's operations, in addition to the funds generated through sales of *WCFL Radio Magazine.* WCFL was opposed in principle to the sale of any of its time to commercial advertisers at the outset. Nockels noted:

> Labor might easily spend a million dollars a year on a radio program and still not overdo it. From where would come this fabulous sum of money? Surely not from radio advertising, for with such a splendid program there would be little airtime to sell to others. Labor would need it all.[10]

In 1926, with the launching of WCFL, Nockels managed to receive donations from 30 percent of the CFL's membership. Unfortunately for Nockels, membership donations did not improve much thereafter, particularly when the FRC limited WCFL to daylight hours in 1928. For the next several years Nockels found himself continually battling membership apathy to the financial needs of WCFL. "Organized labor admits the hostility of the daily press, and yet it voluntarily assesses itself daily to support the enemy," Nockels editorialized in the *Federation News* in 1929.

> The same example of glaring inconsistency is exhibited in organized labor's attitude toward its own radio broadcast station, WCFL, and its revenue producing auxiliary, the WCFL Radio Magazine. . . . This position cannot be maintained indefinitely. Labor must consistently demonstrate its unity by a unified financial support or through its lack be a party to the extinction of these enterprises, with the full knowledge that future regrets will never revitalize the corpse of dead hopes and aspirations.[11]

Nockels was not about to let his vision for a labor station collapse due to a lack of rank and file financial support, his threats to the contrary notwithstanding. By late 1929 Nockels notified the CFL membership that WCFL would turn to commercial advertising to support the station unless CFL members responded to the station's needs. This was a threat that Nockels made good on, although he was quick to observe that people were "kidding themselves" if they thought commercial radio was "free". Within a few years WCFL was actively promoting itself as an advertising medium. Nockels was in need of large quantities of money because he had built a rather substantial enterprise in WCFL. The station spent over $400,000 by the end of 1929 and had twenty-five full-time employees at the time. In 1930 WCFL generated revenues of $200,000, nearly five times as much as the CFL as a whole. In 1928, WCFL purchased 100 acres thirty-two miles west of Chicago in order to install a 50,000 watt transmitter. The new facilities would not be completed for several years after the groundbreaking in 1932.[12]

This point notwithstanding, it would be erroneous to interpret the lack of financial support Nockels was hoping for with a lack of enthusiasm by Chicagoans for WCFL's fare during the station's first few years. Research by Lizabeth Cohen, among others, suggests quite the contrary. From the outset, neither Nockels nor the CFL had any plans to jeopardize this colossal undertaking by alienating WCFL's audience with the type of tedious programming that had undermined some of the educational stations. Long-winded speeches by labor officials were kept to a minimum and CFL officials assured unionists that "music and entertainment will offset the heavy ammunition." In the late 1920s WCFL routinely broadcast dance music, programs in foreign languages, vaudeville and musical comedy, and major league baseball games, as well as maintaining a full-time eleven-member "WCFL Ensemble," which performed both classical and popular music several times each week. The station also covered all major strikes and presented public affairs programming from a labor perspective. In 1926 only a handful of Chicago's working-class households possessed radios, so WCFL's engineers devised an inexpensive five-tube set for a local manufacturer to stimulate radio sales. Nearly half of Chicago's working-class households had radios by 1930, and WCFL had become, for many of them, the station of choice. As Cohen had documented, in Chicago, in the late 1920s, "WCFL was the labor movement."[13]

The trend toward entertainment would become more pronounced in the 1930s as WCFL increasingly sought advertising support to subsidize its operations. In the 1930s when a station sold advertising time, it usually sold an entire time bloc to an advertiser or an advertising agency, which would then provide both the entertainment programming and the explicit commercial messages. Hence, when WCFL sold advertising it was not merely selling random "spots," but it was effectively abandoning an increasing portion of its day to commercial interests. Moreover, this put increased pressure on the remainder of the schedule still controlled by WCFL to provide programming that would continue to attract advertisers to the station. In January 1932 the *Federation News* would boast that WCFL will broadcast "the greatest program of music ever sent out over the air by any radio station."[14] In short, the formula by which WCFL had creatively mixed labor and entertainment programming was short-lived and a casualty of the station's inability to support itself by membership donations, or by any means other than advertising.

Nockels's successful launching of WCFL had put the AFL hierarchy in an uncomfortable position, given the AFL's resolution against establishing a labor station at the 1925 convention and Green's publicly stated antipathy to going outside the existing broadcast structure. At the 1926 AFL convention Nockels and Fitzpatrick sought and received the AFL's endorsement of

WCFL as the "official" labor radio station. Henceforth, Nockels would characterize the CFL as the "trustee" for the entire labor movement and he would continually press to have WCFL become a national clear-channel station that would be under the management of the AFL and other groups sympathetic to labor, and would be subsidized by union contributions. The AFL executive council showed no interest in taking the CFL up on this offer, despite Nockels' repeated overtures.[15]

Moreover, the AFL executive council was unique among organized labor between 1926 and 1935 in its unwillingness to criticize commercial broadcasting. "Certain elements in the labor movement have interested themselves in legislation detrimental to the best interests of the American system of broadcasting," an NBC internal memo observed in 1934. "In the main these activities have been carried on without the encouragement of officials of the American Federation of Labor."[16] Many unions and regional labor federations would pass resolutions during this period condemning the status quo and resolving for the radical reconstruction of the airwaves. The Massachusetts branch of the AFL, for example, resolved for the complete nationalization of broadcasting in 1935. Much of this anticommercial broadcasting momentum came from the activities of newspaper unions, which were concerned with the decrease in employment in their locals with the collapse in newspaper advertising during the depression, all the while broadcasters were enjoying boom times. For example, the International Typographical Union routinely resolved for the nationalization and decommercialization of broadcasting.[17] To dismiss the labor position entirely as one of economic opportunism, however, would be wrong; no small portion of the sentiment sprang from the class-based concerns mentioned earlier.

The AFL conventions between 1925 and 1935 were marked by a running antagonism between the union representatives on the floor and the executive council over broadcast policy. In 1927 the national convention voted to establish a national labor channel to be supported by fees of twenty-five cents per year per AFL member, with the clear intention that WCFL would assume this role. The resolutions committee of the AFL overruled this resolution and, in its place, suggested that the AFL executive council make an "investigation of the entire field of broadcasting" to determine labor's role. The executive council report, issued at the 1928 convention, optimistically concluded that "the abuses necessarily attendant the growth of such an industry are receiving attention" from the FRC. Hence the proposed independent national labor station was unnecessary. Similarly, in 1932, at the urging of the newspaper unions, the AFL convention passed a resolution condemning radio advertising and calling for the executive council to study the matter and recommend legislation to sharply curtail radio commercialism.[18] The executive council's report on its "thorough investigation," issued at the 1933 convention, was a ringing endorsement of advertising and the status quo that left the commercial trade publication *Broadcasting* commending the report for "wisely" concluding that "progress cannot be stopped."[19]

Green had been carefully cultivated by the commercial broadcasters as an ally. He was an active member of the NACRE, the group that advocated that nonprofit organizations work through the auspices of commercial broadcasters. Green was also a member of NBC's Advisory Council, for which he paid $1,000 annually. The ostensible function of the NBC Advisory Council was to counsel the network on its social, political, and cultural programming. Green was the only member of the Advisory Council affiliated with labor or the "common people," and his membership in the body was emphasized by NBC when the legitimacy of the Advisory Council as a "public interest" watchdog organization was called into question.[20] To the broadcast reformers, the NACRE was a questionable enterprise, at best, and the NBC Advisory Council was little more than a public relations ploy.

Hence it was not surprising that Green spoke publicly about how he was "most favorably impressed with the American system of broadcasting" and kept in personal contact with network executives. The primary assistance Green provided WCFL was occasional testimony before the FRC at license hearings; however, even in this regard Green's participation was a mixed blessing. In 1929, for example, WCFL had a hearing before the FRC on its application to be shifted to full-time status on the 970 frequency. Nockels solicited and received support from the entire U.S. labor movement and over ninety unions sent affidavits or representatives to testify before the FRC in April 1929.[21] "This is the greatest free speech fight the world has ever seen," a representative of the Minneapolis Central Labor Council stated before the FRC at WCFL's hearing. "If WCFL's application is denied, it is the end of free speech on the air, as far as labor is concerned." The FRC ruled against WCFL's motion, ironically enough given its stated preference for "general interest" broadcasters with no "axes to grind," on the grounds that although WCFL presented itself as a labor station, it rarely broadcast more than one hour in any twelve-hour broadcast day on labor matters. "Station WCFL has used only a very small portion of time it has at its disposal for broadcasting labor programs," noted the FRC decision, hence "its record does not justify a greater amount of time or power."[22]

Even more damning for WCFL's case was the testimony of their "main witness," AFL President Green. The FRC decision stated,

> The evidence of applicant's main witness at the hearing shows conclusively that more than 100 radio stations in this country are interested in and would broadcast programs in the interest of labor. If 100 radio stations scattered throughout this country are willing to broadcast programs in the interest of labor, such broadcasting would reach millions more than could be hoped to be reached through station WCFL.

Nockels would read this passage to a meeting of the CFL executive board and concentrated on the references to Green. He subjected Green's comments about "100 stations" broadcasting in the interests of labor to a "bath of withering sarcasm" and a "flood of heated words."[23] No mention of this incident was made in public and WCFL would periodically call upon Green for assistance again in the future. Nonetheless, this was a clear example of the rocky relationship between the AFL hierarchy and the CFL on broadcasting matters, and it pointed to the problems Nockels faced as he attempted to provide a uniform labor stance on broadcasting before both the FRC and Congress during these years.

After repeated defeats before the FRC, Nockels and the CFL formally abandoned their campaign to improve WCFL's position through the FRC and turned instead to enacting broadcast reform in Congress. "We no longer have any hope of getting protection through the Commission," he would observe at one point. "We are going back to Congress." Nockels dismissed the FRC as simply acting as "messengers for their masters," the commercial broadcasters or the "radio trust."[24] The most charitable assessment of the FRC provided by the *Federation News* during this period was that the FRC was "utterly lacking in backbone" in dealing with the "radio trust." Nockels felt that, organized labor "has been deliberately gagged" by the FRC.[25]

Moreover, to Nockels the process by which the FRC had established the emerging system had been outside of public view, not having been "possible if the general public was aware of what was being pulled off for the self aggrandizement and enrichment of the plutocratic mob at the public expense."[26] Nockels was calling for Congress to conduct an investigation of the FRC's reallocation by the spring of 1929. "We are sure if this investigation were made," Nockels informed the CFL's executive board, "it would show how these special interests privately and underhandedly held their little conference with the Federal Radio Commission and got their swag, and we are satisfied that if this thing were laid bare there would be another reallocation." As Nockels put it,

Is it in the public interest, convenience and necessity that all of the ninety channels for radio broadcasting be given to capital and its friends and not even one channel to the millions that toil? Will the public interest be served by granting all the channels of communication to those who do the employing and denying even one cleared channel of communication to the vast group of employees?[27]

Nockels saved his greatest criticism for the "Capital-owned stations" that he argued were trying to "monopolize the air." "Never in our history," Nockels wrote to Congress in January 1929, "has there been such a bold and brazen attempt to seize control of the means of communication and to dominate public opinion as is now going on in the field of radio broadcasting.'' He added:

> A few squatters have set up their tents, turned a few furrows, and now ask the nation to confirm in them title to a continent. . . . What do they care for the 'public interest, necessity and convenience'? What they want is to make money, to acquire power and to control in their interest this unparalleled new means of communication.

To Nockels, the commercial stations were ''anxious to eliminate such stations as WCFL'' to have an ''unmolested monopoly'' and be able to ''exploit a deluded and betrayed public for all the traffic will bear.''[28] Nor was this merely an immediate business proposition for the commercial broadcasters, according to Nockels. By ''gagging'' WCFL, the ''forces of reaction'' would be in keeping with their policy of suppressing ''all opinions, and the right and possibility to give expression to them, not in harmony with their own.''[29]

In this spirit, Nockels would become a major figure in the broadcast reform efforts in Washington, D.C., in 1930–1932, and again in 1934, since he was designated the AFL's official radio broadcasting lobbyist by the late 1920s. He brought a strong belief in the importance of the battle for the ether to the fight. In 1930 he said:

> With the exception of the right to organize, there is no goal more important of attainment to the American labor movement than one radio wavelength with a nation-wide network over which it can broadcast Labor's message to all citizens of our country. This is the modern phase of the right of free speech . . . whoever controls radio broadcasting in the future will eventually control the nation.[30]

Throughout the early 1930s, Nockels never abandoned his belief that the status quo was fundamentally and irretrievably flawed and that the solution lay in a radical restructuring, even if that meant out-and-out nationalization of the ether. ''We are heartily in favor of complete government control and operation'' of broadcasting, Nockels noted, ''in preference to complete control and operation by trusts . . . radio networks and their closely allied interests.'' ''WCFL, 'The Voice of Labor,' '' Nockels wrote to the NCER in 1934 to chastise them for not being sufficiently militant on broadcast reform, ''is one station that favors the government ownership and control of radio, in preference to the radio set-up that we now have.''[31]

Father Harney, the Paulist Fathers, and WLWL

The Missionary Society of St. Paul the Apostle was a New York–based order consisting of ninety-three priests in the mid-1920s. This group, generally known as the Paulist Fathers, had been established in the nineteenth century as a distinctly American order dedicated to teaching and democracy.[32] On December 16, 1924, the Paulist General Council approved plans for the Paulist Fathers to establish a radio station. The plans for the station received support and encouragement from Patrick Cardinal Hayes, the archbishop of New York, as well as other church authorities. During 1924 and 1925 the Paulists derived nearly $100,000 in private donations, mostly from Roman Catholic organizations, to get the station off the ground. Western Electric built the station for the Paulists, which was established in their rectory in Manhattan for a cost of $65,000.[33]

The Paulist order had high hopes for their station, WLWL, to become a primary vehicle for their works. Their stated goal with the station was the presentation of ''talks on religious, social and literary subjects and discussions of interest of the present day.'' While Sundays on WLWL would feature Paulist services and sermons by ''distinguished preachers,'' the balance of the programming was meant to be accessible to people of all faiths as well as nonchurch people. In particular, the Paulists identified their desired audience as of the working class.[34] When WLWL went on the air on September 24, 1925, on the 1040 frequency with a license to operate at 5,000 watts power it was among the twenty most powerful stations in the nation. It was also the first Catholic radio station in the United States and would remain the only Catholic radio station in the Northeast throughout its existence. The Paulists worked closely with nearly all the major Roman Catholic organizations as it developed its program for WLWL.[35]

The Paulists and WLWL shortly began to encounter problems with the regulatory authorities. In October 1926 the Department of Commerce ordered WLWL to share its 1040 frequency with a station to be operated by an amusement park based in the Bronx. The superior general of the Paulist Fathers, the Very Reverend John B. Harney, was outraged by this action, terming it ''an overt, deliberate and outrageous discrimination against a high-grade noncommercial radio station with an unrivaled program of cultural entertainment and of instructive talks on religious, ethical, educational, economic and social questions, in favor of a mere dispenser of jazz and cheap amusement.'' WLWL would be reassigned to new frequencies twice in the next nine months until it was eventually placed at the 810 frequency, where they were to share time equally with commercial station WMCA. In December 1927 the FRC notified WLWL that the station's hours had been officially reduced to two daytime hours daily, with WMCA receiving the balance of the air time.[36]

It is curious that when WMCA was granted the lion's share of the hours, it was only operating at 500 watts power and had inferior equipment; indeed, it had been negotiating with the Paulists to obtain the use of WLWL's more powerful transmitter as WLWL was in the process of purchasing an even more expensive transmitter. Father Harney commented that the FRC had discriminated against a nonprofit broadcaster of "high character" and "indubitable cultural and educational value," "in favor of one which unquestionably was not broadcasting for the 'public interest, convenience, or necessity,' but for the fattening of its shareholders' pocketbooks." Harney noted that by 1934, "thanks to the manifold favors of the Radio Commission," WMCA had an estimated market value of $4 million, while WLWL might net $5,000 for the sale of its transmitter and studio equipment.[37]

The FRC's general reallocation of the airwaves through General Order 40 in the autumn of 1928 did not improve matters much for the Paulists. WLWL was shifted to the 1100 frequency, where it was to share time with another 5,000-watt station, WPG, a municipally owned, Atlantic City–based station. Atlantic City, however, soon sold the station to CBS, and the FRC assigned the commercial WPG 110 hours per week on the 1100 band, leaving WLWL 15.5 hours of weekly air time on the frequency. Moreover, WLWL was not assigned any evening hours, which markedly reduced its visibility to its intended adult working class audience.[38]

Concurrent with their problems getting favorable hours assigned to them by the FRC, the Paulists began to face severe problems keeping the station afloat financially. In 1927 WLWL went into debt to build a $38,000 transmitting facility in New Jersey, which the FRC had ordered them to do if WLWL wished to remain at 5,000 watts power. To meet its annual operating budgets, which were lowered from $75,000 in the late 1920s to $40,000–50,000 in the early 1930s, WLWL received loans and grants from the Paulist Fathers and a number of Catholic groups including the Catholic Missionary Union, the Central Verein, the Holy Name Society, and the Knights of Columbus.[39] WLWL, however, faced the same dilemma as the educational broadcasters did who went before their universities and state legislatures to seek funding: Without additional funding they could not hope to receive the type of quality hours that would justify a large investment, and at their present low levels of broadcast time they had difficulty generating or maintaining enthusiasm for their broadcast program in the first place. This placed considerable stress upon WLWL's efforts to maintain funding from Catholic organizations throughout its existence.

To deal with the financial crisis, WLWL attempted with marginal success to sell some time to commercial advertisers. These efforts generated $3,000 per year. In addition, the Paulists would solicit contributions at their masses in their church in Manhattan. As with countless educational broadcasters during this period, the Paulists quickly discovered that there was one surefire way to generate money through their broadcast facilities: They could sell their license to commercial broadcasting interests and discontinue operations. In 1930, CBS offered to purchase WLWL outright so as to establish a clear channel for its WPG. In 1931, Hearst radio interests offered the Paulists

$500,000 for WLWL due to its "excellent frequency." In each case the Paulists refused.[40]

Between 1929 and 1933, the Paulists concentrated their efforts upon reaching some sort of accommodation with CBS and the FRC for increased broadcast hours, and they filed a number of appeals with the FRC to this end. Father Harney, although not practically connected with the day-to-day operations of WLWL, was named the station's director-general in 1929 to give him a title that he could use as he led the efforts before the FRC. In these efforts, the Paulists were continually frustrated by the FRC's policy of favoring "general interest" for-profit commercial broadcasters over nonprofit "special interest" stations. This issue endlessly aggravated Harney and he noted that WLWL

> is not a special interest, unless you want to say that those who are working for public welfare are pursuing special interests and that the gentlemen who are working for their own pockets are not. Why not the other way, with all due respect to Judge Sykes [then chairman of the FRC] and others, why not say that those who are working for their own pocketbooks are the gentlemen who are working for special interests?[41]

The Paulists quickly realized that they would need public support if they were to have any success before the FRC. WLWL listeners, Catholic organizations, and even Catholic parishes in the Archdiocese of New York were asked to write the FRC to voice their support of WLWL. One letter-writing campaign in September 1931 generated 25,000 letters in one week.[42] These efforts all proved fruitless. Finally, when the FRC denied another request by WLWL to share the hours on the 1100 frequency equally with WPG in February 1934, the Paulists disbanded their efforts to seek some satisfactory outcome through the FRC. Father Harney and the Paulist Fathers turned their attention to having broadcast reform legislation passed by Congress.

For three months in the spring of 1934 Father Harney led the campaign on behalf of the Wagner–Hatfield amendment, which called for 25 percent of the channels to be set aside for nonprofit broadcasters. He traveled constantly to Washington, D.C., met frequently with members of Congress, attempted to rally the diverse elements of the broadcast reform movement behind a single program, and seemingly enjoyed a level of success that had eluded the other broadcast reformers.

Pacific-Western Broadcasting Federation and Gross W. Alexander

The Pacific-Western Broadcasting Federation (PWBF) was incorporated on August 17, 1928, to provide "disinterested, cultural broadcasting" under the supervision of an "autonomous, self-perpetuating board." The PWBF was established by four university presidents, and its board of directors included Protestants, Catholics, and Jews. It also enjoyed, in the beginning, the formal support of numerous civic and religious groups including the Federal Council of Churches in America as well as prominent individuals such as Ray Lyman Wilbur, Robert Millikan, John Dewey, Charles A. Beard, Jane Addams, William John Cooper, and Graham Spry, the chairman of the Canadian Radio League, who would be largely responsible for Canada's formal adoption of a noncommercial broadcasting system in 1932.[43]

In its prospectus, the PWBF characterized U.S. radio as an "almost universal Babel of sounds, with a large majority of six or seven hundred stations surcharging the air with triviality, mediocrity, and syncopated noise, not to mention advertising propaganda, buffoonery, quackery and sectarianism." In this vast chasm, the PWBF offered itself as "the only altruistic, comprehensive, cultural broadcasting enterprise in the United States," and as a "Genuine Radio University." The PWBF intended to provide an ambitious range of educational, cultural, political, and entertainment programming that would approximate the broadcast services provided by the BBC to Great Britain. In particular, the PWBF emphasized that

> genuine education carries with it the necessity of discussion of all sides of questions including unpopular, minority views. For example, presentations should be made with utter candor and freedom of such social and economic issues as public ownership of public utilities, birth control, child labor reform, prohibition, religious philosophies, single tax, disarmament, unemployment, etc., etc.[44]

The executive manager of the PWBF and its organizing force was Gross W. Alexander, the son of a prominent Methodist theologian and a Methodist minister in his own right. Alexander was driven by a strident belief in the need for nonprofit broadcast facilities and he was critical of advertising as the means of supporting such broadcasting. "In the United States," he wrote, due to commercialism "the people experience a clever exploitation by private interests, forfeiting culture for commercialized amusement and private advantage." Alexander, however, was no proponent of government broadcasting along the lines of the BBC. Rather, he proposed that private nonprofit groups like the PWBF operate a handful of powerful radio stations and that they be administered like U.S. universities and be supported through philanthropy. "The cooperation of philanthropy is not merely opportune," Alexander argued, "it is imperative."[45]

The PWBF developed plans to construct a 50,000-watt transmitter and to operate on an annual budget in excess of $500,000. In a rare gesture of support for nonprofit broadcasting, the FRC granted the PWBF a construction permit to build a 50,000-watt station in November 1928. "You have been authorized to erect one of the largest broadcasting stations in the world,'' FRC member Harold Lafount wrote to Alexander, adding, ''I sincerely hope you may be able to interest philanthropy, but would advise you to expedite matters as much as possible.'' Alexander later characterized this FRC permit as ''the outstanding achievement'' in the FRC's history.[46] These were heady times for the PWBF. Joy Elmer Morgan wrote in January 1930 that the PWBF was ''the brightest prospect for a large use of radio directly for the public good that I have thus far seen.'' A *New York Times* editorial in May 1930 praised the PWBF, stating that ''there is no question of the need for some such plan as they propose.''[47]

Unfortunately, Alexander did not fare as well when he attempted to gain financing from the major foundations. The PWBF approached the Carnegie Corporation, John D. Rockefeller, Jr., and the J. C. Penney Foundation, along with ''various other philanthropic foundations'' and ''found most of them to be as cold as steel.'' The NACRE's Tyson informed the Carnegie Corporation's Frederick Keppel that Alexander was a ''pest'' and ''against the commercial broadcasters,'' while advising the Carnegie Corporation to stay clear of the PWBF.[48] In addition, Alexander convinced people like Jane Addams and Ray Lyman Wilbur to write to Rockefeller on behalf of the PWBF, to no avail.[49] Much to Alexander's consternation, he found that many of these foundations were ''doing everything apparently in their power to foster the use of commercial facilities for education.'' The lack of financing made it impossible for the PWBF to comply with the FRC's deadlines for purchasing technical equipment, and it was soon engaged in the same sort of combat with the regulatory body as were the other nonprofit broadcasters. ''If this enterprise fails,'' a despondent Alexander wrote to Joy Elmer Morgan in March 1931, ''the commercialization of radio broadcasting in the United States may be anticipated as virtually completed.''[50]

In 1931 the FRC refused to extend the PWBF's license due to their failure to meet deadlines and the organization effectively dissolved without ever going on the air. The ruling was a foregone conclusion as the FRC had never kept a channel vacant for such an extended period and commercial stations were ''eagerly applying'' for the use of PWBF's facilities. The NCER assisted Alexander in his defense, but it regarded the PWBF position as untenable; Armstrong Perry jokingly termed the PWBF's hearing before the FRC a ''funeral.''[51] Alexander attempted unsuccessfully to solicit the support and assistance of the ACLU as he appealed the FRC decision, since ACLU had come to the defense of other nonprofit broadcasters in their hearings before the FRC. ''May I say from some knowledge of the Federal Radio Commission's attitude that I do not think any discrimination whatever has been shown against your station,'' ACLU Director Roger Baldwin informed Alexander. ''You have had generous extensions of time to raise the capital necessary.''[52]

By this time much of the PWBF's initial support from prominent individuals had vanished. "The outside interests who fought us were able to get disharmony within our ranks," Alexander observed in 1933. "Our Board of Directors," he added, "were frightened by what they had received in the way of potential power. They dropped out like overripe fruit from a tree when opposition started." By 1931 Alexander turned to the ACLU's Baldwin, Clarence Darrow, and Upton Sinclair for support. Only Sinclair responded agreeably, arranging meetings, writing letters, and interviewing prospective contributors.[53]

Alexander believed that the PWBF's plans had been actively undermined by two groups. First, by the "reactionary business and commercial interests of Los Angeles" and the "promoters of Los Angeles real estate," whom Alexander believed were frightened by the thought of "the most complete and powerful radio station in the world" offering a "genuine university of the air" to the common people. Alexander claimed to have evidence that major Southern California banking interests went out of their way to discourage people from contributing to the PWBF. He also asserted that the Los Angeles Chamber of Commerce sent a representative in person to Washington, D.C., to oppose the licensing of the PWBF.[54]

Second, Alexander believed that the "power trust"—AT&T, GE, Westinghouse, RCA, and NBC—was threatened by the PWBF's very existence, and had done everything within its substantial power to keep the PWBF from becoming a viable operation. "You see," he would tell a House committee in 1934, "we would have set a precedent in broadcasting for the United States, in addition to taking away listeners from the commercial stations." Alexander had been suspicious of the power trust for some time; in June 1929 he wrote to Secretary Wilbur that since his newly appointed Advisory Council on Education by Radio included representatives of RCA and NBC, it "might not have public confidence." Alexander's hatred for the "power trust" only intensified when AT&T not only refused to sell him the transmitting equipment he needed to satisfy the FRC deadlines at a discount, but it also showed marked indifference, if not hostility, to the PWBF's program. In January 1930 AT&T Vice-President Frank B. Jewett even advised Alexander to work through an existing commercial station "before embarking on any arrangement which would involve . . . a large capital outlay and heavy maintenance expense."[55] Alexander spent much of the early 1930s railing against the domination of broadcasting by the radio trust and he attempted to chronicle how this "unelected oligarchy" had extended its influence right into the heart of educational broadcasting. An essay he wrote on this subject in the summer of 1930 had a great deal of influence on the Payne Fund as it proceeded with its plans to establish the NCER. Ella Phillips Crandall wrote that Alexander had "undeniably evidenced" the intent of RCA, NBC, and the commercial broadcasters to establish "monopolistic" control of the ether.[56]

In particular, Alexander took dead aim at the NACRE as a creation of NBC and the radio trust. To Alexander, the NACRE, which included people like Owen D. Young and David Sarnoff on its board of directors, was

> specifically organized for precluding the support of philanthropy for any large plan of independent educational broadcasting; and for the purpose of obviating legislation looking toward establishment of noncommercial stations in the hands of informed, disinterested, and responsible leaders; and that it aimed to offset and eventually take the place of such of these facilities as now exist.[57]

Alexander was appalled that the NACRE was amply funded by Rockefeller and the Carnegie Corporation, the very foundations that had turned down the PWBF's requests for money, and that these foundations seemingly had their own links to the major electric and power corporations.

Moreover, the president of the NACRE, Cal Tech President Robert Millikan, had given "the most sweeping endorsement" of the PWBF in 1928 and was listed as one of its formal sponsors. In 1929 Millikan praised the noncommercial British radio system for producing programs that were "incomparably superior to anything heard over here."[58] By 1930, however, Millikan wrote to Alexander to dissociate himself from the PWBF, informing Alexander that he believed the PWBF was no longer necessary due to the attitude of the commercial broadcasters. "Owen D. Young," Millikan wrote to Alexander, "informed us that it was possible for any educational group which the council [the NACRE] might set up to obtain all the facilities for nationwide broadcasting that it could possible use." To Alexander it was not necessarily coincidental that Millikan's attitude toward educational broadcasting made this 180-degree turn shortly after AT&T reportedly had donated $3 million and the Rockefeller family had donated $6 million to Cal Tech.[59]

By mid-1930 Alexander had given up hope for a philanthropic-based educational broadcasting system; instead, he became a proponent of broadcast reform. "Philanthropy has failed," he would conclude one speech. "The industry is incompetent. The state must enter the field." Alexander wrote to one U.S. senator in December 1930 that "the only rational control of broadcasting in a democracy is governmental control, and taxation for support of broadcasting."[60]

Alexander would remain on the fringes of the broadcast reform movement between 1930 and 1934, emerging periodically, but almost always working on his own. He was most effective in 1930 when he assisted Armstrong Perry in organizing the Conference on Educational Broadcasting in Chicago in October. Alexander's correspondence continually pushed Perry to adopt a more radical stance vis-à-vis the commercial broadcasters. His isolation was enhanced when, after the PWBF had its permit revoked in 1931, he returned to the ministry and accepted a position with a church in Fresno, California. Nevertheless, Alexander sent nearly a dozen circulars on the subject of broadcast reform to members of Congress and continually pressed all who would listen on the need for well-financed nonprofit broadcasting.[61]

It is unclear how much of Alexander's isolation from the balance of the broadcast reformers and, indeed, the failure of the PWBF to attract philanthropic support, was due to objective circumstances or was a function of his personality and style. "I know Alexander," noted one Department of Agriculture employee in a critical memo to his superior concerning the PWBF in 1930. "He's a promoter." Perry and Morgan both urged Alexander to tone down his rhetoric as he attempted to generate support for the PWBF in 1930. They also suggested that the PWBF "would be more likely to succeed" before the FRC if Alexander did not attend the hearing in 1931.[62] The NCER distanced itself from Alexander after the FRC withdrew the PWBF permit. By 1934, Alexander's isolation was complete and his testimony for broadcast reform in Washington, D.C., consisted as much in conspiratorial attacks upon the NACRE and the power trust as it did upon broadcast reform legislation. If anything, his general contribution to the broadcast reform movement by that time may have been more damaging than helpful.

The ACLU Radio Committee

The emergence of radio broadcasting after 1920 presented a distinct problem for the ACLU. ACLU Counsel Morris Ernst noted: "Nothing has ever divided believers in the Bill of Rights as sharply as the question of radio."[63] With regard to the newspaper industry and the print media in general, the ACLU adhered to a "laissez faire" notion of free speech. This notion countenanced no government interference in the affairs of the press. Furthermore, the government was to provide no obstacles to any person who elected to establish their own newspaper or magazine within extremely broad parameters. In short, the media system should be regulated by the unfettered marketplace and the cause of freedom could only be undermined by government intervention.

This notion of the government removing itself from the affairs of the press was rendered irrelevant for radio broadcasting if only due to the physical scarcity in the number of channels available for use. By the late 1920s virtually everyone agreed that the federal government needed to allocate the limited number of air channels among the contending applicants. Thus, regardless of its intentions, the actions of the government would necessarily determine which groups would have access to American listeners and, conversely, which groups would not. The ACLU recognized this dilemma early on, but it only formalized its concern with the establishment of its Radio Committee in 1933.

Prior to 1933 the ACLU and key figures associated with it played a sporadic role in the debate over broadcast policy. As early as 1926 the ACLU was sympathetic to the criticisms of commercial and private broadcasting as being inimical to the open, robust, and freewheeling debate that a democratic society needed from its media system. The ACLU recognized that the emerging order tended to emphasize trivial programming and that it tended to discount opinions outside the mainstream when it did cover social issues. At the same time, the ACLU could never quite reconcile itself to the role the government would seemingly have to play to counteract the domination of the airwaves by a handful of powerful corporations supported by commercial advertising. This contradiction plagued the entire broadcast reform movement, but was all the more intense for the ACLU given its original mandate as defending political dissidents from government persecution and harassment in the wake of the First World War. It would continually manifest itself in the ACLU Radio Committee's deliberations.

The most active member of the ACLU regarding broadcast policy throughout the 1920s and 1930s was Ernst, who took a rapid interest in the subject and almost immediately adopted an anticommercial broadcasting stance. Ernst testified before Congress regarding the ACLU's "grave misgivings" over what would become the Radio Act of 1927. He also wrote several articles on the subject. Among other things, Ernst was insistent, on free speech grounds, that any broadcast legislation mandate that the regulatory body give preference to nonprofit broadcasters in the allocation of licenses. He was dismayed by the lack of congressional concern for the free speech implications of the legislation and concerned that Congress was neglecting the difficult issue of consciously framing a broadcast policy, which allowed private interests to take over a public resource with minimal public input. "And if you allow these things to grow on the basis of trading for profit," Ernst told the Senate Committee on Interstate Commerce (SCIC), "you are increasing your difficulty in making a change."[64] Ernst argued that Congress needed to prevent chain ownership and that it needed to prohibit letting private broadcasters make a profit by selling their broadcast licenses. It was essential, Ernst argued, to "prevent the domination of the radio stations by two or three large concerns." Unless these steps were taken by Congress, any provisions in the legislation stating "the continued rights of free speech are meaningless." Ernst also testified along these lines at the FRC's open hearings in March 1927, although neither he nor any other representative of the ACLU participated in the subsequent FRC deliberations over how best to implement a reallocation.[65]

The Radio Act of 1927 was also disturbing to Forrest Bailey, then-director of the ACLU, because it failed to provide for adequate record keeping that would permit the public to monitor broadcasters and have an effective voice in the allocation and renewal of broadcast licenses. Ernst stated the ACLU's position on the significance of requiring record-keeping along these lines:

Granted that some censorship of the air is an engineering necessity, those who believe in the right of free speech must see to it that this censorship is controlled so far as possible by the listening millions of the country.[66]

The ACLU was not inactive regarding radio censorship and free expression before 1933, but at best it regarded the efforts to reform U.S. broadcasting as "bearing only indirectly on the question of freedom of communication" until the formation of the Radio Committee. For example, in 1929 the ACLU protested to NBC when it refused to sell air time to a national birth control conference on the grounds that there was insufficient listener interest. In his correspondence with the FRC on the matter, the chairman of the ACLU, Harry F. Ward, was quick to emphasize that NBC was under no legal obligation to carry the broadcast; he emphasized that it was a "moral obligation" that could only be applied "when the service did not conflict in any impressive way with the commercial interests of the Company."[67] In addition to appealing to commercial broadcasters to carry controversial programming during these years, the ACLU also represented New York–based WEVD, a nonprofit and noncommercial radio station sponsored at the time by the Socialist Party, in its constant hearings before the FRC. (WEVD did manage to survive, but, like WCFL, it did so by selling advertising "that is just as bad as that of the big stations," as S. Howard Evans put it.)[68]

By 1931 the ACLU had received numerous complaints of censorship committed by commercial broadcasters to nonmainstream political opinions. The ACLU's National Council on Freedom from Censorship, which was created in 1931, specifically identified radio censorship by commercial broadcasters as "greatly in evidence" and argued that the solution was "to prevent the domination of the industry by two or three large groups." In response to this wave of criticism, the ACLU then sent out a questionnaire to hundreds of commercial broadcasters querying them on their policies with regard to controversial programming.[69] With this information in hand, the ACLU decided to enter the broadcast reform fray and draft legislation to require commercial broadcasters to air at least two sides in any discussion of political or social issues. The legislation was stalled on Capitol Hill.

Ironically, the ACLU recognized that the legislation was hardly any panacea. Socialist party leader and ACLU member Norman Thomas wrote to Roger Baldwin, the director of the ACLU who revealed a keen interest in broadcasting issues, stating that if the legislation passed it would probably lead the radio companies to "drop all discussion of controversial issues" rather than to present two sides, and to "charge an impossible price" to the minority groups that wished to discuss their positions over the air. "I know this will not go far toward freedom of the air," Baldwin responded in frustration to one of many comments along these lines, "but what the devil is the remedy short of public ownership—and is that any remedy?"[70]

By early 1933 Baldwin began to describe the implications of the U.S. broadcasting system for free speech in the starkest of terms.

> Censorship at the stations by the managers is constantly exercised in a most unenlightened fashion, all this with an eye to protecting the status quo. Only a comparatively few small stations voice critical or radical views, and these are in constant danger of either going out of business or being closed up. Protests by the Civil Liberties Union when the larger stations censor programs have resulted in no relief. The Federal Radio Commission pays no attention to such complaints. In only a few cases have station managers been responsive.

By March 1933 Baldwin would concede that efforts to fundamentally re-organize American broadcasting *were* legitimate issues for the ACLU, since "in substance" these efforts were "aimed against the present censorship by the powerful stations."[71] His stance, like that of Ernst, had become that of a radical; he believed that the broadcast system needed fundamental structural change, although he was at a seeming loss to find a viable alternative.

It was in this context that the ACLU established its Radio Committee in the spring of 1933. The Radio Committee was officially created because the ACLU was "vitally concerned with the restrictions on broadcasting inherent in the American system." Its purpose was to study the "whole matter" of broadcasting with the aim of determining a "practical plan we should support." In addition to Baldwin, the Radio Committee was comprised of Ernst, Thomas, New York merchant Henry Eckstein, Bethuel M. Webster, Jr., and Levering Tyson. While Ernst, like Baldwin, was very active, both Thomas and Eckstein played minor roles on the committee, particularly before 1935.[72] Ernst was at all times the most radical of the Radio Committee members, even advocating that the government take over a significant portion of broadcasting and place severe restrictions on the remaining commercial sector.[73]

Thomas was also fundamentally opposed to the status quo. Since "any genuine discussion of great issues" fared badly in a commercially based broadcast system, Thomas stated in 1934, all of broadcasting should be "conducted by a nonprofit-making body set up by the government."[74] Thomas first became alarmed by commercial broadcasting after AT&T canceled a talk he was scheduled to give over WEAF in 1926 because it was "controversial." To Thomas, this was "proof and precedent for the virtual censorship of ideas which the larger radio corporations are establishing." His interest intensified when he worked with the committee to defend and promote WEVD in the late 1920s and early 1930s, which brought him to Baldwin's attention when he was putting the Radio Committee together.[75]

Interestingly, Thomas himself received considerable time on the commercial networks, as least relative to others on the political left, and he was referred to as NBC's "pet radical." As Thomas informed NBC's Aylesworth, "I have been valuable to the N.B.C. as a proof of liberalism."[76] NBC publicized Thomas's participation with NBC as evidence of its commitment to airing all sides on political questions.[77] Thomas acknowledged that "radio censorship is a little less crude, a little less extensive than people think." Nevertheless, he insisted that "it is not therefore less dangerous."[78]

Webster and Tyson were "outsiders" who were added to the Radio Committee due to their experience and expertise in radio matters. Their selection by Baldwin clearly shaped the course of the Radio Committee's activities in a manner that Baldwin, with his admitted ignorance of the controversy surrounding the debate over radio control, had not anticipated. As it would develop, the Radio Committee would experience sharp splits over its policies over the next few years, usually with Ernst and Eckstein on one side, Webster and Tyson on the other side, and Thomas and Baldwin in the middle.

Webster had been the second general counsel for the FRC in the late 1920s; he had resigned in disgust at the group's incompetence and lack of vision. After leaving the FRC in 1929, Webster moved to New York and began advising the ACLU on radio matters on a pro bono basis, thus bringing himself to Baldwin's attention and making himself a logical candidate for the Radio Committee. Webster was distressed that the federal government had failed to develop a coherent plan to utilize broadcasting in the public interest and upset by the manner in which the airwaves had been turned over to commercial broadcasters without any recognition of the problems inherent to the emerging system for free expression.[79] Webster, however, was no radical; he avoided contact with the various reform groups and never revealed much sympathy for their various proposals.

Tyson was even less sympathetic to the other reform groups. As the director of the NACRE, which was formed with the explicit recognition that the status quo was satisfactory for the airing of educational and cultural programming, his inclusion on a committee established to propose and lobby on behalf of structural reform struck some as peculiar. Baldwin received some irate correspondence protesting Tyson's appointment on the grounds that Tyson was too closely allied to commercial broadcasting interests. Nonetheless, Baldwin dismissed these objections, while admitting his failure to understand their basis, and he made it clear that he expected Tyson and Webster to provide expertise in radio matters for the Radio Committee.[80] This was a proposition that Tyson and Webster welcomed; both believed the determination of broadcast policy should be left to neutral experts like themselves rather than be argued by partisan and self-interested politicians.

At Webster's behest, the Radio Committee quickly decided not to generate an alternative model for American broadcasting that would better provide for free and wide-ranging expression, determining that it could not accomplish what the ACLU and Baldwin had intended it to do. Rather, the Radio Committee resolved to have legislation passed calling for the president to appoint a commission to make a thorough study of the "whole radio set-up'' and then suggest specific reforms. Webster saw the study as utilizing "the best possible engineering and legal advice" and as ignoring the "half-baked schemes" of reformers like the NCER.[81] In essence, the Radio Committee was calling for the government to appoint experts to resolve the crisis for civil liberties brought on by the emergence of private, commercial broadcasting.

The ACLU Radio Committee was for the most part isolated from the balance of the broadcast reform movement, despite its similar objectives. In late 1933 Baldwin was urged by the Chicago office of the ACLU to have the Radio Committee begin to work closely with the NCER, which was held in high regard by Chicagoans familiar with the debate over radio policy. This made sense as the NCER had always placed as much emphasis upon what it regarded as the limitations of the status quo for free expression as they had upon its deleterious implications for educational broadcasting. Moreover, in early 1933, the NCER had begun to press hard for legislation to establish a "thorough study" of broadcasting by an independent body that would then suggest fundamental reforms; in short, the NCER was proposing the exact same measure as Webster had encouraged the ACLU Radio Committee to adopt. Baldwin and the NCER's Tracy Tyler began a regular correspondence in late 1933 and they arranged to undertake some lobbying activities together.[82]

This emerging relationship between the NCER and the ACLU was cut off in November 1933. Tyson, whose NACRE was in the midst of a fierce rivalry with the NCER, informed Baldwin that he had a low opinion of the NCER and that he did not believe that the ACLU should work with them. Baldwin then solicited Webster's opinion. In a memorandum that he prefaced by conceding that his views on the NCER were colored by Tyson's opinions, Webster characterized the NCER's efforts as "marked by ineptitude and lack of sufficient basic information and planning." He concentrated his comments on the NCER's original fixed percentage proposal without acknowledging that their platform had been changed for over a year and was presently identical to that of the ACLU. Webster criticized the NCER for failing "to offer a comprehensive scheme for broadcasting in general," without any recognition of irony. Tyson's and Webster's comments were effective. In November Baldwin informed Webster that he would "hold off doing anything directly with them."[83] The two groups would not resume contact again until the late 1930s when the terrain would be radically different.

The ACLU Radio Committee became a significant actor in the deliberations before Congress and the FCC between 1933 and 1935. Moreover, the Radio Committee remained active in its efforts to recast U.S. broadcasting late into the 1930s, after the balance of the broadcast reform movement had fallen by the wayside. By 1940 the ACLU Radio Committee would have made a tortuous transition from a belief that the status quo was fundamentally flawed to a belief that private, commercial broadcasting was fundamentally sound and "American." This point will be elaborated upon in Chapter 9.

American Intellectuals and Commercial Broadcasting

The response of the ACLU to the emergence of network, commercial broadcasting in the United States reflected the larger reaction of U.S. intellectuals. Perhaps the most striking feature of the intelligentsia's response during this period was how *unanimous* the sentiment was in opposition to the status quo. NCER Director Morgan was on the mark when he stated in 1933 that it was impossible to find *any* intellectual in favor of the status quo unless they were receiving money or broadcast time from a commercial broadcaster. Armstrong Perry would comment to the Payne Fund's Crandall that when opinion magazines like *Harper's* sought articles favorable to commercial broadcasting, they "turned to persons on the payroll of RCA or its subsidiaries" in order to locate authors.[84] This does not mean that the issue of broadcast policy was anything close to a preoccupation for the intelligentsia during this period. Numerous prominent social thinkers from the period seem scarcely to have considered the matter; all things considered, this debate did transpire during the depths of the Great Depression, and there were other important issues to consider.

This point notwithstanding, those intellectuals that did consider and comment upon the implications of the emerging capitalist broadcasting set-up for the maintenance of a democratic society regarded the topic as one of the utmost importance. "The radio is the most powerful instrument of social education the world has ever seen," John Dewey announced in a radio address in 1934. "It can be used to distort facts and to mislead the public mind. In my opinion, the question as to whether it is to be employed for this end or for the social public interest is one of the most crucial problems of the present." In 1931 Upton Sinclair wrote:

> The conditions of our radio at the present time constitute a national scandal and disgrace. . . . If they are allowed to continue for another ten years we shall have the most debased and vulgarized people in the world, and the fault will not rest with the people, who are helpless, and have to take what is handed out to them by exploiters and commercialists of the basest type.[85]

Alone among academics and intellectuals, Dr. Herman S. Hettinger of the Wharton School of Finance, published actively throughout this period on the merits of commercial broadcasting over any alternative.[86] Hettinger, however, in accord with Morgan's thesis, had much of his research funded by the NAB. This is not to suggest that Hettinger was some sort of intellectual prostitute whose services were available to the highest bidder; rather, whenever the commercial broadcasters sensed an ally among intellectuals and academics, they appeared eager to support and encourage that scholar's work. In 1935 Hettinger edited a volume on radio for the prestigious *Annals of the American Academy of Political and Social Science*. As one critic noted, since "Hettinger has been a frequent consultant to the broadcasting industry," it was not surprising that he included "in his imposing list of contributors, a substantial number of persons to whom the role of apologist for commercialized radio is not unknown."[87]

Among those notable intellectuals who provided criticism of the status quo during this period, with no discernible immediate financial gain for doing so, were the aforementioned Dewey and Sinclair, Walter Hale Hamilton and Richard Joyce Smith of the Yale Law School, Alexander Meiklejohn, Charles A. Beard, Jane Addams, Frederick Lewis Allen, E. P. Herring, H. L. Mencken, Stuart Chase, Jerome Kerwin, Malcolm Willey, Adolph Berle, and Norman Woeful.[88] Some intellectuals, most notably William Orton of Amherst College, Jerome Davis of the Yale Divinity School, and *New Republic* editor Bruce Bliven, published widely on behalf of broadcast reform and coordinated their activities with elements of the broadcast reform movement.[89]

Two members of the intelligentsia deserve special mention. James Rorty was a former advertising copywriter and social critic who wrote several books and pamphlets criticizing the status quo and who worked closely with the NCER and the ACLU radio committee.[90] Rorty, who was a socialist, enjoyed a lengthy and friendly correspondence with the NCER in which he made it clear that "my own point of view" is "more radical" than that of the other broadcast reformers. Rorty was also the official representative on radio matters of the League of Professional Groups, an association of artists and intellectuals that included Sidney Hook and Edmund Wilson among its members. The battle for the control of the ether was serious business to Rorty:

> At bottom the issue is part of the larger conflict between exploitation for private profit and the increasingly articulate movement for public ownership and operation of essential public services. In this conflict, the citadel of radio is the key position, because the control of radio increasingly means the control of public opinion.[91]

As these comments by Rorty indicate, the battle for broadcast reform was one that could easily attract those with left-wing political outlooks, which probably encompassed a notable segment of the intelligentsia in the early 1930s. This point, however, can easily be overstated. First, most of the organized left avoided the issue entirely. For example, the Communist Party's *Daily Worker*, ignored the issue and only criticized the nature of the broadcast set-up at the end of the decade, long after the system had become politically and ideologically consolidated. Second, much of the support for broadcast reform came not from liberal and reform-minded Democrats, though they were significant, but from Republicans like those connected to the Payne Fund activities. In the early 1930s, commercial broadcasting was not yet synonymous with Americanism in the minds of mainstream America and there was significant room for fundamental criticism, particularly by any subsequent standard. As one telegram to President Herbert Hoover protesting FRC policies in 1930 began, "The loyal patriotic flag loving Republicans of this nation are expecting you to direct a policy that will save the nation from becoming the pawns and chattels of the . . . chain monopolies."[92]

Finally, radio inventor Lee DeForest emerged as one of the most strident critics of the status quo in the early 1930s, which was a source of more than a little embarrassment for the commercial broadcasters. DeForest told one audience:

> To be known as the "Father of Broadcasting" was once an honor of which I was proud, but I'm disgusted and ashamed of my pet child. I will lend to any group of citizens who think as I do every ounce of aid within my power to help drive direct commercial advertising off the air, for I seriously believe it to be a national disgrace.

DeForest routinely attacked the commercial broadcasters for being "greedy to maintain Radio Broadcasting on its present mediocre and moronic basis." His contempt for radio advertising was so great that he devoted much time and energy attempting to create a device he called the "anti-ad." The anti-ad was intended to empower radio listeners to mute radio commercials by remote control, and then alert them when the commercials were over so they could return the volume to an audible level.[93] DeForest applauded the founding of the NCER and hoped that it would arrest "the ever growing tendency to prostitute this magnificent medium in the interests of commercialism and salesmanship." DeForest would be one of only two Americans, along with the NCER's Morgan, to testify before the Special Committee on Radio Broadcasting in Canada in 1932, whose report would call for the nationalization and decommercialization of Canadian broadcasting. DeForest termed U.S. broadcasting "a vulgar, cheapjack show designed solely to coax dollars out of the pockets of the public," and called upon Canadians to "lead radio in North America out of the morass into which it has pitiably sunk."[94]

Harris K. Randall and the American Radio Audience League

Last and least in the pantheon of broadcast reformers comes Harris K. Randall of Chicago. Randall had worked for both the Crosley station WLW of Cincinnati and later as advertising and promotion manager for Silver-Marshall Radio. In 1932, after leaving Silver-Marshall, he established the American Radio Audience League (ARAL). Randall's idea was to eliminate advertising from the airwaves through independent civic groups providing broadcasting to neutral government agencies that would handle the technical aspects of the business rather than through government-supported broadcasting. Randall also thought that if a market had four cleared channels, then each of the channels should concentrate upon a distinct format; for example, one station each would be for classical music, popular music, education and culture, and religious broadcasting.[95]

Randall never had much success with his plan or his organization. His primary problem was explaining where the funds would come from to provide for the programming if the government was not to play an active role. The NCER's Tracy Tyler noted that the plan was "unworkable" and that "if Mr. Randall was honest with himself he would advocate government ownership." Similarly, the Payne Fund's S. Howard Evans informed Randall that "the more I see of your plan," the "more convinced I am that it can never successfully be put across."[96] Nonetheless, Randall gained the attention of numerous intellectuals who were attracted to a plan that spelled out an alternative to the status quo, but did not involve the government in a large role. Randall published and distributed several papers on the subject and managed to gain the formal support of many prominent Chicago area academics, including the likes of Paul Douglas, who provided the ARAL with an impressive letterhead, if nothing else. The ARAL also received the formal endorsement of the American Federation of Teachers in 1932.[97]

Randall's activities quickly attracted the attention of the commercial broadcasting industry. "Mr. Randall is a fanatic and he is bound to draw to his support disgruntled people of all kinds," NBC Vice-President William S. Hedges wrote from Chicago in June 1932.

> He is exceedingly dangerous, inasmuch as he will make his attacks upon the American system of broadcasting through the columns of the newspapers that are hostile to radio. I do not think we should minimize the danger that is possible, providing he secures adequate financing to promote his ideas. The literature that he has issued would indicate that he anticipates a long drawn out fight.

Hedges first encountered Randall in 1930 when he convinced the Silver-Marshall Radio Company not to publish one of Randall's brochures on radio reform, which had already been in galley proof, and which Randall intended to distribute to members of Congress and journalists. In 1932 Merlin Aylesworth would similarly use his influence with the editor of the *National Printer*

Journalist, whose newspaper happened to own an NBC-affiliated radio station, to see that an article submitted by Randall attacking commercial broadcasting not be published.[98]

NBC's concern proved unfounded. By the end of 1932 the ARAL was, as one NBC internal memo observed, "practically defunct," and its "activities had been more or less suspended due to a lack of funds." For the next few years, working out of an office in his home, Randall maintained his efforts to reform U.S. broadcasting. In 1934 the ARAL was formally disbanded and Randall established the Chicago Civic Broadcast Bureau (CCBB).[99] The CCBB had the same basic platform as had the ARAL, except that now Randall was proposing to have his organization, the CCBB, be responsible for acting as a clearing house to get nonprofit groups active in broadcasting over the Chicago area broadcasting stations. The idea fared no better than had the original ARAL proposal.

Randall was active in the efforts to reform U.S. broadcasting between 1931 and 1935, attending conferences and testifying before the FCC. To the average member of Congress or interested citizen, he may well have appeared to have been one of the broadcast reform movement's commanding officers, given his organizational affiliation with its impressive letterhead and his omnipresence at broadcast policy functions.

Randall's major activity throughout the early 1930s was to engage in a prolific correspondence with virtually all others interested in broadcast reform, including members of Congress and the government as well as the NCER's Perry, Tyler, and Morgan, the ACLU's Baldwin, the Payne Fund's Crandall, Bolton, and Evans, University of Chicago President Robert M. Hutchins, and others. Perhaps Randall's only contribution to the broadcast reform movement was to push the ACLU's Baldwin to adopt an explicitly radical stance toward the status quo in their early correspondence in early 1933.[100] Otherwise, the pattern was the same with all of his correspondents. Randall would write a letter of introduction, the other party would respond favorably, and Randall would immediately respond with a several page detailed letter. All future letters to Randall would be met with an immediate and long response. In those cases that Randall had not received a response for a week or so, he would write another long letter to his fellow broadcast reformer, arguing in great detail on behalf of his program and criticizing all other approaches.

Without exception, all of Randall's correspondents eventually tired of him and discontinued relations with the ARAL or the CCBB. For example, the ACLU decided to discontinue working with him after their Chicago office reported to the main New York headquarters that Randall was regarded in his home town as "long winded" and "not very clear headed." Similarly, Allen Miller, director of the University of Chicago Radio Department, would advise Hutchins against working with ARAL because, "Mr. Randall is not the type of man to succeed with the plan even if it were practical.''[101] Morgan ceased responding to Randall's correspondence, terming him "incompetent" and "erratic and impractical." He informed one NCER colleague that "the less we have to do with him the better." Evans tried, without success, to gently encourage Randall to stop writing to him, so Randall could ostensibly "concentrate" his "valuable attention on more promising leads." "This guy, Harris K. Randall, bothers me plenty," Evans wrote to Walter Woehlke at the *Ventura Free Press*. "I wrote him a letter designed to shut him up and the only response was to use it as an excuse for broadcasting a lot more hokum.''[102] Evans, too, simply stopped responding to Randall.

Randall was uniformly unsuccessful as an activist for broadcast reform. His net effect, like that of Gross Alexander, may well have been negative. Even the commercial broadcasters, aside from Hedges, spared Randall from the type of verbal attacks with which they skewered the NCER and the *Ventura Free Press*. "So far as operating a racket is concerned," NBC's Nile Trammell wrote to Aylesworth concerning Randall's intentions, "I don't believe Mr. Randall ever had any intention of shaking anyone down.''[103]

In sum, the broadcast reform movement, aside from the activities of the Payne Fund, was a varied lot with elements from diverse strands of U.S. society. The most significant reformers were those affiliated with displaced and harassed nonprofit broadcasting stations like WCFL and WLWL. Activists like Nockels and Harney launched their stations with compelling visions of nonprofit and noncommercial broadcasting fulfilling social and educational mandates not determined by the need to make profits. Their experiences with the FRC, commercial broadcasters, and, in the case of the PWBF, with philanthropic bodies, soon thrust them into the midst of the campaign to recast U.S. broadcasting. Similarly, intellectuals and groups like the ACLU saw the emergence of commercial broadcasting as undermining core tenets of the laissez faire marketplace of ideas and liberal democratic political theory and reacted accordingly. Finally, the broadcast reformers, like most social movements, attracted their own share of iconoclasts. At best, there was the fiery theologian Alexander, inspired by his great truth about the ignominious implications of commercial broadcasting for a democratic society and fueled by his anger at the demise of the PWBF. At worst, there was the egotist Randall, incapable of working with others and unwilling to grasp his own asininity.

CHAPTER 5

The Broadcast Reform Movement versus the Radio Lobby: Arguments, Proposals, Programs, and Problems

The broadcast reform movement generated an extensive critique of commercial broadcasting and its limitations for the communication requirements of a democratic society. While there was general consensus on the core elements of this critique, the reformers disagreed about alternatives to the status quo. The assorted broadcast reformers had difficulty working in unison, thereby only magnifying the difficulty of their task of reconstructing U.S. broadcasting. This chapter will discuss the basic concerns that united the broadcast reform movement as well as the issues that divided them.

The single greatest obstacle facing the broadcast reformers was the commercial broadcasting industry itself, especially the radio lobby, which emerged full-force by the early 1930s. The commercial broadcasters did not sit idly by as the reformers attacked the legitimacy of their control of the ether. To the contrary, they devoted considerable resources to publicizing their own vision of U.S. broadcasting as innately democratic and American, and superior to all conceivable alternatives. This chapter will examine the radio lobby, its pro–status quo arguments, and the specific measures taken by each of the networks to address weak spots in the emerging system.

The Broadcast Reformers: Critique of the Status Quo, Alternatives, and Problems

The criticism generated by the broadcast reformers of the emerging network, commercial broadcasting system was, at its core, radical criticism. It identified ownership and support as the decisive elements in accounting for the nature of U.S. broadcasting and argued that any meaningful reform of U.S. broadcasting would have to alter the existing patterns of ownership, control, and support. "Ownership of the facilities is the crux of the matter," Gross Alexander stated in 1934. "Whoever controls facilities is bound to control their uses." Moreover, the existing concentrated, private control of the ether gave the U.S. broadcasting system a distinct bias toward preserving and expanding upon the interests of the business class and maintaining the inegalitarian power relations of U.S. society. To Joy Elmer Morgan, the issue was clear:

> The real question at issue is whether the common people, having spent centuries of blood and sacrifice to secure a right to a voice in their own destinies, are now ready to surrender that right to the money-changers or whether they wish to keep their hard-won freedom for themselves. *With its radio broadcasting in the hands of the money-changers, no nation can be free.* [his emphasis]

James Rorty would sum up the situation by stating: "For all practical purposes radio in America is owned by big business, administered by big business, and censored by big business."[1]

This corporate control of the ether was made all the more insidious by the connection of the commercial broadcasters—NBC and CBS—to the power trust of GE, RCA, AT&T, and Westinghouse. "No one familiar with the facts," the NCER's Joy Elmer Morgan informed the Canadian House of Commons in April 1932, "can doubt that there is a close relation between the monopolistic interests which are seeking to control radio and the monopolistic interests involved in the power trust." The alleged power of the radio trust was a sensitive issue in U.S. politics. As H. O. Davis put it, "this inevitable monopoly constitutes the greatest danger American democracy has ever been exposed to." Indeed, the Hoover administration even brought antitrust charges against RCA, which led to the eventual consent decree of November 1932 in which GE and Westinghouse divested their interests in RCA. Even after 1932, RCA, parent company of NBC as well as major manufacturer, was singularly reviled by the broadcast reformers. "The Radio Corporation of America," Armstrong Perry wrote to Ella Phillips Crandall, "is at the bottom of most of the radio troubles in the United States."[2]

Two fundamental themes dominated the reformers' criticism of the status quo. First, the notion that the functioning of the status quo was inimical to the communication requirements of a democratic society was at the center of virtually every critique of commercial broadcasting. This was at once a theoretical and practical concern. "Censorship is inevitable in any broadcasting system," Perry commented, echoing the entirety of the broadcast reform movement, "because there is never enough time for all the programs that might be broadcast. Calling it by other names does not eliminate it." When this assumption was fused with the critique of how U.S. broadcasting was actually structured, the results were explosive. "The existent set-up of the United States is dominated by two monopolistic networks. They decide the types of educational programs that shall do on the air; what social, political, economic, ethical questions shall be discussed; what points of view shall be presented,'' wrote Father John B. Harney in a representative passage.

> None of us would put an axe in the hands of a man who wanted to cut down our most fruitful plum trees, and leave him alone in the orchard for fifteen minutes. Would the managers of commercial stations do an equally foolish thing by giving the use of their facilities to a University professor, however learned, whose economic views clashed with their own? We are not yet in Utopia![3]

Along these lines, E. Pendleton Herring wrote: ''To believe that ideas critical of the existing social and economic order will naturally win a hearing if they are of sufficient importance to the listening public is to ignore the fact that actual programs are drawn up and determined by private interests.'' The NCER's Morgan informed an audience in 1931 that

> there are those that profess to fear the censorship of radio stations operated by local, state, and national government. Do they fail to realize that we already have a censorship—a censorship applied not by government, which is elected and maintained by the people and responsible to their control, but a censorship maintained by powerful private interests who are responsible to no one but their own selfish interests?[4]

Indeed, to Morgan, this private control of broadcasting was not simply a theoretical problem, it rendered ''genuine freedom of thought'' impossible: ''The very points at which facts are most needed if people are to govern themselves wisely are the points at which freedom of speech is most certain to be denied.'' James Rorty observed that due to the corporate control of broadcasting, ''the status quo of business and finance in general'' was protected from any significant criticism.[5] The accuracy of this critique of ''private censorship'' was at the center of the debate over broadcasting in the early 1930s. The reformers and the ACLU produced numerous examples of unpopular political opinions being excluded from the airwaves. To the ACLU, network domination of broadcasting meant that ''the problem of censorship is magnified a thousandfold.'' ''Liberals and the working class movement,'' one ACLU memo in 1935 observed, ''must depend almost entirely, then, on the favors of the large broadcasting companies'' to get on the air. CBS newscaster H. V. Kaltenborn acknowledged that networks only permitted the occasional ''wellbehaved [sic] liberal or radical speaker'' on the air to deflect public criticism.[6]

The second broadcast reform movement theme concerned advertising and its effect upon programming. ''The system of support and how it affects the program,'' stated one educator, ''is the heart of radio.'' An ACLU report on public affairs programming, based upon several years examination, concluded that U.S. broadcasting was typified by "the shameful condition of a public medium on which crooners are commonly considered more important than discussion of vital political and social issues."[7] Father Harney observed that since the "cardinal point" of the commercial broadcasters' programming policy was "to avoid whatever might offend the sensibilities of any of the big advertisers, or might, however unreasonably, give umbrage to any noteworthy percentage of their listeners, they keep off the air whatever is warmly controverted, whether in religion, ethics, or economics." Perry observed that President Hoover had been "humiliated on Lincoln's Birthday" when radio announcers thanked a tobacco company for granting him time for his address. "Do we want our public officials and educators in a position where they can address radio audiences only by becoming adjuncts to commercial advertising?"[8]

It was the tendency of advertising, however, to encourage the airing of seemingly trivial and silly programs that drew the most attention from the broadcast reformers. Arthur Crane argued that "it is unavoidable that a commercial concern catering to the public will present a service as low in standard as the public will tolerate and will produce the most profit." "In order to get large audiences," Morgan observed, "they cultivate the lower appeals." To Morgan, the social implications of this were frightening. "Commercialized broadcasting as it is now unregulated in America may threaten the very life of civilization by subjecting the human mind to all sorts of new pressures and selfish exploitations."[9] Bruce Bliven argued that "real social usefulness for the radio" would be an "impossibility" as long as advertising was the primary means of support, terming commercial programming "moronic drivel and oral garbage." H. L. Mencken characterized U.S. broadcasting as "an almost unbroken series of propaganda harangues by quacks with something to sell, and of idiotic comments upon public events by persons devoid of both information and ideas."[10]

There were two variants to this line of criticism of commercial programming. One variant blamed the situation on the commercial broadcasters and advertisers, who, it was argued, had created an audience for the most profitable programming they could generate. "It may be true, as the broadcasters assert, that the people are satisfied with what they are getting," University of California President Robert G. Sproul observed in 1934, "but that does not prove they would not like something better. The public has been taught to want what it is getting. It has received twelve years of concentrated instruction from an expert corps of teachers."[11] Since advertising and the profit motive had corrupted popular or folk culture, this variant argued, a noncommercial system would therefore generate a more sophisticated audience for a genuine mass culture, which was distinct from a commercially driven mass culture.

The other variant was distinctly elitist, accepting without objection the contention of the commercial broadcasters that they were "giving the people what they want." Bliven was foremost among the elitists, arguing that

> even the so-called entertainment aspects of programs are such that no civilized person can listen to them without nausea. This is often the result of a deliberate policy on the part of the advertiser, who finds that people of low intelligence respond most readily to his commercial appeal, and therefore baits his trap with material intentionally designed to reach those who are not quite bright.

One commentator stated that "the bunkum, the hokum, the vulgarity, the asininity, the crudity, the imbecility of the great majority of commercial programs" was because they were intended for society's " 'hotcha' element." The author described this "hotcha" element as "the vulgar horde, who lack good taste and intelligence and ambition for culture" and "the moronic mob." As another writer stated, his "ideal broadcasting station" would make "no hypocritical pretense" of attempting "to present something for everyone." Rather, all the programming would "be aimed at and above a frankly upper-middle class" audience.[12]

This elitist bias reflected, to some extent, the class basis of the broadcast reform movement, which, with the exception of WCFL and some of the populists associated with the NCER, was constituted by members of the upper-middle and upper classes who were not particularly reflective upon the implications of class for culture. It is not surprising, therefore, that it was only WCFL that took seriously the notion of providing noncommercial entertainment programming for a "mass" audience. Nockels did not regard the commercial entertainment programs as indicative of any desire to "give the people what they want" as much as flat-out bribes so the advertisers and commercial broadcasters could get what *they* wanted.

> How strange that the victims of the system do not see through the game that is being played to bind them hand and foot, possibly forever. The Radio Trust wooing them by "Amos 'n' Andy," or "Thompson's Corner" to listen to the glories of Fleischmann's Yeast or Palmolive soap, of course, may be classed as harmless though silly. But neither harmless nor silly is the determined appropriation of the lanes of the air for the propaganda of Big Biz [sic] for deadening the minds of the masses.[13]

Even the college broadcasters, who regarded their programming as having an explicit educational mission, did not believe they could broadcast whatever they pleased, so long as it met their personal "elite" standards of cultural excellence. Most nonprofit broadcasters regarded themselves as entirely dependent upon cultivating and satisfying their audiences in order to win the budgets necessary to remain on the air. In the minds of many nonprofit broadcasters, it was the commercial broadcasters who had the less direct relationship with their audience, due to the role of advertising.

This point notwithstanding, to some of the broadcast reformers the very notion of entertainment programming was anathema and synonymous with commercial programming. The purpose of noncommercial programming was to provide the cultural uplift that had not been deemed profitable by the commercial broadcasters. This stance left the broadcast reform movement in a precarious position. On one hand, it generated a class-based populist critique of the corporate domination of the ether on free speech grounds that had the potential to appeal to society's dispossessed elements. On the other hand, its cultural critique was aimed largely at an elite audience and, if anything, it repelled potential support from those who welcomed a significant place for entertainment programming on radio.

Although most reformers were not hostile to the marketplace per se, they all rejected it as the appropriate mechanism to regulate broadcasting. In particular, the reformers dismissed the notion that commercial broadcasting had been "selected" in some sort of free market competition for listeners with noncommercial broadcasting. "A license from the Federal Government does more than set the conditions under which broadcasting competition can take place," S. Howard Evans stated. "It actually determines the outcome of the competition." "The American system assumes there is free and fair competition in the business of broadcasting," observed Perry. "This is a false assumption because the number of channels is limited and when one concern secures a channel its competitors are unable to secure the same privilege." E. Pendleton Herring argued that "the populace is actually given little choice when confronted on one hand with the programs of the favored commercial stations and on the other hand with those of special interest stations handicapped by unpopular and inconvenient time schedules and low power."[14]

For the bulk of the population, therefore, little sense existed that there was any viable or fundamental alternative to the relatively narrow range of commercial choices being offered to them in the early 1930s. Moreover, the listeners' "votes" in this marketplace were mediated through the perceived effectiveness of advertising messages rather than cast directly. James Rorty approvingly cited Walter Hale Hamilton's maxim regarding the beauty of the marketplace as an engine of social control: "Business succeeds rather better than the state in imposing restraints upon individuals, because its imperatives are disguised as choices."[15]

The broadcast reform movement also dismissed the notion that a more public-spirited and aggressive federal regulation of the network, commercial system could produce acceptable changes in the system. By the late 1930s, this would become the liberal plank of the dominant paradigm regarding broadcast regulation. In the early 1930s, however, the broadcast reform movement regarded this notion as preposterous, particularly in view of the FRC's less-than-antagonistic relationship with the commercial broadcasters.

Perry concluded that the "point of view" of "our radio officials" was "exactly that of the broadcasting industry." As Father Harney argued, "It was once thought that the Federal Radio Commission could be trusted to make due provision for these human welfare agencies, but the Radio Commission's own acts prove that no such trust can be placed in its hands." The solution seemed obvious: If "Congress wants to protect the radio future of human welfare agencies it must lay down an emphatic law to that effect and give clear, definite mandates" to alter the balance of power in broadcasting.[16]

Beyond criticizing the specific workings of the FRC, the reformers generated a larger critique of the limitations of attempting to regulate the status quo to perform in a fundamentally different manner while leaving the network, commercial system intact. "That kind of arrangement," noted Morgan in reference to the suggestion that a more aggressive regulatory body might force the broadcasters to air unprofitable programming provided by civic and educational organizations, "would result in perpetual warfare, and I do not believe perpetual warfare between our institutions and industries is desirable for either. They are inherently different in purpose, and when you try to drive the two together you are going to have conflict and difficulty. That has been proved over and over again." Moreover, if "perpetual warfare" were to be the result of an aggressive regulatory regime, it was a war that the outsiders and public interest advocates would invariably lose. As S. C. Hooper, a naval officer, who was critical of the lack of coherent federal communications policy, informed President Franklin D. Roosevelt in 1933:

> My experience in government affairs has convinced me that if the large companies in an industry wish to attain a common end they will eventually succeed unless the laws passed by Congress are such to provide adequate barriers. With clever executives and high-priced lawyers, the Government administrators have little chance in the long run to resist such pressure, due to the ever-changing personnel in the Government, regardless of the unquestioned faithfulness of the employees.[17]

Finally, insofar as the purpose of the broadcast reform movement was to exact fundamental change in the structure of U.S. broadcasting, three themes underlay the entirety of the critique of the status quo. First, it was axiomatic that the emerging status quo had not been "selected" by the citizenry in any rational or democratic dialogue. "It is not accurate to describe radio broadcasting in the United States as a system," Morgan wrote. "It is the exact opposite of a system. It is confusion and chaos. From the beginning it has been one mad scramble of powerful commercial interests to gain control of this new means of reaching the human mind." "When I hear people talk of the resulting broadcasting situation as the 'American system,'" William Orton informed a 1935 audience, "I cannot avoid lifting an academic eyebrow. It may be American, but it is not a system. It is," he concluded, an "extension of the reign of ballyhoo."[18]

Second, the broadcast reformers emphatically asserted the right of the public, acting through its elected representatives, to establish whatever type of broadcasting system they deemed desirable, even if this might mean the elimination of the entire capitalist basis of American broadcasting. It was taken for granted that the airwaves were in "the public domain," and not inherently subject to private exploitation on a first come, first serve basis. In this context the issue was quite clear, as Perry argued:

> The question really is, Do we want to submit to the regulation of radio by the people whom we elect to rule over us, or do we want to leave our radio channels in the hands of private concerns and private individuals who wish to use these public radio channels for their own profit?[19]

Indeed, given these presuppositions and the general critique outlined earlier, the entire logic of U.S. broadcasting struck the reform movement as inane and contradictory. "The present American system of broadcasting," University of Wyoming president Crane stated,

> is an almost incredible absurdity for a country that stakes its existence upon universal suffrage, upon the general intelligence of its citizens, upon the spread of reliable information, upon the attitudes and judgments of all the people, and then consigns a means of general communication exclusively to private interests, making public use for general welfare subordinate and incidental. The absurdity becomes more absurd when we deal with a limited resource belonging to all of us and save none of this general resource for our own general use. The absurdity passes comprehension when we not only give up our public birthright but tax ourselves to support commissions, to protect private monopoly in the use and control of what belongs to the nation.

Crane concluded that, "The absurdity becomes tragic when the vital values of radio communication to a democracy are considered."[20]

Accordingly, the broadcast reform movement's third assumption was that reform would necessarily have to address the contradiction between the private, for-profit control of broadcasting and the communication requirements of a democratic society. As William Orton put it, "The profit-motive is fundamentally inconsistent with either technical or cultural excellence in broadcasting service." It is a "fact that the radio channels belong to the people," stated an NCER organizer, "and should not be placed in the hands of private capital." In sum, at the very least the goal of the broadcast reform movement was to remove a significant portion of the radio spectrum from the dictates of the capital accumulation process, with all that this would entail. "Any program of statesmanship in the modern era must take account of radio broadcasting as our major instrument of social communication," James Rorty wrote in this vein. "The object, surely, is to permit the free and adequate use of radio by any and all groups that can legitimately claim to represent the basic needs and functions of society."[21]

Given this logic, it is not surprising that most broadcast reformers had good things to say about the BBC, which had a nonprofit and noncommercial monopoly over Britain's broadcasting services and was subsidized by radio receiver set fees. "After some little study of both systems," Bruce Bliven wrote, "I believe that the British plan is about 1000 percent superior to the American, and the best thing we could do would be to adopt it." Joy Morgan was on record as an enthusiastic proponent of a BBC-type set-up for the United States. "A charge of $1.00 per set would provide America ten times the funds which we would need for a generous program of broadcasting," he proclaimed when the subject came up at the annual convention of the National University Extension Association in 1932.[22]

Nor was this an entirely platonic relationship. Armstrong Perry had visited the BBC several times and enjoyed an extensive and personal correspondence with both Sir John C. W. Reith, managing director of the BBC, and A. R. Burrows, a BBC official who went on to become the executive officer of the International Broadcasting Union. Reith was sympathetic to the U.S. broadcast reform movement, asking Perry in 1931, "Why don't you start at the bottom and clean up your whole system?" He caused a stir on a visit to the United States the same year when he informed members of the FRC that he believed the United States would eventually adopt the British system.[23] Reith subsequently kept his opinions on U.S. broadcasting confidential or nondescript, not wishing to antagonize the commercial broadcasters, whom he increasingly acknowledged as entrenched, and with whom the BBC necessarily cooperated.[24] Moreover, the BBC did not want the U.S. networks to provide assistance to the British proponents of commercial broadcasting anymore than the U.S. broadcasters wanted the BBC to lend its prestige to the cause of broadcast reform in the United States. Hence, the two sides simply agreed to disagree regarding the best way to organize broadcasting.[25] "The whole American system of broadcasting," the BBC politely noted in 1932, lies "outside our comprehension" and "clearly springs from a specifically American conception of democracy." Even without the formal support of Reith, the reformers were enthralled by the BBC's seeming capacity to combine the benefits of a nonprofit, noncommercial monopoly with a lack of overt partisan or government interference. To Perry, the BBC provided the "ideal" example of a "broadcasting service maintained primarily for the benefit of all radio listeners" and was the solution to "the whole world problem of broadcasting."[26]

These sentiments notwithstanding, one of the striking features of the broadcast reform movement's activities is that there was never the slightest effort spent toward accomplishing the nationalization and decommercialization of *all* of U.S. broadcasting. Of the reformers, only the ACLU seemingly rejected the notion of government broadcasting categorically. For the balance of the reformers, it was a pragmatic stance based to some extent on the strength of the commercial broadcasters. "A system of completely government-controlled broadcasting," two reformers acknowledged in 1931, "cannot now be established in the United States unless by economic revolution. The power interests are too firmly entrenched to be pulled loose any other way." In addition, nationalization was regarded as tactical suicide. "Let me advise strongly against sending out as a possible solution of this problem of radio anything that has to do with government ownership or control," Evans advised Walter Woehlke of the *Ventura Free Press*. "The newspapers are afraid of it."[27] Most important, there was a general consensus in the broadcast reform movement that public opinion would not tolerate government radio, monopoly or otherwise. The ideology of enterprise was too deeply entrenched in U.S. culture.

By limiting the government's role in any alternative broadcast scheme, however, the broadcast reformers thereby opened up the pressing question of how then to subsidize adequately nonprofit broadcasting. Crane only affirmed the obvious at a conference in 1933 when he stated that "the question of adequate financial support for public stations must receive more definite and pointed consideration in the near future." The one certainty was that the existing system, whereby the remaining nonprofit broadcasters with restricted daylight hours, low power allowances, dilapidated facilities, and minuscule budgets attempted to generate listener or organizational contributions, had clearly proven ineffectual, particularly with the advent of the Great Depression. As Perry noted, "the weak support of education by radio by the institutions which ought to be most interested is a major problem in the present deplorable radio situation."[28] Moreover, aside from the Payne Fund, the major philanthropies had either elected not to enter broadcasting or had supported activities in conjunction with the commercial broadcasters, like the NACRE.

In this vacuum, the immediate and readily available solution to the financial crisis of nonprofit broadcasters was to sell time to commercial advertisers. In principle, all elements of the broadcast reform movement acknowledged that advertising over the air was a loathsome activity. There was, however, a fundamental split in the opinions of the broadcast reformers regarding advertising's usefulness as a revenue option in the short-term. To the NCER, commercial advertising was despised unconditionally and there were no circumstances that would permit its utilization by nonprofit broadcasters, not to mention in any larger alternative program for U.S. broadcasting. It was self-evident to the NCER that radio advertising was rife with fraudulent claims, far more so than any advertising in other media. In 1933 Perry wrote that "the American system is based largely on advertising in which the statements made do not check with the known facts." Morgan's criticism of advertising was so strident that the business manager of the National Education Association, where Morgan was editor of the advertising-supported *Journal of the National Education Association,* implored him to avoid his "antagonism of national advertisers and advertising agencies" in the *Journal*'s pages, since "our advertising situation is critical."[29]

As Tracy Tyler wrote to one college president in 1932, it was a cornerstone of NCER policy from the outset, "that educational institutions should take every possible step to secure forms of support other than advertising." Morgan wrote to one university president that "when an educational station ties up with the advertisers it loses its claim to preferred consideration." Along these lines, the NCER steadfastly accused the commercial broadcasters of "using every effort to discredit all college and university stations because of the few that are or have gone commercial."[30] A full-page headline announced in *Education by Radio:*

> Not satisfied with having crowded nearly half the educational stations off the air, the commercial monopoly radio interests are seeking to destroy the others by boring from within. The station is approached with the subtle suggestion that it sell time for advertising or that it take the national chain advertising programs originating in New York. Glowing pictures are painted of the profits that can be made. An institution which does not see far ahead is sometimes induced to sell its birthright for a mess of pottage.

The headline concluded that "to turn the college stations commercial is to destroy them, and the monopolists know this." Indeed, *Broadcasting* proclaimed that the presence of advertising on the educational stations discredited any of their claims for preferential treatment.[31] These points notwithstanding, many educational stations found that they had no immediate alternative to accepting advertising if they wished to remain on the air.

Some of the other nonprofit broadcasters, on the other hand, not only accepted advertising, they also defended their right to do so. Nonprofit broadcasters "should have the right to sell some of their time so as to obtain enough to live on," Father Harney told the SCIC in 1934. "Not to make a profit, but enough to support themselves, so they will not be dependent on charity all the while and will not have to be beggars." Far more emphatic were the constant commendations of advertising made by WCFL after it turned to commercial support in the early 1930s. "Advertising," the Chicago Federation of Labor's *Federation News* declared in 1933, "needs no apology from any of us. The force which created the greatest radio system in the world, needs no timid appeal for public condolence."[32] Only a couple of years earlier, the same newspaper had disparaged broadcast advertising in the most uncertain terms.

It was in this context that the broadcast reform movement attempted to develop alternative schemes for the reconstruction of U.S. broadcasting.

Although people like Gross Alexander, H. O. Davis, and Harris Randall each devised their own plans along these lines, only three reform proposals received widespread support by the broadcast reformers. First, there was the fixed-percentage scheme, whereby either 15 percent or 25 percent of the channels would be set aside for nonprofit broadcasters. A variation on this idea called for the government to set aside a specific number of clear channel stations for nonprofit broadcasting. The fundamental limitation of the fixed-percentage measure was that it did nothing to resolve the severe financial crisis facing the nonprofit broadcasters. Even as the NCER was being formed on the basis of lobbying for this measure, Perry informed Crandall that "our problem still is unsolved: the finding of financial support for college and university stations."[33]

This weakness would be exploited by the proponents of the status quo when they argued, with no small amount of logic, that since nonprofit broadcasters were financially ill-equipped to broadcast over the few frequencies they already had, they certainly were in no position to be demanding additional slots on the spectrum. When some broadcast reformers countered that nonprofit broadcasters would sell advertising to support their operations, proponents of the status quo pounced on this admission. Senator C. C. Dill, who led the battle against the fixed-percentage legislation in Congress, stated that his "strongest objection" to the legislation was that these nonprofit stations were not "merely" nonprofit broadcasters, but they would "make use of the stations for advertising purposes." The implication, to Dill, was that "we are simply changing the ownership of the stations" to owners who "call themselves" nonprofit, but were actually indistinguishable from the existing commercial broadcasters.[34] Given the experiences of WCFL and WEVD, there was certainly some truth in Dill's comments.

Accordingly, the NCER was never enamored with the fixed-percentage approach. Perry stated "emphatically" that "any plan dependent upon paid advertising for support was undesirable." Morgan found himself in the position of personally advocating some form of government broadcasting while heading an organization, the NCER, formally chartered to lobby for the fixed-percentage scheme.[35] This hardly lent itself to a victorious lobbying campaign.

The second basic proposal from the broadcast reform movement was for the government to establish an independent body, to be comprised of distinguished individuals with no affiliation to the broadcasting industry, to make a thorough study of broadcasting, and to then suggest fundamental reforms to recreate the system. This measure became the central focus of the reform movement by early 1933. To a certain extent, the reformers hoped that this body would resolve the basic problems that had plagued them regarding the role of the government and generating adequate financial support for nonprofit and noncommercial broadcasting. In short, many reformers believed that a government study by respected experts could call for the government chain they feared to suggest. To the broadcast reformers it was unquestionable that any genuinely independent study of broadcasting would recommend the establishment of a largely nonprofit and noncommercial broadcasting system; the notion that it might recommend the continuation of the status quo was not even considered.

Much of the reform movement's interest in an independent study came from Canada, which had conducted precisely such a study of its broadcasting system before resolving for a strong government, noncommercial broadcasting system along the lines of the BBC in 1932. Canadian Prime Minister R. B. Bennett noted that he could not conceive of a situation in which "any government would be warranted in leaving the air to private exploitation and not reserving it for the use of the people." Even more than with the BBC, the broadcast reformers had an extremely close relationship with Graham Spry, secretary of the Canadian Radio League, which had organized the movement to establish noncommercial and nonprofit broadcasting in Canada. "Your approach to the question of the control of broadcasting," Spry wrote to Gross Alexander, "is precisely my own."[36] Spry saw his major opposition coming from "the American chains" that "were working together and had agents in Ottawa" assisting those Canadian interests, primarily the Canadian Pacific Railway, that wanted to establish a commercial, for-profit system. He solicited the NCER for any information it had on the power trust that he could use against it. "In a word," he wrote to Armstrong Perry, "we fear that the foundation of our national government, the public opinion of our country is being menaced" by the ambitions of RCA and the U.S. commercial broadcasters.[37]

Due to Spry's handiwork, the only Americans to testify before the Special Radio Committee of the Canadian House of Commons during its hearings in the spring of 1932 were Lee DeForest and Joy Elmer Morgan. Spry was effusive in his praise for the impact of Morgan's testimony, noting that it "gave an entirely new complexion to the situation." "Until your appearance," Spry informed Morgan, "the committee had regarded the American situation as largely satisfactory, and at least two members of the committee had become quite wedded to the idea that educational broadcasts were eminently possible through commercial stations." Nor, to Spry, was Canada's victory unimportant to the U.S. broadcast reformers. "If Canada establishes a non-advertising system," he wrote to Morgan, "your whole position in the United States will be strengthened."[38] The NCER's Tracy Tyler concurred. In a memo to educational broadcasters he noted: "Canada's decision in favor of public ownership and operation of radio will serve to strengthen interest in our movement." S. Howard Evans observed that "the action of Canada is a distinct gain for our cause because it is almost a direct slap at the viciousness of our American advertising." Nor were proponents of the

U.S. status quo oblivious to this prospect. Senator Dill warned the commercial broadcasters that if the Canadian plan succeeds and Americans near the Canadian border approve of the noncommercial programming, then it "may easily lead to a nationwide demand for government operation of all radio stations in the United States."[39]

The third and final major program advanced by the broadcast reform movement was for the establishment of a series of noncommercial government stations on a local, state, and national basis, which would be operated semi-autonomously, like public universities or along the lines of the BBC, and be subsidized through tax dollars. Various versions of this program were floated by the broadcast reform movement as early as 1933, but the NCER would not formally resolve for the establishment of a chain of noncommercial government stations until 1935. Its plan included a provision so that existing and potential nonprofit broadcasters could affiliate with the government chain. By this time, however, the possibility for reform was virtually nil. At the same time, public apprehension concerning government ownership was regarded as lessening as the New Deal entered its third year. The NCER plan, like most of the others, was designed to "interfere as little as possible with the existing commercial broadcasting structure."[40]

This third approach had the benefit of seeming to resolve the funding dilemma that plagued the reformers throughout this era: The state was now formally permitted to provide the funds for nonprofit broadcasting through some form of taxation. The quid pro quo was that the commercial broadcasters would be explicitly acknowledged as having a dominant role in broadcasting. Although the fixed-percentage plan had done so as well, it had been framed far more as a "first step" by the NCER and the reform movement with the insinuation that even greater reform would follow. Moreover, the thinking was that this program might satisfy that element of the population that desired the maintenance of the commercial set-up. Thus, the major selling point of this government system proposal was that it would hold out the promise of genuine choice for the listeners. As Bruce Bliven wrote,

> With the government system in operation, the people could choose. If they wanted to listen to advertising as the private broadcasters insist they do, they would certainly have the opportunity. If, on the other hand, there are people like myself, who find advertising so obnoxious that they wish the radio had never been invented, they would be able to listen to the government broadcasts with complete peace of mind.[41]

Unfortunately for the reformers, this was an alternative that the commercial broadcasters had no interest in providing to the American people. Throughout the early 1930s, the commercial broadcasters routinely characterized all of the activities of the broadcast reform as efforts to eliminate private, commercial broadcasting in its entirety. Accordingly, the commercial broadcasters approached all efforts to create space for nonprofit and noncommercial broadcasting during this period as if they were specific efforts to eliminate for-profit, commercial broadcasting; it is virtually impossible during this entire period to find any proponent of the status quo taking seriously the broadcast reform movement's proposals to have a mixed system of for-profit and nonprofit, commercial and noncommercial broadcasting. The various reform proposals that seemingly countenanced some commercial broadcasting were, at best, regarded as inappropriate "legislative chiseling" of the broadcast spectrum, which would lead invariably to the "complete disintegration" of broadcasting. For example, *Broadcasting* would characterize the NCER in 1934 as a group "established on the principle of government ownership of radio," and this was precisely how they framed all of the NCER's reform activities in their pages.[42]

This characterization infuriated the broadcast reformers, who had devoted considerable effort to establishing that they were opposed to a government monopoly. Nevertheless, the commercial broadcasters kept to this position "in spite of official denials" by the NCER and other broadcast reformers. To some extent, the commercial broadcasters' approach may have been justified. After all, the rhetoric of the reformers hardly suggested that they were interested in establishing some sort of truce with the commercial broadcasters. As *Broadcasting* editor Sol Taishoff wrote to Tracy Tyler, the NCER "is constantly sniping at radio without even the courage of coming out flatly and stating that it favors Government ownership."[43]

In a broader sense, however, the commercial broadcasters' stance may have been dishonest, but it reflected astute business and political strategies. Economically, the industry had little interest in losing potential audiences, and advertising dollars, to nonprofit competition not subject to the same market constraints as the commercial broadcasters. Politically, as long as the ether remained entirely commercial, the notion that there was an alternative method for organizing broadcasting would remain abstract and, consequently, the province of the intelligentsia. The population would grow to regard the status quo as an unalterable given. As one NBC executive bluntly informed Perry in 1931, the goal of RCA was to see "that all of the channels be under the control" of "commercial companies."[44] The prospect of providing the listeners with the type of "choice" that Bruce Bliven envisioned may well have opened the proverbial can of worms. For the commercial broadcasters, admitting significant noncommercial broadcasting to the spectrum was a no-win proposition. Moreover, as will be discussed later, this tact proved decisive in uniting all of the commercial broadcasters—large and small—against broadcast reform.

That the broadcast reformers had such difficulty countering the commercial broadcasters on such an elemental point underlines the general lack of coherence in their movement. As a group, the reformers revealed a remarkable lack of political savvy. They rarely agreed to work in unison on a specific program and took years to find a program upon which everyone could agree. One flustered reformer in Washington, D.C., commented that "every son-of-a-gun and his brother has a definite idea about the way it should be handled."[45] Even the two groups funded by the Payne Fund—the NCER and the *Ventura Free Press* radio campaign—could not coordinate their activities. It is possible that this could be attributed to the notion that educators and ministers make lousy political organizers; they are encumbered with the faulty belief that the truth will win out even in the rough and tumble world of politics. Here also the lack of a greater labor or organized left-wing presence in the reform movement may have been most telling. In any case, even under the best of circumstances such ineptitude would have been damaging, and the reformers were in anything but the best of circumstances.

The Radio Lobby: Activities and Arguments in Defense of the Status Quo

The weaknesses in the broadcast reform movement were all the more striking when contrasted to the radio lobby of the commercial broadcasters, which was comprised of NBC, CBS, and the NAB, and also received assistance from the lobbying arms of the great communication firms like GE and AT&T. The broadcast reformers soon became aware of what they were up against. Tracy Tyler characterized the radio lobby as "one of the most powerful here in Washington." One reformer in the Roosevelt administration characterized it as "one of the strongest of the swarming lobbies in Washington—one with substance behind it. Members of Congress are dominated by tactics which are constantly under the direction of private interests."[46] H. O. Davis returned from his first trip to Washington to lobby for broadcast reform impressed by the extent of "the propaganda constantly being peddled on Capitol Hill by the wide-awake lobby of the radio combine."[47]

The radio lobby had a unity of purpose at all times about its activities in Washington. Although fierce competitors in the battle for choice affiliates and advertising accounts, NBC's Merlin Aylesworth and RCA's David Sarnoff met frequently with CBS's William Paley to map strategy in those broad areas, such as communication legislation, where cooperation was opportune. This spirit of cooperation filtered down to the networks' publicity departments and lobbyists.[48] Both NBC and CBS had vice-presidents specifically responsible for lobbying, Harry Butcher and original FRC member Henry A. Bellows for CBS and Frank "Scoop" Russell for NBC. In particular, Bellows, who was awarded Harvard's first doctorate in comparative literature, was a worthy adversary for those who claimed commercial broadcasting denigrated culture and education. As for the Washington-based NAB, it had been established in 1923 with the primary function of serving as the commercial broadcasters' lobbying organization. The NAB executive committee was comprised almost entirely of NBC and CBS executives and included both Russell and Bellows, the latter of whom was the executive committee's chairman throughout the early 1930s.[49] Under the direction of Philip Loucks, it worked closely with the Paley, Aylesworth, and Sarnoff.

The radio lobby was a distinct force if only due to the great and important industry it represented. Owen D. Young could arguably have had a private audience with any president on a moment's notice. Like Bellows, he hardly represented the type of robber baron plutocrat who would be easy prey for reform movement invective. Young was a visionary capitalist with a relatively strong sense of public service. Some of his opinions, as one journalist put it, would have been at home with the "left-wing of the Senate." Although dedicated to private control of the ether, Young evinced a genuine concern for the "fair administration of radio facilities," and much of the public service ethos of NBC's early years may be traced to his influence.[50]

The balance of radio industry executives may not have shared Young's sensibilities, but they enjoyed similar leverage in Washington, D.C. Will Hays, head of the Motion Picture Producers and Distributors of America, telephoned President Hoover in December 1930 to report that Sarnoff "has become the most influential man of his age—only 41 years—in big business. The bankers are sending for him—the older boys. He is in a very important position downtown." Hays advised Hoover to work closely with Sarnoff and to ask him "to come to Washington at an early opportunity." Paley and Aylesworth were also courted by the White House; both enjoyed occasional audiences and dinners with the president.[51] Such privileges were never extended to the leaders of the broadcast reform movement.

Moreover, in critical moments on Capitol Hill, these "big guns of broadcasting," as H. O. Davis called them, could come to Washington to "put on the pressure or make the promises where they would be most effective." These "executives of the chains" were also distinguished by their eloquence and charm. Significant in this regard was Sarnoff. "At the drop of a hat he could make a speech that would just ring the rafters," recalled Sol Taishoff. Even more striking was Aylesworth, who had come to NBC at the recommendation of Owen Young after directing public relations and lobbying for the National Electric Light Association, during what Joy Elmer Morgan termed "its most corrupt period." One of Aylesworth's most important tasks was to do "most of the testifying" in Washington, an assignment for which he was ideally suited. "Only Aylesworth surpassed Sarnoff in eloquence," Taishoff noted. "Aylesworth would testify before these committees and pretty soon he'd have them all crying."[52] Even the broadcast reformers were in awe of Aylesworth's talents. "It was unfortunate that you had to miss the hearing today," Tyler wrote to one educator in 1934. "President Aylesworth's clever and suave presentation was worth the price of admission to all who were there."[53]

In addition to the influence and prestige that normally accompanies great wealth in U.S. politics, the commercial broadcasters also enjoyed the additional influence that accompanied their broadcasting of political affairs. "Nor are the broadcasters without their friends on Capitol Hill," Taishoff assured his readers: "Radio as a campaigning medium is only too valuable to political candidates. They know it for they are regular seekers after favors from the radio people." As Russell noted in 1933, NBC had a policy "which makes our entire system available to any member of Congress, at anytime, for the discussion of any subject."[54] Accordingly, U.S. senators made 298 free appearances and U.S. representatives made 196 free appearances over NBC networks between January 1931 and October 1933.[55] CBS had a comparable policy. Both networks were determined to avoid the charge that they favored a particular major political party, so they seemingly favored both. In addition, the networks studiously avoided political programming that might antagonize members of Congress.

Moreover, it was the two network lobbyists who were also responsible for coordinating the scheduling of the solons on the air.[56] This certainly did not hurt their access to members of Congress when it came time to discuss communications legislation, as the reformers knew all too well. As Perry observed:

> The use of the commercial broadcasting facilities also tends to place administrative and legislative officials who should be independent in representing the people under obligation to the great corporate interests which control broadcasting. . . . It gives the high-powered lobbyists of these corporations a pretext for maintaining contact with influential public officers who can be used to defeat reform measures.

Morgan put it more bluntly: "The politicians are too eager to use radio to come out for reform."[57] This was a weapon that the reformers, with their handful of paltry stations, could scarcely counter.

In addition, the radio lobby could almost always count on the unconditional support of the FRC in its efforts to influence Congress regarding broadcasting legislation; it "enjoyed a particularly amenable and cordial association with" the FRC, as the leading study of the NAB has put it. "NAB leaders felt they had dual capacities" as they acted as an "unofficial liaison between the government and the broadcasters." This relationship had a distinctly material basis. Like Bellows, most FRC members went to careers in some capacity with the commercial broadcasting industry. Even Ira Robinson, the rebel FRC member who refused to support General Order 40, became a commercial broadcasting attorney after leaving the FRC in the early 1930s. As H. O. Davis put it, he "sold out lock, stock and barrel." The balance of the FRC's legal, engineering, and administrative personnel enjoyed similar success finding lucrative employment with the commercial broadcasters after stints in government. To Morgan, the promise of future employment was decisive, providing the radio lobby with "a tactic we could not meet." "Practically all the engineers and commissioners of this first radio commission," he would reflect, "were absorbed by the corporations to whom they had voted privileges worth millions of dollars."[58]

The NAB constantly attempted to arouse support for its activities among the commercial broadcasters in the early 1930s with a strident, almost hysterical, quality to its communications. "The time has come when the broadcasters cannot appear divided against themselves before the American people and the Congress," the NAB warned commercial broadcasters in a newsletter in early 1931. "Today broadcasters must fight organized and powerful opposition," another NAB newsletter proclaimed later that year. "The broadcasters didn't start it, the fight was carried to them. And the fight will be lost unless broadcasters will put aside petty prejudices and join together to defend their own interests." In both its public and private communications, the NAB and the commercial broadcasters revealed nothing but contempt for the broadcast reformers. To the NAB, the opposition to the status quo came from "groups who either have selfish ends to gain by destroying commercial broadcasting or who, having been unwilling to bear the trials of pioneering, now seek to get into the broadcasting business."[59] In a letter to David Sarnoff, Aylesworth described the critics of commercial broadcasting as "people who have an axe to grind or want a job." The NAB routinely dismissed them as "professional agitators."[60]

The NAB was assisted in its drive to mobilize commercial broadcasters by *Broadcasting*, which it helped establish with Sol Taishoff and Martin Codel in 1931. It quickly became recognized as "the voice of the two big chains." The very first editorial laid down the gauntlet:

> Broadcasting in the United States today stands in grave jeopardy. Politically powerful and efficiently organized groups actuated by selfishness and with a mania for power are now busily at work planning the complete destruction of the industry we have pioneered and developed.[61]

To the broadcast reformers, *Broadcasting* "habitually tried to discredit everyone who has not been willing to accept without question the complete commercialization of American radio." Codel and Taishoff "deliberately misstate facts and give one-sided statements," Perry informed Crandall. Given the wide circulation of *Broadcasting* in the nation's capital, however, and the lack of any comparable organ on behalf of reform, its characterizations of the broadcast reform movement were widely cited, which infuriated the reformers. "If and when the American people adopt some other method of supporting broadcasting," Tyler wrote to Taishoff in one of a several letters protesting *Broadcasting*'s treatment of the NCER, "it might be that such a magazine as yours will no longer be necessary."[62]

One of the critical battles between the radio lobby and the broadcast reformers regarded the allegiance of hundreds of small, nonnetwork-affiliated commercial stations in the broadcast reform fight. By 1926 one group, "The American Broadcasters," had been created to mobilize the independent broadcasters to battle "the 'big boys' who have monopolized the air with their chain stations and drowned the small fellow out simply because they monopolize the entire dial." This seemed like a fruitful avenue for the reformers. "I think we can win the support of the average commercial station," an NCER organizer would note after a field trip. Morgan wrote to these stations in December 1930 soliciting their support for the NCER's program; over the next two months he received well over 100 responses, generally of considerable length, critical of the FRC and the networks and sympathetic to the cause of reform. In December 1931 the NCER would protest the FRC's seeming acceptance of the NAB as the representative of all commercial broadcasters, since the smaller stations expressed "dissatisfaction" with the domination over the NAB by the networks.[63]

This strategy had two immediate problems. First, some of these "poorer, minor stations," as Walter Woehlke put it, were responsible for some of the most vulgar commercialism on the air, without any pretense of fulfilling any public interest. In an article written by the BBC's Reith on U.S. broadcasting, when the subject turned to the quality of nonnetwork, independent commercial broadcasting in the United States, he stated "the less one says the better." Second, these stations were every bit as eager for advertising as the more prosperous network affiliates. This made any commitment they might have to broadcast reform tenuous, as well as any alliances with the NCER or the *Ventura Free Press* radio campaign improbable. "These small stations are the worst competitors the newspaper have" for advertising, Woehlke informed S. Howard Evans, in telling him that it would not "be possible for us to come out openly and aggressively on behalf of the small stations."[64]

The NAB worked assiduously with *Broadcasting* to dispel the notion that it was primarily concerned with the networks and disinterested in the plight of the small independent commercial station. "Their principal effort," in this campaign, stated the NCER organizer who had recommended that the commercial stations be solicited, "is to associate our Committee with a group of radicals who are in favor of government ownership of radio." As an NAB official admitted to Perry when he protested the continual misrepresentation of the NCER's position on broadcast reform, "the threat of government ownership always" brings "more stations into its membership." In 1933 approximately one-half of all broadcasting stations belonged to the NAB while the proportion increased to two-thirds one year later.[65] Another factor in undermining potential independent opposition to the status quo was the rapid expansion of the networks. This allowed the larger and more influential independents to hitch their fortunes to the chains, usually with immediate financial rewards. As one New Orleans broadcaster stated in 1932, network affiliation "meant a quick road to better programs, a better class of business, and large financial returns."[66] In sum, the radio lobby won this battle decisively; by 1934 the ranks of the commercial broadcasters would be closed during the Congressional deliberations on broadcast legislation.

While the commercial broadcasters were able to keep their own ranks intact, such a fate eluded the broadcast reformers. The radio lobby closely monitored any and all reform activity and sought "to interpenetrate and paralyze all the groups that are working for radio reform," as Morgan put it. "One of the hardest situations with which I have to deal," an NCER field organizer wrote in a memo to Morgan and Tyler, "arises from the fact that so many organizations are being deliberately cultivated by the commercial companies." The primary mechanism the commercial broadcasters would employ would be to offer educational, religious, and civic groups the use of the air waves. "Practically all these groups have accepted free time from the commercial companies and are therefore more or less under obligation to them," the memo continued. At times, the networks would work through the NACRE in this regard. At other times, they would work on their own. In one striking example, NBC was able to have the president of the National Congress of Parents and Teachers (NCPT) appoint a special committee to work exclusively with NBC, unbeknownst to the NCPT's existing radio committee, which was among the most radical of the reform groups, having resolved for the complete nationalization and decommercialization of U.S. radio broadcasting in 1931.[67]

The commercial broadcasters and the NACRE cultivated religious, civic, and labor organizations with offers of free time, but they courted the educational groups with the greatest fervor. Most if not all of the nine member groups of the NCER were approached by NBC with offers of air time, and many accepted, much to Morgan's dismay. "Every one of the educational organizations connected with his Committee is being besieged by the radio trust outfit," Evans wrote to Woehlke in 1932, "and Brother Morgan knows it very well." Morgan and Crandall conferred over the sort of response to the "attempts of the radio interests to interpenetrate their organization." The radio lobby enjoyed its greatest success in this regard with Morgan's own NEA, which developed a regular program of broadcasting over NBC under NEA official Florence Hale. "Commercial broadcasters began to secure a dominant influence over prominent officials of NEA," Perry observed, leaving the NCER's NEA representative Morgan "constantly in a somewhat ridiculous position, not being supported by his own organization."[68] This interpenetration of the reform groups could only undermine their capacity to provide a sustained opposition to the status quo.

The commercial broadcasters also waged an extensive public relations campaign on behalf of the status quo. For NBC, this campaign was guided by Aylesworth, who was remembered by one long-time commercial broadcasting executive as "the greatest public relations man that broadcasting ever had. He did more than any other individual to sell broadcasting to the American public."[69] For CBS, Paley employed public relations expert Edward Bernays in 1929 to provide counsel on all aspects of CBS's operations.[70] Overall, the two networks and the NAB produced scores of pamphlets, articles, and books that extolled the virtues of private, commercial broadcasting for American society. This campaign was taken no less seriously than were the lobbying efforts in Washington. In early 1931 the trade publication *Radio Music Merchant* editorialized:

> Unless steps are taken by the radio industry and the individuals composing it to combat the impression being created that radio broadcasting is becoming naught but an advertising medium, radio will be harmed to a great extent.

Another trade publication warned the broadcasters in 1932 that unless they engaged in an extensive "public relations" campaign to counteract the "growing dissatisfaction on the part of the American radio audience" with commercialized programming, they would "run the risk of government ownership, or, at least, stricter government control as is exercised in Great Britain."[71]

The amount of material produced by the commercial broadcasters clearly overwhelmed that which the reform movement, with its meager resources, was able to produce and distribute. The reformers found this to be a major obstacle to their being able to generate popular support for their cause. "The commercial companies are very shrewd and seem to have large amounts of money for purposes of propaganda," one NCER memo stated. "They have public relations men in many important centers. They are fighting constantly to continue the present system." In 1933 Morgan noted angrily:

> The privately owned radio monopolies have their own special press bureaus and public relations experts. These highly skilled experts are engaged in flooding the country with misinformation deliberately designed to mislead and prejudice the people.[72]

The centerpiece of the commercial broadcasters' argument on behalf of the status quo was that the system was fundamentally true to American and democratic values. "The United States has an uncanny way of finding for itself what is best for itself," the NAB observed in a 1933 promotional volume.

> People have marveled for years at the astoundingly prophetic minds of the Fathers of this Republic in framing its Constitution and in the practical philosophy laid down in our Declaration of Independence. . . . So in a new means

of communication such as radio broadcasting, he [the American] has evolved a method of control which guarantees freedom of action and at the same time safeguards the public interest.

To emphasize the patriotic nature of for-profit, advertising-supported broadcasting, the commercial broadcasters pointedly referred to the status quo as the "American Plan" or the "American System" for broadcasting, to the point that this became the generally accepted meaning of the terms. This was a source of tremendous frustration for the broadcast reformers. In 1934 S. Howard Evans wrote:

> The phrase 'American system' was coined as a banner with which to glorify the present structure of broadcasting in the United States. The idea seems to have been that whenever the American System was mentioned people were to feel that they had something which was particularly patriotic and which was to be defended against anything and everything which might savor of any other nation.

The NCER resigned itself to the term's currency and tried to seize the patriotic initiative, positing reform as a call for a "New American Plan" for broadcasting.[73]

A related tenet of the commercial broadcasters' defense of the status quo was that a capitalist system of broadcasting was innately democratic, not only through its "Americanism," but more importantly, through its reliance upon the market and the profit-motive as its primary determinants. By this marketplace logic, the commercial broadcasters did not control the airwaves, like the broadcast reformers claimed, as much as they responded to the demands of the real masters, the listeners. One NBC publication framed the debate over broadcasting as:

> [A] basic conflict between two directly contradictory theories of broadcasting. One theory is that the Government, either through an agency of its own or through designated groups of citizens, should give the listeners the programs that the Government thinks it is best for them to hear. The other theory is that private broadcasters, competing freely with one another, will give the listeners the service that the listeners themselves want. The second theory is native to the United States. The first is imported.[74]

It would be difficult to exaggerate the significance the commercial broadcasters attributed to this point; it was simply axiomatic, as one Aylesworth pamphlet was titled, that "The Listener Rules Broadcasting." The very survival of the networks was predicated upon their capacity to "give the people what they want," and they engaged in ferocious competition to accomplish precisely that goal. By this logic, the broadcasters and the listeners had "common interests;" the reformers, on the other hand, rather than being the adversaries of elite, corporate domination of the ether, were cast as attempting to hijack broadcasting from the listeners to use for their own selfish aims.[75] Were there any interest in the programming the reformers wished to provide, this argument went, listeners would make this desire known to the broadcasters who would then find it profitable to provide it.

Clearly the commercial broadcasters were appealing to some deep-seated and important themes in U.S. political culture in their arguments on behalf of the status quo. Nevertheless, they still faced three immediate and important ideological obstacles in the early 1930s before their vision could assume the largely unassailable place on the ideological spectrum it would attain by the end of that decade.

First, the commercial broadcasters faced the considerable dissatisfaction with advertising over radio. While the commercial broadcasters would claim that the public wanted to listen to programs like "Amos 'n' Andy," they never claimed that listeners had any interest in the advertisements on "Amos 'n' Andy." The initial reaction of the public to radio advertising appears to have been quite negative; it was seen as intrusive and obnoxious and quite unlike print advertising. As Perry stated baldly, "there is no demand for it on the part of the listener." Thus, while the commercial broadcasters defended advertising as the necessary basis of support for "free" radio, they did so gingerly. "It is preposterous to put the blame for blatant advertising on the broadcasters," argued Bellows, as the broadcasters' "dream of paradise is a world in which advertisers are content with mere credit announcements at the beginning and end of each program." Moreover, Bellows concluded that, "No advertiser is so foolish as knowingly to offend any considerable part of his audience."[76] Hence, advertising "excesses" would eventually be ironed out through the workings of the marketplace. Public distaste for advertising remained a sensitive issue for the broadcast industry well after the early 1930s, but it was never again regarded as life-threatening as the public became inured to it and resigned to its existence.[77]

Second, the commercial broadcasters had to convince the public and public officials that they were firmly committed to high-grade cultural and educational programming. The emergence of radio broadcasting had given rise to grand expectations of public service, much of which had propelled the reformers' critique of the status quo. In the early 1930s, it was simply not acceptable for anyone to posit that the sole purpose of broadcasting was to serve as an engine for profit-making and that programming should be determined exclusively by market criteria. "One of the big problems facing us is the criticism we get for our so-called lack of educational programs," one NBC internal memo noted. "We are constantly being compared to the British Broadcasting Corporation." Aside from whatever genuine interest may well have existed among the broadcasters along these lines, establishing a commitment to cultural programming was seen as being of fundamental importance in keeping increased government regulation or even radical reform at bay. Any and all network programs along these lines were heavily publicized by the networks; NBC would even publish monthly program guides to its educational shows that it would distribute liberally.[78] Ironically, in the early 1930s the networks broadcast far more noncommercial cultural and educational programming than they would in subsequent years. As the networks were increasingly able to sell all of their available time to advertisers, there was that much less time for unprofitable noncommercial cultural programming.

Both NBC and CBS helped to established organizations to coordinate their noncommercial educational and cultural broadcasts. For NBC, it was the NACRE, funded by the Carnegie Corporation and John D. Rockefeller, Jr., and under the direction of Levering Tyson. Tyson continually negotiated and haggled with NBC executives to keep NACRE programs broadcast in their scheduled evening slots even when the network had been able to subsequently sell the NACRE time slots to advertisers. He understood fully the nature of NBC's commitment to the NACRE's programs. "Broadcasting's position in this country is not overly secure," Tyson wrote to one NBC executive during an especially bitter fight over an NBC plan to shift a NACRE series in 1932. "I have no hesitation in stating to you that many influential members of the Council were supporters of the theory of government broadcasting until the success of our programs convinced them that the American system is and can be workable." Tyson concluded that if the NACRE series was removed from its original time slot, "it will be perfectly apparent to these individuals that American radio will always be relegated to the pure commercial, and that all the public service for which the medium itself gave such promise is mere bunk."[79] Tyson won this particular skirmish, but it portended the fate of noncommercial cultural programming over the networks.

CBS had less success with its attempt to establish a group akin to the NACRE. In 1930 it launched, with great fanfare, the American School of the Air, which consisted of noncommercial programs intended for use in schools. The director of the American School of the Air was Alice Keith, an educator with a decade of experience with radio broadcasting. Keith assembled an advisory board of prominent educators that met twice annually with Paley and other network officials. CBS executives and Keith cited the existence of the American School of the Air as a repudiation of the claims of the broadcast reformers that commercial broadcasters were disinterested in education. "Your arguments in many ways are unjust," she would write the NCER's Morgan. "We have all criticized the commercial stations because they do not put on enough programs. The least that can be done is to recognize worthy efforts."[80]

Keith's reign at CBS was short-lived, however. In the spring of 1932 she had a parting of the ways with the network when CBS made clear its intention to curtail its commitment to the School of the Air for the 1932–1933 school year unless it could find commercial sponsorship for the series. Most of the advisory board resigned in protest, and CBS continued the scaled back School, under the direction of Keith's secretary, whose only experience had been in an advertising agency. To the conductor of the CBS orchestra, the message was clear. "Business is business," Howard Barlow commented. "And when profit and art come into combat with each other, art disappears."[81] Keith then became active in the broadcast reform movement, working closely with the NCER. "The actual control of policy is in the hands of monopolies whose aims are essentially commercial," she wrote in one tract that urged women's organizations to support the NCER. "Is not education more important," she concluded, than "commercial profits for a few?" Prior to Keith's departure, if not afterward, the CBS School of the Air was positively received by many educators. "The worst of it is that a lot of school people are falling for this stuff," the secretary of the Wisconsin Teachers Association wrote to Morgan in December 1931.[82]

The commercial broadcasters were careful to employ the stick as well as the carrot in their defense of the level of cultural programming on the air. "People do not want to be educated," Merlin Aylesworth fulminated in 1934, adding, "they want entertainment." Educational programs, both by the educational stations and the commercial stations, were characterized by one trade publication editor as " 'dry as dust' talks by musty-minded professors who lack a sense of humor and whose main idea seems to be to force their academic opinions on others." Aylesworth cast the critics of the level of cultural and educational programming on the networks as antisocial elitists and snobs. "Radio offers little," he stated, to "only a few persons." They included "the recluse, the intellectually superior person who voluntarily separates himself from the living, breathing, moving America in which he lives."[83] In the long run, this approach proved more successful than was attempting to placate the educators and intellectuals who seemed to constantly complain to the networks over their paucity of cultural fare. Criticism of the cultural and educational limitations of commercial broadcasting remained unrelenting well after the 1930s, but, cast as the concern of the "egghead" set, this criticism hardly augured a threat to corporate, commercial control of the ether.[84]

Third, the commercial broadcasters faced a more problematic obstacle. On one hand, as the NAB put it, they wished to be regarded as "as jealously determined to safeguard the right of free speech by radio as the newspapers are to safeguard their rights in the same field."[85] The broadcasters accepted, even promoted, the notion that they had a responsibility for public affairs similar to the newspapers and were not merely an entertainment medium. Insofar as this entailed granting commercial broadcasters the same independence from government intervention as U.S. newspapers were accustomed to receiving, the cause of free speech would become a great rallying cry for capitalist broadcasting by the end of the decade. In the early 1930s, however, the commercial broadcasters had to establish that they would not exercise their near-exclusive control over the public airwaves to favor any particular political agenda. Indeed, without decisively establishing their social neutrality, the entire legitimacy of a privately owned, network-dominated broadcasting system could quite easily be called into question. Moreover, the "marketplace" defense of giving listeners what they wanted was of little use here. The U.S. tradition in public affairs and journalism placed the responsibility for such content squarely on the shoulders of the media. Hence, on this issue network domination was most sensitive to attacks by the broadcast reform movement.

Considerable attention was devoted to this subject. For example, in 1935 NBC published a four-volume series almost exclusively dedicated to establishing the proposition that U.S. radio was inherently nonpartisan and dedicated to encouraging a rigorous debate on social issues. "American private competitive radio has probably given the world its freest radio forum of open debate on the great controversial political and economic problems of this age," the first volume intoned in a section titled "Democratic Culture." "American radio—without apology—and with definite educational purpose—provides a cultural ladder with *all* rungs" [their emphasis]. The fourth volume consisted entirely of statements from public figures testifying to NBC's commitment to broadcasting their speeches uncensored. This concern with establishing network "social neutrality" also underlay much of the momentum for establishing industry self-regulation.[86]

NBC was the most aggressive in this regard. Concurrent with RCA's creation of NBC, it also announced the establishment of the NBC Advisory Council so that "the public may be assured that the broadcasting is being done in the fairest and best way." Ostensibly comprised of "citizens representative of the country's various interests and aspirations," the NBC Advisory Council was to assist the network as it confronted "questions social and economic and political." Erik Barnouw has observed that the membership of the Advisory Council made it a "unique body, outshining any presidential cabinet of modern times." The Council included Robert M. Hutchins, Elihu Root, and Charles Evans Hughes, among others.[87] Specifically, the NBC Advisory Council would provide a forum for the public to have its grievances with network broadcast policies resolved. In 1927 Merlin Aylesworth informed Congress that the NBC Advisory Council was intended to be a powerful body "to which appeals can be carried over the heads of the operating executives." The existence of the Advisory Council "assures fairness of policy on all matters of public interest," Aylesworth proclaimed. In practice, the members of the Advisory Council, who received $1,000 annually for their services, met for two days every year to "discuss the activities of radio."[88]

The broadcast reformers dismissed the usefulness of the NBC Advisory Council categorically. "They can exercise no real control since the Advisory Council is appointed by the Company and is therefore under its control," Perry informed Crandall in 1929. Morgan was contemptuous, calling it a "smoke screen which seeks to protect the industry from the just and wholesome criticism of an enlightened public." It was a "diabolical practice quite unworthy of the best citizenship of our country." Indeed, there is little in the actual record to indicate it was anything more than "window dressing" for NBC, as Levering Tyson wrote that "a great many people" suspected it of being.[89] Barnouw has termed one NBC Advisory Council meeting as a "festival of congratulations," and he noted: "There is no indication that any citizen ever appealed to this Advisory Council 'over the heads of the operating executives.' Perhaps few knew where to reach it, or even that it existed. Management apparently did not make a practice of relaying complaints to it." Nonetheless, Aylesworth informed the BBC's Reith that his policies "had been approved unanimously by the Council," as if that was some extraordinary accomplishment.[90] The one time Tyson suggested that NACRE resolve a conflict with NBC over scheduling by appealing to the NBC Advisory Council, the network reacted with outrage. Nevertheless, NBC provided ample publicity to the affairs of the Advisory Council, knowing that, as one NBC internal memo put it, "a great deal of weight will be put to it in the public mind."[91]

Just how successful the Advisory Council was as a public relations enterprise is unclear. Although it had a prominent membership, it had a distinctly "establishment" cast, with the AFL's William Green providing the sole representative of the "common masses." "I would like to see some of those on there who represent the common masses of the people," Representative William I. Sirovich, (D-NY) stated when Aylesworth informed him that the Advisory Council would help maintain the network's commitment to all political viewpoints. "I have not found any of them on the list." By the end of the decade, NBC quietly disbanded the Advisory Council. The next phase of industry self-regulation, and one that was received with far less outright cynicism, would be centered around the adoption of the final NAB Code in 1939. Moreover, by the 1940s, with the establishment of network news divisions, network social neutrality would then be assured ostensibly, as it was in the oligopolistic newspaper industry, by professional adherence to journalistic standards of fairness and objectivity.[92] Network control would disappear from the picture.

In sum, the two adversaries in the debate over broadcast policy in the early 1930s presented "directly opposite" visions of democratic radio, as one observer put it.[93] To the reformers, democratic radio meant the explicit formulation of public policy for a vital public resource, a broadcast system accountable to elected representatives, not shareholders beholden to private profit above all else. In the eyes of the reformers, rhetoric about listeners "ruling" through the market masked the selfish aims of the networks and advertisers. To the radio lobby, on the other hand, the market was quintessentially democratic. Hence, government policies to counteract market forces were explicitly antidemocratic, promulgated by self-appointed do-gooders who could not hack it in fair and open competition for the allegiance of American listeners. To the reformers the people had a right to select whatever type of broadcast system they deemed appropriate, be it capitalist or otherwise. To the radio lobby, such a debate was unnecessary as the greatness of the United States was predicated upon its recognition of the market as the superior and natural economic regulator. Moreover, to the extent that such a debate could only take broadcast policy away from a market course, such a debate in itself was both unnecessary and undemocratic.

These adversaries did not approach each other, however, on anything remotely close to the proverbial level playing field. The commercial broadcasters were entrenched and their position grew stronger by the day. Their lobby was lavishly endowed and their cause coherently planned and executed. The broadcast reformers, on the other hand, faced a series of problems far greater than any of those that beckoned the radio lobby, not the least of which was finding a compelling alternative to the status quo that could generate popular support. As such, their strength came in their critique of the status quo. Their threat, in the minds of radio lobby, was always that this critique would find a significant base of support among the citizenry before the system was fully in place and no more susceptible to political challenge than any other major U.S. industry.

CHAPTER 6

1930–Summer 1932: The Battle
on Capitol Hill

The first wave of broadcast reform activity took place between 1930 and 1932 and was directed toward having reform legislation passed by Congress. The reformers came to Washington full of outrage for commercial broadcasting and optimism regarding the prospects for reform. This chapter will chronicle and evaluate their efforts and also discuss the controversy surrounding the ABA Standing Committee on Communications, which emerged as a significant opponent of broadcast reform in Washington during this period.

Public Opinion and Congressional Attitudes
on Broadcasting and Reform

Much of the reform movement's enthusiasm for the eventual success of their cause was fueled by its belief that public opinion was opposed to the status quo and becoming increasingly sympathetic to arguments for structural reform. Walter Woehlke wrote:

> From my contacts with the general public, I know that the dissatisfaction with the present broadcasting system and its results is well nigh universal. Out of one hundred persons you will not find more than five who are satisfied; of the other 95%, more than one-half are ready to support any kind of movement for a drastic change.

Woehlke concluded that the task for broadcast reformers was to convert this distaste for advertising and commercial programming into support for reform, although that support would not necessarily be forthcoming unless the reformers could indicate "a new road leading to better things."[1]

This point was axiomatic to the reformers. As the Radio Committee of the NUEA reported to the 1930 NUEA convention, there was "a growing dissatisfaction with, or lack of interest in, purely commercial programs." After going abroad and making a study of the broadcasting systems in some forty nations, Armstrong Perry stated "there is more dissatisfaction in the United States than in any other country," which was reflected by "so much bitter criticism of their national broadcasting systems and programs."[2] In short, the broadcast reform movement, especially in its first two or three years, regarded itself as the legitimate representative of the vast majority of American listeners; there is no sense yet that it regarded itself as an elite attempting to establish a noncommercial beachhead in the context of a popularly embraced commercial system.

There is no reliable empirical data regarding the public attitude to commercial broadcasting from this era. Both sides claimed to have the support of the public and to represent its interests, and both sides pointed to the amount of mail they received to buttress their cases. It does appear, however, that, at the very least, the response to commercial broadcasting in these years was far more negative than it would be thereafter. The FRC, Congress, and newspaper radio editors were inundated by letters protesting commercialized broadcasting. One Louisiana resident wrote to the FRC in late 1931:

> Can't something be done about the tremendous quantity of rotten advertising coming over the radios? PLEASE! I know beyond all doubt that a very, very large majority of the people of this country do not want the tripe we are getting as entertainment. . . . I will say that I have heard it discussed in many sections, many even going to the extent to trying to arrange community boycotts of products advertised over radio.

"Radio broadcasting," *Business Week* informed its readers in 1932, "is threatened with a revolt of listeners. . . . Newspaper radio editors report more and more letters of protest against irritating sales ballyhoo." In early 1931, a leading newspaper radio editor, who was sympathetic to the status quo, observed, "due to too much advertising talk and to too much mediocre program material," public sentiment was moving toward "Government control."[3]

Indeed, almost all discussion of the public response to commercial broadcasting during these years was centered around the apparent public dissatisfaction with "excessive" commercialism. Even proponents of the status quo countenanced this development. Levering Tyson, whose NACRE defended the capacity of the existing system to meet the educational and cultural needs of the citizenry, informed his group's 1932 convention that "there is increasing evidence of repugnance on the part of the listeners to the invasion of the home by the constant and blatant selling talk." FRC members who built careers around their enthusiasm for the status quo struck notes of caution.

Chairman Charles McKinley Saltzman warned broadcasters that they were in "danger" unless they improved upon the "nauseating" commercialism on the air.[4] Commissioner Harold A. Lafount repeatedly warned the commercial broadcasters of impending doom unless they put their house in order. At the NAB convention in 1932 he stated that "an irate public is besieging Congress to stop overcommercialism of radio in America." In a 1931 interview, Lafount commented that

> [T]he continuance of broadcasting announcements that so obviously offend our ordinary sensibilities is going to lead to a revolt on the part of the listening public. Listeners can, of course, censor their own programs by turning the dial. But I'm afraid many of them will demand that the government take over the radio and operate it, as England does, as a government monopoly.[5]

Nor were the commercial broadcasters unaware of this threat. It is interesting that between 1930 and 1932 the industry tread gently around the subject; there was almost none of the countering that those dissatisfied with the status quo were elitists, a response that would become standard by the middle of the decade. Some measure of the industry's mood is indicated by the 1931 NAB convention, which resolved that "there is not too much advertising on the air," in the face of public criticism. The resolution added, "but there is too much poorly done," and encouraged broadcasters to take steps to defuse the situation. "Broadcasters are themselves well aware of the wave of resentment against excessive advertising," *Broadcasting* acknowledged in December 1931. "The plaint is heard from every quarter. It has been picked up by the reformers as the bludgeon with which to smash the present system of broadcasting."[6]

The nature of public opinion on this matter was certainly made clear to Congress, as Lafount indicated earlier. "There is constant pressure upon those of us interested in radio legislation, to do something to restrict advertising over the air," Senator Wallace H. White, Jr. (R-Maine), told the NAB convention in 1931. "There is restiveness on the part of the public and Congress because of the extent to which broadcasting facilities are today given over to personal or to purely private commercial use." *Broadcasting* observed that, "Many members on both sides of the Capitol are aroused by local conditions," and "have heard protests from constituents" regarding the nature of U.S. broadcasting.[7] The Payne Fund only decided to support the NCER after its president, Frances Payne Bolton, concluded that their "experience in Washington" in 1930 "had clearly indicated the intense resentment and distrust of Congress toward the radio interests." Some indication of the public antipathy toward commercial broadcasting may have been provided by the many members of Congress willing to antagonize the powerful radio lobby by denouncing the status quo. Senator Daniel O. Hastings, (R-Del.) even went so far as to come out "flatly in favor of government ownership of [all] broadcasting stations" in a 1931 speech in Boston.[8]

Whatever general sentiment there was in Congress on behalf of broadcast reform during this period was tempered by three very important considerations. First, from 1930 to 1932 the nation was in the trough of the most severe economic depression in generations. (Indeed, preoccupation with economic recovery partially explains why President Hoover, who played such a decisive role in U.S. broadcasting as secretary of commerce in the 1920s, was almost an incidental player during the final three years of his administration.) "When people are standing in breadlines," one unsympathetic senator commented in late 1931, "why should Congress bother about this propaganda about radio and advertising?" This point resonated throughout the trade publication discussion of the prospects for broadcast reform legislation. "Were it not for the disturbing economic situation," wrote Sol Taishoff in late 1931, "Congress might blunder into the political radio morass camouflaged by these lobbying factions." Another *Broadcasting* report left even less doubt. "Only the fact that Congress has been so vitally concerned with major economic problems and legislation," wrote Capitol Hill correspondent Lynne M. Lamm in early 1932, "has prevented members of the Senate and House from paying more attention to radio matters at this session."[9]

Second, while there was considerable dissatisfaction with the status quo in Congress, it tended to be among those congressmen who had little or nothing to do with the development of broadcast legislation at the committee level. Among the relevant committee leaders in the House and Senate, however, who enjoyed considerable control over the fate of reform legislation, the commercial broadcasters found near unanimous support for the status quo. "We have been fortunate. We have been lucky," observed NAB president Harry Shaw, with perhaps too much modesty, in a speech to the NAB Board of Directors on the legislative situation in January 1932. "We have been content to leave the protection of this industry to a few of our friends in certain places." Given the general lack of emphasis upon broadcast reform issues in Congress due to the economic situation, this made the committee leaders that much more important. The relevant committee leaders prevented any of the reform legislation from getting to the floor of Congress for a vote during this period, and most of it failed to even receive attention at the committee level. "They have done a noble job," Shaw stated.[10]

In the House of Representatives, the most important person was Ewin L. Davis. He was the chairman of the House Merchant Marine, Radio, and Fisheries Committee, which would handle radio legislation during this period. Davis co-authored the Radio Act of 1927 and was responsible for the Davis amendment in 1928, which was intended to force the FRC to make a general reallocation of the broadcast frequencies to give more weight to the under-represented southern and western regions of the nation. For this Davis was unpopular among some commercial broadcasters; *Broadcasting* even termed him an "outspoken opponent of commercial broadcasting." Actually, Davis had little interest in restructuring U.S. broadcasting although he would be sympathetic to measures to limit the extent of advertising on the air. "I am a believer in the American system," Davis would tell the annual convention of the AAAA in 1932. After warning the convention about the need to control "excessive" advertising, he concluded his speech by stating, "Now instead of 'killing the goose that lays the golden egg' let us work together towards the perfecting instead of destroying a great American system of radio control."[11]

In the Senate, the key figures were James Couzens and Clarence C. Dill, who were the ranking members on the Senate Committee on Interstate Commerce, which handled all broadcast legislation, as well as the aforementioned Senator White, who had been a co-sponsor of the Radio Act of 1927. Couzens acknowledged that there was discontent with the status quo, but his major concern was simply to see all communications regulation conducted by one government body. He first introduced such a bill in 1929; it would bring the regulation of radio, cable, telephony, and telegraphy, then spread among the Department of Commerce, the FRC, the State Department, and the Interstate Commerce Commission (ICC), under the heading of a new independent federal commission. This measure, called the "Couzens bill," was supported in principle by the commercial broadcasters. Couzens was an astute politician who would give broadcast reformers an audience and pronounce a degree of sympathy for their aims, although he would invariably oppose their legislation. When H. O. Davis took one of Couzens' proclamations against advertising to heart and cited Couzens as an ally in one of his communications, an irate Couzens wrote to him and demanded a retraction.[12]

In any case, Couzens, White, and Davis were all secondary in importance to Dill, who was generally accepted in Congress as *the* expert on broadcast affairs. Dill, too, had been an author of the Radio Act of 1927; if anything, his interest in broadcasting had grown in subsequent years. By the early 1930s his power over the fate of broadcast legislation was tremendous and unchallenged. *Broadcasting* characterized Dill as "unquestionably" having "the most influential voice in federal radio control of any figure in public life." As Morris Ernst stated emphatically in 1931, "There is no use in drafting material which will not be acceptable to him." Dill was an ambitious politician who had established himself as one of the most powerful members of the Senate by the early 1930s, although he was still in his forties. As one observer commented in 1932, Dill "has made the field of radio policy and control peculiarly his own."[13]

On the surface, Dill had a complex relationship with U.S. broadcasting.

In 1928 and 1929 he was foremost among the senators who attacked the dominance of U.S. broadcasting by RCA and the radio trust. In 1929 he announced with great fanfare that he would support an investigation of the "radio monopoly" and that he might sponsor legislation to force RCA to divest its broadcast holdings.[14] By 1930, however, Dill's stance toward the industry softened considerably. To some extent this may be due to pressure put upon him by Bernard Baruch and other prominent Democratic Party supporters, who impressed upon Dill the political danger in attacking the communication corporations, some of which, like GE and RCA, were managed by important Democrats like Owen D. Young.[15] Thereafter, this rapprochement notwithstanding, Dill continued to cultivate his public persona of being a "trust-busting" progressive who was fundamentally committed to keeping broadcasting *out* of private hands by guaranteeing formal public control of the airwaves through federal licensing and regulation.[16] It is interesting that by accepting his rhetoric at face value and concentrating on his activities in the 1920s, much of the previous scholarship has regarded Dill in precisely this manner.[17]

By the early 1930s Dill was praising U.S. broadcasting as being the finest in the world. It was Dill, for example, who coined the term *American Plan* to refer to the emerging private commercial system of broadcasting. In 1933 he argued that the Radio Act of 1927 "had placed radio in this country far ahead of that of any other country." Dill added that "a forward-looking spirit on the part of most of those engaged in the industry in this country and a liberal policy by Congress, have brought radio to its present place." Nevertheless, Dill could never be confused for an industry spokesperson on the subject of broadcast policy. He was still fully capable of delivering damning criticism of the status quo that was often combined with saber-rattling threats of systematic reform. "The Radio Commission," Dill once stated in one of many sharp attacks on that body, has "put the control of effective radio service in the hands of a few great corporations."[18] As a "result of monopoly and the overcommercialization of radio broadcasting," Dill noted another time, "public opinion" may "compel congress to adopt a government ownership program." Dill also countenanced the concerns of educators. "The greatest weakness in radio today is the lack of educational and informational broadcasting." He even offered educators a tantalizing glimmer of hope. "Education over the radio should be free from commercial interests. It should be independent and free, just as our systems of public education are free and independent," he stated.[19]

Given this rhetoric, it is not surprising that the broadcast reform movement, especially during this period prior to 1933, regarded Dill with ambivalence, and certainly not as an outright opponent. With few exceptions broadcast reformers found Dill "approachable and willing to discuss problems." Dill, far more than Couzens, routinely announced his support for the aims of the broadcast reform movement, although he just as quickly disapproved of any and all specific measures that the reformers might propose, and he never showed the slightest interest in assisting in the development of an acceptable alternative reform program.[20]

These points notwithstanding, the fact remains that whenever the broadcasting industry faced wholesale attack, Dill invariably represented their interests, employing whatever means he deemed necessary. "Senator Dill, rallying to the cause of the broadcasters," noted the NAB after a tough battle over copyright legislation in 1931, "deserves the unstinted thanks of every member of the Association as well as every other station licensee." Dill's public acknowledgment of dissatisfaction with the status quo had no apparent effect upon his treatment of reform legislation, which he routinely stonewalled. A close examination of Dill's "critical" comments during this period reveals that he never actually advocated any structural reform, he merely held it out as the logical direction of public sentiment unless the broadcasters improved their performance. "Unless advertisers and broadcasters clean up their advertising programs," he informed Martin Codel, "the American public will demand that Congress take steps, by the passage of laws, to prevent the abuse of radio privileges." In encouraging the industry to engage in self-regulation in order to undermine the threat of reform, Dill was simply echoing the comments of the FRC and the industry itself. "Self-regulation is the only way to forestall Congressionally imposed regulation, already threatened in the new Congress," *Broadcasting* editorialized in 1931.[21]

Third, the general climate for broadcast reform legislation in the early 1930s was related to the status of communications legislation in general. The giant communications firms—GE, Westinghouse, RCA, and AT&T, with the exception of the latter—were adamant in their support of Couzens bill to establish a unified communications commission to regulate all aspects of the communication industry. As RCA President General James Harbord noted, it was an "urgent need," so that "the United States might be able to compete on an equal basis with the unified interests of the British."[22] Dill and Hoover also both supported the measure. Hoover even issued an executive order in July 1932 tranferring the Radio Division of the Commerce Department to the FRC to expedite the consolidation. At the same time, however, none of the unification supporters had any particular interest in bringing the bill before Congress between 1930 and 1932. The fear was that if Congress considered communication matters, it might "unleash some totally unknown scheme," as historian Philip Rosen observed. In short, the industry was sensitive to any public or congressional examination of its activities, particularly since this was a period in which the government was pursuing antitrust charges against RCA, GE, and Westinghouse. Moreover, broadcasting was the industry's most visible and controversial component. "Broadcasting," Orestes Caldwell wrote in a trade publication in 1932, "is the radio industry's very lifeblood."[23]

Accordingly, this was a period in which the commercial broadcasters were opposed to having Congress consider legislation for the permanent regulation of broadcasting. The industry was also quite content with the manner in which the FRC was stabilizing the airwaves for profitable exploitation. "The Commission is solidly backed by the industry because the industry wants the control in the hands of a small and easily managed group," Armstrong Perry explained to one educator. "It is to be hoped," one *Broadcasting* editorial noted regarding the situation in Congress, "that there will be little more than talk about radio." All the reform proposals were dismissed in principle by the industry as efforts by Congress to kowtow to special interests and establish the "dangerous precedent" of usurping the "power of allocating facilities it had already vested in the Commission." This was the strategy and general situation the broadcast reform movement encountered as it made its way before Congress between 1930 and 1932. "Although much legislation designed to regulate radio has been proposed on both the Senate and House floors," *Education by Radio* observed shortly after the NCER launched its legislative campaign, "Congress seems to have forsaken the field since creating the Federal Radio Commission in 1927."[24]

Edward Nockels and organized labor were responsible for the first resolution on behalf of broadcast reform. Introduced in the spring of 1930 by Representative Frank R. Reid (D-Ill.), it called for the FRC to reserve three clear channels for the use of the Departments of Labor, Agriculture, and Interior (for education purposes), respectively. Each department, in turn, would turn over its clear channel to those nonprofit groups associated with the work of the department. In the case of labor, for example, the AFL would be assigned the channel and it, accordingly, would then have WCFL assume the clear channel. The resolution received the formal backing of the AFL at its 1930 convention. Unfortunately for Nockels, his conscious attempt to gather support for the measure by including education and agriculture failed. Those educators familiar with the resolution were enthusiastic, but most were unaware of its existence because they were still unorganized. Armstrong Perry used the lack of an educational "voice" in support of the resolution as evidence of the need for the Payne Fund to support a group like the NCER.[25] Agriculture produced some support; the Farmers Educational Cooperative Union formally resolved on behalf of the Reid amendment.[26] The Department of Agriculture, however, informed Congress that it had no need or desire for its own broadcast facilities, citing the willingness of NBC to broadcast its programs as making such a measure unnecessary.[27]

In December 1930, Otis Glenn (R-Ill.) introduced this three clear channel resolution in the Senate. Nockels came to Washington to lobby for the measure. He claimed to have the support of 70 percent of the Senate and 80 percent of the House for the measure. The NAB informed its membership that support for the Glenn–Reid resolutions approached 90 percent of the members of Congress. Nonetheless, the Glenn resolution was never even taken up by the SCIC. "If it were not for a little group of reactionary leaders in both branches of Congress," an incensed Nockels wrote in February 1931, "this legislation would have been passed by this time."[28]

Glenn, however, was undaunted. On February 17, 1931, he attached an amendment to a minor radio bill on the Senate floor that called for the FRC to allocate one clear channel to labor organizations. Organized labor was able to use its influence to receive clearance for the motion from the SCIC. "To the great surprise of the entire radio industry," the NAB reported, "the bill as amended passed at a night session without a single dissenting vote." Frantic, the NAB petitioned the House Committee on Merchant Marine, Radio, and Fisheries on February 18 to open immediate hearings on the amendment "because of the important principle involved." They were denied their request. Since the bill, without the labor provision, had already passed the House on April 30, 1930, the matter went to a conference committee chaired by Senator White and including both Dill and Couzens. The NAB's fears were soon alleviated; White elected to let the bill die on the speaker's table. The only consolation for labor was that White warned the FRC to take better care of WCFL or else he would support something similar in the next session. This particular amendment was the closest the broadcast reform movement would ever get to having any of its proposals enacted into law; as the *Federation News* observed, White's action was "disappointing to the liberal and progressive element of Congress."[29]

By this time the NCER had already launched its campaign on behalf of its measure to reserve 15 percent of the channels for educational institutions. Senator Fess introduced the bill that bore his name on January 8, 1931. In an open letter to Congress calling for support for the bill, the NCER characterized American radio as "the dollar sign's mightiest megaphone." The NCER's Morgan and John Henry MacCracken worked the corridors of the Capitol, "disproving the popular notion that educators cannot move promptly," as Armstrong Perry put it.[30] Conversely, calling it "the most vicious piece of legislation before the Congress," the NAB voted unanimously to oppose the Fess Bill at its November 1930 convention, before it even had been introduced. In their newsletters, the NAB repeatedly emphasized how the Fess Bill had "enormous support in Congress."[31]

It quickly became apparent to the NCER, however, "that it would be impossible in the short time remaining in the present session of Congress to put such a bill through." The measure did not even reach the stage of receiving committee hearings in the Seventy-First Congress, which drew to a close in March. The NCER was far from despondent, however, dismissing its initial failure as more the result of logistics than politics. It spent the balance of the spring and summer attempting to "lay a good foundation" for the Fess bill, as Morgan put it, for the upcoming session of Congress, scheduled for December. "We believe that the situation on the next Congress will be more favorable to our proposals than could have been expected earlier," Morgan wrote to Perry in June.[32]

Nockels and organized labor, on the other hand, followed White's admonition to the FRC to treat WCFL better on the heels of the Glenn amendment's defeat. WCFL applied to the FRC for clear channel status on the 720 wavelength of the *Chicago Tribune's* WGN. The FRC set a tentative hearing on the application for May 18, 1931, much to WCFL's delight. The hearing, however, was appealed by Louis Caldwell in April. He criticized this "eleventh hour motion" by WCFL that would cause "a great and unmitigated hardship" upon the *Tribune* company. "The record shows beyond question that the service heretofore rendered by WCFL is of such inferior quality," Caldwell's brief to the FRC concluded, "that by no stretch of the imagination could any 'further testimony' be of such nature as to show WCFL entitled to the granting of its pending application." The FRC agreed with Caldwell, canceling the hearing and denying WCFL's position.[33]

To the *Federation News* this "strange reversal" by the FRC was "of scandalous proportions." It is time, the paper concluded, "the people raised such a clamor as to shake the walls of radio's little Jericho in Washington." The chairman of the Republican National Committee urged the White House to arrange a deal for WCFL before Congress reconvened in December: "There are enough friends of labor on both sides on the Hill to raise Merry Hell about it."[34] Indeed, both the NCER and labor were intending an all-out assault on Congress for broadcast reform that fall. Despite the industry's opposition, it appeared unavoidable, albeit "extremely unfortunate," as one industry analyst put it, "that the whole question of radio regulation will be a subject for consideration in Washington beginning next fall. It is difficult to see how radio can fail to become a political issue."[35]

Louis G. Caldwell and
the American Bar Association

WCFL's interaction with Louis Caldwell before the FRC in April 1931 only highlighted the antagonism that developed between the U.S. legal community and the broadcast reform movement, particularly in the years 1930–1932. Although the ACLU and legal scholars like Walter Hale Hamilton and Richard Joyce Smith of the Yale Law School would be critical of the emerging order, the preponderance of the legal community had few reservations about the capitalist development of the ether. Caldwell, the first FRC general counsel who had devised and implemented the reallocation under General Order 40 in 1928, was the most visible legal authority on broadcast policy and also the most important. At his urging, the ABA had established a Standing Committee on Radio Law in 1928, which would be renamed the Standing Committee on Communications the following year. Caldwell would serve as the Standing Committee's chairman from its inception until 1933. During Caldwell's tenure, the ABA committee would turn out annual reports ranging from 40 to 100 pages in length.[36]

An important purpose of the committee, according to Caldwell, was "the duty of studying and making recommendations on proposed radio legislation." The Standing Committee worked closely with the FRC as well as the relevant legislators on Capitol Hill.[37] The committee's reports were usually authored by Caldwell with the assistance of one or two of the other members of the five-person committee. Although the invariably nondescript resolutions of the committee were voted on and approved each year at the ABA national convention, the actual reports of the committee were not voted upon. Nonetheless, they were presented to the Congress and the public as the expert opinion of the American legal community. Moreover, Caldwell wrote to members of the FRC and Congress routinely to provide his opinion on legislation and policy matters, usually on ABA stationary in his capacity with the Committee on Communications.[38] In short, the opinion of Caldwell was effectively the opinion of the ABA.

In addition to chairing this committee, Caldwell maintained a successful law practice, which featured a clientele comprised almost exclusively of large commercial broadcasters. His law firm's client roster included the *Chicago Tribune,* which had been instrumental in launching Caldwell's career, and he was stated to have annual retainers from RCA and its subsidiaries in excess of $50,000. Caldwell also worked as a top-level legal adviser on behalf of both the NAB and NBC during this period.[39] In one case, for example, the entire industry of "organized broadcasters" hired Caldwell to represent them as their "special counsel" in Congressional hearings on copyright legislation in 1931 and 1932. "The NAB, through Mr. Caldwell," the NAB informed its membership in 1932, "will aid Chairman Sirovich in the preparation of a draft of a bill." To add insult to injury in the minds of broadcast reformers, Caldwell also had represented commercial interests in the critical FRC hearings concerning WCFL, Gross Alexander's Pacific-Western Broadcasting Foundation, and several educational stations. The one exception to this rule was Caldwell's pro bono representation of the Socialist Party's WEVD before the FRC in 1931, which Caldwell pointed to when his neutrality was called into question.[40]

Other members of the Standing Committee enjoyed similarly cordial relations with the commercial broadcasters. John W. Guider, for example, who would eventually succeed Caldwell as chairman of the committee in 1933, was likewise a commercial broadcasting attorney who was active in NAB affairs. "A brilliant young attorney," was how *Broadcasting* characterized him.[41] Among his clients Guider included CBS, which he represented several times before the FRC and, later, before the FCC. Guider would represent a CBS-owned station before the FRC in 1933 when it was challenged for an increased allocation of hours by WLWL, the only Roman Catholic station in the Northeast which had seen its power and hours sharply curtailed as a result of General Order 40. This case generated publicity as "one of the most bitterly contested" cases in "Commission history," and led WLWL to discontinue its appeal before the FRC and, instead, to lead the campaign on behalf of the Wagner–Hatfield amendment in 1934.[42]

Nor were the attorneys on the ABA Standing Committee on Communications the only lawyers taking advantage of this newly emerging field of jurisprudence. Given the ninety-day license term and the constant hearings before the FRC, one trade publication described Washington D.C., as a "happy hunting ground" for commercial broadcasting attorneys, especially "former members of the FRC legal staff." "The lawyer," NBC general counsel A. L. Ashby announced in a speech at the New York University Law School in 1930, "plays as important a role in making radio broadcasting possible as the engineer or the announcer." This emergence of the commercial broadcasting attorney incensed the reformers, whose stations were often the victims of these attorneys' arguments in hearings before the FRC. "The whole system of federal regulation of broadcasting," the NCER's Morgan commented, "has been a golden harvest for lawyers wrangling over litigation." These lawyers were a part of "the parasitic forces that profit from the present set-up" and that, "whenever it appeared that a challenge to the existing radio practice was imminent," they "rushed to the defense of our present privately dominated, advertising-supported system."[43]

Prior to 1928 and the emergence of the status quo, the ABA had shown only marginal interest in the implications for the law suggested by the advent of radio broadcasting. In this period broadcasting matters were covered by the Standing Committee on Air Law. It is interesting that, in its final report, which was published in 1928 and included the topic of radio broadcasting, the Committee on Air Law took a decidedly reformist stance, arguing that, "undoubtedly the public interest will not be served if all available channels are allocated to private use, and for entertainment purposes." The section of the report concluded, "It is believed by your committee that this problem can be solved . . . by allocating a limited number of stations in various parts of the country to be operated as public utilities under appropriate regulations." This sentiment would evaporate with the transfer of broadcast issues to the Caldwell's Standing Committee on Communications. Given Caldwell's role in developing General Order 40, it is not surprising that the ABA committee endorsed the reallocation and the manner in which the FRC had interpreted "public interest, convenience, or necessity." The Radio Act of 1927, the committee wrote, "wisely delegated a wide discretion to the licensing authority subject to the fundamentally sound standard of 'public interest, convenience or necessity.' "[44]

Nor was the private, commercial development of the ether subject to any analysis by Caldwell's committee; it was simply posited as the natural and superior method for organizing the U.S. broadcasting services, the "alpha and omega of broadcasting service as we know it," as one report put it. "I do not think our committee can be fairly criticized," Caldwell informed the ABA convention in 1931, "for holding to the belief that the American plan is better than the European plan for the business of broadcasting." Caldwell's assumptions regarding U.S. broadcasting rendered any debate over the legitimacy of the status quo impossible. In concluding a 1930 law review article Caldwell wrote,

> The fact must not be overlooked that broadcasting is a business, dependent like all other businesses on stability of conditions, a reasonable assurance of continued operation to attract investors, and to permit plans and contracts looking to the future, and freedom from unnecessary Government interference. Argument is unnecessary to show that the interest of the listening public is in the same direction.[45]

Moreover, Caldwell insisted that it was essential that the FRC be left entirely on its own to interpret public interest, convenience, or necessity as it saw fit. "The underlying theory," he wrote, regarding giving the FRC autonomy to act as it wished with minimal statutory guidance, is "perfectly sound; only an indefinite and very elastic standard should be prescribed" by the statute for licensing criteria. Caldwell, both through his own articles and in the ABA reports, resolutely insisted that it would be entirely inappropriate for Congress to "play politics" with broadcast regulation; Congress should "keep its hands off" and let the experts at the FRC scientifically determine what was in the public interest. "While this phrase may seem broad and vague," he wrote in 1930, "any more specific test would have been dangerous." As S. Howard Evans commented, "Mr. Caldwell's interpretation of the law would give a 'whip hand' to the Federal Radio Commission. Any broadcaster who refused to give positive public service or who refused the opportunity for worthy causes to be heard would be liable for the loss of his license."[46]

At times Caldwell was almost dogmatic in his insistence that the regulators must be independent of congressional or public "interference" as they determined licensing criteria. "The radio administration within a nation," he wrote in 1930, "must have a life-and-death power over the radio conduct of its subjects such as it neither has nor desires over their conduct in other matters." The "licensing authority must have a far-reaching power to reject applications for licenses,'' he added. ''Such matters cannot safely be prescribed by statute'' and were ''unsuited for decision by a legislative body.'' As the Committee on Communications observed,

> Involving, as it does, considerations of a legal and technical character, it naturally follows that this regulation must be entrusted to an administrative agency with wide discretionary powers. In an art subject to speedy and far-reaching changes, it is inconceivable that proper regulation could be effected through the medium of inflexible statutes.

Indeed, according to Caldwell, any interference by the public or Congress with the FRC's ability to determine licensing criteria as it pleased would invariably be ''ruinous,'' no matter how well intended, because it would violate the ''sound engineering principles,'' which only the full-time experts on the FRC could comprehend.[47] In short, the capitalist development of the ether was the only system that rationally responded to the technological nuances of the medium, and not a public policy decision.

Caldwell and the ABA Standing Committee were largely unconcerned regarding the possibility that granting the FRC an almost unchecked power to allocate broadcast licenses by any criteria it desired might create a form of censorship, which was specifically prohibited by the Radio Act of 1927. ''If all this be censorship,'' one ABA report commented, ''it seems unavoidable and in the best interest of the listening public.'' Even the commercial broadcasters recognized that contradictory nature of this argument, although they were the primary beneficiaries of it. The FRC was in a ''preposterous situation,'' as Henry Bellows put it. ''The present law,'' he observed in 1929, ''specifically denies the right of censorship and yet makes the whole business of licensing essentially a matter of censorship on a vast scale.''[48] Nevertheless, in 1929 Caldwell informed the SCIC that licensing was not a violation of the clause prohibiting censorship by the FRC in the Radio Act of 1927. The anticensorship clause, Caldwell stated, restricted the FRC only from ''exercising any power to discipline stations'' for any specific programs that contained ''views on questions of public interest or importance.''[49]

Thus it is not surprising that Caldwell and the ABA Standing Committee categorically opposed all of the measures proposed by the broadcast reform movement during this period. The Fess Bill, for example, was attacked as impractical. ''It is difficult to calculate the loss both financially to station owners and in terms of broadcasting service to the listening public'' if the bill were passed, their 1931 report stated. Caldwell dismissed the arguments of the reformers as being based upon ''a great mass of misinformation'' about the ''alleged superiority of European programs.'' Nor were Caldwell and the ABA committee particularly sympathetic with the plight of the displaced nonprofit broadcasters, whom they thought should abandon their disruptive legislative efforts and simply learn to work through the auspices of a very willing, cooperative, and misunderstood commercial broadcasting industry. The 1932 ABA report concluded that "it is safe to say that never in the history of America has any industry had imposed upon it so great an uncertainty as to its continued existence or the enjoyment of its investment, or so great a cost because of government regulation, as has the broadcasting industry."[50]

These sentiments notwithstanding, Caldwell and the ABA Standing Committee were not entirely oblivious to the popular dissatisfaction with commercial broadcasting. They simply posited that structural reform was unnecessary and, moreover, that it would be counterproductive. "There is every reason to hope," the 1932 report stated," that "the self-interest of the broadcaster and the advertiser, combined with the listener's power of censorship by turning away from an offending program, will automatically eliminate excesses."[51]

In general, the articles addressing broadcast policy in the law journals during this period shared the sentiments of the ABA Standing Committee on Communications, partially due, no doubt, to the fact that Caldwell himself was responsible for no small portion of them. He even established and edited the *Journal of Radio Law* in 1931, but the project was abandoned after two years. Both Caldwell's journal and the *Air Law Review* were "dominated by the commercial point of view," in the opinion of Armstrong Perry. Perry even suggested, unsuccessfully, that the NCER might establish a legal committee to read all the law articles on radio in order to "call the attention of editors to omissions or prejudiced statements."[52] Some of the law review articles were unqualified defenses of General Order 40 and the emerging regulatory regime with minimal concern for the free expression implications of such a system.[53] Others, particularly as the system became increasingly entrenched by 1932 and 1933, paid more attention to the threat of censorship implicit in the existing system. Even these articles, however, generally presupposed the superiority of the status quo and acknowledged that the censorship implied by the FRC's reallocation of the airwaves had been a "necessary evil."[54]

Given the importance of Caldwell and the reports of the ABA Standing Committee to the development of broadcast legislation on Capitol Hill, it was only a matter of time until the broadcast reform movement aimed its artillery in their direction. The most obvious area for attack was that of conflict-of-interest. "Perhaps no lawyer in the United States accepts larger retainer fees from commercial broadcasting companies than Mr. Caldwell," the NCER's newsletter *Education by Radio* observed in 1931. "This question should be answered frankly: Is it ethical practice or is it legal racketeering for a man with a selfish interest at stake to use a great civic organization like the American Bar Association to promote his gain contrary to the public good?" S. Howard Evans appeared before an open meeting of the ABA communications committee later that year, stating "I can readily understand that your reports should favor the broadcaster for the very pertinent reason that some of the members of your committee are receiving attractive retainers from broadcasting stations." Even Senator Dill exclaimed at one point that the "public regulation of the growing private monopoly in radio had been obstructed" by the ABA Standing Committee on Communications, which was "made up in part of utility lawyers."[55]

The reformers were also enraged by the argument that broadcast policy was so complex that it could only be understood by legal and engineering "experts" and, therefore, needed to be kept out of "uninformed" public debate. The corollary to this was the notion that efforts to reform the status quo would invariably "violate the facts of radio physics," as Louis Caldwell informed Morgan when the two had a rare confrontation at the May 1931 conference of the NACRE. "I have discovered some very interesting facts," Morgan stated in response to Caldwell's argument that the status quo was the only possible system deemed permissible by experts. "One of them is that engineers do not agree among themselves. Another is that the lawyers do not agree among themselves." Morgan concluded that, "One has to go far beneath any of their assertions or so-called presentations of facts in order to get to the true situation."[56]

The broadcast reform movement's dissatisfaction with the ABA's Standing Committee on Communications reached a crescendo in the summer of 1931 when the committee released a forty-seven-page report disparaging all broadcast reform legislation and praising the status quo unconditionally. Coming only months before the next session of Congress as the reformers were attempting to marshal their forces, the reform movement aggressively reacted to the ABA report, seeing its "intent" as being specifically "to discredit any legislation" on behalf of broadcast reform. The NCER wrote letters to members of Congress and state governors protesting the report and calling Caldwell the representative of "the dominant commercial group in the radio industry."[57] Tracy Tyler and Nockels each wrote to the ABA asking it to repudiate its connection to the Committee on Communications report. Nockels specifically protested "against your association being used for serving the radio trusts," and argued that Caldwell was "subtly and surreptitiously pretending to serve a public cause," while actually working to advance the interests of his clients, the commercial broadcasters. "Mr. Caldwell knows that the licensing bodies are composed of lawyers who will give weight to the expression of the American Bar Association."[58]

When the ABA refused to repudiate the report, the reformers took steps to protest it at the open hearings of the Committee on Communications at the ABA annual convention in Atlantic City, New Jersey in September 1931. S. Howard Evans appeared on behalf of the *Ventura Free Press*. He opened his talk by expressing his displeasure for the manner by which Caldwell and the ABA committee simply presupposed the superiority of the status quo and dismissed the notion that the public even had a right to construct a different system if it so pleased. "Indeed, for anyone who can accept the fundamental assumptions on which your work is based these yearly publications present an almost perfect case," Evans conceded. "Unfortunately, I am one of those to whom your basic assumptions are not acceptable. And I want to call attention to the importance of basic assumptions. They underlie the whole case you have built. If they are false your case is worthless."[59]

Nockels was unable to attend the convention and he arranged for ABA member Frank Walsh to appear on his behalf. Walsh was one of the most prominent utility lawyers in the United States, being chairman of the Power Authority of the State of New York and being appointed by Governor Franklin D. Roosevelt to the New York Commission on the Revision of Public Utility Laws. Moreover, Walsh had spent two years as editor and publisher of the *Kansas City Post* and had served as chairman of the Federal Commission on Industrial Relations during the Wilson administration.[60] In short, while the unknown and young nonattorney Evans could be easily dismissed, Walsh was a formidable critic for the Committee on Communications.

Walsh began his comments before the Standing Committee on Communications by observing that "there is a very great danger of monopolization of the air" which "might not be best for public welfare, or at least might interfere with a free discussion upon the air." In particular, due to the "inhibition of free speech and free interchange of thought," incumbent to the emerging broadcast system, and due to the opposition to the system by "many persons who have given it very careful consideration," Walsh stated that "what I am here for today is to suggest that the influence of the American Bar Association should not be given to any one side of this controversy at this time." Caldwell immediately denied that the committee was partisan in its approach or that it compromised the integrity of the ABA. "We have felt that our chief mission was to collect information, primarily on scientific facts, and such facts are not readily accessible to the average lawyer. We have regarded the forming of conclusions as rather a secondary mission. The Association can take them or leave them." Walsh was not content with Caldwell's explanation of the report's essential neutrality, nor of its function being primarily educational. "Can that not be used as a very powerful propaganda before senate committees and the like, without any action of our association upon it, no opportunity to argue it from both sides, but merely a report of 47 pages; can it not be used as very strong propaganda?"[61]

At this point the interchange turned to the ethical question of how Caldwell and two of the other five committee members supported themselves as commercial broadcasting attorneys. Caldwell admitted the basis of the criticism but denied that it effected the committee's judgment. Walsh, unconvinced by Caldwell's response, persisted in his attack. Finally, Caldwell stormed out of the hall "flushed and angry." The following week he sent a letter to *The New York Times* explaining his actions and defending his conduct. Despite the brouhaha, the NAB assured its members that the "attacks on the report" had been "effectively answered during the meeting."[62] Indeed, the report of the Standing Committee was not altered as a result of the uproar at the convention. As a concession to the critics, however, Frank Walsh was appointed to the Standing Committee for a one-year term, and the NCER, the *Ventura Free Press,* and WCFL were solicited in April 1932 to provide the Committee on Communications with statements of their positions if they so desired. Nevertheless, the three commercial broadcasting attorneys on the committee, including Chairman Caldwell and Guider, remained.[63]

These steps were far from satisfactory to the reformers. Nockels declined Caldwell's invitation to submit his position on broadcast legislation to the Standing Committee in early 1932, terming it "an idle gesture." He wrote, "until a committee on communications is composed of lawyers who are not influenced, directly or indirectly, by retainer for or against radio legislation, we must decline to participate." The 1932 committee report was indistinguishable in tone from the committee's earlier efforts. Caldwell authored the sixty-five-page report and Guider was the only committee member who appeared to defend it at the 1932 ABA convention, as Caldwell was in Madrid representing the NAB at the International Radio Telegraphic Conference. The NCER characterized the 1932 report as another example of the "nationwide scheme among radio trust lawyers to dominate the sources of legal opinion in America with relation to radio by controlling committees within the American Bar Association, legal periodicals given to radio, and radio law courses in universities."[64]

The 1932 report would be the last major opus for the ABA Standing Committee on Communications. In 1933 Louis Caldwell would leave the committee, to be replaced as chairman by John W. Guider, and become chairman of the ABA's new Standing Committee on Administrative Law, which he had been instrumental in getting established. The reports of the Standing Committee on Communications became considerably shorter (e.g., only nineteen pages in 1934), far less sweeping, and somewhat less partisan in tone. After 1934 the committee would be but a shadow of its former self and it would not even present a report in 1938. Finally, in 1939, the Standing Committee announced its plans to disband as it had been largely superseded by the Federal Communications Bar Association (FCBA), which was a professional association for commercial broadcasting attorneys. It is interesting that the FCBA had been established in the aftermath of the Communications Act of 1934 with the encouragement of Louis G. Caldwell, who served as the organization's president in 1936 and 1937.[65]

It is unclear what precise effect Caldwell and the ABA Standing Committee on Communications had upon Congress as it contemplated broadcast reform legislation in 1931 and 1932. Nor is it clear what effect the furor surrounding the Committee on Communications report at the 1931 ABA convention might have had toward undermining the group's credibility. This much, however, is certain. The refusal of the ABA Standing Committee to even countenance the arguments of the broadcast reform movement made the reformers' task on Capitol Hill that much more difficult when dealing with legislators who often relied upon the ABA for neutral and expert advice on legislative matters such as this. This was especially true for a subject like radio law, of which most members of Congress had little knowledge or experience upon which to draw. The word of the ABA would tend to carry considerable weight in such a case.

SR 129 and *Commercial Radio Advertising*

Following the ABA convention in September, the broadcast reformers turned their attention back to Congress, "where the situation is growing daily more favorable to our cause," as one educator put it in November. "You will be glad to know," Morgan wrote to one NCER member, "that Senator Fess is planning to reintroduce our radio bill with more interest and zeal than ever."[66] Bolton, who was "an active advocate" of the NCER radio program and "lost no opportunity to talk with senators and congressmen alike on all possible occasions" regarding broadcast reform, tempered the NCER's enthusiasm that autumn. She "regretted" the selection of Fess as the bill's sponsor, as he "does not command much confidence," and argued that the bill was probably doomed if only for that reason. Indeed, Fess seemed singularly out of touch with the political exigencies of broadcast reform; for example, in February 1932, he wrote an irate letter to Armstrong Perry thinking that Perry was the editor of the commercial broadcasting trade publication, *Radio Digest,* much to Perry's bewilderment.[67]

Moreover, Bolton was alarmed, as she informed the NCER, that none of the members of congress that she had spoken with "had even heard of your legislative campaign in view of the fact that . . . you were sending bulletins to all of them." She discovered that the bulletins had been sent in voluminous quantities, but without cover letters; "therefore their secretaries had not brought it to their attention." Morgan immediately wrote personal letters to members of Congress and informed Bolton that he had received "the most remarkable collection of replies that I have ever seen in a life of experience in connection with legislative matters. There isn't the slightest doubt as to the growing concern of Congress over this issue." Bolton remained pessimistic and informed the NCER that from her "direct Congressional contacts" it was clear that while there was sizable support for reform, there were too many objections to the fixed-percentage concept to pass the Fess bill. "I am forced to the opinion that a complete reconsideration should be given the matter," although she conceded she had no alternative measure to suggest.[68]

Bolton and the Payne Fund increasingly looked to the *Ventura Free Press* radio campaign, which it launched that summer with several tasks, including that of lobbying for broadcast reform. Evans was dispatched to Washington by the Payne Fund to serve as the official representative of the *Ventura Free Press* that fall. He plunged into the congressional waters in a manner that had eluded the more temperate officers of the NCER. Unlike the NCER, Evans was not wed to the Fess bill and his initial mission was simply to gauge the level of congressional enthusiasm for any type of reform legislation. In a December memo he noted that "practically all [members of Congress] agree on undesirable features of commercial advertising," and that many were "heartily in sympathy with our efforts." He cautioned, however, that some members seemed unconcerned or unfamiliar with reform legislation and that several warned him that there would be "plenty of opposition" to reform legislation from the commercial broadcasters in their districts. Walter Woehlke asserted to Senator Dill that the *Free Press* campaign had received "assurances" from all of the members of the Oklahoma congressional delegation "that they will support progressive radio legislation during the next session." After only a few weeks in Washington, Evans concluded "things look awfully good here."[69]

This sentiment was also apparent to the commercial broadcasters. "This structure is in very serious danger," Henry Bellows informed the NAB convention in late October. "More people are after our scalps than in any other industry." As one conference participant noted, Bellows spent much of the conference imploring the broadcasters to contribute for lobbying in Washington, and warning them that, otherwise, "some morning they'd wake up and find that they had no stations from which to broadcast." It is unclear how much of Bellows's "bellowing," as the participant described it, was genuine and how much was bombast intended to strengthen the position of the NAB. At the same conference Bellows conceded the power of the radio lobby to undercut reform legislation before it could even get to the stage of committee hearings, let alone to the floor for a vote. "Our greatest danger," he commented in this vein, "is through the passage by Congress in the form of amendments or riders of legislation which will not be adequately considered and which will slide through without much opportunity to oppose it."[70] In short, Bellows feared that the reformers might skillfully maneuver to outflank the powerful radio lobby on the floor of Congress, bypass the committee leadership, and play on their strength among the rank and file members, as almost happened with the Glenn amendment in the spring.

In any case, admonitions that the industry's very existence was in jeopardy like those made by Bellows understandably left some commercial broadcasters little short of hysterical. Rumors were rampant by December, many suggesting that the FRC and/or Congress were going to prohibit advertising over the air or perhaps even nationalize all of U.S. broadcasting. As H. O. Davis cackled, "The Washington radio pot is beginning to boil." At the urging of Senator Dill, the FRC released a statement on December 21 titled "In Re The Use of Radio Broadcasting Stations for Advertising Purposes," meant to assure the broadcasters that nothing drastic was planned.[71]

The FRC statement noted:

> The Commission believes that the American system of broadcasting has produced the best form of radio entertainment that can be found in the world. This system is one which is based entirely upon the use of radio broadcasting stations for advertising purposes. It is a highly competitive system and is carried on by private enterprise. There is but one other system—the European system.

The statement added that "there is no practical medium between the two systems. It is either the American system or the European system," thereby repudiating the claims of the broadcast reform movement. The statement concluded by reprinting and lauding the NAB's eight-point "Code of Ethics," citing it as "an avenue by which the industry can regulate itself." That the FRC was far from neutral on the topic of broadcast reform was no surprise. In November FRC member Lafount had released his own statement defending the educational output of commercial broadcasters, proclaiming that "Commercialism has developed radio to an amazing degree of perfection within an incredibly short space of time."[72]

On the same day that the FRC released its statement defending commercial advertising, Representative Ralph A. Horr (R. Wash.) introduced a resolution requiring an independent investigation of both the FRC and the broadcasting companies, specifically mentioning NBC. This had been the product of Evans's labors, who had concluded that no specific "legislative plan for remedying our situation can be jammed through this year," and opted for the independent investigation to draw attention to the issue. "If we are successful in stirring up news and building a case which shows that the present system is unsound, we can undoubtedly get somewhere next session." By this time Bolton and Crandall were "seeing eye to eye" with Evans, regarding the Fess bill as a lost cause and probably not a long-run solution for broadcasting in any case. Crandall noted that the Fess Bill had "served to open up the subject" at the previous session and "to arouse the educators," and therefore had "fulfilled a certain purpose." The great advantage of the Horr resolution, in the minds of Evans, Crandall, and Bolton, was that it would permit members of Congress to make a tentative vote for reform without having to commit themselves to a specific program that might in itself be difficult to defend. "Mr. Average Congressman is undoubtedly dissatisfied with the present condition of radio," Evans explained to Woehlke. "But I doubt if he will be likely to give up the present system for one the merits of which cannot be definitely ascertained in advance."[73]

Given the general sentiment in Washington, it appeared increasingly questionable that warnings by Congress and the FRC to the commercial broadcasters to clean up their acts and "eliminate the bad material" were going to be acceptable. Even Senator Couzens informed *Broadcasting* that "I am wholly disgusted with the whole broadcasting situation." In another talk Couzens demanded that "either advertising must be eliminated entirely or limited to a single statement concerning sponsorship of the program." Otherwise, he said, the "whole radio industry" would be subject to radical restructuring at the public's insistence.[74] Some remedial legislation stood a decent chance of getting passed, be it the Horr resolution, the Fess bill, or something else. Couzens introduced Senate Resolution (SR) 129 into this chasm on January 7, 1932: "Whereas there is growing dissatisfaction with the present use of radio facilities for the purposes of commercial advertising," the resolution stated: "Be it resolved, That the Federal Radio Commission is hereby authorized and instructed to report to the Senate on the following questions." Seven questions by Couzens followed addressing, among other things, whether government ownership was a viable option for U.S. broadcasting, how might the level of advertising be reduced if not eliminated, and whether foreign systems might provide some ideas for how the U.S. might organize its broadcasting. "The inspiration back of this resolution was the criticism by the public of many of the programs now being broadcast," Couzens explained to *Printers' Ink*. "I reached the conclusion that the whole radio industry, outside of communications, was in danger of being permanently damaged."[75]

The broadcast reformers were taken by complete surprise by Couzens's resolution. Evans had been in close contact with Couzens, noting in early December that "he has the whole situation pictured in a nutshell," but "he disagrees with our plans." When Evans confronted Couzens regarding SR 129 the following day, Couzens told him it was a victory for the reformers, an interpretation Evans accepted. "Couzens and the boys are ready to go just as far as public opinion will support them," Evans wrote to Woehlke on January 8. "The decks are cleared for a real measure. Now all we have to do is get public opinion clamoring for it."[76] Nor was SR 129 complete. On January 9 Senator Dill, with the permission of Couzens, amended it with eight more questions specifically querying the FRC to discuss its treatment of educational stations and to defend the level of educational programming on the commercial stations. These questions were prepared by Dill with the assistance of Morgan, who termed their addition to SR 129 "very helpful to the cause." Perry gleefully reported to Evans that one radio writer sympathetic to the status quo confided to him "that the radio industry made the mistake of its life in letting the fight get into Congress." The revised

SR 129, also called the Couzens–Dill resolution, passed the Senate on January 12.[77]

Any enthusiasm for SR 129 on behalf of the broadcast reform movement faded quickly, though, particularly when it was realized that it was the FRC that had been charged with making the investigation. Given the FRC statement of December 21, not to mention the entire corpus of its work, the results of an FRC study were foregone conclusions. "I am wondering whether this request for information to the Radio Commission has been made for the purpose of drawing a herring across a trail," Woehlke wrote to Evans on January 11.

> You and I know that the Commission as at present constituted will tell Couzens that there is an overdose of direct advertising at the present time, but that the broadcasters themselves are beginning to remedy the situation and that they should be given more time for improvement. They will report that European programs are unsatisfactory, that the American competitive and selective system produces a greater variety and a higher quality of programs at no cost to the listener than is provided by the European state monopolies through a tax on receiving sets. They will report that under the American system—much flag waving at this point—government ownership and operation is not feasible and they will prove their viewpoint, at least to the satisfaction of most members of Congress. In other words, it will be the Commission's advice that Congress do nothing, and it will reinforce this advice with all the well known assertions provided by the bright RCA boys.[78]

Perhaps even more unsettling to the reformers, Couzens made it clear that with the passage of SR 129, he would use his influence to see that Congress not consider any reform legislation until the FRC had filed its report in response to the measure. In short, SR 129 provided committee chairmen a legitimate reason to postpone reform legislation until the next session of Congress in the fall. In this light, SR 129 appeared more as a ringing defeat than a victory. As Woehlke so quickly grasped, it was a grand defensive maneuver by the allies of the industry that left the reformers immobilized. "Needless to say," one educator wrote in February on the apparent demise of reform legislation, "I am quite discouraged over the whole radio situation as it looks at the present time." H. O. Davis argued that it would be fatal for the reformers to accept Couzens's agenda. "I have a feeling that we should make every possible effort to get action at this session of Congress," he advised Crandall in February, "for it would be very difficult to keep the radio matter alive through another year."[79] All the active elements of the broadcast reform movement concurred with Davis's sentiments, recognizing the impossibility of a favorable report from the FRC in response to SR 129, and each attempted at having reform legislation considered in the spring of 1932.

The *Ventura Free Press*'s Evans was most active in this regard. "I am going down to Washington this afternoon for the express purpose of finding out just what sort of legislation we can get introduced into Congress,'' he wrote to Woehlke on February 9. He quickly ruled out the Horr resolution; SR 129 was the only radio investigation bill for that session even if the study was to be conducted by the FRC. Evans concentrated his efforts on Ewin Davis and Dill, as their cooperation would be essential for any legislation to get through the relevant committees, and Couzens had already made known his opposition to any hearings for radio bills at that session. Dill gave Evans the run-around. ''Dill is the only man actively promoting stuff in radio of whom I would be afraid. I wouldn't trust him anywhere,'' he told Woehlke.[80]

Ewin Davis, on the other hand, was willing to add a provision limiting the amount of advertising on stations with over 1,000 watts power to an omnibus radio bill that he was bringing to the floor of the House for a vote. Davis attempted unsuccessfully to convince the commercial broadcasters that this measure was in their best interest, ''a case of using the pruning knife in order to ward off the guillotine.''[81] This was probably the aspect of commercial broadcasting that was most sensitive to criticism and, therefore, most likely to pass Congress. ''Our whole effort should be to get the Ewin L. Davis advertising restriction across,'' Evans wrote to Woehlke in March. ''That is going to be the purpose of my agitation from now on.''[82] The *Ventura Free Press* rallied newspaper publishers and editors to support the measure in their frequent mailings. The Radio Omnibus Bill passed the House with practically no opposition and went to Dill's SCIC. Evans was encouraged about the support he found for the measure in Congress.

Quite unexpectedly to Evans, however, Dill immediately introduced a number of minor and controversial amendments to the Radio Omnibus bill, watered down the anti-advertising provisions, and arranged to keep the bill from having public hearings. ''The radio boys injected their jokers into the Davis bill,'' Evans explained to Woehlke. ''They certainly know how to operate. It also shows how nearly impossible it is for any man to sufficiently protect his legislation so the smart boys like the N.B.C. outfit cannot render it worthless.'' The result of Dill's amendments was to make the bill virtually unpassable or, if it was passed, to have it sent to a conference in which the committee leadership could largely control the wording of the agreed-upon legislation; it ''renders the chance of passage of any bill eliminating or limiting advertising absolutely impossible,'' as Evans put it. ''The result of Senator Dill's'' amendments, H. O. Davis highlighted in a letter to publishers, ''is bound to be the death of all radio-reform legislation at this session.''[83]

To the *Free Press,* this episode cast Dill in unambiguous terms. Evans concluded that ''Dill is very close to the radio crowd and is trying to hide this fact by constantly making a large noise about minor radio matters.'' Woehlke agreed, seeing Dill as ''working hand and glove with RCA.'' ''It is at least well to have him definitely pigeonholed and out in the open,''

H. O. Davis wrote to Crandall.[84] The *Ventura Free Press* strategy at this point turned to putting pressure on Dill by alerting Washington state newspaper publishers to his hypocrisy vis-à-vis the power trust and having them pressure Dill to support Ewin Davis's restriction on advertising. "In order to get anywhere we have to blow hell out of Dill," Evans stated. Dill was outraged by this tactic, but he skillfully defused the situation by passing the responsibility for the amendments to other senators and shifting the discussion to other provisions of the Radio Omnibus bill. Evans tried to patch up relations in Dill in June when he saw that the tactic had failed.[85] The bill did not pass the Senate in that session.

The NCER also caught some of the fallout from the *Free Press's* campaign on behalf of the advertising restriction. H. O. Davis repeatedly implored Crandall to have the Payne Fund pressure the NCER to lobby for the Ewin Davis provision since the Fess bill was clearly dead in the water. Perry agreed with H. O. Davis, believing the Ewin Davis bill the only reform legislation with any hope for passage. Morgan not only refused to endorse the advertising restriction provision but he cryptically informed H. O. Davis that the only reform program he was interested in lobbying for was the NCPT 1931 resolution calling for the complete public ownership and decommercialization of broadcasting. "Mr. Joy Elmer Morgan," Davis wrote to Crandall incredulously, "does not even approve the campaign he is conducting."[86] By now the NCER's lobbying had assumed an almost surreal quality. It discontinued all work on Capitol Hill in January when Fess informed them it would be "ill-advised" to press ahead with the Fess bill after the passage of SR 129. Nevertheless, Tyler continued to solicit support for the Fess bill among educators throughout the spring while Morgan spoke optimistically of how the corner was being turned in Congress and the NCER was poised to "push forward with greater confidence during the next winter."[87]

All of this was not lost on the Payne Fund, which had regarded the *Free Press* radio campaign as the only lobbying effort with any promise. Crandall convened a confidential meeting with Morgan, Perry, and Bolton in late March to, as she informed Davis, "get a better understanding of their ways of working," particularly the NCER's confusing legislative activities, although she was doubtful by now "if this can bring about any significant change in their program." In a postmortem of the NCER's legislative activities made that summer, Crandall noted that the NCER's notion of lobbying seemed "to have begun and ended with the introduction of the Fess bill. Apparently no work has been done upon it" beyond that, she added. Her analysis of the NCER concluded that "no effort has been made to understand the entire political situation in Congress and out of it regarding radio legislation and no attempt at collaboration with the established committees of the two houses of Congress under whose auspices radio legislation is necessarily formulated nor with other agencies operating to the same general purpose.''[88] In sum, as a lobbying agency, the Payne Fund regarded the NCER as an abject failure.

One element of the broadcast reform movement that the *Ventura Free Press* made no effort to associate with was WCFL and organized labor. Woehlke dismissed the CFL's Nockels as a "bull-necked low-browed radical." Woehlke wrote to Evans that spring that

> The entire Chicago labor situation is honeycombed with graft and corruption. It is a racket instead of a labor movement. . . . My impulse was to denounce the Chicago labor outfit and to maintain that they were not fit to be allowed to operate any kind of a radio station even with 5 watts, but that would not be good politics.

He concluded that the wise move was to avoid "even seeming to be allied with the outfit.''[89] This erroneous impression of the CFL, based, at best, on the regime that Nockels and John Fitzpatrick had replaced some twenty-five years earlier, prevented the *Free Press* from linking up with the group that was best positioned to have reform legislation passed in the spring of 1932, and the group that had the most effective lobby working on behalf of reform. Since the FRC had rejected even granting a hearing for WCFL in April 1931, after having been advised by Senator White to do something to assist WCFL, organized labor was on very solid ground in Congress in the spring of 1932, the passage of SR 129 notwithstanding.

Hence, Nockels had little difficulty convincing Senator Henry Hatfield (R-WVa) to introduce a bill that would establish a clear channel for organized labor in January 1932. A similar measure was introduced in the House. Nockels and labor pushed hard for the amendment and the SCIC established a special subcommittee to hold public hearings on the proposed legislation. Subcommittee member Senator Smith W. Brookhart (R-Iowa) pigeonholed Perry in March and he urged the NCER to support the Hatfield bill, "as the granting of a channel for labor would open the way for a similar reservation for education." Brookhart also confided to Perry, as he had to Evans in December, that "if I had my way the government would take over full control and do away with all commercial aspects.''[90] Despite the advice, the disorganized NCER made no appreciable contribution on the bill's behalf, other than a few proclamations of moral support. *Broadcasting* noted that the industry regarded the Hatfield bill "as perhaps the most objectionable legislation introduced." It soon became clear that a majority of the subcommittee, which Brookhart chaired, was "unalterably in favor of giving Labor a clear channel," and even the NAB conceded that the bill "was practically sure of passage.''[91] CBS, NBC, and the NAB linked forces and used their considerable leverage to stall the hearings.

Finally, in early May, WCFL reached an agreement with NBC that would let the labor station broadcast full-time on the 970 frequency it shared with

NBC affiliate KJR of Seattle and to increase its wattage from 1,500 to 5,000. NBC even arranged for WCFL to begin to transmit some NBC programs. In return, the CFL and organized labor agreed to drop their campaign for the Hatfield bill. WCFL received unlimited hours in exchange for abandoning the fight for broadcast reform. The deal was struck in secret, high-level negotiations involving the FRC as well as the broadcasters that caught Congress by surprise, as members had convened for subcommittee hearings on the Hatfield bill the morning the deal was announced. The FRC approved the deal immediately, the legislation was withdrawn, and the hearings were canceled.[92]

This was a major triumph for the commercial broadcasters in what was probably the most serious threat they faced that tumultuous spring. As Perry somberly noted, the networks were able "to prevent the establishment of the principle of allocation of frequencies by act of Congress." A "precedent" has been set, Evans immediately informed the NCER after the deal was announced, "which will make it practically impossible for you people to get to first base without doing the same thing, having N.B.C. make a deal with you and you know as well as I that the N.B.C. people will never make any concession to education." It is possible that Nockels reached his accord with NBC and the FRC because he realized the broadcast reform movement was getting nowhere in Congress and the time was ripe to take the best deal he could find. More likely, however, Nockels was simply made the proverbial offer he could not refuse; WCFL had been in severe financial straits for at least two years and this was probably Nockels's best chance to make the station solvent and keep his dream for labor radio alive.[93]

With the collapse of the various broadcast reform bills by May, all attention turned to the FRC, which was scheduled to issue its report in response to SR 129 by early summer. The FRC's study was conducted by its secretary, James W. Baldwin, who would happen to advance to an executive position with the NAB in 1933. Called "young and capable" by *Broadcasting,* Baldwin's study essentially consisted of sending out a three-page questionnaire to every station inquiring as to how much of each station's time was dedicated to advertising and how much to education, along with a request for a copy of the station's advertising rate card.[94]

In response to Baldwin's questionnaire, the NAB established an emergency fund to provide member stations with "the material to provide the American public with the real facts about the American broadcasting industry." "The entire American Plan of broadcasting, based on private ownership and advertising support, is now definitely under fire," stated a letter to NAB members soliciting funds for this emergency fund by Harry Shaw. It "presents the most serious danger which the American broadcasting system has ever faced." For its part, NBC, prepared a bulletin advising all of its affiliates how best to answer the questionnaire. In keeping with standard FRC policy,

Baldwin elected to accept the responses on the questionnaires at face value, since the FRC regarded its task as that of a "neutral purveyor of information."[95] When ACUBS was tipped off to this "inside information," they immediately notified their member stations, in answering the FRC questionnaire, to "interpret as educational broadcasting everything they do except any time sold commercially."[96]

The FRC formally responded to SR 129 on June 9, 1932, in the form of a report titled *Commercial Radio Advertising*. In addition to Baldwin's survey of existing stations, the report relied upon old FRC dockets and consultations with the NAB and leading commercial broadcasters. Baldwin had solicited and received extensive material from Armstrong Perry regarding the nature of foreign broadcasting systems, but little of Perry's influence was to be found in *Commercial Radio Advertising*.[97] A more emphatic statement on behalf of the status quo would be difficult to imagine. As *Broadcasting* noted, it was "a report that unequivocally favors commercial broadcasting, without further government interference." Among other things, the FRC concluded that conditions in Europe were so different from those in the United States, that any attempt to learn from their experience with government-operated networks "would probably lead one to entirely wrong conclusions." The report rejected any attempt to limit advertising as illogical: "The American system of broadcasting is predicated upon the use of radio facilities as a medium for local and national advertising." Furthermore, the report dismissed the claims of the broadcast reform movement that educators needed their own independent stations: "The present attitude of broadcasters, as indicated herein, justifies the commission in believing that educational programs can be safely left to the voluntary gift of the use of facilities by commercial stations."[98]

Proponents of the status quo responded to *Commercial Radio Advertising* enthusiastically, and accorded the report great prominence in their communications. "The report," stated the NAB in a press release, "presents, for the first time, an accurate picture of American broadcasting." The NAB newsletter observed that "it answers with facts all the unfair charges which have been made against American broadcasting by certain groups of educators and others selfishly interested in changing our system of broadcasting."[99] *Broadcasting* was even less guarded in its assessment of the report. "A huge dose of antitoxin that should effectively check the epidemic of wild and irresponsible criticism," was how an editorial characterized *Commercial Radio Advertising*. "Critical politicians, jealous competitors and calamity-howling reformers won't be so careless in their attacks on commercial radio hereafter. Facts, for the first time are available." Louis Caldwell's ABA Committee on Communications regarded the FRC's findings as "based on a careful and exhaustive study of fact." The "facts and conclusions presented by the report are of the greatest importance to the proper determination of legislative issues which face Congress."[100]

The broadcast reformers, on the other hand, were unimpressed by the FRC report. Members of the ACUBS angrily wondered if the FRC was getting a "rake-off" from the commercial broadcasters or if they owned stock in AT&T. H. O. Davis dismissed it as "a joke." Arthur Crane, politely informed the annual convention of the National Association of State Universities that "the Commission evaded some of the questions."[101] Perry termed it "a weak report" in which the FRC "attempted to justify its support of the commercial monopolies." "It was to be expected," the NCER's Tyler explained to Crandall, "that when a Federal body is asked to investigate itself it would do its best to make its investigation a defense of its own activities." Tyler argued that *Commercial Radio Advertising* was "so clearly unfair that no one seems satisfied with it."[102] He was only partially correct.

That summer H. O. Davis despondently observed how the situation had changed in less than six months, since the start of the most recent session of Congress. "We expected to get several bills," he commiserated to Woehlke, "and failed to get any." The immediate effect of *Commercial Radio Broadcasting*, as *Broadcasting* noted, would be to make the prospects for reform on Capitol Hill all the more unlikely in the coming year. As Evans noted, "all of the arguments we have used to date will be pretty much in the discard" in the minds of many public officials. Indeed, NBC's chief lobbyist, Frank Russell, wrote to the White House that summer to draw their attention to the FRC report showing that the concerns of the educators were unwarranted.[103]

The plight of the broadcast reform movement was laid out starkly in a "confidential" letter by Representative Thomas R. Amlie (R-Wisc.) to the NCER on May 24, 1932. Amlie was a first-term member of Congress who had sponsored legislation to prohibit any radio advertising on Sundays. He had attempted without success to get the support of both the NCER and Evans, who had dismissed Amlie as "so far outside the picture he cuts no ice at all."[104] "I came to Congress last fall as a new member. I wanted to do something that would call attention to the inherent evils of our present commercialized form of broadcasting," Amlie informed the NCER. After describing his initial efforts at broadcast reform, Amlie added:

> I have found the Radio interests are well organized. At a convention in my state, the eleven stations assembled adopted a very bitter resolution condemning me in most outspoken terms for my stand . . . it indicates what any representative is running up against if he attempts to regulate or control the private broadcasters.

Amlie noted that once the commercial broadcasters aimed their fire at his bill, it was dropped "without as much a voice of protest on the Floor of the

House." Amlie attributed this to the fact that "Members of Congress are dependent upon these stations for many favors," not the least of which was the broadcasting of their speeches on a regular basis. "This is a factor you must overcome," he informed the NCER in his conclusion, "if you are to get anywhere with your program."[105]

The summer of 1932 was one of reflection for the various elements of the broadcast reform movement. "The professional agitators," noted the NAB, have provided "a rather quiet summer." The recently adjourned session of Congress seemingly confirmed the prediction of the CBS executive who had confided to Perry late in 1930 that the broadcast reformers "would fail because the political cards were stacked against them."[106] To many it appeared that the reformers had missed what would be their best opportunity to generate reform legislation in Washington. The first great encounter in the battle for the control of U.S. broadcasting was won decisively by the commercial broadcasters, leaving the reformers wounded, though by no means dead.

CHAPTER 7

Autumn 1932–December 1933: The Battle for Public Opinion and the White House

The collapse of the efforts to have broadcast reform legislation considered and passed by Congress in the spring of 1932 marked the beginning of an eighteen-month period in which Congress barely considered any communications legislation. During this interregnum, the broadcast reform movement basically came to abandon lobbying on Capitol Hill and directed its attention and resources in other directions. Perhaps most important, the reformers attempted to generate public recognition of and support for broadcast reform. This chapter will chronicle the various efforts of the reformers along these lines, with particular emphasis upon the battle for the allegiance of the newspaper industry and the efforts to gain favorable press coverage of the debate over radio broadcasting. In addition, the reformers attempted to win the newly elected Roosevelt administration to its cause, engaging in a ferocious fight with the commercial broadcasters for the president's allegiance. After analyzing this confrontation, this chapter will conclude by discussing the steps taken by the Roosevelt administration in the final months of 1933 to lay the groundwork for legislation to establish the permanent regulation of radio broadcasting and all of communications.

Shifting Currents in Autumn 1932

The immediate response of the NCER to the devastating effect the FRC's *Commercial Radio Advertising* was having on the prospects for broadcast reform on Capitol Hill was to approach the ACUBS and ask it to prepare a response that would repudiate the FRC report. Although the ACUBS was sympathetic, it was despondent about what good any counterreport would accomplish. "The position of the FRC in view of the way they have treated educational broadcasters is absurd,'' the educator commissioned by the ACUBS to make the study noted, ''but it is not so easy to make facts clear to those who are on the outside.'' The ACUBS was unable to complete the study, leaving the NCER, in its effort to repudiate *Commercial Radio Advertising*, to rely in part upon a pamphlet on college and university broadcasting by Tracy Tyler that drew from his earlier doctoral research at Columbia University.[1] Unfortunately for the NCER, the report's publication in early 1933 was unrecognized beyond educational circles and had no discernible impact upon congressional or public opinion.

The *Ventura Free Press* radio campaign, on the other hand, resumed its campaign ''to silence Dill,'' as S. Howard Evans put it, in the summer of 1932. Dill had indicated no change that summer in his opposition to reform legislation, yet any campaign for reform would have to deal squarely with his immense power over radio legislation. Evans wrote to Walter Woehlke that ''we have definitely broken with him. We must discredit Dill and keep his influence . . . at a minimum.''[2] Woehlke and H. O. Davis attempted to ''start a hot fire under the seat of Brother Dill's pants in his home state,'' mostly by alerting newspaper publishers and editors of his work on behalf of commercial broadcasting interests. ''Dill is constructing a noisy, radical front by going through the motions of attacking the broadcasting monopoly for home consumption,'' H. O. Davis wrote to the editor of the *Spokane Spokesman-Review* in a representative letter, ''while behind this front he is working hand and glove with the broadcasters themselves.''[3]

It soon became apparent that this effort to discredit Dill would prove no more successful than the similar attempt made by the *Ventura Free Press* in the spring, unless the *Free Press* could establish that Dill had engaged in corrupt practices, as was rumored in Washington state. This approach proved fruitless. ''This guy Dill,'' a frustrated Evans wrote to Woehlke in December, ''has been just careful enough of his record so that there is nothing which can be pinned upon him.''[4] The *Ventura Free Press* discontinued the attacks on Dill thereafter, as it was clear that, if anything, they were becoming counterproductive.

The reformers hoped that the coming fall elections would put a more sympathetic body of legislators in Congress. Without success, the NCER used its contacts among educators to attempt to convince the Democratic and Republican parties to include planks on broadcast reform in their party platforms.[5] That fall, in letters to congressional candidates, Morgan pleaded for making the ''undemocratic and unfair'' commercial broadcasting system and the consequent need for broadcast reform issues in the campaign.[6] Not only did Morgan's call go unheeded, the 1932 elections would prove disastrous for almost all of the members of Congress who had been active on behalf of broadcast reform and who stood for re-election. Representative Ralph Horr and Senator Smith Brookhart were defeated in primaries, while Senator Otis

Glenn and Representative Thomas Amlie were defeated in the general election.

More disastrously for the broadcast reform movement, Representative Ewin Davis was defeated in his primary election in a major upset. Davis specifically cited the radio industry as providing the cash to have him defeated, although he admitted he could not produce enough evidence to go public with his claim. There is no evidence to suggest that these other members of Congress were done in by their stated opposition to commercial broadcasting, although the message may have seemed clear to the members of Congress who assembled that winter. Horr's successor, liberal Democrat and ACLU member Marion Zioncheck, for example, would refuse to take a position on broadcast reform legislation until he had "referred the bills to the local director of the CBS station in Seattle for his opinion," as ACLU Director Roger Baldwin noted despondently.[7]

Ironically, just as the situation in Congress appeared more unpromising than ever, the Payne Fund was able to convince Morgan and the NCER to formally abandon its work on behalf of the Fess bill and work with the *Ventura Free Press* radio campaign on behalf of legislation for an independent "investigation of the whole field of radio broadcasting," with the aim of laying the groundwork for the construction of a new system of broadcasting. The NCER so resolved at its November 1932 meeting, much to the approval of Evans, H. O. Davis, and Woehlke.[8] In its literature the NCER stressed the democratic nature of such a study and pointed to Canada, which in the spring of 1932 had resolved for a nonprofit and noncommercial system after an extensive study by a Royal Commission.[9] Representative Hampton P. Fulmer (D-SC) agreed to introduce the NCER study proposal as a bill in the House of Representatives. In November 1932 Evans returned to the corridors of the Capitol to mobilize support for the bill. "If the federal investigation of radio fails," he wrote to H. O. Davis, "we are practically sunk anyway." The commercial broadcasters were opposed to the idea. Any further study of radio, *Broadcasting* wrote in early 1933, citing the existence of *Commercial Radio Advertising*, "is entirely unnecessary."[10]

It was soon evident that there was little interest in Congress in broadcast reform legislation. To some extent this was due to the unwillingness of Congress to consider any major legislation in the session preceding the inauguration of Franklin Roosevelt as president and, also, to Congressional preoccupation with economic issues as the Depression was entering its darkest months. In addition, however, with the defeat of those members of Congress outspoken on behalf of reform, especially Ewin Davis, there was simply nobody on Capitol Hill willing to champion the cause. "In both Houses of Congress there is no one," Evans informed Woehlke after a month of lobbying, "with whom we can play ball to get ahead in radio."[11]

In January 1933 Evans appeared before a subcommittee of the SCIC to argue for an independent study of broadcasting. After the *Ventura Free Press* campaign to present him as a pawn of the radio trust or as a politician on the take, Dill dispensed with the cordiality with which he normally greeted the broadcast reformers in public. Dill's response to Evans was antagonistic, immediate, and emphatic. "There is no need of investigation," Dill informed Evans. "Everybody knows the situation. And the report to the Senate gives the complete picture of the situation in the United States. I do not think anyone doubts the truth of the report." Hence *Commercial Radio Advertising,* which had derailed the momentum for reform measures in 1932, would now eliminate the rationale for any further study of broadcasting. This marked the end of the active lobbying for Evans for the foreseeable future. "I must say that the situation has developed to a point," Evans wrote to the NCER on January 25, "where I am convinced that further radio agitation in Washington is futile at the present time."[12]

The reform activities subsidized by the Payne Fund were not alone in this perception. Independently, the ACLU began to lobby for legislation in late 1932 that would require all broadcasters to air at least two sides to any discussion they carried of controversial social and political issues. The Radio Act of 1927 had called for this "privilege of reply," but it only pertained to candidates in a race for public office. The ACLU was far from oblivious to the problems inherent to this proposal, and it had few illusions that its passage would improve upon the amount of social affairs broadcasting. Nevertheless, the ACLU worked as closely as possible with Senator Dill, whom they believed was in favor of the legislation, based upon their interaction with him. They were disappointed when the version of the bill that left his committee was "in a form that is not even recognizable." The ACLU was dismayed further by Dill's withdrawal of support for their legislation in December 1932, which effectively doomed it. "Senator Dill has unaccountably weakened during the past couple of months," the ACLU secretary noted in January 1933, "and our letters to him come back with little explanation and no encouragement." This experience led the ACLU to reevaluate its radio program and to establish its Radio Committee, with its explicitly radical mandate, in the spring of 1933. It also taught the ACLU that, rhetoric notwithstanding, Senator Dill was a "weak sister" who would provide no assistance to the movement for broadcast reform.[13]

Given the status of reform legislation in Congress, the winter of 1932–1933 constituted a crossroad for the broadcast reform movement. In November 1932 Evans prepared a confidential memorandum for the Payne Fund concerning whether the Payne Fund should drop its campaign for reform, accept the status quo, and cooperate with the commercial broadcasters. Evans acknowledged that the strength of the commercial interests was such that the reformers would probably never be able to "successfully undermine commercial broadcasting in this country." At the same time he emphasized that "the fundamental structure of broadcasting" was "absolutely unsound," that the commercial system was inherently undemocratic and inimical to free speech, and that the public remained dissatisfied with the "excessive commercialism which characterizes our radio programs." He urged the Payne Fund to stay the course, as "the whole broadcasting structure needs to be reorganized."[14] The Payne Fund accepted Evans's counsel, electing to maintain its stance vis-à-vis commercial broadcasting for the foreseeable future.

In this context, the broadcast reformers pursued two distinct strategies over the next year or so in addition to what lobbying they continued to pursue on Capitol Hill and, more importantly, at the White House. First, the reformers attempted to influence policy at an elite level. The NCER and its member group ACUBS launched an aggressive campaign late in 1932 to have President Herbert Hoover appoint an educator to the FRC to fill the post being vacated by Chairman Charles McKinley Saltzman. The educator promoted by the NCER was Professor John C. Jensen of Nebraska Wesleyan University, who had served a term as ACUBS president and was a confirmed opponent of the status quo. For years Nebraska Wesleyan's radio station, WCAJ, had been entrenched in expensive litigation with commercial station WOW of Omaha to increase its allocation from one-seventh of the available hours on the frequency they shared. Nebraska Wesleyan finally shut down WCAJ in 1933 when the combination of the Depression and the legal expenses made continued operation too costly. Considerable effort was expended on this campaign and President Hoover even submitted Jensen as his nominee. In February 1933, however, the NCER determined that "there is absolutely no chance of his being confirmed." The Democratic leaders in Congress decided to keep the position unfilled until the new administration began in March.[15]

Another tactic to influence policy at an elite level was far more ambitious. In the autumn of 1932 Armstrong Perry attended the International Radio Telegraphic Conference in Madrid as the representative of the NCER. The conference was intended, among other things, to divide the ether among the nations of the world. Perry discovered there was considerable concern among foreign governments that the U.S. commercial radio interests were attempting to dominate the world broadcasting spectrum.[16] The conference failed to resolve the problem of allocation and a separate North American Radio Conference was called for the summer of 1933 in Mexico City, where it was hoped that the United States, Mexico, Canada, Cuba, and the Central American governments could agree to a regional allocation of the spectrum by the North American countries.

In several discussions in the beginning of 1933, Perry, Evans, and Tracy Tyler agreed that "an extensive reallocation is bound to occur as a result of the North American Conference." By all accounts, the United States, which had complete or partial control over ninety of the ninety-six available channels would be a certain loser in any accord. Thus, the federal government would be forced to address the structure of its broadcasting system whether it wanted to or not when the Mexico City conference required the United States to turn over several of the channels it controlled to the other North American nations.[17] NBC officials agreed with this analysis. Regardless of the outcome of the Mexico City conference, one memo stated, "there unquestionably will be a more or less general reallocation of broadcasting stations in this country." Another NBC memo noted that "it is this reallocation which contains the greatest potential danger to the NBC."[18] The NCER began to participate actively in the planning sessions that were convened to determine the U.S. negotiating position for the Mexico City conference, with the aim of establishing its credibility with policymakers for the future moment when the plans for the ultimate domestic reallocation were going to have to be made.[19]

Perry and the NCER found a surprising ally in these planning sessions in the early months of 1933 in Navy Captain Stanford C. Hooper. Hooper represented the "mobile group," which included the U.S. Navy and Army, and other interests that wanted space on the spectrum for point-to-point and ship-to-shore radio communication. Hooper, the director of naval communications and a trained radio engineer, was arguably the most knowledgable and experienced federal official on radio.[20] He was also a charter member of the executive branch's Interdepartmental Radio Advisory Committee, which coordinated the government's usage of radio. In 1928 the navy lent Hooper to the FRC for six months where he single-handedly devised the allocation of short-wave frequencies while the balance of the FRC occupied itself with the broadcasting reallocation.[21]

Regarding radio policy, Hooper was obsessed with two issues throughout the late 1920s and early 1930s. First, he believed that the United States needed to develop a coherent national communications policy, similar to Britain, to be competitive internationally. Second, Hooper was a strident proponent of having strong U.S. communications corporations that were "100% American and under American control." Hooper was in regular and amiable contact with the chief executive officers and other top officers at GE, AT&T, and RCA throughout this period in his capacity with the navy.[22] To no surprise, Hooper emerged as an advocate of network-dominated, advertising-supported broadcasting between 1927 and 1931.[23] As Perry informed Crandall in March 1932, Hooper was "strongly inclined toward the commercial interests."[24]

By the end of 1932, however, Hooper had become appalled by what he regarded as the overabundance of advertising in U.S. broadcasting. He even suggested to President-elect Roosevelt in November 1932 that a campaign to limit or eliminate broadcast advertising "would appeal to the public."[25] Although he was never a proponent of nationalized broadcasting, Hooper confidentially expressed his enthusiasm for broadcast reform on numerous occasions between 1932 and 1935. He termed the NCER's campaign to mobilize opposition to commercial broadcasting "just what is needed," and referred to one anticommercial broadcasting tract by William A. Orton of Smith College as "the best thing on the subject that I have read." "Somehow I have the feeling that the next three or four years are going to witness some real results of your efforts," Hooper wrote to Tyler. "I hope so." At the same time, however, Hooper remained a proponent of strong corporate control for the overall communications industry. For example, he opposed the government's actions leading to the 1932 consent decree requiring GE and Westinghouse to divest their interests in RCA, saying it "would bring disaster, and good to no one," on the grounds that it would weaken the U.S. position in international communications.[26]

The major argument in the planning sessions for the Mexico City conference concerned where in the spectrum the United States would be willing to offer additional channels to the other North American countries. The commercial broadcasters insisted that the channels below 550 kilocycles used by the "mobile group" were the logical choice, so that the broadcasters who occupied the range from 550 to 1500 kilocycles would remain undisturbed, to the benefit of U.S. listeners. Hooper rejected that notion and, finally, when the broadcasters persisted, he proposed in March that "the whole subject of the broadcasting band be opened up and studied from the point of view of the listener," rather than from the point of view of advertisers and commercial broadcasters, in the planning sessions.[27] Perry, who had been lobbying Hooper for three months for such a move was ecstatic; Evans, Morgan, Tyler, and the other reformers associated with Payne Fund activities were in almost daily contact with Hooper during the last two weeks of March. Not only did a reallocation appear probable, but a dominant government official who was central to communications policymaking was explicitly attacking the commercial basis of U.S. broadcasting.[28]

The enthusiasm, however, was short-lived. The broadcasters caved in almost immediately, agreeing that the band below 520 kilocycles was inviolate. Hooper then withdrew his request for a "study of the broadcast situation." He explained to Evans that he remained sympathetic to broadcast reform, but that he felt obligated to do "what is necessary to protect our mobile group."[29] In his capacity with the navy, he wrote to Perry, it was his job to "keep friends with everyone," and he was only justified in taking up the reform cause when "the invasion of our part of the spectrum is concerned."[30]

In Mexico City that July Perry was kept out of all the official sessions, but he established cordial contacts with the Latin American delegations, whom he discovered "were incensed over the attitude of the U.S. delegation." Perry funneled broadcast reform literature and U.S. government pub-

157

lications to the foreign delegations, with whom he shared antagonism toward the U.S. radio interests. Moreover, Perry "had a hand in drafting the proposals of the Latin American countries," as he admitted "very confidentially" to Joy Elmer Morgan. The conference ended without an agreement when Mexico insisted upon twelve clear channels whereas the U.S. delegation was only willing to relinquish three or four at most.[31]

The commercial broadcasters were outraged by Perry's actions in Mexico City, even without being aware of his role in assisting the Latin Americans draft their proposal. "The insidious propaganda opposing American commercial broadcasting spread by Armstrong Perry . . . had the effect of stimulating Latin opposition to the proposals of the American delegation," *Broadcasting* editorialized. The magazine chastised Perry for working "against the objectives of an official delegation from his own country," and suggested Congress might want to investigate Perry's conduct for possible criminal charges. This became a major crisis for the NCER, which sent out several mailings to defend Perry's conduct and to explain the NCER position.[32] Nonetheless, the immediate result of the NCER's venture into diplomacy had proven a public relations disaster on the highly sensitive issue of patriotism. Moreover, it only reaffirmed what the broadcast reform movement had learned elsewhere: Behind closed doors, where decisions were made by the powerful with minimal public participation, they were hopelessly overmatched by the commercial broadcasters.

Accordingly, the second strategy adopted by the broadcast reform movement in the wake of the demise of any hope for reform on Capitol Hill was, as Evans put it, "to concentrate its attention on arousing public interest throughout the country in radio matters." This theme dominated the correspondence of the Payne Fund, the NCER, and the *Ventura Free Press* during the final months of 1932 and the beginning of 1933. "After all, the problem is more one of public opinion than anything else, hence the more public discussion the better," Tyler noted. "Our only hope is in wakening the public opinion so that a new system will be established here."[33] "My trying to do anything further in Washington," Evans emphasized, "is useless until sufficient pressure has been brought from the provinces to make Congress feel that it really must act." The Payne Fund's Crandall concurred, stating that lobbying efforts should be "abandoned for the time being," while the reformers "concentrate all their forces on creating local opinion which would later be reflected in Congress."[34]

In this spirit the NCER, with the approval of the Payne Fund and the assistance of the *Ventura Free Press* radio campaign, launched three major campaigns in order to stimulate public interest in broadcast reform beginning in the autumn of 1932. First, in November 1932 the NCER formally established the American Listeners Society (ALS) which was meant to be a "nationwide organization of listeners committed to the improvement of radio in America.'' The ALS would be a grassroots organization, supported by annual dues of $1 per member, that would effectively adopt the platform of the NCER as its mandate, including ''the improvement of laws and governmental administration affecting broadcasting.'' Its first mailing stated that the ALS would fight to represent the interests of listeners in their conflict with broadcasters, who were ''actuated only by the profit-making motive.'' The ALS planned to publish a mass circulation monthly magazine ''containing no advertising and free to tell the truth,'' as Joy Elmer Morgan put it.[35]

This was a bold plan by the NCER to establish a mass-based listeners group that would eventually become self-governing and independent of the NCER and which would become the main actor in the broadcast reform movement. Although not made explicit, the nature of the ALS recreated the listener-supported model of broadcasting provided by the BBC, which was much admired by many in the NCER. *Broadcasting* was unimpressed, editorializing that the ALS had been formed by the NCER simply ''to justify the existence'' of the NCER since its legislative work had failed. The ALS never really got off the ground; although a handful of people joined and quarterly meetings were held for several years, the NCER effectively stopped promoting it only a few months after it had been launched. An unsympathetic Levering Tyson observed in 1934 that the ALS ''was launched with usual hullabaloo, was an immediate failure, and has not been heard of since.'' To some extent the failure of the ALS may have been due to to the NCER's inability to publicize its existence to the intended mass audience. In addition, the prospects of the ALS were not helped by the formation of other ''listeners groups'' at the same time, including one launched by Chicago reformer Harris K. Randall and another one associated with Tyson's NACRE. These, like the ALS, also flopped.[36]

The second program launched by the NCER in the autumn of 1932 was intended to directly stimulate grassroots awareness of the broadcasting situation. In September 1932 the NCER hired Eugene J. Coltrane as its special representative with the primary aim of traveling the country to gain support for broadcast reform. Coltrane was the president of the North Carolina Education Association and had a long career as an educational administrator. In his first few months on the job, Coltrane met with educators across the nation to gauge their level of understanding of the broadcasting situation and to see what level of support there was for broadcast reform. He quickly discovered that most of the people who had been receiving the NCER's *Education by Radio* ''admitted they were not reading it.''[37] In November Coltrane wrote to Tyler that ''there is an amazing lack of information about radio and its problems,'' along with ''a certain amount of indifference and skepticism.'' ''I find that the people are not informed about radio, and certainly not about its problems,'' Coltrane wrote to Morgan. ''We can never hope to do the whole job by publications, and private conferences. People must come together, and discuss these issues and problems.''[38]

Between December 1932 and December 1933 Coltrane aggressively pursued this strategy. He crossed the nation, holding one- and two-day conferences on college campuses, giving speeches, writing letters, and distributing NCER literature. For example, in one representative month Coltrane traveled 4,400 miles, gave eleven conferences, made three speeches, and was interviewed approximately 100 times. Although he concentrated his attention upon meeting with educators, he also attempted to contact other influential people, usually lawyers, ministers, and other professionals. His monthly reports to the NCER were at times hopeful and at other times strikingly pessimistic. ''I have no doubt that it will be possible to get the necessary moral support for the program of the'' NCER, if we can ''acquaint the people with the issues'' and ''explain the numerous problems that are involved,'' he wrote in September 1933. ''A great many accept the position that a fundamental change in the present system is necessary and that legislation should be the end in view,'' his June 1933 report concluded.[39]

Yet Coltrane was almost glum in a special memorandum written for Morgan and Tyler in the autumn of 1933, noting the ''indifference'' that typified the educational and the professional communities' responses to his efforts to rally support for reform.

> I find that men are paying very little attention to radio, and most of them are rather commercially minded. The average man seems to think that it is perfectly legitimate to make money and that the support of radio by advertising is justifiable.

Coltrane scaled down his travels by the end of 1933, and curtailed them altogether in 1934 when he became seriously ill. He formally left the NCER in April 1934 to assume the presidency of Brevard College in North Carolina.[40] This was the NCER's most concerted effort to organize support for broadcast reform across the nation and while Coltrane's work exposed a great deal of people to the issues, it seems to have been largely ineffectual, at least to the extent that it was designed to significantly increase the level of mass support for broadcast reform.

The third NCER public awareness campaign launched may well have been the most ambitious. In the summer and fall of 1932 Tracy Tyler convinced both the Virginia State High School Debate League and the Western Conference Debating League to officially debate whether the United States should reserve channels for nonprofit broadcasters or whether ''radio broadcasting stations in the United States should be governmentally owned and operated.'' In December 1932 buoyed by these successes and working with other sympathetic educators, Tyler convinced the NUEA to adopt the radio issue as its official debate topic for all U.S. colleges, universities, and high schools for the 1933–1934 school year. To Tyler's disappointment, the final wording of the NUEA debate topic was "Resolved: That the United States should adopt the essential features of the British system of radio control and operation." As such, Tyler and the NCER thought the debate placed too much emphasis on Britain and not enough on the existing conditions in the United States.[41]

Any disappointment with the wording was tempered, however, by the prospects of having broadcast policy and legislation become the object of study and debate for millions of high school and college students nationwide. The NCER, Tyler wrote to one educator, "feels that the decision of the schools of America to debate the radio question is one of the most important decisions which has been made since the radio problem became acute." "There is no other single factor that can be promoted that will better bring the radio problem directly to the attention of the American homes than the sponsoring of this debate subject," one educational broadcaster wrote to Tyler. We need to "make it the biggest event in the history of organized debating in America," he concluded. The topic would be debated by some 1,500 colleges and 6,000 high schools in thirty-three states during the school year. Approximately 2.5 million people would be exposed to the debates.[42]

Nor were the educators and the NCER alone in their enthusiasm for the potential these school debates held. "The more I think about the possibilities in these school debates on radio, the more excited I get," S. Howard Evans wrote to Tyler in July 1933. H. O. Davis wrote to one publisher to argue that "it is important that the debates this fall and winter should be given the widest possible publicity by the newspapers." Davis concluded that "the debates will arouse an enormous amount of interest in the radio problem and will bring home the nature of this problem to millions of people who have so far given it very little thought except to curse the character of the radio programs and to swear at the sales talks." Evans proposed that the reformers not publish any debate materials but, rather, that the students be told to contact their congressmen to get further information. "Can you imagine one of these lazy Congressmen being repeatedly asked for information by every high-school in his district?" Evans asked Woehlke. "He would simply have to find out what radio was all about and that, after all, is exactly what we want."[43] As it developed, the NCER devoted much of its space in *Education by Radio* to the debate and assisted in the preparation of the official debate materials.

In addition to the official debate guide, several other handbooks were published to assist the student debaters that presented statements both pro and con.[44] Furthermore, the NAB published and distributed its own 191-page defense of the status quo, which was purportedly in response to "thousands of requests supporting the negative side of the issue" that "began pouring into the headquarters of the National Association of Broadcasters'' from ''public school officials, debate coaches and college and high school students from all parts of the nation.'' The NCER, which relied upon the official debate handbooks to present the affirmative position, was incensed by the lavish contribution of the NAB to the debate. ''Our high school debaters for whom this publication was prepared,'' *Education by Radio* stated in January 1934, ''will soon discover that most of the material in this pamphlet has been prepared by or at the instance of those who are reaping profits from the present American broadcasting practices.'' Tyler recommended that the NCER flood the NAB with requests for the NAB debate guide in order to deplete its stock. Evans reminded him that such a strategy would fail since the ''N.A.B. will have sufficient money to print enough copies to supply all the high school debaters regardless of how many other outside requests may come in.''[45]

Indeed, the commercial broadcasters were terrified by the debate. ''The Radio Industry was led into these debates through an error of judgment'' by an NBC executive, ''who innocently enough subscribed to the idea,'' admitted Merlin Aylesworth in a letter to David Sarnoff. The broadcasters shifted the debate, as much as possible, to a discussion of the limitations of the BBC rather than discuss the merits and demerits of the status quo in the United States. This approach was unpopular in Britain, where BBC Director Sir John Reith was outraged by the ''misrepresentation and distortion of facts about our system'' in the NAB debate guide and other commercial broadcasting debate material. NBC's London representative wired Aylesworth that the BBC indicated the ''deepest resentment'' and was considering ''severing relations'' with U.S. commercial broadcasters. *The Listener,* a BBC publication, devoted twelve pages in its January 31, 1934, issue to a repudiation of the claims in the NAB debate guide.[46] The commercial broadcasters did not want Reith or the BBC to make a public issue of the matter in the United States. Aylesworth moved quickly to defuse the situation by minimizing the significance of the debates. ''We consider the whole matter of little importance in this country,'' Aylesworth noted in one of several letters on the subject to Reith, describing the debates as ''just a lot of fun between school children who have a good time debating the subjects for which there are two good sides.''[47] The issue eventually went away, but the industry became more sensitive to the BBC's feelings. In April 1934 Aylesworth asked Senator Dill ''to go easy on the British'' in a radio talk on the debate question for fear of antagonizing Reith any further.[48]

The emphasis on Britain also left people like Morgan, Tyler, and Perry making strong arguments on behalf of the BBC, while the U.S. broadcasting situation received less attention than the reformers might have hoped. The debate became more an academic exercise than a threat to the existing commercial broadcasting set-up, particularly since the NCER representatives were quick to acknowledge that the NCER was not formally in favor of having the United States adopt the BBC model for broadcasting. The debates had no apparent impact upon public opinion. "We were able to comply with the objective without damage," Aylesworth informed Sarnoff.[49]

The Battle for the Press

The problems encountered by the NCER in the three preceding attempts to generate popular support for broadcast reform were accentuated by the publicity vacuum in which they operated. The major battle for public opinion in the early 1930s, therefore, which dwarfed the preceding NCER ventures by comparison, was the fight to gain the allegiance of the newspaper industry and U.S. journalists. This had been the specific twofold mandate given to H. O. Davis when the Payne Fund agreed to subsidize his *Ventura Free Press* radio campaign in 1931: The radio campaign was (1) to get newspaper publishers to lobby on behalf of reform through the ANPA, their trade organization, in Washington, D.C., and (2) to encourage extensive and sympathetic treatment of the broadcast reform struggle in the nation's newspapers. "The need of enlightening the public by giving space to the spot news concerning the fight against the attempted monopolization of the air," must be "relentless," Davis wrote to newspaper publishers in 1931. This was indispensable to the "final objective," which was "the creation of a popular sentiment to early Congressional action" to reform the status quo.[50]

For their part, the commercial broadcasters had little incentive to publicize the broadcast reform debate as their control of the ether became more entrenched with each passing year. This rendered more "difficult" the task of generating popular consciousness of broadcast reform, as one Yale law professor stated in 1932. "The radio industry has the first command of public opinion in the country," he observed. "If it is ever necessary, the industry is strategically situated for a campaign of propaganda." As it was, the issue of broadcast reform was rarely mentioned on commercial radio broadcasts; the most comprehensive examination of what remains of network news and public affairs broadcasts and transcripts from this period has found no instances in which the topic was even broached on the air.[51]

The closest that the debate over broadcast policy got to the network airwaves came in two brief episodes. First, for a brief period in the spring of 1932 NBC broadcast denunciations of the *Ventura Free Press* radio campaign, much to the Payne Fund's surprise. When Davis informed NBC that he was planning to make a transcript of these reports, NBC "contracted a bad case of cold feet" and discontinued them immediately. "I am inclined to think," Davis wrote to Crandall, that "they suddenly awoke to the fact that they were giving us a lot of good advertising." The only other known instance occurred when there were a couple of broadcasts of debates of the 1933–1934 official debate topic on whether the U.S. should adopt the British system of broadcasting. These debate broadcasts were carried annually by the networks.[52] This lack of coverage incensed the broadcast reformers, particularly when the commercial broadcasters repeatedly argued that the American people were adamant in their preference for the status quo. "The National Association of Broadcasters has absolutely no warrant for declaring it speaks in the name of millions of radio listeners," WLWL's Father John B. Harney testified before a Senate committee in 1934, when it "is absolutely certain that they have never told their listeners the contents" of the broadcast reform proposals.[53]

Indeed, to the reformers, the broadcasters engaged in a self-serving censorship on the subject. For example, in 1933 both NBC and CBS refused to give or even sell time to the National Religion and Labor Foundation, a nondenominational and nonsectarian organization, for a "series of talks on religion in action." NBC claimed that its policy was to "give time to Catholics, Jews, and Protestants separately, but never to religious organizations including all three," while CBS said it was "impossible to find the time." As Jerome Davis, the group's chairman, noted, the "series covered such controversial issues as public ownership of utility companies and radio itself."[54]

The networks did manage to find some time for treatment of related issues. In late 1933 CBS launched a weekly program, "A Message from the Executive Offices of the Columbia Network," to provide a "better understanding of both the future possibilities and present problems of . . . broadcasting." An analysis of the program's scripts, however, reveals that the program was a weekly salute to commercial broadcasting; not a word was uttered regarding the deliberations concerning the Communications Act of 1934 taking place in Washington, D.C., concurrent with the program's tenure, nor of the movement on behalf of the Wagner–Hatfield amendment, which would have set aside 25 percent of the channels for nonprofit broadcasters. In the fall of 1933, over 200 commercial stations nationwide broadcast fifteen weekly "Short Talks on Advertising," prepared by the Advertising Federation of America. This celebratory series was intended to "promote a better understanding" of this "characteristically American institution" that was a "champion of progress," and which was instrumental in bringing "complete security and universal happiness" to the nation.[55]

NBC was arguably most active in this regard. It broadcast a series of weekly talks in 1932 that were prepared in conjunction with the NAB. The talks were read by local radio personalities at each of their affiliates, and their purpose was to indicate how U.S. commercial broadcasting was "the everlasting glory of the American people and their business ingenuity." In 1933 Aylesworth and Sarnoff engaged in confidential correspondence to determine "the best method of presenting to the American radio audience the purpose of the sponsored program and who pays for radio broadcasting." Aylesworth confided that NBC's national advertisers "are all very interested in this idea" and that "it will be a wonderful thing for radio's prestige." The purpose of the campaign would be to show how "the sponsor is responsible for all radio broadcasting programs," even the sustaining shows that were unsponsored.[56] The end result was a special nationwide Sunday evening broadcast, "The History of Advertising," on November 12, 1933. The program's purpose was to indicate NBC's "appreciation of the vital part advertising has played in the success of radio broadcasting in this country." The program characterized radio broadcasting as a "natural development" in the history of advertising.[57]

This enraged the broadcast reformers. In 1932 Morgan stated:

> Commercial interests who wish to control radio broadcasting in the United States, . . . have not hesitated to use the radio broadcasting privileges granted them by the government as a means of indoctrinating the people in the so-called advantages of commercialized broadcasting.[58]

It also made the need for extensive and positive coverage of the broadcast reform campaign in the nation's newspapers all the more pressing, perhaps even essential, if there was any hope for eventual success.

The reformers certainly had reason to expect a sympathetic reaction from newspaper publishers, who were concerned with the competitive threat posed by the new medium, both for advertisers and circulation. In Britain and Canada, newspapers were cornerstones in the movements to establish non-profit and noncommercial broadcasting systems.[59] Moreover, many of the activists for broadcast reform were working journalists, like Perry, Woehlke, and Morgan, who regarded their colleagues as natural allies. For example, when Perry encouraged the Payne Fund to support the NCER in 1930, he informed Crandall that his broadcast reform activities received "unqualified and unlimited support from his colleagues at the Press Club" in Washington, D.C. To many broadcast reformers, it was nearly axiomatic, as one educator put it, that "almost 100 percent of the papers are against the present radio set-up."[60]

When the ANPA first established its radio committee in 1923, its purpose was to "thoroughly investigate the entire subject" and see how the newspaper industry could profitably exploit the new medium; radio was not regarded as a particular threat. By the beginning of the 1930s, however, elements of the newspaper industry had become alarmed by the rapid growth of the networks and commercial broadcasting. Radio enjoyed a 90 percent increase in advertising revenues between 1929 and 1931 while newspaper advertising sales dropped dramatically. By the beginning of 1931 the ANPA determined that 60 cents were being spent by advertisers on radio for every dollar being spent on newspapers, whereas the ANPA had officially recorded no direct advertising on radio whatsoever as recently as 1927. An ANPA membership survey in 1931 discovered that over 90 percent of its members believed that the emergence of radio was responsible for some loss in newspaper advertising revenues.[61] Newspaper trade publication *Editor & Publisher* lauded the BBC in an editorial and praised the British system for adequately financing "programs without thrusting strident sales talks into homes." The president of the ANPA informed one audience in 1931 that "we can learn something from the conduct of radio abroad," especially in Britain, where the "frantic scramble for the air" had been eliminated primarily by "the interdiction of all forms of commercial exploitation of radio."[62]

This was the context in which H. O. Davis launched his bid to mobilize newspaper opposition to commercial broadcasting in the summer of 1931. Davis, Evans, and Woehlke established contacts with major publishers nationwide and pushed the trade associations, particularly the ANPA, to adopt platforms calling for sweeping broadcast reform. Despite the clear material conflict between the two media, however, the *Ventura Free Press* radio campaign quickly discovered that it had work to do. "The majority of newspaper publishers," one early *Free Press* memorandum reflected, "while resenting the inroads of radio on their advertising revenue, knew very little of the social dangers of completely commercialized broadcasting." Moreover, many publishers were suspicious of the *Free Press* for offering to bankroll the antiradio campaign without any apparent material incentive. This "suspicion" of the *Free Press* was encouraged by the "conservative metropolitan dailies with strong radio affiliations" that dominated the ANPA. At the 1931 ANPA convention, for example, the reception accorded the *Free Press* was "less than cold, it was arctic in its frigidity," as Davis remembered.[63]

The *Ventura Free Press* campaign was not altogether unsuccessful, however. With its active encouragement, many press associations, including the Michigan League of Home Dailies, the California Press Association, and the Illinois Press Association adopted anticommercial broadcasting platforms in 1931 and 1932.[64] To the untrained eye, it may well have appeared that the newspaper industry was rabidly anticommercial broadcasting. More important, the *Free Press* campaign established very close ties with the ANPA radio committee chairman, Elzey Roberts, publisher of the *St. Louis Star*. Roberts regarded Davis and Evans as having "a better grasp of this problem than almost anyone I have come in contact with, either personally or by correspondence." Roberts credited the *Ventura Free Press* radio campaign for being responsible for "waking up" newspapers to the radio problem. Before it "tackled this proposition," Roberts wrote to Evans, "the publishers as a whole were sound asleep." Roberts informed the New York State Publishers meeting in 1931 that the newspapers' ally in the fight against commercial broadcasting would be "the great army of radio listeners who are disgusted with the blatant advertising blurbs" that "are rammed down their throats with monotonous regularity." Roberts concluded that "it is not unreasonable to suppose that a demand may be created to cease commercialization of the radio in the United States and put it on the basis of broadcasting in Britain."[65]

The radio committee's report to the ANPA national convention in 1931 was sharply critical of radio advertising as the newspaper industry's "greatest competitor" and praised the BBC, but stopped short of suggesting radical reform of the status quo. Newspaper opposition to commercial broadcasting reached its zenith in 1931, the *Ventura Free Press* campaign notwithstanding. The industry came rather quickly to accept the status quo and eschew efforts to link newspaper concerns about lost revenues to broader calls for the structural reform of the ether. This transition was encouraged by the NAB and the two networks, understandably concerned that the newspaper industry might link up with the broadcast reformers and dismantle an industry still in its infancy. The NAB's newsletter harped on the threat to commercial broadcasting posed by the newspaper industry. In particular, NBC took the lead in defusing this situation. One of Aylesworth's primary duties, as he informed one press executive, was to "solve" the "rather delicate problems" that "pertain to the relationship of the press and the radio" and to do so "in the joint interest of the press and radio." Aylesworth devoted considerable attention to maintaining extensive correspondence with publishers and editors, many of whom were close friends; he also attended ANPA conventions for personal discussions with publishers.[66]

The commercial broadcasters approached the newspaper publishers on three distinct levels. First, they disputed the argument that radio was taking advertising away from newspapers. *Broadcasting* accused *Editor & Publisher* of "twisting figures to suit a thesis." "Broadcasting has not diverted funds" from newspapers and magazines, Aylesworth wrote in 1930. "Rather, it has earned additional funds for use on this new method of promoting business." Although recent scholarship suggests that the broadcasters may have been accurate in this appraisal, the newspaper industry had little patience for this argument, as the ANPA survey cited earlier indicated.[67]

Second, broadcasting industry representatives emphasized the newspaper industry's traditional opposition to government regulation of the press; in short, commercial broadcasters attempted to affix themselves to the ideological coattails of the newspaper industry vis-à-vis the state. "I for one see no more reason why a government bureau should be permitted to run American broadcasting than why a government bureau should be permitted to run American newspapers," Henry Bellows informed the Kansas City Chamber of Commerce in 1931. Bellows added: "When we are willing to follow Soviet Russia to the point of letting government functionaries tell us what we shall and shall not read, then and then only we can consider letting government functionaries tell us what we shall and shall not hear.'' ''O.K. gentlemen of the press,'' one commercial broadcaster wrote in an open letter to newspaper publishers that opposed commercial broadcasting in early 1932, ''We are willing to have the European system of broadcasting, provided you agree to the same government regulation of your newspapers as experienced by European newspapers at present.''[68]

These arguments apparently struck a sensitive chord among the newspaper publishers, both on ''free speech'' grounds and because of traditional U.S. business hostility to government regulation that impedes, rather than assists, profitability. ''Although the press bears the radio no love,'' one AT&T executive wrote in January 1933, ''it could hardly see with equanimity an ultimate classification of public utility placed upon so close a relative.'' *Nation's Business,* the publication of the U.S. Chamber of Commerce, addressed the issue squarely in a March 1932 editorial:

> Radio is a serious—we almost said dangerous—competitor of the advertising in this magazine. For that reason, perhaps, we should encourage the . . . campaign to eliminate radio advertising. But we don't . . . we object to any increased government control of, or interference with, functions of business.

One NBC vice-president informed the San Francisco Advertising Club in early 1932 that he and newspaper publisher William Randolph Hearst had discussed the matter and had agreed that ''any threat to commercial advertising on the radio is a threat to all forms of advertising.''[69]

The third method of generating support for commercial broadcasting involved actively encouraging newspaper ownership of stations and, moreover, the affiliation of these stations with the networks. This solution seemed obvious because it had been those newspapers with radio affiliations that had held off the antiradio offensive at the 1931 ANPA convention. The networks wasted little time promoting this strategy. ''Columbia regards it as highly important that its affiliates become valuable assets to the areas they serve,'' William Paley told an interviewer in 1932. ''Whenever the station is owned or closely associated with a newspaper this cooperation is accomplished per se.'' Thirty-five of the ninety CBS network stations were owned by or affiliated with newspapers by 1932. ''We only know here that newspaper-owned stations have increased their revenues through network broadcasting,'' Paley commented, citing instances of newspapers tripling their broadcast revenues in a single year. ''Nor are these example exceptions.'' CBS was not alone in this regard, as NBC had nearly as many newspaper affiliations and, moreover, tended to affiliate with the leading newspaper in each market.[70]

Broadcasting calculated that 139 U.S. radio stations were owned by or affiliated with newspapers in late 1931. ''We note with gratification the intelligence being displayed toward radio by such important newspapermen as William Randolph Hearst,'' the trade publication observed, ''nearly every one of whose newspapers has a radio affiliation where possible.'' *Broadcasting* noted that ''so long as a goodly array of journalists are close corporate allies of radio,'' the broadcasting industry could ignore ''the tempest in the teapot that certain press interests have been trying to create.'' During 1932 *Broadcasting* estimated that another 100 newspapers affiliated with commercial broadcasting stations. ''We know of instances during this depression where the tail has actually been wagging the dog,'' *Broadcasting* enthused, ''where radio properties have been profitable enough to carry losing newspaper properties.'' Major chains including those of Hearst, Scripps, and Gannett were all active in acquiring broadcast properties.[71]

Several newspaper publishers with broadcasting interests quickly became active in undermining opposition to commercial broadcasting in their ranks. In October 1932 Walter J. Damm, manager of the *Milwaukee Journal*'s WTMJ and a former president of the NAB, organized an ad hoc group of newspaper-owned radio stations to represent their interests before the NAB and ANPA.[72] Some half-dozen editors and publishers with NBC radio affiliations corresponded surreptitiously with Aylesworth regarding the activities and communications of H. O. Davis, whom they queried as fellow journalists regarding the broadcast reform movement's strategy and tactics. More important, in 1932, when the ANPA established a series of state radio committees to assist the national radio committee, several of these informants became state committee chairmen.[73]

This third approach paid the most immediate benefits. The 1932 ANPA convention ignored radio altogether, much to the dismay of the reformers. ANPA radio committee chairman Roberts then quit in disgust at his inability to have the ANPA resolve for a program that would set distinct limits on commercialism in U.S. broadcasting. ''The ANPA seems to be divided into two groups,'' Roberts stated in his letter of resignation, ''newspapers having radio station interests on the side and newspapers independent of radio connections, and the dominant policy of the association is that of the newspaper–radio combination, not owing to numbers but to activity.'' Roberts concluded: ''Until these two groups admit the dissimilarity of their interests and desire to go their separate ways, I see no hope of protective action on radio by the ANPA.'' As *Business Week* summed up the situation later that year in a piece titled ''Radio vs. Newspaper,'' the ''public expects a grudge fight between natural rivals for a big purse, but insiders know better. It's really newspaper vs. newspaper.'' ''The big interests are too closely tied up,'' a despondent Evans concluded in April 1932, ''with the radio industry to be aggressive in any attack made upon the present commercial setup.''[74]

The conflict between newspapers and commercial broadcasting did not disappear immediately. In late 1932 tempers flared as newspapers became increasingly concerned with broadcasters usurping their news function. "The ultimate extent of radio competition with the press," an ANPA *Bulletin* observed in October 1932, "will depend in large measure on the effect which the broadcasting of news may have on circulation." This concern was accentuated by the round-the-clock coverage of the 1932 presidential election and the Lindbergh baby kidnapping, which opened the publishers' eyes to the possibility of radio becoming the public's news medium of choice.[75] In the spring of 1933 the newspaper industry returned to the rhetoric of 1930 and 1931. Roberts's replacement as chairman of the ANPA radio committee, E. H. Harris, denounced the status quo before the National Editorial Association. In a speech that emphasized the limitations of private, commercial broadcasting for "free speech," Harris stated:

> It is quite possible that the whole broadcast system in the United States is on the wrong basis and that some other form of organization must be developed to control radio broadcasting. . . . It is not within my province to recommend to you that there should be government ownership of radio, but I am urging every editor to study the points which I have attempted to present today. . . . There are many dangers apparent in private ownership of radio.

The assembled editors resolved for "more rigid control of radio broadcasting by the Government."[76]

The *Ventura Free Press* worked its contacts to fan the flames of newspaper antagonism toward radio news and convert it to support for reform, although their influence was admittedly limited with Roberts's resignation. "Our job is to make them see that the silencing of radio must come as a matter of public policy and not as a defense action of an accredited newspaper association," Evans wrote to Woehlke. The ANPA and the Associated Press (AP) declared war on the radio industry at their national conventions in April 1933. Newspapers were to discontinue running free radio listings. The Southern Newspaper Publishers Association resolved that AP subscribers should not provide the radio chains with news. At the same time, one observer noted "subtle press agitation" in 1933 on behalf of the broadcast reform legislation before Congress.[77] Initially, the commercial broadcasters fought back with apparent success; CBS even established its own news service while the newspapers were unable to refrain entirely from providing the publicly demanded radio listings. On the surface, this looked like a contest that would go to the broadcasters.

Behind the scenes, however, intense negotiations were going on throughout the autumn between Aylesworth, Sarnoff, and Paley on one hand and the AP Executive Director Kent Cooper and United Press Associations (UPA) President Karl Bickel to resolve the crisis. Considerable pressure was brought to settle the matter by the newspapers that owned radio stations, particularly the Hearst and Scripps-Howard chains, which had significant broadcast interests.[78] Finally, in early December, when NBC and CBS reached an agreement on a position, the broadcasters made an "urgent appeal" to the ANPA radio committee to settle the matter. The resulting whirlwind negotiations culminated in the "Biltmore agreement" of December 1933, whereby, among other things, the broadcasters agreed to sharply restrict their broadcasting of news in return for newspaper resumption of their publication of radio listings.[79] Proponents of broadcast journalism were dismayed. "The first great battle between the Fourth and Fifth Estates," CBS newscaster H. V. Kaltenborn commented, "has ended with the complete defeat of radio." O. H. Caldwell congratulated Roy Howard, chairman of the Scripps-Howard chain, on coming "out of that meeting with the broadcasters' shirts, scalps, and shoelaces." "There is no longer any question," H. O. Davis chortled in the aftermath of the Biltmore agreement, that "the commercial broadcasters are in full retreat." Evans recommended that the *Ventura Free Press* radio campaign, which was effectively discontinued by the Payne Fund in the summer of 1933, be formally terminated with a declaration of victory.[80]

On the surface this was a defeat for the commercial broadcasters as they appeared to be sacrificing their news operations with little concrete in return. The "main reason" why the broadcasters were willing to "retreat" although "in the midst of victory," according to *The New Republic,* was the broadcasters' "fear of newspaper agitation" against commercial broadcasting. "If you ask why the broadcasters accepted such an unsatisfactory and humiliating arrangement," H. V. Kaltenborn informed a group of educators in the spring of 1934, "the answer is simple. They feared the power of the press. That power was ready to swing into action against them." *Editor & Publisher* hailed the Biltmore agreement as resolving "the troublesome, wasteful and ramifying antagonism between the newspaper press and radio broadcasting." *Broadcasting* highlighted the real benefit of the deal for broadcasters:

> Broadcasting, by this agreement, concedes to journalism that news-gathering is merely incidental to radio's prime function of entertaining and educating, and radio secures from the press a plainly implied acceptance of the fact that sponsor-support is the proper American way of broadcast operation.[81]

In short, the broadcasters would forego active competition in news if the newspapers would discontinue the threat of opposition to commercial broadcasting in Washington, D.C., where Congress was about to take up legislation for the permanent regulation of broadcasting.

The Biltmore agreement did not resolve all the tensions between the newspaper and commercial broadcasting industries, but it placed them on fraternal ground. Any enthusiasm that Davis and Evans had for the Biltmore agreement disappeared in short order; by April 1934 Evans was unable to convince any publisher who had been active in the anticommercial broadcasting campaign to attend an NCER conference in Washington, D.C. After December 1933 the industry never again threatened to use its influence to challenge the legitimacy of commercial broadcasting. The incendiary rhetoric of 1933 disappeared. Harris even agreed to replace David Sarnoff in a debate with *New Republic* editor Bruce Bliven about the nationalization of U.S. broadcasting in October 1934. "If we accept dictation and domination of radio programs by those in government power," Harris argued, "conceivably it will not be a far step until our government leaders may seek to influence our presentation, or prevent our presentation, of news in our daily press." Aylesworth observed, "From a newspaper man, who was once very prejudiced against Radio Broadcasting, this is some speech and should have great weight at the proper time and the proper place." Sarnoff concurred, terming Harris's speech "very illuminating."[82]

Although the *Ventura Free Press* was vanquished in its campaign to have the newspaper industry support the lobbying campaign for broadcast reform, the second part of its mandate, to encourage extensive and favorable coverage of the broadcast reform movement in the press itself, was another matter. At the outset of the *Free Press* campaign in August 1931, H. O. Davis lamented that the reform movement's "fight" had been "almost unnoticed by the press—in every part of the country." Davis found it "astonishing" that the 1931 resolution of the NCPT calling for the complete decommercialization of broadcasting was ignored almost universally by the nation's newspapers.[83]

Davis did what he could, providing between 300 and 700 newspapers with anticommercial broadcasting columns on a regular basis between 1931 and the summer of 1933. Almost all of the newspapers that ran the *Ventura Free Press* copy were admittedly quite small, and they may have been every bit as enthusiastic about free copy to fill their pages as they were about broadcast reform. Nor did the effects of this *Free Press* campaign escape the attention of the commercial broadcasters. The trade publication *National Broadcast Reporter* editorialized in late 1932 about the frequency of antiradio columns in "a large number of small-town newspapers." Accurately terming it as "a deliberately planned and executed campaign to undermine the public about advertising on the radio," the editorial concluded that if the campaign continued "without definite steps being taken to counteract it, the present system inevitably will be wrecked."[84] Nevertheless, this was one of the few instances in which the broadcasters expressed any concern; otherwise, the *Ventura Free Press*'s efforts notwithstanding, the broadcast reform struggle never caught on as a significant issue in the balance of the newspapers, especially among the medium- and large-circulation metropolitan dailies.

For all but the largest daily newspapers that maintained Washington bureaus, news coverage of the debate concerning broadcast policy would come from a syndicated news service or one of the three wires services: the AP, the UPA, or Hearst's International News Service (INS). The major news service that covered radio regularly from Washington, D.C., during these years was the North America Newspaper Alliance (NANA), which provided continual coverage to sixty major U.S. dailies, including the *Chicago Daily News,* the *Des Moines Register,* and the *Detroit News,* among others. The chief radio correspondent for the NANA was Martin Codel, who maintained his position with the NANA even after he cofounded *Broadcasting* in 1931. The only other newspaper or service that had a full-time radio beat correspondent in Washington, D.C., was the *U.S. Daily,* under its editor David Lawrence, a friend of Merlin Aylesworth and confirmed advocate of commercial broadcasting. Lawrence's radio correspondent from 1927–1931 was Sol Taishoff, Codel's partner in the founding of *Broadcasting* and its managing editor. Although Codel's and Taishoff's dispatches regarding broadcast matters were less florid for the NANA and the *U.S. Daily* than they would be in *Broadcasting,* the basic tenor was the same. The industry position dominated and industry sources provided the basis for most stories; it was simply assumed that commercial broadcasters and listeners had identical interests. The reformers, on the other hand, were presented sporadically and mostly as a nuisance.[85]

Most daily newspapers had to rely, therefore, upon the wire services for anything close to balanced news coverage of the debate over broadcast policy. The wire services, however, did not even have specific radio correspondents in Washington, D.C., like the NANA. Moreover, the wire services had their own institutional constraints that impeded their capacity to provide extensive or sympathetic treatment of the radio debate. The Scripps-Howard UPA and the INS were both affiliated with newspaper chains with broadcasting holdings. The AP was a cooperative averse to anything that might antagonize the major daily newspapers that were its most important members. The AP's Cooper found himself in a delicate position as "many of his dominant members" were "actively broadcasting" while the majority of AP members were unaffiliated and "probably against broadcasting."[86]

In addition, both Bickel and Cooper were Aylesworth's close friends, and neither had qualms about the commercial basis of U.S. broadcasting. Aylesworth worked closely with them as he orchestrated the negotiations that led to the Biltmore agreement. Bickel, in particular, was an outspoken advocate of commercial broadcasting. He published a book in 1930 advocating, among other things, that newspapers accept the commercial basis of the industry and not engage in a futile war over advertising and the news. Bickel's boss, Scripps Chairman Roy W. Howard, no strident foe of commercialism, even threatened to fire Bickel in August 1932 for working so closely with the broadcasters and not protecting the distinct interests on the newspaper industry. In extensive and intimate personal correspondence with Aylesworth, Bickel provided whatever assistance he could to NBC's efforts to undercut the *Ventura Free Press* campaign.[87] In any case, the most striking aspect of press coverage of the broadcast reform debate throughout the early 1930s was that it was ignored. One analysis of ten randomly selected daily newspapers found that there was, at best, brief wire service coverage of some but not all of the major events in the development of broadcast policy during these years.[88]

Were this the only salient aspect of the coverage, it might only establish that broadcast policy was not considered a particularly important issue by the professional news standards of the period. On the surface, this seems a highly plausible explanation. In addition to the paucity of coverage, however, most of what little coverage there was, which was in the form of feature stories rather than news stories, tended to present the industry's position in a favorable light while downplaying or ignoring the arguments and activities of the broadcast reformers. This difficulty getting its activities and positions publicized in the nation's newspapers weighed heavily upon the broadcast reformers. The NCER's *Education by Radio* featured no less than five feature articles on this topic between 1933 and 1935. One article insisted:

> To secure accurate and unbiased knowledge about the radio systems of countries where governments control programs in the interest of the listener rather than in the interest of minority groups which wish to exploit the listener, is virtually impossible in the United States. The present dictators of American radio are using every possible device to prevent the real truth from reaching the American public. Every Englishman—and they are few—who has a word of praise for the radio practices in the United States, makes the front page in all the metropolitan newspapers, while the tens of thousands of cultured Englishmen who point out the fundamental unsoundness of our system and the disgraceful level of our programs, usually fail to be quoted at all.[89]

This assessment was not disputed by the commercial broadcasters. Conspicuously absent from their records is any indication of dissatisfaction with the manner by which the press covered the debate over broadcasting during these years. Quite to the contrary a radio fan magazine noted in 1932 that "somehow newspapers that theoretically should be their strongest advocates have not been altogether kind" to the broadcast reform movement. "The newspaper correspondents here in Washington have been very generous to radio," NBC's chief lobbyist and top Washington, D.C., executive wrote to NBC's New York headquarters in early 1934, in a letter urging the network to provide free entertainment for the upcoming White House Correspondents dinner. It would be "an expression of our appreciation for the manner in which the . . . important people at the dinner here have given us their generous support, not only to our Company, but to the operation of radio in this country under private control."[90]

By 1934, thanks to the Biltmore agreement, any ambivalence that may have existed was replaced by outright enthusiasm. The entertainment trade publication *Variety* assured its readers not to worry about the Wagner–Hatfield amendment in 1934:

> Industry counterattack presents novel aspect in that strong press support has been enlisted. Press associations and local bureaus appear to have tacit understanding to play down news about educators' activities and give far more prominent attention to stories about objectionable phases of Wagner–Hatfield amendment.

Behind the scenes, however, newspaper publishers were far from inactive. For example, Frank Gannett told Wagner that the Wagner–Hatfield amendment would cause great "injustices and accomplish nothing."[91]

Three explanations for the pro–status quo bias were offered at the time. Nockels took a class-based, almost conspiratorial approach and emphasized the close affiliation of many prominent newspapers with the commercial broadcasters, which it characterized as a marriage of the newspaper trust and the power trust. To Nockels, the press had treated the debate over broadcasting

> with the thunders of press silence so that their own and their master's interests might be more easily protected and advanced than would be possible if the general public was aware of what was being pulled off for the self-aggrandizement and enrichment of the plutocratic mob at public expense.[92]

The NCER, on the other hand, shied away from conspiracy and gave the nation's journalists the benefit of the doubt, regarding the press as a natural ally. The NCER's analysis emphasized the public relations efforts of the commercial broadcasters. "The chain stations and the larger stations," noted *Education by Radio,* "all maintain high-powered public relations staffs. From these grist mills are turned out daily an endless mass of words and pictures, much of which the companies hope will find its way into the newspapers and magazines of the country." Indeed, NBC maintained what one internal memo characterized as "a large and expensive Press Department to handle contacts with newspapers and the information given to them." The NBC press department had particularly cordial relations with the NANA, which, to the delight of the network, sometimes even effectively ran NBC press releases as the work of the NANA staff.[93] "Most of the printed material concerning radio," concluded the NCER, "appearing in American publications, originates with the chain companies, the individual broadcasting stations, or writers with the commercial point of view." One educator argued that the broadcast reformers needed to counterattack by providing their own "barrage" of material to newspapers and press associations. "Not just an article once every three or four months, but every week or so." Apparently this was easier said than done, and the experience of the *Ventura Free Press* suggests even doing that might not have guaranteed eventual publication.[94]

The NCER also emphasized that coverage of the debate over broadcasting was largely the province of the newspaper's radio editor. By the early 1930s this was a standard position for even medium-circulation newspapers; one study at the time found that over 80 percent of dailies with circulations over 10,000 carried regular radio sections with listings, columns, and features. One standard feature was "Radiograms from NBC," courtesy of the NBC press department, which offered humorous anecdotes, information, and gossip regarding NBC programs. The thrust of most radio reporting was much closer to the entertainment journalism of Hollywood than it was to the canons of professional journalism ostensibly found in the newsroom. By the early 1930s, for example, radio editors were electing annual "All-America" teams of star radio entertainers. In short, radio editors shamelessly adopted a dependent relationship to the commercial broadcasters, who provided them with the raw material upon which their jobs were predicated. "Is it any wonder," the NCER asked, "that radio editors in newspapers are sometimes biased in their viewpoints?"[95]

Perhaps most visible in this regard was Orrin Dunlap, Jr., radio editor of *The New York Times*. Dunlap wrote several uncritical books on commercial broadcasting, including one "how-to" manual for advertisers on how best to utilize the medium that featured a foreword by Aylesworth. Dunlap's *New York Times*'s radio section was among the most news-oriented in the nation; however, while it provided lavish and often flattering coverage of the annual conventions of the NACRE and the NBC Advisory Council, it devoted all of two column inches to the NCER between 1933 and 1935.[96] Perry characterized Dunlap as "a faithful handmaiden of the industry," whose weekly column provided a direct pipeline to whatever network executives wanted to communicate to the public. Indeed, unbeknownst to Perry, top NBC executives, working outside the knowledge of the network's own press department, had an arrangement with Dunlap in 1934 whereby they secretly funneled him "an exclusive story once a week."[97] Nor were Dunlap's sympathies unusual. In 1930 several radio editors formed the National Radio Editors Association (NREA), which was designed to meet in conjunction with the NAB's annual conventions. Sol Taishoff was the NREA's first secretary-treasurer. To no surprise an NREA survey of 200 radio editors in 1931 found that the journalists overwhelmingly favored the "American plan of private enterprise in broadcasting."[98]

The influence of these radio editors over the public perception of broadcasting issues appalled the reformers. In 1934 Joy Elmer Morgan opened testimony before the new FCC by demanding, unsuccessfully, that the FCC or the Senate investigate the "relation between news writers, certain of the news writers, for radio broadcasting and corporations interested in broadcasting." This insidious relationship that produced "dishonest" stories, Morgan argued, "concerns fundamentally the ability of democracy to safeguard the public policy and its ability to get the facts about great institutions before the public.''[99]

In sum, the battle for the press was won decisively on both counts by the commercial broadcasters. Only those that regularly read broadcast reform publications, radio trade publications, or the handful of small circulation opinion magazines that occasionally published articles on the topic could have had any sense of what was transpiring with regard to broadcast policy. As such, the range of participants in the debate was severely constricted and kept, for the most part, at an elite level, where the commercial broadcasters had established themselves as largely invulnerable to attack.

The Battle for the White House, 1933

If Congress and the press had proved difficult to enlist for broadcast reform, and if public opinion remained largely undeveloped on the issue, all was not lost for the movement. Franklin D. Roosevelt was inaugurated as president in March 1933 amid much fanfare about a "New Deal" that would address fundamental social and economic institutions with an urgency perhaps unprecedented in U.S. political history. The reformers were encouraged, regarding radio broadcasting as a natural candidate for the type of systemic reform the New Deal seemed to promise. "Unless the big business [sic] has somehow entrenched itself with President Roosevelt," Arthur Crane noted, "the program of protecting radio for its best public purpose would fit admirably into his entire program."[100]

Both the reformers and the broadcasters worked furtively to determine the administration's position on radio. Evans informed Frances Payne Bolton that "high Democratic circles are very much in confusion as to what should be done in radio." "Every group seems to have had assurances," Evans wrote to Woehlke. "What is actually in the wind, however, is still a mystery." Nonetheless, Evans also noted that the networks "anticipate that there will be some important upheavals in the radio situation."[101] Rumors were rampant that the FRC was to be abolished and replaced in a massive reorganization, although few details were known. In short, there was great confusion regarding the status of broadcasting in the spring and summer of 1933. This confusion was accentuated by Roosevelt's reticence to discuss the subject of broadcast reform. "The unanimous opinion here," Woehlke noted, is that "Roosevelt would not touch the issue with a ten-foot pole."[102]

It soon became clear that without some indication of support by the president, the prospects for reform in the new Congress would be no better than they had been in the past. If anything, Senator Dill was more powerful than ever as he assumed the chairmanship of the SCIC in the wake of the Democratic landslide. In February Representative Fulmer reintroduced the resolution for a study of broadcasting and Eugene Coltrane was called in from the field by the NCER to lobby on behalf of the measure on Capitol Hill.[103] Coltrane may have been an effective educator, but he was a novice in politics. He quickly proclaimed Dill ''as being somewhat friendly to our cause'' after one brief chat, and he informed Evans that he thought he could get Dill to support the study resolution. Evans worked the Capitol to see what sort of interest there was in reform and found Coltrane's optimism unjustified. ''There just doesn't seem to be a person who really knows anything about radio and who will become active or energetic anywhere in either house of Congress,'' he wrote to Woehlke in late March.[104] Conceding the impossibility of reform for the time being, the Payne Fund discontinued the *Ventura Free Press* radio campaign that summer, although Evans remained active as a member of the Payne Fund staff. There was no further congressional lobbying by Evans or the NCER for the balance of 1933.

All was not constant, however, with regard to broadcasting. By the end of 1932, the shakeup of the airwaves that had followed the reallocation resulting from General Order 40 in 1928 had been completed. By 1933, as Erik Barnouw has written, ''almost all forms of enterprise that would dominate radio and television in decades to come had taken shape.'' The NAB's chief researcher, economist Herman Hettinger, located the economic consolidation of the industry as having taken place by the summer of 1932. Most of the frequencies were occupied by the stations that would utilize them through the balance of the century by the end of 1932, with only marginal alterations. By 1932 the number of contested license hearings before the FRC had dropped sharply from previous years.[105]

The NCER also found that the commercial broadcasters were beginning to reveal a greater willingness to have harmonious relations with the few dozen educational stations that had survived the restructuring of the ether. Moreover, the NCER was now reconciled to the fact that, potential broadcast reform notwithstanding, the educational stations were permanently relegated to a subordinate role in U.S. broadcasting, particularly given the seeming increased public acceptance of commercial broadcasting fare. ''Educational stations are weakening,'' Perry wrote to Morgan in April 1933. ''I doubt if the public can be led to look to educators as administrators of a national system that includes entertainment.''[106] In sum, the private, commercial system of broadcasting had been installed as an industry.

In this context, the commercial broadcasters were becoming less enthralled with the uncertain legislative status of U.S. broadcasting. Although opposed to any legislation (''congressional interference'') during the period that the FRC consolidated the ether for profitable commercial exploitation before 1933, the economic stabilization encouraged the industry to seek permanent legislation that would crystallize the status quo and remove broadcasting from annual political contemplation on Capitol Hill. The latent support among broadcasters and the radio industry as a whole for the unification of communications regulation under one new independent federal commission moved to the fore. In early 1933, the NAB, in a major policy shift, generated funds from member stations for "war plans" to fight off "attacks by unfriendly groups" and to "speed up the movement toward a thoroughly stabilized broadcasting industry."[107]

Three additional developments encouraged this push for permanent legislation along these lines. First, the 1932 RCA consent decree, which GE, RCA, and Westinghouse regarded as the best possible solution to the antitrust suit brought against them by the government, clarified the relationship of the radio corporations to each other, and removed some of the basis for political opposition to the radio trust on Capitol Hill. Second, the International Telecommunication Union was established in 1932. It combined the international regulation of radio, telephony, and telegraphy in one body, thus putting pressure upon the United States to do likewise to be able to negotiate at full strength. Third, Ewin Davis's replacement as the relevant communications committee chairman in the House, Representative Sam Rayburn (D-Tex.), was friendly to commercial broadcasting and a pronounced advocate of unification. Hence all the necessary congressional leaders were in step with the industry's legislative agenda.[108]

In essence, the commercial broadcasters wanted to see the Radio Act of 1927 reenacted and a new unified regulatory body similar to the FRC established on a permanent basis. A fundamental problem facing the industry was that while it wanted permanent legislation enacted by Congress, it had no desire for Congress to debate or discuss how best to organize U.S. broadcasting, let alone have any general public discussion of the issues involved.[109] This would prove to be a difficult, though not necessarily impossible, path. For the broadcasters, as with the reformers, the Roosevelt administration was the one great remaining independent variable with the capacity to affect the course of events.

Although the reformers were never able to have direct discussions with the president concerning broadcasting, despite repeated efforts to do so, they were heartened by the presence of several outspoken opponents of the commercial broadcasting within the Roosevelt administration. For example, Eddie Dowling, who had been in charge of the Stage, Screen, and Radio Division of the Democratic Campaign Committee in 1932, emerged as a vocal critic of network and commercial broadcasting. In an article titled "Radio Needs a Revolution," Dowling advocated breaking up the two major networks and establishing numerous smaller networks on a regional basis. Dowling, who was appointed to the Code Authority by Roosevelt in 1933, also professed confidence in the president's sympathies for broadcast reform.

> Our nation faces more pressing problems than the reorganization of radio, but none more in need of attention when the proper time arrives. And it is reasonably

sure that the great and good man in the White House will take constructive steps when his calendar permits. The president's attitude in the matter of public utilities is well known, and radio is a public utility, with proper emphasis on each descriptive word.[110]

Another broadcast reform sympathizer prominent in the New Deal was economist Adolph A. Berle, one of three charter members of Roosevelt's much-publicized "Brain Trust," and co-engineer with Raymond Moley of the Roosevelt administration's "Hundred Days" program to resurrect the economy in the spring of 1933. The most radical New Dealer may well have been Dr. Arthur Morgan, chairman of the Tennessee Valley Authority (TVA). Radio, as well as newspapers and motion pictures "should not be operated for profit," Dr. Morgan stated in a 1934 speech. "They should be operated as social services and not for commercial profit just as are the public schools."[111]

The most significant opponent of the status quo in the Roosevelt administration was Josephus Daniels, the ambassador to Mexico, who had served over Roosevelt as secretary of the navy in the Wilson administration. As naval secretary, Daniels led the unsuccessful fight to have radio communication kept as a governmental monopoly. Roosevelt and Daniels were very close and they maintained a regular and intimate correspondence.[112] Daniels's interest in broadcasting was rekindled by the North American Radio Conference in Mexico City in the summer of 1933. His opposition to the private, commercial development of the ether was stoked by Armstrong Perry, who remained in Mexico City a full week after the conference ended to continue discussions on the matter with Daniels. "Ambassador Daniels is so interested in the radio situation that he has invited me to the Embassy repeatedly for conferences," Perry wrote to Morgan in August, and he "has read much material that I have given him."[113]

Daniels immediately began writing a series of personal letters to "Franklin," sometimes handwritten, urging him in no uncertain terms to nationalize radio broadcasting. This correspondence would continue for two years. One such letter stated:

> We must take over communications. The Government should own and control them all the time. There is no more reason why other communications should be privately owned than the mails. Radio and telephone are as important parts of communications as the mail was when Benjamin Franklin was Postmaster General.

Nonetheless, Daniels, as one of Roosevelt's most trusted political advisers, periodically emphasized the need for caution:

> I am not suggesting that at this time you should propose this plan. You have too many other plans that must be carried out now to justify you in digging up

more snakes than you can kill promptly, and the controllers of the telegraph and telephone and radio and cable are powerful.[114]

The presence of Daniels, Dowling, Morgan, and others notwithstanding, President Roosevelt elected not to become involved in the fight for radio reform. Instead of even paying lip service to the criticism surrounding commercial broadcasting, he maintained his stance of ignoring it, following his well-honed political instincts. "It is now perfectly evident," Evans wrote to Davis in October, "that Roosevelt does not want to make any declarations on public policy if he can avoid such declarations."[115] His rare public statements on broadcasting were decidedly ambiguous, employing language that could be interpreted in any number of ways. "To permit radio to become a medium for selfish propaganda of any character would be shamefully and wrongfully to abuse a great agent of public service," he stated in one speech, which could be cited approvingly by both the NCER and the commercial broadcasters. "Despite the splendid advancement made in recent years in the science of radio," Roosevelt stated in a speech over NBC in 1933, "I do not concede that it has yet been developed to the point where it approaches a full utilization of the opportunities that it has in store for service to mankind." Language like this was far from the emphatic vote of confidence that network executives would have preferred.[116]

Almost all of Roosevelt's activities regarding communications legislation were conducted through his secretary, Louis McHenry Howe, and Howe's two assistants, Stephen Early and Marvin H. McIntyre. Howe, a former journalist who had worked for Roosevelt since 1912, was arguably the president's single closest adviser until he was struck ill in 1935. As one historian puts it, Howe met with Roosevelt whenever he pleased, "in private to discuss anything." "Howe may have been the only man in the world," another scholar observes, who could "say no to the President with impunity." With "unerring instincts," this scholar adds, Howe "could not have cared less about issues or policies or the clash of ideologies; the well-being of Franklin Roosevelt was all that mattered." As Josephus Daniels put it, Howe "would have laid on the floor and let Franklin walk all over him."[117] Perhaps Howe's most important function was to coordinate the administration's press coverage, and to attempt to generate favorable attention for the New Deal in the media. Howe was well aware of the importance of radio; he was the White House official who monitored FRC activities, and the FRC secretary's frequent memoranda to Howe were addressed to "Boss." Howe's importance was widely known. "Howe is certainly closer to Roosevelt than even the Governor's 'brain trust,' " Evans wrote to Woehlke in February. "He will without doubt have tremendous influence during the coming administration."[118]

The networks and the NAB went out of their way to cultivate a healthy relationship with the Roosevelt administration, often working through Henry A. Bellows, a Democrat and a Harvard classmate of the president. The great trump card the networks had at their disposal, which the broadcast reformers could never match, was the ability to grant the president access to a national audience at no charge whenever he pleased. The day after Roosevelt's inauguration, the networks and the NAB announced jointly that "on an instant's notice, the wires of all the networks or all American broadcasting stations are at his notice . . . no matter what is on the air."[119] In his first year in office, Roosevelt made fifty-one network broadcasts, significantly more than any year's output by his predecessor Herbert Hoover. The commercial broadcasters were not bashful about bringing this to the president's attention. The president's wife, Eleanor Roosevelt, also became a regular speaker over the airwaves. For example, in 1934 she was paid $4,000 for hosting a series of thirteen weekly shows over NBC.[120]

Perhaps most important, Louis Howe began a weekly Sunday evening radio broadcast over NBC in March 1933, which "gave an inside story of the administration's actions," and put forth "useful trial balloons" on administration proposals, as one scholar politely puts it. This program, which was sponsored by RCA Victor and Cunningham Radio Tube Companies, consisted of fluff pieces on the president and his policies, in which Howe would answer selected questions from listeners. "Mr. Howe, prime minister to Mr. Roosevelt, is playing ball in every respect with the big chains," Evans informed Bolton. Moreover, Howe was paid a weekly $900 fee for his program, much to the outrage of the reformers and many newspapers. "It is patent that NBC lost no time in buying the White House," Woehlke noted in June.[121] By the fall he continued the program on a less regular basis and, due to the controversy surrounding his NBC stipend, Howe was no longer paid for his services.[122]

Broadcasting historian Philip Rosen has argued that Roosevelt was determined to maintain cordial relations with the commercial broadcasting industry to "ensure his ready access to the airwaves." Considering Roosevelt's and Howe's legitimate concerns regarding the New Deal's treatment by the largely Republican newspaper industry, this is certainly a powerful argument. In 1932 Roosevelt was supported by only 41 percent of U.S. dailies despite getting 57 percent of the popular vote. The gap widened in 1936 when his support among dailies dropped to 37 percent and his popular vote reached 60 percent. Moreover, these figures fail to convey the bitterness with which New Deal policies were greeted by a significant number of U.S. dailies. "A lot of people say we can expect nothing in radio from Roosevelt," Evans wrote to Davis in October. "As long as he can use the broadcasters he will let them exist as they are."[123]

Moreover, the radio lobby was not to be taken lightly. Roosevelt was probably in no hurry to take on an uphill battle with the radio industry when the fruits of an unlikely victory did not promise much immediate political payback and when the cost of a defeat or even a protracted victory could be immense. As even Daniels acknowledged, he had more important battles to fight. Also, as much recent scholarship suggests, the radio industry was representative of the capital-intensive and internationalist branch of the business community that was sympathetic to the overarching aims of the New Deal. Owen D. Young, accordingly, was a Democrat and Roosevelt supporter. This was all the more reason for Roosevelt to support the aims of the commercial broadcasters.[124]

Consequently, Roosevelt never supported any challenge to the status quo, while never taking a public stand on the issue. The opponents to the status quo within the Roosevelt administration were placed in positions far away from the FRC or any place where broadcast policy decisions were made. Dowling was considered for a post on the FRC in early 1934, but the idea was quickly scotched when the commercial broadcasters indicated their extreme displeasure with the idea. Indeed, when Dowling was able, after much effort, to have an audience with Roosevelt to explain his ideas on broadcast reform, Howe, Early, and McIntyre let the broadcasters know almost immediately that his proposals were "unsought," being "pigeonholed," and "not being considered seriously in any fashion."[125] Berle, who as a Brain Trust member gave the president policy recommendations across the spectrum of issues, acknowledged to Perry in December 1933 that he regarded government ownership of radio broadcasting as desirable, but that he held little sway on the issue. "That is one Department with which I have nothing to do." Daniels, too, whose correspondence indicates he had the president's ear on most any subject, admitted to Perry that "the Administration is afraid" of him, "so far as radio is concerned."[126]

Perhaps some indication of the administration's position was revealed when Roosevelt took office in March and there were two expired positions on the FRC. President Roosevelt immediately reappointed Judge Eugene O. Sykes (D-Miss.) to become the new FRC chairman, replacing the retiring General Charles McKinley Saltzman. Sykes was adored by the commercial broadcasters; *Broadcasting* noted his "excellent record on the Commission and almost universal support throughout the industry." The reappointment of Sykes sent a strong message to the commercial broadcasters concerning the Roosevelt administration's intentions. "Whatever else the new administration does with the control of radio, it is reassuring to know that Judge Sykes," a *Broadcasting* editorial pronounced, "will now remain as the government's radio 'anchor man.' "[127]

It was the other FRC position, that opened up by Saltzman's retirement, that the reformers attempted to fill. This was the slot to which they had managed to get President Hoover to appoint educator J. C. Jensen in the waning days of his administration, only to have Congress decide to let the new administration fill the post. The NCER then threw their support to Dr. Bruce Mahan of the University of Iowa and an "ardent Democrat." They worked furiously but without success to have Roosevelt appoint Mahan. Rather, the Roosevelt administration gave Nebraskan Arthur F. Mullen, vice-chairman of the Democratic National Committee, who had served as floor leader for Franklin Roosevelt at the 1932 Democratic National Convention, the option of either taking the post himself or of naming his candidate for the job. Mullen selected his Omaha law partner, James Hanley, for the job and Hanley was confirmed by the Senate in April. Mullen then moved to Washington, D.C., where he became an attorney and lobbyist for a range of corporate clients including RCA.[128] To the reformers, Roosevelt's appointments to the FRC were disappointing. "Mr. Hanley is not a very prominent man and furthermore knows nothing about radio," Tracy Tyler informed Crandall. "The recent appointments indicate," ACLU radio committee member Bethuel M. Webster, Jr., commented, "that this, like previous administrations, will use the Radio Commission as a means of satisfying secondary claims to political patronage."[129]

Yet, while the administration elected not to challenge the commercial basis of the industry, Roosevelt himself appears to have given the issue little thought, and there is no evidence to suggest that, in principle, he was either enthusiastic or troubled about the nature of commercial broadcasting. He merely deferred to Howe's judgment, his own political instincts, and the Democratic congressional leadership, most notably Senator Dill, in this area. Moreover, while the New Deal may have had ambitious plans in other areas, broadcasting does not appear to have been a special area of concern.

Upon taking office, President Roosevelt had Secretary of Commerce Daniel Roper appoint a committee to prepare recommendations for reorganizing the Department of Commerce. The committee of four, which was headed by former FRC chairman Saltzman, elected to incorporate communications into their recommendations since the Department of Commerce still maintained a portion of the government responsibility for radio regulation. In April 1933 Saltzman's committee decided that the FRC should be abolished and its functions returned to the Department of Commerce, along with those communications functions of the ICC. The idea was dropped when opposition to the idea emerged, largely on the grounds that while a consolidated body to regulate communications was a good idea, it was not a good idea to have the body under the control of the Secretary of Commerce. Hence, radio was not included in the subsequent reorganization legislation that Roosevelt had introduced in the session of Congress that ended in June 1933.[130]

Broadcasting could not be permitted to languish in a legislative limbo forever; there was pressure to resolve the matter, not the least of which was now coming from the industry. It was generally understood, as ANPA radio committee chairman Harris put it, "that President Roosevelt will take up the subject of revamping the radio set-up during the summer months and be ready to present a concrete program to Congress in the fall." It was during the summer that the president received the first wave of impassioned letters from Ambassador Daniels in Mexico. One such letter, dated July 14, stated forthrightly that "I strongly believe that all communications should be governmentally owned and operated." Perry's influence was also evident.

> In countries where the broadcasting is controlled by the government, they send out semi-annual questionnaires and put on the air what the people want. In the United States largely we put on what somebody pays for. In such countries as control the radio there is much more educational broadcasting than with us. If our government owned the radio and operated it as part of the post-office Department, we could make it a greater educational institution than is possible under the present arrangement.

Daniels implored Roosevelt to take action. "If the government is ever to take over radio and broadcasting, it should be done in your administration and next winter if possible. Every year makes it more difficult."[131]

In late July President Roosevelt turned over the Daniels July 14 letter to Secretary Roper and directed Roper to appoint a committee to study Daniels's recommendation that radio broadcasting be nationalized.[132] Roper appointed another committee of four, once again chaired by Saltzman, who had been chairman of the FRC when it prepared *Commercial Radio Advertising* in 1932. Roosevelt's request and the subsequent study were kept completely confidential; their existence would not become known for decades.

On September 8, 1933, Saltzman's committee submitted an eight-page, single-spaced report that described in no uncertain terms the impracticality of government ownership of communications. The report stressed the fundamental soundness of the Radio Act of 1927 and the regulatory system that emerged out of it. The report also emphasized the immense opposition that would confront any effort to eliminate private broadcasting—particularly from the commercial broadcasters and the newspapers, which "after losing much advertising revenue due to radio advertising are becoming interested in owning radio stations." The report then asked: "Under the present unfortunate economic conditions, is the time ripe to incur the opposition that would arise?" The report, in keeping with the general sentiment on Capitol Hill and in the industry, recommended the consolidation of all communication regulatory functions under one federal agency. Yet the report was also critical of the lack of planning that had characterized the development of broadcasting and communications regulation in the United States. Thus the report concluded by recommending that the president establish a group under the direction of the secretary of commerce to make "a careful survey of existing facilities and conditions with a view to the formation of a national communications policy."[133]

The president was not entirely satisfied with the Saltzman committee's report. On September 12 he gave Secretary Roper another letter from Daniels calling for government ownership and operation of radio, and he told Roper that he "wished" the Commerce Department "would go into it a little further" with the FRC. At this point the matter died, as the FRC informed Roper that the FRC had already dismissed the notion of government ownership in *Commercial Radio Advertising*. Otherwise, Roosevelt did accept the recommendations of Saltzman's ad hoc committee. He advised Roper to assemble an interdepartmental committee "to make a study for me of the entire communications situation" that would provide the basis for the subsequent "construction of the needed legislation" in the area. In September and October Roper gradually assembled representatives from eleven federal agencies and departments, including Captain Hooper, for weekly meetings to discuss the matter of communications regulation and policy. Senator Dill and Representative Rayburn were also formal members of this "Roper Committee," since their congressional committees would be responsible for the eventual legislation. The Roper Committee was supervised by the vice-chairman, the seemingly ubiquitous General Saltzman.[134]

The Roper Committee met in complete secrecy during the fall and did not solicit any form of public testimony. Roper later would justify this secrecy by explaining that the committee was conducting a "study," not an "investigation," and therefore had not sought the opinions of "outsiders." According to Roper, these "outsiders" would have their opportunity to provide input on the eventual recommended legislation during the upcoming congressional committee hearings. A frustrated Evans found it impossible to determine what the Roper Committee was doing. "In connection with the radio re-organization committee," he wrote to Woehlke on November 24, after weeks of probing, "nobody could say anything. Every time I tried to finesse, the answer was 'I'm very sorry but I can't say a thing.' "[135] The secrecy of the Roper Committee's activities was broken in a NANA story by Martin Codel in late October. He reported that his sources indicated that the committee would recommend unification of communication regulation in a new independent body and that the broadcast system be maintained status quo. Perhaps this explains why the broadcasters appeared unusually relaxed about the potential recommendations of this top-secret governmental committee that was ostensibly pondering their very fate. Drew Pearson and Robert S. Allen were less sanguine about the Roper Committee in their "Washington Merry Go-Round" column of November 30. They wrote:

> A secret move is on foot to perpetuate the present monopoly which the big broadcasting companies have on the choice wave lengths. It is being worked out behind closed doors by the so-called Roper radio committee. Appointed by the Secretary of Commerce originally to bring a new deal for radio, the committee is actually working to continue the old deal.[136]

Matters did not look much better for the reform movement in Congress. For a lobbyist prone to alarmism, Bellows was noticeably assured as he told the NAB convention in October that chances of broadcast reform legislation getting through Congress were "slim." The only hope of getting Fulmer's broadcasting study bill, or any reform legislation, through Congress was to have President Roosevelt publicly endorse it, and this was where all of the reformers' efforts focused in the fall of 1933. The NCER sought an audience with the president in December, only to be denied. The NCER also combined forces with the ACLU to convince Berle to use his influence with Roosevelt to push for his support of the Fulmer bill. Berle discussed the issue with the president, but was unable to get Roosevelt's commitment on behalf of the legislation. In January 1934 Baldwin noted the lack of White House support and concluded: "The bill is therefore dead."[137]

As 1933 drew to a close things could hardly have appeared gloomier for the reformers nor rosier for the commercial broadcasters. Congress appeared unalterably under the control of its pro–status quo committee chairmen while the White House had been enlisted as a tacit, if not vocal or enthusiastic, ally for the industry's program. The reform movement was splintered and without a sense of direction. The ACLU radio committee stopped working with the NCER in December on the recommendation of Bethuel Webster and Levering Tyson, and neither group had any idea concerning how best to proceed.[138] Organized labor had long since abandoned the fight and the *Ventura Free Press* radio campaign was, for all intents and purposes, defunct. Moreover, the only group that truly frightened the commercial broadcasters and appeared to have the capacity to put the kibosh on the broadcasters' legislative ambitions—the newspaper publishers—had been brought into the fold with the signing of the Biltmore agreement in December. "You can tell the Chief that we have arrived at an amicable understanding," Aylesworth notified Howe in a confidential letter on December 16. "The friction between the press and radio is a thing of the past."[139] In short, the president would not get caught in any media crossfire by supporting the broadcasters' legislation on Capitol Hill.

Finally, despite the concerted efforts of the broadcast reformers, the preponderance of the public appeared oblivious to the very existence of the debate. If anything, the sense among some reformers was that commercial broadcasting was more accepted among the populace than it had been only two years earlier when they had mounted their first assault on Washington, D.C. All signals pointed to the rapid and quiet passage of permanent communications legislation that would crystallize the status quo.

CHAPTER 8

December 1933–January 1935: The Statutory Consolidation of the Status Quo

Although the network-dominated, advertising-supported system of U.S. broadcasting largely had stabilized in an economic sense as an industry by 1932 or 1933, its legal status remained indeterminate considering the temporary basis of regulation mandated by the Radio Act of 1927 through the FRC. Given the generally accepted nature of the ether as a public resource subject to public control, this was hardly a tenable situation for the two major chains and the other major beneficiaries of what was routinely termed the status quo. These groups wished to see permanent legislation enacted that would crystallize commercial broadcasting, thereby removing substantive broadcast policy issues from the range of legitimate topics that could be addressed by Congress and the public in subsequent years.

During the course of 1934 the broadcasting industry accomplished its legislative agenda, primarily with the enactment of the Communications Act of 1934, which is still the primary regulatory broadcast and telecast statute in the United States. The route to statutory consolidation, however, proved to be far from the primrose path that might have been thought likely in the autumn and early winter days of 1933. Although seemingly battered into oblivion and outmaneuvered on every front by the commercial broadcasters, the broadcast reform movement found new and mostly unanticipated sources of support in 1934. As the commercial broadcasters feared, the road to permanent legislation required a brief window of opportunity for public hearings and debate over the nature of commercial broadcasting; their goal was to see this window opened for as brief a historic moment as possible and to assure that as little of Congress or the public as possible could take advantage of its existence. It was during this brief "window-opening" that the reformers mounted an assault on the status quo that revealed surprising ferocity. This chapter will chronicle and analyze this last great battle for the control of U.S. broadcasting.

Jockeying for Position in Early 1934

Although the broadcast reformers entered 1934 scattered and despondent about the immediate prospects for reform, they were no less hostile to commercial broadcasting nor any less committed to their belief that the system would necessarily collapse of its own weaknesses in the long run. The reformers accordingly remained active throughout 1934. Congress still held little promise, however, for reform activities. After surveying Capitol Hill in January 1934, the Payne Fund's S. Howard Evans, who now was working more closely with the NCER, concluded that "with regard to radio legislation the chance of getting anything significant through this legislature is practically nil. The House will do nothing which does not come directly from the White House." As for the Senate, Evans observed that "the Democrats clear everything through Dill. The Republicans are practically quiescent." This analysis led the NCER in two directions. First, at its annual meeting in January, the NCER voted to assemble "national leaders to enter into a frank discussion of the radio question from the point of view of the public interest" in the springtime in Washington. If the government would not provide the platform upon which to debate fundamental broadcast issues, the NCER resolved that it would sponsor such a confab with the hope of stimulating public and congressional activity. Second, the experience on Capitol Hill only reaffirmed the importance of working through the White House if the reformers were to have any success in Congress. "Nothing will be passed by the present Congress unless it is initiated by the president," Tyler informed Roger Baldwin.[1]

Regarding the White House, the new year brought fresh hope to the reformers that the administration's apparent resolve to support the legislative agenda of the commercial broadcasters might be lessening. The Roper Committee, under the de facto chairmanship of Charles McKinley Saltzman, informally regarded its mandate as that of simply providing a report that would justify the passage of legislation calling for the unification of communications regulation without otherwise changing the existing laws or industrial structures.[2] Their closed and unpublicized deliberations accordingly had been superficial; members Dill, Representative Sam Rayburn, and Secretary of Commerce Daniel C. Roper never attended the weekly sessions in October and November. Any hope that the Roper Committee would be able to fulfill this function were disrupted by the Drew Pearson and Robert S. Allen newspaper column of November 30, 1933, in which they suggested that the Roper Committee was in cahoots with the "big broadcasting companies" and was trying "to get their report adopted by the White House before the general public knows about it, before opposition can develop."[3]

This put the Roper Committee on the defensive. The NCER and sympathetic members of Congress immediately wrote Roper, Dill, and other committee members to express their concerns that the Roper Committee was attempting to "crystallize the status quo" before there was a "thorough-going impartial Congressional study of broadcasting." Roper and Saltzman wrote to Tyler to assure him he was misinformed and that his concerns would be brought before the Roper Committee. "I can say there is absolutely no foundation to the suggestion that anything is going to be put over in the way of legislation on the subject of radio," Dill wrote to Tyler on December 11, "without full and complete public hearings."[4] In a major shift, the Roper Committee now defended its conduct by stating that it had "not taken into consideration the question of radio broadcasting," as one member wrote to Representative Hampton Fulmer, despite the mandate from President Roosevelt to the contrary when the group was formed.[5] In mid-December, the committee informally sent its completed report, which came to be known as the Roper Report, to the president. The fourteen-page report simply called for the continuation of private ownership and operation as well as the unification of communications regulation into a new federal agency, independent of the Department of Commerce. There was little else in the report; it merely stated "the problems of broadcasting are not being considered in this study." The NCER urged Roper to launch a "thorough study of the whole field of radio broadcasting" to supplement the Roper Report.[6]

The NCER was mild in its response to the Roper Report compared to other broadcast reformers. James Rorty termed it "mumbling, evasive, and futile." The ACLU's Bethuel M. Webster, Jr., attacked the Roper Report as "inept," and noted that "it appears on analysis that the administration has no program or policy at all, except to consolidate communications control." He observed that "It takes no courage to recommend the consolidation of communications control in a communications commission. The necessity for such consolidation has been known for years." Indeed, most reformers professed little opposition to the consolidation proposal per se. Webster concluded that anyone who had read

> almost any report prepared by almost any committee or commission which had taken the trouble, with the assistance of specialists, to gather and organize the facts and to formulate statesmanlike conclusions and recommendations, will blush at the sight of the Roper Report.[7]

Had dissatisfaction with the Roper Report been limited to the broadcast reformers, it probably would not have been enough to derail the Roper Report from its political function of providing enough of a study to justify the pushing of permanent communications legislation through Congress with minimal congressional examination. In addition, however, Roper Committee member Captain Stanford C. Hooper emerged as a dissident voice. Hooper had been advocating the need for an in-depth federal study of communications to determine a national policy for a decade. He took seriously Roper's admonition to the committee to provide the president with a detailed analysis of "the pro and con of the present policy." Much to Hooper's dismay the other Roper Committee members followed Saltzman's lead and indicated less interest in tackling major long-term communications policy issues. Hooper met and corresponded with most leading communications company presidents to determine the core principles that should be the basis of U.S. communications policy.[8]

Hooper's disenchantment with his fellow committee members was soon extended to U.S. communications corporations, which he determined were quite satisfied with the lack of a deliberate federal study of communications because they were the immediate beneficiaries of the procorporate status quo. Indeed, Hooper came to regard Saltzman's position on the Roper committee as that of representing the interests of the giant communication firms. "I am absolutely appalled by the power of these corporations," he wrote to Josephus Daniels on November 22, in a letter chronicling the plight of the Roper Committee.[9]

Hooper refused to sign the Roper Report, submitting instead his own fifty-page "minority report" on communications to the president. Hooper was especially displeased by the superficial examination the Roper Committee had made of broadcasting as

> the subject of regulation of broadcasting, mentioned so prominently in the directive given to the committee, and of such great importance to the communication facilities of the nation, has not been considered by the committee, although their report recommends the regulation of the communication service of the country, *without excluding broadcasting*, by a single body. The minority member feels that any study of Federal relationship to communications is incomplete unless a thorough study of radio broadcasting has been included. [his emphasis]

Hooper also rejected Saltzman's argument in Roper Committee deliberations that any study of broadcasting should be left to the "experts" on the to-be-created communications commission. "I believe that unlimited discretion should not be given to any regulatory body, on matters of broad policy," he concluded.[10]

Hooper also remained in close contact with Ambassador Daniels, who had been Hooper's boss when Daniels served as secretary of the navy in the Wilson administration. While Daniels agreed with Hooper on the need for a coherent federal communications policy, he was primarily interested in the nationalization and decommercialization of radio broadcasting. In December and January Daniels wrote the president to push him in this direction. He also wrote to Roper:

> The matter with which your Committee is dealing is one of the highest importance.... It may be that the water has already gone over the dam and we cannot call back what has been done. However, the more I have thought about it ... the more I have been convinced that if Congress had been wise enough in 1919 to listen to the advice of the Wilson administration and make radio a government monopoly, we would have been saved from the things that trouble us now, and the people would have had the use of radio at a very small price.

Roper quickly replied: "It is true that much water has gone over the dam—apparently so much that it cannot be called back." Because "centralization has gone so far in the corporate control of communication agencies," and "the vested interests are so great, and so much capital is invested, there would be such interminable controversies as to value of such capital that Government Ownership and Operation, at the present time, does not appear possible."[11]

In early January, 1934, Roper and Saltzman met with Dill and Rayburn to show them the Roper Report and to discuss its implications for legislation. Both Dill and Rayburn announced that they were in accord with the recommendations of the report and that they each intended to submit communications bills to Congress in the near future, which would cover broadcasting in addition to other branches of communication. The NAB noted that "it is probable that identical bills will be introduced in both Houses of Congress at the same time," and that they would be based upon the idea of consolidating all communications regulation into one body. One internal NBC memo observed that "it has been decided to keep the president's hands out of Communications and let the initiative be taken by members of Congress."[12] Dill, Rayburn, and the broadcasters intended to stay with their original legislative strategy despite the fact that the Roper Report admittedly did not provide the "study" of broadcasting that was planned to be the justification for pushing through permanent legislation.

Such a course faced a major hurdle: The administration was sending out conflicting messages regarding its strategy for broadcasting legislation. "There seems no doubt that an administration bill will be presented," Armstrong Perry wrote to Evans, with an interpretation differing from NBC's, but "the feeling around Washington is that broadcasting will not be included in it." This confusion regarding the administration's position was only enhanced when, at the "special request" of the president, Roper announced after his meeting with Saltzman, Dill, and Rayburn that the Roper Committee would remain together to conduct a separate study of broadcasting, as the president's original directive had requested.[13] In sum, whatever hope may have existed that the Roper Report might have provided the necessary momentum to push prostatus quo communications legislation through Congress with minimal opposition had been squashed before the report was even made public on January 23. Radio broadcasting had proven to be the Roper Report's Achilles' heel.

During the next two weeks, the NCER and its allies in Congress and the administration worked furtively to see that Roper followed up on the broadcasting investigation. The matter came up in a cabinet meeting, where there was support for conducting such a study. On January 25, Roper wrote to the president and formally requested that a new committee be formed to conduct this study of broadcasting that would include representatives of the Office of Education, the FRC, and the State Department, with the aim of providing the basis for permanent legislation for the regulation of broadcasting. Roosevelt approved the request immediately and the plans for this "Federal Committee to Study Radio Broadcasting" (FCSRB) were announced to the public within a week.[14] Saltzman was disheartened by the turn of events, noting that Roosevelt was showing a new-found "personal interest" in broadcasting.[15] NCER representatives wrote to Roper on several occasions to offer their input and to plead for as thorough and independent a study as possible. Much to the delight of the NCER, the FCSRB was to be chaired by Cline M. Koon, who had succeeded Armstrong Perry as the radio specialist at the Office of Education and had revealed some sensitivity to the problems faced by educational broadcasters. Koon had written for the NCER's *Education by Radio* and, in 1930, he wrote a flattering report on the BBC, although he did have cordial relations with the commercial broadcasters in his capacity with the Office of Education.[16]

Recognizing the controversial nature of the topic, Koon's initial plan for the FCSRB was to have groups and individuals submit briefs on the matter, but for no hearings to be held. Koon worked closely with Perry and Evans as he drafted the plans for the FCSRB in February. The NCER was cautiously ecstatic with the establishment of the FCSRB. On one hand, for the first time since Perry was in the employ of the Office of Education, the reformers apparently had struck success in the corridors of power, and with the stakes considerably higher than Perry could have hoped for back in 1930 and 1931. "It would appear now," reported Eugene Coltrane to an educational broadcaster, "that we are going to get some breaks from the Roosevelt Administration on the radio situation."[17] "I believe there are men in the present Administration, including the President, who want to see the right thing done," Coltrane wrote to Tyler. On the other hand, the NCER was aware that the study would face opposition. The "thorough-going study of the whole broadcasting situation," Tyler wrote to Ella Phillips Crandall on February 20, "will need all of the influence of those interested in better radio, since the selfish interests will throw every possible stumbling block in the way."[18]

Tyler had accurately gauged the sentiments of the commercial broadcasters. "Because the report will be used as a basis for legislation," the NAB newsletter noted when the FCSRB was initially announced, "the broadcast survey is looked upon with great importance by the broadcast industry." The trade publication *Broadcasting* pronounced the study unnecessary and that it would provide a forum for "the usual parade of calamity-howling reformers, jealous competitors and other self-serving critics." In short order, the commercial broadcasters determined that the study had the potential to be very damaging, particularly when it became clear that "antibroadcasting groups" intended to use the proposed study as an opportunity to present their case. The industry made clear its displeasure with the proposed study to the White House.[19]

Similarly dissatisfied with the proposed study were Senator Dill and Representative Rayburn. Like Saltzman, they could not understand why the president would authorize a study of broadcasting that could only undermine the administration's stated goal of having permanent communications legislation passed in the current session of Congress.[20] Dill met with Roosevelt in early February and informed him that he intended to go ahead with his proposed communications bill, which included broadcasting, regardless of the activities of the FCSRB. Dill and Rayburn made it clear to the president that it was absurd to continue with the FCSRB since it would hardly finish its study in time to be of value in the current session of Congress and, moreover, "that the committee's report, even if submitted, probably would not be considered." They reminded the president that there was no need for a study since the FRC had conducted one in 1932, the oft-cited *Commercial Radio Advertising*. Given this position by Dill and Rayburn, there was little rationale for conducting the study and plans for the FCSRB were dropped quietly in late February.[21] Secretary Roper informed interested parties that the committee had been terminated and "this matter, for the time being, will be entirely handled by the Congress." "Apparently the National Association of Broadcasters worked to have the investigation called off," Perry informed Evans in early March, and "their strategy was to bring pressure to bear through members of Congress."[22]

In view of the sensitivity of broadcasting as a political issue, the legislative strategy of Dill and Rayburn was to avoid anything that might incite controversy. Both Dill and Rayburn prepared their respective communications bills during February in consultation with the president and White House aides. They both planned to rush their bills through committee hearings and have the measures brought to the floors of the House and Senate as quickly as possible. To minimize the need for comprehensive committee hearings, the Roper Report was now characterized as the result of "a very painstaking study of communications," as Roper informed Congress. Moreover, Dill and Rayburn hoped to stem any opposition to the proposed legislation by authorizing the to-be-created communications commission, the FCC, to make its own thorough study of communications and report back to Congress with any suggestions for additional legislation by the beginning of 1935. Dill's bill specifically cited broadcasting, the one area where the Roper Report was admittedly weak, as a subject the new FCC should examine. "If we leave out the controversial matters," Dill stated, "the bill can be passed at this session."[23]

Dill said his desire was that broadcasting not even be discussed during the upcoming committee hearings on the communications legislation, since the unresolved broadcasting issues would now be taken up by the FCC. "It is far wiser to let the proposed commission have the power to make these studies than to have Congress legislate on intricate and complex aspects of the communications program at this time," Dill explained. This approach was received with unconditional enthusiasm by the commercial broadcasting industry. As David Sarnoff approvingly told some senators, "The commission itself must, after careful study and investigation, help in determining its legislative needs."[24] In short, the study of broadcasting that was not conducted by the Roper Committee or by the FCSRB would *not* then become the province of the pertinent congressional committees in the form of hearings, despite Dill's promise to Tyler to the contrary in December 1933. Rather, whatever public examination of fundamental broadcast questions would take place would be delegated to the new FCC to do with as it saw fit, after permanent legislation had passed Congress.

In late February Dill and Rayburn each introduced their respective bills to the Senate and the House. Both of the bills essentially reenacted the wording of the Radio Act of 1927, while abolishing the FRC and creating the new FCC to regulate all of communications. On February 26 President Roosevelt issued a formal statement to Congress announcing his support for the legislation and urging its passage. He also reiterated Dill's argument: "The new body [the proposed FCC] should, in addition, be given full power to investigate and study the business of existing companies and make full recommendations to the Congress for additional legislation at the next session." FRC Chairman Eugene O. Sykes immediately announced the FRC's support for the proposed legislation and added that the "Federal Radio Commission desires to express its endorsement of the creation of a Federal Communications Commission." With the collapse of the FCSRB, the NCER withdrew from active lobbying to concentrate its attention upon its upcoming conference on radio, scheduled for early May. Meanwhile the other reformers, including Evans and the ACLU, effectively stopped their lobbying activities out of frustration for the foreseeable future, thereby leaving no organized opposition on the horizon. Hooper, never one to put the navy in an awkward position, announced his support for the legislation, proclaiming his hope that the prospective FCC investigation would provide the basis for a comprehensive "national communications policy."[25] Daniels alone did his best, writing members of Congress throughout the spring to urge radical broadcast reform, without any specific legislation in mind. Much to his dismay, however, Daniels was unable to get away from Mexico City to make a personal lobbying campaign in Washington, D.C. Isolated and removed, Daniels could no longer influence the president, let alone Congress. As Philip T. Rosen has observed, given the support and popularity of the president and given the clout of Dill and Rayburn, "all signs pointed to a quick passage."[26]

The Wagner–Hatfield Amendment and the Communications Act of 1934

The SCIC hearings on S. 2910, as the Dill communications bill was numbered, took place in the second week in March. True to Dill's wishes, only five of the nineteen witnesses dealt with broadcasting, and then in only the most cursory fashion, with one notable exception that will be discussed shortly. The commercial broadcasters were not enthralled with Dill's bill. They enthusiastically endorsed Rayburn's House bill, which, aside from creating the FCC, maintained the Radio Act of 1927 verbatim and stated that any other changes made down the road should be recommended by the FCC. Dill's bill was similar but it also included, what one broadcaster termed, "every pet radio measure Senator Dill has endeavored to have enacted during the past seven years." Nonetheless, Sarnoff and Bellows were conciliatory in their testimony before the SCIC; they concentrated their opposition to one specific clause, which summed up their concerns. "Our essential objection with this bill concerns itself with just exactly 10 words out of its total of 100 pages," Henry Bellows informed the senators. "They are 'The Radio Act of 1927, as amended, is hereby repealed.' " Sarnoff strenuously voiced the same objection, in the process of otherwise commending the proposed legislation.[27]

Dill later explained the inclusion of the clause repealing the Radio Act of 1927 as "it seemed important to us that we should enact new legislation rather than merely transfer the existing powers in present law."[28] Given the disrepute of the FRC, this was a fairly astute, albeit cosmetic, political move by Dill to gather support for the legislation from those who might be opposed to simply ratifying the Radio Act of 1927, without any discussion of defects in the U.S. broadcasting set-up. It was by no means evident that the commercial broadcasters would oppose this legislation once it reached the floor for a vote were it the only possibility for permanent legislation during the session; rather, it is only certain that they were pressuring the committee, unsuccessfully as it developed, to drop the "repeal" clause before the bill was reported out of the committee.

In both the Senate and the House committee hearings in early May, radio broadcasting matters were "largely overshadowed by the telephone and telegraph regulatory matters," as *Broadcasting* put it. The major reform suggested by the Roper Report and both the Dill and Rayburn communications bills was to transfer the regulation of telephony and telegraphy from the ICC to the new FCC. The general consensus, as Dill stated, was that since "railroads and other transportation take most of the attention of the" ICC, telephony and telegraphy should be shifted to the new FCC, where they might receive more satisfactory attention. In addition, Rayburn's House committee commissioned economist and railroad regulation expert Walter W. M. Splawn to prepare a report on communications companies to assist in the development of legislation, which made the same recommendation. Splawn's 331-page report devoted only twelve pages to broadcasting, which consisted of listing chain ownership holdings. Splawn indicated that broadcasting would be taken up in a future study. Splawn's report criticized AT&T, which received the bulk of the report's attention. AT&T, unlike RCA, opposed the creation of the new FCC on the grounds that shifting telephone and telegraph regulation from the ICC was unnecessary.[29] "The telephone business is now, in our opinion, adequately regulated," AT&T president Walter Gifford informed the SCIC. "There has been no evidence that any change is necessary."[30]

Given AT&T's influence on Capitol Hill, even within the SCIC, Dill quickly determined that unless he could work out a deal with AT&T, it would be impossible to get the communications bill passed. When negotiations failed, Dill took the offensive. In March he introduced a resolution that called for the Senate to conduct a special investigation of AT&T, particularly its "acquisition of patents," a subject where Dill claimed to have evidence suggesting possible impropriety. Morever, the resolution specifically authorized the investigation to take place only if communications legislation failed to pass that session of Congress, in order "to furnish the necessary facts upon which to base legislation with broader powers over communications at the next session." The resolution captured AT&T's attention. Gifford immediately came to Washington to meet with Dill and other members of the SCIC. After intense negotiations, AT&T agreed to support having the regulation of telephony and telegraphy shifted to the new FCC in return for Dill dropping the investigation resolution. At the House committee hearings in May, Gifford formally supported the unification legislation, although he asserted that the legislation should otherwise assign the task of determining if any other reforms were necessary to the new FCC, and not Congress.[31]

Precisely as AT&T abandoned the fight, the commercial broadcasters reconsidered the Dill bill following the March SCIC hearings and determined that the unsatisfactory aspects of the bill were worth fighting. An NBC memo cited seven clauses in Dill's bill that were against network interests. Dill has "dumped everything into the new bill excepting the cook-stove," one broadcaster complained. These were admittedly far from life-threatening; the ACLU's Webster termed them Dill's "harmless hobbies." They would, however, perhaps establish a precedent for congressional tinkering with the statute in future years. The NAB announced its opposition to Dill's bill, which seemingly sounded its death knell.[32] *Broadcasting* forecast a "slim chance of passage for the bill," while NBC's chief lobbyist doubted "very much its opportunity of passage."[33]

In late March Dill appointed a five-member subcommittee to iron out a final draft of the bill. The commercial broadcasters threw their weight behind a move by subcommittee member Wallace White (R-Maine) to rewrite the bill to be identical with Rayburn's House bill.[34] When White's effort failed, the industry's opposition to the Dill bill gradually diminished. By the end of April the industry supported the passage of the Dill bill wholeheartedly, reflecting its desire to see permanent legislation passed. Moreover, if both the Dill and Rayburn bills passed their respective houses, any differences between them would have to be resolved in conference, where the commercial broadcasters had traditionally fared quite well.

Perhaps most important, by the middle of April the Dill bill, its peccadillos notwithstanding, was beginning to look more than adequate to the industry as the general picture for broadcast legislation had become far more treacherous than they could have anticipated only a few months or even weeks earlier. This was mostly due to the work of WLWL's Father John B. Harney, who entered the fray when WLWL lost a hearing before the FRC in February. Harney demanded that the SCIC permit him an opportunity to testify, unlike the other reformers who accepted Dill's argument that it was unnecessary. In his testimony on the final day of the hearings, March 15, Harney submitted an amendment to S. 2910 that would require the new FCC to allocate 25 percent of the channels to nonprofit broadcasters after ninety days. Harney's proposal was challenged by committee members on two points. First, Senator James Couzens asked Harney to explain how these nonprofit broadcasters would support themselves. Harney responded that the nonprofit broadcasters would have to be able to sell advertising, "not to make a profit, but enough to support themselves." Second, Senator Dill stepped in and tried to impress upon Harney his idea of having the new FCC study his fixed percentage proposal and then report back to Congress with recommendations for new legislation, if deemed necessary, the following year. Harney rejected this idea categorically, noting the FRC's dismal record with nonprofit broadcasters and emphasizing that it was Congress's duty, not that of a regulatory agency, to determine fundamental broadcast policy.[35]

The SCIC voted against Harney's amendment; only Robert Wagner (D-NY) and Henry Hatfield (R-W. Virginia) supported it. To defuse sentiment developing in the Senate for what was now called the "Harney amendment," Dill had the subcommittee insert a clause into the legislation that specifically instructed the new FCC to study and evaluate Harney's fixed percentage proposal and report back to Congress in early 1935 with any recommendations for new legislation reserving channels for nonprofit broadcasters. This would become section 307(c) of the Senate bill, and later of the Communications Act of 1934. Dill reported the revised bill, now numbered S. 3285, to the Senate on April 19, calling it a "good bill." The White House indicated that it was committed to seeing S. 3285 passed.[36]

Harney was in no mood to abandon the fight. Dissatisfied by the amendment's treatment by the SCIC, Harney and the Paulists launched an extensive campaign to gain public support for the Harney amendment. In particular, the Paulists attempted to mobilize Roman Catholic organizations to the cause of broadcast reform. By the end of April the Senate received over 60,000 signatures on petitions supporting the amendment in addition to thousands of letters and telegrams. The Paulists also inundated Wagner, who had supported the Harney amendment in the committee vote, with petitions to emphasize the level of popular support for the measure. One such petition was titled, "Save Catholic Radio." Another concluded:

> Our children listen to the radio and if there were some restrictions on some of the junk commercialized over the various stations, we would have a better country to live in. We think it is about time we Catholics of America get some representation and protection from our government.[37]

Most of the petitions, however, were formal representations of the "Harney amendment" and were signed by chapters of such groups as the Knights of Columbus, the Ancient Order of Hibernians, the Catholic Ladies' Relief Society, and the National Council of Catholic Women. One speaker informed the Catholic Daughters of America, for example, that WLWL was "being crowded off the air" and that the fight for "good clean radio programs" was a "serious part of the program of Catholic action."[38]

Both the White House and the FRC also received thousands of signatures on petitions, letters, and telegrams supporting the proposed legislation. In April the Paulists published 20,000 copies of a pamphlet by Harney titled, "Education and Religion vs. Commercial Radio." This was a ringing denunciation of the status quo, indistinguishable in tone from the critique of the status quo generated by the balance of the broadcast reform movement, which was mailed to Catholic parishes across the nation.[39] Given the lack of coverage the Harney campaign was receiving in the mass media, the ability of this ad hoc grassroots campaign to generate such a rapid and enormous response, from groups and individuals previously inactive in the movement for broadcast reform no less, is noteworthy. The activities of Harney and the Paulists captured the attention of Congress in a manner that had eluded the previous broadcast reform lobbying campaigns. By early April Wagner, who had eschewed all previous attempts by reformers to have him introduce reform legislation, agreed to co-sponsor the Harney legislation in the Senate.[40] The commercial broadcasters appeared to have been caught flat-footed; whereas the industry had carefully cultivated allies willing to swear allegiance to the status quo with educators, organized labor, and even the ACLU, this was not the case with the Catholic organizations that responded to Harney's pleas without any apparent hesitation.

Harney also met individually with several Catholic members of Congress in early April to press his argument. His eloquence carried the day; an April 12 meeting with some two dozen House members, not exclusively Catholics, generated unanimous sentiment for the measure. When Representative Stephen Rudd (D.NY) introduced the ''Harney Amendment'' to the House in April, he attributed it directly to Father Harney. On April 27 Senators Wagner and Hatfield introduced a slightly revised version of the same amendment to the Senate; henceforth, the 25 percent proposal would be referred to as the Wagner–Hatfield amendment.[41] By the end of April the momentum seemingly had shifted to the side of the reformers; *Variety* observed that the sentiment on Capitol Hill was that the Wagner–Hatfield amendment stood ''better than a 50–50 chance of being adopted.'' The NAB proclaimed that the amendment ''brings to a head the campaign against the present broadcasting set-up which has been smoldering in Congress for several years.''[42]

Harney found two important allies for his campaign to reform U.S. broadcasting. First, organized labor, specifically Edward N. Nockels, ended a two-year hiatus from broadcast reform activities and came out squarely for the Wagner–Hatfield amendment. Nockels helped Harney draft the legislation, coming to Washington to lobby on the bill's behalf where he was assisted by the AFL's chief lobbyist, Michael Flynn. Unlike his activities prior to 1932, Nockels appears to have entered the fray in 1934 as much for idealistic motives as to advance the specific position of WCFL, which was fairly secure by then. This was most fortuitous for Harney; of all the previous broadcast reform lobbies, organized labor had been most successful on Capitol Hill.

Nockels also wrote to all the member unions of the AFL urging them to support the bill. Nockels did not enjoy as much success with the AFL unions, however, as Harney did with the Catholic organizations. While he would inform Congress that organized labor was ''solidly behind'' the Wagner–Hatfield amendment, he would confess in a meeting of the CFL that, ''It is often very discouraging and disappointing to find how little response we get from our affiliated organizations when we call upon them for cooperation.'' Nevertheless, the alliance of labor and the Paulists alarmed the commercial broadcasters. As Bellows later recounted, given the support of labor, it "appeared probable that the amendment would be adopted in the Senate'' by late April.[43]

The second ally was found, in all places, on the FRC. James Hanley, President Roosevelt's "patronage'' appointment to the FRC in 1933, had developed into what *Broadcasting* termed a radio "radical.'' Much to their surprise, Hanley indicated a sympathy for broadcast reform in a series of meetings with NCER officials in the fall of 1933.[44] In February 1934 Hanley was the only FRC member to support WLWL in its efforts to be granted increased time over the air in its clash with CBS-affiliated WPG. His dissent noted that WLWL "started as a full-time station on a good frequency and has been reduced practically to radio poverty, while a commercial station on the same channel is given the lion's share of 110½ hours out of the 126-hour broadcast week.'' The WLWL hearings were marked by vicious exchanges between Hanley and the CBS attorneys, John Guider of the ABA's Standing Committee on Communications, and Duke Patrick, formerly an FRC administrator.[45]

During the course of the hearings, Hanley developed a working relationship with Father Harney. On April 14, 1934, Hanley issued a statement marking his first anniversary on the FRC that called for setting "aside a liberal number of channels for the exclusive use of educators and educational institutions.'' The reformers then claimed, perhaps out of optimism as much as reason, that Hanley "is believed to represent the administration's point of view in the Federal Radio Commission,'' as Armstrong Perry wrote in a letter to Sir John W. Reith.[46] Any breakthrough along these lines was nipped in the bud, however, as Hanley's statement was immediately repudiated by White House aides Louis Howe and Stephen Early and the balance of the FRC. Nonetheless, Father Harney became a "frequent visitor'' to Hanley's office, according to *Broadcasting*, which characterized Hanley as a "staunch supporter'' of the amendment.[47] The reformers had an ally in the FRC for the first time since Judge Ira Robinson promoted their cause in 1929 and 1930.

Unfortunately for Harney, however, he was unable to get the NCER to lobby actively on behalf of what would become the Wagner–Hatfield amendment, but not due to any lack of effort on his part. Harney telegrammed the NCER to solicit its assistance on March 29. In a letter to Harney the following day, Tracy Tyler wrote that he had spoken to Senator Dill about the matter and that Dill "thought there was considerable merit in the proposal.'' Dill nonetheless informed Tyler that it would be best to leave the measure out of the bill so that the new FCC could "study the whole question and make recommendations for legislation.'' Tyler accepted Dill's analysis and informed Harney that any lobbying would be a waste of time as he was "convinced" by Dill that the measure "would not be passed by the Senate." Tyler encouraged Harney to keep up his impressive lobbying work as it would "bear fruit" when the new FCC was "appointed" and would "give careful and impartial study to the whole matter of priority of broadcasting rights."[48]

Harney found Tyler's response entirely unsatisfactory. He was astounded to find that Tyler regarded Dill as "at all in sympathy with the Amendment." He dismissed the notion that Dill and the other senators on the Senate Committee on Interstate Commerce who opposed his measure sincerely wanted to have the new FCC make a "careful" study of broadcasting as "naïve to the point of childishness." These senators, he wrote,

> know that history will repeat itself in this connection, and that a new Commission created to control the distribution of radio facilities will pay no more heed to the needs of education than the soon to expire Federal Radio Commission, unless Congress emphatically reserves a portion of radio facilities for educational stations, and leaves it to the new Commission to merely work out the details.[49]

In addition, Harney sent letters to other members of the NCER in an effort to generate sentiment to override Tyler's lethargic stance and convince the NCER "to work energetically for the adoption of this amendment." To NCER lobbyist Eugene Coltrane he wrote:

> Some of our opponents would like to create the impression that this is a "special interest bill"; that it is drawn up only in favor of religion, and to be more specific, only in favor of a Catholic radio station. Nothing can be farther from the truth or more palpably against it than any such assertion.[50]

Harney "purposely made" the legislation "broad" and inclusive of education and other nonprofit groups, he argued,

> not merely or mainly to secure the help of others, but because deep down in my soul I am convinced that commercial interests if allowed to dominate the radio field will hamper and prevent that full, free, many-sided discussions of our varied social, economical, ethical and educational problems which are necessary for their wise solution. For me it is a question of human welfare, not a question of the welfare of the Catholic Church, which will live and thrive and march steadily onward no matter how the Congress of the United States may rule with regard to radio.

Harney argued accordingly that "it would be a sorry thing to let the impression get abroad that Catholics alone are interested" in the amendment. Harney implored the NCER to give the amendment "earnest and outspoken support" rather than the "silent sympathy" that Tyler was promising. If the NCER would join Catholics and organized labor, Harney wrote to Armstrong Perry on April 4, "it is almost unthinkable" that Congress would not pass the measure. "We must not let this opportunity knock at our door in vain. A better day will hardly come in our lifetime."[51]

Unfortunately, "silent sympathy" is exactly what the NCER provided. Several NCER members, most notably Perry, agreed with Harney's analysis but were unable to alter NCER policy. The college broadcasters affiliated with the NCER that voiced opinions were adamant on behalf of the Wagner–Hatfield amendment, regarding it as the logical extension of the NCER's original mandate to lobby for legislation that would set aside 15 percent of the channels for educational purposes. Coltrane conducted a brief survey of senators in early April and agreed with Tyler that the amendment could not pass. Tyler continued in his belief that Dill's inclusion of section 307(c) constituted a victory for the NCER's legislative ambition of having an independent study of broadcasting.[52] Tyler wrote to Harney on April 25 to offer moral support for the Wagner–Hatfield campaign, as well as to inform him that the NCER would not be able to assist with the lobbying as all of its attention was to be devoted to its upcoming conference on radio on May 7 and 8. Similarly, the ACLU radio committee had no interest in lobbying on behalf of the Wagner–Hatfield amendment; committee members Webster and Levering Tyson were opposed to the bill in principle. To the extent that the ACLU lobbied at all, it was to attempt to convince Dill to support legislation for a full-blown study of broadcasting, not the FCC study mandated by section 307(c).[53]

The radio lobby attacked the Wagner–Hatfield amendment between April 27 and May 15 as if, as Henry Bellows later put it, its passage "obviously would have destroyed the whole structure of broadcasting in America." One NAB official characterized the Wagner–Hatfield debate as "a fight between life and death." Telegrams were sent to every broadcaster informing them that, if passed, the Wagner–Hatfield amendment "would cancel your license in 90 days." Broadcasters were provided no other explanation or information about the legislation but they were urged in no uncertain terms to contact their representatives in Congress to voice their severe opposition to the measure. As *Broadcasting* put it, all broadcasters were "aroused to a white heat when faced with the threat of an unprecedented upheaval."[54] "Practically every Senator and Congressman," Bellows later observed, "learned much during May about the operation of broadcasting stations in his state." In addition, "a very large number of senators and congressmen were seen personally" by Bellows and other network executives to set forth their "objections" to the amendment. *Variety* noted that the NAB was "in panic checking off names of senators and trying to pull wires and get votes." Emergency plans were made to enlist newspaper and press service support for an anti-Wagner–Hatfield campaign if its passage appeared imminent.[55]

The industry called upon its allies in the executive branch to assist in the fight. FRC Chairman Sykes wrote and spoke with undecided members of

Congress to express his support for Dill's section 307(c) and his opposition to the Wagner–Hatfield amendment. While the White House formally took no position on the amendment, all the while supporting Dill's S. 3285, Philip Rosen has noted that it played a critical behind-the-scenes role: "Quick action from the Roosevelt administration overwhelmed its opposition." Indeed, when Father Harney and the AFL's Michael Flynn spread the word that the White House "saw no objection" with the Wagner–Hatfield amendment, White House aide Stephen Early refuted this in a public statement, noting that the lack of formal opposition to the amendment could not be interpreted as a sign of tacit support.[56]

CBS, which had been haggling with Harney's WLWL for years over how WLWL and CBS affiliate WPG would share air time on the same frequency, also became actively involved in the fight. At the end of April, prominent public relations agent Ivy Lee, representing CBS, approached the WLWL attorney and indicated that CBS was willing to grant WLWL more air time at the expense of WPG, as much as five hours per day, with the implication that such a gift would be in exchange for the Paulists agreeing to withdraw their support for the Wagner–Hatfield amendment. CBS was opting to cut the same sort of deal with the Paulists that NBC had made with WCFL in May 1932. Harney and his advisers interpreted the move to mean that the networks were "scared" and that the wise move would be "to let them worry somewhat longer." A few days later, Harney advised his attorney to inform CBS that WLWL rejected the offer, finding it "seriously unsatisfactory." He suggested, however, that he would be open to further negotiations on the matter.[57]

Nevertheless, on May 2 Harney discovered on a trip to Washington that a rumor had surfaced that WLWL had accepted the proposition made by CBS. Senator Wagner told Harney that a government official had told the senator to take no further steps on the Wagner–Hatfield amendment "in view of the fact that the difficulties between Columbia Broadcasting System and WLWL were at the point of settlement." Although Harney quickly informed Wagner of the true state of affairs and told him to push on with the bill, it is difficult to gauge how much damage this did the reform effort. In any case, after the Wagner–Hatfield amendment was defeated, CBS did not attempt to resume negotiations with WLWL.[58]

The NCER was far from inactive during these tumultuous days. On May 7 and 8, 1934, the NCER convened its first and only national conference in Washington, D.C., to discuss the "problem of radio use and control." Some 100 leaders in education were invited to participate and, although sponsored by the NCER, it was an "entirely self-determining conference." In addition to scores of educators, the participants included Dr. Arthur Morgan of the TVA, James Rorty, Jerome Davis, and Gross Alexander. Father Harney had planned to attend but he had to pass on the conference when he fell ill.[59]

The NCER had truly ambitious plans for the conference: It hoped that the participants would reach a consensus on a tangible program to unite behind to reform U.S. broadcasting and then have everyone proceed to work toward that end. The sentiment of Joy Elmer Morgan, Perry, and others active in the NCER had long been that the ultimate program for broadcast reform was to see the establishment of a chain of nonprofit and noncommercial government stations supported by tax revenues to complement the existing commercial chains. The NCER as a whole, however, had a few members who resisted any call for an increased role for the government in broadcasting. With this "self-governing" conference, the more radical element of the NCER hoped to break through the impasse and establish the dominance of the sentiment for a noncommercial government radio chain. Indeed, one of the two conference subcommittees called for the establishment of a series of state and regional noncommercial public stations to be funded by the federal government. The proposal was roundly applauded by the preponderance of the conference participants. When an effort was made to have the conference adopt this report, however, limited but vociferous opposition rapidly emerged. A few of the participants were opposed to anything critical of the status quo. The NCER had apparently not been very selective when it sent out the invitations. Even more damaging, some of the participants claimed that the NCER had told them upon receiving invitations that the conference would *not* be making any specific recommendations.[60]

Hence the final report of the conference refrained from calling for the series of public broadcasting stations, and recommended, instead, that the conference appoint a committee to meet with the president and urge him to appoint an independent committee to study broadcasting and make suggestions for systemic reform. The only difference between this and all the earlier "study" proposals was that the reformers planned to bypass Congress and appeal directly to the president. Representatives of this NCER conference tried repeatedly and without success to gain an audience with President Roosevelt for the next six weeks. They eventually gave up when the passage of the Communications Act of 1934 with section 307(c) seemingly rendered moot their request for a presidential study.[61]

Many of the conference participants were appalled by the futility of the ultimate conference recommendation. Perry dismissed the conference categorically, noting despondently that "following a well-established habit of educators," it called for "another study instead of action." He was increasingly convinced that some members of the NCER, although none of the key figures like Morgan, Tyler, or Coltrane, "were interested in preventing it from taking a definite position concerning broadcasting."[62] Indeed, NBC records indicate that one NCER conference participant, James Francis Cooke, was secretly keeping the network posted on the NCER's activities. Cooke led the fight to keep the NCER conference from adopting the call for a government network. Cooke was the president of a music publishing house that had dealings with NBC who had long since decided that broadcast reform was not only unnecessary, but would be harmful. "I am still a member of the National Committee on Education by Radio," he informed an NBC executive as he turned over some NCER internal documents, because "I desire to have other bulletins especially as they might be very interesting, even vital, to you."[63]

It is highly questionable whether a resolution in favor of a government chain at this late date would have had any impact upon the legislative picture. The NCER planners seemed mostly unconcerned with linking the conference to any immediate or even foreseeable campaign for reform legislation. In Father Harney's absence at the conference, it was left to Gross Alexander to be the only participant to acknowledge the impending vote on the Wagner–Hatfield amendment. "I wish the conference were minded not to adjourn until we had taken action to commit ourselves," Alexander remarked, in favor "of the pending legislation which is to be voted on in the Senate tomorrow or the next day."[64]

It also remains doubtful whether support by the NCER conference at this late stage would have done much for the Wagner–Hatfield amendment's prospects. By the time that the House Committee on Interstate and Foreign Commerce commenced its hearings on the Rayburn communications bill on May 8, NBC's vice-president in charge of legislative matters, Frank Russell, had already reported confidently to headquarters that the Wagner–Hatfield amendment did not have "the slightest chance of enactment into law" and that he "had taken every opportunity to work against it." Likewise, on May 12, the NAB noted that "the Wagner–Hatfield amendment vote, if its proponents permit it to come to a vote, will be overwhelmingly against its adoption." The Dill communications bill, on the other hand, faced certain passage, according to the NAB.[65]

By May 10 it was clear to the commercial broadcasters that they could do as they pleased with the legislation. Some, like Merlin Aylesworth, wished to have the legislation withdrawn for fear that "too many victories go wrong on a vote." Russell argued, on the other hand, that it would be a "danger" if the proponents of the amendment were able to return the legislation to committee to mount another campaign in the next session of Congress. Russell convinced Aylesworth of the soundness of his argument and his approach carried the day. "Some of our friends in the Senate," Russell informed Aylesworth on May 11, "have indicated they will force a vote in order to dispose of this matter for all time."[66]

The Senate took up consideration of S. 3285 and the Wagner–Hatfield amendment on May 15. As Bellows later commented, Senator Dill "splendidly assumed" the floor leadership against the amendment. After Senator Wagner offered his amendment and briefly argued on its behalf, Dill interjected that the amendment was flawed because it permitted "so-called" nonprofit broadcasters to sell advertising time to support themselves. Another senator responded to the spirit of this criticism and added that the amendment "would open the door and allow many stations, under the guise of religious and educational enterprises, to come in to compete with business enterprises."[67] This inability to account for an effective means to subsidize nonprofit broadcasting aside from advertising was the central weak spot of the fixed-percentage proposal. In 1931 this argument undermined much of the sentiment on behalf of the NCER's fixed-percentage proposal, which had been introduced by Senator Simeon Fess.

Dill then proceeded to recite many of the other criticisms of the Wagner–Hatfield amendment, much of which had been liberally disseminated by the commercial broadcasters in the preceding two weeks. He then added a new twist, drawing attention to the NCER conference that had been held in Washington only one week earlier. "They do not recommend the adoption of this amendment," Dill stated. "They recommend, rather, a study." Dill then provided his own interpretation of why the NCER was "not ready to recommend that 25 percent of the facilities be set aside for educational and religious institutions":

> Let me call to the attention of the senator why what they [NCER] say is so. It costs a tremendous amount of money to build large radio stations. The religious and educational and cultural organizations do not have the money necessary, *and they are trying to work out a system whereby existing stations may be used,* probably in addition to the sixty-three stations which are already in operation, of an educational and nonprofit nature, and still not be burdened with the great expense of building stations. [author's emphasis]

Senator Wagner then took the floor and attempted to clarify the position of the NCER by citing an *Education by Radio* article from 1932 that came out foursquare for the fixed-percentage principle.[68]

At this time Dill returned to the podium and continued with his arguments against the amendment, emphasizing, in particular, how section 307(c) would essentially let the principle involved be examined in detail by the new FCC. Dill also stressed in no uncertain terms his commitment to educational broadcasting. Dill concluded his case by delving into some of the conceivable administrative problems involved with the amendment. In the following exchange with Senator M. M. Logan, (D. Utah) he stressed the problem of allocating the 25 percent to the various nonprofit broadcasters.

> Dill: "If we should provide that 25 percent of the time shall be allocated to nonprofit organizations, someone would have to determine—Congress or somebody else—how much of that 25 percent should go to education, how much of it to religion, and how much of it to agriculture, how much of it to labor, how much of it to fraternal organizations, and so forth. When we enter this

field we must determine how much to give to the Catholics probably and how much to give to the Protestants and how much to the Jews.''
Logan: "And to the Hindus.''
Dill: "Yes, and probably the infidels would want some time.''
Logan: "Yes; there is a national association of atheists. They perhaps would want some time.''

Wagner was clearly flustered by this tidal wave of no-holds-barred opposition to the amendment. "This amendment does not in any way interfere with the larger stations. They may continue to use all their time for purely profit-making purposes," he stated. "To me the proposition that at least 25 percent should be allocated to nonprofit ventures seems so fair that I cannot understand the opposition to it.''[69] Wagner's protests notwithstanding, the amendment was defeated shortly thereafter on a vote of 42–23.

Armstrong Perry noted that Senator Dill's citing of the NCER conference resolutions "had much to do with the defeat of the amendment." Ironically, Tyler had rushed a copy of the resolutions to Dill on May 14 to help him evaluate the "numerous bills and amendments to bills concerning radio which are being proposed these days."[70] At the same time Tyler was assuring WCFL's Edward Nockels that he thought the "principle" of the Wagner–Hatfield bill "fundamentally sound," that it would eventually triumph, and "you can count on us to continue the fight." That Dill took license with the actual sentiments of the NCER, turning them into both opponents of the Wagner–Hatfield amendment and proponents of section 307(c), if not the status quo, in order to thwart the Wagner–Hatfield amendment is beyond question; likewise, that Tyler and the NCER played directly into his hands is obvious. Questions of ethics aside, Dill's efforts won the battle. Dill's inclusion of section 307(c) was seemingly the decisive factor that stemmed the tide of sentiment on the bill's behalf. "Without his active cooperation," Bellows informed the NAB convention that September, "the Wagner–Hatfield amendment would probably have passed."[71]

Immediately following the defeat of the Wagner–Hatfield amendment, the Senate approved Dill's S. 3285 on a voice vote. After the intense debate concerning broadcast reform in the Senate, the debate over the communications legislation in the House, where stricter rules prevented the introduction of amendments on the floor, was brief and anticlimatic. There, Representative Rayburn kept the "Harney amendment" from being attached to his bill, and he managed, through "complex parliamentary maneuvering," to limit the floor debate over his bill to two hours and keep the subject of broadcast reform off the agenda. Rayburn's bill passed on a voice vote on June 2.[72] The bill then went to conference where the differences between the Senate and House bills were ironed out.

Almost all of the clauses objectionable to the commercial broadcasters were dropped in conference in exchange for keeping section 307(c), which was nonnegotiable given its role in getting support for the legislation in the Senate. In addition, the final bill kept the clause repealing the Radio Act of 1927, probably for the same reason the bill kept section 307(c), but the conference report assured congressional supporters of the status quo that while it did so, the bill "in effect reenacts it [the Radio Act of 1927] in Title III." When the conference committee completed its work, Senator Dill informed Henry Bellows over the telephone: "We have been very generous to you fellows." Bellows would later comment: "When we read it, we found that every major point we had asked for was there."[73] After the conference report was adopted by both houses, the bill was submitted to President Roosevelt on June 14. He signed the Communications Act of 1934 into law on June 18.

For the most part, the passage of the bill was buried by the news media in the coverage of the plethora of bills passed and signed into law that June as the session of Congress ended. When the Communications Act of 1934 was covered, the legislation was characterized as a major "New Deal in Radio Law" reform measure aimed at "curbing monopoly in radio," and asserting public control of the medium.[74] Although one scholar has noted that the Communications Act did "mark the beginning of serious federal regulation" of telephony and telegraphy, much as AT&T feared, and others have commented that the Act launched an adversarial regulatory climate toward AT&T that lasted for several years, such claims were bogus when applied to radio broadcasting.[75] Nonetheless, neither Dill nor Rayburn nor the Roosevelt administration did anything to discourage this interpretation.[76] This notion of the Communications Act of 1934 being representative of New Deal legislation that boldly harnessed antagonistic private power and forced it to act in the public interest has been a theme in some of the broadcasting histories heretofore.[77]

Proponents of the status quo were uniformly delighted with the legislation. The ABA Committee on Communications characterized the Communications Act of 1934 as providing "the best method of evolving a sound and sensible body of law for communications control." Henry Bellows stated that "the entire broadcasting industry is deeply indebted" to both Dill and Rayburn, for their roles in getting the "wise and reasonable" legislation passed.[78] Conversely, the broadcast reformers had little comment on the law, not seeming to know how precisely to regard it at the time. The implications of the Communications Act of 1934 for the reform movement seemed lost to it.

The crystallization of capitalist broadcasting was now on the home stretch; the major hurdle had been overcome. All that stood between the industry and the statutory consolidation of the status quo were the FCC hearings mandated by section 307(c) that had been the price paid to assure the defeat of the Wagner–Hatfield amendment and the passage of the Communications

Act of 1934. "There is, after all, little point in discussing theoretical conditions," CBS newscaster H. V. Kaltenborn informed a group of educational broadcasters in the summer of 1934 after listening to comments criticizing the status quo by Tyler and Perry, among others. "We are confronted with a definite radio system in the United States which is not going to be transformed in the immediate future. We shall have commercial stations, and they are going to dominate the radio situation."[79]

The FCC Hearings in Autumn 1934

While the commercial broadcasters were delighted by the passage of the Communications Act of 1934, *Broadcasting* cautioned that the extent of this "victory" would be dependent upon whom President Roosevelt appointed to the new FCC. There were grounds for concern. In early June the navy department, Daniels, Roper, and broadcast reform sympathizers in the Senate launched a campaign to have Roosevelt appoint Hooper to the FCC. Roosevelt even had Hooper on his initial list of appointees, but he removed Hooper's name when it was met by what Hooper characterized as the "most intensive opposition" of the communications firms that no longer regarded him as sufficiently loyal to their interests.[80] Any other concerns were erased when the president announced his seven appointees on June 30. Two members of the old FRC were retained on the new FCC: Chairman Sykes and Vice-Chairman Thad H. Brown. Hanley, the radio "radical" who had been the FRC's sole supporter of the Wagner–Hatfield amendment, was not carried over.[81]

At its first meeting on July 11, the new FCC voted to "retain the status quo insofar as broadcasting regulation is concerned," and to move "cautiously" toward any reform. The FCC also created a special Broadcast Division, which would be solely responsible for all broadcast regulatory matters. This Broadcast Division was comprised of FRC holdovers Sykes and Brown in addition to newcomer Hampson Gary (D-Tex.). "Any fears harbored by those in broadcasting that an immediate upheaval of radio might result from the creation of the new FCC are dispelled with the organization of that agency into divisions," *Broadcasting* assured its readers. "The Broadcasting Division," it explained, "is a conservative group. It can be expected to carry on the basic policies of the old Radio Commission, for, indeed, two of its members were on the former agency."[82]

At its first meeting, the Broadcast Division announced that the hearings mandated by section 307(c) would be held in October. It also made clear that these hearings were meant to "secure the facts in order to make the study." Hence, there would be no "adverse parties," and the hearings would not become a "forum for argumentative discussion." Moreover, the Broadcast Division insisted that the purpose of the hearings was specifically to consider the merits of reserving 25 percent of the channels for nonprofit broadcasters, as it had been directed by section 307(c), and not to make an overall evaluation of the merits and demerits of the status quo.[83]

In August the NCER consulted with each of its nine member organizations to determine "what position . . . it should take in connection with these hearings." The NCER received encouragement from its member organizations to take part in the FCC hearings. "We have long been fighting for the reservation of certain channels for the exclusive use of educational stations," one ACUBS officer wrote. "Now the matter is definitely scheduled for official consideration." Joy Elmer Morgan informed the FCC that the NCER would testify on behalf of the "pro-fixed percentage" side, despite the fact that the NCER "had not suggested the enactment of the specific legislation under discussion."[84] The NCER "had hoped for something more far-reaching in its effect on American broadcasting practice," Tracy F. Tyler informed the Broadcast Division, "something which would arrive at the very heart of the ills effecting broadcasting in this country; something which would consider fearlessly not only the educational aspects of radio but the numerous other problems, some of which, though known to the former Radio Commission, were left unsolved." As Tyler wrote to Senator Dill in June, the FCC hearings "would be better than no study at all." Not all NCER officials were reconciled to the FCC hearings as any sort of acceptable alternative; Armstrong Perry, for one, dismissed them as "one step in an elaborate plan for keeping radio under commercial control and censorship."[85]

The NCER soon discovered that there was a great difference of opinion among its nine member groups as to what its testimony should be. Some groups desired to appear conciliatory toward the status quo in the hope of working out a compromise, while others, like the ACUBS, wished to propose to the FCC that it call for the creation of a noncommercial government network to supplement, not replace, the commercial chains.[86] The NCER, therefore, decided to have each of the nine groups make separate presentations before the FCC in the October hearings. There would be no effort to coordinate the statements or have the different groups agree on a specific platform; for all intents and purposes, each group would be on its own.

The discussion concerning the proper approach for the ACLU to take with regard to the FCC hearings led to a major rift on its radio committee. That rift reflected some of the tensions appearing elsewhere in the broadcast reform movement as the prospects for reform began to disintegrate. It recognized early on that the passage of the Communications Act of 1934 meant that "it would be rather difficult to stir up interest" in Congress for their own legislation, leaving the FCC hearings as the only forum for debate open to them for the being. Nevertheless, committee member Webster was convinced that the hearings were going to be strictly a formality to satisfy section 307(c), and that it was a foregone conclusion that the new FCC would recommend against the fixed-percentage notion.[87] "It is too much to expect that Judge Sykes or Thad Brown will deal energetically or constructively with the communications situation," Webster informed radio committee member Henry Eckstein. The publicity director of the ACLU concurred; he noted that the hearings were "called simply to satisfy the squawks of educators" and that they were a "set-up for the broadcasters" since the educators were in no position to defend the fixed percentage principle.[88]

Moreover, Webster thought the fixed-percentage principle was indefensible. In early September he argued that the ACLU should distance itself from the educators in the hearings, repudiate the fixed-percentage notion, and attempt to work out a separate deal with the networks and the NAB whereby the commercial broadcasters would set aside time for the broadcast of noncommercial public affairs programming under the guidance of the FCC. Tyson announced that he was in "hearty accord" with Webster's suggestion, adding that he thought the proposal would be "welcomed" by the networks and the FCC.[89]

The remaining Radio Committee members were opposed to the suggestion. Eckstein argued that "anticommercial" forces should keep a "united front" to the commercial broadcasters and he did not see why, if the anticommercial groups were ineffectual and in disarray, the commercial broadcasters would have anything to gain by negotiating with the ACLU. Morris Ernst was opposed to Webster's proposal categorically. He argued that the ACLU should not only advocate that 25 percent of the channels be turned over to nonprofit broadcasters in the FCC hearings, but, furthermore, that 25 percent of the time on commercial stations should be set aside for the uncensored use of nonprofit groups.[90] It was left to Roger Baldwin to settle this "sharp" split on the Radio Committee. He wired that he favored Ernst's proposal because "it demands maximum." He added, "I think it is unwise for us to make any deal with broadcasters."[91] A few days later, Baldwin told the Radio Committee that "anything that breaks up the monopoly and gets noncommercial stuff across is our meat, because only thus do we escape advertisers' pressure and open up controversial discussion." He advised Ernst and Webster to work out a compromise between their two positions for the ACLU's presentation to the FCC. We "should ask for what we want, not what we might get," Baldwin reminded the radio committee in a telegram a few days later. We "should stand on principle."[92]

Ironically, the two elements of the broadcast reform movement—the NCER and the ACLU—that had not worked for the Wagner–Hatfield amendment earlier that year spent the most time preparing for the FCC hearings on the desirability of the fixed-percentage notion. Concurrently, the two groups most responsible for the Wagner–Hatfield campaign that forced Congress to include section 307(c)—the Paulist Fathers and organized labor—

paid little, if any, attention to the FCC hearings during the summer of 1934. Neither group had any faith in the hearings, dismissing them categorically. This sentiment was widespread among reformers. *New Republic* editor Bruce Bliven rejected the NCER's request that he testify before the FCC, stating that "to do so would be a waste of time; the Federal Communications Commission will do nothing to improve radio." Likewise, *The Christian Century* editorialized that the FCC hearings had the earmarks of "a pro formal affair, designed to entrench the commercial interests in their privileged position."[93]

There were certainly grounds for skepticism on the part of the broadcast reformers. Sykes, the FCC chairman, was an unvarnished proponent of the status quo who enjoyed cordial relations with the commercial broadcasters. The other two members of the Broadcast Division made it equally clear, in their public statements prior to the October hearings, that they had no interest in implementing any reform of the status quo. "Let me reassure you," Hampson Gary told the NAB convention in September, that "nothing revolutionary is in view. Naturally we will bend every effort to improve the existing set-up for the benefit of the public's reception and for your benefit." FCC Vice-Chairman Thad Brown told the same gathering of commercial broadcasters that

> [I]t is our steadfast desire to vest in the broadcaster all powers of control properly belonging to him. It is rightly your job, and you are the ones properly qualified to do the job of directing broadcasting for the benefit of and to protect the rights of millions of American listeners.[94]

Despite these assurances, the commercial broadcasting industry's approach to the upcoming FCC hearings was not imbued with an air of overconfidence. Quite to the contrary, Henry Bellows took a leave-of-absence from his position as a vice-president at CBS, for example, to devote all of his attention to preparing the NAB case. Bellows told the NAB convention in September 1934 that:

> It is one of the most important events in the entire history of American broadcasting. . . . It is up to us, not merely to present a case which will justify the Commission in recommending no material changes in the law as it affects broadcasting, but far more to establish so strong a record that we shall have a conclusive answer to every attack which can be made on our industry.[95]

NBC Washington lobbyist Frank Russell had been emphatic throughout the summer in his correspondence to NBC's New York headquarters about the need for a "definite campaign" in defense of the status quo before the FCC that October. "The need for undertaking work along this line has been very evident here in Washington during the past three months." He argued that NBC needed to work closely with Bellows and the NAB so that the industry presented a coherent position on all the issues that would be raised by the opponents of commercial broadcasting. In mid-August NBC assigned Russell to devote all of his attention to directing its case before the FCC, as "this might very well be the most important survey of the American broadcasting system yet undertaken."[96] Russell quickly determined that the case for NBC would be much stronger if it was publicly led by "an important outside man who can give us detached assistance from an editorial standpoint." Russell then hired journalist William Hard to be the formal leader of the NBC case before the FCC. Hard would be paid $2,000 plus his expenses for his efforts over the next two months.[97]

In addition, NBC and CBS both began what *The New York Times* characterized as a "strenuous clean-up campaign" that summer to put more culturally enriched programming on the air in advance of the FCC hearings. Henry Bellows acknowledged the existence of this "clean-up campaign," but claimed it was simply a response to a shift in public demand: "The radio public wanted jazz programs, got them and became tired of them. Now there is a definite swing in the other direction."[98] Behind the scenes, however, industry executives conceded that the purpose of the clean-up campaign was "to go far toward spiking the guns of those ardent and voluble critics of broadcasting."[99] In any case, the industry was leaving nothing to chance. This would be its opportunity to deliver the proverbial "knockout punch" to the broadcast reformers, and eliminate any further possibility for structural criticism of the status quo to be legitimately debated before either the FCC or Congress. Hence the degree of preparation, which may have seemed absurdly unnecessary on the surface, made all the sense in the world.

When the FCC hearings began on October 1, the NCER coordinated the first three days of witnesses who were ostensibly in favor of reserving 25 percent of the channels for nonprofit broadcasters. Ironically, none of the NCER witnesses spoke on the measure's behalf. The NCER's first witness, Joy Elmer Morgan, simply said the NCER was in favor of the vague principle that "public welfare stations" be "protected in their present privileges" and that the FCC give them "due and favorable weight." Later the same day the ACUBS representative made the proposal for the sort of government chain referred to earlier. The following day S. Howard Evans denounced the fixed-percentage proposal and refused to offer any substitute.[100] Shortly thereafter, the representative of the NUEA similarly shied away from the fixed-percentage proposal and argued that the FCC should convene a broader study of broadcasting. The educators provided no coherent program to the FCC whatsoever. On the evening of October 2, in a memo to NBC's New York headquarters, Russell described the various proposals being offered by the educators at the hearings and concluded, "I do not think we have anything particularly to worry about because all of these could be done without any impairment of our present system."[101]

In this context, the commercial broadcasters were feeling fairly secure in their position following the conclusion of the NCER testimony on October 3. "The presentation of their case was entirely temperate and there was very little in the way of a serious attack upon the business as now conducted," one NBC memo observed. Indeed, on the evening of October 3, NBC's Frank Russell met privately with Commissioners Gary and Brown and reported to NBC's New York headquarters that

> the commissioners are inclined to feel that, unless the circumstances are radically altered, they will not be under any pressure to recommend new legislation in their report to Congress. They think they might use their good offices to have the educational groups concerned appoint a committee to work with the broadcasters for an amicable solution of this problem instead of trying to solve it through Congress.

Russell advised his superiors that "we should go along with this point of view, confident that the gradual adjustment of the whole matter can be handled in a way which would not be detrimental to our business."[102]

If possible, those who testified on "behalf" of the fixed-percentage proposal in the days following the NCER did even more damage to the reform movement's prospects. Nearly one-third of the scheduled witnesses, including Gross Alexander, failed to appear, and many of those that did praised commercial broadcasting. Bethuel M. Webster, Jr.'s, testimony on behalf of the ACLU on October 5 was contradictory. In the first half of his statement he politely reiterated his idea of having the networks voluntarily set aside time for the airing on noncommercial public affairs programming. In the second part of his statement, he presented Morris Ernst's radical critique of the status quo and suggested that the FCC consider establishing a government owned and operated network on a five-year trial basis.[103] Father Harney, who had not planned to testify before the hearings, appeared on October 8 to refute a vitriolic attack on Catholicism that had been made by the representative of the Jehovah's Witnesses on October 4. He made no additional statement concerning broadcast policy, explaining later that since the hearings were "confined strictly to factual data," there was nothing for him to add to what "had already been submitted to the Federal Communications Commission" by WLWL.[104]

Finally, to add insult to injury, as the "proponents" of the fixed-percentage proposal completed their testimony on October 8, the NACRE was holding a relatively well-publicized national convention in Chicago on October 8 and 9, where the tenor of the conclave was stridently in favor of the status quo. In the eyes of the public, let alone the FCC Broadcast Division, the educators could have easily appeared as a house divided, if not actually in favor of the status quo. As the headline of *Broadcasting* gleefully announced: "Educators Drop Nationalized Radio Plea [sic]; Offer Wide Variety of Vague

Proposals at FCC Hearing; NAB Opens Factual Case for Radio Industry.'' Frank Russell reported back to New York confidently on October 9: ''I believe the Industry will go on the stand with its case under most favorable circumstances.''[105]

Between October 11 and October 20, the NAB, NBC, and CBS paid the ''expenses'' for seventy-two witnesses to come to Washington to testify against the fixed-percentage principle and in favor of the status quo. *Broadcasting* was hardly exaggerating when it commented that ''The roster of witnesses who testified in support of the existing system read like a 'Who's Who' of education, music, literature, and broadcasting.'' Some of these witnesses were celebrities like musician Paul Whiteman and comedians Freeman Gosden and Charlie Correll, who starred in the hit show ''Amos 'n' Andy.'' More important, several prominent educators and cultural figures testified on behalf of the industry to attest to the suitability of the status quo for cultural and educational programming. The networks had solicited and paid for these appearances since, as one memo observed, they ''have used our facilities in the last two years.'' That these educators ''were induced to appear because they were enjoying the use of facilities made available to them by commercial broadcasters,'' as Tracy Tyler later put it, gave the hearings an inaccurate representation of the real situation to the broadcast reformers.

> Those that had satisfactory relations with the commercial broadcasters were unwilling to jeopardize their future activities thru [sic] aligning themselves in favor of a change in the status quo. Those who had unsatisfactory relations with the commercial broadcasters were unable to secure the funds with which to finance an appearance at the hearing.[106]

Probably most damaging to the reformers was the testimony of the NEA's Florence Hale, who as NEA radio director had coordinated educational programming over NBC for several years. Hale professed to the FCC ''great belief in the efficiency of American broadcasting'' and that ''the cooperative enterprise of NEA and NBC represent an ideal set-up for this type of educational work.'' Hale's sympathies had long been known and disparaged by the NCER and educational broadcasters, who had regarded her for years privately as little more than an agent of NBC in their midst. In her testimony, which was accorded lavish publicity by the network public relations staffs and *Broadcasting* magazine, Hale also claimed that educators were incapable of managing their own stations and therefore needed to permit the commercial broadcasters to control the ether. Her testimony outraged educational broadcasters, many of whom wrote to the NEA in protest. Hale's testimony was ''a direct insult'' to college broadcasters, one wrote, and ''proof of her utter lack of knowledge'' of their efforts over the preceding fifteen years.[107]

In addition to the witnesses, the NAB produced 286 statements from individual stations, which comprised some 10,000 pages and required sixteen volumes, all swearing to the commitment of commercial broadcasters to air all the educational and cultural fare the public could desire or that educators could produce. In sum, the case put forth by the industry was everything that the case by the reformers had not been: coordinated, well-planned, lavishly financed, and crisply executed. Frank Russell could barely contain his enthusiasm for the case the commercial broadcasters made before the FCC:

> The thing was done to perfection. Everything went off like clockwork, and as the evidence on point after point was heaped up before the Commission, the effect was not only vastly impressive so far as they were concerned, but was simply overwhelming so far as the opposition's case was concerned.[108]

Nevertheless, the industry faced three distinct and mostly unexpected threats during the balance of the FCC hearings, each of which required different levels of intervention to be successfully defused.

The most serious of these threats came from the TVA, a New Deal administrative body established to encourage economic development in the depressed Tennessee River valley that encompassed portions of some seven states in the U.S. South. The NCER had great admiration for the TVA both in principle and in practice; Tracy Tyler wrote to the TVA in September 1933, noting approvingly that it reminded him of the BBC and "that the next step should be the creation of a similar authority to handle all of our radio broadcasting here." Moreover, TVA Chairman Dr. Arthur Morgan, a prominent educator, advocated the radical reconstruction of U.S. broadcasting. Dr. Morgan presented a speech at the NCER conference in May 1934 in which he argued that not only radio broadcasting but the entirety of the mass media were too important to be left to the control of capitalists and, accordingly, should be operated on a nonprofit and noncommercial basis, "just as are the public schools." Nor was this a slip of the tongue; Dr. Morgan held up the publication of the NCER proceedings in June 1934 specifically to "correct" this paper for publication.[109]

It was at the urging of the NCER that the TVA assigned Dr. Floyd W. Reeves to testify on its behalf at the FCC hearings in the sessions. The NAB permitted Reeves, like Dr. Morgan a prominent educator, to appear during its allotted time, on October 19, because he was to be out of town at the TVA's later scheduled date. Much to the industry's and the FCC's surprise, Reeves delivered a sharply worded critique of the limitations of the status quo and called for the creation of a federally subsidized noncommercial network to supplement the commercial networks and to be operated along the lines of the BBC. As *Broadcasting* observed, Reeves' unexpected proposal "brought sharp cross-examination from the three members of the Broadcast Division."[110]

The NAB and the two networks immediately attempted to defuse this potential crisis. On October 20, they expressed their concern about Reeves's TVA testimony to the White House; as H. M. McIntyre reported to Stephen Early, "the broadcasters seem very perturbed." Early then contacted Dr. Arthur Morgan and told him to withdraw Reeves's statement and replace it with one that rejected government ownership of radio. Dr. Morgan responded with the following telegram to the FCC on October 23:

> In view of the fact that its brief statement to the Federal Communications Commission was misinterpreted, the Tennessee Valley Authority prefers to withdraw its former statement and restate its position as follows: The Tennessee Valley Authority has not urged or favored government administration of radio stations. It is the opinion of the board of directors that the educational and cultural agencies of the country should have a reasonable use of the radio facilities of the country but that all such programs should be under nongovernmental and nonpartisan control and direction.

Broadcasting observed that Arthur Morgan's telegram was "promptly interpreted in political circles" as a move by the Roosevelt administration to "squelch the whole incident" and make it absolutely clear that the New Deal had no interest in government ownership of radio stations. The NAB insisted that Dr. Morgan's telegram repudiated Reeves' testimony and therefore rendered it irrelevant and forgettable.[111]

The incident was far from over, however. Joy Elmer Morgan, who had seen his side battered during these hearings, seized the initiative and interpreted Reeves's testimony as an indication of the New Deal position on radio. He insisted that Dr. Morgan's October 23 statement had not formally repudiated Reeves' testimony but, rather, had simply restated the TVA proposal, since the commercial broadcasters had "misinterpreted" it. On October 26 Morgan sent the text of Reeves's testimony to hundreds of educators and civic leaders and encouraged them to notify the FCC of their support for the measure. Unfortunately for Morgan, other elements of the broadcast reform movement failed to respond to his clarion call. The ACLU, for example, quickly decided that "at present it is not a fight we want to get into," although one member confessed that Reeves's "argument for a federal chain seems sound to me."[112] Nevertheless, the FCC would receive several hundred letters—many of considerable length and thought—endorsing Reeves's TVA proposal over the next few weeks.[113]

The commercial broadcasters responded forcefully, writing to the Payne Fund and all of the educators associated with the NCER to notify them that Joy Elmer Morgan was going against the expressed wishes of the TVA in its October 23 statement and the White House in pursuing this campaign for government radio. James Francis Cooke turned over to NBC all the NCER documents on the matter that he could get his hands on to assist them in their campaign to derail Joy Morgan's TVA-based offensive. Moreover, the FCC wrote to each of the persons who had written to them on behalf of the TVA proposal to inform them that since the TVA had formally withdrawn the proposal, the FCC could no longer consider the proposition of a government network. Robert G. Sproul, who had written such a letter to the FCC in support of the Reeves's TVA proposal at the urging of the NCER, was incensed with Joy Morgan for apparently misleading him with regard to the TVA position. "I am now informed by Mr. Gary [of the FCC] that I have misrepresented the position of the Tennessee Valley Authority, which, according to him, is opposed to a federal chain of radio stations," Sproul wrote to Joy Elmer Morgan. "May I ask for an explanation?"[114]

Joy Morgan's gambit had quickly turned into a disaster, as he was now regarded as having misinterpreted the TVA's real position in addition to promulgating an NCER position in favor of government broadcasting that had never been formally adopted by the group. If this was an example of how "trustworthy" the NCER was "in all its efforts to obtain its objective," one newspaper editor wrote to Joy Morgan on October 29, "then the country would profit by your committee's silence." One NCER board member promised the NAB "that at the next meeting of the Committee I shall be glad to take up this whole matter in detail." Another stated that "this matter has come up more than once during our committee meetings and I am certain that we have never decided that radio should be owned and controlled by the Government." A distraught Tracy Tyler implored one NCER member, who had written angrily to Joy Morgan after receiving an NAB letter, to remember the "selfish interests" that profited from the NCER's disharmony. "Nothing would please the commercial broadcasters' lobby any more than to drive a wedge between members of the committee."[115]

Unfortunately for Joy Elmer Morgan, Dr. Morgan refused to publicly clarify his position on the initial TVA proposal, nor to meet with representatives of the NCER to discuss the matter. Hence, it was the industry's and the FCC's interpretation of the matter that carried the day. "Probably none of us will ever know what happened," Joy Elmer Morgan wrote in a postmortem on the incident shortly thereafter. "If one were to hazard a guess, it would be that the radio 'big-wigs' decided that their best strategy lay in misrepresenting the TVA proposal." "We have reached a sad state in America," Joy Morgan wrote to one NCER member, "when public men like the directors of the Tennessee Valley Authority cannot state their honest convictions without being forced by commercial interests to withdraw their statements."[116]

The second threat to the commercial broadcasters came from organized labor. In contrast to the TVA episode, this was far from unexpected. In September 1934 Edward Nockels resumed negotiations with RCA's Sarnoff and NBC's Aylesworth to provide WCFL with greater power as it presently shared the 970 frequency with NBC affiliate KJR, which was based in Seattle. Nockels was desperate to do whatever he could to keep the financially strapped labor station in existence.[117] During the course of these negotiations, Nockels informed both NBC and the FCC that he intended to support a resolution to the upcoming AFL convention in October calling for no less than 50 percent of the airwaves to be reserved for nonprofit broadcasters. The AFL convention in San Francisco approved of the "50 percent" resolution as well as three others, two similar to it and one, which was submitted by Nockels, calling for the FCC to reserve the 970 frequency exclusively for the use of organized labor. The tenor of the AFL convention was decidedly radical with regard to broadcasting; it considered adopting a resolution for the complete nationalization of broadcasting submitted by delegates from the Pacific Northwest.[118] Nockels apparently viewed the FCC hearings as useful mostly to enhance WCFL's bargaining position with the FCC and the networks; no attempts were made to coordinate labor's position before the FCC with any of the other broadcast reform groups.

On November 8 AFL National Legislative Representative William C. Hushing appeared before the FCC hearings, which reconvened after a two-week recess, to submit the three "radical" AFL convention resolutions for the FCC's consideration. Nevertheless, he was hardly interested in presenting any radical critique of commercial broadcasting. After reading the resolutions into the record, Hushing explained that they were the result of WCFL's "endeavor to get more time on the air and greater distance." The FCC members requested that Hushing go and ask AFL President William Green to come before the hearings to discuss the resolutions. On the following Monday, November 12, Green appeared before the FCC with Nockels. In his capacity as AFL president, Green informed the commissioners that "I now wish to formally withdraw these resolutions from formal consideration by this Commission, and I ask you to disregard the testimony presented by Mr. Hushing when he met with you a few days ago." Green then entered the AFL resolution calling for giving labor sole rights to the 970 frequency into the record and commented that he "would think it a fine gesture" if the FCC would help them reach this goal. The FCC informed Green and Nockels that it would be willing to meet with labor to discuss the matter.[119]

More important, behind the scenes NBC had agreed to immediately resume its negotiations with WCFL to help the station remain solvent in return for the withdrawal of the radical resolutions by organized labor. A tentative agreement making WCFL an NBC affiliate, on unusually generous terms, and granting labor exclusive rights to the 970 frequency was quickly reached by NBC's Frank Russell and Nockels. A refined version of the deal would be put in writing by the first week in December.[120] "This is a great victory for American radio," Russell informed NBC headquarters after Green withdrew the radical AFL radio resolutions. The quid pro quo for NBC in its deal with WCFL, which on the surface seemed to be a total victory for the labor station, was the promise "that no element of Labor will participate in legislation against the existing system when Congress convenes in January."[121] Hence, organized labor, the one remaining element of the reform movement that threatened the commercial broadcasters on Capitol Hill, was now reconciled to the status quo. By 1936 WCFL was broadcasting five hours of NBC programming daily. Nockels remained outspoken in his contempt for commercial broadcasting until his death in 1937, but he kept his word to the broadcasters and discontinued all lobbying for reform legislation.[122]

The third threat to the commercial broadcasters was the least troublesome. Alice Keith, who had served as educational director for RCA in the late 1920s and in a similar capacity for CBS in the early 1930s, testified before the FCC on November 7. Keith was one of the pioneers of the field, having directed radio use for the Cleveland public schools between 1926 and 1928 and having written the first textbook on using radio for education.[123] Keith left CBS in 1932 to protest what she regarded as the network's insincerity about fulfilling its much-ballyhooed commitment to educational broadcasting.[124] After leaving CBS, Keith traveled extensively in Europe, where she studied educational broadcasting in state-run broadcasting systems. She returned to the United States, conducted graduate research at Columbia University, and eventually accepted a position directing radio education at American University in 1935. Keith wrote to the FCC's Gary in late August requesting the right to appear at the hearings to present her views on the capacity of commercial broadcasters to accommodate the educational requirements of the nation. "Personal politics, advertising agency politics, and above all, a profit motive dominate in such a way that a stable, well-organized system of educational programs," she wrote Gary, "is impossible."[125]

In her November 7 testimony, Keith quickly dismissed the claims of the commercial broadcasters that they were deeply concerned with educational programming. "Educational activities were not occupying the minds of the executives who were in authority—and do not mistake, they were in authority. They were much too busy with matters of high finance." Keith explained her experience with the proposed "American School of the Air," which CBS had mentioned prominently in the period immediately following the publication of the Wilbur Report in 1930. "In spite of the many public-relations articles extolling the virtues of a University of the Air, in private council the idea of organized school broadcasting was quashed."[126]

Keith acknowledged that she could not offer a "well-worked out scheme," but she did not hesitate to immediately propose a federal noncommercial educational network supported by a 25-cent annual fee on radio receivers. "Strange as it may seem," she explained, "I am not afraid of government control, not as afraid of government control as of a government controlled."

Keith argued that it was essential "that control of the budget should be in the hands of those whose motives are primarily social and not commercial." Keith's admonitions regarding the status quo were received politely by the commissioners, but were otherwise ignored. The FCC showed no interest in pursuing the inconsistencies between the testimony of the NEA's Hale and the commercial broadcasters on one hand, and Keith on the other hand. The commercial broadcasters did not need to take any action to counteract Keith's testimony as it had no impact and received virtually no publicity.[127]

By the time Keith and organized labor testified, even before the FCC concluded its hearings in the second week of November, there was no doubt in anyone's mind that the FCC would report back to Congress against the fixed-percentage proposal and in favor of the status quo. "We will not upset the applecart," the FCC's Brown informed Martin Codel in an interview over NBC in November.[128] "Things do not look any too rosy," Tyler conceded to Eugene Coltrane. In late November Henry Bellows confidently informed the White House's Early that due to the "widely publicized" FCC hearings, "the criticisms directed against the administration and the old Federal Radio Commission which were occasionally made last year in Congress ought to be pretty well killed off." An editorial in *The Christian Century* of November 14 captured the frustration of the broadcast reform movement.

> After all, it is quite possible that the public may not be convinced of the wisdom of the 25 percent proposal while at the same time it is profoundly dissatisfied with the radio situation as it now stands. And by lining up the testimony at Washington "for" or "against" one specific bill, the commission may have unwittingly (?) given quite a false impression as to whether public opinion is "for" or "against" the present advertising-saturated state of the air.

The editorial concluded, "Of one thing, however, we are convinced. The present situation is thoroughly unsatisfactory."[129]

The FCC Broadcast Division set a November 26 deadline for those hearings participants that wished to submit briefs restating their positions. The NAB submitted a 55,000-word treatise while the NCER and the ACLU elected to pass on this opportunity. WLWL, which had not testified before the FCC on behalf of the fixed-percentage proposal, did submit a forty-two-page brief to the FCC on November 26 that was sharply critical of broadcasting for "private profit." The Paulists were not content to wait for the FCC's report in January to pass judgment on the quality of the just-concluded hearings. In December, the Paulists sent copies of their brief to Catholic parishes and organizations nationwide with a cover letter stating that the FCC

> for the first time in the history of the United States, has recommended to Congress [sic] that a public property—radio broadcasting—be controlled by the power trust for their enrichment rather than have some of those facilities possessed by those not seeking private profit.

In November and December the Paulists also generated 60,000 signatures on a petition demanding that the transcripts of the FCC hearings be published and mailed to each of the signatories. Given the length of the transcripts— nearly 14,000 pages—such a demand was absurd and the issue collapsed.[130]

The final two months of 1934 were gloomy days for the NCER, in view of the impending FCC report. "It seems to me that the commercial broadcasters have got such a firm grip on the situation," the president of the University of Arkansas, a long time NCER loyalist, wrote to Tracy Tyler in December, "that it is going to be difficult for it ever to be broken up." Moreover, the controversy surrounding Morgan's attempt to capitalize on the TVA testimony was hardly the sort of episode that would enthrall the publicity-shy Payne Fund, and it only accentuated the weaknesses of the NCER as a lobbying organization. In a confidential memo to Frances Payne Bolton in November, secretary Ella Phillips Crandall concluded that "the organization and administration of the committee from the beginning has been unsatisfactory." Crandall recommended that the Payne Fund stop its funding of the NCER at the end of its initial five-year grant in 1935 as long as the NCER continued under its existing leadership.[131] The November 20 meeting of the NCER was marked by severe criticism of Morgan, with Morgan responding by shouting "insults," as Perry phrased it, at the assembled educators amid threats to resign. By this time Morgan's health had deteriorated markedly, and he effectively discontinued his role at the NCER after the November 20 meeting. As a result of the meeting, Tyler wrote to educators around the nation to see if they believed there was a need for group like the NCER and, moreover, to determine the nature of that need.[132]

On January 22, 1935, the FCC submitted its report on the study mandated by section 307(c) to Congress. The report stated that the present system was functioning successfully and that there was no need for legislation to set aside channels for the exclusive use of nonprofit and educational broadcasters. At the same time, the report noted that relations were somewhat strained between the broadcasters and educators and, therefore, the report also stated:

> The Commission proposes to hold a national conference at an early date in Washington, at which time plans for mutual cooperation between broadcasters and nonprofit organizations can be made, to the end of combining the educational experiences of the educators with the program technic of the broadcasters, thereby better to serve the public interest.

"I am entirely satisfied with the recommendation and have no concern about any part of it," Frank Russell informed NBC's New York headquarters, noting "the complete justification which the Commission has given to the American System of Broadcasting." Indeed, the FCC had recommended precisely the type of conference Gary and Brown had told Russell they were hoping to convene back at their private meeting as the hearings got underway in October. "I look forward to the Commission's conference with considerable enthusiasm," Russell concluded.[133]

The NCER announced in *Education by Radio* that it would "cooperate wholeheartedly in the conference." It could not fail to notice the irony in the similarity of the FCC report's recommendation to that of the Wilbur Committee over five years earlier, which similarly proposed that educators learn to work through the commercial broadcasters, and where "the clash between the educators and broadcasters was such that the principal recommendations have never been put into effect." In their internal communications, the NCER was less charitable concerning the FCC report. "The report is essentially a 'straddle'—a device for killing time while the commercial interests become more firmly entrenched," Tracy Tyler wrote to the NCER's member organizations.[134]

Indeed, the FCC report had essentially restated the recommendations of the Wilbur Report of January 1930. In this sense, the immediate legacy of the broadcast reform movement was that it had delayed the consolidation of the status quo for five years. Whereas the futility of the Wilbur Report had only given birth to the NCER, the FCC report would seemingly mark the death of the movement for broadcast reform. With the FCC report of January 1935 the statutory consolidation of the status quo was complete. Congress would never again consider fundamental structural questions in its communications deliberations. The legitimacy of network-dominated, advertising-supported broadcasting was now off-limits as a topic of congressional scrutiny. Congress effectively washed its hands of broadcast policy for all time, deeming future debate to be the province of the FCC. The FCC, on the other hand, regarded the status quo as the officially authorized system unless informed otherwise by Congress. This point was not immediately apparent to the NCER or the other reformers, although it would be in short order. When the FCC "recommended against the reservation of radio channels exclusively for the use of education," a 1939 NCER memo would observe, "the long fight of the Committee was ended and a new program had to be developed."[135]

The opportunity for legitimate debate regarding the suitability of a network-dominated, advertising-supported broadcasting system for a democratic society had been successfully postponed from the Roper Committee to the FCSRB to the congressional committee hearings to the FCC Broadcast Division, where the debate took place under circumstances that were far from advantageous to the forces for reform. These FCC hearings still remain the sole instance in which fundamental criticism of the status quo was formally considered by a policymaking body, with all that that suggests about the extent of popular involvement in the formation of U.S. broadcast policy.

In sum, the economic consolidation of commercial broadcasting by 1932 or 1933 was followed by the thorough-going statutory consolidation of the status quo by January 1935. Only one great task remained for the industry, that of establishing ideological closure (i.e., of elevating commercial broadcasting to the point where it was entrenched in the dominant political culture as a natural and benevolent U.S. institution that was both immune to fundamental attack and at the level at which fundamental attack would be unthinkable). With the collapse of organized opposition by 1935, the route to ideological consolidation would prove rapid, even inexorable.

CHAPTER 9

January 1935 and Beyond:
The Ideological Consolidation
of the Status Quo

In the period following the FCC report to Congress in January 1935 the remainder of the broadcast reform movement lost its momentum and collapsed. Moreover, with this collapse, there was little opposition to the widely disseminated promotional claims of the commercial broadcasters that their control of the ether was innately democratic and American; indeed, that no other system could even be conceivable to a freedom-loving people.

A critical new component to this mid- to late–1930s campaign by the networks and their allies was the argument that any government regulation of the status quo whatsoever held the potential to degenerate into a heinous state-censored system with the most ignominious implications for democratic rule. In effect, the industry sought to eliminate any regulation of radio broadcasting whatsoever. Although this campaign was not entirely successful, it laid the way for the emerging dominant paradigm regarding broadcasting in the United States that deemed the control of the ether by commercial broadcasters as inviolable and outside the boundaries of legitimate discussion.

Concurrently, liberal thinkers, who had reacted to the emergence of commercial broadcasting at the beginning of the decade with considerable skepticism if not outright hostility, came to accept commercial broadcasting as the appropriate media structure for the United States. This chapter will evaluate the deregulation campaign of the later 1930s in the context of the overall sanctification of the status quo.

The Collapse of the Broadcast Reform Movement

It is ironic that precisely as the possibility for broadcast reform had been eliminated on Capitol Hill, Senator C. C. Dill, the broadcast reform movement's long-time nemesis, announced in the summer of 1934 that he would not run for re-election for a third term that fall. After this surprise announcement, Dill immediately embarked on a controversial plan to establish a radio news service for the major networks in which he would be an investor and chief executive officer. The newspaper industry was incensed with what it regarded as Dill's brazen attempt to capitalize upon his popularity with the broadcasters following his leading the fight against the Wagner–Hatfield amendment and for the passage of the Communications Act of 1934. After some negotiation with NBC, CBS, and RCA in August and September, 1934, Dill dropped his plans. He then established a private law practice that included several commercial broadcasters as clients. Dill even authored a textbook on radio law in the late 1930s.[1]

Moreover, Dill's replacement as chairman of the SCIC, which considered all radio broadcasting legislation, was Senator Burton Wheeler (D-Mont.), an outspoken critic of commercial broadcasting who had voted for the Wagner–Hatfield amendment. As lobbyist Henry Bellows informed the NAB board of directors in December 1934, "the make-up of the new Congress plays directly into the hands of those who advocate drastic changes in broadcasting." The NCER's Tracy Tyler informed members that the replacement of Senator Dill with "the able" Senator Wheeler would lead to "progressive legislation" on the broadcasting front. "Now that the Commission's report is in," Tyler wrote, "it appears that the next fight will occur in the halls of Congress."[2]

In January 1935, Wheeler even hired the Payne Fund's S. Howard Evans as a "special investigator" on radio for the SCIC to prepare a "Report on Radio Broadcasting." Evans completed his forty-page report for Wheeler in April, in which he noted that given the "small likelihood" that any reform of the status quo was possible, his report would concern itself with "possible improvements which can be made [with]in the present broadcasting structure." As Evans conceded to his old cohort from the *Ventura Free Press* radio campaign, Walter Woehlke, Wheeler had made it clear that he would not be able "to do anything about radio" in Congress. Wheeler's goals were simply to pressure the broadcasters to act more responsibly and to encourage the FCC to regulate the commercial broadcasters more strenuously.[3] Accordingly, the NCER, which was in contact with Wheeler through Evans, did not attempt to lobby for broadcast reform legislation at all during 1935.

This state of affairs soon became apparent to the balance of the reformers. Organized labor was nowhere to be found, having abandoned the fight after labor station WCFL reached an accord with NBC following the FCC hearings in the fall of 1934. Likewise, at about the same time, H. O. Davis notified the Payne Fund that he was formally disbanding the long moribund *Ventura Free Press* radio campaign, informing Ella Phillips Crandall how much he "regretted" that it had been "impossible for us to carry the campaign to a successful end."[4]

Paulist radio station WLWL did remain active into 1935. It first responded to the FCC's January 1935 report by applying to the FCC for a minor reallocation that would have provided WLWL full-time at the 810 frequency, but would have necessitated that several other stations shift frequencies as well. On May 1, 1935, the FCC ruled against WLWL's application and word circulated, as the commercial trade publication *Broadcasting* put it, that "because of the FCC decision" the Paulist lobby would return to Congress and "resume its anti-FCC and anti-network operations at once." By now this was a hollow threat and the Paulists stopped their futile efforts at legislative reform midway through 1935. They continued to use whatever influence they could to pressure the White House, the networks, and the FCC improve the status of WLWL, but to no avail. In 1937 the Paulists sold WLWL to Arde Bulova, the watch manufacturer, for $275,000 and discontinued their broadcasting program.[5] In retrospect, perhaps the Paulists should have agreed to a deal with CBS to give WLWL more broadcast hours in the spring of 1934 in exchange for discontinuing their activity on behalf of the soon-defeated Wagner–Hatfield amendment.

This left the NCER and the Radio Committee of the ACLU as the two remaining standard bearers for broadcast reform. Late in 1934, the NCER had appointed a subcommittee under the direction of Arthur G. Crane to determine a "definite future procedure" and program for the group. The subcommittee made a preliminary report on January 21, 1935, calling for the NCER to formally adopt the government establishment of a series of nonprofit and noncommercial stations as its platform. The call for government-subsidized broadcasting was no great surprise; it had been the overwhelming sentiment at the NCER conference in May 1934 and had been precisely what Floyd Reeves of the TVA had proposed to Joy Elmer Morgan's delight at the FCC hearings in October. On March 25, 1935, the NCER formally approved of the subcommittee's plan for a "national supplemental public broadcasting system." The NCER plan was for the federal government to subsidize a series of local, regional, and national stations that would be managed by independent advisory boards of civic leaders. Nonprofit groups and educational institutions would have access to these governmental facilities, and existing nonprofit stations would be permitted to hook up with the new system.[6]

At long last, the NCER had resolved for a system that addressed the sensitive issues of funding and the role of the government. Arthur Crane became the main advocate for the new NCER plan, informing the Institute for Education by Radio conference in May 1935 that it

> would give America a threefold system of broadcasting: first, the present one open to those wishing to pay the price; second, the government system; and

third, the local stations. Such an opportunity would go far toward protecting the vital thing we call freedom of speech, far toward protecting the voice of minorities so that all sides of controversial issues may be heard.

Crane estimated that the NCER plan would require 10–20 percent of the channels to accommodate the NCER system and that the commercial broadcasters could maintain their control over the remainder. This was hardly any consolation to the broadcasting industry. *Broadcasting* lambasted the NCER proposal as "another hare-brained scheme," while NBC's Frank Russell termed it "the most dangerous thought today on the subject."[7]

Given the inhospitable climate in Congress for broadcast reform, the NCER turned to the FCC for a forum. The FCC announced in March that it would convene a conference to bring educators and commercial broadcasters together in mid-May in Washington, D.C. This conference was the primary recommendation in the FCC's January 1935 report to Congress in response to the hearings mandated by section 307(c) of the Communications Act of 1934. Unfortunately for Crane and the NCER, the FCC's May conference was not designed for any criticism of the status quo or suggestions for reform. At a planning session on May 10 with a few government officials and representatives of NBC, CBS, and the NAB, FCC Chairman Eugene O. Sykes stated that he would "rule out of order any recommendations or suggestions" to alter the status quo because "as a result of the hearings held in October and November . . . there was no need for any change in the present broadcasting structure." This is precisely what Sykes did, informing Crane and the other reformers present that the conference was strictly to work out a plan for educators to utilize existing facilities because the structural issues had already been addressed by the FCC.[8]

Hence, although the FCC permitted Crane to present his scheduled address on May 16, it was inconsequential. As Russell concluded in his memo to NBC's New York headquarters, "I have a very definite feeling that this conference is proceeding in the right direction." Tracy Tyler took the opposite position, noting the rules prohibiting discussion of the NCER proposal: "In reality it could hardly be called a conference." Armstrong Perry observed that the FCC was "friendly" toward the educators, but that "the Commission's point of view" was "essentially that of the broadcasting industry."[9] In any case, the NCER briefly continued to attempt to arouse support for the measure into the summer of 1935, when the plan was quietly abandoned and quickly forgotten as it became obvious that the plan had no chance to be considered seriously, let alone come into existence.[10]

By this time, the NCER, mostly through Crane's subcommittee, was preoccupied with whether it would even exist after the end of 1935, as its initial five-year grant from the Payne Fund was soon to expire. After the FCC hearings, Joy Elmer Morgan was only a titular head of the group. He formally resigned as the NCER's chairman in August 1935 to be replaced by Crane. Morgan's replacement from the NEA on the NCER was Dr. Willis Sutton, who was characterized by an NBC memo as "friendly" to commercial broadcasting. Likewise, the new president of the NEA, Agnes Samuelson, was favorably described in the same memo as "on the conservative side." Perry wrote to Tyler that Samuelson "has accepted so many favors from the commercial stations that she may not be in favor of the point of view of our Committee." These developments also reflected the considerable sentiment gaining ground among educators that the time had come to concede victory to the commercial broadcasters and accept the status quo for better or for worse. As the president of Ohio State University, a staunch advocate of university broadcasting stations, informed Crane in a letter opposing the NCER government radio plan, "attempts to secure a sizable percentage of the existing channels" would precipitate "an open and declared fight with the commercial interests in broadcasting," which would be "unsound and dangerous" for "the whole cause of education by radio."[11] In this context Crane was charged with negotiating another grant from the Payne Fund to continue the NCER.

Nor were the commercial broadcasters content to let the NCER and Payne Fund determine a new path without providing some encouragement of their own. This certainly did not surprise the NCER; in 1934 Perry had written to Evans that "the industry fully understands that if it can get the Fund to withdraw its support commercial radio will have an almost clear field." In early September 1935, two NBC executives met with Frances Payne Bolton and Crandall "to educate them on what the radio industry has actually done to increase the educational habits of our people." One week later, U.S. Representative Clarence E. Hancock (R-NY), a respected acquaintance of Bolton and her husband, Representative Chester C. Bolton, confidentially informed her that if the Payne Fund continued to subsidize a group that lobbied so that "the present broadcasting structure be scrapped," the Payne Fund would no longer be regarded as "acting with the sincere motive of improving the educational status of the youth of America." Rather, he informed her, the Payne Fund might be regarded as "highly controversial" in Washington and, therefore, "the Fund might be in some danger."[12]

When the NCER met two weeks later to discuss its future, the Payne Fund informed the NCER that it might continue to fund the group, at a greatly reduced level, for another year provided the purpose of the NCER be changed to "cooperate with established radio stations and networks." In October, Crandall recommended to Bolton that the Fund continue to support the NCER as long as it would be directed by Crane and Evans, rather than by Tyler or Perry, who were regarded as part of the unsuccessful old regime. Evans took up the cue, preparing a memo for the Payne Fund in November that proposed that the NCER should "change its emphasis during the next two years."[13]

Any conflict with Tyler and Perry was avoided. Tyler announced that he was leaving the NCER to accept a grant from the Rockefeller Foundation to study educational broadcasting in Europe. His position was not filled. By the end of the decade Tyler would accept a position as an associate professor of education at the University of Minnesota, where he developed a graduate curriculum in radio education. In December Perry also resigned and the NCER's Service Bureau and Washington headquarters were shut down. Perry returned to his career as a freelance writer until his death by heart attack in 1938.[14]

On January 18 and 19, 1936, the Payne Fund Executive Committee met with Crane to discuss the future of the NCER. "One thing is clear," Bolton informed Crane. "We can't get into anything which means the violent kind of battle." Crane concurred, stating that the new NCER "should refrain from controversy or an attack," and that its function "should be restricted to educational" work. The Payne Fund agreed to assign Evans to the NCER indefinitely to replace Tyler and to assist Crane in the day-to-day operations of the committee, although he would remain on the Payne Fund payroll. On January 20, 1936, the NCER voted to accept a two-year $15,000 grant from the Payne Fund, on the terms agreed upon by Crane the previous day. The NCER formally moved its headquarters to New York where it would share office space with the Payne Fund. Dr. Arthur Crane was re-elected chairman. On January 23, the Payne Fund's Crandall informed Crane in writing that the Payne Fund grant to the NCER was under the explicit condition that "the Fund does not wish to contribute to political propaganda."[15] The original NCER, adversary of the status quo, was officially dead. The Payne Fund maintained its funding for the NCER until the early 1940s.

In May 1936 the revamped NCER announced a new program for broadcasting that called for the creation of "American Public Radio Boards." These were to be citizen panels that would develop noncommercial educational programs to be aired over the existing commercial facilities.[16] While Crane acknowledged that the plan was far from perfect, he contended that the commercial broadcasters "are anxious to cooperate with educational agencies and groups." Crane generally prefaced his public statements with commendations for the status quo. He introduced one NCER pamphlet by noting that "private enterprise has succeeded in making exceptionally fine broadcasts available to American listeners." In early 1936 *Education by Radio* was even congratulating Owen D. Young, president of General Electric and mentor of the insidious power trust and radio trust in earlier editions of the NCER newsletter, for "making another significant contribution to broadcasting" and "free speech." NBC certainly enhanced the legitimacy of this new-found spirit of cooperation when it hired retiring Yale president, James Rowland Angell, as its educational counselor in 1937 at a salary of $37,000 per year.[17]

In this vein, the NCER discontinued all lobbying efforts. Instead, it became active in the Federal Radio Education Committee (FREC), which was established by the FCC after its May 1935 conference to facilitate educational programming on commercial stations. The FREC held its first meeting in December 1935 and numerous educators were invited to participate along with representatives of the major broadcasting companies. The commercial broadcasters played a prominent role in its development. The NAB agreed to cover one-half of the FREC's expenses. "It does not seem to me," the NBC representative reported back to New York after the first meeting of the FREC, "that we have anything to fear from the Committee." Tracy Tyler expressed the skepticism of the old NCER when he commented that there was "a great deal of dissatisfaction relative to the personnel" of the FREC. "It is heavily loaded with representatives of the broadcasting industry and educators whose connection with the industry," he noted, "may make it difficult for them to assume an impartial attitude." Crane obviously could not accept such a tact. He became chairman of the FREC's Subcommittee on Conflicts and Cooperation. "There is a growing attitude of cooperation," he stated in 1936, "between the Federal Communications Commission, the commercial broadcasters, and the educational groups."[18]

Unfortunately for Crane, the FREC never accomplished its mandate. One prominent educational broadcaster, Harold Engel of the University of Wisconsin, noted after one FREC conference that its function was simply to satisfy the commercial broadcasters and to "bring educational broadcasting into their folds." "As usual the commercial broadcasters painted a rosy picture of what they were doing," he observed, "but most people took that with a grain of salt." The FREC held several conferences in the following years, but, as broadcasting historian George Gibson has observed, the group "got bogged down in planning expensive studies," and "little was done as a result of the conferences." "The activity went on for years," Erik Barnouw has noted. "To some it seemed that educators had skillfully been shunted into busy work."[19]

Unlike Crane, Evans never abandoned his thorough dislike of commercial broadcasting. "A psychology has been created in this country under which the business of broadcasting is recognized to be a commercial enterprise," he wrote to Crane in 1936. "If only we will stay away from the fundamental problem and not disturb the commercial boys or the other educators, everybody will be happy." Evans concluded this memorandum by describing himself as "advocating Christianity in a world that is decidedly pagan." Evans nonetheless eventually reconciled himself to the futility of reform, accepted the status quo begrudgingly, and proceeded accordingly. His primary activity as NCER secretary in the late 1930s was to encourage the FCC to engage in more vociferous regulation of the status quo. By 1939 even this stance put Evans at odds with the dominant sentiment within the Payne Fund, not to mention the political culture writ large. In 1939 he was asked by the Payne Fund secretary to defend his position that the FCC had the right to regulate the programming of commercial broadcasters, which she now regarded as perhaps constituting a violation of the commercial broadcasters' First Amendment rights. A discouraged Evans acknowledged that "a disagreement seems to have developed which promises to be both fundamental and continuing."[20] Evans subsequently resigned his position; if the NCER was no longer in favor of aggressive regulation of commercial broadcasting in the public interest, then there was little for him to do. By this time, however, the NCER was a group of little significance. When the Payne Fund terminated the NCER at the end of 1941, the event received almost no notice.

Indeed, the late 1930s and early 1940s were far from halcyon days to many educators concerned with broadcasting. By 1936, only thirty educational stations remained, and most of these were still enmeshed in dire financial straits that were seemingly inescapable. This was a period of coming to grips with the marginal situation of educational and nonprofit broadcasters, acknowledging the dominance of commercial broadcasting, and hoping, with minimal leverage, to exact concessions from the FCC and the networks.[21] The major development during this period was the plan to place educational broadcasters on the new, experimental ultrahigh frequency band. A similar proposal had been floated by Senator Dill and the old FRC in early 1934, which would have put educators on a new experimental band between 1,500 and 1,600 kilocycles, a band that few existing radio receivers could pick up. At that time, the proposal was dismissed categorically. "The administration felt the need of shutting up every discordant element in broadcasting," Armstrong Perry explained at the time, "and is just trying to find the easy way out." As Perry put it then, the FRC "would let the educational stations do the experimental work," just like the college stations had largely pioneered radio broadcasting in the early 1920s, "and then perhaps would take away the channels and allocate them for commercial use."[22]

Given the irreversible nature of the commercial broadcasting on the AM band, however, and given the seeming impotence of the FREC, this alternative appeared increasingly attractive as time passed, and would eventually become the only viable option for educators to pursue. Finally, in 1940, the FCC announced that educational stations would be given exclusive right to develop the new FM band, which would be authorized to begin operations in 1941.[23] This was characterized as "educational radio's second chance," and educators were warned not to botch this opportunity as they had with AM broadcasting in the 1920s and 1930s.[24] This and all subsequent campaigns to reserve a space for nonprofit broadcasting in the United States, however, were pale comparisons to the movement of the early 1930s. To paraphrase Marx, if the experience of the NCER and the other 1930s reformers was tragic, the later campaigns appear mostly as farce. They could be successful or secure only to the extent that they did not interfere with the profitability, existing or potential, of commercial broadcasters (i.e., to the extent they were ineffectual).[25]

The demise of the broadcast reform movement and the creation of the FREC seemed to constitute a decisive victory for the NCER's primary competitor for the allegiance of the educational community, the NACRE, which had championed the plausibility of cooperation between educators and commercial broadcasters since its inception in 1930. As Armstrong Perry observed in one of his final memos for the NCER, the NACRE "is well advanced in its plans to secure quasi-official standing with the United States government and place itself in a position to control, to a considerable extent, the use of public radio channels for educational purposes."[26] Not far below the surface, however, the long-festering antagonism between the industry and the NACRE was growing more intense. In the summer of 1934 NBC and CBS executives confidentially informed the Carnegie Corporation that the NACRE was held in low regard and there was no longer a great need for such an organization. One industry observer commented that NACRE officials seem most interested in "the keeping of their jobs with the salaries that go with them."[27] The feelings were mutual. Indeed, precisely as the NCER found itself embracing the status quo and rejecting structural reform, the NACRE released a major study denouncing cooperation as unworkable and failed.

This study, *Four Years of Network Broadcasting,* was produced by the Committee on Civic Education by Radio, which was co-sponsored by the NACRE and the American Political Science Association. The report evaluated the relationship of the NACRE and NBC between 1932 and 1936. The fifteen-member Committee on Civic Education was mostly comprised of academics, including Charles A. Beard and Charles E. Merriam, and was chaired by Professor Thomas Reed of the University of Michigan. The report observed:

> Our experience has demonstrated a conflict between the commercial interests of the Broadcasting Company and the educational uses of radio which threatens to become almost fatal to the latter. Educational broadcasting has become the poor relation of commercial broadcasting, and the pauperization of the former has increased in direct proportion to the growing affluence of the latter.

The report concluded:

> [I]n view of the double conflict between the commercial and educational interests and between the chains and their individual stations, it is useless at this time to attempt systematic education by national network broadcasting at hours when it will be available to large adult audiences.[28]

NBC was incensed by the report. Even more upsetting to NBC, the report in December 1936 was officially submitted to the first National Conference

on Education Broadcasting (NCEB), which had been organized by the Institute for Education by Radio in conjunction with the FCC and the U.S.
Office of Education. The report was scheduled to be published as part of the
proceedings of the NCEB conference. NBC Vice-President John Royal wrote
to NCEB Chairman and former U.S. Commissioner of Education George
Zook demanding that the NACRE report not be published in the proceedings,
as it contained a "very serious attack on NBC" due to "malicious intent on
the part of those who put it together." David Sarnoff also protested to Zook,
noting that "this does not seem in accordance with the spirit and purpose of
the meeting." Zook immediately wired back that he had decided not
to include the NACRE report in the published proceedings after all. The
NACRE's director, Levering Tyson, wrote to Zook repeatedly demanding
that *Four Years of Network Broadcasting* be published as originally planned.
"If *now* the document is *not* included in the proceedings, I am confident that
its omission will stir up quite a storm. For it is already known," Tyson
warned Zook, that NBC "is trying to move heaven and earth the prevent its
publication" [his emphasis]. Zook refused to budge, claiming that NBC had
no influence over his decision.[29]

Tyson also wrote to NBC to protest the aspersions they were casting
regarding the report's credibility. He noted the thoroughness of the Committee on Civic Education by Radio's research and demanded that NBC
provide him with a written statement of any alleged "inaccuracies." Tyson
then arranged to have the report published by the University of Chicago Press
in 1937. One NBC executive termed it "Tyson's last dying kick." The
executive went on to note that "nearly everyone in educational circles knows
that the report was malicious, because Professor Reed has no standing."
Reed's credibility, however, was held in much higher regard by the broadcasting industry when he testified on behalf of the status quo at the FCC
hearings in October 1934. In his relatively well-publicized testimony, Reed
commended NBC unequivocally for being "helpfully cooperative and thoroughly sympathetic with our purposes."[30]

This episode ushered in the demise of the NACRE. Tyson resigned almost
immediately thereafter, at the urging of NBC, and accepted the position of
president at Muhlenberg College in Pennsylvania. The NACRE would disband as well in the summer of 1937. "I have only one regret," Tyson wrote
to NBC on his last day at the NACRE in July 1937. "It is that I was so
dense that I didn't recognize six or seven years ago the futility of trying to
mix oil and water." Ironically, in December 1937 Tyson came out for having
the government conduct a sweeping "royal commission" study of U.S.
broadcasting, similar to the one proposed by the NCER and the ACLU in
the early 1930s, which would establish a viable nonprofit and noncommercial
sector on the broadcast spectrum.[31] Tyson, however, was anything but re-
pentant otherwise. He insisted thereafter that the demise of the NACRE and

its cooperation approach was due mostly to the NCER, which Tyson claimed had antagonized the commercial broadcasters irreparably with its radical rhetoric in the early 1930s. As a result, Tyson asserted, when the industry was still in its infancy and pliable, the NCER had soured it on cooperating with educators. Tyson maintained a debate in correspondence with the NCER's Evans over this point for several years.[32]

The NCER could not help but take notice of Tyson's resignation and the collapse of the NACRE, although it failed to see its responsibility for the events. "In spite of Dr. Tyson's efforts," *Education by Radio* observed regarding the NACRE's cooperation doctrine, "the experiment failed." The NCER also noted that the findings of *Four Years of Network Broadcasting* clearly "repudiated" the evidence upon which the FCC had ruled against reserving frequencies for educational institutions in 1934 and 1935. Evans even suggested in early 1937 that the FCC might wish to reconsider its findings from those hearings.[33] By this time, however, any possibility of structural reform had long since passed. Although the NACRE had an inglorious conclusion to its brief career, it was hardly an abject failure. It had served a vital function for the commercial broadcasters. It was perhaps not entirely coincidental that the NACRE's demise corresponded precisely to the historical moment that the industry no longer needed such a group.

In contrast to the rather sudden transformation of the NCER, and the quick collapse of the NACRE for that matter, the transformation of the ACLU's attitude toward commercial broadcasting was more gradual, yet no less compelling. Indeed, the adaptation of the ACLU from a position of hostility to the status quo to one eventually of defending the status quo is extremely important to understanding the emerging liberal acceptance of commercial broadcasting as the best possible, if not only imaginable, broadcasting set-up for a democratic society. Moreover, the ACLU Radio Committee was the last element of the broadcast reform movement to abandon the fight; it explicitly lobbied for broadcast reform legislation for several more years, despite the readily apparent futility of the cause.

The ACLU Radio Committee also was unimpressed by the FCC's January 1935 report and proposed conference, particularly when it was rebuffed in its efforts to have the FCC's conference make a broad evaluation of what they regarded as the defects in U.S. broadcasting. In March 1935 the Radio Committee concluded that the FCC's conference "will probably not get very far," and concluded that any reform would have to come through legislation. This sentiment was reinforced when the FCC informed the ACLU that it was powerless to deal with ACLU complaints of station censorship and, furthermore, that the FCC could not even consider these incidents of censorship at an individual station's license renewal hearing. "There's no redress at all except through legislation," ACLU publicity director Clifton Read informed one Radio Committee member.[34]

The ACLU Radio Committee prepared three bills and one resolution for congressional consideration in the spring and summer of 1935. The bills called for: (1) Requiring commercial broadcasters to set aside time for non-commercial, uncensored discussion of social and political problems, with the program to be administered by an independent advisory committee; (2) That stations not be liable for civil or criminal action for anything said during these nonprofit periods; and (3) That each station be required to maintain strict and accurate records of all its dealings with groups requesting access to its frequency. The resolution called for the establishment of a "Broadcasting Research Commission" to conduct a thorough study of U.S. broadcasting that would provide the basis for reform legislation. The resolution suggested many areas to be studied, including the feasibility of a government-owned and/or -operated network.[35]

The ACLU quickly discovered that there was little interest in broadcast reform on Capitol Hill, to the point that it took it several months even to find a congressional sponsor for their bills. The traditional liberal allies of the ACLU showed no interest in being connected to the legislation. Senator Robert F. Wagner, for example, showed initial interest, but decided not to act as a sponsor after consulting David Sarnoff. The Radio Committee became so desperate that they even put the matter to their arch-enemy, conservative Representative Hamilton Fish (R-NY), with no more success. Finally, Representative Byron Scott (D-Cal.) agreed to be the sponsor, and he introduced the legislation in August 1935. Clifton Read described Scott as a "liberal though unimportant congressman."[36]

Even equipped with a sponsor, the bills failed to receive hearings at the committee level, let alone reach the floor for a vote. The Radio Committee attempted to generate popular support for the measures with press releases and pamphlets, but they enjoyed very little success. Read would complain that "the many advocates of government ownership of radio don't seem to get excited" over the bills, while other sympathetic forces "who recognize that radio presents a certain problem are by and large unwilling to risk offending the broadcasters by even backing these bills." The ACLU only received seven acknowledgments when it sent out a sixteen-page pamphlet on behalf of their legislation to 535 members of Congress in January 1936. A desperate Roger Baldwin even tried to gain support for the measures from Merlin Aylesworth; he asked for a meeting "to determine how far apart we are." Russell advised Aylesworth to inform Baldwin that "we will have to oppose all these bills," with the possible exception of the bill reducing the liability of the commercial broadcasters for statements made over the air.[37]

By the end of 1935, radio committee member Henry Eckstein acknowledged the futility of the group's efforts in Congress and admitted to Read, "it looks like we had no job." Eckstein confessed to Bethuel M. Webster, Jr., a few months later that, "we are certainly not getting any real interest or excitement in this whole thing."[38] By 1937 the ACLU's chief Washington, D.C., lobbyist informed the New York headquarters that Scott "has not done anything or intends to do anything with these bills." The lobbyist concluded that Scott appeared to have a strong desire to "avoid any kind of real fight" with the "radio monopolies." A few months later the radio committee, noting that "the big broadcasting chains are very strong with the administration," concluded that their legislation had no future. "The whole radio picture looks very sad." In desperation, the Radio Committee dropped its resolution calling for an independent study of broadcasting and emphasized that their remaining bills would not affect "the present radio set-up."[39]

This last gambit failed. In a few months the radio committee gave up all hope of having any of their bills considered by Congress. Key members of congress informed Morris Ernst that the only hope for the ACLU was to have the FCC take up some of their issues in their proposed study of chain broadcasting, which had been announced to much fanfare in March 1938. Eckstein observed that the FCC study made it "totally impossible" to press ahead with the legislation and leaves "us almost nothing to do on the subject."[40] As Eckstein noted in 1938, perhaps "we have reached a point where we have to decide that our whole radio work is futile and stop making meaningless gestures."[41]

Rather than dispense with any efforts in the area of broadcasting, however, the Radio Committee merely adapted to the seemingly irreversible contours of U.S. commercial broadcasting and attempted to make the best of the existing situation. It was only a matter of time for the ACLU, which at all times was a practical and activist group operating in the political mainstream, albeit on the liberal wing, to shed what had become largely an academic critique of commercial broadcasting that had no bearing on the operations of the industry.

By 1938 both Bethuel M. Webster, Jr., and Levering Tyson had resigned from the Radio Committee, while Norman Thomas was a titular member at best. The ACLU decided to replace them on the Radio Committee with representatives of the broadcasting and advertising industries, and thus earn credibility for their concerns regarding free expression issues. They found little immediate interest. Well-known professional broadcasters with liberal sympathies like Edward R. Murrow and Raymond Gram Swing were then asked to join the committee, but they declined. Murrow was an obvious choice. *Education by Radio* called him "the most sympathetic friend education has had in the network offices." "He is definitely liberal in personal viewpoints," Eckstein enthused, and "he takes rather great pride in his membership in the ACLU." Unfortunately, though, Murrow was off to Europe to become the CBS European director. As for Swing, he admitted that if he accepted the position his reputation "in the minds of the commercial chains as anything from a liberal to a dangerous radical'' would ''perhaps become insurmountable'' and end his career.[42]

Undaunted, the ACLU decided in May 1938 to establish a confidential advisory board to the Radio Committee that would be comprised of industry people ''who can aid us from their experience in our efforts to gain greater freedom of the air.'' Representatives of the networks and the AAAA, as well as David Sarnoff, were approached to suggest candidates. All interested parties were informed that their identities would not be ''publicized in any way.''[43] At the same time, the ACLU formally repudiated any interest in reform legislation, and professed that the radio committee was very much concerned with the free speech concerns of the commercial broadcasters. This stratagem worked; the Radio Committee found a permanent niche upon accepting the status quo, with an agenda as focused on protecting commercial broadcasters from government harassment as with protecting the public interest from the consequences of having a network-dominated, advertising-supported broadcasting set-up.

Free Speech and Ideological Closure

The ACLU Radio Committee's transformation from a stance that regarded commercial broadcasting as fundamentally flawed to one of regarding the status quo as fundamentally sound becomes more understandable in the context of the broader ideological developments regarding U.S. broadcasting in the second half of the 1930s. For it was in the period immediately following the passage of the Communications Act of 1934 that the commercial broadcasters became enshrined in the dominant culture as, in the words of broadcast historian Philip Rosen, ''the purveyors of the unqualified truth, a sort of holy grail, if you will, of good judgment and sound vision.''[44] The commercial broadcasters actively cultivated the notion that the status quo was innately democratic and that even the consideration of alternatives was absurd, if not dangerous. With no broadcast reform movement in existence to dispute these claims, they went from being unchallenged to unchallengeable.

Many of the themes in this ideological campaign, particularly the emphasis on Americanism and the power of listeners effectively to control broadcasting through the marketplace, had been stressed prior to 1934, when the commercial broadcasters had struggled to establish the legitimacy of their control of the ether in the face the broadcast reform movement's challenge. A primary purpose of this campaign was to assure that the broadcasters would have minimal governmental or public interference with their affairs. ''Self-regulation,'' David Sarnoff informed the FCC in 1938, ''is the American answer to an American problem.'' The other legitimate regulator of broadcasting, Sarnoff asserted, was the body of radio listeners, who "by their control of the Nation's radio dials . . . decide the ultimate fate of the broadcaster. Here we find legitimate censorship by public opinion." He concluded that these two mechanisms constituted "the democratic way in a democratic country."[45]

A major new theme, however, was the emphasis on the need for commercial broadcasters to be protected from the threat of government censorship, which was now argued to be implicit in any form of government regulation.[46] In 1936 Sarnoff stated:

> I believe that a free radio and a free democracy are inseparable; that we cannot have a controlled radio and retain a democracy; that when a free radio goes, so also goes free speech, free press, freedom of worship, and freedom of education.[47]

Suddenly, the right of the government to regulate broadcasting, which had been accepted, if not demanded, by the commercial broadcasting industry in the years before 1934, was being questioned, primarily due to its being a threat to the First Amendment rights of broadcasters and the general communication requirements of a democratic society.

Louis G. Caldwell, the foremost commercial broadcasting attorney in the United States, emerged as the most prolific figure in the group of writers who would publicize the threat to free speech implicit in government regulation of broadcasting. He threw down the gauntlet in a speech before the ACLU in December 1934 in which he attacked the group for

> advocating what seems to me an inconsistent and indefensible view on radio censorship. The evil to be avoided—if we have any regard for the lessons of history—is *governmental* restraint on liberty of expression, whether imposed by hereditary monarchs or democratic majorities. [his emphasis]

In an article published in the *Annals of the American Academy of Political and Social Science* the following month, Caldwell rejected the ACLU's concern with "private censorship" as entirely unfounded. He claimed it was simply the same thing as the "editorial selection" exercised by newspapers and magazines.

> In a word, the alternative is between so-called private censorship, and actual government censorship, and the latter is the evil against which the First Amendment is directed.[48]

The *Annals* article reflected a strong concern for the free expression needs of a democratic society. "With the present governmental power to regulate speech by radio, the clock of liberty has been set back three hundred years," Caldwell stated. The article cited no less than John Stuart Mill, Tolstoy, Mr. Justice Holmes, and Voltaire ("I do not agree with a word you say, but I will defend to the death your right to say it.'') in Caldwell's effort to emphasize the significance of his argument:

> The scope of freedom of speech by radio should be no whit less than the scope of freedom of the press, not only for the sake of the broadcaster and his listening public, but as well for the sake of the publisher and his reading public.

In another article Caldwell noted that ''the ordinances of the Star Chamber were strikingly like the radio title of the Communications Act of 1934 as it has been interpreted.''[49]

This concern with government censorship was not simply a fear that the FCC might harass specific broadcasters or specific programs, it went to the very notion that the licensing of stations was a particularly foreboding violation of the First Amendment. Through the right to license, the FCC held a ''Damoclean sword'' over the conduct of every broadcaster, Seymour N. Siegel, a protege of Caldwell, noted in the *Air Law Review*. ''The net result,'' Siegel concluded, ''is that every broadcaster awaits with fear and trembling, the action of the Federal Communications Commission.'' Caldwell, and indeed most of the authors advancing this argument, recognized that this concern with FCC harassment of private broadcasters was largely theoretical, as actual instances of government censorship and license revocation were few and far between. The actual track record was unimportant to Caldwell. Merely granting the government the right to regulate broadcasting, he argued, was similar to ''the erection of a guillotine,'' which, were ''a state of national hysteria'' to emerge, would almost certainly develop into a situation similar to what had transpired with broadcasting in Nazi Germany.[50]

Moreover, there was no continued justification for broadcast regulation on the grounds of the ether being a scarce resource, thereby restricting access to those citizens willing to pay the price but unable to find a frequency. Caldwell acknowledged:

> It is true that scientifically there is a limit to the total facilities available for radio stations. Yet in most of the large cities there are actually more broadcast stations in operation than there are newspapers, so that apparently the physical limitations are not more serious than the economic.

Linking the situation of broadcasters to newspapers was a staple insight of these articles. In effect, Caldwell, Siegel, and the commercial broadcasting industry were attaching broadcasting to the ideological and legal coattails of the unchallengable newspaper industry.[51]

Nor was the newspaper industry of any mind to contest the broadcasters' claims in this regard. The so-called press–radio war of the early 1930s was a distant memory by now, with harmonious and mutually beneficial relations the order of the day. In 1937 an eleven-part series on ''Radio and the Newspapers'' in the newspaper trade publication *Editor & Publisher* proclaimed that the concerns of the two industries were "inseparable," that "the continuance of the American system of broadcasting is vital," and that maintaining commercial broadcasting "is an obligation the industry must meet." That same year the ANPA resolved that the two industries needed to coordinate their activities in their mutual self-interest. If only of symbolic importance, Merlin Aylesworth left NBC and soon became director of the Scripps–Howard newspaper chain's broadcasting properties.[52]

Caldwell and the mid–1930s deregulationists made several fundamental revisions from the positions of Caldwell and the ABA Standing Committee on Communications in the period from 1929–1932. First, the FCC was now criticized for having the audacity to engage in "making regulations and issuing orders," thereby inappropriately "exercising legislative functions." Second, the phrase "public interest, convenience, or necessity" was now denounced for providing a "vague and variable standard of conduct." "The phrase public interest, convenience, or necessity," Caldwell observed in 1935, "has proven to be the Achilles' heel by which a serious wound has been inflicted upon the First Amendment to the constitution."[53]

This was the same Louis G. Caldwell who, in 1930, stated that his "ideal law" for "regulating radio communication within the United States" would recognize that "the licensing authority must have a far-reaching power to reject applications for licenses." This radio administration "must have a life-and-death power over the radio conduct of its subjects such as it neither has or desires over their conduct in other matters." Caldwell insisted in 1930 that "such matters cannot safely be prescribed by statute" and were "unsuited for decision by a legislative body." He would conclude that the Radio Act of 1927 came very close to being precisely this "ideal law," particularly due to the vagueness of the only criteria the law gave the FRC to evaluate potential broadcasters, that of public interest, convenience, or necessity. "While this phrase may seem broad and vague," Caldwell concluded at the time, "any more specific test would have been dangerous."[54]

Third, the true intent of the Radio Act of 1927, it was now argued, was to establish mere "traffic regulation," to prevent interference, for an already existing private, commercial system. That the FRC had failed to recognize this limited mandate, according to Caldwell in 1935, was due to the un- fortunate vagueness of the term public interest, convenience, or necessity, which let the FRC assume far more power than it was intended to have.[55] In short, U.S. broadcasting was now deemed to have been profit-driven and advertising-oriented since its inception. The previous fifteen years of struggle and debate over the control and structure of U.S. broadcasting had been erased from history along with the entire reallocation of the ether engineered by the FRC in 1928, as had been demanded by Congress when it created and funded the FRC.

This historical revisionism took two forms. The dominant form, and the one preferred by Caldwell and the industry, asserted that commercial broadcasting was not the conscious result of public policy deliberation as much as it was the only conceivable manner to organize the ether in the context of American democracy. Public policy debate had been unnecessary as there was nothing for the public to discuss. In 1938 David Sarnoff informed a nationwide audience over an NBC network that

> Our American system of broadcasting is what it is because it operates in the American democracy. It is a free system because this is a free country. It is privately owned because private ownership is one of our national doctrines. It is privately supported, through commercial sponsorship of a portion of the program hours, and at no cost to the listener, because ours is a free economic system. No special laws had to be passed to bring these things about. They were already implicit in the American system, ready and waiting for broadcasting when it came.[56]

The same year, NAB researcher and University of Pennsylvania economist Herman S. Hettinger noted that "the fundamental assumptions underlying American broadcasting have been clear since the very beginning of radio." He concluded that all subsequent discussion and legislation regarding broadcasting "proceeded from one premise: the desirability of a privately owned, competitively operated system of broadcasting." For Louis G. Caldwell this notion that U.S. broadcasting adopted its modern structure by acclamation from its very beginning seemingly was the result of considerable rethinking on his part. In 1931 his ABA communications committee had conceded that as late as the mid–1920s, "the conception of broadcasting as a business, with sale of time as its economic basis, was held by only a few."[57]

The second bit of revisionism was less common, but no more accurate. This form asserted that commercial broadcasting was the result of a comprehensive and exhaustive examination of all the options available to the American people. As FCC member Thad H. Brown put it, both the Roper Committee and Congress had given "careful consideration of every phase" of communications and broadcasting in 1933 and 1934 and there were "extensive hearings" to develop the suitable statute for broadcast legislation. Proponents of the status quo seemingly could adopt both of these two contrasting interpretations with little concern for consistency. Hence, at another point in the previously cited article, Hettinger also claimed that the private, commercial basis of U.S. broadcasting "was selected from a number of alternative forms of economic organization, including government ownership, because it was believed that it would contribute most to the public good."[58] Apparently, once any possibility for debate had been foreclosed, in the wake of the FCC report to Congress in January 1935, those that had battled with all their might to prohibit or render impotent any public or congressional debate regarding broadcasting could then assert that the system was the result of precisely such a debate, thereby rendering any further debate unnecessary.

Both of these interpretations removed the very existence of any formal opposition to the status quo in the late 1920s and early 1930s from the history of the industry, replacing it with a dominant "consensus" vision of an inherently democratic and popularly embraced commercial system. This erasure of the broadcast reform movement from broadcasting history was more than the handiwork of the industry and its allies, although their work was critical.[59] It was also expedited by the refusal of important reformers to insist on their place in history, which left the story to be told by those who were gainfully cooperating with the commercial broadcasters in the late 1930s and beyond. For example, Henry Ewbank who attacked commercial broadcasting at the FCC hearings in October 1934, would go on to write a leading textbook on broadcasting in the early 1950s that ignored the broadcast reform movement and accepted commercial broadcasting as the natural American system.[60] The NCER, in three separate histories it prepared of itself between 1936 and 1942, refused to acknowledge the group's radical critique of the status quo and twice flatly ignored the proposal for a government network in 1935. Indeed, these authorized histories, which in one instance eliminated the role played by Joy Elmer Morgan altogether, made the NCER seem much more like the NACRE than the NCER. One educator wrote a historical review of educational broadcasting in 1939 that characterized the NCER's early years as "colorful." It then noted that they "laid the foundation necessary for the present-day spirit of cooperation in which many commercial broadcasters seek out the assistance of educational interests in the production of programs."[61]

What makes this deregulation campaign all the more remarkable is that there were no instances of the FCC revoking a broadcaster's license due to programming during this period. As mentioned earlier, the FCC had gone on record in 1935 as saying that it *could not* take a station's programming into consideration when license renewal applications were reviewed, and that it did not countenance the notion of "private censorship." Moreover, the entire thrust of the criticism of the status quo by the broadcast reform movement was that the natural inclination of the commercial broadcasters was to air trivial programming and to ignore less profitable, and more controversial, serious social and political programming. "Amos 'n' Andy" seemed to typify commercial broadcasting far more than the images of James Franklin and John Peter Zenger that Caldwell and the deregulationists were providing. A 1936 ACLU study concluded that U.S. broadcasting was typified by "the shameful condition of a public medium on which crooners are commonly considered more important than discussion of vital political and social issues."[62] It was this assessment that kept the ACLU in the battle for broadcast reform long after it had become obvious that the commercial broadcasters were immune to political challenge.

The question that becomes inescapable, then, is why this sudden concern about broadcasters' First Amendment rights? Furthermore, why the sudden 180-degree shift on the value of having a high-powered regulatory agency with minimal congressional, public, or statutory direction? To some extent, this may be attributed to the emergence by 1933 of the Nazis in Germany and fascist movements worldwide.[63] To a greater extent, however, without trivializing the very legitimate issue of government censorship or questioning the sincerity of those making the deregulation argument, its seems plausible that this sudden interest in free expression was fueled by a desire to remove any government intervention that could inhibit profitability. When the FRC applied the vague concept of public interest, convenience, or necessity to stabilize the ether and provide a profitable climate for capitalist broadcasters, not a word was uttered by Louis Caldwell or the commercial broadcasters equating the FRC to the Star Chamber. Nor did Caldwell express much concern for the First Amendment rights of the displaced nonprofit broadcasters and the listeners that would no longer be able to hear them.

Once the important task of establishing a profitable and stable industry had been completed, and private broadcasting was on a secure and unchallengable basis, however, further regulation in the "public interest" increasingly held the potential of infringing upon the interests of the commercial broadcasters. Hence the First Amendment was appropriated as trade legislation and brandished to remove the last vestiges of public control of the airwaves. Indeed, to have engaged in a no-holds-barred discussion of the free speech implications of the broadcasting set-up *prior* to the economic and legislative consolidation of the status quo would have played right into the hands of the broadcast reform movement; hence, prior to 1934 the issue of the free speech implications of licensing and regulation was mentioned mostly in passing by proponents of capitalist broadcasting.

This assault on the right of the government to regulate broadcasting did not go unanswered. The ACLU Radio Committee's Webster responded to Caldwell's arguments in a series of letters, speeches, and memos between 1934 and 1937. "There are few evidences of governmental interference and so many evidences of abuse of the power of 'editorial selection' by network and station owners," Webster informed the 1935 annual meeting of the ACLU, thereby explaining the Radio Committee's decision to continue to "tackle vigorously" the issue of private censorship. Webster was singularly unimpressed with Caldwell's claims and he could not help but notice the contradictory shifts in Caldwell's positions. Moreover, he was not afraid to note how Caldwell's opinions had been "shaped," albeit "unconsciously," by his legal work on behalf of commercial broadcasters. "I have to fight a tendency to swallow this kind of language hook, line, and sinker,'' Webster admitted to Henry Eckstein regarding Caldwell's invective, "for it sounds grand and I like it.'' Having said that, Webster added, "I think that in this respect Mr. Caldwell is tilting at a windmill, that interference by network and station owners is a daily reality, whereas the interference Mr. Caldwell seems chiefly to oppose is a phantom.''[64]

Nevertheless, as Webster's own language indicates, this campaign by Caldwell and the commercial broadcasters struck a very sensitive chord among ACLU members and found an increasingly sympathetic response. The ACLU received correspondence in the mid- and late 1930s asking, incredulously, if it was in favor of government censorship of broadcasting. In 1936 the ACLU's chief Washington lobbyist wrote to Webster that most of the arguments he encountered against the ACLU broadcast reform legislation were on the basis of the feeling that the bills would permit the government to dictate radio content. "I confess,'' he concluded, "that I am somewhat troubled by the thought that the bills possibly represent in part a principle which is essentially false to civil liberty.''[65] As the private, commercial basis of U.S. broadcasting became almost sacrosanct in the later 1930s, these arguments gained an enormous amount of momentum. Indeed, as the status quo became accepted as fundamentally democratic and "American,'' the government moved inexorably to its logical position as the primary threat to free speech in broadcasting.

By 1938, for both philosophical and practical reasons, the ACLU repudiated the notion that society had a right, through government action, to be concerned about "private'' censorship in an oligopolistic broadcasting set-up:

> With respect to the material presented, it is a private enterprise in the same respect in which newspapers, magazines and motion pictures and theatrical producing organizations are private enterprises and radio stations should have the same discretion in refusing to anyone the use of their facilities.

Two weeks later the ACLU restated this position in a widely distributed press release: "Radio stations are private institutions. It is only when the federal licensing authority interferes that a clear issue of censorship arises.'' For a group that had been founded upon a fear of repressive government intervention, and which had that fear visited upon it repeatedly, it was probably not especially difficult for it to increasingly accept the notion that government intervention portended more evil than good.[66]

For several years members of the ACLU even maintained a healthy critique of the limitations of the status quo all the while suggesting reforms that scarcely challenged and often enhanced the status quo. In 1946, for example, Morris Ernst would attack commercial broadcasting for depriving "large sectors of society'' a chance to "get through the bottlenecks of the air.'' He would conclude that, "Radio has not given listeners the diversity of points of view to which a democratic society is entitled." Ernst would go so far as to proclaim that reform of broadcasting was impossible, not because it was necessarily undesirable, but because "the cohesion of business sentiment of the press and radio has never allowed these ideas to filter out to a forum of public discussion or wide consideration." Yet Ernst, always the most radical member of the Radio Committee in the 1930s, was not immune to the shifting ideological currents. In the same chapter he described commercial broadcasting as an example of "the genius of freedom in the United States."[67]

Nevertheless, the campaign for the complete deregulation of broadcasting was not entirely successful. What emerged as the dominant paradigm for U.S. broadcasting by the end of the 1930s was the notion of an industry that was subject to government regulation, but only after self-regulation and the marketplace had proven to be abject failures. FCC Vice-Chairman Irvin Stewart presented the theoretical justification for the government to play a significant regulatory role in a seminal law review article in 1937. After acknowledging that the basis of U.S. radio was quite properly private and commercial, Stewart noted that since the "primary consideration" of the broadcaster is "financial return," then the government had to reserve the right to protect the public interest.

> "Public interest" is more than a phrase to which an applicant for broadcast facilities must give lip service. It is a constant reminder that the station licensee has the temporary use free of all charge of an invaluable facility which belongs to all the people. The American people control the frequencies which are the sine non qua of broadcasting; they have made a temporary and condition loan of those frequencies to the present licensees of broadcast stations. The condition is that the operation of these stations will be in the public interest.[68]

Following Stewart's lead, the ACLU gravitated to the left flank of the dominant paradigm. Henry Eckstein observed:

> However public-spirited and sincere the broadcasting companies may be, they cannot be representative of the public interest; that if there is to be any control by anyone, there is no reason why the public should entrust itself to even the most altruistic and idealistic industrial group than to a government agency.[69]

By the end of the decade, the commercial broadcasters as well as Caldwell and Siegel had come to represent the right flank of the dominant paradigm, albeit begrudgingly in Caldwell's case. They accepted the legal right of the government to regulate broadcasting in the most extreme cases of private abuse, but insisted that these instances were few and far between. The sole legitimate function of government regulation, as Hettinger put it, was to provide conditions that would make the commercial stations sufficiently profitable, and advertisers sufficiently content, such that the broadcasting system would be able to provide "program service of a standard that is in the public interest." After 1934 this meant keeping a very low profile, mostly protecting broadcasters from illegal encroachment on their channels by pirate broadcasters.[70]

The deregulationists, however, had not been vanquished entirely. Within the dominant paradigm the private and commercial basis of the U.S. broadcasting was now beyond challenge; the control of the frequencies by the networks and the role of advertising were no longer open to debate. Given this rather fundamental proviso, the call for deregulation would always be able to muster considerable theoretical and emotional power, while calls for an activist role for the government would always be suspect. Once the possibility of transcending the status quo was removed from the range of legitimate policy options and discussion topics, the newly emerging "liberal" position found itself in disjointed, even contradictory, positions. For example, in 1938 Roger Baldwin would chastise FCC Chairman Frank R. McNinch for the FCC's new policy of reviewing program content at license renewal hearings, precisely what the ACLU had been lobbying for, without success, between 1934 and 1937. By the end of the decade the ACLU came to the defense of two private broadcasters who were being monitored by the FCC after numerous complaints regarding their anti-Semitic and anti-Catholic programming.[71] At the same time ACLU radio committee members like Eckstein and Ernst were adamant regarding the limitations of commercial broadcasting, although incapable of providing solutions that were plausible.

This conundrum facing those attempting to act as liberals within the status quo weighed heavily on the NCER's Evans. In 1939, at the invitation of Henry Eckstein, he attended an ACLU Radio Committee meeting in order to see if there were ways that the two groups could coordinate their activities. To Evans's dismay, "this committee took the position that what was needed in radio was complete freedom," including "so far as possible freedom from regulation by government." The ACLU Radio Committee, Evans noted, "was almost completely in agreement with the position that the industry has taken and was opposed to the whole program of the National Committee [on Education by Radio]. A representative of the National Association of Broadcasters was present and the [ACLU Radio] Committee offered to back him in any way it could." The ACLU Radio Committee, Evans's concerns notwithstanding, never did come to regard the commercial broadcasters as indistinguishable from newspaper publishers as far as their relationship with the government, although much confusion marked their efforts to determine a coherent position, a confusion that would seem endemic to the assignment. Years later, it became the ACLU Radio–TV Committee with a membership that included Hans V. Kaltenborn and Paul Lazarsfeld.[72] The committee became an active proponent of what would become the Fairness Doctrine; it would become a leading, if not the leading, proponent of liberal reform within the context of the status quo.

Hence the system that emerged, with the government a regulator of last resort, has been one of "weak regulation." License revocation, Stewart's theoretical stick so necessary to make regulation in the public interest a viable concept, has been disregarded as a legitimate policy option, much as the broadcast reform movement argued would be the case in the early 1930s. In effect, there has been a de facto privatization of the airwaves; what Philip Rosen has termed the "myth of regulation."[73] In this informal sense, then, Caldwell's and the commercial broadcasters' campaign to eliminate government regulation in the mid-1930s was decisively triumphant.

The ideological consolidation of the status quo was abetted by the ongoing efforts of the commercial broadcasters to establish their social neutrality, and thereby justify their domination of the public airwaves. In 1939 the NAB established the NAB Code which specified how, through self-regulation, the commercial broadcasters would provide a forum for the entire range of legitimate political opinion. Of more importance were the political stabilization of the industry following the passage of the Communications Act of 1934 and the stabilized, harmonious relations with the newspaper industry, which together permitted the networks to actively develop news divisions in the late 1930s. By World War II these news divisions were active, almost omnipresent, broadcasting on a daily basis, and they brought considerable prestige to NBC and CBS. The emergence of broadcast news also reinforced network claims that radio broadcasting deserved the same respect, if not the exact same First Amendment protection, as the print media received. In 1945 the NAB formed the Council on Radio Journalism (CRJ) in conjunction with the American Association of Schools and Departments of Journalism. The purpose of the CRJ was to establish the same professional standards for radio news that were applied to print journalism.[74] As the content of radio news broadcasts was increasingly ascribed to independent, expert, professional news values, the issue of how the broadcasting system was owned, operated, and subsidized decreased markedly in importance.

The path to thoroughgoing consolidation was not without its bumps. Under James Lawrence Fly in the early 1940s, the FCC even assumed, as much by accident as by design, an adversarial stance toward network, commercial broadcasting. One FCC member commented in 1944 that radio was "rapidly becoming less free" to the extent it was devoted to being "an effective and extremely profitable advertising medium."[75] The FCC's 1941 *Report on Chain Broadcasting* and 1946 *Public Service Responsibilities of Broadcast Licensees* (commonly referred to as the "Blue Book") included critiques of network control and the influence of advertising over content that echoed reform movement criticism of the early 1930s. In perhaps the most daring move in its history, the FCC even forced NBC to sell one of its two networks, thus leading to the formation of the American Broadcasting Company in 1943.[76]

This criticism and action was nevertheless bounded at all times by the acknowledged impossibility of tampering with the profit-motivated, network-dominated, and advertising-supported basis of U.S. broadcasting. Even the FCC's strongest criticism was combined with homages to commercial broadcasting that would have been unthinkable to a 1930s broadcast reformer. As Evans commented regarding the FCC's investigation of network monopoly, there was no chance that the FCC would "propose any constructive changes in the present setup" as a result.[77] Fly conceded that the structure of the industry was off-limits as well; his goal was simply to regulate the commercial system to act more in the public interest. The broadcasters successfully removed Fly and the reform threat, and used their immense resources thereafter to assure that the FCC remained faithful to industry needs. Those dissident voices that happened to positions on the FCC in later years, such as Frieda Hennock, Newton M. Minow, and Nicholas Johnson, were easily marginalized and unable to accomplish even minor reforms, let alone the types of changes that Fly envisioned.[78]

The Second World War brought with it the commercial broadcasters' well-publicized collaboration with the government's war effort, thus permitting the industry to consolidate its position on patriotic grounds. "The American system of broadcasting had enormous prestige as the war ended," Barnouw notes. "It was holding the nation spellbound."[79] Any lingering sentiment for structural reform was purged by the frenzied hysteria of the Cold War. For the first time, advocacy of nonprofit broadcasting as well as criticism of commercial broadcasting were then routinely dismissed as "socialistic" and therefore treasonous. Indeed, in the 1930s the specter of communism had been decidedly absent from the commercial broadcasters' critiques of the broadcast reform movement.[80]

In the 1940s and 1950s, the FCC effectively devised all its plans for the development of television to suit the needs of the major communications corporations, particularly RCA. Unlike the uproar that followed the FRC's radio allocation of 1928, there was little public dissent to the FCC's television allocation. This does not mean, however, that people accepted commercial broadcasting uncritically. As William Boddy chronicled, by the end of the 1950s more than a few Americans were displeased with the nature of advertising-based and profit-driven television.[81] This discontent remained amorphous and unthreatening, perhaps because it was presented with an unsavory set of choices. Critics could either abide by an unsatisfactory commercial system or they could call for undesirable government regulation of an unsatisfactory commercial system. It was difficult to mount much enthusiasm for the latter, and those campaigns that did call for increased regulation ran head-on into public misgivings about the possibility of government censorship.[82]

This stunted set of options for U.S. broadcasting critics had its origins in the 1930s with the collapse of the broadcast reform movement. By the 1940s the private and commercial nature of U.S. broadcasting was both outside the parameters of legitimate debate and there was not even the notion that the public had the right to determine the type of broadcast system it deemed appropriate, after political study, discussion, and debate. The status quo had been internalized in toto by the dominant political culture. The ante for taking part in the debate over broadcast policy was the belief that for-profit, network-dominated, advertising-supported broadcasting was fundamentally sound, rather than fundamentally flawed. "He who attacks the fundamentals of the American system" of broadcasting, William S. Paley informed a conference of educators in 1937, "attacks democracy itself."[83] Only a few years earlier, such a statement would have been met with derision; by the late 1930s such proclamations barely received comment. The broadcast reform movement had been defeated and eliminated ideologically as well as politically.

It was no surprise then, in 1946, that Paul Lazarsfeld concluded his study of broadcasting by observing that the American people seemed to approve of the private and commercial basis of the industry. "People have little information on the subject," he added, "they have obviously given it little thought."[84]

CHAPTER 10

Conclusion

Rethinking U.S. Broadcasting History

A major objective of this study has been to indicate the extent to which there was organized popular opposition to commercial broadcasting in the United States, and to discredit the notion that the American people went along with the establishment of the status quo with barely a glimmer of dissent. The deterministic stance is based upon an assessment of the popular response to radio by the mid-1920s, which follows from the presupposition that the network-dominated, advertising-supported system was intact and beyond political or ideological challenge by 1927 at the very latest. The status quo, however, only came into existence between 1927 and 1930; prior to those years, few if any imagined U.S. broadcasting would assume the traits it quickly adopted. Once the contours of the new system became apparent, many Americans, from a variety of backgrounds, reacted with utter disgust and devoted considerable energy to public campaigns to restructure the broadcasting set-up to allow for significant nonprofit and noncommercial development. Far from being entrenched in the mid-1920s, before it even came into existence, the status quo was only economically consolidated by 1932, legislatively consolidated by 1934, and ideologically consolidated by the end of the decade. On all three fronts, the broadcast reform movement challenged the industry with impunity prior to consolidation.

This is not to deny that the radio corporations were immensely powerful by the mid-1920s, not to mention a few years later, nor that they had an intimate relationship with those government officials and legislators who could affect broadcast policy. If anything, previous scholarship may not have sufficiently appreciated these points. Nor do I claim that the commercial system was ever threatened with imminent extinction due to the activities of the broadcast reform movement; rather, I claim that the reformers existed to a far greater extent than has been recognized, that the industry took their threat quite seriously, and that understanding this conflict is indispensable toward any effort to develop a meaningful understanding the manner in which the U.S. system actually did consolidate and the context in which broadcast law and policy actually were developed. The network-dominated, advertising-supported U.S. system of broadcasting is better understood in the context of social conflict than as the result of social consensus.

The Radio Act of 1927, generally regarded as ordaining the status quo and closing the book on any and all public debate on the nature of U.S. broadcasting, is better characterized in less apocalyptic terms. Although of clear importance to the crystallization of the status quo, the Radio Act of 1927 was emergency legislation that provided temporary regulation to bring order to the airwaves. It was a particularly vague statute, with its meaning and intent unclear to most members of Congress. Nobody at the time regarded the regulation emanating from the Radio Act as the final word on the subject. While there may well have been a consensus for the "private" or "non-governmental" development of radio among Congress or the public-at-large in 1927, there is no evidence that anyone conceived of private development in terms of the system that was to emerge. "Broadcasting today is not what it was expected to be," broadcast reformer S. Howard Evans noted in passing in 1932. "The amount of advertising on the air is beyond any expectation that could have existed five years ago."[1] This point was accepted by observers of all stripes in the early 1930s.

Moreover, legislation to establish the permanent basis for broadcast regulation was introduced and considered at every session of Congress until the eventual passage of the Communications Act of 1934. It is striking how the entire legislative process for radio law in the period connecting the Radio Act to the Communications Act has been so inadequately studied, particularly in comparison to the research conducted on broadcasting and communications law prior to 1927 and after the Second World War. Such critical developments as the FRC's *Commercial Radio Advertising*, the Roper Committee, the Federal Committee to Study of Radio Broadcasting, and the FCC's autumn 1934 hearings either have been discussed superficially and out of context, or were simply ignored outright. At the very least, I hope this study has shed light on these overlooked topics and will stimulate further research in this area. The Communications Act of 1934, far from constituting an addendum to the Radio Act of 1927, was promulgated and passed on its own terms and in its own context. That the radio title of Communications Act of 1934 restated the Radio Act verbatim was not a "given," but, rather, the consequence of the political fight over broadcasting in the early 1930s.

These points highlight the apologetic nature of some of the scholarship concerning the origins and nature of U.S. broadcasting. Although this analysis fails to stand up to much scrutiny, it seems to enjoy a certain half-life, perhaps due to the interest of the commercial broadcasting industry to keep alive the mythical interpretation of its origins. Thus, some still characterize the Radio Act of 1927 as some sort of ''progressive victory'' that was ''passed in the best interest of the citizenry.'' This was the interpretation of the Radio Act of 1927 that C. C. Dill dedicated his life to promoting after his retirement from the U.S. Senate in 1935. Likewise, the Communications Act of 1934 is still occasionally represented as an enlightened ''New Deal'' measure that, as Walter B. Emery put it, constituted a ''Magna Charta for broadcasting'' in its heroic advancement of ''democratic concepts and values.''[2] These interpretations survive to the extent that they infuse their historical observations with their unvarnished belief in the greatness of a regulated, commercial broadcasting set-up, while they studiously avoid all historical evidence that does not neatly confirm this prejudice. Fortunately, few scholars accept such apologia; nonetheless, the dominant broadcasting historiography still has a limited perspective on the critical events of the 1920s and 1930s.

One fundamental oversight of much U.S. broadcasting history is that of devaluing the substantial nonprofit sector of U.S. broadcasting in the 1920s. To some extent this may be due to the general inaccessibility of archival material on these stations, particularly in comparison to the early commercial stations that went on to prosper. For the most part, though, it seems the consequence of the general bias in U.S. broadcasting historiography to regard capitalist broadcasting as the ''natural'' system in the United States, for better or for worse. Werner Severin is not far off the mark when he terms these nonprofit broadcasters the ''true pioneers'' of American broadcasting.[3] Literally hundreds of these stations commenced operations between 1920 and 1926. They began with lofty ambitions and grand aspirations for public service. Most of these stations quickly collapsed, their economic plight magnified by an aggressive and hostile commercial broadcasting industry, an unresponsive FRC, and the Great Depression. Nevertheless, their existence constitutes what could almost be termed a ''hidden history'' of American radio. At the very least, acknowledging the depth of the nonprofit broadcasters' history requires that one repudiate the notion that the ether was inherently and naturally subject to private, for-profit exploitation. This is a step that the commercial broadcasters have not encouraged, nor is it one that proponents of the status quo have shown any inclination to pursue.[4]

The inability or unwillingness to consider the nonprofit sector of U.S. broadcasting in the 1920s may explain why the FRC's General Order 40 has been dealt with as such an inconsequential measure by much of U.S. broadcasting history. It was General Order 40, far more than the Radio Act of 1927, that specifically laid the foundations for the network-dominated, advertising-supported U.S. broadcasting system. As Chapter 2 discussed at some length, General Order 40 was the mostly secretive product of the FRC working in conjunction with the commercial broadcasting industry, with minimal, if not nonexistent, congressional or public participation. It merits more than passing mention. (Barnouw, for example, neglects General Order 40 altogether.) Stripped of any sense of the contest between nonprofit and capitalist broadcasters, those who do discuss General Order 40 tend to characterize it as a technical engineering mechanism, rather than as a provision of a striking set of policy assumptions that had never been considered in any public deliberation. Indeed, those commentators especially enthralled by commercial broadcasting have tended to regard General Order 40 glowingly, although never giving any sense that they recognize who were the casualties of the measure, other than the standard free market "losers."[5]

Only by appreciating the role of nonprofit broadcasting and the significance of General Order 40 can one comprehend the upheaval created by the reallocation of 1928. General Order 40 specifically signaled to the struggling nonprofit sector that the FRC was oblivious to its plight, if not actively working with the commercial broadcasters to bring about its imminent demise. It was these nonprofit broadcasters who formed the backbone of the emerging broadcast reform movement of the 1930s, to be joined by intellectuals, civic activists, elements of the labor movement, and elements of the press.

In the historical vacuum that frames most of the scholarship, the broadcast reform movement has been marginalized and distorted beyond recognition, with two discernible patterns. First, many scholars either ignore the reformers altogether or lump them in with the "propagandists, religious zealots, and demagogues seeking to influence listeners with their peculiar brand of publicity," as Emery puts it. In this perspective, the rebels of note are the medicine-selling quacks and radio preachers who either wanted to purchase time from commercial stations or who wanted to establish their own stations, but who at no time participated in the debate over broadcast policy or developed a principled critique of the status quo. Perhaps most significant along these lines was the Reverend Charles E. Coughlin, the Detroit-based priest who used the commercial airwaves to disseminate his controversial right-wing views. Coughlin mostly ignored the debate over the broadcast reform in the early 1930s; to the extent he did acknowledge it, Coughlin expressed support for the status quo and little sympathy for the principles upon which the reform movement was predicated. As one broadcast reformer wrote to Coughlin to protest an article by Coughlin disparaging nonprofit broadcasting, "the commercial chain has lifted you from comparative obscurity to a place of prominence."[6] That this notion of radio "rebels" survives, particularly when they were nowhere to be found in the early 1930s, is probably explained by the fact that their free speech claims fully accepted the capitalist basis of U.S. broadcasting, which renders them suitable for the dominant paradigm.

The second treatment of the reform movement has been more accurate and far more charitable, as many historians are sympathetic with its critique and aims. Nevertheless, the reform movement has been dealt with out of context and in a piecemeal fashion. Most of the discussion, accordingly, centers around the Wagner–Hatfield amendment of 1934, where, it usually goes, educator opposition to the status quo suddenly appears for a few brief months as an anomaly, gets defeated, and goes quietly into the night.[7]

As it was, the Wagner–Hatfield campaign in 1934 was the proverbial "tip of the iceberg," and no indication whatsoever of the extent of principled opposition activity to commercial broadcasting that existed throughout the early 1930s. In concrete terms, the legacy of the reform movement is that it delayed the consolidation of the status quo for five years, from 1930 to 1935. In a broader sense, the existence of the reform movement puts the lie to the notion that the American people were entirely ignorant or apathetic, not to mention enthusiastic, about the emergence of the status quo. While most Americans never engaged in the debate over broadcasting in the early 1930s, those that did were mostly dissatisfied with the emerging order, unless, of course, they were receiving some sort of material benefit from commercial broadcasting. The existence of the reform movement also highlights the extent to which many Americans reacted negatively to the commercialized programming delivered by the networks between 1928 and 1934. This is not to say that most Americans supported broadcast reform; rather, it points out that many more Americans disliked the commercialized basis of the new medium than has been acknowledged, although most were unaware that it was within their power to alter the situation through public policy.

Moreover, this broadcast reform movement generated a thorough and compelling critique of the limitations of a regulated capitalist broadcasting set-up for a democratic society. The existence of this body of criticism instantly discredits the notion that criticism of a capitalist media system is a recent development in the United States, or that it is innately "foreign" and dependent upon "imported ideologies." In fact, with little exception the entire body of criticism sprang from a variety of American intellectual traditions, ranging from populism and transcendentalism to pragmatism and natural rights philosophy. In the early 1930s, at least, the nature of the commercial broadcasting system seemed inimical to several strains of American liberal thought, and it was not yet anti-American to criticize the status quo. It is even arguable that criticism of a capitalist media structure has some right to claim to be a true inheritor of American democratic traditions. At the very least, the reform movement provides a distinctly American tradition of no-holds-barred media criticism.

The defeat of the broadcast reform movement was much more than a victory for oligopolistic, commercial broadcasting; in fact, it was a defeat for the very notion that the public had the right to determine how best to structure its broadcasting services. For the real dilemma that plagued the reformers was their inability to even initiate widespread public discussion of the issue, let alone mobilize support for sweeping broadcast reform. If this study has demarcated anything, it is the extent to which the commercial broadcasters and their allies in Washington, D.C., continually postponed, eliminated, or defused any public examination of the American broadcasting system or any discussion of alternative models. In 1934 the NCER stated that the commercial broadcasters "tremble at the thought of a nonpolitical, fearless audit."[8] The radio lobby even managed to keep Congress from any substantial consideration of broadcasting issues, for the most part. Hiding behind the rhetoric that only "experts" were capable of understanding "complex" policy issues, the proponents of the status quo were successful in their campaign to keep the preponderance of the American people ignorant of their right to dictate broadcast policy. The network-dominated, advertising-supported basis of U.S. broadcasting was anything but the product of an informed public debate.[9]

Interestingly, the mythical notion that the U.S. airwaves were inherently subject to capitalist exploitation and that this is the only "natural" and "democratic" method by which a society can organize its broadcasting services, is still credible, even axiomatic, for the very respectable contemporary broadcasting deregulation movement. These authors, who not surprisingly are embraced by the commercial broadcasting and advertising industries, argue that commercial broadcasters merit the same relationship with the government as that enjoyed by newspaper publishers, and that any licensing or regulation is a heinous violation of the First Amendment and a direct threat to the continued existence of democratic government in the United States. Much of their work has a strong historical component, which outlines the irrelevance of the communications laws to the contemporary media situation.[10] In effect, these critics argue for granting the existing capitalist broadcasters property rights to the channels they occupy.

Their proposals parallel the first great wave of deregulation arguments that emerged in the middle 1930s, after the system was consolidated and beyond challenge, serving mostly as a weapon to eliminate or reduce government regulation that might inhibit profitability. Indeed, prior to the 1934, the mid-1930s proponents of deregulation and the commercial broadcasters were mostly silent regarding the free speech implications of licensing because they were most satisfied with the manner by which the FRC was rather arbitrarily clarifying the spectrum for profitable exploitation. It was the broadcast reform movement that obsessively attempted, without success, to bring questions of free expression to the forefront of any discussion regarding broadcast policy. The dominant theory regarding the meaning of free speech for radio broadcasting did not emerge until after the private, commercial basis of the industry had become sacrosanct. The First Amendment and free speech barely influenced policy in the formative stages; rather, they were only utilized later and then to protect the commercial broadcasting industry from any public intervention in its affairs once the system was beyond political or ideological challenge.[11]

The contemporary deregulation movement uses history selectively to illustrate the only relationship it deems significant: the commercial broadcaster, who by definition should rule the ether to make as much money as humanly possible, and the government regulator, who, regardless of intent, can only portend evil. All other aspects of U.S. broadcasting history are relegated to the margins, which is necessary to maintain the untenable "immaculate conception" notion of the origins of commercial broadcasting. This is an extraordinary bias that provides a dubious foundation for the entire deregulation argument. The manner by which any society organizes its broadcasting system is hardly something that can be presupposed as a given. In fact, it is a political decision that each society makes, sometimes through democratic means and sometimes, as in the U.S. case, not in the most democratic manner imaginable. When proponents of deregulation are forced to dispense with its notion that a capitalist media system is "natural" and "unalterable," much like a mountain range or the solar system, the basis for the deregulation argument begins to crumble. When the public is not forced to accept the status quo as a given, the possibilities for protecting and promoting free expression can extend far beyond the narrow range of alternatives that the deregulationists (and commercial broadcasters) presuppose and countenance. Within their narrow range, the deregulationists can always make a strong case, but, arguably, only within their narrow range.

Even if the historical foundations of the deregulation argument are dubious, it has vaulted to prominence in recent years due to the emergence of satellite technologies, video cassette recorders and cameras, cable television, remote control devices, and a host of other new technologies. Deregulationists argue that these technologies have reduced the power of the broadcast networks over their audiences and have permitted a wave of vigorous competition to enter previously uncompetitive markets. Moreover, they hold that the next generation of technological innovations will further this process, thereby rendering moot traditional concerns, like those held by the 1930s broadcast reformers, about corporate domination of communications media. The deregulationists contend that governments must abdicate any role in communications policy-making and permit the market to allocate resources and direct investment where most profitable. There is one important truth in these observations. Revolutionary developments in communications technology have changed the media landscape dramatically. In particular, human societies are poised, for the first time, to be able to develop decentralized and democratic communications systems that would have been unthinkable to earlier generations. The critical question, however, is whether such developments will be possible in a market-driven system, as the deregulationists presuppose.

Three weak spots in the deregulationist argument spring to mind. First, the ability of consumers to benefit by the new communications marketplace is strictly determined by how much money they have. Hence, the market will be skewed toward providing numerous choices to those with larger incomes and tend to neglect those who are poor. In view of the general decline of living standards in the United States and elsewhere in the past decade, particularly among the lower half of the population, there is reason to suspect that the communications revolution will be aimed primarily at the more affluent sectors of the population, with all that this suggests about its democratic effect. In this context, the communications revolution will probably enhance inequality in the population.

Second, there is little historical evidence for the argument that the new technologies will break up oligopolistic markets and create a competitive marketplace. It seems more likely that whatever shake-up in the corporate applecart is brought on by the new communications technologies will eventually stabilize with a handful of corporations establishing dominant and mostly unchallengable control of the market, probably on an international basis. Third, all the consumer "choices" in the new communications marketplace are bounded by what is profitable for the providers. This seems to be a fundamental constraint, implicit to a market-based system, and one which is inherently problematic for a democratic society. Furthermore, many of these "choices" will be influenced, if not determined, by the advertising and marketing needs of giant corporations in pursuit of desirable target audiences. In sum, the fundamental concerns of the 1930s broadcast reformers are not necessarily answered by the advent of the new technologies. Rather, they are transformed. Indeed, the majesty of the new technologies may well be that they permit societies to actually develop alternative forms of nonprofit, noncommercial media that would have been impossible until recently. Only the public, consciously acting to counteract the marketplace, can bring this promise into existence.

Finally, there are those who contend that with the eventual establishment of educational stations on the FM band, with the creation of the Public Broadcasting Service in the 1960s, and with the development of the NAB Code and the Fairness Doctrine, that the broadcast reform movement was actually victorious in achieving its goals.[12] It would probably be unfair to say that the reformers were entirely vanquished. The activities of the NCER did help to preserve what little remained of educational broadcasting by the early 1930s, and the activities of the entire reform movement did make the commercial broadcasters, Congress, and the regulators more sensitive to the need to air educational and cultural programs and to provide access to a broader range of political opinions than they might have otherwise. However, even the most superficial analysis of the broadcast reform movement of the early 1930s reveals that all of the preceding would constitute a "victory" in only the shallowest sense of the term. The reformers sought fundamental structural transformation, not enlightened regulation or self-regulation of a capitalist system (if one accepts that that is, indeed, what fell into place). In this fundamental sense, the reformers were unmercifully crushed, with their activities and arguments mostly banished from the historical record.

Failure of the 1930s Reform Movement and Media Reform Efforts Thereafter

Could the broadcast reform movement actually have been victorious in the 1930s, or was it a doomed, quixotic venture from the outset? Why precisely did the broadcast reform movement fail in its campaign to restructure U.S. broadcasting? If, in fact, the concentration and commercialization of broadcasting, not to mention the entire mass media, have increased since the 1930s with similarly negative implications for democracy, why has a new broadcast or media reform movement not emerged to carry the fight to a new generation? Why, indeed, does this 1930s episode stand out starkly as the sole instance in which fundamental questions of ownership, support, and control of the media could be broached in legitimate public discourse in the United States?

The conventional wisdom, of course, is that the reformers never stood much of a chance. It is true that the broadcast reform movement was almost hopelessly overmatched from the outset; in this sense the conventional wisdom is virtually unimpeachable.

To leave the analysis at this point, however, does a certain injustice to history. Legislation passed Congress in 1931 that would have established a national, nonprofit, 50,000-watt labor station to be operated by the CFL, and was only eliminated by allies of the industry behind the closed doors of a congressional conference meeting. Moreover, the Wagner–Hatfield amendment found an astonishing degree of support in 1934, which was all the more incredible given that the support was generated by an ad hoc campaign thrown together by an obscure and impoverished Roman Catholic order with virtually no coverage in the mass media. Had either of these measures become law, they would have established precedents that may well have been carried over to television in the 1940s and 1950s. At the very least they would have accomplished an important task for the reform movement of the 1930s by making nonprofit (and noncommercial) broadcasting a viable prospect for millions of American listeners, and given the notion of broadcast reform an immediacy that it lacked throughout its existence. Nonprofit broadcasting would no longer have been merely an abstract issue, the province of intellectuals, civic activists, upper-class tourists returning from Europe, and the marginalized nonprofit sector. In short, had either measure passed it is by no means clear what other developments may have followed down the road.

At least two short-term factors, specific to the early 1930s experience, undermined the broadcast reform movement. Had either of these factors been absent, something along the lines of the preceding measures may well have come into existence. First, and perhaps foremost, was the political incompetence of the broadcast reform movement itself. As a movement that was directly challenging the legitimacy of an entrenched and powerful industry, the reformers above all else needed to coordinate their activities and to generate broad based popular support for their movement. While lip service was paid to this strategy, for the most part the elements of the reform movement went their own ways and made only sporadic efforts to work in unison. To some extent this weakness is attributable to the composition of the broadcast reform movement; it was basically a cross-section of mainstream or "establishment" figures who had little capacity for engaging in the type of full-scale political battle that was necessary. In particular, the NCER, proved to be an especially feeble lobbying force, which was all the more damaging given the relatively lavish resources it had been provided by the Payne Fund.

In addition, much of the reform movement had elitist sympathies, which mitigated against organizing the sort of popular base that was so essential. Many of the reformers were content to have existing authorities dictate broadcasting policy; they simply thought the task was better delegated to university presidents and intellectuals rather than capitalist broadcasters and commercial advertisers. In this vein, much of the broadcast reform movement was convinced that any neutral audit of broadcasting by Congress or anyone not affiliated with the radio industry would invariably reach the same conclusion. There were only a few broadcast reformers, most notably Edward Nockels and Father John B. Harney, who had some grasp of the nature of the political fight in which the reform movement was engaged. It is not surprising that they enjoyed the most success on Capitol Hill. Moreover, only Nockels and the CFL were unwilling to concede that entertainment programming was the natural province of advertisers, and insisted that entertainment shows were a legitimate aspect of the nonprofit station's programming. Many of the other proponents of nonprofit broadcasting were seemingly content to provide a diet of programming that would not have mass appeal, and at times even dismissed the idea contemptuously, thus making the task of organizing mass support for reform to create more nonprofit and noncommercial broadcasting all the more problematic.

Second, the economic depression of the 1930s hurt the cause of broadcast reform. Bear in mind that the establishment of the status quo and the creation of the broadcast reform movement began in earnest in 1929, before the onset of the Depression. The Depression sounded the death knell for the budgets of many nonprofit broadcasters, making it impossible for the reformers to have an existing group of stations it could hold up to the public as providing a markedly better service than the commercial broadcasters. The Depression also undercut the financial capacity of the reformers to challenge the status quo and turned public and congressional attention to the pressing need for economic recovery. The Depression made the willingness of the advertising industry to bankroll U.S. broadcasting far more attractive than it might have been had the government coffers been brimming with tax dollars and had one-quarter of the work force not been unemployed. In this context, it was difficult to mount enthusiasm for a fight against one of the few industries that was actually prospering in the early 1930s. In short, the Depression put a series of obstacles before the broadcast reform movement that may have been insurmountable in combination.

Of course, the Depression is also regarded as having legitimated the sort of anticorporate politics that the broadcast reformers were espousing. While the Depression finally made increased government participation in the economy legitimate, this only developed meaningfully in the years after 1935, when commercial broadcasting was entrenched and impervious to political challenge. Likewise, while the Depression fueled a class-based politics that might have provided the foundation for a movement to undercut the radio industry, this too came about later in the 1930s. It was typified by the emergence of the Congress of Industrial Organizations (CIO), which took an explicitly radical stance toward radio and all of the media from its inception that was reminiscent of the CFL.[13] Once again, however, the battle was already over by the time the CIO got started. In short, the broadcast reform movement had the misfortune of experiencing the negative fallout of the Depression for the cause, and then collapsed before it could take advantage of any possible benefits.

Even had these two short-term factors been different, however, it is not certain that any radical reform would have taken place. Indeed, there were also at least three other important long-term factors that can account for the failure of the broadcast reform movement in the early 1930s, factors that remain in place to this day. These factors, which will be examined next, go a long way toward explaining why no subsequent campaign to reconstruct the U.S. broadcasting or general media system has emerged, and why there is little reason to believe that one is in the offing.

First, the U.S. political culture does not permit any discussion of fundamental weaknesses in capitalism. In a certain sense, deference to private property and the market can be traced to the earliest European settlements in North America; these are deep-seated American cultural traits in any calculation. Nevertheless, there is also a history of opposition to dominant economic relations in U.S. history prior to the twentieth century. Capitalism has been an off-limits topic of political discussion since at least the First World War, and arguably as far back as the 1890s. As one historian hyperbolically noted: "After World War I, capitalism was made a part of the constitution.'' In the case of the broadcast reformers, it was probably easier to criticize capitalism in the early 1930s than at any other time since the First World War, particularly in intellectual circles, but this point is often exaggerated.[14] It was still far from legitimate in political debate to question the capitalist basis of the political economy as was evidenced by the deference to the principle of private property elicited by most members of the broadcast reform movement.

It lies outside the scope or capacity of this discussion to explain why capitalism became off-limits for critical discussion by the second decade of the century; suffice it to say that this coincided in broad historical terms with the maturation of corporate capitalism as the reigning political economic model, and, moreover, with the ascension of U.S. capitalism to its position as the dominant force in the world economy. In addition, this removal of capitalism from the range of legitimate debate corresponded to the elimination of the left as a viable factor in U.S. political life since the First World War. This removal has also made it that much more difficult for a left critique of U.S. society to re-emerge in subsequent years. For the most part, the left has struggled to maintain an identity and a presence on the margins of academia, divorced from any popular base, with all the pitfalls that entails for radical social theory and analysis.[15]

The absence of a viable left has proven to be a critical factor accounting for the lack of debate over the control and structure of the mass media. For example, in much of Western Europe the groups that have tended to politicize the media often have been groups that tend to take a critical stance toward capitalism, such as the Labour Party in Britain and the Social Democrats in Scandinavia.[16] These groups have tended to recognize that concentrated private control and reliance upon advertising have effectively meant control by members of the capitalist class, which was inimical to their notion of a socialist democracy. Conversely, the political right has generally led the fights to dismantle public service broadcasting systems or to prevent their establishment, often on the grounds that such services provide undesirable political perspectives. The right seemingly understands the inherent capacity of the profit-motive and advertising support to imbue media programming with what it regards as an acceptable range of political debate.[17] This comparison should not be applied categorically, however; there is also a tradition for media policy to become resolved less on ideological lines than simply along logistical lines, as evidenced by the French Socialist ''privatization'' of broadcasting in the 1980s on the belief that the state system had been dominated by Gaulist party cronies. In any case, the United States has not had any broad-based left political force since the demise of the Socialists after the First World War that would, by definition, be hostile to the suitability of a capitalist media set-up.

Beyond this lack of any agency that has been organized to fundamentally challenge the prerogatives of capital, this inability to criticize capitalism has translated into two specific ideological problems for those inclined to bring the legitimacy of the corporate media structure into the political arena. First, capitalism being off-limits means, almost by definition, that the propriety of private control for selfish purposes of society's productive resources is generally unassailable. In the 1930s debate over broadcasting, for example, the broadcast reform movement was willing to challenge the private control of radio, but not the private control of society; the reformers were willing to accept the marketplace as a satisfactory social arbiter elsewhere, but not in the realm of broadcasting. Although this distinction was quite logical, it put them in a bind when they encountered the arguments of the commercial broadcasters. If the private marketplace was essentially good and democratic elsewhere, why not in radio? This may have seemed an arbitrary distinction to all but some committed reformers. The same dilemma has haunted the efforts of would-be reformers ever since.

Second, to the extent that capitalism has been removed from critical public evaluation, it has been characterized in the dominant culture in a highly sanitized fashion. The legitimate vision of capitalism is not that of an economic system that rests on a highly skewed class basis and that, in fact, recreates a class system by its very operations. Rather, the sanitized and accepted version of capitalism is one of free and equal individuals voluntarily entering into exchange in the marketplace. This is not an entirely inaccurate description of capitalism; rather, it is merely incomplete and therefore misleading when presented as the whole picture. Conspicuously absent is an acknowledgment of the class basis of production that is the heart of the system, as even neoclassical economic theory acknowledges in the form of presupposition.[18]

It was a sanitized vision of capitalism that the commercial broadcasters emphasized in their ideological campaign in the 1930s. They strove to attach commercial broadcasting to the ideological wagon that equated capitalism with the free and equal marketplace, the free and equal marketplace with democracy, and democracy with "Americanism." The status quo, therefore, easily became the "American Plan," where the public interest was assured, as it always was, by the machinations of the marketplace. Challengers to the efficacy of the marketplace in broadcasting drew the raised eyebrows of the dominant culture as malcontent "special interests," incapable of meeting the public's needs in the marketplace. They were, therefore, dispensers of essentially worthless "propaganda."

This was the powerful logic staring at the broadcast reform movement in the 1930s. As Philip T. Rosen concluded: "Any attempt to challenge or criticize the arrangement [commercial broadcasting] represented a direct assault on the larger society as well as a rejection of the nation's past."[19] The inability, therefore, if not the unwillingness, to present an alternate vision of capitalism and American society left the broadcast reform movement in a tenuous position. This is not to say a "radical" approach to the debate would have been successful, let alone possible; rather, it says that a "mainstream" approach was by definition in the contradictory position of having to accept dominant ideological mores that seriously handicapped any reform efforts. In particular, an argument that private commercial radio undermined democracy necessitated an understanding of U.S. capitalism as a class system to be effective. This contradiction has plagued all subsequent efforts to politicize the issue of media control in the United States.

The second factor accounting for the failure of the broadcast reform movement, and the subsequent lack of debate over the control and structure of the media, is that the corporate media have actively and successfully cultivated the ideology that the status quo is the only rational media structure for a democratic and freedom-loving society. The corporate media have encouraged the belief that even the consideration of alternatives was tantamount to a call for totalitarianism. In the 1930s, the proponents of commercial broadcasting spared no expense or effort to popularize this position. With the demise of the broadcast reform movement it quickly became unchallenged (and unchallengable) in the dominant discourse.

In the 1930s the commercial broadcasters worked incessantly and successfully to hold onto the ideological coattails of the newspaper industry, which had built up a largely impenetrable ideological armor to protect its role in U.S. society. The depth of this laissez faire ideology, which prevents public discussion of, examination of, and intrusion into the affairs of the newspaper industry, is truly staggering. A fundamental argument used by the commercial broadcasters to demand deregulation—in the late 1930s through the present—is that despite the physical scarcity of the ether, broadcasting is in fact more competitive than the largely monopolistic newspaper industry. They argue, therefore, that there is no longer any meaningful justification to single out broadcasters for regulation in the public interest.

Jerome Barron and others have taken this acknowledgment that the competitive market is no longer an accurate description for the newspaper industry to what, on the surface, would seem to be a logical conclusion: Since the laissez faire model based on access in a competitive market was no longer appropriate, and the marketplace was therefore an ineffective regulator, the state has a right to intervene as it has in broadcasting to assure that the press system act in the best interests of a democratic polity. Barron's effort to promote this idea was dismissed categorically. Proponents of the status quo will even acknowledge the legitimacy of Barron's arguments, but they simply refuse to countenance any alteration of the laissez faire ideology, regardless of the empirical evidence. Even media critic Ben Bagdikian, whose work has been seminal in bringing attention to the antidemocratic implications of the corporate, commercial media system, simply presupposes the superiority of a capitalist media set-up, despite all his evidence to the contrary.[20] The laissez faire media ideology has been internalized to such an extent that it has become an article of faith for anyone committed to democracy.

Furthermore, given the oligopolistic basis of the modern media industries, an additional problem has presented itself to the commercial broadcasters and the major media corporations. They have to both establish the capitalist media set-up as the best possible system and, moreover, establish that the status quo is innately nonpartisan and committed to the truth rather than any sort of ideological axe-grinding. This is a critical point that must be established by a highly concentrated media system, capitalist or otherwise; the very legitimacy of the system as a primary dispenser of political information is quickly, and rightfully, suspect unless it can establish social neutrality. In the early 1930s, therefore, the commercial broadcasters placed a great deal of emphasis on establishing their social neutrality and debunking the broadcast reform movement's charges of "private censorship." The major media corporations have found two invaluable allies as they go about their ideological chores.

The first is found in the hundreds of departments and schools of journalism and communications that have arisen over the past few generations in colleges and universities across the nation. These departments were frequently established at the behest of commercial media and rely upon maintaining close and cordial relationships with the commercial media. Even the most hard-hitting critic tends to pull punches when the legitimacy of the corporate media is challenged. As one media educator recently acknowledged in a trade publication:

> We all know, whether we're candid enough to acknowledge it or not, that the advertising, news and public relations industries that provide employment for our students—plus other benefits—expect us to follow the "company line" on issues involving the special interests of mass communication.[21]

Until quite recently, and then only in a handful of instances, these departments of journalism have had little difficulty accepting the corporate line that attacks on a corporate media system are attacks on a free press. Generations of students have been and are being trained that this is the best possible and only conceivable media system available to the U.S. people. The issue is generally not even open to contemplation.

The second is found in the ideology of professional journalism, which, regardless of its merits, is indispensable for the legitimation of an oligopolistic media system. It is not entirely coincidental that professional journalism emerged precisely as the newspaper industry was becoming a mature and concentrated industry. Moreover, despite the ostensible claim that the ideology of professional journalism protects the news product from the pressures of advertisers and media owners attempting to cast undue influence over the news, the ideology of professional journalism clearly internalized the commercial dictates of the newspaper enterprise as it developed. It also internalized the class structure and values of the emerging modern capitalist political economy. Professional journalism was a far-more complementary than antagonistic development to the emergence of the modern capitalist media set-up and modern capitalism itself. As Ben Bagdikian has noted, professional journalism effectively made journalists oblivious to the compromises with authority they constantly make as they go about their jobs.[22]

Professional journalism serves as a critical agent for legitimation as it shifts responsibility for media performance from the broader economic context to the specific conduct of reporters and editors following a set of professional standards and operating within a presupposed broader context. The logic of the ideology is such that the actual ownership and support mechanisms become incidental to explaining news media performance. Working journalists do not object to this mystification, perhaps because it inflates their role in the journalistic process. Concurrently, professional journalists, despite long-standing and deep-seated conflicts with corporate media management, have accepted the corporate line that attacks on the corporate control of the industry are the equivalent to attacks on free speech and a free press as well as on their professional prerogatives. For example, in the 1930s the Newspaper Guild, unlike many labor unions and newspaper-related industries at the time, showed almost no interest in the debate over radio policy. They did pass a resolution, however, denouncing one clause in the Communications Act of 1934 that permitted the president the right to censor the news during a national emergency. The balance of the debate over broadcasting apparently had nothing to do with free speech issues, at least to the trained professionals in America's newsrooms.[23]

Finally, the third long-term factor explaining the collapse of the broadcast reform movement of the 1930s is related to the nature of the broadcasting networks and the corporate media themselves. By this I do not mean the political and economic muscle that accompanies any powerful industry in the United States, but rather two additional benefits that broadcasting networks and the media corporations enjoy beyond those generally enjoyed by other wealthy and powerful institutions. Indeed, in the following respects, the corporate media are no doubt the envy of the balance of the corporate community.

First, given the media's control over the flow of information, few politicians have any desire to antagonize the media industry as a whole, with the conceivable repercussions that might entail for their political careers and agendas. "Politicians fear the media," Ben Bagdikian commented regarding the manner by which media firms were able to circumvent business regulations with greater ease than other firms, "and the bigger the media, the greater the fear."[24] This was a crucial factor in the demise of the broadcast reform movement in the early 1930s. The politicians of the early 1930s grasped what is axiomatic to the modern politician: To challenge the economic position of the major media firms is to write one's own political obituary, particularly in the absence of a broad-based popular movement in support of media or broadcast reform.[25]

Second, the corporate media are in an ideal position to control the public perception of any possible debate regarding the control and structure of the mass media. The media have shown two basic responses to efforts to challenge their legitimacy. They either simply ignore the issue or provide it minimal coverage, which is standard operating procedure, or the corporate mass media distort the issues to suit their own purposes. Hence, challenges to the corporate media, which are generally predicated upon the desire to open up the channels of communication, are invariably framed as threats to free speech, democracy, and The Rights of Man rather than as challenges to corporate rule. The best recent example is the media coverage of the campaign to have the United States withdraw from UNESCO in the early 1980s. The real issues in this example were distorted and ignored, shrouded behind much flowery rhetoric about free speech and free press, mostly because of U.S. media corporate concerns that UNESCO was overly sympathetic to Third World nations regarding communication issues, and might support measures to hamper their activities. More recently, the media have covered the social and political implications of their 1980s consolidations and mergers with what Bagdikian characterizes as "close to total silence."[26] The implication of this news blackout and/or news distortion for any campaign to alter the status quo is self-evident.

This was a central dilemma for the broadcast reformers of the early 1930s. Facing an entrenched industry that had no incentive to publicize the debate over its existence, the reformers needed to receive ample, sympathetic coverage in the print media to generate popular momentum for their cause. Instead the debate received minimal coverage that was skewed tremendously toward the proponents of the status quo. Indeed, the newspaper industry, which in other nations had forcefully led the fight to decommercialize broadcasting, quickly became defenders of the commercial broadcasters as their corporate brethren, and opposed broadcast reform with only a handful of exceptions. As a disconsolate Morris Ernst noted in the 1940s, the corporate media who benefited most by the antidemocratic basis of the U.S. mass media, "are the very forces which can swing the mind of America against finding any remedies for the situation."[27] In the early 1930s, the corporate media provided a roadblock to the communication needs of the broadcast reform movement, a roadblock that proved insurmountable.

These three long-term factors go a long way toward explaining the lack of debate over the control and structure of the media in modern U.S. political life and, further, in accounting for the plight of the broadcast reform movement in the early 1930s. Although these are distinctly powerful phenomena, I do not mean to suggest that any alteration of existing conditions will be forever impossible. Countervailing forces may be on the horizon and their development may eventually signal a shift in the status of the debate over the fundamental contours of the U.S. media system.

Most important, the "American century" is literally and figuratively nearing an end and the halcyon days of a bustling capitalism may well be in America's past. This may eventually undermine the inability to criticize capitalism in U.S. political culture. This is clearly a decisive factor. If no other lesson emerges from the early 1930s, then let it be that any viable campaign to reconstruct the media system must be part of a broad-based mass movement that is attempting to reform the basic institutions of U.S. society.[28] Left as the province of elites, any effort at media reform will quickly be washed up on the same shores that received the broadcast reformers in the early 1930s. The centerpiece of any viable alternative political movement in the U.S. must be the shared belief that contemporary capitalism is working effectively for only a minority of the citizenry and, moreover, that its core tendencies are frequently at odds with democratic ideals. Contemporary U.S. politics are typified by perhaps the narrowest range of legitimate debate of any democratic nation in the world, with an attendant degree of citizen apathy, cynicism, and ignorance that, arguably, is unsurpassed. When U.S. political culture begins to address fundamental issues of power, much as politics should do by definition, questions regarding the media will and must be where they belong: on the agenda.

In the short run, however, those committed to extending the democratic foundations of U.S. society must continue the impressive growth in critical media scholarship. As Thomas Paine wrote in 1776, "a long habit of not thinking a thing wrong, gives it the superficial appearance of being right."[29] Scholars must relentlessly debunk the myths that provide a buttress for the existing media and social structure. Moreover, scholars must strive to develop a vision of a more democratic media system as well as a more democratic society. This will be no easy task, as the efforts of the 1930s reformers suggest. It has yet to be adequately explained how to create such a more democratic system without merely substituting state domination for corporate domination. Nevertheless, this does not mean the task cannot be accomplished, nor does it make the need to do so any less pressing. It is certain, however, that it never will happen if people do not recognize it as a legitimate goal. It is the duty of intellectuals to press ahead with this task regardless of the immediate prospects for reform.

Some may protest that, the preceding factors notwithstanding, there is little evidence that Americans are dissatisfied with their media set-up or that they will have reason to become dissatisfied in the future. Moreover, even if they are dissatisfied, there is no evidence that they regard the issue as serious enough to warrant political activity. In short, people are complacent with the status quo, or at least they are apathetic, which in itself reflects a degree of acceptance that must be acknowledged. By this line of reasoning, the preceding discussion may be dismissed as an academic exercise or a utopian digression. This is an important criticism, for its currency if not its analytic rigor, and it deserves a response. First, it is probably true that most do accept the status quo, after all that is what the three preceding factors also explain. The question remains, however, if this reflects the informed consent of a self-governing people or, as Alexander Meiklejohn put it, the "pseudo consent" of a people who become reconciled to their submission before a "ruling force" that is "overwhelming."[30] If it is the latter, as the evidence suggests, then to accept this explanation as satisfactory is to accept a fairly undemocratic and elitist basis for U.S. society as legitimate.

Second, the notion that the American people are simply apathetic about media policy, or politics in general for that matter, is an issue of the utmost importance for contemporary U.S. scholars and citizens. This observation, however, is at best a description of a situation; it explains nothing and it begs a number of critical intellectual questions that cut across a variety of academic disciplines. It is untenable to lob forth "apathy" as some sort of accounting of the present world situation as if it is the product of an immutable human nature. The "apathy" thesis is only useful if it initiates vital research and debate. When offered as the final word on this subject, or any other subject for that matter, one has left the realm of explanation and entered the domain of apologetics.

Indeed, the first line of defense of any inegalitarian social order is to cultivate the conviction in the subordinate subjects that any fundamental change for the better is impossible, if not undesirable, and therefore unworthy of consideration, let alone action. The responsibility of the intellectual, on the other hand, can be defined as that of making "a ruthless criticism of everything existing," which "must not be afraid of its own conclusions, nor of conflicts with the powers that be." Even in the darkest moment when the possibility of altering existing social relations for the better appears most remote, the intellectual must maintain this commitment. Otherwise, intellectual activity loses its raison d'être and logically becomes a weapon for the powerful or a toy for privileged. Either way, this abdication of responsibility is an open invitation to barbarism in the context of the great crises before the human species. Scholars need to maintain a historical perspective on the present and the future, and reassert the optimism that is necessary for meaningful human existence. "The future is still open," Samir Amin noted recently. "It is still to be lived."[31]

Notes

Please note: Many of the notes have been combined to provide less distraction in the text. When more than one citation is listed in a single note, the citations are presented sequentially and separated by a semicolon. There are rarely more than three citations in a single note, and the notes never pertain to more than a single paragraph.

Sources Frequently Cited in Notes

ABA 1928 *Report of the Fifty-First Annual Meeting of the American Bar Association, 1928* (Baltimore: The Lord Baltimore Press, 1928).

ABA 1929 *Report of the Fifty-Second Annual Meeting of the American Bar Association, 1929* (Baltimore: The Lord Baltimore Press, 1929).

ABA 1930 *Report of the Fifty-Third Annual Meeting of the American Bar Association, 1930* (Baltimore: The Lord Baltimore Press, 1930).

ABA 1931 *Report of the Fifty-Fourth Annual Meeting of the American Bar Association, 1931* (Baltimore: The Lord Baltimore Press, 1931).

ABA 1932 *Report of the Fifty-Fifth Annual Meeting of the American Bar Association, 1932* (Baltimore: The Lord Baltimore Press, 1932).

ABA 1939 *Report of the Sixty-Second Annual Meeting of the American Bar Association, 1939* (Baltimore: The Lord Baltimore Press, 1939).

ACER *Advisory Committee on Education by Radio, Report of the Advisory Committee on Education by Radio Appointed by the Secretary of the Interior* (Columbus, OH: The F. J. Heer Printing Company, 1930).

ACLU Mss   American Civil Liberties Union Papers, Princeton University Library, Princeton, NJ.

AFL 1926   *Report of the Proceedings of the Forty-Sixth Annual Convention of the American Federation of Labor Held at Detroit, Michigan October 4 to 14, Inclusive 1926* (Washington, D.C.: The Law Reporter Printing Company, 1926).

AFL 1927   *Report of the Proceedings of the Forty-Seventh Annual Convention of the American Federation of Labor Held at Los Angeles, California October 3rd to 14th, Inclusive 1927* (Washington, D.C.: The Law Reporter Printing Company, 1927).

AFL 1928   *Report of the Proceedings of the Forth-Eighth Annual Convention of the American Federation of Labor Held at New Orleans, Louisiana November 18 to 28, Inclusive 1928* (Washington, D.C.: The Law Reporter Printing Company, 1928).

AFL 1929   *Report of the Proceedings of the Forty-Ninth Annual Convention of the American Federation of Labor Held at Toronto, Ontario, Canada October 7th to 18th, Inclusive 1929* (Washington, D.C.: The Law Reporter Printing Company, 1929).

AFL 1930   *Report of the Proceedings of the Fiftieth Annual Convention of the American Federation of Labor Held at Boston Massachusetts October 6th to 17th, Inclusive 1930* (Washington, D.C.: The Law Reporter Printing Company, 1930).

AFL 1931   *Report of the Proceedings of the Fifty-First Annual Convention of the American Federation of Labor Held at Vancouver, B. C., Canada October 5th to 15th, Inclusive 1931* (Washington, D.C.: The Law Reporter Printing Company, 1931).

AFL 1932   *Report of the Proceedings of the Fifty-Second Annual Convention of the American Federation of Labor Held at Cincinnati, Ohio November 21st to December 2nd, Inclusive 1932* (Washington, D.C.: The Law Reporter Printing Company, 1932).

AFL 1933   *Report of the Proceedings of the Fifty-Third Annual Convention of the American Federation of Labor Held at Washington, D.C. October 2 to 13, Inclusive 1933* (Washington, D.C.: Judd & Detweiler, Inc., 1933).

AFL 1934   *Report of the Proceedings of the Fifty-Fourth Annual Convention of the American Federation of Labor Held at San Francisco, California October 1 to 12, Inclusive 1934* (Washington, D.C.: Judd & Detweiler, Inc., 1934).

Annals 1935   *Radio—The Fifth Estate*, Edited by Herman S. Hettinger (Philadelphia: The Annals of the American Academy of Political and Social Science, Volume 117, January 1935).

AT&T   American Telephone and Telegraph Archives, Warren, NJ.

AT&T Mss American Telephone and Telegraph Corporate Papers, AT&T Archives, Warren, NJ.

CC Mss Carnegie Corporation of New York Papers, Columbia University, New York, NY.

COHC Columbia Oral History Collection, Columbia University, New York, NY.

Control *Radio Control and Operation,* Edited by E. R. Rankin (Chapel Hill: University of North Carolina Extension Bulletin, 1933).

Current *Current Conflicting Views on American vs. British Broadcasting,* Edited by T. H. Hall (Chicago: National Research Bureau, 1933).

Daniels Mss Josephus Daniels Papers, Library of Congress, Washington, D.C.

Debate *A Debate Handbook on Radio Control and Operation,* Edited by Bower Aly and Gerald D. Shively (Columbia, MO: Staples Publishing Company, 1933).

DoA Mss Department of Agriculture Papers, National Archives, Washington, D.C., Record Group 16.

DoC Mss Department of Commerce Papers, National Archives, Washington, D.C., Record Group 40.

FCC Digest *Digest of Hearings. Federal Communications Commission Broadcast Division, under Sec. 307(c) of the "Communications Act of 1934" October 1–20, November 7–12, 1934* (Washington, D.C.: Federal Communications Commission, 1935).

FCC 1934 *Official Report of Proceedings Before the Federal Communications Commission on Section 307(c) of the Communications Act of 1934,* Smith & Hulse, Official Reporters (Washington, D.C.: Federal Communications Commission, 1935).

FCC Mss Federal Communications Commission Papers, National Archives, Suitland, Md., Record Group 173.

FDR Mss Franklin Delano Roosevelt Papers, Franklin D. Roosevelt Presidential Library, Hyde Park, NY.

FRC 1929 *Third Annual Report of the Federal Radio Commission to the Congress of the United States Covering the Period from October 1, 1928 to November 1, 1929* (Washington, D.C.: United States Government Printing Office, 1929).

FRC 1932 *Commercial Radio Advertising* (Washington, D.C.: United States Government Printing Office, 1932).

Future *Radio and Its Future,* Edited by Martin Codel (New York: Harper and Brothers, 1930).

Harney *In the Matter of Section 307(c) of the Federal Communications Act of 1934; Brief on behalf of Radio Station WLWL Submitted by the Very Reverend John B. Harney, C.S.P.* (Washington, D.C.: 1934).

HH-C Mss Herbert Hoover Papers. Commerce Series. Herbert Hoover Library, West Branch, IA.

HH-P Mss Herbert Hoover Papers. Presidential Subject Series. Herbert Hoover Library, West Branch, IA.

Hooper Mss Stanford C. Hooper Papers, Library of Congress, Washington, D.C.

House 1928 United States House of Representatives, Seventieth Congress, First Session, *Hearings Before the Committee on the Merchant Marine and Fisheries on H.R. 8825* (Washington, D.C.: United States Government Printing Office, 1928).

House 1929 United States House of Representatives, Seventieth Congress, Second Session, *Hearings Before the Committee on Merchant Marine and Fisheries on H.R. 15430 Part 1* (Washington, D.C.: United States Government Printing Office, 1929).

House 1934a United States House of Representatives, Seventy Third Congress, Second Session, *Federal Communications Commission Hearings Before the Committee on Interstate and Foreign Commerce on H.R. 8301* (Washington, D.C.: United States Government Printing Office, 1934).

House 1934b United States House of Representatives, Seventy Third Congress, Second Session, *Radio Broadcasting, Hearings Before the Committee on Merchant Marine, Radio and Fisheries on H.R. 7986* (Washington, D.C.: United States Government Printing Office, 1934).

Howe Mss Louis McHenry Howe Papers. Franklin D. Roosevelt Library, Hyde Park, NY.

IER 1930 *Education on the Air: First Yearbook of the Institute for Education by Radio,* Edited by Josephine H. MacLatchy (Columbus: Ohio State University, 1930).

IER 1931 *Education on the Air: Second Yearbook of the Institute for Education by Radio,* Edited by Josephine H. MacLatchy (Columbus: Ohio State University, 1931).

IER 1932 *Education on the Air: Third Yearbook of the Institute for Education by Radio,* Edited by Josephine H. MacLatchy (Columbus: Ohio State University, 1932).

IER 1933 *Education on the Air: Fourth Yearbook of the Institute for Education by Radio,* Edited by Josephine H. MacLatchy (Columbus: Ohio State University, 1933).

IER 1934 *Education on the Air: Fifth Yearbook of the Institute for Education by Radio,* Edited by Josephine H. MacLatchy (Columbus: Ohio State University, 1934).

IERTV Mss   Institute for Education by Radio and Television Manuscripts,
University Archives, The Ohio State University, Columbus, OH.

Illinois Mss   Public Affairs Director's Office Papers, University of Illinois
Archives, Urbana, IL.

JEM Mss   Joy Elmer Morgan Papers, National Education Association,
Washington, D.C.

NAB *1931*   *Proceedings of the Ninth Annual Convention of the National*
Association of Broadcasters, October 26–28, 1931, Detroit,
Mich. (Washington, D.C.: National Association of Broadcasters,
1931).

NACRE   *Radio and Education: Proceedings of the First Assembly of the*
1931   *National Advisory Council on Radio in Education, 1931,* Edited
by Levering Tyson (Chicago: University of Chicago Press, 1931).

NACRE   *Radio and Education: Proceedings of the Second Annual*
1932   *Assembly of the National Advisory Council on Radio in*
Education, Inc., 1932, Edited by Levering Tyson (Chicago:
University of Chicago Press, 1932).

NACRE   *Radio and Education: Proceedings of the Third Annual Assembly*
1933   *of National Advisory Council on Radio in Education, Inc., 1933,*
Edited by Levering Tyson (Chicago: University of Chicago Press,
1933).

NACRE   *Radio and Education: Proceedings of the Fourth Annual*
1934   *Assembly of National Advisory Council on Radio in Education,*
Inc., 1934, Edited by Levering Tyson (Chicago: University of
Chicago Press, 1934).

NACRE   *Education on the Air . . . and Radio and Education 1935,* Edited
1935   by Levering Tyson and Josephine H. MacLatchy (Chicago:
University of Chicago Press, 1935).

NAEB Mss   National Association of Educational Broadcasters Papers, State
Historical Society of Wisconsin, Madison, WI.

NANA   North American Newspaper Alliance scrapbooks, 1927–1934.
Daily newspaper clippings provided to sixty U.S. daily
newspapers. Organized sequentially in volumes in the Martin
Codel Papers, State Historical Society of Wisconsin, Madison,
WI. Dates given are the dateline, not the date of publication.
Approximated dates are based upon surrounding datelines and are
broad enough to allow for a margin of error.

NASU *1931*   *Transactions and Proceedings of the National Association of State*
Universities in the United States of America 1931, Volume 29,
Edited by A. H. Upham (National Association of State
Universities, 1931).

275

NASU *1933*   *Transactions and Proceedings of the National Association of State Universities in the United States of America 1933, Volume 31,* Edited by A. H. Upham (National Association of State Universities, 1933).

NASU *1934*   *Transactions and Proceedings of the National Association of State Universities in the United States of America 1934, Volume 32,* Edited by A. H. Upham (National Association of State Universities, 1934).

NASU *1937*   *Transactions and Proceedings of the National Association of State Universities in the United States of America 1937, Volume 35,* Edited by Herman G. James (National Association of State Universities, 1937).

NBC Mss   National Broadcasting Company Papers, State Historical Society of Wisconsin, Madison, WI.

NCEB *1936*   *Educational Broadcasting 1936,* Edited by C. S. Marsh (Chicago: University of Chicago Press, 1937).

NCEB *1937*   *Educational Broadcasting 1937,* Edited by C. S. Marsh (Chicago: University of Chicago Press, 1937).

NCER *1934*   *Radio As A Cultural Agency: Proceedings of a National Conference on the Use of Radio as a Cultural Agency in a Democracy,* Edited by Tracy F. Tyler (Washington, D.C.: National Committee on Education by Radio, 1934).

NUEA *1927*   *Proceedings of the Twelfth Annual Convention of the National University Extension Association 1927, Volume 10* (Boston: Wright & Potter Printing Company, 1927).

NUEA *1930*   *Proceedings of the Fifteenth Annual Convention of the National University Extension Association 1930, Volume 13* (Bloomington: Indiana University Press, 1930).

NUEA *1931*   *Proceedings of the Sixteenth Annual Convention of the National University Extension Association 1931, Volume 14* (Bloomington: Indiana University Press, 1931).

NUEA *1932*   *Proceedings of the Seventeenth Annual Convention of the National University Extension Association 1932, Volume 15* (Bloomington: Indiana University Press, 1932).

NUEA *1933*   *Proceedings of the Eighteenth Annual Convention of the National University Extension Association 1933, Volume 16* (Bloomington: Indiana University Press, 1933).

NUEA *1934*   *Proceedings of the Nineteenth Annual Convention of the National University Extension Association, Volume 17, 1934* (Bloomington: Indiana University Press, 1934).

OoE Mss   Office of Education Papers, National Archives, Washington, D.C., Record Group 12.

Sources Frequently Cited in Notes

Paulist Mss   Society of St. Paul the Apostle Papers, Catholic University, Washington, D.C.

PFI Mss   Payne Fund, Inc. Papers, Western Reserve Historical Society, Cleveland, OH.

RMH I Mss   The Presidents' Papers, ca 1925–1945, University of Chicago Library, Chicago, IL.

RMH II Mss   R. M. Hutchins Papers Addenda, University of Chicago Library, Chicago, IL.

Roper Report   *Study of Communications by an Interdepartmental Committee, Letter of Transmittal from the President of the United States to the Chairman of the Committee on Interstate Commerce Transmitting a Memorandum from the Secretary of Commerce Relative to a Study of Communications by an Interdepartmental Committee* (Washington, D.C.: United States Government Printing Office, 1934).

Senate 1926   United States Senate, Sixty-Ninth Congress, First Session, *Radio Control, Hearings Before the Committee on Interstate Commerce on S. 1 and S. 1754* (Washington, D.C.: Government Printing Office, 1926).

Senate 1928   United States Senate, Seventieth Congress, First Session, *Hearings Before Committee on Interstate Commerce on the Confirmation of Federal Radio Commissioners* (Washington, D.C.: United States Government Printing Office, 1928).

Senate 1929   United States Senate, Seventieth Congress, Second Session, *Hearings Before the Committee on Interstate Commerce on S. 4937* (Washington, D.C.: United States Government Printing Office, 1929).

Senate 1933   United States Senate, Seventy-Second Congress, Second Session, *Fees for Radio Licenses, Hearings Before a Subcommittee of the Committee on Interstate Commerce on S. 5201* (Washington, D.C.: United States Government Printing Office, 1933).

Senate 1934   United States Senate, Seventy-Third Congress, Second Session, *Hearings Before the Committee on Interstate Commerce on S. 2910 1934* (Washington, D.C.: United States Government Printing Office, 1934).

SHSW   State Historical Society of Wisconsin, Madison, WI.

Thomas Mss   Norman Thomas Papers, New York Public Library, New York, NY.

Tyler Mss   Tracy F. Tyler Papers, University of Minnesota Archives, Minneapolis, MN.

Wagner Mss   Robert F. Wagner Papers, Georgetown University, Washington, D.C.

Wilbur Mss   Ray Lyman Wilbur Papers, Hoover Institution on War, Revolution and Peace, Stanford University, Stanford, CA.

Young Mss   Owen D. Young Papers, St. Lawrence University, Canton, NY.

Chapter 1

1. See Robert W. McChesney, "Off Limits: An Inquiry into the Lack of Debate Over the Ownership, Structure and Control of the Mass Media in U.S. Political Life," *Communication* 13 (1992): 1–19.

2. See, for example, Ben H. Bagdikian, *The Media Monopoly* (Boston: Beacon Press, 1990); Edward S. Herman and Noam Chomsky, *Manufacturing Consent: The Political Economy of the Mass Media* (New York: Pantheon, 1988). See also Robert W. McChesney, "An Almost Incredible Absurdity for a Democracy," *Journal of Communication Inquiry* 15:1 (Winter 1991):89–114.

3. Gleason L. Archer, *Big Business and Radio* (New York: American Historical Society, 1938). Reprinted by Arno Press, 1971.

4. See Walter B. Emery, *Broadcasting & Government: Responsibilities and Regulations* (East Lansing: Michigan State University Press, 1961); Walter B. Emery, *National and International Systems of Broadcasting* (East Lansing: Michigan State University Press, 1969), pp. 5–15. For another classic statement from this period see Frederick W. Ford, "The Meaning of the Public Interest, Convenience and Necessity," *Journal of Broadcasting* 8 (Winter 1964):8.

5. Erik Barnouw, *A History of Broadcasting in the United States* (New York: Oxford University Press, 1966, 1968, 1970). See also Erik Barnouw, *The Sponsor: Notes on a Modern Potentate* (New York: Oxford University Press, 1978).

6. Mary S. Mander, "The Public Debate About Broadcasting in the Twenties: An Interpretive History," *Journal of Broadcasting* 25 (Spring 1984): 185.

7. Susan J. Douglas, *Inventing American Broadcasting 1899–1922* (Baltimore: The Johns Hopkins University Press, 1987), p. 317.

8. James Schwoch, *The American Radio Industry and Its Latin American Activities. 1900–1939* (Urbana and Chicago: University of Illinois Press, 1990), p. 76. See also, Michele Hilmes, *Hollywood and Broadcasting: From Radio to Cable* (Urbana and Chicago: University of Illinois Press, 1990), p. 49.

9. Lee C. Bollinger, *Images of a Free Press* (Chicago: University of Chicago Press, 1991), p. 63; Robert Britt Horwitz, *The Irony of Regulatory Reform* (New York: Oxford University Press, 1989), p. 127.

10. Perhaps the best treatment has been Philip T. Rosen, *The Modern Stentors: Radio Broadcasting and the Federal Government 1920–1934* (Westport, Conn.: Greenwood Press, 1980), pp. 161–78.

11. Four recent works that share this perspective and develop it in varying ways are: Edward Herman, "Democratic Media," *Z Papers 1992* 1(1): 23–30; John Keane, *The Media and Democracy* (Cambridge, U.K.: Polity, 1991), especially pp. 159–60; Martin A. Lee and Norman Solomon, *Unreliable Sources: A Guide to Detecting Bias in News Media* (New York: Lyle Stuart, 1990), especially pp. 355–58; Charlotte

Ryan, *Prime Time Activism: Media Strategies for Grassroots Organizing* (Boston: South End Press, 1991), especially pp. 235–37.

12. See Horwitz; Hugh G. J. Aitkin, *The Continuous Wave: Technology and American Radio, 1900–1932* (Princeton: Princeton University Press, 1985); Alan Stone, *Public Service Liberalism* (Princeton: Princeton University Press, 1991).

13. See Robert W. McChesney, "Press-Radio Relations and the Emergence of Network, Commercial Broadcasting in the United States, 1930–1935," *Historical Journal of Film, Radio and Television* 11:1 (1991):41–57.

14. See Robert W. McChesney, "Free Speech and Democracy: Louis G. Caldwell, the American Bar Association, and the Debate Over the Free Speech Implications of Broadcast Regulation, 1928–1938," *The American Journal of Legal History* 35 (October 1991):351–92.

Chapter 2

1. For discussions of the formation of RCA and the radio group see Hugh G. J. Aitkin, *The Continuous Wave: Technology and American Radio, 1900–1932* (Princeton: Princeton University Press, 1985), ch. 5; Susan J. Douglas, *Inventing American Broadcasting, 1899–1922* (Baltimore: Johns Hopkins University Press, 1987), ch. 8; N. R. Danielian, *A.T. & T.: The Story of Industrial Conquest* (New York: The Vanguard Press, 1939), ch. 5.

2. Harry Mount, "Interview for Cleveland Plain Dealer," summer 1925, HH-C Mss, Radio Correspondence, 1925 May–September, Box 490; Herbert Hoover to Karl Broadley, November 24, 1925, HH-C Mss, Radio.

3. Cited in James L. Baughman, *Television's Guardians* (Knoxville, TN: University of Tennessee Press, 1985), p. 5.

4. See Aitkin, ch. 5; Douglas, ch. 8.

5. See, for example, C. M. Jansky, "The Problem of the Institutionally Owned Station." In *NACRE 1932*, pp. 214–17; Edward F. Sarno, "The National Radio Conferences," *Journal of Broadcasting* 13 (Spring 1969): 189–202; Carl J. Friedrich and Jeanette Sayre, *The Development of the Control of Advertising on the Air* (New York: Radiobroadcasting Research Project, 1940); Joy Elmer Morgan, "The National Committee on Education by Radio." In *IER 1931*, p. 10.

6. Werner J. Severin, "Commercial Vs. Non-Commercial Radio During Broadcasting's Early Years," *Journal of Broadcasting* 20 (Fall 1978): 491–504; Eugene E. Leach, *Tuning Out Education; The Cooperation Doctrine in Radio, 1922–38* (Washington D.C.: Current, 1983), p. 2; S.E. Frost, Jr., *Education's Own Stations* (Chicago: University of Chicago Press, 1937), p. 4; *FCC Digest*, pp. 180–249.

7. Jansky, "Institutional Station." In *NACRE 1932*, p. 214.

8. "Report of the Standing Committee on Communications." In *ABA 1931*, p. 385.

9. *House 1928*, p. 129; Martin Codel, "Who Pays for Your Radio Program?" *Nation's Business* 17 (August 1929): 39 ff; see also "Federal Control of Radio Broadcasting," *Yale Law Journal* 32 (1929), p. 250.

10. Broadcasting Station Survey, January 1, 1926, pp. 3, 11, Edwin H. Colpitts Papers, AT&T, 07 01 02, Box 77.

11. *FCC Digest*, pp. 180–249; See also, "Statement of Mr. David Sarnoff to Third National Radio Conference," HH-C Mss, Radio: Conferences, National, Third, Box 496.

12. See *Mass Communications*, edited by Wilbur Schramm (Urbana: University of Illinois Press, 1960), p. 43; David Sarnoff, "Address to Chicago Chamber of Commerce, April 1924." In Samuel L. Rothafel and Raymond Francis Yates, *Broadcasting Its New Day* (New York: Arno Press, 1971), pp. 171–84; David Sarnoff, "Letter to E. W. Rice, Jr., Honorary Chairman of the Board, General Electric Company, June 17, 1922." In *American Broadcasting: A Source Book on the History of Radio and Television*, Edited by Lawrence W. Lichty and Malachi C. Topping (New York: Hastings House, 1975), pp. 163–64.

13. H. D. Kellogg, Jr., "Who is to Pay for Broadcasting—and How." In *American Broadcasting*, pp. 208–10.

14. *The Reminiscences of Phillips Carlin*, p. 13., COHC; Memorandum on Proposed Methods of Supporting Broadcasting, September 11, 1924, AT&T Mss, Box 61.

15. Levering Tyson to Frederick P. Keppel, February 2, 1925, CC Mss, NACRE Box 1, NACRE 1929.

16. H. A. Bellows, "Broadcasting: A New Industry." In *American Broadcasting*, p. 229; "Report of the Committee on Radio," *American Newspaper Publishers Association Bulletin*, No. 5374, May 5, 1927, p. 285; see also John W, Spalding, "1928: Radio Becomes a Mass Advertising Medium," *Journal of Broadcasting* 8 (Winter 1963–1964): 31–44.

17. *The Reminiscences of William Harkness*, pp. 63, 44, COHC; *The Reminiscences of Mark Woods*, p. 19, COHC.

18. William Harkness to J. J. Carty, September 30, 1925, John J. Carty Papers, AT&T, 83–10–01, Box 106; "The Use of Radio Broadcasting as a Publicity Medium," undated AT&T pamphlet, sometime in 1926 before founding of NBC, E. P. H. James Papers, SHSW, Container 1, Folder 8; *The Reminiscences of Walter Evans*, p. 30, COHC.

19. Merlin H. Aylesworth, "Radio's Accomplishment," *Century* 118 (June 1929): 214–21; for an analysis of how commercial values permeated WEAF programming even during the era of indirect advertising, see Julie D'Acci, "Early Radio and the Industrialization of Culture: WEAF 1922–1929," unpublished research paper, presented to research colloquium, Department of Communication Arts, University of Wisconsin–Madison, 1991. See also assorted correspondence, HH-C Mss, 1925 October–December, Box 490; Herbert Hoover to Donald D. Davis, December 26, 1924, HH-C Mss, Radio Correspondence, 1924 October–December, Box 490; Alfred N. Goldsmith to Herbert Hoover, November 24, 1925, for similar sentiments see Henry A. Bellows to Herbert Hoover, November 24, 1925, HH-C Mss, Radio Conferences, National, Fourth, Box 496.

20. Mount, HH-C Mss, Box 490; Herbert Hoover to Wallace H. White, December 4, 1924, HH-C Mss, Radio Correspondence, 1924, October–December, Box 490.

21. "Opening Address by Herbert Hoover." In *Proceedings of the Fourth Na-*

tional Radio Conference and Recommendations for Regulation of Radio (Washington, D.C.: Government Printing Office, 1926), p. 5; Herbert Hoover to Harold G. Ingham, December 13, 1924, Herbert Hoover to Col. Arthur Woods, December 10, 1924, "Hoover Advocates Tax on Radio Sales," *The New York Times,* December 22, 1924, in HH-C Mss, Radio Correspondence, 1924 October–December, Box 490.

22. This legislative history is reviewed in Eliot C. Lovett, "The Antitrust Provisions of the Radio Act," *The Journal of Radio Law* 2 (January 1932):1–44.

23. Department of Commerce Press Release, July 9, 1926, AT&T Mss, Box 2002; see also Stephen B. Davis, "The Law of the Air." In *The Radio Industry: The Story of Its Development,* Edited by Anton de Haas (Chicago: A. W. Shaw Company, 1928), p. 169; Daniel E. Garvey, "Secretary Hoover and the Quest for Broadcast Regulation," *Journalism History* 3 (Autumn 1976): 66–70, 85; Marvin R. Bensman, "The Zenith-WJAZ case and the Chaos of 1926–27," *Journal of Broadcasting* 14 (Fall 1970): 423–40; "Pending Litigation Marks Beginning of Radio Jurisprudence," *American Bar Association Journal* 15 (March 1929): 173–78.

24. See, for example, C. W. Pugsley to Calvin Coolidge, February 11, 1927, HH-C Mss, General 1927–1928, Box 500; Christian Grell to President Calvin Coolidge, February 1, 1927, FRC Legislation, HH-C Mss, Box 501; see Donald G. Godfrey, "Senator Dill and the 1927 Radio Act," *Journal of Broadcasting* 23 (1978): pp. 477–89; *The Reminiscences of Herbert Clark Hoover,* p. 15, COHC.

25. See "Report of the Committee on Radio Broadcasting." In *NUEA 1927,* p. 182; Morris L. Ernst, "Who Shall Control the Air," *The Nation* 122 (April 21, 1926): 444; Donald G. Godfrey, "The 1927 Radio Act: People and Politics," *Journalism History* 4 (Autumn 1977):78. Godfrey's article was based on his dissertation research concerning the congressional debate surrounding the passage of the Radio Act of 1927. See Donald G. Godfrey, "A Rhetorical Analysis of the Congressional Debates on Broadcast Regulation in the United States, 1927" (Ph.D. dissertation, University of Washington, 1975); Erik Barnouw, *A Tower in Babel* (New York: Oxford University Press, 1966), p. 281; Carl J. Friedrich and Evelyn Sternberg, "Congress and the Control of Radio-Broadcasting I," *The American Political Science Review* 37 (October 1943):799–800.

26. Statement by Secretary Herbert Hoover regarding the radio situation, February 24, 1927, HH-C Mss, Radio Correspondence, 1927 January–April, Box 490; Ed Craney, "Interview with C. C. Dill," July 21, 1964, pp. 8–9, Erik Barnouw Papers, Columbia University, New York, NY, Box 32, Miscellaneous Background Documents.

27. See Louis G. Caldwell, "The Standard of Public Interest, Convenience or Necessity as Used in the Radio Act of 1927," *Air Law Review* 1 (July 1930): 295–330; Willard D. Rowland, Jr., "The Meaning of 'The Public Interest' in Communications Policy—Part I: Its Origins in State and Federal Regulation," paper presented to International Communication Association, 1989 Annual Meeting, San Francisco, CA.

28. Clarence C. Dill, "Safe-Guarding the Ether—The American Way," *Congressional Digest,* August–September 1933, p. 196; second quote from Lucas A. Powe, Jr., *American Broadcasting and the First Amendment* (Berkeley: University of California Press, 1987), p. 60.

29. FRC press release, March 15, 1927, Text of Radio Talk by Judge Eugene O. Sykes, March 17, 1927, HH-C Mss, FRC Clippings, 1926–1928 and undated, Box 501; C. M. Jansky to I. L. Lenroot, February 21, 1927, HH-C Mss, FRC General, 1927–28, Box 500.

30. Minutes of Conference Before the Federal Radio Commission, March 29–April 1, 1927, pp. 1–4, HH-C Mss, Radio Conference 3/29/27, Box 491; Robert Mack, "Confidence is Felt by Large Broadcasters," April 1, 1927, NANA, Vol. 58; Memorandum on Hearings Before the Federal Radio Commission, April 5, 1927, Edwin H. Colpitts Papers, AT&T, 07–01–02, Box 77.

31. FRC Minutes, March 29–April 1, 1927, pp. 163, 359, 374, 154, HH-C Mss, Box 491.

32. This is discussed at length in the "Report of the Standing Committee on Radio Law." In *ABA 1929*, pp. 404–506; see also Laurence F. Schmeckebier, *The Federal Radio Commission* (Washington, D.C.: The Brookings Institution, 1932), pp. 22–23; Federal Radio Commission Minutes, April 29, 1927, p. 27, FCC Mss, FRC Minutes, Microfilm reel 1.1; Federal Radio Commission Minutes, November 2, 1927, p. 227, FCC Mss, FRC Minutes, Microfilm reel 1.1.

33. Robert Mack, "Success of Plan Depends on Test," May 25, 1927, NANA, Vol. 58; Robert Mack, "Only Change in Policy of Board," October 14, 1927, NANA, Vol. 58.

34. *House 1928*, January 27, 1928, p. 68.

35. *Ibid.*, January 31, 1928, pp. 108–9.

36. *Ibid.*, January 27, 1928, p. 74; *Senate 1928*, p. 192.

37. President, National Association of Broadcasters to Harold Lafount, January 23, 1928, FCC Mss, RG 173, General Correspondence 1927–1946, 89–6, NAB, Box 395.

38. "Inquiry Looming on Radio Policies," undated, late December 1927, NANA, Vol. 58; "Breaking of Chain Dominance Likely," undated, early January 1928, NANA, Vol. 58; "High-Power Radio May Be Curtailed," undated, late March 1928, NANA, Vol. 58.

39. *ABA 1929*, pp. 404–506; Murray Edelman, *The Licensing of Radio Services in the United States, 1927 to 1947* (Urbana: University of Illinois Press, Illinois Studies in the Social Sciences, 1950), pp. 38–39; L. S. Baker to Ira E. Robinson, August 31, 1928, FCC Mss, RG 173, FCC General Correspondence 1927–1946, 89–6, NAB, Box 395; NAB press release, April 23, 1928, FCC Mss, RG 173, FCC General Correspondence 1927–1946, NBC, Box 398.

40. Federal Radio Commission Minutes, March 19, 1928, pp. 383–85, FCC Mss, RG 173, FRC Minutes, Microfilm reel 1.1; Federal Radio Commission Minutes, March 26, 1928, FCC Mss, RG 173, FRC Minutes, Microfilm reel 1.1; *House 1929*, p. 275.

41. Armstrong Perry to S. H. Evans, January 6, 1931, PFI Mss, Container 56, Folder 1071; "Harold A. Lafount, Former Utahn, Dies," October 21, 1952, *Desert News & Telegraph*, in HH-C Mss, FRC, Endorsements J-N, Box 150.

42. O. H. Caldwell Endorsers, HH-C Mss, FRC Endorsements, Lists-Zone 1, Box 501; "Speech of Commissioner O. H. Caldwell." In *Proceedings of the Fifth*

Annual Convention of the National Association of Broadcasters, September 19–21, 1927, in HH-C Mss, 5th Annual Assoc. of Broadcasters, Box 491; Harold Lafount to Paul Wooten, June 11, 1931, HH-P Mss, FRC, 1931 June-July, Box 148.

43. *Senate 1928*, Part One, pp. 151, 191; *Senate 1929*, p. 142; "And All Because They're Smart," June 1935, p. 13, Columbia Broadcasting System Corporate Press Services, New York, NY.

44. "Confidential Memorandum: Allocation of Broadcasting Channels to Zones and States," March 30, 1928, FCC Mss, FCC General Correspondence 1927–1946, 66–4, Frequencies, Box 275; Federal Radio Commission Minutes, April 5, 1928, p. 441, FCC Mss, RG 173, FRC Minutes, Microfilm reel 1.1; Federal Radio Commission Minutes, March 30, 1928, p. 427, FCC Mss, RG 173, FRC Minutes, Microfilm reel 1.1; "Proposals Made to Radio Board Taken to Task," April 11, 1928, NANA, Vol. 58.

45. Federal Radio Commission Minutes, April 11, 1928, pp. 461–63, FCC Mss, RG 173, FRC Minutes, Microfilm reel 1.1; George McClelland to O. H. Caldwell, January 4, 1928, NBC Mss, General Correspondence, Box 3, Folder 34. The findings of the engineers committee were nearly identical to those provided in a November 1927 report by RCA's and NBC's chief engineer, Alfred Goldsmith, who was on the FRC's committee of consulting engineers. Indeed, the report reflected the general consensus of the corporate radio engineering community as had emerged during 1927. See Alfred N. Goldsmith, "Analysis of Network Broadcasting," paper presented to 1927 Mid-Winter meeting of the Radio Division of the National Electrical Manufacturers Association, in HH-C Mss, Radio Correspondence, 1927 May–December, Box 490.

46. David F. Noble, *America By Design: Science, Technology and the Rise of Corporate Capitalism* (New York: Oxford University Press, 1979), p. 97.

47. J. H. Dellinger, "Engineering Aspects of the Work of the Federal Radio Commission." In *Proceedings of the Institute of Radio Engineers* 17:8 (August 1929): 1333; Alfred N. Goldsmith, "Cooperation Between the Institute of Radio Engineers and Manufacturers' Associations." In *Proceedings of the Institute of Radio Engineers* 16:8 (August 1928): 1071; see also A. Michal McMahon, *The Making of a Profession: A Century of Electrical Engineering in America* (New York: Institute of Electrical and Electronic Engineers, Inc., 1984), pp. 133–73.

48. M. H. Aylesworth to Ira E. Robinson, September 25, 1928, E. O. Sykes to M. H. Aylesworth, May 21, 1928, O. H. Caldwell to M. H. Aylesworth, August 17, 1928, FCC Mss, RG 173, FCC General Correspondence 1927–1946, 89–6, NBC, Box 398; Agreements and Differences Which Appear to Prevail at Present Regarding Broadcast License Allocations, April 24, 1928, p. 2, FCC Mss, RG 173, FCC General Correspondence 1927–1946, 66–4, Frequencies, Box 275.

49. O. H. Caldwell to M. H. Aylesworth, May 14, 1928, FCC Mss, RG 173, FCC General Correspondence 1927–1946, 89–6, NBC, Box 398.

50. Robert Mack, "Await Echoes From Speech of Caldwell," May 2, 1928, NANA, Vol. 58.

51. Edelman, pp. 38–39; Federal Radio Commission Minutes, April 22, 1928–July 30, 1928, pp. 579–645, FCC Mss, RG 173, FRC Minutes, Microfilm reel 1.1;

Memorandi, July 24, 1928, July 26, 1928, FCC Mss, RG 173, FCC General Correspondence 1927–1946, 20–2, Memos to Commission, Box 128; *House 1929*, pp. 248, 256, 273.

52. Louis G. Caldwell, "Summary of Recommendations," August 1928, FCC Mss, RG 173, FCC General Correspondence 1927–1946, 20–2, Memos to Commissioners, Box 128; Rosen, p. 135; Barnouw, pp. 215–19.

53. "At Large with Sol Taishoff." In *The First Fifty Years of Broadcasting* (Washington, D.C.: Broadcasting Publications Inc., 1982), p. vi.; Frank C. Waldrop, *McCormick of Chicago* (Englewood Cliffs, NJ: Prentice-Hall, Inc., 1966), p. 201; "Station Revision Called Justified," *The New York Times*, July 8, 1928, Section 9, p. 15; Louis G. Caldwell, "Memorandum to the Federal Radio Commission," August 17, 1928, FCC Mss, RG 173, FCC General Correspondence 1927–1946, Memos to Commission, Box 128.

54. *House 1929*, pp. 75, 56; J. H. Dellinger, "Analysis of Broadcasting Station Allocation." In *Proceedings of the Institute of Radio Engineers* 16:11 (November 1928): p. 1478.

55. "FRC Interpretation of Public Interest." In *Documents of American Broadcasting*, fourth edition, edited by Frank J. Kahn (Englewood Cliffs, N. J.: Prentice-Hall, Inc., 1984), pp. 57–62.

56. *ABA 1929*, p. 459; *Federation News*, May 9, 1931, p. 9; Powe, Jr., p. 65.

57. See *ABA 1929*, pp. 459, 470, 491.

58. *FRC 1929*, p. 32.

59. *Ibid.*, p. 34.

60. *Ibid.*, p. 34.

61. *Ibid.*, pp. 35, 36.

62. *Ibid.*, p. 32.

63. Christopher H. Sterling, *Electronic Media, A Guide to Trends in Broadcasting and Newer Technologies 1920–1983* (New York: Praeger, 1984), p. 12; Thomas Porter Robinson, *Radio Networks and the Federal Government* (New York: Columbia University Press, 1943), pp. 26–27; "The Menace of Radio Monopoly," *Education by Radio*, March 26, 1931, p. 27; "The Power Trust and the Public Schools," *Education by Radio*, December 10, 1931, p. 150; "Radio Censorship and the Federal Communications Commission," *Columbia Law Review* 39 (March 1939): p. 447; 97 percent figure cited in William Boddy, *Fifties Television: The Industry and Its Critics* (Urbana and Chicago: University of Illinois Press, 1990), p. 36.

64. Josephine Young Case and Everett Needham Case, *Owen D. Young and American Enterprise* (Boston: David R. Godine, 1982), p. 356.

65. *The Remininscences of William C. Hedges*, p. 32, COHC; *The Remininscences of Frank Atkinson Arnold*, p. 66, COHC; *Woods*, p. 38, COHC.

66. Martin Codel, "Networks Reveal Impressive Gains," undated, January 1931, NANA, Vol. 61; Herman S. Hettinger, "Some Fundamental Aspects of Radio Broadcasting," *Harvard Business Review* 13 (1935): 14–28; "Chain Income From Time Sales," *Variety*, January 8, 1935, p. 40; *Hearings Before the Committee on Interstate Commerce United States Senate on Commission on Communications* (Washington, D.C: United States Government Printing Office, 1930), January 18, 1930, pp. 1790–92.

67. "Neither Sponsors Nor Stations Heed Radio Listeners' Grumbling," *Business Week*, February 10, 1932, pp. 18–19; *Education by Radio*, January 5, 1932, p. 2; Rosen, p. 158; J. Fred MacDonald, *Don't Touch That Dial: Radio Programming in American Life, 1920–1960* (Chicago: Nelson-Hall, 1979), pp. 29–34; Michele Hilmes, *Hollywood and Broadcasting: From Radio to Cable* (Urbana and Chicago: University of Illinois Press, 1990), p. 52.

68. Rosen, p. 12; Barnouw, p. 270; Henry Volkening, "Abuses of Radio Broadcasting," *Current History* 33 (December 1930): 396–400.

69. *FCC Digest*, pp. 180–249; *Congressional Record*, 78 (May 15, 1934): 8830–34; "Superpower," *Education by Radio*, May 7, 1931, p. 50.

70. W. S. Gregson to B. B. Brackett, February 25, 1932, NAEB Mss, Box No. 1a, General Correspondence, 1932; Rosen, p. 136.

71. J. Wright to Frank R. Reid, May 26, 1930, PFI Mss, Container 41, Folder 796; Armstrong Perry to Ella Phillips Crandall, September 23, 1930, p. 3, PFI Mss, Container 56, Folder 1070; "Personal and Strictly Confidential," B. B. Brackett to T. M. Beaird, December 15, 1931, NAEB Papers, Box No. 1a, General Correspondence 1929–1931; B. B. Brackett to Joseph F. Wright, November 28, 1932, NAEB Papers, Box No. 1a, General Correspondence 1932; "Federation Hears Radio Situation," *Federation News*, June 8, 1929, p. 8.

72. "A Report on Stewardship," *Education by Radio*, December 1937, p. 61; "Discussion." In *IER 1930*, p. 251; B. B. Brackett to T. M. Beaird, February 2, 1932, NAEB Mss, Box No. 1a, General Correspondence 1932.

73. *Senate 1929*, February 4, 1929, p. 24; *House 1929*, p. 258.

74. Interview between author and Bethuel M. Webster, Jr., February 18, 1987; also Bethuel M. Webster, Jr., "Notes on the Policy of the Administration with Reference to the Control of Communications," *Air Law Review* 5 (April 1934): 107–31.

75. "Superpower," *Education by Radio*, May 7, 1931, p. 49; see also "The Committee on Radio Broadcasting," *Transactions and Proceedings of the National Association of State Universities in the United States of America, Volume 27, 1929,* Edited by A. H. Upham, p. 37.

76. This point has been revealed in several places. See Walter V. Woehlke to S. Howard Evans, October 1, 1931, PFI Mss, Container 60, Folder 1163; testimony of Father John B. Harney, *Hearings Before the Committee on Interstate Commerce United States Senate 73rd Session on S. 2910 1934* (Washington D.C.: United States Printing Office, 1934), March 13, 1934, p. 186; John Henry McCracken, "The Fess Bill for Education by Radio," *Education by Radio*, March 19, 1931, p. 21; George H. Gibson, *Public Broadcasting: The Role of the Federal Government, 1919–1976* (New York: Praeger Publishers, 1976), p. 8; "Discussion following speech by Joy Elmer Morgan." In *IER 1931*, p. 24; Armstrong Perry, "The College Station and the Federal Radio Commission." In *IER 1931*, p. 33.

77. Louis G. Caldwell, "Radio and the Law." In *Future*, p. 231; "Statement of Mr. S. Howard Evans." In *FCC 1934*, Volume One, p. 202.

78. "Superpower," *Education By Radio*, May 7, 1931, p. 49; E. N. Nockels, "The Tribune, Caldwell and Property Rights," *The Federation News*, September 5, 1931, p. 6; Herman S. Hettinger, "The Future of Radio as an Advertising Medium,"

The Journal of Business of the University of Chicago 7:4 (October 1934): 284; Lafount to Wooten, June 11, 1931, HH-P Mss, Box 148.

79. Martin Codel, "Expert Approves Reallocation Plan," undated, October 1928, NANA, Vol. 58.

80. Charles McKinley Saltzman, "Commercial Broadcasting and Education." In *NACRE 1931*, p. 26; Harold A. Lafount, "Contributions of the Federal Radio Commission." In *IER 1931*, p. 23.

81. Perry, *IER 1931*, p. 40.

82. Harold A. Lafount, "Educational Programs in Radio Broadcasting," *School and Society* 34 (December 5, 1931); 758–60; Lafount, *IER 1931*, p. 14; *Senate 1929*, February 4, 1929, p. 24.

83. Statement by Radio Commissioner Harold A, Lafount, August 5, 1929, HH-P Mss, FRC, 1929, Box 147; Lafount to Wooten, HH-P Mss, Box 148.

84. Ira E. Robinson to Armstrong Perry, December 20, 1930, PFI Mss, Container 43, Folder 841.

85. Ira E. Robinson, "Memorandum for the General Counsel," October 19, 1928, FCC Mss, RG 173, FCC General Correspondence 1927–1946, 20–2, Memos to Commission, Box 129; Ira E. Robinson, "Memorandum for the Commissioners," October 16, 1928, FCC Mss, RG 173, FCC General Correspondence 1927–1946, 20–2, Memos to Commission, Box 129; Federal Radio Commission Minutes, October 12, 1928, p. 96, FCC Mss, RG 173, FRC Minutes, Microfilm reel 1.1; Ira E. Robinson to Ray Lyman Wilbur, February 18, 1930, Ray Lyman Wilbur Manuscripts, Hoover Institution on War, Revolution and Peace, Stanford University, Palo Alto, CA, Box 63, Folder 1.

86. *House 1929*, January 8, 1929, p. 44; "Commissioner Robinson Stands Firm," *Radio Broadcast* 14 (January 1929): 163–64; Martin Codel, "Evils of Radio Aired at Hearing," undated, late October 1929, NANA, Vol. 60.

87. Walter H. Newton memo, October 18, 1929, Sam Pickard to Lawrence Richey, February 21, 1929, HH-P Mss, FRC, 1929, Box 147; Walter H. Newton memo re: Couzens and Robinson, January 20, 1930, HH-P Mss, FRC, Endorsements O-R, Box 150; Sol Taishoff, "Session of Radio-Minded Congress Nears," *Broadcasting*, December 1, 1931, p. 5.

88. Ira E. Robinson, "Who Owns Radio?" In *IER 1930*, pp. 16–17.

Chapter 3

1. Information taken from description of Payne Fund, Inc., Records in the Western Reserve Historical Society Manuscript Collections, John J. Grabowski, editor; for discussion of Payne Fund's work in motion picture effects studies, see Garth Jowett, "Social Science as a Weapon: The Payne Fund's Film Studies, 1927–1930," *Communication*, forthcoming.

2. Information taken from description of Payne Fund, Inc., op. cit.; Information on Frances Bolton taken from description of Frances Payne Bolton Papers in the Western Reserve Historical Society Manuscript Collections, John J. Grabowski and Kermit J. Pike, editors. The analysis of the Payne Fund in these opening paragraphs

has been assisted by Garth Jowett and Ian Jarvie, both of whom have researched the Payne Fund's involvement with motion pictures.

Following her husband's death in 1939, Mrs. Bolton was elected to replace him in the House of Representatives. She remained in office for twenty-nine years.

3. Armstrong Perry, "Summary of the Payne Fund's Activities in Radio," undated, late 1933, PFI Mss, Container 40, Folder 768; Olive M. Jones and B. H. Darrow, "Report of the Preliminary Committee on Educational Broadcasting," undated, early 1928, PFI Mss, Container 51, Folder 981.

4. Armstrong Perry, "Memorandum for Mrs. Bolton," April 23, 1931, PFI Mss, Container 56, Folder 1072; Armstrong Perry to H. M. Clymer, May 29, 1929, PFI Mss, Container 56, Folder 1068.

5. "Statement of Mr. Armstrong Perry," First National Radio Conference Minutes, pp. 120–24, HH-C Mss, Radio Conference, National, First, Box 496; H. M. Clymer to Mrs. Chester C. Bolton, December 27, 1927, PFI Mss, Container 56, Folder 1067; H. M. Clymer, "Memorandum to Miss Davies," April 1, 1929, PFI Mss, Container 56, Folder 1067.

6. Armstrong Perry, *Radio in Education: The Ohio School of the Air and Other Experiments* (New York: The Payne Fund, 1929); "Praises Commercial Stations," *Broadcasters' News Bulletin,* February 21, 1931.

7. Armstrong Perry, "The Ohio School of the Air and Other Experiments in the Use of Radio in Education," May 29, 1929, PFI Mss, Container 69, Folder 1353; "The Report of B. H. Darrow, February 1928," March 7, 1928, PFI Mss, Container 70, Folder 1368.

8. Armstrong Perry to Ella Phillips Crandall, July 3, 1929, PFI Mss, Container 56, Folder 1068; "Report of Ohio Conferences on Radio Broadcasting for the Schools, March 18–20, 1929," PFI Mss, Container 70, Folder 1368; Perry, "Memorandum for Mrs. Bolton," April 23, 1931, PFI Mss, Container 56, Folder 1072.

9. Armstrong Perry to H. M. Clymer, April 6, 1929, PFI Mss, Container 56, Folder 1067; H. M. Clymer to Executive Committee, Department of Superintendence, National Education Association, April 6, 1929, PFI Mss, Container 56, Folder 1067.

10. Armstrong Perry, "The Status of Education by Radio in the United States." In *NUEA 1931,* p. 16; Eugene E. Leach, *Tuning Out Education: The Cooperation Doctrine in Radio, 1922–38* (Washington, D.C.: Current, 1983), p. 5; Ray Lyman Wilbur, "The Radio in Our Republic." In *NACRE 1931,* pp. 85, 89.

11. Leach, p. 8; *ACER,* p. 7; "Minutes of Conference on Radio Education," June 13, 1929, OoE Mss, Box 31.

12. John C. Jensen to L. A. Kalbach, August 13, 1929, OoE Mss, RG 12, Box 31.

13. Armstrong Perry to Ella Phillips Crandall, September 2, 1929, PFI Mss, Container 56, Folder 1068; Ella Phillips Crandall to Armstrong Perry, November 18, 1929, PFI Mss, Container 56, Folder 1069; *ACER,* p. 51.

14. Armstrong Perry to C. M. Koon, October 4, 1929, PFI Mss, Container 56, Folder 1069; Armstrong Perry to Ella Phillips Crandall, August 3, 1929, PFI Mss, Container 56, Folder 1068.

15. Armstrong Perry to Ella Phillips Crandall, "Report on the Present Status of Radio in Education," October 6, 1929, PFI Mss, Container 56, Folder 1069; Arm-

strong Perry to Ella Phillips Crandall, July 9, 1929, PFI Mss, Container 56, Folder 1068; Armstrong Perry to J. L. Clifton, August 21, 1929, PFI Mss, Container 56, Folder 1068.

16. Armstrong Perry to Ella Phillips Crandall, October 25, 1929, PFI Mss, Container 56, Folder 1069.

17. Armstrong Perry, "The College Station and the Federal Radio Commission." In *IER 1931,* pp. 16–17; Armstrong Perry to Ella Phillips Crandall, November 24, 1929, PFI Mss, Container 56, Folder 1069.

18. *ACER,* pp. 35–37.

19. "Meeting of the National Advisory Committee on Education by Radio," December 30, 1929, OoE Mss, Box 32, p. 3; "Some Notes on the Trip," OoE Mss, Box 2, Miscellaneous General Correspondence; *ACER,* pp. 66–67, 26.

20. Leach, p. 6; *ACER,* p. 76.

21. W. John Cooper to H. Robinson Shipherd, March 31, 1930, OoE Mss, Box 31; Armstrong Perry to Ella Phillips Crandall, March 17, 1930, PFI Mss, Container 56, Folder 1069.

22. Ray Lyman Wilbur to Charles McKinley Saltzman, May 29, 1930, June 12, 1930, FCC Mss, Box 104, General Correspondence; Charles McKinley Saltzman to Ray Lyman Wilbur, June 7, 1930, PFI Mss, Container 59, Folder 1135.

23. Armstrong Perry to Ella Phillips Crandall, March 17, 1930, PFI Mss, Container 56, Folder 1069; W. John Cooper to Presidents of Land Grant Institutions having Broadcasting Stations, undated, summer 1930, OoE Mss, RG 12, Box 32; Armstrong Perry, "The Status of Education by Radio in the United States." In *IER 1930,* pp. 80–81.

24. Ira E. Robinson, "Who Owns Radio?" In *IER 1930,* pp. 8–18; Armstrong Perry to Ella Phillips Crandall, July 5, 1930, PFI Mss, Container 56, Folder 1070.

25. Armstrong Perry to Margaret Walker, July 5, 1930, PFI Mss, Container 56, Folder 1070; R. C. Higgy and B. B. Brackett to the Governors of Various States, July 1, 1930, NAEB Mss, Box 68a, Printed Materials, 1930s; Armstrong Perry, "Radio and Education." In *Biennial Survey of Education 1928–1930* (Washington, D.C.: United States Printing Office, 1932), p. 634.

26. Ella Phillips Crandall to Armstrong Perry, July 17, 1930, PFI Mss, Container 56, Folder 1070; Ella Phillips Crandall, "Memorandum of Conference with Mr. Perry," July 23, 1930, PFI Mss, Container 69, Folder 1352.

27. "Proposed Plan of Action," October 2, 1930, PFI Mss, Container 69, Folder 1352; "Memoranda re Conferences October 9 to 12, 1930," October 12, 1930, PFI Mss, Container 69, Folder 1352.

28. Letter of Transmittal of Commissioner Cooper, undated, 1930, OoE Mss, Box 31; Armstrong Perry to Ella Phillips Crandall, July 21, 1930, PFI Mss, Container 56, Folder 1070; Tracy F. Tyler, "The National Committee on Education by Radio." In *Debate,* p. 118; From discussion in *NCER 1934,* p. 38.

29. "Minutes of the Conference on Educational Radio Problems Stevens Hotel, Chicago, October 13, 1930, At the Invitation of the U.S. Commissioner of Education," OoE Mss, Box 31.

30. Tyler, *Debate,* pp. 119–20; Minutes, October 13, 1930, OoE Mss, Box 31.

31. "Record of Committee Meeting," December 30, 1930, PFI Mss, Container 38, Folder 743.

32. Ella Phillips Crandall to Armstrong Perry, December 2, 1930, PFI Mss, Container 56, Folder 1071.

33. Tracy F. Tyler, "Brief Summary Report of the National Committee on Education by Radio, 1931–1935," pp. 1–5, Tyler Mss, NCER file.

34. See correspondence in HH-P Mss, FRC, 1930 July–August, Box 148; Henry A. Bellows to Walter H. Newton, November 26, 1930, William John Cooper to Ray Lyman Wilbur, December 8, 1930, HH-P Mss, FRC, 1930 November–December, Box 148.

35. "Summary of Miss Crandall's Discussions with Dr. Charters," March 14, 1931, PFI Mss, Container 69, Folder 1352; B. H. Darrow to H. M. Clymer, February 3, 1931, PFI Mss, Container 68, Folder 1343.

36. Armstrong Perry to Edward Klauber, March 9, 1931, PFI Mss, Container 55, Folder 1052.

37. A. G. Crane to B. B. Brackett, April 27, 1934, NAEB Mss, Box 1a, General Correspondence 1934.

38. Joy Elmer Morgan, "Education's Rights on the Air." In *NACRE 1931*, p. 128.

39. See Joy Elmer Morgan and E. D. Bullock, *Selected Articles on Municipal Ownership* (Minneapolis, MN: Wilson, 1911); Joy Elmer Morgan, *The American Citizens Handbook* (Washington, D.C.: National Education Association, 1941); for an example of his populist sentiment, see Joy Elmer Morgan, "The Corporation in America," *Journal of the National Education Association* 23 (December 1934):227–29; Armstrong Perry to Ella Phillips Crandall, October 26, 1930, PFI Mss, Container 56, Folder 1070.

40. Martin Codel, "Editor Sponsors Broadcast Plan," October 15, 1928, NANA, Vol. 58.

41. Avis Roberts, "The Battle to Save Radio for the People," March 8, 1962, JEM Mss, NEA, FCB 1, Drawer 1; Morgan, *NACRE 1931*, pp. 123, 128.

42. *Ibid.*, pp. 120–21.

43. Joy Elmer Morgan, "The Radio in Education." In *NUEA 1932*, p. 79; Joy Elmer Morgan to Dr. William McAndrew, September 20, 1932, JEM Mss, NEA, 1932 correspondence, FCB 2, Drawer 3.

44. Joy Elmer Morgan, "The National Committee on Education by Radio." In *IER 1931*, p. 25.

45. See, for example, Morgan, *NACRE 1931*, p. 124; Joy Elmer Morgan, "Radio and Education." In *Future*, pp. 76–77; Joy Elmer Morgan, "Should the U.S. Adopt the British System of Radio Control?" *Congressional Digest*, August–September 1933, p. 206; Morgan, *NUEA 1932*, p. 83; Joy Elmer Morgan to H. O. Davis, March 8, 1932, PFI Mss, Container 47, Folder 901.

46. Tracy F. Tyler to C. C. Cunningham, November 2, 1933, PFI Mss, Container 47, Folder 916; Armstrong Perry to Gross W. Alexander, December 18, 1930, PFI Mss, Container 59, Folder 1135.

47. "The Fittest Survive," *Broadcasting*, January 15, 1933, p. 16; " 'Listeners

Society'," *Broadcasting*, April 1, 1933, p. 14; "When Educators Differ," *Broadcasting*, June 1, 1933, p. 20; "Mass Action is Imperative," *Broadcasters' News Bulletin*, February 14, 1931; "Exit Mr. Morgan," *Broadcasting*, September 15, 1935, p. 30.

48. Joy Elmer Morgan, "Report of the Chairman," April 9, 1931, PFI Mss, Container 38, Folder 743; see, for example, Tracy F. Tyler, *Some Interpretations and Conclusions of the Land-Grant Radio Survey* (Washington, D.C.: National Committee on Education by Radio, 1933).

49. Morgan, *IER 1931*, p. 10; "Distribution Sheet . . . Education by Radio," May 1934, PFI Mss, Container 39, Folder 751; see also "Report of the NUEA Committee on Radio for the Year." In *NUEA 1934*, p. 83.

50. Armstrong Perry to Ella Phillips Crandall, October 28, 1932, PFI Mss, Container 68, Folder 1344.

51. "Confidential Report of Armstrong Perry on the International Radiotelegraphic Conference in Madrid, September 3 to December 9, 1932," p. 19, PFI Mss, Container 68, Folder 1344.

52. Joy Elmer Morgan to William John Cooper, January 8, 1931, PFI Mss, Container 43, Folder 838; Armstrong Perry, "Conference Increases International Difficulty," *Education by Radio*, September 28, 1933, p. 45.

53. "Report of the Committee on Radio." In *NUEA 1931*, p. 57; Armstrong Perry, "Weak Spots in the American System of Broadcasting." In *Annals 1935*, p. 26; Armstrong Perry, "Report of the Service Bureau," March 1931, PFI Mss, Container 38, Folder 743.

54. Minutes of the Meeting of the NCER, May 2, 1932, PFI Mss, Container 39, Folder 744; Horace L. Lohnes to Tracy F. Tyler, January 10, 1933, PFI Mss, Container 44, Folder 854.

55. Ella Phillips Crandall to Armstrong Perry, June 9, 1931, PFI Mss, Container 56, Folder 1072; Frances Payne Bolton to Joy Elmer Morgan, June 17, 1932, PFI Mss, Container 42, Folder 812.

56. Ella Phillips Crandall to Armstrong Perry, February 17, 1933, PFI Mss, Container 56, Folder 1076; Ella Phillips Crandall, "Memorandum Re Conference with Dr. Joy Elmer Morgan," October 1, 1932, PFI Mss, Container 42, Folder 812.

57. Ella Phillips Crandall, "Memorandum Re Radio to Mrs. Bolton and Mr. Maxfield," November 5, 1934, PFI Mss, Container 69, Folder 1352; "Education Demands Freedom of the Air," *Education by Radio*, April 28, 1932, p. 64; Eugene J. Coltrane, "A Brief Statement in Support of Representative Fulmer's Resolution for a Study of Radio Broadcasting," March 2, 1933, PFI Mss, Container 54, Folder 1034.

58. C. W. Warburton to R. A. Pearson, December 13, 1930, DoA Mss, General Correspondence, 1930, Radio; Higgy quote in B. B. Brackett to T. M. Beaird, December 15, 1931, NAEB Mss, Box No. 1a, General Correspondence 1932; Frank M. Russell to R. C. Patterson, Jr., January 31, 1935, NBC Mss, Box 36, Folder 38, FCC, Federal Educational Committee 1935.

59. For role of Young and network officials see assorted correspondence, CC Mss, NACRE Box 1, NACRE 1929; *NUEA 1934*, p. 86.

For a discussion of the Carnegie Corporation and the founding of the AAAE, see

Ellen Condliffe Lagemann, *The Politics of Knowledge: The Carnegie Corporation, Philanthropy, and Public Policy* (Middletown, CT: Wesleyan University Press, 1989), pp. 106–8.

60. Erik Barnouw, *A Tower in Babel* (New York: Oxford University Press, 1966), p. 261; Robert K. Avery and Robert Pepper, "An Institutional History of Public Broadcasting," *Journal of Communication* 30 (Summer 1980), p. 127.

61. Leach, pp. 5–10.

62. Resolution of the Advisory Group on Radio Education of the American Association for Adult Education, November 18, 1929, Minutes of Conference between Mr. Cooper, Mr. Cartwright and Mr. Tyson, September 20, 1929, OoE Mss, Box 2, Miscellaneous General Correspondence; Levering Tyson, *Education Tunes In* (New York: American Association for Adult Education, 1930), p. 9.

63. Tyson, *Education Tunes In*, p. 58.

64. Levering Tyson to Armstrong Perry, September 25, 1929, Levering Tyson, "Memorandum to Dr. H. Robinson Shipherd," September 25, 1929, PFI Mss, Container 56, Folder 1069.

65. Armstrong Perry, "National Broadcasting Company," December 1935, PFI Mss, Container 52, Folder 986; Merlin H. Aylesworth, "Broadcasting Today," *Dun's Review*, March 5, 1932, p. 3.

66. Leach, p. 7; Wm. John Cooper to Levering Tyson, September 29, 1930, OoE Mss, RG 12, Box 32, File on Conference on Education by Radio; William John Cooper, "Memorandum for the Secretary," October 20, 1930, Wilbur Mss, Box 63, Folder 1; Cited in Tracy F. Tyler, "The Joint Survey of Radio in Land-Grant Colleges and Separate State Universities." In *IER 1932*, p. 16.

67. "Proceedings of the Conference on Radio Education Problems, October 13, 1930, Stevens Hotel, Chicago," p. 122, FCC Mss, Docketed Case Files, #1112, Box 225; Minutes of the Meeting of the Executive Board of the National Advisory Council on Radio in Education, December 17, 1930, Wilbur Mss, Box 63, Folder 1.

68. Levering Tyson, "Report of the Director to the Board of Directors." In *NACRE 1933*, pp. 18–19.

69. " 'Listeners Society'," *Broadcasting*, April 1, 1933, p. 14; "When Educators Differ," *Broadcasting*, June 1, 1933, p. 20.

70. Tracy F. Tyler to Dr. Levering Tyson, December 28, 1931, PFI Mss, Container 45, Folder 881.

71. See, for example, Herman S. Hettinger, "A Defense of the American System of Broadcasting." In *Debate*, p. 80; Tracy F. Tyler to James N. Rule, May 23, 1932, PFI Mss, Container 42, Folder 807.

72. Levering Tyson, "Where is American Radio Heading?" In *IER 1934*, p. 15; Levering Tyson, *"Educational Static"* (Washington, D.C.: National Association of Broadcasters, 1931), p. 2.

73. Levering Tyson to F. P. Keppel, January 2, 1934, CC Mss, NACRE Box 1, NACRE 1934.

74. Armstrong Perry to Ella Phillips Crandall, May 31, 1934, PFI Mss, Container 56, Folder 1079; Tracy F. Tyler to J. O. Keller, February 9, 1933, PFI Mss, Container 41, Folder 798.

75. S. Howard Evans to E. H. Harris, October 8, 1934, PFI Mss, Container 69, Folder 1350; Comments of I. Keith Tyler, cited in Calvin Fredrick Ruskaup, "The Other Side of Broadcasting: A History of Challengers to the Use of the Airwaves," Ph.D. dissertation, Ohio State University, 1979, p. 60.

76. Armstrong Perry, "National Advisory Council on Radio in Education," December 1935, PFI Mss, Container 52, Folder 986; Morgan, *NUEA 1932,* p. 79.

77. Ella Phillips Crandall, "Memorandum to Mr. Perry Re General Situation of Radio in Education," December 29, 1930, PFI Mss, Container 69, Folder 1352.

78. Morgan, *NUEA 1932,* p. 79; Joy Elmer Morgan to J. McKeen Cattell, September 28, 1931, JEM Mss, NEA, 1931 Correspondence, FCB 2, Drawer 3; "Shall Foundations Control Educational Radio?" *Education by Radio,* May 25, 1933, p. 27.

79. Levering Tyson to F. P. Keppel, October 28, 1930, CC Mss, NACRE Box 1, NACRE 1930; Tyson to Keppel, January 2, 1934, CC Mss, NACRE Box 1, NACRE 1934.

80. Levering Tyson to Mrs. Chester C. Bolton, November 18, 1930, PFI Mss, Container 68, Folder 1337.

81. Ella Phillips Crandall to Dr. W. W. Charters, November 26, 1930, PFI Mss, Container 69, Folder 1352; Ella Phillips Crandall to Mrs. Chester C. Bolton, June 23, 1932, PFI Mss, Container 52, Folder 983.

82. Armstrong Perry to Ella Phillips Crandall, September 23, 1930, PFI Mss, Container 56, Folder 1070; Levering Tyson to John W. Elwood, December 12, 1932, NBC Mss, Box 12, Folder 15, NACRE 1932.

83. Levering Tyson to F. P. Keppel, December 22, 1933, CC Mss, NACRE Box 1, NACRE 1933.

84. Levering Tyson to F. P. Keppel, December 4, 1929, CC Mss, NACRE Box 1, NACRE 1929; F. P. Keppel Memorandum on N.A.C.R.E., May 5, 1931, CC Mss, NACRE Box 1, NACRE 1931.

85. "Meeting of the Radio Committee," February 1932, Allen Miller Papers, SHSW, small envelope; *IER 1934,* p. 53.

86. Franklin Dunham to R. C. Patterson, Jr., May 12, 1934, NBC Mss, Box 30, Folder 16; Merlin H. Aylesworth to John W. Reith, October 8, 1934, NBC Mss, Box 24, Folder 27.

87. Frank E. Mason to E. W. Harden, July 25, 1934, NBC Mss, Box 30, Folder 16; "Director's Report," p. 3, NBC Mss, Box 39, Folder 38.

88. Tyson, *IER 1934,* p. 17; M. H. Aylesworth to David Sarnoff, August 20, 1934, NBC Mss, Box 32, Folder 7, David Sarnoff 1934.

89. H. O. Davis to Ella Phillips Crandall, September 20, 1934, PFI Mss, Container 59, Folder 1148.

90. William H. Short, "Memorandum to Miss Crandall regarding proposal of Mr. H. O. Davis," February 1, 1930, PFI Mss, Container 59, Folder 1141; Lloyd E. Yoder to Don E. Gilman, September 30, 1931, NBC Mss, Box 5, Folder 65, Ventura Free Press; "H. O. Davis, 87, Dies; Early Moviemaker," *The New York Times,* August 29, 1964, p. 21.

91. H. O. Davis to Mrs. Chester C. Bolton, June 11, 1930, PFI Mss, Container 59, Folder 1141; Ella Phillips Crandall to H. O. Davis, August 1, 1930, PFI Mss,

Container 59, Folder 1141; Ella Phillips Crandall to H. O. Davis, April 15, 1931, PFI Mss, Container 59, Folder 1142.

92. Crandall to Davis, April 15, 1931, PFI Mss, Container 59, Folder 1142; H. O. Davis to H. L. Williamson, September 25, 1931, NBC Mss, Box 5, Folder 65, Ventura Free Press; H. O. Davis to Berton L. Maxfield, June 12, 1931, June 22, 1931, PFI Mss, Container 59, Folder 1142.

93. Davis to Maxfield, June 12, 1931, PFI Mss, Container 59, Folder 1142; S. Howard Evans to Edward L. Bernays, March 3, 1932, PFI Mss, Container 69, Folder 1350.

94. Ella Phillips Crandall to H. O. Davis, October 13, 1931, PFI Mss, Container 59, Folder 1143; S. Howard Evans to W. O. Dapping, March 19, 1932, PFI Mss, Container 60, Folder 1172.

95. S. Howard Evans to Cranston Williams, December 9, 1932, PFI Mss, Container 60, Folder 1174; H. O. Davis to Karl Thiesing, undated, summer 1931, PFI Mss, Container 59, Folder 1142; H. O. Davis to S. Howard Evans, July 30, 1931, PFI Mss, Container 59, Folder 1142.

96. Walter V. Woehlke, "Memorandum," undated, summer 1931, PFI Mss, Container 49, Folder 945.

97. Walter Woehlke, "Memorandum Concerning the Radio Campaign of the Ventura Free Press," undated, summer 1931, PFI Mss, Container 49, Folder 945; Davis to Williamson, September 25, 1931, NBC Mss, Box 5, Folder 65, Ventura Free Press.

98. "Summary of Expenditures on Ventura Free Press Radio Project," June 1932, PFI Mss, Container 59, Folder 1145; "Free Press Most Widely Quoted Newspaper West of the Rockies," *Ventura Free Press*, July 28, 1932, pp. 1, 3; "Ventura Crusader Now Asks Editors to Pay for Anti-Radio Screeds," *Broadcasting*, August 15, 1933, p. 47.

99. H. O. Davis, *Empire of the Air* (Ventura, CA: Ventura Free Press, 1932); A. R. Williamson to Frank E. Mason, March 1, 1932, NBC Mss, Box 15, Folder 5, Ventura Free Press; " 'The Empire of the Air'," *Broadcasters' News Bulletin*, January 16, 1932; Ventura Free Press, *American Broadcasting: An Analytic Study of One Day's Output of 206 Commercial Radio Stations Including Program Contents and Advertising Interruptions* (Ventura, CA: Ventura Free Press, 1933); Frances P. Bolton to H. O. Davis, September 1, 1931, PFI Mss, Container 59, Folder 1143.

100. "A Vicious Fight Against Broadcasting," *Broadcasting*, December 1, 1932, p. 10.

101. *Broadcasting*, August 15, 1933, p. 47; "An Unholy Alliance," *Broadcasting*, February 1, 1932, p. 16; "More Ventura," *Broadcasting*, December 15, 1931, p. 18.

102. David Sarnoff to M. H. Aylesworth, October 21, 1931, NBC Mss, Box 5, Folder 65, Ventura Free Press.

103. Gene Huse to Frank E. Mason, January 23, 1932, February 23, 1932, NBC Mss, Box 15, Folder 5, Ventura Free Press; Frank E. Mason to Gene Huse, January 27, 1932, NBC Mss, Box 15, Folder 5, Ventura Free Press; Gene Huse to J. B. Mayland, February 1, 1932, J. B. Mayland to Gene Huse, February 7, 1932, February 19, 1932, NBC Mss, Box 15, Folder 5.

104. M. H. Aylesworth to George Harris, October 24, 1931, M. H. Aylesworth to H. L. Williamson, October 6, 1931, NBC Mss, Box 5, Folder 65, Ventura Free Press.

105. *Empire of the Air,* p. 99.

106. Walter Woehlke to S. Howard Evans, September 1, 1931, PFI Mss, Container 60, Folder 1163; S. Howard Evans to H. O. Davis, September 5, 1931, PFI Mss, Container 59, Folder 1143; Walter Woehlke to S. Howard Evans, December 2, 1932, PFI Mss, Container 60, Folder 1159.

107. "Discussion on Radio," *American Newspaper Publishers Association Bulletin,* No. 5919, November 21, 1931, p. 522; H. O. Davis to Charles A. Webb, January 5, 1932, NBC Mss, Box 15, Folder 5, Ventura Free Press; H. O. Davis to Ella Phillips Crandall, September 14, 1931, PFI Mss, Container 59, Folder 1143.

108. H. O. Davis to Mrs. Frances P. Bolton, September 9, 1931, PFI Mss, Container 40, Folder 764; S. Howard Evans, "Memorandum Re Payne Fund Relationship with Davis Radio Campaign," September 18, 1931, PFI Mss, Container 49, Folder 945.

109. Davis to Bolton, September 9, 1931, PFI Mss, Container 40, Folder 764.

110. Ella Phillips Crandall to Armstrong Perry, June 3, 1931, PFI Mss, Container 56, Folder 1072.

111. S. Howard Evans to Walter V. Woehlke, October 14, 1931, PFI Mss, Container 60, Folder 1163; H. O. Davis to Ella Phillips Crandall, October 2, 1931, PFI Mss, Container 59, Folder 1143.

112. Walter Woehlke to S. Howard Evans, November 25, 1931, PFI Mss, Container 60, Folder 1164.

113. Ella Phillips Crandall to H. O. Davis, October 1, 1931, PFI Mss, Container 59, Folder 1143; "Memorandum Re Discussion at Board Meeting Held October 30, 1931 Regarding the Ventura Free Press Campaign Against Radio Monopoly," October 30, 1931, PFI Mss, Container 61, Folder 1178.

114. H. O. Davis to Berton L. Maxfield, November 10, 1931, Berton L. Maxfield to H. O. Davis, December 19, 1931, PFI Mss, Container 68, Folder 1339.

Chapter 4

1. "History of WCFL," in *Program for Dedication of Radio Stations WCFL, W9XAA and W9XFL* (Chicago, 1931). In Chicago Historical Society, Chicago, IL; Nathan Godfried, "The Origins of Labor Radio: WCFL, the 'Voice of Labor', 1925–1928," *Historical Journal of Film, Radio and Television,* 7 (1987): 143; "Radio Broadcasting," in *AFL 1928,* p. 115.

2. Barbara Warne Newell, *Chicago and the Labor Movement: Metropolitan Unionism in the 1930s* (Urbana: University of Illinois Press, 1961), pp. 20–24; Dale Fetherling, *Mother Jones, The Miners' Angel* (Carbondale and Edwardsville: Southern Illinois University Press, 1974), pp. 199–208; Newell, p. 25.

3. Mike Davis, *Prisoners of the American Dream* (London: Verso, 1986), p. 49;

Lizabeth Cohen, *Making a New Deal: Industrial Workers in Chicago, 1919–1939* (Cambridge: Cambridge University Press, 1990), pp. 39, 49–50; Newell, p. 44.

4. Godfried, pp. 144, 145; Newell, p. 25.

5. "History of WCFL," in *Program;* Godfried, p. 145; Erling S. Jorgenson, "Radio Station WCFL: A Study in Labor Union Broadcasting," M.A. thesis, University of Wisconsin, 1949, pp. 31, 91.

6. Cohen, p. 136; "Cites Radio Story in Condensed Form," *Federation News,* April 27, 1929, p. 2; "Report of the Committee on Radio Broadcasting Station." In *Illinois State Federation of Labor Proceedings Forty-Sixth Annual Convention November 8–14, 1928 Herrin, Illinois* (Illinois Federation of Labor, 1928), pp. 71–76.

7. Godfried, pp. 146–47, 150; Jorgenson, pp. 45–51.

8. "Press Bulletin of the Central Bureau of the Central Verein," May 11, 1927, ACLU Mss, 1927, Volume 328.

9. "Cites Radio Story in Condensed Form," *Federation News,* April 27, 1929, p. 2; "Control Air We Breathe," *Federation News,* January 5, 1929, p. 4; *FRC 1929,* pp. 35–36.

10. "Radio and Press Twin Publicity Agents," *Federation News,* September 2, 1929, p. 35; Godfried, p. 151.

11. "Radio Value," *Federation News,* March 6, 1929, p. 4.

12. "The Radio Situation," *Federation News,* August 24, 1929, p. 4; *Federation News,* September 7, 1929, p. 16; *Federation News,* April 27, 1929, p. 2; "Chicago Federation of Labor and WCFL. Profit and Loss Statement for the Year 1930," in FCC Mss, FCC Docketed Case Files #1231, Box 266.

13. Cohen, pp. 133–38; Godfried, p. 149; Jorgenson, pp. 59, 73–78, 90, 95, 104.

14. *Federation News,* January 2, 1932, p. 1.

15. *Federation News,* April 27, 1929, p. 2; Godfried, p. 151; "Supplemental Reports," in *AFL 1929,* pp. 214–15; "Resolution No. 30," in *AFL 1930,* pp. 241–42.

16. Frank M. Russell to R. C. Patterson, Jr., November 13, 1934, NBC Mss, Box 26, Folder 29, FCC Hearings 1934.

17. "Massachusetts Urges Government Radio," *Education by Radio,* September 19, 1935, p. 47; "Government Operation Proposed," *Education by Radio,* October 17, 1935, 51; Charles P. Howard to George E. Graff, July 22, 1932, PFI Mss, Container 60, Folder 1159; Armstrong Perry to S. Howard Evans, September 19, 1934, PFI Mss, Container 56, Folder 1080.

18. *AFL 1928,* pp. 115–16; "Resolution No. 53," in *AFL 1932,* p. 389.

19. *Ibid.,* p. 389; "Radio Advertising," in *AFL 1933,* pp. 111–12; "Labor Speaks Out," *Broadcasting,* October 15, 1933, p. 26.

20. See *House 1934b,* pp. 132–36.

21. William Green to Lenox Lohr, February 26, 1936, NBC Mss, Box 46, Folder 47, Wm. Green, 1936; "Commission Denies Requests of WCFL," *Federation News,* May 25, 1929, p. 1.

22. "Unbiased Account of Radio Hearing Told," *Federation News,* May 4, 1929,

p. 17; "Chicago Federation of Labor v. Federal Radio Commission," FCC Mss, FCC Docketed Case Files #342, Box 70, p. 10.

23. *Ibid.*, p. 9; "Radio Commission's Inconsistency Plain," *Federation News,* July 13, 1929, pp. 1, 3, 8.

24. "Air Monopoly Threatens, Says Nockels of WCFL," *Federation News,* January 31, 1931, p. 9; "Radio's Influence in Shaping the Future," *Federation News,* December 7, 1929, pp. 1, 7.

25. "WCFL Representatives Put Force in Truth," *Federation News,* February 1. 1930, p. 2; "A Raw Deal," *Federation News,* January 12, 1929, p. 4.

26. Edward N. Nockels, "Labor's Experience in Radio," *American Federationist,* 44 (1937), p. 280; "Organized Labor's Battle Cry of Freedom," *Federation News,* September 7, 1929, p. 1.

27. "Federation Hears Radio Situation," *Federation News,* June 8, 1929, p. 8; Edward N. Nockels, *Public Interest, Convenience and Necessity, and the Last of the Public Domain* (Washington, D.C., 1936), p. 13.

28. "Press Bulletin," ACLU Mss, 1927, Volume 328; *Federation News,* September 7, 1929, p. 1; Edward N. Nockels to Senator, January 5, 1929, HH-P Mss, FRC, Public Opinion & Relations, 1929, January–March, Box 151; E. N. Nockels, "Appeals to Honor of American Bar," *Federation News,* June 6, 1929, p. 8.

29. *Federation News,* January 12, 1929, p. 4; "Press Bulletin," ACLU Mss, 1927, Volume 328.

30. Edward N. Nockels, "The Voice of Labor," *American Federationist,* 37 (1930), p. 414.

31. Nockels, *Public Interest,* p. 23; E. N. Nockels to Tracy F. Tyler, May 24, 1934, Illinois Mss, Subject File (RS 39/1/1), 1919–1984, Box 3, National Committee on Education by Radio.

32. For discussions of the theological and intellectual origins of the Paulist order see, John Farina, *An American Experience of God* (New York: Paulist Press, 1981); and John Farina, *Hecker Studies* (New York: Paulist Press, 1983).

33. James McVann, *The Paulists, 1858–1970* (New York: Society of St. Paul the Apostle, 1983), p. 875; C. Joseph Pusateri, *Enterprise in Radio* (Washington, D.C.: University Press of America, 1980), p. 167; McVann, *Paulists,* p. 876; Pusateri, *Enterprise,* p. 167.

34. Pusateri, *Enterprise,* p. 167; *Harney,* p. 27.

35. McVann, *Paulists,* p. 877; *Harney,* p. 25.

36. *Harney,* pp. 25, 26.

37. *Ibid.,* p. 26.

38. *Ibid.,* p. 26.

39. McVann, *Paulists,* pp. 882, 890–91; *House 1934a,* p. 160.

40. *House 1934a,* p. 166; "Paulists Seeking Radio Aid," *The New York Times,* November 11, 1929, p. 32; "Hearst Negotiating to Acquire WLWL," *Broadcasting,* November 15, 1931, p. 16.

41. *House 1934a,* p. 161.

42. "25,000 Praise WLWL, Asking for More Time," *The New York Times,* September 29, 1931, p. 23; "Catholic Aid Asked for Station WLWL," *The New York Times,* September 28, 1931, p. 26; "WLWL Asks More Time," *The New York*

Times, November 5, 1931, p. 30; "Protest WLWL Decision," *The New York Times,* June 14, 1932, p. 2; for an example of the concern WLWL raised among FRC members, see Charles McKinley Saltzman to Theodore G. Joslin, October 8, 1931, HH-P Mss, FRC, 1931 October–November, Box 149.

43. Pacific-Western Broadcasting Federation, *For a Genuine Radio University* (Los Angeles: Pacific-Western Broadcasting Federation, 1930), pp. 28, vii, 12; *House 1934a,* p. 285; Gross W. Alexander, "Statement Concerning Radio Control." In *NCER 1934,* p. 107; Pacific-Western Broadcasting Federation, *"A Race Between Education and Catastrophe"* (Pasadena: Pacific-Western Broadcasting Federation, undated, either 1930 or 1931).

44. *Genuine Radio University,* pp. 1, 65; Gross W. Alexander to the Chicago Conference on Educational Broadcasting, October 11, 1930, OoE Mss, Box 31, Conference on Education by Radio, Letters.

45. *Genuine Radio University,* p. 14; Gross W. Alexander, *Ownership of Facilities—The Determinative Factor in the Control of Broadcasting* (Pasadena: Pacific-Western Broadcasting Federation, 1930), p. 11.

46. Harold A. Lafount to Gross W. Alexander, PFI Mss, Container 59, Folder 1135; *House 1934a,* p. 286.

47. Joy Elmer Morgan to G. F. Angne, January 10, 1930, JEM Mss, 1930 Correspondence, FCB 2, Drawer 2; *The New York Times,* May 4, 1930. Reprinted by Pacific-Western Broadcasting Foundation. In Wilbur Mss, Box 63, Folder 1.

48. See, for example, Gross W. Alexander to Ray Lyman Wilbur, February 7, 1930, F. P. Keppel to Gross W. Alexander, January 28, 1930, Robert W. Bruere to Gross W. Alexander, January 28, 1930, E. K. Wickham to Gross W. Alexander, January 28, 1930, Wilbur Mss, Box 63, Folder 1; Tyson's comments in Levering Tyson to F. P. Keppel, August 19, 1930, CC Mss, NACRE Box 1, NACRE 1930.

49. Ray Lyman Wilbur to Mr. Fosdick, January 30, 1931, Jane Addams to Mr. Rockefeller, March 19, 1931, PFI Mss, Container 46, Folder 890.

50. Alexander, "Supplemental Statement." In *NCER 1934,* p. 111; Gross W. Alexander to Joy Elmer Morgan, March 24, 1931, PFI Mss, Container 46, Folder 890.

51. *FCC Digest,* p. 191; Federal Radio Commission Docket 1112, ACLU Mss, 1931–1933, Volume 510; Armstrong Perry, "Summary Report of the Trip to the Pacific Coast," August 7, 1931, PFI Mss, Container 56, Folder 1073; Armstrong Perry to Ella Phillips Crandall, April 4, 1931, PFI Mss, Container 56, Folder 1072.

52. Roger N. Baldwin to Gross Alexander, July 13, 1931, ACLU Mss, 1931–1933, Volume 510.

53. Gross W. Alexander to Winifred L. Chappell, February 1, 1933, ACLU Mss, 1931–1933, Volume 510.

54. *House 1934a,* p. 287; Alexander to Chappell, February 1, 1933, ACLU Mss, 1931–1933, Volume 510.

55. *House 1934a,* p. 287; Gross W. Alexander to Ray Lyman Wilbur, June 2, 1929, PFI Mss, Container 59, Folder 1135; Frank B. Jewett to H. D. Pillsbury, January 31, 1930, Frank B. Jewett Papers, AT&T, 75–03–03, Box 87.

56. Alexander, *Ownership of Facilities;* Ella Phillips Crandall, "Memorandum of Conference with Dr. Perry," July 23, 1931, PFI Mss, Container 69, Folder 1352.

57. *House 1934a*, p. 287.

58. Alexander to Chappell, February 1, 1933, ACLU Mss, 1931–1933, Volume 510; Cited in *The New York Times*, May 4, 1930. Reprinted by Pacific-Western Broadcasting Federation. In Wilbur Mss, Box 63, Folder 1.

59. Alexander, "Statement." In *NCER 1934*, pp. 112, 109; Walter Woehlke to S. Howard Evans, November 12, 1932, PFI Mss, Container 60, Folder 1167.

60. Alexander, "Statement." In *NCER 1934*, pp. 122, 124; Gross W. Alexander to Robert F. Wagner, December 29, 1930, Wagner Mss, Legislative Files, Box 195.

61. Armstrong Perry to Gross W. Alexander, August 22, 1930, Gross W. Alexander to Armstrong Perry, August 6, 1930, Gross W. Alexander to Armstrong Perry, July 16, 1930, PFI Mss, Container 59, Folder 1135; Gross W. Alexander to Ruth Roberts, July 17, 1931, PFI Mss, Container 59, Folder 1136; Alexander to Chappell, February 1, 1933, ACLU Mss, 1931–1933, Volume 510.

62. Morse Salisbury to Mr. Eisenhower, February 18, 1930, DoA Mss, General Correspondence 1930, Radio; Armstrong Perry to Mrs. Chester C. Bolton, March 24, 1931, PFI Mss, Container 68, Folder 1343; Armstrong Perry to Gross W. Alexander, July 31, 1930, PFI Mss, Container 59, Folder 1135.

63. Morris Ernst and Alexander Lindey, "Freedom of the Air," *Saturday Review of Literature*, January 6, 1940, p. 15.

64. Forrest Bailey to C. C. Dill, January 31, 1927, ACLU Mss, 1927; Testimony of Morris Ernst, *Senate 1926*, pp. 128, 133.

65. ACLU Press Release, February 3, 1927, ACLU Mss, 1927, Volume 318; Morris Ernst, "Radio Censorship and the 'Listening Millions' ", *The Nation* 122 (April 28, 1926): p. 475; See Minutes of Hearings Before the Federal Radio Commission, March 29–April 1, 1927, pp. 359–76, HH-C Mss, Radio, Conference, 3/29/27, Box 491.

66. Memo on "The Radio Bill" by Forrest Bailey, undated, ACLU Mss, 1927, Volume 318; Ernst, *The Nation*, pp. 473–75.

67. Gordon W. Moss to Harris K. Randall, February 25, 1933, ACLU Mss, 1931–1933, Volume 513; Harry F. Ward to Carl H. Butman, December 18, 1929, ACLU Mss, 1929, Volume 375.

68. Charles Lam Markham, *The Noblest Cry: A History of the American Civil Liberties Union* (New York: St. Martin's Press, 1965), pp. 89–92; "National Committee to Fight for WEVD," *American Civil Liberties Union Press Service*, January 22, 1931, ACLU Mss, 1931, Volume 44; see also Nathan Godfried, "Legitimizing the Mass Media Structure: The Socialists and American Broadcasting, 1926–1932." In *Culture, Gender, Race and U.S. Labor History*, edited by Ronald Kent, et al. (Westport, CT: Greenwood Press, 1993); Evans quote in HLR to Roger Baldwin, November 4, 1937, ACLU Mss, 1937, Volume 1011.

69. American Civil Liberties Union, *Announcing the National Council on Freedom From Censorship* (New York: American Civil Liberties Union, 1931), p. 5. In PFI Mss, Container 46, Folder 885; Form letter, Roger Baldwin to Station Manager, March 12, 1931, ACLU Mss, 1931–1933, Volume 513.

70. Norman Thomas to Roger Baldwin, December 8, 1932, Roger Baldwin to Harris K. Randall, February 28, 1933, ACLU Mss, 1931–1933, Volume 513.

71. Roger Baldwin, "Memorandum on Radio in Relation to Free Speech," May

19, 1933, ACLU Mss, 1933, Volume 599; Roger Baldwin to Harris K. Randall, March 22, 1933, ACLU Mss, 1931–1933, Volume 513.

72. Harry F. Ward to Federal Communications Commission, August 24, 1934, ACLU Mss, 1934, Volume 694; Roger Baldwin to Harris K. Randall, April 4, 1933, ACLU Mss, 1931–1933, Volume 513; Roger Baldwin to Harris K. Randall, October 30, 1933, ACLU Mss, 1933, Volume 510.

73. Clifton Read to Norman Thomas, September 19, 1934, Thomas Mss, Series II, Reel 56.

74. "Wants Impartial Radio," *The New York Times*, March 30, 1934, p. 19.

75. Norman Thomas to George F. McClelland, April 21, 1926, NBC Mss, Box 4, Folder 49; Godfried, "Socialists."

76. Norman Thomas to M. H. Aylesworth, October 2, 1931, NBC Mss, Box 4, Folder 1.

77. National Broadcasting Company, *Broadcasting, Volume IV* (New York: National Broadcasting Company, 1935), p. 64; see also H. V. Kaltenborn, "The Future of Radio," *Education by Radio*, May 14, 1931, p. 53.

78. Norman Thomas to Clifton Read, December 18, 1935, Thomas Mss, Series II, Reel 56.

79. Based on interview between author and Bethuel M. Webster, Jr., February 18, 1987. See, also, Bethuel M. Webster, Jr., "Our Stake in the Ether," *American Bar Association Journal* 17 (January 1931):364–73.

80. See, for example, Harris K. Randall to Roger Baldwin, September 9, 1933, ACLU Mss, 1933, Volume 599; Roger Baldwin to Harris K. Randall, September 13, 1933, ACLU Mss, 1933, Volume 599.

81. *Ibid.;* Bethuel M. Webster, Jr., "Memorandum for Mr. Baldwin Re: National Committee on Education by Radio," November 18, 1933, ACLU Mss, 1933, Volume 599.

82. Helen Ascher to Roger Baldwin, November 6, 1933, ACLU Mss, 1933, Volume 599; Roger Baldwin to Tracy Tyler, October 24, 1933, Tracy Tyler to Roger Baldwin, October 26, 1933, assorted additional letters between Tyler and Baldwin, November–December 1933, ACLU Mss, 1933, Volume 599.

83. Roger Baldwin to Bethuel M. Webster, Jr., November 14, 1933, ACLU Mss, 1933, Volume 599; Webster, "Memorandum re: NCER," ACLU Mss, Volume 599; Roger Baldwin to Bethuel M. Webster, Jr., November 20, 1933, ACLU Mss, 1933, Volume 599.

84. Joy Elmer Morgan, "The New American Plan for Radio." In *Debate*, p. 82; Armstrong Perry to Ella Phillips Crandall, April 15, 1933, PFI Mss, Container 56, Folder 1077.

85. Cited in *School and Society*, December 15, 1934, p. 805; Cited in *Education by Radio*, December 24, 1931, p. 156.

86. See, for example, Herman S. Hettinger, *A Decade of Radio Advertising* (Chicago: University of Chicago Press, 1933); Herman S. Hettinger, "A Defense of the American Plan for Radio." In *Debate*, pp. 56–80; Herman S. Hettinger, "Broadcasting in the United States." In *Annals 1935*, pp. 1–14; Herman S. Hettinger & Walter J. Neff, *Practical Radio Advertising* (New York: Prentice-Hall, 1938); Herman S. Hettinger, "The Personal Interview." In *IER 1933*, pp. 195–208; Herman

S. Hettinger, "Some Fundamental Aspects of Radio Broadcasting," *Harvard Business Review* 13 (1935):14–28; Herman S. Hettinger, "The Economic Factor in Radio Regulation," *Air Law Review* 9 (April 1938): pp. 115–28; Herman S. Hettinger, "A Commentary on Radio Regulation," *Air Law Review* 10 (January 1939):28–44.

87. L. Ingram, "Review of 'Radio: The Fifth Estate'," *Survey Graphic*, May 1935, p. 251.

88. For Hamilton's influence, see Richard Joyce Smith, "The Ultimate Control of Radio in the United States." In *NACRE 1932*, pp. 181–94; E. Pendleton Herring, "Politics and Radio Regulation," *Harvard Business Review* 13 (1935): pp. 167–78; Alexander Meiklejohn, *Political Freedom* (New York: Harper & Brothers, 1948), pp. 86–87; John Dewey, "Radio—for Propaganda or Public Interest." In *Education by Radio*, February 28, 1935, p. 11; John Dewey, "Our Un-Free Press," *Common Sense*, November 1935, pp. 6–7; For Sinclair's position see *Education by Radio*, December 24, 1931, p. 156; Frederick Lewis Allen, "Radio City: Cultural Center?" *Education by Radio*, May 12, 1932, pp. 65–68; Norman Woeful, *Molders of the American Mind* (New York: Columbia University Press, 1933); "H. L. Mencken," *Education by Radio*, August 27, 1931, pp. 101–2.

89. Bruce Bliven, "Shall the Government Own, Operate, and Control Radio Broadcasting in the United States?" In *NACRE 1934*, pp. 76–83, 106–15; Bruce Bliven, "An English Miscellany," *The New Republic*, August 8, 1934, p. 342; Bruce Bliven, "The Future of Free Speech." In *Problems of Journalism; Proceedings of the Twelfth Annual Convention of the American Society of Newspaper Editors*, April 19–21, 1934, pp. 124–31.

Jerome Davis, *Capitalism and Its Culture* (New York: Farrar & Rinehart, 1935), Chapter XVII; Jerome Davis, "The Radio, A Commercial or an Educational Agency?" In *NCER 1934*, pp. 3–9.

William Orton, *Memorandum on Radio Policy* (Northampton, MA, 1934); William Aylott Orton, *America in Search of Culture* (Boston: Little, Brown, and Company, 1933), Chapter XIII; William A. Orton, "Education by Radio." In *NACRE 1935*, pp. 63–70; William Orton, "The Level of Thirteen Year-Olds," *Atlantic Monthly* 147(1931):1–10; William Orton, "Unscrambling the Ether," *Atlantic Monthly* 147(1931):429–38; William Orton, "Radio and the Public Interest," *Atlantic Monthly* 157(1936):351–59; William A. Orton, "A Future American Radio Policy," *Education by Radio*, December 20, 1934, pp. 61–61; William A. Orton, "Planned Radio Vital to a Better Civilization," *Education by Radio*, June 13, 1935, pp. 25–27.

90. See James Rorty, *Order on the Air!* (New York: The John Day Company, 1934); James Rorty, *Our Master's Voice: Advertising* (New York: The John Day Company, 1934); James Rorty, "Order on the Air,' *The Nation*, May 9, 1934, pp. 529–32; James Rorty, "Free Air; A Strictly Imaginary Educational Broadcast," *The Nation*, March 9, 1932, pp. 280–82; James Rorty, "The Impending Radio War," *Harper's Monthly* 163 (1931):714–26; James Rorty, *Pandora's Tube* (Westport, Connecticut, undated, approximately 1930–1932).

91. James Rorty to Armstrong Perry, May 12, 1931, Armstrong Perry to James Rorty, March 23, 1931, PFI Mss, Container 58, Folder 1128; See *NACRE 1933*, pp. 35–37; James Rorty to Tracy Tyler, December 15, 1933, PFI Mss, Container 44, Folder 859; Rorty, *Harper's Monthly*, pp. 714–15.

92. See Mike Gold, "Change the World," *New York Daily Worker*, October 12, 1938; M. L. Mott to President, May 16, 1930, HH-P Mss, FRC, Public Opinion & Relations, 1930 March–May, Box 151.

93. "DeForest Ashamed of 'Child'," *Broadcasters' News Bulletin*, November 14, 1931; Lee DeForest to Tracy F. Tyler, April 19, 1934, PFI Mss, Container 44, Folder 847; Arthur Kittredge, "DeForest Devises Radio Ad Quietus," undated, October 1930, NANA, Vol. 60.

94. Lee DeForest to Joy Elmer Morgan, February 26, 1931, *Education by Radio*, March 5, 1931, p. 14; Lee DeForest, "An Appeal to Canada," *Education by Radio*, June 23, 1932, p. 73; unlike many other 1930s critics, DeForest never abandoned or forgot his hatred of commercial broadcasting, even calling for a significant government-owned, noncommercial radio sector as late as 1950, when few dared challenge the capitalist foundations of the industry. "To this extent I am a socialist, knowing how anathemic is that suggestion to the radio hucksters of America." In Lee DeForest, *Father of Radio* (Chicago: Wilcox & Follett, 1950), p. 448.

95. Niles Trammell to M. H. Aylesworth, December 10, 1932, NBC Mss, Box 15, Folder 60, April 1933; William S. Hedges to Niles Trammell, June 10, 1932, NBC Mss, Box 15, Folder 60, April 1933; "Another Listeners League," *Broadcasters' News Bulletin*, June 4, 1932; "Radio Audience League Formed to Effect Changes in Industry," *Editor & Publisher*, June 11, 1932, p. 22.

96. Tracy F. Tyler to J. O. Keller, April 10, 1933, PFI Mss, Container 41, Folder 798; S. Howard Evans to Harris K. Randall, April 7, 1932, PFI Mss, Container 68, Folder 1338.

97. Harris K. Randall, "Don't Fight Radio: Help Rescue it From its Rackets," undated, sometime in 1932, Harris K. Randall, "A Plan for the Establishment of Healthier Conditions of Competition Between the Publishing and Radio Broadcasting Industries," NBC Mss, Box 6, Folder 4, American Radio Audience League; "American Radio Audience League," *The American Teacher*, October 1932, p. 29.

98. William Hedges to Niles Trammell, June 10, 1932, NBC Mss, Box 15, Folder 60, April 1933; H. L. Williamson to M. H. Aylesworth, December 1, 1932, NBC Mss, Box 6, Folder 4, American Radio Audience League.

99. Niles Trammell to M. H. Aylesworth, December 10, 1932, NBC Mss, Box 15, Folder 60, April 1933; "Chicago 'Civic Bureau' Would Transfer Stations Of City to 'Better Hands'," *Broadcasting*, April 1, 1934, p. 36.

100. Assorted Correspondence, Harris K. Randall to Thomas Amlie, Thomas R. Amlie Papers, SHSW, Box 3; S. C. Hooper to Joe, June 30, 1933, Hooper Mss, Box 15; Assorted correspondence, Harris K. Randall to Roger Baldwin, Roger Baldwin to Harris K. Randall, ACLU Mss, 1931–1933, Volume 513; 1933, Volume 510; 1933, Volume 599; Assorted correspondence, Harris K. Randall to Robert M. Hutchins, Robert M. Hutchins to Harris K. Randall, RMH I Mss, Box 7, Folder 9; Assorted correspondence, Harris K. Randall and S. Howard Evans and the NCER, PFI Mss, Containers 41 and 68.

101. Helen Ascher to Roger N. Baldwin, November 6, 1933, ACLU Mss, Volume 599, 1933; Allen Miller to Robert M. Hutchins, April 29, 1931, RMH I Mss, Box 7, Folder 9.

102. Joy Elmer Morgan to James N. Rule, May 2, 1933, PFI Mss, Container 42,

Folder 807; Joy Elmer Morgan to John H. McCracken, May 4, 1933, PFI Mss, Container 42, Folder 801; S. Howard Evans to Harris K. Randall, May 15, 1933, PFI Mss, Container 68, Folder 1338; S. Howard Evans to Walter V. Woehlke, May 12, 1933, PFI Mss, Container 60, Folder 1169.

103. Trammell to Aylesworth, December 10, 1932, NBC Mss, Box 15, Folder 60, April 1933.

Chapter 5

1. Gross W. Alexander, "Supplemental Statement." In *NCER 1934*, p. 119; Joy Elmer Morgan, "The New American Plan for Radio." In *Debate*, p. 110; James Rorty, "Order on the Air," *The Nation*, p. 529.

2. Joy Elmer Morgan, "Memoranda on Radio Broadcasting," April 14, 1932, JEM Mss, NEA, Folder Writings 1931, FCB 1, Drawer 3; H. O. Davis to E. H. Lighter, December 1, 1931, PFI Mss, Container 59, Folder 1143; Armstrong Perry to Ella Phillips Crandall, October 24, 1931, PFI Mss, Container 68, Folder 1343.

3. Armstrong Perry, "Weak Spots in the American System of Broadcasting." In *Annals 1935*, p. 26; *Harney*, pp. 21, 32.

4. E. P. Herring, "Politics and Radio Regulation," *Harvard Business Review* 13 (1935): pp. 72–173; Joy Elmer Morgan, "Education's Rights on the Air." In *NACRE 1931*, p. 128.

5. Joy Elmer Morgan, "A National Culture—A By-Product or Objective of National Planning." In *NCER 1934*, pp. 26, 28; James Rorty, *Order on the Air!* (New York: The John Day Company, 1934), pp. 24–25.

6. Minna F. Kassner and Lucien Zacharoff, *Radio is Censored!* (New York: American Civil Liberties Union, 1936), p. 7; Clifton Read to Miss Kirchwey, September 11, 1935, ACLU Mss, 1935, Box 770; H. V. Kaltenborn, "The Future of Radio," *Education by Radio*, May 14, 1931, p. 53; see also, Mitchell Dawson, "Censorship on the Air," *American Mercury* 15 (March 1934):257–68; Vita Lauder and Joseph H. Friend, "Radio and the Censors," *The Forum* 86 (December 1931):359–65;

7. Eugene J. Coltrane, "A System of Radio Broadcasting Suited to American Purposes," In *Control*, p. 32; Kassner and Zacharoff, pp. 5–7.

8. *Harney*, p. 16; Armstrong Perry to educational stations, March 30, 1931, PFI Mss, Container 55, Folder 1040.

9. "Report of the Committee on Radio Broadcasting." In *NASU 1931*, p. 150; Morgan, *NACRE 1931*, p. 130; Morgan, *Debate*, p. 93.

10. Cited in "Gleanings from Varied Sources," *Education by Radio*, September 19, 1935, p. 97; "Federal Dictation Opposed for Radio," *The New York Times*, October 10, 1934, p. 23; Cited in *Education by Radio*, August 27, 1931, p. 102.

11. Cited in George Henry Payne, *The Fourth Estate and Radio and Other Addresses* (Boston: The Microphone Press, 1936), p. 65.

12. Bruce Bliven, "For Better Broadcasting," *The New Republic*, October 3, 1934, p. 201; "The Dominant Moron," *Catholic World*, May 1934, pp. 135–37; Anonymous, "I'm Signing Off," *The Forum*, February 1932, p. 114.

13. "Keeping Public Opinion for Big Biz," *Federation News*, May 30, 1931, p. 4.

14. Testimony of S. Howard Evans, *FCC 1934*, p. 200; Armstrong Perry, "Merits and Demerits of American & British Systems." In *Current*, p. 265; Herring, *Harvard Business Review*, pp. 172–73.

15. Rorty, *Order*, p. 10.

16. For the classic statement of this position see Irwin Stewart, "The Public Control of Radio," *Air Law Review* 8 (1937):131–52; Armstrong Perry, "The Present Status of Radio Broadcasting," p. 2, undated internal document, PFI Mss, Container 57, Folder 1086; *House 1934a*, p. 162.

17. Morgan, *NACRE 1931*, p. 122; Comments on Report of Majority Members of Committee and Discussion of Position of Minority Member, FDR Mss, OF 859a, 1933–45.

18. Morgan, *Debate*, p. 82; William A. Orton, "Education by Radio." In *NACRE 1935*, p. 64.

19. See, for example, Richard Joyce Smith, "The Ultimate Control of Radio in the United States." In *NACRE 1932*, pp. 181–94; See Armstrong Perry, "The Status of Education by Radio in the United States." In *NUEA 1931*, p. 22; Armstrong Perry, Comments following talk by C. M. Jansky, Jr. In *NACRE 1932*, p. 223.

20. Arthur G. Crane, "Safeguarding Educational Radio." In *NACRE 1935*, pp. 118–19.

21. William A. Orton, "A Future American Radio Policy," *Education by Radio*, December 20, 1934, p. 61; Coltrane, *Control*, p. 36; James Rorty, *Order on the Air!* (New York: The John Day Company, 1934), p. 10.

22. Bruce Bliven, "An English Miscellany," *The New Republic*, August 8, 1934, p. 342; Morgan, *NUEA 1932*, p. 83.

23. Armstrong Perry, "A. R. Burrows," December 1935, PFI Mss, Container 52, Folder 986; Armstrong Perry to Sir John C. W. Reith, August 28, 1935, PFI Mss, Container 58, Folder 1110; "Predicts Federal Radio," *The New York Times*, May 28, 1931, reprinted and distributed by the NCER, June 8, 1931, PFI Mss, Container 47, Folder 910.

24. J. W. Quigley to Tracy F. Tyler, June 13, 1935, PFI Mss, Container 45, Folder 868.

25. R. H. Coase, *British Broadcasting: A Study in Monopoly* (London: Longmans, Green & Company, 1950), pp. 130–46; Assorted memoranda, May 1934, NBC Mss, Box 24, Folder 25.

In 1935, after the reformers had been vanquished in the United States, NBC and RCA did agree to work surreptitiously with a move by elements of the British Post Office to commercialize British broadcasting. See John Royal to Richard C. Patterson, Jr., February 14, 1935, NBC Mss, Box 34, Folder 52.

26. "American Broadcasting." In *B.B.C. Year-book* (London: The British Broadcasting Corporation, 1932), p. 47; Owen D. Young to Sir John Reith, August 25, 1931, Young Mss, 11–14–116; Armstrong Perry to British Broadcasting Corporation, December 17, 1935, PFI Mss, Container 58, Folder 1110.

27. Lauter and Friend, *The Forum*, p. 364; S. Howard Evans to Walter V. Woehlke, February 1, 1932, PFI Mss, Container 60, Folder 1165.

28. Arthur G. Crane, "Interpretations of the Land-Grant College and University Radio Survey." In *IER 1933*, p. 25; Armstrong Perry to Arthur G. Crane, September 21, 1934, PFI Mss, Container 55, Folder 1053.

29. Armstrong Perry to H. H. Johnson, January 3, 1933, PFI Mss, Container 59, Folder 1136; H. A. Allan to Joy Elmer Morgan, January 20, 1932, JEM Mss, 1932 correspondence, FCB 2, Drawer 3.

30. Tracy F. Tyler to Dr. Herman G. James, January 7, 1932, NAEB Mss, Box No. 1a, General Correspondence 1932; Joy Elmer Morgan to J. J. Tigert, March 3, 1931, PFI Mss, Container 44, Folder 863; Tyler to James, NAEB Mss, Box 1a, General Correspondence 1932.

31. "Boring From Within," *Education by Radio*, August 18, 1932, p. 92; "Education Stations Turn Commercial," *Broadcasting*, January 1, 1932, p. 19.

32. Testimony of Father John B. Harney, *Senate 1934*, p. 186; "Advertising is Basis of Radio Existence," *Federation News*, August 5, 1933, p. 6.

33. Armstrong Perry to Ella Phillips Crandall, July 5, 1930, PFI Mss, Container 56, Folder 1070.

34. *Congressional Record*, 78 (May 15, 1934):8843.

35. Armstrong Perry to Ella Phillips Crandall, March 8, 1932, PFI Mss, Container 59, Folder 1144; H. O. Davis to Ella Phillips Crandall, March 15, 1932, PFI Mss, Container 59, Folder 1144.

36. Cited in "Air Not for Private Exploitation," *Education by Radio*, March 28, 1935, p. 15; "Nationally-Owned Radio System for Canada," *Education by Radio*, July 7, 1932, pp. 81–82; Martin Codel, "Canadian Broadcasting to be Nationalized," *Broadcasting*, May 15, 1932, pp. 7–8; Graham Spry to Gross W. Alexander, May 12, 1931, PFI Mss, Container 59, Folder 1136.

37. Graham Spry to Joy Elmer Morgan, April 7, 1932, JEM Mss, 1932 correspondence, FCB 2, Drawer 3; Graham Spry to Armstrong Perry, April 9, 1931, May 12, 1931, PFI Mss, Container 58, Folder 1122.

38. Graham Spry to Joy Elmer Morgan, May 2, 1932, PFI Mss, Container 42, Folder 822; Spry to Morgan, April 7, 1932, JEM Mss, FCB 2, Drawer 3.

39. Tracy F. Tyler to educational broadcasters, May 16, 1932, PFI Mss, Container 39, Folder 747; S. Howard Evans to H. O. Davis, May 16, 1932, PFI Mss, Container 59, Folder 1144; "Canadian Radio Proposal is Challenge to U.S. Broadcasters, Dill Tells Senate," *Broadcasting*, May 15, 1932, p. 8.

40. H. O. Davis to W. V. Woehlke, March 30, 1933, PFI Mss, Container 49, Folder 945.

41. Cited in "Gleanings from Varied Sources," *Education by Radio*, April 18, 1935, p. 20.

42. "Legislative Chiseling," *Broadcasters' News Bulletin*, August 15, 1931; Sol Taishoff, "Class Wave Plan Overwhelmingly Opposed," *Broadcasting*, November 1, 1934, p. 6.

43. Armstrong Perry, "National Association of Broadcasters," December 1935, PFI Mss, Container 52, Folder 986; Sol Taishoff to Tracy F. Tyler, December 14, 1933, PFI Mss, Container 45, Folder 868.

44. Armstrong Perry memo, June 19, 1931, PFI Mss, Container 68, Folder 1343.

45. S. Howard Evans to Walter V. Woehlke, February 15, 1932, PFI Mss, Container 60, Folder 1165.

46. Tracy Tyler to Roger Baldwin, October 26, 1933, ACLU Mss, 1933, Volume 599; Eddie Dowling, "Radio Needs a Revolution," *The Forum,* February 1834, p. 69.

47. H. O. Davis to E. H. Lighter, December 1, 1931, PFI Mss, Container 59, Folder 1143.

48. M. H. Aylesworth to David Sarnoff, April 1, 1933, David Sarnoff to M. H. Aylesworth, March 30, 1933, NBC Mss, Box 21, Folder 48; Jesse S. Butcher to Frank Mason, December 10, 1931, NBC Mss, Box 8, Folder 17.

49. *NACRE 1931,* p. 40; "Legislative Program is Planned by NAB Executive Committee," *Broadcasting,* December 1, 1931, p. 6.
The eclectic Bellows also served as a professor of rhetoric at the University of Minnesota, was a published music critic who had written program notes for the Minnesota Symphony Orchestra, had translated some of the classics from Latin to English, and had authored several published volumes of poetry. See "We Pay Our Respects to Henry Adams Bellows," *Broadcasting,* October 15, 1932, p. 17; "Changes Made in Staff of Gold Medal Station," *The Eventually News,* May 1925, p. 9; "Henry Adams Bellows 1885–1939," *The Modern Millwheel,* December 1939, p. 2; James Gray, *Business Without Boundary: The Story of General Mills* (Minneapolis: University of Minnesota Press, 1954), pp. 281–83.

50. Josephine Young Case and Everett Needham Case, *Owen D. Young and American Enterprise* (Boston: David R. Godine, 1982), p. 561; see also Owen D. Young to Harry F. Ward, December 3, 1929, Young Mss, 11–14–101; Owen D. Young to Karl A. Bickel, July 19, 1932, Young Mss, 11–14–116.

51. Memorandum on Will Hays telephone call, December 11, 1930, HH-P Mss, Sec'y Papers, Sari-Sarr, Box 835; Lawrence Richey to William S. Paley, August 24, 1932, HH-P Mss, Sec'y Papers, Palet-Paley, Box 777; M. H. Aylesworth to Herbert C. Hoover, March 15, 1929, George Arson to M. H. Aylesworth, December 20, 1929, HH-P Mss, Sec'y Files, Aylesworth, Box 423.

52. H. O. Davis, "Bulletin No. 13," July 1932, p. 5, PFI Mss, Container 60, Folder 1160; Sol Taishoff, " 'The First Fifty Years Were the Hardest'." In *The First 50 Years of Broadcasting* (Washington D.C.: Broadcasting Publications Inc., 1982), pp. x, vii; see also Joy Elmer Morgan to George W. Norris, May 8, 1933, JEM Mss, NEA, 1933 correspondence, FCB 2, Drawer 3.

53. Tracy F. Tyler to Cline M. Koon, October 18, 1934, PFI Mss, Container 43, Folder 830.

54. Sol Taishoff, "Session of Radio-Minded Congress Nears," *Broadcasting,* December 1, 1932, p. 5; Frank M. Russell to Stephen Early, March 13, 1933, Early Mss, Box 16.

55. Paul F. Peter, NBC Chief Statistician, "Appearances by U.S. Federal Officials Over National Broadcasting Company Networks, 1931–1933," November 1933, NBC Mss, Box 16, Folder 26.

56. Frank M. Russell to Lawrence Richey, September 25, 1931, HH-P Mss, FRC, 1931 August–September, Box 148.

57. Perry, *Current*, p. 267; Joy Elmer Morgan to John Henry McCracken, August 2, 1932, PFI Mss, Container 42, Folder 801.

58. David R. Mackey, "The National Association of Broadcasters—Its First Twenty Years" (Ph.D. dissertation, Northwestern University, 1956), pp. 342, 345; Memo on Federal Radio Commission, undated, PFI Mss, Container 55, Folder 1057; H. O. Davis to Ella Phillips Crandall, October 2, 1931, PFI Mss, Container 59, Folder 1143; Joy Elmer Morgan, unpublished memoirs, pp. 19–20, JEM Mss, NEA, FCB 1, Drawer 1.

59. "Broadcasters Must Organize," *Broadcasters' News Bulletin*, February 14, 1931; "Is Organization Necessary?" *Broadcasters' News Bulletin*, October 10, 1931; "Rates," *Broadcasters' News Bulletin*, February 27, 1932; " 'Mass Action is Imperative'," *Broadcasters' News Bulletin*, February 14, 1931.

60. M. H. Aylesworth to David Sarnoff, April 11, 1934, NBC Mss, Box 32, Folder 7, David Sarnoff 1934; "The Curtain Rises," *Broadcasters' News Bulletin*, September 24, 1932.

61. Taishoff, *50 Years*, p. v; H. O. Davis to R. J. Dunlap, February 10, 1932, PFI Mss, Container 59, Folder 1149; Cited in Taishoff, *50 Years*, pp. v, vi.

62. S. Howard Evans to George F. Zook, October 21, 1936, PFI Mss, Container 42, Folder 821; Armstrong Perry to Ella Phillips Crandall, February 9, 1932, PFI Mss, Container 56, Folder 1074; Tracy F. Tyler to Sol Taishoff, December 13, 1933, PFI Mss, Container 45, Folder 868.

63. "The American Broadcasters," May 22, 1926, WHA Papers, University of Wisconsin Archives, Madison, Wis., Box 1, File 11, General Business, A–L, 1925–28; Eugene J. Coltrane to Joy Elmer Morgan, June 17, 1933, PFI Mss, Container 41, Folder 783; Joy Elmer Morgan to all broadcasting stations in the United States, December 6, 1930, PFI Mss, Container 47, Folder 910; responses in PFI Mss, Container 54, Folder 1035; NCER Press Release, December 22, 1931, PFI Mss, Container 39, Folder 744.

64. Walter Woehlke to S. Howard Evans, December 14, 1931, PFI Mss, Container 60, Folder 1164; J. C. W. Reith, "Broadcasting in America." In *American vs. British System of Radio Control; The Reference Shelf, Volume 8, Number 10*. Compiled by E. C. Buehler (New York: H. W. Wilson Company, 1933), p. 298.

65. Eugene J. Coltrane, "Special Memorandum for Mr. Morgan and Mr. Tyler," undated, PFI Mss, Container 40, Folder 774; Perry, "N.A.B.," PFI Mss, Container 52, Folder 986; "All Set to Go," *Broadcasting*, October 15, 1933, p. 26; "Networks and NAB Dominate Radio," *Education by Radio*, February 15, 1934.

66. Cited in James L. Baughman, *Television's Guardians: The FCC and the Politics of Programming, 1958–1967* (Knoxville: University of Tennessee Press, 1985), p. 8.

67. Joy Elmer Morgan to E. J. Coltrane, November 22, 1932, PFI Mss, Container 41, Folder 783; Coltrane, "Special Memo," PFI Mss, Container 40, Folder 774; Armstrong Perry, "National Broadcasting Company," December 1935, PFI Mss, Container 52, Folder 986; "Education Demands Freedom of the Air," *Education by Radio*, April 27, 1932, p. 64.

68. S. Howard Evans to Walter V. Woehlke, October 18, 1932, PFI Mss, Con-

tainer 60, Folder 1167; Memorandum Re Conference, Dr. Joy Elmer Morgan and Miss Crandall, October 1, 1932, PFI Mss, Container 42, Folder 812; Armstrong Perry, "National Education Association," December 1935, PFI Mss, Container 52, Folder 986.

69. *The Reminiscences of William C. Hedges*, p. 71, COHC.

70. Sally Bedell Smith, *In All His Glory: The Life of Willism S. Paley* (New York: Simon and Schuster, 1990), pp. 70–71, 132; Edward L. Bernays, *Biography of an Idea: Memoirs of Public Relations Counsel Edward L. Bernays* (New York: Simon and Schuster, 1965), pp. 426–37.

71. Cited in "Combat Harmful Propaganda," *Broadcasters' News Bulletin*, February 21, 1931; F. X. W., "Will American Broadcasting become Classified and Regulated as a Public Utility?' *Public Utilities Fortnightly* 10 (August 4, 1932): p. 155; for a discussion of Merlin Aylesworth and the National Electric Light Association P.R. campaign, see Andrew Feldman, "Selling the 'Electrical Idea' in the 1920s: A Case Study in the Manipulation of Consciousness," M.A. thesis, University of Wisconsin-Madison, 1989.

72. Coltrane, "Special Memo," PFI Mss, Container 40, Folder 774; Morgan, *Debate*, p. 82.

73. *Broadcasting in the United States* (Washington D.C.: National Association of Broadcasters, 1933), p. 7; S. Howard Evans, Memorandum on Radio, October 18, 1934, PFI Mss, Container 69, Folder 1352; See Morgan, *Debate*.

74. Herman S. Hettinger, "Broadcasting in the United States." In *Annals 1935*, p. 12; See Henry A. Bellows, "The Right to Use Radio," *Public Utilities Fortnightly* 3 (June 27, 1929): pp. 770–74; *Broadcasting. Volume I* (New York: National Broadcasting Company, 1935), p. 5.

75. Merlin Hall Aylesworth, "The Listener Rules Broadcasting," *Nation's Business*, September 1929, pp. 23, 122–28; "Broadcasters on Their Guard," *Radio Digest*, March 1931, p. 61.

76. Armstrong Perry, "Advertising," December 1935, PFI Mss, Container 52, Folder 986; for treatment of "Amos 'n' Andy," see Melvin Patrick Ely, *The Adventures of Amos 'n' Andy* (New York: The Free Press, 1991); Bellows cited in Rorty, *Order*, p. 9.

77. For a discussion of public distaste of broadcast advertising in the 1960s, see Baughman, *Television's Guardians*, pp. 130, 170.

78. John F. Royal to Richard C. Patterson, Jr., May 21, 1935, NBC Mss, Box 34, Folder 52; "Radio Groups Open Wave Length Fight," *The New York Times*, September 10, 1934, p. 19. Examples of network promotional material in PFI Mss, Container 68, Folder 1337.

79. Levering Tyson to Richard C. Patterson, November 29, 1932, NBC Mss, NACRE 1932, Box 12, Folder 15.

80. William S. Paley, *As It Happened: A Memoir* (Garden City, NY: Doubleday & Company, 1979), p. 116; Alice Keith to Joy Elmer Morgan, February 27, 1931, March 7, 1931, PFI Mss, Container 45, Folder 875.

81. Alice Keith to Tracy Tyler, July 29, 1932, PFI Mss, Container 44, Folder 853; *The Reminiscences of Howard Barlow*, p. 127, COHC.

82. Alice Keith, "A Statement of Facts and Recommendations for Educational Radio," December 1932, PFI Mss, Container 55, Folder 1059; B. B. McCormick to Joy E. Morgan, December 24, 1931, PFI Mss, Container 39, Folder 744.

83. "Education 'Time' on Radio Opposed," *The New York Times*, October 19, 1934, p. 6; Charles R. Tighe to Tracy F. Tyler, June 7, 1934, PFI Mss, Container 44, Folder 862; Merlin H. Aylesworth, "Broadcasting in the Public Interest." In *Annals 1935*, p. 118.

84. For a discussion of this phenomenon in the 1950s, see William Boddy, *Fifties Television: The Industry and Its Critics* (Urbana and Chicago: University of Illinois Press, 1990), pp. 236–38.

85. *House 1934a*, p. 162.

86. *Broadcasting. Volume I*, p. 9; "Industry Viewpoints on Radio Regulation," *Education by Radio*, December 1938, pp. 37–38.

87. Francis D. Farrell, *Brief History of the Advisory Council of the National Broadcasting Company* (New York: National Broadcasting Company, 1939), p. 2; *Broadcasting. Volume I*, p. 36; Erik Barnouw, *A Tower in Babel* (New York: Oxford University Press, 1966), p. 204.

88. *Ibid.*, p. 204; Orrin E. Dunlap, Jr., "Council Reviews Effect of Radio on American Life," *The New York Times*, April 29, 1934, section IX, p. 9.

89. Armstrong Perry, "Report on the Present Status of Radio in Education," October 9, 1929, PFI Mss, Container 56, Folder 1069; Joy Elmer Morgan, "The National Committee on Education by Radio." In *NACRE 1931*, p. 13; Confidential Memorandum from Levering Tyson to Dr. Robert M. Hutchins, January 14, 1933, RMH II Mss, Volume 99.

90. Barnouw, *Tower*, pp. 205–6; M. H. Aylesworth to Sir John C. W. Reith, June 14, 1935, NBC Mss, Box 34, Folder 53.

91. Levering Tyson to Richard C. Patterson, December 1, 1932, NBC Mss, Box 12, Folder 15; Suggested Memorandum to Mr. Aylesworth from Mr. Patterson, 1933, RMH II Mss, Volume 99.

92. *House 1934b*, p. 133; Mackey, "The NAB," chapter IX; see, for example, Council on Radio Journalism, *Report on Radio News Internships* (Washington, D.C.: National Association of Broadcasters, 1946).

93. Agnes H. Shough to H. M. Beville, Jr., May 17, 1935, NBC Mss, NACRE 1935, Box 39, Folder 38.

Chapter 6

1. Walter V. Woehlke to S. Howard Evans, December 22, 1932, PFI Mss, Container 60, Folder 1167.

2. George B. Zehmer, "Report of the Radio Committee." In *NUEA 1930*, p. 167; Armstrong Perry, "Weak Spots in the American System of Broadcasting." In *Annals 1935*, pp. 23–24.

3. C. B. Haddon to Federal Radio Commission, December 3, 1931, FCC Mss, 63–2, Advertisements-Radio, FCC General Correspondence, Box 270; "Neither Sponsors Nor Stations Heed Radio Listeners' Grumbling," *Business Week*, February

10, 1932, pp. 18–19; In "From the Newspapers," *Education by Radio,* March 5, 1931, p. 14.

4. Levering Tyson, "Report of the Director." In *NACRE 1932,* p. 13; "Radio Men Warned on Advertising Evil," *The New York Times,* May 22, 1931, p. 27.

5. Orrin E. Dunlap, Jr., "Broadcasters Warned Listeners Want a New Deal— Drastic Action is Expected," *The New York Times,* November 20, 1932, Section 8, p. 6; "Lafount Sees Listener Revolt," *Broadcasters' News Bulletin,* March 28, 1931.

6. Sol Taishoff, "Session of Radio-Minded Congress Nears," *Broadcasting,* December 1, 1931, p. 6.

7. "As Senator White Sees It," *Broadcasters' News Bulletin,* November 21, 1931; Taishoff, *Broadcasting,* December 1, 1931, p. 6.

8. "Memorandum for Interview with D. Carters," March 14, 1931, PFI Mss, Container 69, Folder 1352; "Favors Government Ownership," *Broadcasters' News Bulletin,* June 27, 1931.

9. "Congress," *Broadcasting,* December 1, 1931, p. 18; Taishoff, *Broadcasting,* December 1, 1931, p. 5; Lynne M. Lamm, "Many Radio Bills Introduced But Other Matters Delay Action," *Broadcasting,* February 1, 1932, p. 10.

10. "President Shaw Warns," *Broadcasters News Bulletin,* January 11, 1932.

11. "Ewin Davis Loses Reelection Contest," *Broadcasting,* August 15, 1932, p. 6; Armstrong Perry, "Hon. Ewin L. Davis," December 1935, PFI Mss, Container 52, Folder 986; "Ewin Davis Address to American Association of Advertising Agencies," *Broadcasters' News Bulletin,* April 15, 1932, pp. 6, 9.

12. James Couzens, "The Channels of Information," *Public Utilities Fortnightly* 4 (August 22, 1929):216–20; Philip T. Rosen, *The Modern Stentors: Radio Broadcasters and the Federal Government, 1920–1934* (Westport, Conn.: Greenwood Press, 1980), p. 178; H. O. Davis to Our Cooperating Editors, October 27, 1931, H. O. Davis to Our Cooperating Editors, November 17, 1931, NBC Mss, Box 5, Folder 65, Ventura Free Press.

13. Martin Codel, "Dill and Davis Seen Powers in Radio Rule Under Roosevelt," *Broadcasting,* November 15, 1932, p. 8; Morris Ernst to Gordon W. Moss, November 19, 1931, ACLU Mss, 1931–1933, Volume 513; "To Investigate The Radio," *The Christian Century,* February 3, 1932, p. 141.

14. Martin Codel, "Radio Leaders Targets for Senator Dill," November 25, 1929, NANA, Vol. 60; Martin Codel, "Cleared Channels Appear to be Safe," undated, November 1929, NANA, Vol. 60; "Dill Again Assails Acts of Radio Board," *The New York Times,* September 22, 1929, p. 12, in John J. Carty Papers, AT&T, 83–10–01, Box 106.

15. Josephine Young Case and Everett Needham Case, *Owen D. Young and American Enterprise: A Biography* (Boston: David R. Godine, 1982), pp. 474–77.

16. Dill, "American Plan," p. 253; "The Weakness of American Radio," *Education by Radio,* February 4, 1932, p. 17; H. O. Davis to H. W. Parish, April 2, 1932, PFI Mss, Container 59, Folder 1144.

17. Donald G. Godfrey, "Senator Dill and the 1927 Radio Act," *Journal of Broadcasting* 23 (1978):486; Donald G. Godfrey, "The 1927 Radio Act: People and Politics," *Journalism History* 4 (Autumn 1977):74–78; see also William Fay Chamberlin, "A History of Public Issues Programming Regulation by the Federal Com-

munications Commission: More Rhetoric than Action," Ph.D. dissertation, University of Washington, 1977, p. 23.

18. Clarence C. Dill, "Radio by the American Plan." In *Future*, pp. 251–57; Clarence C. Dill, "Safe-Guarding the Ether—The American Way," *Congressional Digest*, August–September 1933, p. 196; "Senator Dill Flays Radio Commission," *Federation News*, October 19, 1929, p. 13.

19. "Canadian Government Wants Radio Control," *Federation News*, September 28, 1929; "Dill Warns Public Radio May Replace Private Operation," *Federation News*, May 21, 1932, p. 6; Cited in Werner J. Severin, "Commercial vs. Noncommercial Radio During Broadcasting's Early Years," *Journal of Broadcasting* 22 (Fall 1978):496; "Senator Dill Discusses Education," *Broadcasters' News Bulletin*, January 16, 1932.

20. Armstrong Perry, "Hon. Clarence C. Dill," December 1935, PFI Mss, Container 52, Folder 986.

21. "The Vestal Bill," *Broadcasters' News Bulletin*, January 12, 1931; "Better Business," *Broadcasting*, December 15, 1931, p. 18; see also, Martin Codel, *Senator Dill Is Interviewed* (Washington D.C.: National Association of Broadcasters, 1931), p. 4.

22. General J. G. Harbord, "Communications Legislation," January 8, 1930, p. 4, Young Mss, 11-14-55. AT&T was less enthusiastic about unification because it was satisfied with the manner it was being regulated by the ICC and not especially eager to gamble on how it would be regulated by a new unified commission. See E. S. Hawley, "Memorandum for J. H. Ray," March 8, 1930, AT&T Mss, Communication Act of 1934 series, Box 30.

23. Philip T. Rosen, *The Modern Stentors: Radio Broadcasting and the Federal Government, 1920–1934* (Westport, CT.: Greenwood, 1980), pp. 172–73; O. H. Caldwell, " 'American Plan' Broadcasting Goes Under Fire," *Electronics*, February 1932, p. 62.

24. Armstrong Perry to Jos. F. Wright, June 23, 1932; *Broadcasting*, December 15, 1931, p. 18; "Congress Active on Radio Regulation," *Broadcasting*, April 1, 1932, p. 25; Henry Adams Bellows, "Danger Signals Ahead of the Broadcasters," *Broadcasting*, October 15, 1931, p. 9; "The Seventy-Second Congress," *Education by Radio*, April 23, 1931, p. 41.

25. "Memorandum for Mr. Richey, Secretary to the President, from Chairman Saltzman, January 28, 1931, FCC Mss, 15-2, Legislation, FCC General Correspondence, Box 38; "Resolution No. 30." In *ABA 1930*, pp. 241–42; William Green to Robert F. Wagner, December 18, 1930, Wagner Mss, Legislative Files, Box 195; Joseph Wright to Frank R. Reid, May 26, 1930, PFI Mss, Container 41, Folder 796; Armstrong Perry to Ella Phillips Crandall, April 15, 1930, PFI Mss, Container 56, Folder 1070.

26. Martin Codel, "Radio Changes for 1931 Limited," undated, January 1931, NANA, Vol. 60.

27. Arthur W. Hyde to Senator Wesley L. Jones, January 29, 1931, DoA Mss, General Correspondence 1931, Radio; Arthur W. Hyde to Lawrence Richey, January 30, 1931, HH-P Mss, FRC, 1931 January 1–30, Box 148; Armstrong Perry to Ella Phillips Crandall, November 20, 1930, PFI Mss, Container 56, Folder 1070.

28. Edward N. Nockels, "Labor's Rights on the Air," *Federation News*, February 7, 1931, p. 2; "Labor Resolution Presented," *Broadcasters' News Bulletin*, January 12, 1931.

29. "Legislation," *Broadcasters' News Bulletin*, March 21, 1931, p. 9; "Labor Bill Headed for Congress," *Broadcasters' News Bulletin*, February 21, 1931; "Labor's Big Fight for Freedom of the Air," *Federation News*, March 21, 1931, p. 9.

30. "Congress is Asked for Radio Freedom," *The New York Times*, December 6, 1931, Section 2, p. 8; Armstrong Perry to Ella Phillips Crandall, January 8, 1931, PFI Mss, Container 56, Folder 1071.

31. "Legislation," *Broadcasters' News Bulletin*, March 21, 1931, p. 9; "Education Bill by Fess," *Broadcasters' News Bulletin*, January 10, 1931; "Fight Looms on Fess Bill," *Broadcasters' News Bulletin*, February 7, 1931.

32. Armstrong Perry to Joy Elmer Morgan, February 25, 1931, PFI Mss, Container 56, Folder 1071; Joy Elmer Morgan to H. M. Clymer, January 8, 1931, PFI Mss, Container 42, Folder 811; Joy Elmer Morgan to Armstrong Perry, June 16, 1931, PFI Mss, Container 55, Folder 1062.

33. Louis G. Caldwell, "Argument on Motion to Reconsider Commission's Action in Granting Reopening Hearing of WCFL," p. 15, April 15, 1931, "Motion of the Tribune Company," April 15, 1931, FCC Mss, Docketed Case Files #881, Box 167.

34. "Radio, A Red Hot Issue," *Federation News*, May 9, 1931, p. 4; Bill Murray memorandum, April 15, 1931, HH-P Mss, FRC, 1931 March–April, Box 148.

35. Levering Tyson, "The Radio Situation," March 18, 1931, CC Mss, NACRE Box 1, NACRE 1931.

36. For a longer exposition on the activities of the legal community during this period see Robert W. McChesney, "Free Speech and Democracy! Louis G. Caldwell, the American Bar Association, and the Free Speech Implications of Broadcast Regulation, 1928–1938," *The American Journal of Legal History* XXXV (October 1991): pp. 351–92.

37. "Discussion following Friday Morning Session, May 21, 1931." In *NACRE 1931*, p. 144; *ABA 1929*, pp. 406–7.

38. Examples include Louis G. Caldwell to Eugene O. Sykes, February 8, 1930, FCC Mss, General Correspondence 1927–1946, 89–6, American Bar Association, Box 317; Louis G. Caldwell to Robert F. Wagner, May 20, 1930, Wagner Mss, Legislative Files, Box 195.

39. Armstrong Perry to Mrs. Chester C. Bolton, August 7, 1931, PFI Mss, Container 68, Folder 1343; Frank M. Russell to A. L. Ashby, September 6, 1934, NBC Mss, Box 26, Folder 28, FCC Hearings 1934; "NAB Board," *Broadcasting*, March 1, 1933, p. 5; "Caldwell Off to Madrid," *Broadcasters' News Bulletin*, July 30, 1932.

40. "NAB Copyright Proposals," *Broadcasters' News Bulletin*, February 20, 1932; "Hearings Begin on Copyrights; Mills Rejoins American Society," *Broadcasting*, February 15, 1932, p. 8; "Copyright," *Broadcasters' News Bulletin*, March 21, 1931; "Dill Offers Copyright Measure With Guards for Radio Industry," *Broadcasting*, March 15, 1932, p. 10; Notes on Bar Association Communications Committee, September 16, 1931, PFI Mss, Container 45, Folder 866.

41. "NAB Convention Launches New Era," *Broadcasting,* October 15, 1933, pp. 14, 40; "Reorganizing Regulation," *Broadcasting,* September 1, 1933, p. 20.

42. *FCC 1934,* p. 198; Sol Taishoff, "Commission Shakeup Seen After March 4," *Broadcasting,* February 15, 1933, p. 5; "Hearing on WLWL Plea is Continued," *Broadcasting,* September 15, 1933, p. 29; "WLWL Request Denied," *Broadcasting,* February 15, 1934, p. 32.

43. Cited in "Radio's Legal Racket," *Education by Radio,* May 10, 1934, p. 19; "Lawyer Plays Important Part in Radio Broadcasting," *American Bar Association Journal,* 16 (June 1930):347; Joy Elmer Morgan, "The New American Plan for Radio." In *Debate,* pp. 103–4.

44. *ABA 1928,* p. 323; *ABA 1929,* p. 470.

45. *ABA 1932,* p. 145; *ABA 1931,* pp. 102–3; Louis G. Caldwell, "Principles Governing the Licensing of Broadcasting Stations," *University of Pennsylvania Law Review* 79 (December 1930):157.

46. Louis G. Caldwell, "The Standard of Public Interest, Convenience or Necessity as Used in the Radio Act of 1927," *Air Law Review* 1 (July 1930):296; Louis G. Caldwell, "Radio and the Law." In *Future,* p. 231; S. Howard Evans, "The Crisis in Radio Regulation," October 1931, PFI Mss, Container 51, Folder 978.

47. Caldwell, "Radio and the Law," p. 227; *ABA 1932,* p. 145; "Discussion." In *NACRE 1931,* p. 147.

48. *ABA 1929,* p. 459; Henry A. Bellows, "The Right to Use Radio," *Public Utilities Fortnightly,* June 27, 1929, p. 773.

49. Cited in Joel Rosenbloom, "Authority of the Federal Communications Commission." In *Freedom and Responsibility in Broadcasting,* Edited by John E. Coons (Evanston: Northwestern University Press, 1961), pp. 144–145.

50. *ABA 1931,* pp. 384, 102; *ABA 1932,* pp. 147–48.

51. *ABA 1931,* p. 103; *ABA 1932,* p. 477.

52. See, for example, Louis G. Caldwell, "The New Rules and Regulations of the Federal Radio Commission," *Journal of Radio Law* 2 (January 1932):66–99; Armstrong Perry to Joy E. Morgan, July 13, 1932, PFI Mss, Container 55, Folder 1062.

53. In addition to the Caldwell pieces cited earlier, see James M. Herring, "Public Interest, Convenience or Necessity in Radio Broadcasting," *Harvard Business Review* 10 (April 1932): pp. 280–291; James M. Herring, "Equalization of Broadcast Facilities Within the United States," *Harvard Business Review* 9 (July 1931):417–30.

54. See, for example, "The Freedom of Radio Speech," *Harvard Law Review* 46 (March 1933): pp. 987–93; Edward C. Caldwell, "Censorship of Radio Programs," *Journal of Radio Law* 1 (October 1931):441–76; Leland L. Chapman, "The Power of the Federal Radio Commission to Regulate or Censor Radio Broadcasts," *George Washington Law Review* 1 (March 1933):380–85; Byron Pumphrey, "Censorship of Radio Programs and Freedom of Speech," *Kentucky Law Journal* 22 (May 1934):634–41.

55. "Legal Racketeering?" *Education by Radio,* August 27, 1931, p. 101; "Radio From the Citizen's Point of View," *Education by Radio,* October 8, 1931, p. 12;

Cited in "Canadian Government Wants Radio Control," *Federation News*, September 28, 1929, p. 10.

56. "Discussion." In *NACRE 1931*, pp. 144–48.

57. Armstrong Perry to John Carson, August 7, 1931, PFI Mss, Container 68, Folder 1343; Joy Elmer Morgan to Governors, August 7, 1931, PFI Mss, Container 55, Folder 1040.

58. E. N. Nockels, "Appeals to Honor of American Bar," *Federation News*, September 19, 1931, p. 1; Tracy F. Tyler to Charles A. Boston, August 15, 1931, PFI Mss, Container 45, Folder 866.

59. *Education by Radio*, October 8, 1931, p. 112.

60. *Who's Who in America, 1934–35*, Volume 18, Edited by Albert Nelson Marquis (Chicago: The A. N. Marquis Company, 1934), p. 2446.

61. *ABA 1931*, pp. 107–13.

62. "Property Rights in Air Racket Puts Bar Meeting in Turmoil," *Federation News*, September 26, 1931, p. 3; "Mr. Caldwell Explains," *The New York Times*, September 25, 1931, p. 24; "Bar Report Criticized," *Broadcasters' News Bulletin*, September 19, 1931.

63. Louis G. Caldwell to National Committee on Education by Radio, April 8, 1932, PFI Mss, Container 39, Folder 744; Louis G. Caldwell to S. Howard Evans, April 8, 1932, PFI Mss, Container 60, Folder 1172; "Bar Committee Appointed," *Broadcasters' News Bulletin*, November 7, 1931.

64. "Labor Declines Caldwell Offer," *Federation News*, May 7, 1932, p. 6; Martin Codel, "Bar Group Opposes Critical Report," *Broadcasting*, October 15, 1932, p. 12; "Caldwell Off to Madrid," *Broadcasters' News Bulletin*, July 30, 1932; "Radio Report to Bar Association," *Broadcasters' News Bulletin*, September 3, 1932; "Bar Committee Repudiated," *Education by Radio*, November 10, 1932, p. 104.

65. *ABA 1939*, pp. 184–89.

66. J. O. Keller to Joy Elmer Morgan, November 5, 1931, PFI Mss, Container 41, Folder 797; Joy Elmer Morgan to Charles N. Lischka, November 12, 1931, JEM Mss, NEA, 1931 correspondence, FCB 2, Drawer 3.

67. Ella Phillips Crandall to Joy Elmer Morgan, September 9, 1931, PFI Mss, Container 47, Folder 903; Mrs. Chester C. Bolton to Dr. John H. MacCracken, October 9, 1931, PFI Mss, Container 40, Folder 768; Simeon D. Fess to Armstrong Perry, February 26, 1932, Armstrong Perry to Simeon D. Fess, March 2, 1932, PFI Mss, Container 58, Folder 1129.

68. Crandall to Morgan, September 9, 1931, PFI Mss, Container 47, Folder 903; Ella Phillips Crandall to H. O. Davis, October 1, 1931, PFI Mss, Container 59, Folder 1143; Bolton to MacCracken, October 9, 1931, PFI Mss, Container 40, Folder 768.

69. S. Howard Evans, "Report on Members of Congress," December 1931, PFI Mss, Container 43, Folder 826; Walter V. Woehlke to Hon. C. C. Dill, October 20, 1931, PFI Mss, Container 59, Folder 1143; S. Howard Evans to Walter V. Woehlke, October 14, 1931, PFI Mss, Container 60, Folder 1163.

70. "Radio's Friends Get Ready for Its Foes," *Printers' Ink*, November 15, 1931,

p. 71; Tracy F. Tyler to J. O. Keller, November 3, 1931, PFI Mss, Container 41, Folder 797; *NAB 1931*, p. 52.

71. H. O. Davis to Editors, December 24, 1931, NBC Mss, Ventura Free Press, Box 5, Folder 65; S. Howard Evans to Walter V. Woehlke, December 22, 1931, PFI Mss, Container 60, Folder 1164.

72. Federal Radio Commission, "In Re The Use of Radio Broadcasting Stations for Advertising Purposes," December 21, 1931, PFI Mss, Container 60, Folder 1159; "Commission Commends NAB Code," *Broadcasters' News Bulletin*, December 24, 1931; "A Report of Stewardship," *Education by Radio*, December 1937, p. 60; Harold A. Lafount, "Radio and Education," November 12, 1931, PFI Mss, Container 47, Folder 910.

73. S. Howard Evans to Walter V. Woehlke, December 24, 1931, PFI Mss, Container 60, Folder 1164; Ella Phillips Crandall to H. O. Davis, October 2, 1931, PFI Mss, Container 59, Folder 1143; S. H. Evans to Walter Woehlke, February 29, 1932, PFI Mss, Container 69, Folder 1358.

74. Taishoff, *Broadcasting*, December 1, 1931, p. 6; "Radio Inquiry Welcomed by Broadcasters," January 16, 1932, NANA, Vol. 61.

75. *FRC 1932*, p. v; "Radio Advertising Goes Before United States Senate," *Printers' Ink*, January 14, 1932, p. 10.

76. S. Howard Evans to Walter Woehlke, December 9, 1931, PFI Mss, Container 60, Folder 1164; S. Howard Evans to Walter Woehlke, January 8, 1932, PFI Mss, Container 60, Folder 1165.

77. *FRC 1932*, p. vi; Joy Elmer Morgan to Ella Phillips Crandall, January 13, 1932, PFI Mss, Container 42, Folder 812; Armstrong Perry to S. Howard Evans, February 9, 1932, PFI Mss, Container 56, Folder 1074; *Congressional Record* 75 (January 4, 1932): pp. 1194–95; *Congressional Record* 75 (January 7, 1932): pp. 1412–13; Sol Taishoff, "Commission Opens Sweeping Radio Inquiry," *Broadcasting*, February 1, 1932, pp. 5, 28.

78. Walter V. Woehlke to S. Howard Evans, January 11, 1932, PFI Mss, Container 60, Folder 1165.

79. Martin Codel, "Radio Advertising Inquiry Proposed," *Broadcasting*, January 15, 1932, p. 8; T. M. Beaird to Joseph F. Wright, February 25, 1932, NAEB Mss, Box No. 1a, General Correspondence 1932; H. O. Davis to Ella Phillips Crandall, February 23, 1932, PFI Mss, Container 59, Folder 1144.

80. S. Howard Evans to Walter V. Woehlke, February 9, 1932, PFI Mss, Container 60, Folder 1165; S. Howard Evans to Walter V. Woehlke, February 1, 1932, PFI Mss, Container 60, Folder 1165.

81. Davis comment in NBC memo on 1932 AAAA convention. See E. P. H. James to Roy C. Witmer, April 19, 1932, NBC Mss, Box 5, Folder 103.

82. S. Howard Evans to Walter V. Woehlke, March 21, 1932, PFI Mss, Container 60, Folder 1165.

83. S. Howard Evans to Walter V. Woehlke, March 23, 1932, March 25, 1932, PFI Mss, Container 60, Folder 1165; H. O. Davis to H. L. Bras, March 29, 1932, PFI Mss, Container 59, Folder 1144.

84. Walter V. Woehlke to S. Howard Evans, May 3, 1932, PFI Mss, Container 60, Folder 1166; Walter V. Woehlke to S. Howard Evans, March 26, 1932, PFI

Mss, Container 60, Folder 1165; H. O. Davis to Ella Phillips Crandall, March 28, 1932, PFI Mss, Container 59, Folder 1144.

85. Evans to Woehlke, March 23, 1932, PFI Mss, Container 60, Folder 1165; C. C. Dill to H. O. Davis, April 4, 1932, April 6, 1932, PFI Mss, Container 59, Folder 1149; S. Howard Evans to John Carson, April 6, 1932, PFI Mss, Container 60, Folder 1172; S. Howard Evans to Walter V. Woehlke, June 4, 1932, PFI Mss, Container 60, Folder 1166.

86. Ella Phillips Crandall to H. O. Davis, March 24, 1932, PFI Mss, Container 59, Folder 1144; Report of the Service Bureau, January 15–31, 1932, PFI Mss, Container 68, Folder 1344; Telegram, Joy Elmer Morgan to H. O. Davis, March 8, 1932, PFI Mss, Container 47, Folder 901; H. O. Davis to Ella Phillips Crandall, PFI Mss, March 8, 1932, Container 59, Folder 1144.

87. Ella Phillips Crandall, "Review of the Program of the National Committee on Education by Radio," August 11, 1932, PFI Mss, Container 56, Folder 1075; Tracy F. Tyler to Arthur L. Marsh, April 7, 1932, PFI Mss, Container 39, Folder 744; Joy Elmer Morgan to Mrs. Bolton, June 6, 1932, PFI Mss, Container 42, Folder 812.

88. Ella Phillips Crandall to H. O. Davis, March 16, 1932, PFI Mss, Container 59, Folder 1144; Ella Phillips Crandall to Armstrong Perry, March 15, 1932, PFI Mss, Container 56, Folder 1074; Crandall, August 11, 1932, PFI Mss, Container 56, Folder 1144.

89. Walter Woehlke to S. Howard Evans, April 17, 1933, PFI Mss, Container 60, Folder 1169; Walter Woehlke to S. Howard Evans, May 4, 1932, PFI Mss, Container 60, Folder 1166.

90. "Bill for Labor Channel," *Broadcasters' News Bulletin*, January 23, 1932; "Labor Fighting for Channel," *Broadcasters' News Bulletin*, March 19, 1932; Armstrong Perry to Ella Phillips Crandall, March 11, 1932, PFI Mss, Container 56, Folder 1074; Evans, "Report," PFI Mss, Container 43, Folder 826.

91. "Radio Legislation," *Broadcasting*, April 1, 1932, p. 25; Armstrong Perry to Ella Phillips Crandall, May 11, 1932, PFI Mss, Container 56, Folder 1075; "Labor Station Promises Fight," March 26, 1932, NANA, Vol. 61.

92. "Labor Wins Victory in Long Air Fight," *Federation News*, June 4, 1932, p. 6; Armstrong Perry to Joseph Wright, June 23, 1932, Illinois Mss, Box 3, National Committee on Education by Radio; Perry to Crandall, May 11, 1932, PFI Mss, Container 56, Folder 1075.

93. Perry to Wright, June 23, 1932, Illinois Mss, Box 3, National Committee on Education by Radio; S. Howard Evans to Armstrong Perry, May 2, 1932, Armstrong Perry to S. Howard Evans, May 1, 1932, PFI Mss, Container 56, Folder 1075.

94. Taishoff, *Broadcasting*, February 1, 1932, pp. 5, 28; "NAB, 1933 Model," *Broadcasting*, December 1, 1932, p. 18; James Baldwin to Meyer Broadcasting Company, March 12, 1932, FCC Mss, North Dakota, 15–4, FCC General Correspondence, Box 47.

95. "Commercial Broadcasters to Intensify Lobby," *Education by Radio*, March 10, 1932, p. 38; Paul F. Peter, "FRC Questionnaire to all Stations," NBC Mss, Box 9, Folder 50, FRC, January–April 1932; Susan Renee Smulyan, " 'And Now a Word From Our Sponsors': Commercialization of American Broadcast Radio,

1920–1934.'' Ph.D. dissertation, Yale University, 1985, pp. 223–25; Harold A. Lafount, ''Contributions of the Federal Radio Commission.'' In *IER 1931*, p. 21.

96. ''What's Going on Here?'' *Broadcasters' News Bulletin*, February 13, 1932.

97. Joseph F. Wright to B. B. Brackett, November 29, 1932, T. M. Beaird to B. B. Brackett, December 8, 1932, NAEB Mss, Box No. 1a, General Correspondence 1932; James W. Baldwin to Armstrong Perry, January 18, 1932, January 19, 1932, PFI Mss, Container 55, Folder 1057; Armstrong Perry, ''Federal Radio Commission Questionnaire of January 18, 1932,'' March 9, 1932, Armstrong Perry, ''Federal Radio Commission Questionnaire of January 19, 1932,'' March 9, 1932, PFI Mss, Container 68, Folder 1344.

98. Sol Taishoff, ''Limit on Advertising Called Dangerous,'' *Broadcasting*, June 15, 1932, p. 5; *FRC 1932*, pp. 2, 33–36, 101.

99. ''Couzens–Dill Report Completed,'' *Broadcasters' News Bulletin*, June 11, 1932; ''Congress Adjourns,'' *Broadcasters' News Bulletin*, July 23, 1932.

100. ''Indisputable Facts,'' *Broadcasting*, June 15, 1932, p. 20; *ABA 1932*, p. 144.

101. Cited in Harold E. Hill, *The National Association of Educational Broadcasters: A History* (Urbana, IL: The National Association of Educational Broadcasters, 1954), p. 14; H. O. Davis to Walter H. Brooks, October 5, 1932, PFI Mss, Container 59, Folder 1145; ''Report of the Committee on Radio Broadcasting.'' In *NASU 1933*, p. 38.

102. ''Memorandum of Progress of the National Committee on Education by Radio,'' September 15, 1932, PFI Mss, Container 47, Folder 904; Tracy F. Tyler to Ella Phillips Crandall, September 7, 1932, PFI Mss, Container 42, Folder 812; Tracy F. Tyler, ''Radio Broadcasting By The American Plan,'' *The Torch* 6 (April 1933):31–35.

103. H. O. Davis to Walter Woehlke, undated, summer 1932, PFI Mss, Container 60, Folder 1167; ''*Broadcasting*, June 15, 1932, p. 20; S. Howard Evans to Walter V. Woehlke, June 22, 1932, PFI Mss, Container 60, Folder 1166; Frank M. Russell to Walter Newton, HH-P Mss, FRC, July–August 1932, Box 149.

104. Thomas R. Amlie to Joy Elmer Morgan, December 28, 1931, PFI Mss, Container 39, Folder 744; Evans to Woehlke, February 1, 1932, PFI Mss, Container 60, Folder 1165.

105. Thomas R. Amlie to Tracy F. Tyler, May 24, 1932, PFI Mss, Container 43, Folder 825. The Wisconsin League of Radio Stations formally condemned Amlie for his ''thoughtless and inconsistent tactics in disparaging a medium of communication,'' in February 1932. Resolution in NBC Mss, Box 13, Folder 72.

106. ''The Curtain Rises,'' *Broadcasters' News Bulletin*, September 24, 1932; Armstrong Perry, ''Columbia Broadcasting System,'' December 1935, PFI Mss, Container 52, Folder 986.

Chapter 7

1. Internal NCER Memorandum, November 18, 1932, PFI Mss, Container 54, Folder 1028; B. B. Brackett to Joseph F. Wright, December 13, 1932, NAEB Mss,

Box No. 1a, General Correspondence 1932; Tracy F. Tyler, *Some Interpretations and Conclusions of the Land Grant Radio Survey* (Washington D.C.: National Committee on Education by Radio, 1933).

2. S. Howard Evans to Walter V. Woehlke, June 29, 1932, PFI Mss, Container 60, Folder 1166; S. Howard Evans to Walter V. Woehlke, November 30, 1932, PFI Mss, Container 60, Folder 1167.

3. Walter V. Woehlke to S. Howard Evans, August 19, 1932, PFI Mss, Container 60, Folder 1167; H. O. Davis to W. H. Cowles, June 24, 1932, PFI Mss, Container 59, Folder 1145.

4. Walter V. Woehlke to S. Howard Evans, November 15, 1932, PFI Mss, Container 60, Folder 1167; S. Howard Evans to Walter V. Woehlke, December 1, 1932, PFI Mss, Container 60, Folder 1167.

5. Joy Elmer Morgan to Delegate, June 15, 1932, PFI Mss, Container 39, Folder 747; Armstrong Perry to Jos. F. Wright, June 25, 1932, Ruth Roberts to Jos. F. Wright, June 21, 1932, Jos. F. Wright to Armstrong Perry, July 1, 1932, Illinois Mss, Box 3, National Committee on Education by Radio.

6. Joy Elmer Morgan to members of Congress, candidates for Congress, and members of national committees of all political parties, October 20, 1932, PFI Mss, Container 47, Folder 910.

7. S. Howard Evans to Walter V. Woehlke, November 12, 1932, PFI Mss, Container 60, Folder 1167; Roger N. Baldwin to Henry J. Eckstein, ACLU Mss, July 17, 1935.

8. Memorandum re: Conference between Joy Elmer Morgan and Miss Crandall, October 1, 1932, PFI Mss, Container 42, Folder 812; "A Congressional Investigation of Radio," *Education by Radio,* December 8 1932, p. 105; S. Howard Evans to Walter V. Woehlke, October 4, 1932, PFI Mss, Container 60, Folder 1167; S. Howard Evans to Walter V. Woehlke, October 7, 1932, PFI Mss, Container 60, Folder 1167.

9. Joy Elmer Morgan, "Radio and the Home," *Education by Radio,* January 19, 1933, p. 8; *Education by Radio,* October 13, 1932, p. 98; "Nationally Owned Radio System for Canada," *Education by Radio,* July 7, 1932, p. 81; "A Proposal for Public Ownership of Radio; Report of the Canadian Royal Commission on Radio Broadcasting," *Education by Radio,* May 26, 1932, pp. 69–72.

10. S. Howard Evans to H. O. Davis, November 18, 1932, PFI Mss, Container 59, Folder 1145; "Educator Protests," *Broadcasting,* February 1, 1933, p. 34.

11. S. Howard Evans to Walter V. Woehlke, December 19, 1932, PFI Mss, Container 69, Folder 1358.

12. S. Howard Evans to H. O. Davis, January 8, 1933, PFI Mss, Container 59, Folder 1146; *Senate 1933,* p. 25; S. Howard Evans to Eugene J. Coltrane, January 25, 1933, PFI Mss, Container 41, Folder 783.

13. Gordon W. Moss to Bethuel M. Webster, Jr., December 15, 1932, ACLU Mss, 1931–1933, Volume 513; Gordon W. Moss to Edmund Campbell, January 4, 1933, ACLU Mss, 1931–1933, Volume 513; Tracy Tyler to Roger Baldwin, October 26, 1933, ACLU Mss, 1933, Volume 599.

14. Memorandum Concerning Payne Fund Cooperation with Commercial Radio Stations, November 15, 1932, PFI Mss, Container 69, Folder 1352.

15. Tracy F. Tyler, "Educational Broadcasting Station Succumbs to Commercial Attack," *Education by Radio,* August 31, 1933, pp. 41–42; "Education Loses, Listeners Betrayed," *Education by Radio,* July 11, 1935, p. 31; Joseph F. Wright to B. B. Brackett, February 13, 1933, NAEB Mss, Box No. 1a, General Correspondence 1933; James Couzens to B. B. Brackett, February 13, 1933, NAEB Mss, Box No. 1a, General Correspondence 1935.

The commercial broadcasters also attempted to fill the vacant FRC spot with NBC executive William Hedges. This movement was stopped when Senator James Couzens (R-Mich.) informed the White House that "it would be a very grave error" to put an NBC representative on the FRC. See James Couzens to Herbert Hoover, August 13, 1932, HH-P Mss, Sec'y Papers, National Broa-Brot, Box 756.

16. Confidential Report of Armstrong Perry on the International Radiotelegraphic Conference in Madrid, September 3 to December 9, 1932, PFI Mss, Container 68, Folder 1344.

17. Tracy F. Tyler to Armstrong Perry, April 19, 1933, PFI Mss, Container 56, Folder 1077.

18. Armstrong Perry to Glenn Frank, January 6, 1933, Henry Ewbank Papers, University of Wisconsin Archives, Madison, WI, Box 1, WHA Radio Committee 1933; Frank M. Russell to M. H. Aylesworth, July 11, 1933, C. W. Horn to Richard C. Patterson, Jr., February 24, 1933, NBC Mss, Box 20, Folder 19.

19. Joy Elmer Morgan to T. A. M. Craven, March 13, 1933, PFI Mss, Container 57, Folder 1090.

20. See Susan J. Douglas, *Inventing American Broadcasting, 1899–1922* (Baltimore: The Johns Hopkins University Press, 1987) for treatment of Hooper's important role in the development of radio prior to broadcasting.

21. "Record of Captain S. C. Hooper, U. S. Navy," undated, 1934, Hooper Mss, Box 16.

22. S. C. Hooper, Memorandum on Communications, November 14, 1928, Hooper Mss, Box 9; S. C. Hooper to Owen D. Young, May 11, 1928, November 21, 1927, Young Mss, 11–14–66.

23. For Hooper's early sentiments toward commercial broadcasting, see S. C. Hooper to Robert D. Heinl, December 14, 1927, Hooper Mss, Box 8; S. C. Hooper, "Communications," January 10, 1930, p. 15, Hooper Mss, Box 11; S. C. Hooper, "Radio Communications,' November 20, 1930, pp. 3–4, Hooper Mss, Box 12; S. C. Hooper, "How to Reduce Over-Advertising in Broadcasts," February 24, 1931, Hooper Mss, Box 13.

24. Armstrong Perry to Ella Phillips Crandall, March 11, 1932, PFI Mss, Container 56, Folder 1074.

25. S. C. Hooper to Louis McHenry Howe, November 21, 1932, Hooper Mss, Box 14.

26. S. C. Hooper to Armstrong Perry, March 31, 1933, PFI Mss, Container 43, Folder 838; Tracy F. Tyler to William A. Orton, June 15, 1935, PFI Mss, Container 44, Folder 857; S. C. Hooper to Tracy F. Tyler, June 15, 1934, PFI Mss, Container 68, Folder 1345.

For Hooper's position on the antitrust case against RCA see S. C. Hooper, Memorandum for the Assistant Secretary on the Radio Situation, October 31, 1931, Hooper Mss, Box 13.

27. Martin Codel, "North America to Settle Own Wave Length Disputes," December 3, 1932, NANA, Vol. 61; S. C. Hooper to Armstrong Perry, March 24, 1933, Hooper Mss, Box 15.

28. Armstrong Perry to S. C. Hooper, March 22, 1933, April 1, 1933, PFI Mss, Container 43, Folder 838; Armstrong Perry to Joy Elmer Morgan, March 28, 1933, PFI Mss, Container 56, Folder 1077; Armstrong Perry to Tracy F. Tyler, April 4, 1933, PFI Mss, Container 57, Folder 1090.

29. S. C. Hooper to Armstrong Perry, March 31, 1933, S. C. Hooper to S. Howard Evans, April 3, 1933, Hooper Mss, Box 15.

30. S. C. Hooper to Armstrong Perry, March 24, 1933, PFI Mss, Container 43, Folder 838.

31. Activities of Armstrong Perry in connection with the North and Central American Radio Conference, September 6, 1933, PFI Mss, Container 43, Folder 838; Armstrong Perry to Joy Elmer Morgan, August 16, 1933, PFI Mss, Container 55, Folder 1062; Sol Taishoff, "Mexico's Demands Break Up Wave Parley," *Broadcasting,* August 15, 1933, p. 5.

32. "Failure in Mexico," *Broadcasting,* August 15, 1933, p. 18; Tracy F. Tyler to Broadcasting Station Manager, October 13, 1933, PFI Mss, Container 47, Folder 911.

33. Evans to Coltrane, January 25, 1933, PFI Mss, Container 41, Folder 783; Tracy F. Tyler to Jos. F. Wright, October 11, 1932, PFI Mss, Container 42, Folder 820; Tracy F. Tyler to Herman Roe, December 13, 1932, PFI Mss, Container 46, Folder 885.

34. S. Howard Evans to Walter V. Woehlke, December 19, 1932, PFI Mss, Container 60, Folder 1167; Ella Phillips Crandall to William John Cooper, February 19, 1933, PFI Mss, Container 68, Folder 1337.

35. An Invitation for the American Listeners Society, March 25, 1933, PFI Mss, Container 42, Folder 813; Tracy F. Tyler to John Smith, September 1932, PFI Mss, Container 47, Folder 913; Joy Elmer Morgan to McAndrew, September 20, 1932, JEM Mss, 1932 correspondence, FCB 2, Drawer 3.

36. " 'Listeners Society'," *Broadcasting,* April 1, 1933, p. 14; Levering Tyson to F. P. Keppel, January 2, 1934, p. 2, CC Mss, NACRE Box 1, NACRE 1934; for the NACRE's listeners society, see Levering Tyson, "Report of the Director to the Board of Directors." In *NACRE 1933,* p. 19.

37. Joy Elmer Morgan to State Presidents, PTA, June 6, 1932, PFI Mss, Container 39, Folder 747; Report of Eugene J. Coltrane, October 1932, PFI Mss, Container 39, Folder 749.

38. Eugene J. Coltrane to Tracy F. Tyler, November 18, 1932, PFI Mss, Container 41, Folder 783; Eugene J. Coltrane to Joy Elmer Morgan, October 20, 1932, PFI Mss, Container 41, Folder 783.

39. Report of Eugene J. Coltrane, December 1932, PFI Mss, Container 39, Folder 749; Report of Eugene J. Coltrane, August 1933, PFI Mss, Container 39, Folder 750; Report of Eugene J. Coltrane, June 1933, PFI Mss, Container 40, Folder 773.

40. Special Memorandum for Mr. Morgan and Dr. Tyler, Autumn 1933, PFI Mss, Container 40, Folder 774; Memorandum concerning Mr. Coltrane, April 23, 1934, PFI Mss, Container 40, Folder 773.

41. Tracy F. Tyler, "Brief Summary Report of the National Committee on Education by Radio, 1931–1935," pp. 16–18, Tyler Mss, NCER file.

42. Tracy F. Tyler to T. M. Beaird, April 14, 1933, PFI Mss, Container 47, Folder 916; T. M. Beaird to Tracy Tyler, April 11, 1933, PFI Mss, Container 47, Folder 916; "Radio Question Popular," *Education by Radio*, June 22, 1933, p. 24.

43. S. Howard Evans to Tracy F. Tyler, July 21, 1933, PFI Mss, Container 42, Folder 813; H. O. Davis to Cranston Williams, July 27, 1933, PFI Mss, Container 59, Folder 1147; S. Howard Evans to Walter Woehlke, October 16, 1933, PFI Mss, Container 60, Folder 1170.

44. *Debate; Current; Control; American Vs. British System of Radio Control: The Reference Shelf Volume 8, Number 10*, Compiled by E. C. Buehler (New York: The H. W. Wilson Company, 1933); *University Debaters' Annual, 1932–33*, Edited by Edith M. Phelps (New York: The H. W. Wilson Company, 1933), chapter III; *University Debaters's Annual, 1933–34*, Edited by Edith M. Phelps (New York: The H. W. Wilson Company, 1934), Chapter I.

45. National Association of Broadcasters, *Broadcasting in the United States* (Washington D.C.: National Association of Broadcasters, 1933), p. 3; "Let's Have the Facts," *Education by Radio*, January 18, 1934, p. 1; S. Howard Evans to Tracy F. Tyler, November 1, 1933, PFI Mss, Container 68, Folder 1346.

46. Merlin H. Aylesworth to David Sarnoff, August 20, 1934, NBC Mss, Box 32, Folder 7; See J. C. W. Reith, "Broadcasting in America." In Buehler, pp. 287–88; Bate to Aylesworth, January 10, 1934, NBC Mss, Box 24, Folder 25; Sir John Reith to Armstrong Perry, February 24, 1934, PFI Mss, Container 58, Folder 1110.

47. M. H. Aylesworth to Sir John C. W. Reith, January 27, 1934, NBC Mss, Box 24, Folder 27.

48. John F. Royal to M. H. Aylesworth, April 9, 1934, NBC Mss, Box 25, Folder 51.

49. See, for example, Joy Elmer Morgan, "The Radio in Education." In *NUEA 1932*, p. 84; Tracy F. Tyler, "The British System of Radio Control, Speech delivered to First Annual Conference for Senior High School Students, April 13, 1934, PFI Mss, Container 42, Folder 815; Aylesworth to Sarnoff, August 20, 1934, NBC Mss, Box 32, Folder 7, David Sarnoff 1934.

50. H. O. Davis to Mr. L. Lea, August 8, 1931, NBC Mss, Box 5, Folder 65, Ventura Free Press. For a longer discussion of the press–radio conflict of the early 1930s, see Robert W. McChesney, "Press–Radio Relations and the Emergence of Network, Commercial Broadcasting in the United States, 1930–1935," *Historical Journal of Film, Radio and Television* 11 (1991): 41–57.

51. Richard Joyce Smith, "The Ultimate Control of Radio in the United States," *NACRE 1932*, p. 186. For the most thorough examination of 1930s network newscasts, see Gwenyth Jackaway, "The Press–Radio War, 1924–1937: The Battle to Defend the Professional, Institutional, and Political Power of the Press," (Ph.D. dissertation, University of Pennsylvania, 1992).

52. H. O. Davis to Ella Phillips Crandall, April 27, 1932, PFI Mss, Container

59, Folder 1144; Text of debate on broadcast reform proposal which was broadcast over NBC on November 1, 1933 later published as *Debate: Resolved: That the United States Should Adopt the Essential Features of the British System of Radio Control and Operation* (Chicago: University of Chicago Press, 1933); See also "Radio Control Debate November 1," *NAB Reports*, October 28, 1933, p. 207.

53. *House 1934a*, p. 162.

54. Jerome Davis to Federal Communications Commission, October 10, 1934, PFI Mss, Container 44, Folder 847.

55. Scripts provided author courtesy of Corporate Press Services, Columbia Broadcasting System, New York, NY; Texts for the fifteen talks in PFI Mss, Container 55, Folder 1050.

56. Frank Russell to M. H. Aylesworth, March 11, 1932, NBC Mss, Box 12, Folder 18; M. H. Aylesworth to David Sarnoff, March 15, 1933, NBC Mss, Box 21, Folder 48.

57. National Broadcasting Company, "The History of Advertising," November 12, 1933, pp. 1, 22. Script located in E. P. H. James Papers, SHSW, Box 4, Folder 7.

58. Joy Elmer Morgan, "The New American Plan for Radio," in *Debate*, pp. 81–82.

59. William Leiss, Stephen Kline, and Sut Jhally, *Social Communication in Advertising* (New York: Metheun, 1986), p. 78; Asa Briggs, *The Birth of Broadcasting* (London: Oxford University Press, 1961), pp. 172–75, 302–4; R. H. Coase, *British Broadcasting: A Study in Monopoly* (London: Longmans, Green and Company, 1950), pp. 103–16, 192–93; P. P. Eckersley, *The Power Behind the Microphone* (London: Jonathan Cape, 1941), p. 144.

Regarding Canada, see Frank W. Peers, *The Politics of Canadian Broadcasting 1920–1951* (Toronto: University of Totonto Press, 1969), p. 77.

60. Memorandum of Conference with Mr. Armstrong Perry, July 23, 1930, PFI Mss, Container 56, Folder 1070; Jos. F. Wright to Tracy F. Tyler, February 3, 1934, Illinois Mss, Box 3, NCER.

61. Editors of Broadcasting Magazine, *The First 50 Years of Broadcasting* (Washington D.C.: Broadcasting Publications, Inc., 1982), p. 2; "Report of the Radio Committee," *American Newspaper Publishers Association Bulletin*, No. 5856, May 6, 1931, p. 179; "Results of Radio Questionnaire," *American Newspaper Publishers Association Bulletin*, No. 5848, April 9, 1931, p. 113; Buel W. Patch, "Radio Competition With Newspapers," *Editorial Research Reports* 1 (May 21, 1931):331–47.

62. Robert S. Mann, "After All, Why Radio Advertising?" *Editor & Publisher*, June 6, 1931, p. 12; Cited in *Education by Radio*, June 4, 1931, pp. 63–64; "Want Government Ownership," *Broadcasters' New Bulletin*, November 28, 1931.

63. The Ventura Free Press Radio Project, June 1932, PFI Mss, Container 59, Folder 1145; The Ventura Free Press Radio Campaign, Its Results and Suggested Final Program, July 1933, PFI Mss, Container 59, Folder 1147.

64. "A.N.P.A. Fails to Renew Radio Attack, California Body Urges European System," *Broadcasting*, December 1, 1931, p. 8; H. O. Davis to Ella Phillips Crandall, October 30, 1931, PFI Mss, Container 59, Folder 1143; Illinois Press

Association Indorses [sic] Fess Bill, February 27, 1932, PFI Mss, Container 39, Folder 744.

65. Elzey Roberts to A. R. Graustein, November 26, 1932, PFI Mss, Container 60, Folder 1174; Elzey Roberts to S. Howard Evans, December 12, 1932, PFI Mss, Container 60, Folder 1174; "Asserts Radio 'Ads' Disgust Listeners," *The New York Times,* January 14, 1931; "And Now for the Facts," *Broadcasters' News Bulletin,* April 4, 1931.

66. "Broadcasting and Newspapers," *Broadcasters' News Bulletin,* April 25, 1931; *ANPA Bulletin,* No. 5856, May 6, 1931, p. 209; "Broadcasting Under Attack," *Broadcasters' News Bulletin,* April 11, 1931; M. H. Aylesworth to Karl Bickel, March 26, 1932, NBC Mss, Box 114, Folder 69, United Press Association, 1932; S. Howard Evans to Walter V. Woehlke, April 27, 1932, PFI Mss, Container 60, Folder 1166.

67. "Facts Prove Editor & Publisher Wrong in Conclusions on Radio Advertising," *Broadcasting,* June 14, 1934; Merlin Hall Aylesworth, "National Broadcasting." In *Radio and Its Future,* Edited by Martin Codel (New York: Harper & Brothers, 1930), p. 37; Stephen Lacy, "The Effect of Growth of Radio on Newspaper Competition, 1929–1948," *Journalism Quarterly* 64 (Winter 1987):775–81.

68. "Bellows Answers Critics," *Broadcasters' News Bulletin,* February 28, 1931; Virgil Evans, "Let's Make It Fifty-Fifty," *Broadcasting,* February 1, 1932, p. 24.

69. Harry K. Schauffler, "Why Radio Broadcasting is Not a Public Utility Service," *Public Utilities Fortnightly* 7 (January 8, 1933):44; "Ruin of Radio Broadcasting," *Nation's Business,* March 1932, pp. 13–14; "Radio Threat Concerns Press, Says Don Gilman," *Broadcasting,* February 15, 1932, p. 8.

70. Caleb Johnson, "Newspapers Share Radio Revenues," *Broadcasting,* May 15, 1932, p. 17; *FRC 1932,* pp. 158–60.

71. "Radio and the Press," *Broadcasting,* November 15, 1931, p. 18; "Welcome Press Inquiry," *Broadcasting,* December 1, 1932, p. 18; "Sees Radio as Supplement to Press," *American Newspaper Publishers Association Bulletin,* No. 6054, December 22, 1932, p. 516.

72. Report of Meeting, Newspaper-Owned Radio Stations, October 19, 1932, William S. Hedges to Frank Knox, October 20, 1932, William S. Hedges Papers, SHSW, Box 1, Correspondence 1926–35.

73. Much of this correspondence is in NBC Mss, Box 5, Folder 65, Ventura Free Press and Box 15, Folder 5, Ventura Free Press. See also "State Radio Committees Appointed," *American Newspaper Publishers Association Bulletin,* No. 6045, November 18, 1932, pp. 467–69.

74. Memorandum on Radio Situation, January 1933, PFI Mss, Container 49, Folder 945; "Elzy Roberts Quits Press Radio Post," *Broadcasting,* May 15, 1932, p. 17; "Radio vs. Newspapers," *Business Week,* December 21, 1932, p. 12; S. Howard Evans to Harris K. Randall, April 11, 1932, PFI Mss, Container 68, Folder 1338.

75. "Radio and Circulation," *American Newspaper Publishers Association Bulletin,* No. 6033, October 28, 1932, p. 427; Alfred McClung Lee, *The Daily Newspaper in America* (New York: The Macmillan Company, 1937), p. 562; T. R. Carskadon, "The Press–Radio War," *The New Republic,* March 11, 1936, p. 133.

76. E. H. Harris, *Radio, The Newspapers and the Public* (Nashville: Southern School of Printing, 1933), pp. 10–11; "Editors Urge Rigid Radio Control," *NAB Reports,* June 10, 1933, p. 63.

77. S. Howard Evans to Walter V. Woehlke, May 3, 1933, PFI Mss, Container 60, Folder 1169; "A.P. and A.N.P.A. Declare War on Radio," *Broadcasting,* May 1, 1933, p. 5; "Five Point Program Urged on Radio," *Editor & Publisher,* April 29, 1933, pp. 14, 74; Barnet Charles Shapiro, "The Press, The Radio and the Law," *Air Law Review* 4 (April 1935):133; Llewellyn White, *The American Radio* (Chicago: University of Chicago Press, 1947), p. 46.

78. William S. Paley, *As It Happened: A Memoir* (Garden City, NY: Doubleday & Company, 1979), pp. 125–28; Kent Cooper to M. H. Aylesworth, September 20, 1933, NBC Mss, Box 15, Folder 75.

79. "Report of Radio Committee," *American Newspaper Publishers Association Bulletin,* No. 6266, May 3, 1934, p. 283; Martin Codel, "News Plan to End Press-Radio War," *Broadcasting,* January 1, 1934, p. 10; S. Howard Evans to James Rorty, August 15, 1938, PFI Mss, Container 44, Folder 859.

80. H. V. Kaltenborn, *Radio Bows to the Press* (New York, 1933), p. 1; O. H. Caldwell to Roy Howard, December 22, 1933, NBC Mss, Box 21, Folder 53; Circular letter by H. O. Davis, December 26, 1933, PFI Mss Container 59, Folder 1147; S. Howard Evans to Walter V. Woehlke, December 13, 1933, December 18, 1933, PFI Mss, Container 60, Folder 1170.

81. Carskadon, *The New Republic,* p. 133; H. V. Kaltenborn, "Radio's Place in Distributing News." In *IER 1934,* p. 207; "Propose Press–Radio Agreement," *NAB Reports,* December 23, 1933, p. 261; "Peace With the Press," *Broadcasting,* January 1, 1934, p. 22.

82. S. Howard Evans to Tracy F. Tyler, April 20, 1934, PFI Mss, Container 47, Folder 905; E. H. Harris, "Shall the Government Own, Operate, and Control Radio Broadcasting in the United States?" In *NACRE 1934,* p. 96; M. H. Aylesworth to David Sarnoff, October 10, 1934, NBC Mss, Box 32, Folder 6, David Sarnoff 1934.

83. H. O. Davis to Lea, August 8, 1931, NBC Mss Box 5, Folder 65, Ventura Free Press; H. O. Davis to Joy Elmer Morgan, November 3, 1931, PFI Mss, Container 47, Folder 901.

84. Reprinted in "Fears Opposition to Radio Advertising," *American Newspaper Publishers Association Bulletin,* No. 6028, October 21, 1932, p. 413.

85. "Codel to Edit New Magazine," September 19, 1931, NANA, Vol. 61; see NBC Mss, Box 30, Folder 38. The entire collection of the NANA pieces from 1927 to 1934 is in six volumes of scrapbooks in the Martin Codel Papers, SHSW. They have been employed in the writing of this book.

86. Karl A. Bickel to Roy W. Howard, August 18, 1932, Roy W. Howard Papers, Library of Congress, Washington, D.C., Box 71.

87. See Kent Cooper, *Kent Cooper and the Associated Press: An Autobiography* (New York: Random House, 1959), p. 288; Karl A. Bickel, *New Empires: The Newspaper and the Radio* (Philadelphia: J. B. Lippincott Company, 1930); Aylesworth correspondence with Bickel in NBC Mss, Box 14, Folder 69; Roy W. Howard to Karl Bickel, August 15, 1932, Roy W. Howard Papers, Indiana University, Bloomington, Ind.

88. Research conducted by Cate Steele, Andrew Feldman and Robert W. Mc-Chesney of University of Wisconsin–Madison in 1991. The newspapers studied include: Portland *Oregonian,* Philadelphia *Public Ledger,* Sacramento *Bee,* Memphis *Commercial Appeal,* Roanoke *Times,* Wichita *Daily Eagle,* Buffalo *Evening News,* Detroit *News,* Galveston *Daily News,* and Des Moines *Register.*

89. "Can America Get the Truth About Radio?" *Education by Radio,* March 15, 1934, p. 9.

90. "A New York Newspaper Derides Government Control of the Air," *Radio Digest,* February 1932, p. 47; Frank M. Russell to R. C. Patterson, Jr., February 10, 1934, NBC Mss, Box 90, Folder 52, Frank Russell.

91. "Air Enemies Unite Forces," *Variety,* May 8, 1934, p. 37; Frank E. Gannett to Robert F. Wagner, May 1, 1934, Legislative Files, Box 223, Robert F. Wagner Papers, Georgetown University, Washington D.C.

92. "Control Air We Breathe," *Federation News,* January 5, 1929, p. 4; *Federation News,* September 7, 1929, p. 1.

93. "Wanted—An Honest Radio Writer," *Education by Radio,* May 16, 1935, p. 23; Wayne L. Randall to Frank E. Mason, July 3, 1934, NBC Mss, Box 25, Folder 58; Frank Mason to Merlin H. Aylesworth, January 9, 1934, NBC Mss, Box 30, Folder 38. For a candid discussion of what one network executive wanted from his press department, see James E. Pollard, "Newspaper Publicity for Radio Programs." In *IER 1934,* pp. 222–23.

94. "Radio Censorship in America and England," *Education by Radio,* February 15, 1934, p. 5; Jos. Wright to Tracy F. Tyler, February 3, 1934, Illinois Mss, Box 3, NCER.

95. Pollard, *IER 1934,* p. 218; "All-American Team, Radio Editors Popularity Poll Reveals Several Repeaters," *Broadcasting,* March 1, 1933, p. 17; *Education by Radio,* May 16, 1935, p. 23.

96. Orrin E. Dunlap, Jr., *Advertising by Radio* (New York: The Ronald Press, 1929); The two column inch notice on the NCER was "Radio in Education Subject for Conference," *The New York Times,* April 29, 1934, section IX, p. 9. Interestingly, this was on the same page as a lengthy feature story on the NBC Advisory Council, "Council Reviews Effect of Radio on American Life."

97. Armstrong Perry to Ella Phillips Crandall, May 9, 1933, PFI Mss, Container 56, Folder 1077; John F. Royal to Frank E. Mason, July 6, 1934, NBC Mss, Box 25, Folder 58.

98. A. R. Williamson to Wayne L. Randall, August 8, 1934, NBC Mss, Box 30, Folder 31; "Editors Favor American Plan," *Broadcasters' News Bulletin,* June 13, 1931.

Most adamant in the defense of the status quo were the radio fan magazines that began to proliferate as radio became a mass medium. Here the dependence upon the networks for editorial and, at times, financial support was explicit. See NBC Mss, Box 31, Folders 30, 37; NBC Mss, Box 40, Folders 56, 60, 61. For a more accessible discussion, see McChesney, *Historical Journal of Film, Radio and Television,* pp. 51–52.

99. Testimony of Joy Elmer Morgan, *FCC 1934,* pp. 22–23.

100. See Roger Biles, *A New Deal for the American People* (DeKalb, Ill.: Northern

Illinois University Press, 1991); *Education by Radio,* December 8, 1932, p. 105; A. G. Crane to Tracy F. Tyler, March 19, 1934, PFI Mss, Container 41, Folder 785.

101. S. Howard Evans to Mrs. Chester C. Bolton, February 15, 1933, PFI Mss, Container 49, Folder 945; S. Howard Evans to Walter Woehlke, June 19, 1933, PFI Mss, Container 60, Folder 1169; S. Howard Evans to Walter V. Woehlke, February 18, 1933, PFI Mss, Container 60, Folder 1168.

102. Tracy F. Tyler to Eugene J. Coltrane, April 8, 1933, PFI Mss, Container 40, Folder 773; Walter V. Woehlke to J. Noel Macy, August 17, 1931, PFI Mss, Container 59, Foler 1142.

103. Martin Codel, "Dill and Davis Seen Powers in Radio Rule Under Roosevelt," *Broadcasting,* November 15, 1932, p. 8; Eugene J. Coltrane, "A Brief Statement in Support of Representative Fulmer's Resolution for a Study of Radio Broadcasting," March 1933, PFI Mss, Container 39, Folder 750.

104. Report of an Interview with Senator Dill, January 11, 1933, PFI Mss, Container 40, Folder 774; Eugene J. Coltrane to S. Howard Evans, February 28, 1933, PFI Mss, Container 42, Folder 813; S. Howard Evans to Walter V. Woehlke, March 25, 1933, PFI Mss, Container 60, Folder 1168.

105. Erik Barnouw, *A Tower in Babel* (New York: Oxford University Press, 1966), p. 270; Herman S. Hettinger, "The Future of Radio as an Advertising Medium," *The Journal of Business of the University of Chicago,* 7 (October 1934): p. 284; "Report of the Standing Committee on Communications." In *ABA 1932,* p. 452; Report of the Service Bureau, January 1932, p. 6, PFI Mss, Container 68, Folder 1344.

106. Armstrong Perry to Ella Phillips Crandall, December 20, 1932, PFI Mss, Container 56, Folder 1076; Armstrong Perry to Joy Elmer Morgan, April 15, 1933, PFI Mss, Container 56, Folder 1077.

107. Sol Taishoff, " 'War Plans' Laid to Protect Broadcasting," *Broadcasting,* March 1, 1933, p. 5; See *Senate 1934,* pp. 53–55; Henry Bellows stressed this point in a letter to White House aide Stephen Early in February 1934. Bellows to Early, February 28, 1934, FDR Mss, OF 859a, 1933–45.

108. Alan Stone, *Public Service Liberalism: Telecommunications and Transitions in Public Policy* (Princeton: Princeton University Press, 1991), pp. 282–83; George Arthur Codding, Jr., *The International Telecommunication Union* (Leiden, Netherlands: E. J. Brill, 1952), p. 1; "Bar Group Sees New Air Control," undated, August 1933, NANA, Vol. 61.

109. See Philip T. Rosen, *The Modern Stentors: Radio Broadcasters and the Federal Government 1920–1934* (Westport, CT.: Greenwood Press, 1980), pp. 173–74.

110. Eddie Dowling, "Radio Needs a Revolution," *Forum* 91 (February 1934):70.

111. Biles, p. 29; Armstrong Perry to S. H. Evans, April 15, 1933, PFI Mss, Container 56, Folder 1077; Arthur E. Morgan, "Radio as a Cultural Agency in Sparsely Settled Regions and Remote Areas." In *NCER 1934,* p. 81.

112. Douglas, pp. 268–84; See *Roosevelt and Daniels, A Friendship in Politics,* Edited by Carroll Kilpatrick (Chapel Hill: University of North Carolina Press, 1950);

Josephus Daniels, *Tar Heel Editor* (Chapel Hill: University of North Carolina Press, 1939); Josephus Daniels, *Editor in Politics* (Chapel Hill: University of North Carolina Press, 1941).

113. Perry to Morgan, August 16, 1933, PFI Mss, Container 55, Folder 1062.

114. Josephus Daniels to Franklin D. Roosevelt, July 12, 1933, Daniels Mss, (A.C. 18416), Container 95, Reel 59; Josephus Daniels to Franklin D. Roosevelt, January 15, 1935, FDR Mss, PPF 86, 1935.

115. Roosevelt only mentioned radio policy once during this period in his many presidential press conferences, and then it was only in the vaguest of senses. See *Complete Presidential Press Conferences of Franklin D. Roosevelt Volumes 1–2* (New York: DeCapo Press, 1972), pp. 541–43; S. Howard Evans to H. O. Davis, October 3, 1933, PFI Mss, Container 59, Folder 1147.

116. "Keep Radio Free, Roosevelt Urges," *The New York Times,* June 14, 1934, p. 21; "Gleanings from Varied Sources," *Education by Radio,* July 19, 1934, p. 32; "Address of President Roosevelt," November 8, 1933, Merlin Aylesworth to Franklin D. Roosevelt, November 11, 1933, NBC Mss, Box 21, Folder 35, FDR 1933.

117. Betty Houchin Winfield, *FDR and the News Media* (Urbana and Chicago: University of Illinois Press, 1990), pp. 79–80; George Wolfskill, *Happy Days Are Here Again! A Short Interpretive History of the New Deal* (Hinsdale, IL: The Dryden Press, 1974), pp. 29–30; Daniels quote cited in Nathan Miller, *FDR: An Intimate History* (Lanham, MD: Madison Books, 1983), p. 105.

118. Several memoranda to Howe from FRC secretary Herbert L. Pettey are found in Howe Mss, Boxes 89, 90, 91; S. Howard Evans to Walter V. Woehlke, February 11, 1933, PFI Mss, Container 60, Folder 1168. See also Alfred B. Rollins, *Roosevelt and Howe* (New York: Alfred A. Knopf, 1962).

119. Martin Codel, "President Aided by Radio Chains," undated, March 1933, NANA, Vol. 61.

120. "F.D.R.'s Radio Record," *Broadcasting,* March 15, 1934, p. 8; Merlin H. Aylesworth to Ed Kobak, September 25, 1934, NBC Mss, Box 31, Folder 58. See also Maureen H. Beasley, *Eleanor Roosevelt and the Media: A Public Quest for Self-Fulfillment* (Urbana: University of Illinois Press, 1987).

121. Winfield, p. 80; Several scripts of the Howe program, which were released to the press (often after being edited by the president), are found in Howe Mss, Boxes 89, 90, 91; Evans to Bolton, February 15, 1933, PFI Mss, Container 49, Folder 945; Walter V. Woehlke to S. Howard Evans, June 1933, PFI Mss, Container 60, Folder 1169.

122. "Broadcasting for Pay," undated, June 1933, NANA, Vol. 61; Tracy Tyler to Eugene J. Coltrane, December 4, 1933, PFI Mss, Container 40, Folder 773.

123. Rosen, p. 174; Winfield, pp. 127–28; Evans to Davis, October 3, 1933, PFI Mss, Container 59, Folder 1147.

124. See Thomas Ferguson, "Industrial Structure and Party Competition in the New Deal: A Reply to Webber," *Sociological Perspectives* 34 (1991): 493–526; Thomas Ferguson, "Industrial Conflict and the Coming of the New Deal: The Triumph of Multinational Liberalism in America." In *The Rise and Fall of the New Deal Order, 1930–1980,* edited by Steve Fraser and Gary Gerstle (Princeton: Prince-

ton University Press, 1989); Michael Patrick Allen, "Capitalist Response to State Intervention: Theories of the State and Political Finance in the New Deal," *American Sociological Review* 56 (October 1991): 679–89.

125. "Starbuck's Job Sought by Eddie Dowling, et al., As End of Term Nears," *Broadcasting,* January 1, 1934, p. 16; "President Ignores Dowling Proposals," *Broadcasting,* March 1, 1934, p. 15; "Unsought Advice," *Broadcasting,* March 1, 1934, p. 24.

126. A. A. Berle, Jr., to Armstrong Perry, December 13, 1933, PFI Mss, Container 56, Folder 1078; Perry to Morgan, August 16, 1933, PFI Mss, Container 55, Folder 1062.

127. "Sykes Reappointed to Commission," *NAB Reports,* March 18, 1933, p. 5; see, also, Edwin E. Meek, "Eugene Octave Sykes, Member and Chairman of Federal Communications Commission and Federal Radio Commission, 1927–1939," *Journal of Mississippi History* 36 (1974):377–86; "Sykes is Renamed, J. H. Hanley Slated for Commissioner," *Broadcasting,* March 15, 1933, p. 6; *Broadcasting,* March 15, 1933, p. 16.

128. Joseph F. Wright to B. B. Brackett, February 14, 1933, Joseph F. Wright to J. C. Jensen, March 8, 1933, NAEB Mss, Box No. 1a, General Correspondence 1933; "Mullen, Nebraska Attorney Considers Commission Post," *Broadcasting,* March 1, 1933, p. 6; *Broadcasting,* March 15, 1933, p. 6; "Mullen Denies Profiting By Hanley Appointment," *Broadcasting,* February 1, 1934, p. 12.

129. Tracy F. Tyler to Ella Phillips Crandall, March 29, 1933, PFI Mss, Container 42, Folder 813; "Notes of Discussion at a Conference on Educational Broadcasting Held on April 14, 1934 at the Century Club, New York City, Called by Dr. F. P. Keppel of the Carnegie Corporation of New York," p. 13, In RMH I Mss, Volume 99.

130. "Report of the Committee on Reorganization of the Department of Commerce," May 2, 1933, DoC Mss, General Correspondence, File 80553; Daniel C. Roper to Lewis W. Douglas, May 2, 1933, DoC Mss, Office of the Secretary, General Correspondence, File 84053, Radio Division; "Government Reorganization," *NAB Reports,* May 1933, p. 50; *NAB Reports,* June 17, 1933, p. 68.

131. E. H. Harris to S. Howard Evans, June 2, 1933, PFI Mss, Container 61, Folder 1176; Josephus Daniels to Franklin D. Roosevelt, July 14, 1933, Daniels Mss, (A.C. 18416), Container 95, Reel 59.

132. Daniel C. Roper to Franklin D. Roosevelt, August 15, 1933, DoC Mss, NARG 40, General Correspondence, File 80553/13-D.

133. "Report of a Committee on Communications Appointed by the Secretary of Commerce," September 8, 1933, National Bureau of Standards Manuscripts, National Archives, Washington, D.C., National Archives Record Group 167, J. Howard Dellinger File, 1933.

134. Memo from President to Secretary Roper, September 12, 1933, FDR Mss, Box 1, X Refs 1933; See Letter of Transmittal to *Roper Report;* C. C. Dill to Daniel C. Roper, January 9, 1934, FDR Mss, OF 859a, 1933–1945; Bethuel M. Webster, Jr., "Notes on the Policy of the Administration with Reference to the Control of Communications," *Air Law Review* 5 (April 1934):109–10.

135. "Control Board Planned for All Communications; With Mergers Permitted," *The New York Times,* December 14, 1933, p. 2; S. Howard Evans to Walter V. Woehlke, November 24, 1933, PFI Mss, Container 60, Folder 1170.

136. Martin Codel, "Change in Control of Radio Looming," October 23, 1933, NANA, Vol. 61; "Daily Washington Merry-Go-Round," November 30, 1933, in DoC Mss, General Correspondence, File 80553/13-G.

137. "NAB Convention Launches New Era," *Broadcasting,* October 15, 1933, p. 40; John H. MacCracken to Marvin H. McIntyre, December 14, 1933, M. H. McIntyre to John Henry MacCracken, December 18, 1933, PFI Mss, Container 39, Folder 751; Tracy Tyler to Roger Baldwin, October 26, 1933, Assorted letters between Tyler and Baldwin, November–December 1933, ACLU Mss, 1933, Volume 599; Roger Baldwin to Bethuel M. Webster, Jr., January 13, 1934, ACLU Mss, 1934, Volume 699.

138. Roger Baldwin to Bethuel M. Webster, Jr., November 20, 1933; Bethuel M. Webster, Jr., "Memorandum for Mr. Baldwin Re: National Committee on Education by Radio," November 18, 1933; Roger Baldwin to Bethuel M. Webster, Jr., November 20, 1933; all found in ACLU Mss, 1933, Volume 599.

139. M. H. Aylesworth to Louis McHenry Howe, December 16, 1933, FDR Mss, OF 859, 1933–1945.

Chapter 8

1. S. Howard Evans to H. O. Davis, February 19, 1934, PFI Mss, Container 59, Folder 1148; Minutes of the Seventeenth Meeting of the National Committee on Education by Radio, Washington, D. C., January 15, 1934, PFI Mss, Container 39, Folder 751; Tracy F. Tyler to Roger N. Baldwin, January 12, 1934, PFI Mss, Container 45, Folder 866.

2. Charles McKinley Saltzman to Frederick Keppel, February 20, 1934, Frederick Keppel Papers, Columbia University, New York, NY, Box 61.

3. "Daily Washington Merry-Go-Round," November 30, 1933, DoC Mss, General Correspondence, File 80553/13-G.

4. Tracy F. Tyler to Daniel C. Roper, December 5, 1933, Daniel C. Roper to Tracy F. Tyler, December 8, 1933, Charles McK. Saltzman to Tracy F. Tyler, December 11, 1933, DoC Mss, NARG 40, General Correspondence, File 80553/13-G; C. C. Dill to Tracy F. Tyler, December 11, 1933, PFI Mss, Container 43, Folder 824.

5. Herbert L. Pettey to H. P. Fulmer, December 8, 1933, PFI Mss, Container 40, Folder 773; Daniel C. Roper to Tracy F. Tyler, December 13, 1933, PFI Mss, Container 43, Folder 827.

6. "Wash. Omits Radio From Fed. Control of Communication," *Variety,* January 30, 1934, p. 37; Joy Elmer Morgan and Tracy F. Tyler to Daniel C. Roper, December 19, 1933, DoC Mss, Office of the Secretary, General Correspondence, File 80553/13-G, Communications Committee.

7. James Rorty, "Order on the Air," *The Nation,* May 9, 1934, p. 529; Bethuel

M. Webster, Jr., "Notes on the Policy of the Administration with Reference to the Control of Communications," *Air Law Review* 5 (April 1934):108, 117.

8. Comments on Report of Majority Members of Committee and Discussion of Position of Minority Member, December 7, 1933, FDR Mss, OF 859a, 1933–1945; Several memoranda and letters between Hooper and executives, including Western Union's R. B. White and David Sarnoff, are in Hooper Mss, Box 15.

9. Hooper comment and letter cited in Josephus Daniels to S. C. Hooper, December 4, 1933, Hooper Mss, Box 15.

10. Comments on Report of Majority Members of Committee and Discussion of Position of Minority Member, FDR Mss, OF 859a, 1933–45.

11. Josephus Daniels to Daniel C. Roper, December 4, 1933, DoC Mss, General Correspondence 80553/13-G, Communications Committee; Daniel C. Roper to Josephus Daniels, December 16, 1933, DoC Mss, General Correspondence 80553/13-G, Communications Committee.

12. "Communications Bills Loom," *NAB Reports,* January 13, 1934, p. 271; "Dill Writing Communications Bill," *NAB Reports,* January 20, 1934, p. 279; Mrs. Murphy to Frank M. Russell, January 19, 1934, NBC Mss, Box 90, Folder 52, Frank Russell.

By 1933 radio legislation had been shifted from the House Committee on Merchant Marine, Radio and Fisheries to the House Committee on Interstate and Foreign Commerce. These shifts often are the result of industry pressure and it is unclear if the broadcasters had any connection to the shift. The former committee had been chaired by Ewin Davis (D-Tenn.), who the industry had regarded as a foe, but Davis was defeated in a primary election in 1932. Otherwise, both House committees were solid supporters of the industry, far more than Dill's SCIC. For an example of this, see *Congressional Record* 78 (June 2, 1934):10984–90.

13. Armstrong Perry to S. H. Evans, January 2, 1934, PFI Mss, Container 56, Folder 1076; *NAB Reports,* January 13, 1934, p. 271.

14. Tracy F. Tyler to Jos. F. Wright, February 6, 1934, Illinois Mss, Subject File (RS 39/1/1), 1919–1984, Box 3, NCER; S. Howard Evans to Armstrong Perry, March 2, 1934, PFI Mss, Container 56, Folder 1079; Sol Taishoff, "Roosevelt Demands Communications Bill," *Broadcasting,* February 15, 1934; Robert S. Mack, "Survey of Broadcasting Requested by President," February 5, 1934, NANA, Vol. 63.

15. Saltzman to Keppel, February 20, 1934, Keppel Mss, Box 61.

16. Daniel C. Roper to Tracy F. Tyler, February 15, 1934, Tracy F. Tyler to Daniel C. Roper, February 12, 1934, Kerlin to Joy Elmer Morgan, February 26, 1934, DoC Mss, NARG 40, General Correspondence, File 80553/13-D; Armstrong Perry to B. B. Brackett, January 6, 1933, Joseph F. Wright to B. B. Brackett, January 12, 1933, NAEB Mss, Box No. 1a, General Correspondence 1933; Cline M. Koon, "The Radio in Supervision," *Education by Radio,* July 21, 1932, p. 85; Cline M. Koon, *The Growth of British Broadcasting* (Columbus: Ohio State University, 1930).

17. Cline M. Koon to Daniel C. Roper, February 21, 1934, DoC Mss, NARG 40, General Correspondence, File 80553/13-D; Eugene J. Coltrane to Joseph F.

Wright, February 21, 1934, Illinois Mss, Subject File (RS 39/1/1), 1919–1984, Box 3, NCER.

18. Eugene J. Coltrane to Tracy F. Tyler, February 9, 1934, PFI Mss, Container 40, Folder 773; Tracy F. Tyler to Ella Phillips Crandall, February 20, 1934, PFI Mss, Container 47, Folder 905.

19. "President Orders Broadcast Survey," *NAB Reports*, February 3, 1934, p. 287; "If Facts Prevail," *Broadcasting*, February 15, 1934, p. 20; "Broadcasting Survey Postponed," *NAB Reports*, February 24, 1934, p. 309.

20. Saltzman to Keppel, February 20, 1934, Keppel Mss, Box 61; Robert S. Mack, "New Radio Set-up is Being Pushed," February 12, 1934, NANA, Vol. 63.

21. "Dill Will Push Communications Bill," *NAB Reports*, February 10, 1934, p. 299; "Broadcast 'Study' Shelved as Futile; Roper-Proposed Investigation Discouraged by Congress," *Broadcasting*, March 1, 1934, p. 15; Taishoff, "Roosevelt Demands," *Broadcasting*, February 15, 1934, p. 5.

22. Daniel C. Roper to Hohenstein, March 6, 1934, DoC Mss, NARG 40, General Correspondence, File 80553/13-G; Armstrong Perry to S. Howard Evans, March 3, 1934, PFI Mss, Container 56, Folder 1079.

23. "U.S. to Regulate Air Adv.," *Variety*, February 13, 1934, p. 1; Assorted memos between Dill, Rayburn, Roosevelt, and McIntyre, January–February 1934, FDR Mss, OF 859, 1933–1945; Roper comment in *House 1934a*, April 10, 1934, p. 2; "Communications Bill Speeded," *NAB Reports*, March 10, 1934, p. 323; Dill comment in "Roosevelt Approves Communications Board to Rule Radio, Telephone, Telegraph, Cable," *The New York Times*, February 10, 1934, p. 12.

24. Taishoff, "Roosevelt Demands," *Broadcasting*, February 15, 1934, p. 5; *The New York Times*, February 10, 1934, p. 12; *Senate 1934*, March 13, 1934, p. 106.

25. "Asks Body to Rule Wires and Radio," *The New York Times*, February 27, 1934, p. 1; "Judge Sykes Approves Unification," *NAB Reports*, March 10, 1934, p. 323; Hooper's position in *House 1934a*, April 10, 1934, p. 20.

26. Josephus Daniels to C. C. Dill, Josephus Daniels to S. C. Hooper, February 24, 1934, Josephus Daniels to S. C. Hooper, April 4, 1934, Hooper Mss, Box 16; Philip T. Rosen, *The Modern Stentors: Radio Broadcasting and the Federal Government, 1920–1934* (Westport, CT: Greenwood Press, 1980), p. 177.

27. "Broadcasters to War on Dill Communications Bill," *Heinl Radio Business Letter*, March 2, 1934, p. 2; *Senate 1934*, March 10, 1934, pp. 53–54, March 13, 1934, p. 106.

28. *Congressional Record*, 78 (May 15, 1934):8822.

29. "Radio Submerged at Capital Hearings," *Broadcasting*, April 15, 1934, p. 11; Sol Taishoff, "FCC Replaces Radio Commission July 1," *Broadcasting*, June 15, 1934, p. 6; "Communications Commission Bill Believed Blocked for Year," *Broadcasting*, May 1, 1934, p. 17; Alan Stone, *Public Service Liberalism: Telecommunications and Transitions in Public Policy* (Princeton, NJ: Princeton University Press, 1991), p. 278; Glen O. Robinson, "The Federal Communications Act: An Essay on Origins and Regulatory Purpose." In *A Legislative History of the Communications Act of 1934*, edited by Max D. Paglin (New York: Oxford University Press, 1989), p. 4.

30. Statement of Walter S. Gifford, president of the American Telephone and Telegraph Company Before Committee on Interstate Commerce of the Senate in Opposition to Communications Bill S. 2910, p. 5, AT&T Mss, Communication Act of 1934 series, Box 9, Volume 3.

31. Ed Craney, "Interview with C. C. Dill," July 21, 1964, pp. 18–22, Erik Barnouw Papers, Columbia University, New York, NY, Box 32, volume of miscellaneous background documents; Clarence C. Dill, "Telephone Monopoly Investigation," undated, AT&T Mss, Communication Act of 1934 series, Box 9, Vol. 3; Martin Codel, "Passage of Radio Bill is Held Up," March 19, 1934, NANA, Vol. 63; "New Commission May Undertake A. T. & T. Investigation," *Heinl Radio Business Letter,* March 27, 1934, p. 7; *House 1934a,* May 10, 1934, pp. 167–68.

32. R. C. Patterson, Jr. Memo on the Dill–Rayburn Communication Bills, undated, NBC Mss, Box 25c, Folder 51; *Heinl Radio Business Letter,* March 2, 1934, p. 2; Webster, *Air Law Review,* p. 108; "The Dill Bill," *NAB Reports,* April 7, 1934, p. 351.

33. "Communications Bill Pushed; Slim Chance of Passage Seen," *Broadcasting,* April 1, 1934, p. 14; Frank M. Russell to R. G. Patterson, Jr., April 4, 1934, NBC Mss, Box 90, Folder 53.

34. "Dill is Speeding Radio Measure," March 26, 1934, NANA, Vol. 63; "Dill Hopes to Report Communications Bill in Two Weeks," *Heinl Radio Business Letter,* March 23, 1934, p. 7.

35. *Senate 1934,* March 15, 1934, p. 186.

36. Henry A. Bellows, "Report of the Legislative Committee," *NAB Reports,* November 15, 1934, p. 618; "Wire-Radio Bill Up to President," *The New York Times,* April 14, 1934, p. 7; "Air Enemies Unite Forces," *Variety,* May 8, 1934, p. 45.

37. James McVann, *The Paulists, 1858–1970* (New York: Society of St. Paul the Apostle, 1983), p. 896; Petitions and letters found in Wagner Mss, Legislative Files, Box 223; United States SCIC Papers, National Archives, Washington, D.C., Sen 73A-J28, tray 155.

38. "Plea for Radio Station," *The New York Times,* March 26, 1934, p. 26.

39. See FCC Mss, National Archives Record Group 173, Box 38, File 15–3a; John B. Harney, *Education and Religion vs. Commercial Radio* (New York: Paulist Fathers, 1934); "WLWL Seeks New Law," *The New York Times,* April 11, 1934, p. 15.

40. The NCER, the *Ventura Free Press,* and the ACLU never had any luck getting Wagner to consider their legislation, although not for any lack of effort on their parts. As he finally telegramed the ACLU on March 21, 1934, after not responding to several letters, "I am too overwhelmed with duties at the present time to assume additional ones." See Robert F. Wagner to Roger N. Baldwin, March 21, 1934, Wagner Mss, Legislative Files, Box 223.

41. William P. Connery, Jr., et al, to Colleagues, April 12, 1934, Wagner Mss, Legislative Files, Box 223; *Congressional Record,* 78 (April 19, 1934):6898; "Another Radio Bill Introduced," *NAB Reports,* April 7, 1934, p. 351; *Congressional Record,* 78 (April 27, 1934):7509.

42. *Variety,* May 8, 1934, pp. 37, 45; "Wagner Amendment Up Next Week," *NAB Reports,* May 5, 1934, p. 375.

43. "Labor Aids Bill for Free Radio," *Federation News,* April 7, 1934, p. 6; "Labor Toils for Radio Freedom," *Federation News,* May 26, 1934, pp. 1, 3; Bellows, *NAB Reports,* November 15, 1934, p. 618.

44. Sol Taishoff, "Fate of FCC Measure Hangs in Balance," *Broadcasting,* June 1, 1934, p. 6; Tracy F. Tyler to Eugene J. Coltrane, November 23, 1933, PFI Mss, Container 40, Folder 773; Tracy F. Tyler to James H. Hanley, November 27, 1933, PFI Mss, Container 43, Folder 841.

45. Federal Radio Commission Dockets #2080, 2129, p. 9, FCC Mss, Docketed Case Files, Box 454; "Hearing on WLWL Plea is Continued," *Broadcasting,* September 15, 1933, p. 29; "WLWL Request Denied," *Broadcasting,* February 15, 1934, p. 32.

46. "One Year on the Federal Radio Commission by Commissioner James H. Hanley," April 14, 1934, p. 6, DoC Mss, NARG 40, Office of the Secretary, General Correspondence, File 84053, Radio Division; Armstrong Perry to Sir John W. Reith, April 29, 1934, PFI Mss, Container 58, Folder 1110.

47. "Hanley Criticism of Broadcasting Setup Denied by Administration, Colleagues," *Broadcasting,* May 1, 1934, p. 22; Sol Taishoff, "Powerful Lobby Threatens Radio Structure," *Broadcasting,* May 15, 1934, pp. 5, 6.

48. Tracy F. Tyler to John B. Harney, March 30, 1934, PFI Mss, Container 44, Folder 850.

49. John B. Harney to Tracy F. Tyler, April 3, 1934, PFI Mss, Container 44, Folder 850.

50. John B. Harney to Eugene J. Coltrane, April 24, 1934, PFI Mss, Container 44, Folder 850; John B. Harney to Joseph F. Wright, April 5, 1934, Illinois Mss, Subject File (RS 39/1/1), 1919–1984, Box 3, NCER.

51. Harney to Tyler, April 3, 1934, PFI Mss, Container 44, Folder 850; John B. Harney to Eugene J. Coltrane, April 4, 1934, PFI Mss, Container 40, Folder 744; John B. Harney to Armstrong Perry, April 4, 1934, PFI Mss, Container 59, Folder 1132.

52. Edward Bennett to H. Umberger, April 21, 1934, K. L. Hatch to H. W. Umberger, April 25, 1934, PFI Mss, Container 68, Folder 1340; Tracy F. Tyler to Arthur G. Crane, April 19, 1934, PFI Mss, Container 42, Folder 822.

53. Tracy F. Tyler to John B. Harney, April 25, 1934, PFI Mss, Container 44, Folder 850; Roger Baldwin to C. C. Dill, April 22, 1934, C. C. Dill to Roger Baldwin, April 25, 1934, Henry Eckstein to Clifford Read, May 17, 1934, ACLU Mss, 1934, Volume 699.

54. Henry A. Bellows, "Report of the Legislative Committee," *NAB Reports,* November 15, 1934, p. 618; *Broadcasting,* May 15, 1934, pp. 5, 6; *House 1934a,* pp. 116, 345; "Meeting Vital Issues," *Broadcasting,* June 1, 1934, p. 26.

55. Bellows, *NAB Reports,* November 15, 1934, p. 618; *Variety,* May 8, 1934, pp. 45, 37.

56. Francis T. Maloney to Eugene Sykes, April 25, 1934, Eugene Sykes to Francis T. Maloney, April 28, 1934, FCC Mss, NARG 173, Legislation, Acts-Radio, FCC General Correspondence, Box 38; Rosen, *Stentors,* p. 179; *Broadcasting,* May 15, 1934, p. 6.

57. McVann, *Paulists,* p. 897; Harney to Harry, May 2, 1934, Harney to MacDonald, May 3, 1934, Paulist Mss, WLWL file.

58. Harney to Gillespie, May 3, 1934, Gillespie to Harney, May 17, 1934, Paulist Mss, WLWL file.

59. *NCER 1934,* p. v; "Washington Conference Charts Radio's Future," *Education by Radio,* May 24, 1934, p. 22; "U.S. Radio System Scored and Lauded at Educators' Meet," *Broadcasting,* May 15, 1934, p. 16.

60. *NCER 1934,* pp. 91, 106, 93.

61. Tracy F. Tyler to Stephen Early, May 16, 1934, FDR Mss, OF 136, 1934; Dr. McCracken to H. M. McIntyre, May 25, 1934, FDR Mss, PPF 2447; Frank Ernest Hill, *Tune in for Education* (New York: National Committee on Education by Radio, 1942), p. 65.

62. Armstrong Perry, "NCER Radio Education Conference," December 1935, Armstrong Perry, "Federal Communications Commission Hearing," December 1935, PFI Mss, Container 52, Folder 986; Armstrong Perry to A. G. Crane, August 30, 1934, PFI Mss, Container 55, Folder 1053; Armstrong Perry to Ella Phillips Crandall, May 22, 1934, PFI Mss, Container 56, Folder 1079.

63. *NCER 1934,* p. 106; James Francis Cooke to Walter Koons, October 31, 1934, James Francis Cooke to Walter Koons, November 14, 1934, NBC Mss, Box 26, Folder 29, FCC Hearings 1934.

64. *NCER 1934,* p. 122.

65. Frank Russell to R. G. Patterson, May 5, 1934, NBC Mss, Box 90, Folder 53; "Senate to Pass Dill Bill," *NAB Reports,* May 12, 1934, p. 387.

66. Frank Russell to Merlin Aylesworth, May 11, 1934, Merlin Aylesworth to Frank Russell, May 15, 1934, NBC Mss, Box 90, Folder 53.

67. Bellows, *NAB Reports,* November 15, 1934, p. 617; *Congressional Record,* 78 (May 15, 1934): p. 8830.

68. *Ibid.,* pp. 8831, 8833.

69. *Ibid.,* pp. 8843, 8828.

70. Perry, "FCC Hearing," December 1935, PFI Mss, Container 52, Folder 986; Tracy F. Tyler to Clarence C. Dill, May 14, 1934, PFI Mss, Container 43, Folder 824.

71. Tracy F. Tyler to E. N. Nockels, May 28, 1934, PFI Mss, Container 47, Folder 912; Bellows *NAB Reports,* November 15, 1934, p. 618.

72. Rosen, *Stentors,* p. 178; *Congressional Record,* 78 (June 2, 1934): pp. 10315–23.

73. "House–Senate Writing Compromise Communications Bill This Week; Will Determine Govt's Air Policy," *Variety,* June 5, 1934, p. 34; *Congressional Record,* 78 (June 9, 1934):10987; Bellows, *NAB Reports,* November 15, 1934, p. 618.

74. "Hanley Suggests a New Deal," *The New York Times,* May 13, 1934, section IX, p. 7; "New Communications Bill is Aimed at Curbing Monopoly in Radio," *The New York Times,* May 20, 1934, section IX, p. 9; Orrin E. Dunlap, Jr., "New Deal in Radio Law to Regulate All Broadcasting," *The New York Times,* June 24, 1934, section XIII, p. 19.

75. John Brooks, *Telephone: The First Hundred Years* (New York: Harper & Row, 1975), p. 196; Harry M. Shooshan III, "The Bell Breakup: Putting It In

Perspective.'' In *Disconnecting Bell: The Impact of the AT&T Divestiture*, edited by Harry M. Shooshan III (New York: Pergamon Press, 1984), p. 12; Peter Temin, *The Fall of the Bell System: A Study in Prices and Politics* (Cambridge and New York: Cambridge University Press, 1987), pp. 12–14.

76. For Rayburn's view of the progressive nature of the Communications Act of 1934, see Sam Rayburn, *Speak, Mr. Speaker* (Bonham, TX: Sam Rayburn Foundation, 1978), p. 59.

77. For an extreme example, see Walter B. Emery, ''Broadcasting Rights and Responsibilities in Democratic Society,' *The Centennial Review* 8 (1964): 306–22. The characterization of the Communications Act of 1934 as representative of progressive New Deal legislation is more widespread among scholars who do not specialize in communications issues. For example, one historian clumps it with the other New Deal bills, terming them ''not at all to the liking of most businessmen.'' See Frank A. Freidel, *Franklin D. Roosevelt: A Rendezvous with Destiny* (Boston: Little, Brown and Company, 1990), p. 139.

78. ''Report of the Standing Committee on Communications.'' In *Report of the Fifty-Seventh Annual Meeting of the American Bar Association 1934* (Baltimore: The Lord Baltimore Press, 1934), p. 469; Bellows, *NAB Reports*, November 15, 1934, pp. 617, 618.

79. ''Co-operation of Commercial Stations and Educational Organizations.'' In *IER 1934*, p. 45.

80. Taishoff, *Broadcasting*, June 15, 1934, p. 5; Navy Department press release, June 9, 1934, S. C. Hooper to Paul Shoup, July 19, 1934, Hooper Mss, Box 16.

81. For this characterization of Hanley and a discussion of his campaign to be appointed to the new FCC, see Sol Taishoff, ''Fate of FCC Measure Hangs in Balance,'' *Broadcasting*, June 1, 1934, p. 6.

82. Sol Taishoff, ''Radio Status Quo as FCC Convenes,'' *Broadcasting*, August 1, 1934, p. 5; ''Three-Man Control,'' *Broadcasting*, August 1, 1934, p. 22.

83. ''FCC Hearings on Facility Demands to Require Two Weeks for Testimony,'' *Broadcasting*, October 1, 1934, p. 34; ''Opening Statement by Hampson Gary.'' In *FCC 1934*, Volume 1, p. 4.

84. Tracy F. Tyler to B. B. Brackett, August 16, 1934, NAEB Mss, Box 1a, General Correspondence 1935; Josef F. Wright to ACUBS members, August 3, 1934, NAEB Mss, Box 1a, General Correspondence 1935; ''Federal Communications Commission Reports to Congress,'' *Education by Radio*, January 31, 1935, p. 5.

85. *FCC 1934*, Volume 25, pp. 13622–23; Tracy F. Tyler to Clarence C. Dill, June 5, 1934, PFI Mss, Container 43, Folder 824; Perry, ''FCC Hearing,'' December 1935, PFI Mss, Container 52, Folder 986.

86. Willis E. Phillips to Harold Ingham, September 4, 1934, H. L. Ewbank to Harold G. Ingham, September 6, 1934, NAEB Mss, Box No. 1, Correspondence, 1925–1949; ''College and University Broadcasters Meet,'' *Education by Radio*, September 13, 1934, p. 37.

87. Henry Eckstein to Roger Baldwin, June 19, 1934, ACLU Mss, 1934, Volume 699; Bethuel M. Webster, Jr., to Henry Eckstein, July 16, 1934, ACLU Mss, 1934, Volume 699.

88. Bethuel M. Webster, Jr., to Henry J. Eckstein, July 16, 1934, ACLU Mss, Volume 699, 1934; Clifton Read to Hadley Cantril, October 25, 1934, ACLU Mss, 1934, Volume 699.

89. Clifton Read, "Memorandum for Members of Radio Committee," September 12, 1934, ACLU Mss, 1934, Volume 699; Levering Tyson to Clifton Read, September 14, 1934, ACLU Mss, 1934, Volume 699.

90. Henry Eckstein to Clifton Read, September 13, 1934, ACLU Mss, 1934, Volume 699; Clifton Read to Norman Thomas, September 19, 1934, Thomas Mss, Series II, Organizational Records, Reel 56; Morris Ernst to Clifton Read, September 14, 1934, ACLU Mss, 1934, Volume 699.

91. Clifton Read to Morris Ernst, September 19, 1934, Telegram from Roger Baldwin to Clifton Read, September 19, 1934, Day letter from Roger Baldwin to Clifton Read, September 19, 1934, ACLU Mss, 1934, Volume 699.

92. Roger Baldwin to Clifton Read, September 24, 1934, Roger Baldwin to Clifton Read, September 28, 1934, ACLU Mss, 1934, Volume 699.

93. Bruce Bliven to Tracy F. Tyler, October 18, 1934, PFI Mss, Container 46, Folder 886; "Commercial Control of the Air," *Christian Century,* September 26, 1934, pp. 1196–97.

94. "Government Interference Fear Groundless, Say Commissioners," *Broadcasting,* October 1, 1934, p. 18.

95. "Bellows to Assist in Hearings," *NAB Reports,* August 22, 1934, p. 509; Sol Taishoff, "Roosevelt Gives Broadcasters Confidence," *Broadcasting,* October 1, 1934, p. 10.

96. Frank M. Russell to R. C. Patterson, Jr., July 11, 1934, NBC Mss, Box 30, Folder 19, National Association of Broadcasters 1934; R. C. Patterson, Jr., to Frank M. Russell, August 17, 1934, NBC Mss, Box 26, Folder 34, FCC; Federal Radio Education Committee, 1934.

97. Frank M. Russell to R. C. Patterson, Jr., August 13, 1934, NBC Mss, Box 26, Folder 34, FCC; Federal Radio Education Committee, 1934. Hard had already established himself as one of the relatively few writers not in the pay of commercial broadcasters in favor of the status quo. See William Hard, "Europe's Air and Ours," *Atlantic Monthly* 150 (1932): 499–509.

98. "Radio Groups Open Wave Length Fight," *The New York Times,* September 10, 1934, p. 19.

99. Sol Taishoff, "Stations Start 'Clean-Up' of Objectionable Programs," July 16, 1934, NANA, Vol. 63.

100. "Statement by Joy Elmer Morgan on Behalf of the National Committee on Education by Radio and the National Education Association." In *FCC 1934,* Volume 1, pp. 19–48; "Statement of Josef F. Wright, On Behalf of the National Association of Educational Broadcasters and the University of Illinois." In *FCC 1934,* Volume 1, pp. 131–50; "Statement of Mr. S. Howard Evans, on Behalf of the Ventura, California Free Press." In *FCC 1934,* Volume 1, pp. 199–206.

101. "Statement of Mr. James A. Moyer." In *FCC 1934,* Volume 1, pp. 234–60; Frank M. Russell to William Hard, October 2, 1934, NBC Mss, Box 40, Folder 54, Frank Russell 1934.

102. Henry K. Norton to R. C. Patterson, Jr., October 4, 1934, NBC Mss, Box 26, Folder 28, FCC Hearings 1934.

103. "Statement of Bethuel M. Webster, Jr. on Behalf of the American Civil Liberties Union." In *FCC 1934*, Volume 2, pp. 536–51; "Educators Drop Nationalized Radio Plea," *Broadcasting*, October 15, 1934, p. 9.

104. *Broadcasting*, October 15, 1934, p. 9; "J. P. Kiernan to Herbert L. Pettey, November 6, 1934." In *FCC 1934*, Volume 25, p. 13674.

105. "Educators Show Friendly Attitude," *Broadcasting*, October 15, 1934, p. 15; Robert A, Millikan, "Greetings From London." In *NACRE 1934*, p. 5; *Broadcasting*, October 15, 1934, p. 9; Frank M. Russell to William Hard, October 9, 1934, NBC Mss, Box 26, Folder 28, FCC Hearings 1934.

106. *New Republic*, November 28, 1934, p. 59; *New Republic*, January 9, 1935, p. 233; Sol Taishoff, "Class Wave Plan Overwhelmingly Opposed," *Broadcasting*, November 1, 1934, p. 5; *Broadcasting*, November 1, 1934, p. 5; H. K. Norton to William Hard, October 1, 1934, NBC Mss, Box 26, Folder 28, FCC Hearings 1934; Tracy F. Tyler, "Brief Summary Report of the National Committee on Education by Radio," p. 24, Tyler Mss, NCER file.

107. "Statement of Miss Hale read by S. D. Shankland." In *FCC 1934*, Volume 23, pp. 12596–600; Tracy F. Tyler to Frank F. Nalder, November 3, 1934, PFI Mss, Container 47, Folder 912; Memorandum re: Conference between Dr. Joy Elmer Morgan and Miss Crandall, October 1, 1932, PFI Mss, Container 42, Folder 812; "Highlights of Educational Testimony," *Broadcasting*, November 1, 1934, p. 6.

108. *FCC 1934*, Volumes 2–22; Frank Russell to William Hard, October 23, 1934, NBC Mss, Box 26, Folder 28, FCC Hearings 1934.

109. Tracy F. Tyler to Arnold Kruckman, September 26, 1933, PFI Mss, Container 43, Folder 842; Arthur E. Morgan, "Radio as a Cultural Agency in Sparsely Settled Regions and Remote Areas." In *NCER 1934*, p. 81; Tracy F. Tyler to Jerome Davis, June 22, 1934, PFI Mss, Container 44, Folder 847.

The TVA had pursued establishing its own radio station in 1933 and 1934, working with the NCER and hiring J. C. Jensen, administrator of the defunct Nebraska Wesleyan University station, as a consultant. See Tracy F. Tyler to A. E. Morgan, December 6, 1933, PFI Mss, Container 43, Folder 842; assorted correspondence, PFI Mss, Container 55, Folders 1058–59.

110. Tracy F. Tyler to Arthur E. Morgan, September 25, 1934, Arthur E. Morgan to Tracy F. Tyler, September 28, 1934, PFI Mss, Container 43, Folder 842; "Tennessee Valley Authority Urges Chain," *Education by Radio*, October 25, 1934, p. 45; "A 5-Point Plan for Radio," *The New York Times*, October 28, 1934, section IX, p. 11; *Broadcasting*, November 1, 1934, p. 5; *FCC 1934*, Volume 23, pp. 12687–90.

111. Early Memo, McIntyre Memo, October 20, 1934, October 22, 1934, FDR Mss, OF 136, 1934; "More About TVA Proposal," *Education by Radio*, November 22, 1934, p. 53; *Broadcasting*, November 1, 1934, p. 5.

112. *Education by Radio*, November 22, 1934, p. 54; *Education by Radio*, November 22, 1934, p. 53; Clifton Read to Henry Eckstein, November 1, 1934, ACLU Mss, 1934, Volume 699.

113. These letters can be found in FCC Mss, NARG 173, Box 497, File 201–4.

114. For example, Philip G. Loucks to Ella Phillips Crandall, November 10, 1934, PFI Mss, Container 68, Folder 1340; See FCC Mss, NARG 173, Box 497, File 201–4; Robert G. Sproul to Joy Elmer Morgan, November 21, 1934, PFI Mss, Container 44, Folder 861.

115. Verne Marshall to Joy Elmer Morgan, October 29, 1934, PFI Mss, Container 44, Folder 855; J. O. Keller to Philip G. Loucks, November 2, 1934, Chas. A. Robinson, S. J., to Philip G. Loucks, November 3, 1934, NBC Mss, Box 26, Folder 28, FCC Hearings 1934; Tracy F. Tyler to Charles A. Robinson, November 21, 1934, PFI Mss, Container 42, Folder 805.

116. Arthur G. Crane, "Radio Broadcasting." In *NASU 1934*, p. 201; *Education by Radio*, November 22, 1934, p. 53; Joy Elmer Morgan to A. G. Crane, November 20, 1934, PFI Mss, Container 41, Folder 785.

117. David Sarnoff to E. T. Cunningham, September 25, 1934, NBC Mss, Box 32c, Folder 6, David Sarnoff 1934; Day letter from Merlin H. Aylesworth to Edward N. Nockels, September 25, 1934, NBC Mss, Box 26, Folder 28, FCC Hearings 1934.

I am indebted to Nathan Godfried for assisting me with my analysis of Nockels and WCFL. Professor Godfried is in the process of completing a book-length manuscript, tentatively titled *The Tragedy of Labor Radio Station WCFL: Labor, Capital, the State, and the Mass Media, 1925–1978*. It should be in print by 1994.

118. Herbert L. Pettey to Edward N. Nockels, October 20, 1934, FCC Mss, NARG 173, Box 497, Folder 201–4, 1934, Allocation of Broadcast Facilities, FCC, General Correspondence; *AFL 1934*, pp. 274–77.

119. "Statement of Mr. William C. Hushing." In *FCC 1934*, Volume 25, pp. 13667–73; "Statement of Mr. William Green." In *FCC 1934*, Volume 25, pp. 13744–57.

120. Memorandum of Agreement between Chicago Federation of Labor and NBC, December 5, 1934, NBC Mss, Box 24, Folder 60.

121. Frank Russell to R. C. Patterson, Jr., November 12, 1934, Frank M. Russell to R. C. Patterson, Jr., November 13, 1934, NBC Mss, Box 26, Folder 29.

122. See Robert W. McChesney, "Labor and the Marketplace of Ideas: WCFL and the Battle for Labor Radio Broadcasting, 1928–1934," *Journalism Monographs*, No. 134, August 1992.

123. Ben H. Darrow, *Radio, The Assistant Teacher* (Columbus: F. G. Adams & Company, 1932), pp. 24–25; see also Alice Keith, "Broadcasting Educational Programs Over a National Network." In *IER 1930*, pp. 227–32.

124. See discussion of Keith on pp. 116–17 for an account of this episode.

125. Alice Keith, "Why British Educational Programs are Successful," *Education by Radio*, June 21, 1934, pp. 25–26; "Gleanings from Varied Sources," *Education by Radio*, July 11, 1935, p. 32; Alice Keith to Hampson Gary, August 29, 1934, FCC Mss, Office of the Executive Director, General Correspondence 1927–1946, 201–2, Box 497.

126. "Statement of Miss Alice Keith." In *FCC 1934*, Volume 25, pp. 13601–16.

127. *Ibid.*, pp. 13601–16.

128. " 'We Will Not Upset the Applecart', Says Colonel Brown," *Heinl Radio Business Letter,* December 7, 1934, p. 2.

129. Tracy F. Tyler to Eugene J. Coltrane, November 6, 1934, PFI Mss, Container 40, Folder 773; Henry A. Bellows to Stephen Early, November 26, 1934, FDR Mss, OF 136, Box 1, 1934; "Is the Nation Satisfied With the Radio?" *The Christian Century,* November 14, 1934, p. 1446.

130. "Cooperation Urged as Solution to Educational Radio Problems," *Broadcasting,* December 1, 1934, p. 16; See *Harney;* Form letter, Paulist Mss, WLWL file; United States SCIC Papers, National Archives, Washington, D.C., Sen 73A–J28, Tray 155.

131. J. C. Futrall to Tracy F. Tyler, December 15, 1934, PFI Mss, Container 49, Folder 941; Miss Crandall memorandum to Mrs. Bolton, Mr. Maxfield, November 5, 1934, PFI Mss, Container 69, Folder 1352.

132. Armstrong Perry to S. H. Evans, November 28, 1934, PFI Mss, Container 56, Folder 1080; Tracy F. Tyler to E. O. Holland, December 8, 1934, PFI Mss, Container 49, Folder 944.

133. From "Federal Communications Commission Reports to Congress," *Education by Radio,* January 31, 1935, p. 5; Frank M. Russell to R. C. Patterson, Jr., January 31, 1935, NBC Mss, Box 36c, Folder 38, FCC, Radio Education Committee 1935.

134. *Education by Radio,* January 31, 1935, p. 5; National Association of Educational Broadcasters Bulletin, February 18, 1935, NAEB Mss, Box 1a, General Correspondence 1935.

135. Memorandum Concerning National Committee on Education by Radio, October 17, 1939, p. 5, PFI Mss, Container 49, Folder 945.

Chapter 9

1. "Dill Ponders News Group for Stations," *Broadcasting,* June 15, 1934, p. 14; "Dill is Undecided," *Broadcasting,* July 1, 1934, p. 20; "Friends Think Dill Will Run for Seat," *Broadcasting,* August 1, 1934, p. 8; F. X. W., "Radio News Competition with the Daily Press Projected," *Public Utilities Fortnightly,* September 27, 1934, pp. 420–21; "Dill to Await NAB Conclave Reaction Before Deciding on Press–Radio Service," *Broadcasting,* September 1, 1934, p. 101; "Dill Plans Big Radio News Service," *Editor & Publisher,* August 18, 1934, p. 17; "The Press and Senator Dill," *Variety,* August 21, 1934, p. 31; "Senator Dill's Big Idea," *Editor & Publisher,* August 18, 1934, p. 22; "Radio Survey Public Business, Says Dill," *Editor & Publisher,* August 25, 1934, p. 6; "Dill Addresses L.A. Broadcasters; Denies Self Tie-Up With Air News," *Variety,* September 4, 1934, p. 34; Merlin H. Aylesworth to C. C. Dill, September 7, 1934, W. A. Winterbottom to David Sarnoff, September 11, 1934, Frank E. Mason to R. C. Patterson, Jr., September 21, 1934, NBC Mss, Box 25, Folder 51, C. C. Dill, 1934; "Dill Calls Press–Radio Program Failure," *Broadcasting,* October 1, 1934, pp. 15, 48, 49, 51; Clarence C. Dill, *Radio Law* (Washington, D. C.: National Law Book Company, 1938).

2. Henry A. Bellows, "Memorandum to the Board of Directors of the National Association of Broadcasters," December 7, 1934, William S. Hedges Manuscripts, State Historical Society of Wisconsin, Madison, Wis., Box 2; NAEB Bulletin, February 18, 1935, NAEB Mss, Box 1a, General Correspondence 1935.

3. S. Howard Evans to E. H. Harris, February 4, 1935, PFI Mss, Container 69, Folder 1350; S. Howard Evans, "Report on Radio Broadcasting prepared for Senator Burton K. Wheeler," April 1935, PFI Mss, Container 69, Folder 1351, p. 17; S. Howard Evans to Walter V. Woehlke, May 6, 1935, PFI Mss, Container 69, Folder 1358.

4. H. O. Davis to Ella Phillips Crandall, September 20, 1934, PFI Mss, Container 59, Folder 1148.

5. "WLWL to Resume Lobbying Campaign," *Broadcasting,* May 15, 1934, p. 50; For greater detail regarding the demise of WLWL, see Robert W. McChesney, "Crusade Against Mammon: Father Harney, WLWL and the Debate Over Radio in the 1930s," *Journalism History* 14 (Winter 1987): 118–30.

6. Frank Ernest Hill, *Tune In for Education* (New York: National Committee for Education by Radio, 1942), p. 75; NAEB Bulletin, February 18, 1935, NAEB Mss, Box 1a, General Correspondence 1935; W. I. Griffith to B. B. Brackett, June 14, 1935, NAEB Mss, Box 68a, File: Printed Materials, 1930s; Arthur G. Crane, "Safeguarding Educational Radio." In *NACRE 1935,* p. 123.

7. *Ibid.,* pp. 124; "Arthur Crane Comments." In *NACRE 1935,* p. 99; "Educated Education," *Broadcasting,* April 1, 1935, p. 30; Frank M. Russell to R. C. Patterson, May 18, 1935, NBC Mss, Box 36, Folder 38, FCC; Federal Education Committee 1935.

8. "Education Conference May 15," *NAB Reports,* March 22, 1935, p. 759; Personal and Confidential Memorandum from Frank M. Russell to R. C. Patterson, Jr., May 10, 1935, NBC Mss, Box 36, Folder 38, FCC; Federal Education Committee 1935; "Joint Committee to Develop Plan for Cultural Broadcasts," *Broadcasting,* June 1, 1935, p. 5.

9. Russell to Patterson, Jr., May 10, 1935, NBC Mss, Box 36, Folder 38; Tracy F. Tyler, "Can Clubwomen Aid in Solving the Radio Problem?" *Education by Radio,* August 8, 1935, p. 35; Armstrong Perry, "Federal Communications Commission," December 1935, PFI Mss, Container 52, Folder 986.

10. Arthur G. Crane to Charles A. Robinson, May 16, 1935, PFI Mss, Container 42, Folder 821; J. O. Keller to NUEA members, June 20, 1935, PFI Mss, Container 47, Folder 912.

11. R. C. Patterson, Jr., to Henry K. Norton, September 5, 1935, NBC Mss, Box 36, Folder 38, FCC; Federal Educational Committee 1935; Armstrong Perry to Tracy F. Tyler, August 5, 1935, PFI Mss, Container 57, Folder 1090; George W. Rightmire to A. G. Crane, May 2, 1935, PFI Mss, Container 48, Folder 922.

12. Armstrong Perry to S. Howard Evans, March 18, 1934, PFI Mss, Container 56, Folder 1079; Patterson, Jr., to Norton, September 5, 1935, NBC Mss, Box 36, Folder 38, FCC; Federal Educational Committee 1935; Memorandum to Mrs. Chester C. Bolton from S. Howard Evans, September 16, 1935, PFI Mss, Container 69, Folder 1351.

13. Memorandum for Mrs. Bolton from Miss Crandall, October 24, 1935, PFI

Mss, Container 49, Folder 945; Memorandum by S. H. Evans, November 1, 1935, PFI Mss, Container 69, Folder 1152.

14. Frank Russell memo on the National Committee on Education by Radio, September 1935, R. C. Patterson, Jr., to H. K. Norton, September 20, 1935, NBC Mss, Box 36, Folder 38, FCC: Federal Educational Committee 1935; *Education by Radio*, March 1939, p. 11; *Education by Radio*, October 1939, p. 31; "New Program for NCER," *Education by Radio*, January–February 1936, p. 1; *Education by Radio*, August–September 1938, p. 25.

15. Excerpt from Minutes of Executive Committee Meeting on National Committee on Education by Radio, January 18, 19, 1936, PFI Mss, Container 69, Folder 1147; Ella Phillips Crandall to Arthur G. Crane, January 23, 1936, PFI Mss, Container 69, Folder 1147.

16. "An American Public Radio Board Plan," *Education by Radio*, May 1936, p. 13; see also Arthur G. Crane, *A Plan for an American Broadcasting Service and Proposals for the Immediate Establishment of Two Regional Units* (Laramie, WY: National Committee on Education by Radio, 1937); Arthur G. Crane, "Co-operative Radio Councils." In *NCEB 1937*, pp. 306–25.

17. "Report of the Committee on Radio Broadcasting." In *NASU 1937*, p. 118; Crane, *A Plan for an American Broadcasting Service*, p. 1; "Mr. Young's Service to Free Speech," *Education by Radio*, March 1936, p. 5; *Education by Radio*, December 1937, p. 44.

18. James W. Baldwin to Dr. J. W. Studebaker, October 24, 1935, NBC Mss, Box 36, Folder 38; Judith C. Waller to Major Lenox R. Lohr, February 20, 1936, NBC Mss, Box 45, Folder 76, FREC 1936; Tracy F. Tyler, "Brief Summary Report of the National Committee on Education by Radio, 1931–1935," December 1935, Tyler Mss, NCER file, pp. 25–26; *Education by Radio*, December 1936, pp. 43, 44.

19. Harold A. Engel to Carl Menzer, December 18, 1936, NAEB Mss, Box No. 1, Correspondence 1925–1949; Harold A. Engel to B. B. Brackett, December 18, 1936, NAEB Mss, Box No. 22, File: NCER; George H. Gibson, *Public Broadcasting: The Role of the Federal Government, 1919–1976* (New York: Praeger Publishers, 1977), p. 40; Erik Barnouw, *The Golden Web* (New York: Oxford University Press, 1968), pp. 26–27.

20. S. Howard Evans to A. G. Crane, June 19, 1936, PFI Mss, Container 69, Folder 1147; S. Howard Evans to Mrs. Chester C. Bolton, July 6, 1939, S. H. Evans to Mrs. Walker, August 10, 1939, PFI Mss, Container 69, Folder 1350.

21. "Emergence of the Educational Stations," *Education by Radio*, June 1936, p. 18; See Gibson, *op. cit.;* Harold E. Hill, *The National Association of Educational Broadcasters: A History* (Urbana, IL: The National Association of Educational Broadcasters, 1954); Willard D. Rowland, "Continuing Crisis in Public Broadcasting: A History of Disenfranchisement," *Journal of Broadcasting and Electronic Media* 30 (Summer 1986):251–74; Robert J. Blakely, *To Serve the Public Interest: Educational Broadcasting in the United States* (Syracuse, NY: Syracuse University Press, 1979); Eugene E. Leach, *Tuning Out Education; The Cooperation Doctrine in Radio, 1922–38* (Washington, D.C.: Current, 1983).

22. *Education by Radio,* March 1938, p. 9; Round Table Discussion, "The Problems of College and University Stations." In *IER 1934,* pp. 200, 201.

23. *Education by Radio,* March 1938, p. 9; *Education by Radio,* Second Quarter, 1940, p. 12; Don V. Erickson, *Armstrong's Fight for FM Broadcasting* (University, AL: University of Alabama Press, 1973).

24. C. M. Jansky, Jr., "FM—Educational Radio's Second Chance—Will Educators Grasp It," August 5, 1946, in Edwin H. Armstrong Papers, Columbia University, New York, NY, Box 59, Folder on Educational FM.

25. Karl Marx, "The Eighteenth Brumaire of Louis Bonaparte." In *The Marx–Engels Reader,* edited by Robert C. Tucker (New York: W. W. Norton & Company, 1972), p. 436; William Boddy, *Fifties Television: The Industry and Its Critics* (Urbana and Chicago: University of Illinois Press, 1990), p. 36.

26. Armstrong Perry, "National Advisory Council on Radio in Education," December 1935, PFI Mss, Container 52, Folder 986.

27. Confidential memorandum for Frederick P. Keppel, July 13, 1934, CC Mss, NACRE Box 1, NACRE 1934.

28. Committee on Civic Education by Radio of the National Advisory Council on Radio in Education and the American Political Science Association, *Four Years of Network Broadcasting* (Chicago: University of Chicago Press, 1937), pp. 49, 73.

29. John F. Royal to Lenox R. Lohr, February 20, 1937, NBC Mss, Box 55, Folder 48, NACRE 1937; Telegram from David Sarnoff to George Zook, March 18, 1937, Telegram from George Zook to David Sarnoff, March 19, 1937, NBC Mss, Box 55, Folder 48, NACRE 1937; Levering Tyson to George F. Zook, March 5, 1937, PFI Mss, Container 46, Folder 882; George F. Zook to Levering Tyson, March 9, 1937, PFI Mss, Container 42, Folder 821.

30. Levering Tyson to Franklin Dunham, April 14, 1937, NBC Mss, Box 55, Folder 48, NACRE 1937; John F. Royal to David Sarnoff, October 21, 1937, NBC Mss, Box 55, Folder 48, NACRE 1937; "Statement of Dr. Thomas A. Reed." In *FCC 1934,* Volume 23, pp. 12505–10; "Educational Leaders Join Broadcasters in Defense of Radio ..," *Broadcasting,* November 1, 1934, p. 15.

31. Levering Tyson to John Royal, July 31, 1937, NBC Mss, Box 55, Folder 48, NACRE 1937; Levering Tyson, "The Need for Standards and How They Might be Established." In *NCEB 1937,* pp. 78–79.

32. Levering Tyson to S. Howard Evans, February 16, 1938, PFI Mss, Container 46, Folder 882; Levering Tyson to S. Howard Evans, November 28, 1938, S. Howard Evans to Levering Tyson, November 29, 1938, Levering Tyson to S. Howard Evans, November 30, 1938, PFI Mss, Container 44, Folder 863; see also, Minutes of Meeting of Board of Directors of National Advisory Council on Radio in Education, Inc., Held in the Council's Board Room, 60 East 42nd Street, New York, N. Y. on Wednesday, February 10, 1937 at 2 P. M., RMH II Mss, Volume 99, pp. 4–5.

33. "Dr. Tyson Retires from the Radio Field," *Education by Radio,* February 1937, p. 8; *Education by Radio,* December 1937, p. 61; S. Howard Evans, "National Conference on Educational Broadcasting," *Public Opinion Quarterly,* 1 (April 1937):127.

34. Roger Baldwin to the Federal Communications Commission, January 25,

1935, ACLU Mss, 1935, Volume 770; "Agenda for Meeting of Radio Committee," March 7, 1935, ACLU Mss, 1937, Volume 1011; Herbert Pettey to American Civil Liberties Union, August 28, 1935, Morris Ernst to Clifton Read, September 6, 1935, Clifton Read to Henry Eckstein, September 17, 1935, Clifton Read to Mr. Barnes, September 4, 1935, Clifton Read to Henry Eckstein, September 17, 1935, ACLU Mss, 1935, Volume 770.

35. *Scott Bills and Supporting Memoranda* (New York: American Civil Liberties Union, 1935), ACLU Mss, 1935, Volume 770.

36. Henry Eckstein to Clifton Read, December 6, 1935, ACLU Mss, Frederick Ballard to Clifton Read, June 17, 1935, Roger Baldwin to Frederick Ballard, June 19, 1935, ACLU Mss, 1935, Volume 770; Clifton Read to Henry Eckstein, September 7, 1935, ACLU Mss, 1935, Volume 769.

37. Clifton Read to Milton Kaufman, February 10, 1936, ACLU Mss, 1936, Volume 913; American Civil Liberties Union, *Bills in Congress for Freedom of the Air* (New York: American Civil Liberties Union, 1936); Clifton Read to Henry J. Eckstein, February 18, 1936, ACLU Mss, Volume 913, 1936; Roger Baldwin to Merlin H. Aylesworth, October 25, 1935, Frank M. Russell to M. H. Aylesworth, November 7, 1935, NBC Mss, Box 33, Folder 58, ACLU, 1935.

38. Henry Eckstein to Clifton Read, September 6, 1935, ACLU Mss, 1935, Volume 769; Henry Eckstein to Bethuel M. Webster, Jr., February 26, 1936, ACLU Mss, 1936, Volume 913.

39. M. J. Wilsie to Roger Baldwin, May 26, 1937, ACLU Mss, 1937, Volume 1011; Hazel Rice to Henry Eckstein, December 22, 1937, ACLU Mss, 1937, Volume 1011; Form letter: Harry F. Ward to United States Senator, November 1, 1937, ACLU Mss, 1937, Volume 1011.

40. Morris Ernst to Hazel Rice, May 24, 1938, Henry J. Eckstein to Hazel L. Rice, March 24, 1938, ACLU Mss, 1938, Volume 2013.

41. See David Sarnoff, *Network Broadcasting* (New York: National Broadcasting Company, 1938); "Investigation of Monopoly," *Education by Radio,* April 1938, p. 13; "The Monopoly Investigation," *Education by Radio,* Third Quarter 1940, pp. 15–16; Leo Huberman, "Monopoly Control of Radio," *U.S. Week,* May 31, 1941, p. 16; Henry Eckstein to Hazel Rice, May 18, 1938, ACLU Mss, 1938, Volume 2013.

42. Roger Baldwin to Thomas L. Stix, November 16, 1937, ACLU Mss, 1937, Volume 1011; *Education by Radio,* April 1937, p. 16; Henry J. Eckstein to Clifton R. Read, October 1, 1935, ACLU Mss, 1935, Volume 769; Raymond Gram Swing to Roger Baldwin, February 7, 1938, ACLU Mss, 1938, Volume 2012.

43. Hazel L. Rice to David Sarnoff, May 17, 1938, Hazel L. Rice to John Benson, May 18, 1938, Hazel L. Rice to Henry J. Eckstein, May 27, 1938, ACLU Mss, 1938, Volume 2014; Minutes of meeting of Radio Committee, May 11, 1938, ACLU Mss, 1938, Volume 2013; Hazel Rice to T. C. Streibert, May 18, 1938, ACLU Mss, 1938, Volume 2014.

44. Philip T. Rosen, *The Modern Stentors: Radio Broadcasting and the Federal Government 1920–1934* (Westport, CT: Greenwood Press, 1980), p. 180.

45. David Sarnoff, "Proposed Voluntary Self-Regulation of Radio," *Congressional Digest,* December 1938, p. 296.

46. See, for example, Henry Adams Bellows, "Is Radio Censored?" *Harper's Monthly*, 171 (1935):702; For a detailed discussion of this middle 1930s deregulation campaign, see Robert W. McChesney, "Free Speech and Democracy! Louis G. Caldwell, the American Bar Association and the Debate over the Free Speech Implications of Broadcast Regulation, 1928–1938," *The American Journal of Legal History* 35 (1991):351–92.

47. David Sarnoff, "Broadcasting in the American Democracy." In *NCEB 1936*, p. 154.

48. Louis G. Caldwell, "Freedom of the Air for Broadcasters," *Broadcasting*, December 15, 1934, p. 45; Louis G. Caldwell, "Freedom of Speech and Radio Broadcasting." In *Annals 1935*, pp. 179–81, 207.

49. *Ibid.*, pp. 179–81, 207; Louis G. Caldwell, "Comment on the Current Problems of the Law of Communication," *American Bar Association Journal*, December 1936, p. 852.

50. Seymour N. Siegel, "Censorship in Radio," *Air Law Review* 7 (January 1936): 18, 24; Caldwell, "Freedom of Speech," pp. 203, 180; see also Bellows, "Is Radio Censored," p. 702; Irwin Stewart, "The Public Control of Radio," *Air Law Review* 8 (1937):149.

51. Caldwell, "Freedom of Speech," p. 204; Seymour N. Siegel, "A Realistic Approach to the Law of Communications," *Air Law Review* 8 (April 1937):83.

52. Frank A. Arnold, "Radio and the Newspapers," *Editor & Publisher*, April 17, 1937, p. 48; "Newspapers End Antagonism to Radio," *Broadcasting*, May 1, 1937, p. 15; "Aylesworth joins Scripps–Howard," *The Literary Digest*, February 13, 1937, p. 28.

53. Siegel, "Realistic Approach," p. 96; Caldwell, "Freedom of Speech," p. 206.

54. Louis G. Caldwell, "Radio and the Law." In *Future*, pp. 226, 227, 221, 231.

55. Caldwell, "Freedom of Speech," p. 197; Siegel, "Censorship," pp. 9–12.

56. Cited in "In Their Own Behalf," *Education by Radio*, June–July 1938, p. 21.

57. Herman S. Hettinger, "The Economic Factor in Radio Regulation," *Air Law Review* 9 (April 1938):115, 120; "Report of the Standing Committee on Communications." In *ABA 1931*, p. 385.

58. Thad H. Brown, *The Federal Communications Law* (Cleveland: Western Reserve University, 1937), pp. 19–20; Hettinger, "Economic Factor," pp. 118–19.

59. Rosen, *Stentors*, p. 180; For the classic statement along these lines see Sydney W. Head, *Broadcasting in America* (Boston: Houghton-Miflin, 1956); for a discussion of David Sarnoff's work to recast broadcasting history see Tom Lewis, *Empire of the Air: The Men Who Made Radio* (New York: HarperCollins, 1991), Chap. 13.

60. Henry Ewbank and Sherman P. Lawton, *Broadcasting: Radio and Television* (New York: Harper & Brothers, 1952); Henry Ewbank, *Conservation of Radio Resources* (Madison, WI: WHA, 1934).

61. "A Report on Stewardship," *Education by Radio*, December 1937, pp. 55–62; "The National Committee on Education by Radio, 1930–1941," *Education by Radio*, Fourth Quarter 1941, pp. 35–40; Hill, *Tune In op. cit.;* Carroll Atkinson,

Development of Radio Education Policies in American Public School Systems (Edinboro, PA: Edinboro Educational Press, 1939), pp. 5, 8.

62. Stewart, "Public Control," p. 149; Pettey to ACLU, August 28, 1935, ACLU
Mss, Volume 770; Minna F. Kassner and Lucien Zacharoff, *Radio is Censored!*
(New York: American Civil Liberties Union, 1936), pp. 5–7.

63. One of the first works to emphasize this point was O. W. Riegel, *Mobilizing
for Chaos: The Story of the New Propaganda* (New Haven: Yale University Press,
1934). This book was received warmly by the commercial broadcasters upon its
publication in December. See Martin Codel, "Federal Radio Dangers Cited," December 10, 1934, NANA, Vol. 63.

64. Bethuel M. Webster, Jr., "Report on Radio Censorship to the Annual Meeting
of the American Civil Liberties Union," April 24, 1935, ACLU Mss, 1935, Volume
774; Bethuel M. Webster, Jr., to Henry Eckstein, February 13, 1935, ACLU Mss,
1935, Volume 769.

65. John W. Love to American Civil Liberties Union, December 23, 1937, ACLU
Mss, 1937, Volume 1011; Frederick Ballard to Bethuel M. Webster, Jr., April 4,
1936, ACLU Mss, 1936, Volume 913.

66. Memorandum of a meeting of the Committee on Free Speech of the National
Council on Freedom from Censorship, December 9, 1938, ACLU Mss, 1938, Volume
2012; Statement by the American Civil Liberties Union on the relation of Reverend
Charles E. Coughlin to Radio Censorship, December 21, 1938, ACLU Mss, 1938,
Volume 2011. For a general discussion of the origins and aspirations of the ACLU,
see Charles Lam Markham, *The Noblest Cry: A History of the American Civil
Liberties Union* (New York: St. Martin's Press, 1965); Samuel Walker, *In Defense
of American Liberties: A History of the ACLU* (New York: Oxford University Press,
1990).

67. Morris L. Ernst, *The First Freedom* (New York: The Macmillan Company,
1946), pp. 126–41; see also Morris L. Ernst, "Freedom to Read, See, and Hear,"
Harper's Monthly 191 (July 1945): pp. 51–53.

68. Stewart, "Public Control," pp. 128, 138.

69. Henry Eckstein to Hazel Rice, November 16, 1938, ACLU Mss, 1938, Volume 2013.

70. Hettinger, "Economic Factor," p. 120; See also Seymour N. Siegel, "Radio
and Propaganda," *Air Law Review* 10 (April 1939):141; Louis G. Caldwell, "Legal
Restrictions on the Contents of Broadcast Programs," *Air Law Review* 9 (July
1938):232; James M. Herring, "Broadcasting and the Public Interest," *Harvard
Business Review* 18 (1940):356.

71. Roger N. Baldwin to Frank R. McNinch, February 7, 1938, ACLU Mss,
1938, Volume 2012; Roger Baldwin to Frank McNinch, November 23, 1938, ACLU
Mss, Volume 2012.

72. Memorandum by S. Howard Evans, June 7, 1939, PFI Mss, Container 69,
Folder 1152; See H. V. Kaltenborn Manuscripts, State Historical Society of Wisconsin, Madison, WI, Box 153, ACLU 1943–1960.

73. For example, see Joy Elmer Morgan, "Education's Rights on the Air." In
NACRE 1931, p. 122. This point was also emphasized by naval Captain Stanford
Hooper in a memo to President Roosevelt. See Comments on Report of Majority

Members of Committee and Discussion of Position of Minority Member, FDR Mss, OF859a, 1933–1945; Rosen, *Stentors,* p. 180.

74. See David R. Mackey, *The National Association of Broadcasters—Its First Twenty Years* (Ph.D. dissertation, Ohio State University, 1956), Chapters IX and X; Council on Radio Journalism, *Report on Radio News Internships* (Washington, D.C.: National Association of Broadcasters, 1946).

75. See James L. Baughman, *Television's Guardians: The FCC and the Politics of Programming, 1958–1967* (Knoxville, TN: University of Tennessee Press, 1985), p. 3; see also J. Fred MacDonald, *One Nation Under Television* (New York: Pantheon, 1990), pp. 25–27; FCC commissioner quoted in J. Frank Beatty, "Ohio Institute Opens With Freedom Debate," *Broadcasting,* May 8, 1944, p. 14; James Lawrence Fly, "Free Speech—An Exploration of the Broadcaster's Duty," October 7, 1943, Commission on Freedom of the Press Papers, Columbia University, New York, NY, Box 12, Speeches/Articles.

For an overview of the FCC during the Second World War and the formation of ABC, see Christopher H. Sterling and John M. Kittross, *Stay Tuned: A Concise History of American Broadcasting* (Belmont, CA: Wadsworth, 1978), Chap. 6.

76. Boddy, pp. 97, 114; Baughman, pp. 9–10; Federal Communications Commission, *Report on Chain Broadcasting* (Washington, D.C.: Government Printing Office, 1941); Federal Communications Commission, *Public Service Responsibilities of Broadcast Licensees* (Washington, D.C.: Federal Communications Commission, 1946).

77. S. Howard Evans to Frank Schooley, June 24, 1938, NAEB Mss, Box No. 22, File: NCER.

78. Robert Britt Horwitz, *The Irony of Regulatory Reform* (New York: Oxford University Press, 1989), pp. 170, 331; Baughman, p. 74; Boddy, p. 224; see also Erwin G. Krasnow, Lawrence D. Longley and Herbert A. Terry, *The Politics of Broadcast Regulation,* third edition (New York: St. Martin's Press, 1982).

FCC reformers generally found themselves in the position that the only tact they could opt for that would not bring severe consternation was to advocate increased competition in the marketplace. Ironically, as my colleague James L. Baughman has brought to my attention, the FCC's role in the creation of ABC may have been counterproductive. NBC unloaded its less profitable Blue network, which carried the most sustaining programs. The new ABC, starting way behind NBC and CBS, quickly became the most aggressively commercial of the networks and, some have argued, thereby forced NBC and CBS to lower their standards in order to compete. The deregulation movement of the 1980s, predicted upon a blind faith in the marketplace, arguably has had similar consequences. What cannot be broached, of course, is the notion that the marketplace itself is inappropriate as the dominant regulator of broadcasting.

79. Erik Barnouw, *The Sponsor: Notes on a Modern Potentate* (New York: Oxford University Press, 1978), p. 41.

80. See, for example, " 'Socialism'; Broadcasters Protest Trend in Wisconsin," *Broadcasting,* March 15, 1948, p. 36; Boddy, p. 52.

81. Boddy, pp. 31, 48, 253.

82. For how this dilemma plagued Newton Minow's reform efforts in the early

1960s, see Baughman, p. 80. This was certainly the way the broadcasters wanted the choice to be seen by the public. See Boddy, p. 222.

83. William S. Paley, "The Viewpoint of the Radio Industry." In *NCEB 1937*, p. 6.

84. Paul F. Lazarsfeld, *The People Look at Radio* (Chapel Hill: The University of North Carolina Press, 1946), p. 89. This survey was commissioned and paid for by the NAB. As the industry increasingly subsidized communications research, it could only lessen the chance that scholars would take up questions of how the industry was structured and controlled from a critical perspective. In his preface Lazarsfeld, one of the founders of mass communication research, noted:

> The fact that the National Association of Broadcasters sought out independent research experts to prepare and report such a survey is a sign that the industry is doing its best to mold a constructive program of action from the great variety of forces which impinge upon it. (p. ix)

Chapter 10

1. S. Howard Evans to Walter V. Woehlke, February 29, 1932, PFI Mss, Container 69, Folder 1358; for some examples of recent scholarship that regard the system at entrenched in the 1920s and/or the Radio Act of 1927 as decisive, see Michele Hilmes, *Hollywood and Broadcasting* (Urbana and Chicago: University of Illinois Press, 1990); James Schwoch, *The American Radio Industry and Its Latin American Activities, 1900–1939* (Urbana and Chicago: University of Illinois Press, 1990); Susan J. Douglas, *Inventing American Broadcasting, 1899–1922* (Baltimore: The Johns Hopkins University Press, 1987).

2. For example, see Joseph P. McKerns, "Industry Skeptics and the Radio Act of 1927," *Journalism History* 3 (Winter 1976–77):128–31, 136; Donald G. Godfrey, "Senator Dill and the 1927 Radio Act," *Journal of Broadcasting* 23 (1978):477–89; Walter B. Emery, "Broadcasting Rights and Responsibilities in Democratic Society," *The Centennial Review* 8 (1964):306–22.

3. Werner J. Severin, "Commercial vs. Non-commercial Radio During Broadcasting's Early Years," *Journal of Broadcasting* 20 (Fall 1978):491–504.

4. One account of the history of radio programming eliminates the role of nonprofit stations altogether. See J. Fred MacDonald, *Don't Touch That Dial! Radio Programming in American Life from 1920 to 1950* (Chicago: Nelson-Hall, 1979).

5. Erik Barnouw, *A Tower in Babel* (New York: Oxford University Press, 1966), pp. 211–19; Christopher H. Sterling and John M. Kitross, *Stay Tuned: A Concise History of American Broadcasting* (Belmont, CA: Wadsworth, 1978), pp. 127–30; Robert Britt Horwitz, *The Irony of Regulatory Reform* (New York: Oxford University Press, 1989), pp. 120–22; Andrew F. Inglis, *Behind the Tube: A History of Broadcasting Technology and Business* (Boston: Focal Press, 1990), pp. 80–82; Lucas A. Powe, Jr., *American Broadcasting and the First Amendment* (Berkeley: University of California Press, 1987), pp. 61–67.

6. Walter B. Emery, *National and International Systems of Broadcasting* (East Lansing, MI: Michigan State University Press, 1969), p. 7; William B. Ray, *FCC: The Ups and Downs of Radio–TV Regulation* (Ames, IA: Iowa State University

Press, 1990), ch. 5, 6; Harold A. Engel to Charles E. Coughlin, January 9, 1932, WHA Papers, University of Wisconsin Archives, Madison, Wisc., Box 2, Folder 12, C-F, 1931–1933.

7. For example, see Erik Barnouw, *The Sponsor* (New York: Oxford University Press, 1978), pp. 27–32; Robert Sobel, *RCA* (New York: Stein and Day, 1986), pp. 110–12. An example of this phenomenon is found in Douglas Kellner, *Television and the Crisis of Democracy* (Boulder, CO: Westview Press, 1990), pp. 34–36, where the author discusses the "Hatfield–Wagner Act."

8. "Radio Censorship in America and England," *Education by Radio*, February 15, 1934, p. 5.

9. To some proponents of the market, it is *undemocratic* even to have a public debate over whether the media might best be operated on nonmarket principles. Since the market is quintessentially democratic, any debate that leads away from a market system is antidemocratic. Therefore, it is best in a democratic society to keep this issue off-limits. For an example of this type of reasoning, see Lucas A. Powe, Jr., *The Fourth Estate and the Constitution: Freedom of the Press in America* (Berkeley: University of California Press, 1991), p. 282.

This reasoning, when looked at closely, sometimes reveals a distinctly elitist position: It is alright for intellectuals to ponder the big issues as long as they keep their opinions in the academy and do not act upon them, but not for the masses who might act irresponsibly if given the opportunity to exercise any real power. The purpose of political democracy in this view is to handle a narrow range of administrative tasks, while the important decisions are made in the marketplace or by government officials responding to the needs of business. The power relations of society are off-limits, effectively written into the constitution and hidden behind rhetoric about the market. A recent statement along these lines is David Kelley and Roger Donway, "Liberalism and Free Speech." In *Democracy and the Mass Media,* edited by Judith Lichtenberg (Cambridge and New York: Cambridge University Press, 1990), p. 95. To the extent that this vision characterizes U.S. political culture, is it any wonder that political apathy is so prevalent?

10. See Powe, op. cit.; Ithiel de Sola Pool, *Technologies of Freedom* (Cambridge, MA: Belknap Press of Harvard University Press, 1983); Jonathan W. Emord, *Freedom, Technology, and the First Amendment* (San Francisco: Pacific Research Institute for Public Policy, 1991); Craig R. Smith, *Freedom of Expression and Partisan Politics* (Columbia, SC: University of South Carolina Press, 1989); David Kelley and Roger Downey, "Liberalism and Free Speech." In *Democracy and the Mass Media,* edited by Judith Lichtenberg (New York: Cambridge University Press, 1989), pp. 66–101.

11. See Robert W. McChesney, "Free Speech and Democracy! Louis G. Caldwell, the American Bar Association and the Debate over the Free Speech Implications of Broadcast Regulation, 1928–1938," *The American Journal of Legal History* 35 (October 1991):351–92.

12. David Paul Nord, "The FCC, Educational Broadcasting, and Political Interest Group Activity," *Journal of Broadcasting* 22 (Summer 1978):321–38; one recent work credits the NCER with the passage of the Communications Act of 1934, although it quickly points out that the NCER did not get the reform they anticipated thereafter.

See Tom Lewis, *Empire of the Air: The Men Who Made Radio* (New York: HarperCollins, 1991), p. 240.

13. For example, see "Press and Publicity." In *Proceedings of the First Constitutional Convention of the Congress of Industrial Organizations Held in the City of Pittsburgh, Pennsylvania November 14 to November 18, 1938, Inclusive* (Congress of Industrial Organizations, 1938), p. 42; "Radio Facilities." In *Daily Proceedings of the Second Constitutional Convention of the Congress of Industrial Organizations October 10, 11, 12, 13, 1939 San Francisco, California* (Congress of Industrial Organizations, 1939), p. 192; C. I. O. Political Action Committee, *Radio Handbook* (Washington, D. C.: Congress of Industrial Organizations, 1945), pp. 4, 5.

14. Comment of the late Professor William E. Ames, who served as the author's dissertation supervisor at the University of Washington; see Istvan Meszaros, *The Power of Ideology* (New York: New York University Press, 1989), pp. 399–400.

15. See Martin J. Sklar, *The Corporate Reconstruction of American Capitalism, 1890–1916* (New York: Cambridge University Press, 1988); Gabriel Kolko, *The Triumph of Conservatism* (Chicago: Quadrangle Books, 1967); James Weinstein, *Ambiguous Legacy; The Left in American Politics* (New York: New Viewpoints, 1975); Christopher Lasch, *The Agony of the American Left* (New York: Vintage Books, 1969); James Weinstein, *The Decline of Socialism in America, 1912–1925* (New York: Monthly Review Press, 1967); William Appleman Williams, *The Great Evasion* (Chicago: Quadrangle Books, 1964); Paul Buhle, *Marxism in the USA* (London: Verso, 1987); Russell Jacoby, *The Last Intellectuals: American Culture in the Age of the Academe* (New York: Basic Books, 1987).

16. For example, see Tony Benn and Eric Heffer, "A Strategy for Labour: Four Documents," *New Left Review*, July–August 1986, pp. 60–75; for a historical perspective on the left and the British media policy, see Communist Party of Britain, *The B.B.C.* (London: The Communist Party, 1945), p. 2; for some general reference material on this topic see, for example, John Whale, *The Politics of the Media* (Atlantic Highlands, N.J: Humanities Press, 1977); *The Politics of Broadcasting*, Edited by Raymond Kuhn (New York: St. Martin's Press, 1985).

17. For example, see H. H. Wilson, *Pressure Group: The Campaign for Commercial Television* (London: Secker & Warburg, 1961); see also Boddy, p. 142.

In 1992 the political right in the United States led an abortive campaign to reduce or even eliminate the federal subsidy to the Corporation for Public Broadcasting, mostly on the grounds that the Public Broadcasting Service was broadcasting too much material that the right considered left-wing. See Martin Tolchin, "Senate Rejects Efforts to Cut Fund for Public Broadcasting," *The New York Times*, June 4, 1992, p. 1. Ironically, PBS, with its dependency upon corporate financing, is a pale imitation of the type of public service broadcasting envisioned by the 1930s' reformers or found elsewhere in the world. Its political range is generally as narrow as that of the commercial stations, with the exception of a handful of programs that draw the consternation of the right. The right's campaign seems best understood, like most right-wing media criticism, as an effort to harass and intimidate PBS to eliminate or markedly reduce anything more than superficially critical of the status quo. For a discussion of PBS's political leanings that you will not find in the commercial media or on PBS, see "PBS' Missing Voices," *Extra!*, June 1992, pp. 15–18.

18. See Robert L. Heilbroner, *The Nature and Logic of Capitalism* (New York: W. W. Norton, 1985); Stuart Hall, "Culture, Media and the Ideological Effect." In *Mass Communications and Society*, Edited by James Curran, Tony Bennett, Michael Gurevitch and Janet Woolacott (Beverly Hills: Sage, 1979), p. 323.

19. Philip T. Rosen, *The Modern Stentors: Radio Broadcasters and the Federal Government 1920–1934* (Westport, CT: Greenwood Press, 1980), p. 181.

20. Jerome A. Barron, "Access to the Press—A New First Amendment Right," *Harvard Law Review* 80 (1967):1641–78; Stephen L. Carter, "Technology, Democracy, and the Manipulation of Consent," *Yale Law Journal* 93 (1984): pp. 561–607; Powe, op. cit., pp. 248–57; Ben H. Bagdikian, *The Media Monopoly*, third edition (Boston: Beacon Press, 1990), p. 223.

21. John DeMott, " 'Company Line' raises ethical dilemma," *Media Law Notes*, Spring 1990, p. 9.

22. For example, see Herbert J. Gans, *Deciding What's News* (New York: Pantheon, 1979); W. Lance Bennett, *News: The Politics of Illusion* (New York: Longmans, 1983); Gaye Tuchman, *Making News* (New York: Basic Books, 1978); Mark Fishman, *Manufacturing the News* (Austin: University of Texas Press, 1980); David L. Paletz and Robert M. Entman, *Media Power Politics* (New York: Free Press, 1981); Michael Schudson, "The Profession of Journalism in the United States." In *Professions in American History*, edited by N. O. Hatch (Notre Dame, In.: Notre Dame University Press, 1988), pp. 145–61; James W. Carey, "A Plea for the University Tradition," *Journalism Quarterly* 55 (Winter 1978):846–55; Bagdikian, op. cit., ch. 10, 12.

23. "Newspaper Guild Attacks Wires Bill," *The New York Times*, June 7, 1934, p. 21.

24. Ben H. Bagdikian, "American Mass Media and the Future," paper presented to 1990 Annual Convention, Association for Education in Journalism and Mass Communication, Minneapolis, Minn., August 1990.

25. While politicians can never attack the economic basis of the media industries, they can attack the alleged liberal biases of editors and journalists. Indeed, the two U.S. presidents who made the strongest attacks in this area and who also did the most to prevent press and public access to government information—Nixon and Reagan—were also the presidents who did the most to enhance corporate media profitability. It is telling that they each received as much, if not more, support from the media in their re-election campaigns as any other recent presidential candidate. For a longer discussion of conservative media criticism, see Robert W. McChesney, "Off Limits: An Inquiry into the Lack of Debate Over the Ownership, Structure, and Control of the Mass Media in U.S. Political Life," *Communication* 13 (1992): 1–19.

26. C. Anthony Giffard, *UNESCO and the Media* (New York: Longman, 1988); Edward S. Herman, "U.S. Mass Media Coverage of the U.S. Withdrawal from UNESCO." In *Hope & Folly: The United States and UNESCO, 1945–1980*, edited by William Preston, Jr., Edward S. Herman, and Herbert I. Schiller (Minneapolis: University of Minnesota Press, 1989), pp. 203–84.

27. Morris Ernst, "Freedom to Read, See, and Hear," *Harper's Magazine*, July 1945, p. 53.

28. For more on this point see Noam Chomsky, *Necessary Illusions: Thought Control in Democratic Societies* (Boston: South End Press, 1989), p. 136; Herbert I. Schiller, *Culture, Inc.* (New York: Oxford University Press, 1989), pp. 157–74.

29. Thomas Paine, "Common Sense." In *The Thomas Paine Reader* (New York: Penguin Books, 1987), p. 65.

30. Alexander Meiklejohn. *Political Freedom* (New York: Harper & Brothers, 1960), pp. 14–15.

31. Karl Marx, "For a Ruthless Criticism of Everything Existing." In *The Marx-Engels Reader,* edited by Robert C. Tucker (New York: W. W. Norton & Company, 1972), p. 8; Samir Amin, *Eurocentrism* (New York: Monthly Review Press, 1989), p. 152. For an analysis of the duty of the intellectual and the present world situation that is opposed to my own, see Richard Rorty, "The Intellectual at the End of Socialism," *The Yale Review* 80 (April 1992): 1–17. Richard Rorty is James Rorty's son.

Selected Bibliography

Books and Monographs (Since 1940)

Aitkin, Hugh G. J. *The Continuous Wave: Technology and the American Radio, 1900–1932* (Princeton: Princeton University Press, 1985).

Ashmore, Harry S. *Unseasonable Truths: The Life of Robert Maynard Hutchins* (Boston: Little, Brown and Company, 1989).

Bagdikian, Ben H. *The Media Monopoly*, third edition (Boston: Beacon Press, 1990).

Barnouw, Erik. *The Golden Web* (New York: Oxford University Press, 1968).

———. *The Sponsor* (New York: Oxford University Press, 1978).

———. *A Tower in Babel* (New York: Oxford University Press, 1966).

Baughman, James L. *Televison's Guardians: The FCC and the Politics of Programming* (Knoxville: University of Tennessee Press, 1985).

Beasley, Maureen. *Eleanor Roosevelt and the Media: A Quest for Self-Fulfillment* (Urbana: University of Illinois Press, 1987).

Bennett, W. Lance. *News: The Politics of Illusion* (New York: Longman, 1983).

Bergreen, Laurence. *Look Now, Pay Later* (Garden City, NY: Doubleday & Company, 1980).

Bernays, Edward L. *Biography of an Idea: Memoirs of Public Relations Counsel Edward L. Bernays* (New York: Simon and Schuster, 1965).

Beuick, Marshall. *Bibliography of Radio Broadcasting* (New York: Marshall Beuick, 1947).

Biles, Roger. *A New Deal for the American People.* (DeKalb, IL: Northern Illinois University Press, 1991).

Blakely, Robert J. *To Serve the Public Interest; Educational Broadcasting in the United States* (Syracuse: Syracuse University Press, 1979).

Bliss, Edward, Jr. *Now the News: The Story of Broadcast Journalism* (New York: Columbia University Press, 1991).

Boddy, William. *Fifties Television: The Industry and Its Critics* (Urbana and Chicago: University of Illinois Press, 1990).

Bollinger, Lee C. *Images of a Free Press* (Chicago: University of Chicago Press, 1991).

Briggs, Asa. *The BBC—the First Fifty Years* (New York: Oxford University Press, 1984).

———. *The History of Broadcasting in the United Kingdom* (New York: Oxford University Press, 1961).

Brooks, John. *Telephone: The First Hundred Years* (New York: Harper & Row, 1975).

Buhle, Paul. *Marxism in the USA: Remapping the History of the American Left* (London and New York: Verso, 1987).

Case, Josephine Young, and Case, Everett Needham. *Owen D. Young and American Enterprise* (Boston: David R. Godine, 1982).

CBS Reference Library, *Radio and Television Bibliography* (New York: Columbia Broadcasting System, 1941).

Charnley, Mitchell V. *News By Radio* (New York: The Macmillan Company, 1948).

Chomsky, Noam. *Necessary Illusions: Thought Control in Democratic Societies* (Boston: South End Press, 1989).

C.I.O. Political Action Committee. *Radio Handbook* (Washington, D.C.: Congress of Industrial Organizations, 1945).

Coase, R. H. *British Broadcasting: A Study in Monopoly* (London: Longmans, Green and Co., 1950).

Codding, George Arthur, Jr. *The International Telecommunication Union* (Leiden, The Netherlands: E. J. Brill, 1952).

Cohen, Lizabeth. *Making a New Deal: Industrial Workers in Chicago, 1919–1939* (Cambridge and New York: Cambridge University Press, 1990).

Communist Party of Britain. *The B.B.C.* (London: Communist Party, 1945).

Complete Presidential Press Conferences of Franklin D. Roosevelt Volumes 1–2 (New York: DeCapo Press, 1972).

Coons, John E., ed. *Freedom and Responsibility in Broadcasting* (Evanston: Northwestern University Press, 1960).

Cooper, Isabella. *Bibliography on Educational Broadcasting* (Chicago: University of Chicago Press, 1942).

Cooper, Kent. *Kent Cooper and the Associated Press: An Autobiography* (New York: Random House, 1959).

Council on Radio Journalism. *Report on Radio News Internships* (Washington, D.C.: National Association of Broadcasters, 1946).

Covert, Cathy, and Stevens, John L. *Mass Media Between the Wars* (Syracuse: Syracuse University Press, 1984).

Curran, James, Bennett, Tony, Gurevitch, Michael, and Woolacott, Janet, eds. *Mass Communications and Society* (Beverly Hills: Sage, 1979).

Daniels, Josephus. *Editor in Politics* (Chapel Hill: University of North Carolina Press, 1941).

Davis, Mike. *Prisoners of the American Dream* (London: Verso, 1986).

Davis, Robert Edward. *Response to Innovation: A Study of Popular Argument About New Media* (New York: Arno Press, 1976).

De Forest, Lee. *Father of Radio: The Autobiography of Lee de Forest* (Chicago: Wilcox & Follett Co., 1950).

Dewey, John. *The Later Works, 1925–1954. Volume 11: 1935–1937,* Jo Ann Boydston, ed. (Carbondale and Edwardsville: Southern Illinois University Press, 1991).

Donahue, Hugh Carter. *The Battle to Control Broadcast News* (Cambridge, MA: The MIT Press, 1989).

Douglas, Susan J. *Inventing American Broadcasting 1899–1922* (Baltimore: The Johns Hopkins University Press, 1987).

Eckersley, P. P. *The Power Behind the Microphone* (London: Jonathan Cape, 1941).

Edelman, Murray. *The Licensing of Radio Services in the United States, 1927 to 1947* (Urbana: University of Illinois Press, Illinois Studies in the Social Sciences, 1950).

Editors of Broadcasting Magazine. *The First 50 Years of Broadcasting* (Washington, D.C.: Broadcasting Publications, Inc., 1982).

Ely, Melvin Patrick. *The Adventures of Amos 'n' Andy: A Social History of an American Phenomenon* (New York: The Free Press, 1991).

Emerson, Thomas I. *Toward a General Theory of the First Amendment* (New York: Random House, 1963).

Emery, Edwin. *History of the American Newspaper Publishers Association* (Minneapolis: University of Minnesota Press, 1950).

Emery, Walter B. *Broadcasting & Government; Responsibilities and Regulations* (East Lansing: Michigan State University Press, 1961).

———. *National and International Systems of Broadcasting* (East Lansing: Michigan State University Press, 1969).

Emord, Jonathan W. *Freedom, Technology, and the First Amendment* (San Francisco: Pacific Research Institute for Public Policy, 1991).

Erickson, Don V. *Armstrong's Fight for FM Broadcasting* (University, AL: University of Alabama Press, 1973).

Ernst, Morris L. *The First Freedom* (New York: The Macmillan Company, 1946).

Ewbank, Henry and Lawton, Sherman P. *Broadcasting: Radio and Television* (New York: Harper & Brothers, 1952).

Farina, John. *An American Experience of God* (New York: Paulist Press, 1981).

———. *Hecker Studies* (New York: Paulist Press, 1983).

Fetherling, Dale. *Mother Jones, The Miners' Angel* (Carbondale and Edwardsville: Southern Illinois University Press, 1974).

Fishman, Mark. *Manufacturing the News* (Austin: University of Texas Press, 1980).

Fowler, Gene and Crawford, Bill. *Border Radio* (Austin: Texas Monthly Press, 1987).

Fraser, Steve, and Gerstle, Gary, eds. *The Rise and Fall of the New Deal Order, 1930–1980* (Princeton: Princeton University Press, 1989).

Freidel, Frank. *Franklin D. Roosevelt: A Rendezvous with Destiny* (Boston: Little, Brown, and Company, 1990).

Friedrich, Carl J., and Sayre, Jeanette. *The Development of the Control of Advertising on the Air* (New York: Radiobroadcasting Research Project, 1940).

Friedrich, Carl J., and Smith, Jeanette Sayre. *Radiobroadcasting and Higher Education* (New York: Radiobroadcasting Research Project, 1942).

Gans, Herbert J. *Deciding What's News* (New York: Pantheon, 1979).

Gibson, George H. *Public Broadcasting; The Role of the Federal Government, 1919–1976* (New York: Praeger Publishers, 1977).

Giffard, C. Anthony. *UNESCO and the Media* (New York and London: Longmans, 1989).

Gray, James. *Business Without Boundary: The Story of General Mills* (Minneapolis: University of Minnesota Press, 1954).

Hatch, Nathan O., ed. *Professions in American History* (Notre Dame: University of Notre Dame Press, 1988).

Head, Sydney W. *Broadcasting in America*. Boston: Houghton-Miflin, 1956.

Headrick, Daniel R. *The Invisible Weapon: Telecommunications and International Politics 1851–1945*. New York: Oxford University Press, 1991.

Herman, Edward S. and Chomsky, Noam. *Manufacturing Consent: The Political Economy of the Mass Media* (New York: Pantheon, 1988).

Hill, Frank Ernest. *Tune in for Education* (New York: National Committee on Education by Radio, 1942).

Hill, Frank Ernest, and Williams, W. E. *Radio's Listening Groups* (New York: Columbia University Press, 1941).

Hill, Harold E. *The National Association of Educational Broadcasters: A History.* (Urbana: The National Association of Educational Broadcasters, 1954).

Hilmes, Michele. *Hollywood and Broadcasting: From Radio to Cable* (Urbana and Chicago: University of Illinois Press, 1990).

Hogan, Michael J. *Informal Entente: The Private Structure of Cooperation in Anglo-American Economic Diplomacy, 1918–1928* (Chicago: Imprint Publications, 1991).

Horwitz, Robert Britt. *The Irony of Regulatory Reform* (New York: Oxford University Press, 1989).

Inglis, Andrew F. *Behind the Tube: A History of Broadcasting Technology and Business* (Boston: Focal Press, 1990).

Jacoby, Russell. *The Last Intellectuals: American Culture in the Age of the Academe* (New York: Basic Books, 1987).

Kahn, Frank J., ed. *Documents of American Broadcasting*, fourth edition (Englewood Cliffs, NJ: Prentice-Hall, Inc., 1984).

Keane, John. *The Media and Democracy* (Cambridge, U.K.: Polity Press, 1991).

Kellner, Douglas. *Television and the Crisis of Democracy* Boulder, CO: Westview Press, 1990).

Kent, Ronald, et al., eds. *Culture, Gender, Race, and U.S. Labor History* (Westport, CT: Greenwood Press, 1993).

Kilpatrick, Carroll, ed. *Roosevelt and Daniels, A Friendship in Politics* (Chapel Hill: University of North Carolina Press, 1950).

Kittross, John M., comp. *A Bibliography of Theses and Dissertations in Broadcasting: 1920–1973* (Washington D.C.: Broadcast Education Association, 1978).

Koenig, Allen E., ed. *Broadcasting and Bargaining* (Madison: University of Wisconsin Press, 1970).

Kolko, Gabriel. *The Triumph of Conservatism* (Chicago: Quadrangle Books, 1967).

Krasnow, Erwin G., Longley, Lawrence D., and Terry, Herbert A. *The Politics of Broadcast Regulation,* third edition (New York: St. Martin's Press, 1982).

Kuhn, Raymond, ed. *The Politics of Broadcasting* (New York: St. Martin's Press, 1985).

Lagemann, Ellen Condliffe. *The Politics of Knowledge: The Carnegie Corporation, Philanthropy, and Public Policy* (Middletown, Conn.: Wesleyan University Press, 1989).

Lasch, Christopher. *The Agony of the American Left* (New York: Vintage Books, 1969).

Lazarsfeld, Paul F. *The People Look at Radio* (Chapel Hill: The University of North Carolina Press, 1946).

Leach, Eugene E. *Tuning Out Education: The Cooperation Doctrine in Radio, 1922–38* (Washington D.C.: Current, 1983).

Lee, Martin A., and Solomon, Norman. *Unreliable Sources: A Guide to Detecting Bias in the News Media* (New York: Lyle Stuart, 1990).

Leiss, William, Kline, Stephen, and Jhally, Sut *Social Communication in Advertising* (New York: Metheun, 1986).

Lewis, Tom. *Empire of the Air* (New York: HarperCollins, 1991).

Lichtenberg, Judith, ed. *Democracy and the Mass Media* (Cambridge and New York: Cambridge University Press, 1990).

Lichty, Lawrence W., and Topping, Malachi C., eds. *American Broadcasting: A Source Book on the History of Radio and Television* (New York: Hastings House, 1975).

Lyons, Eugene. *David Sarnoff* (New York: Harper & Row, 1966).

MacDonald, J. Fred. *Don't Touch That Dial! Radio Programming in American Life, 1920 to 1960* (Chicago: Nelson-Hall, 1979).

———. *One Nation Under Television* (New York: Pantheon, 1990).

Maclaurin, W. Rupert. *Invention and Innovation in the Radio Industry* (New York: The Macmillan Company, 1949).

Markham, Charles Lam. *The Noblest Cry: A History of the American Civil Liberties Union* (New York: St. Martin's Press, 1965).

McMahon, Michal. *The Making of a Profession: A Century of Electrical Engineering in America* (New York: Institute of Electrical and Electronic Engineers, Inc., 1984).

McVann, James. *The Paulists, 1858–1970* (New York: Society of St. Paul the Apostle, 1983).

Meiklejohn, Alexander. *Political Freedom* (New York: Harper & Brothers, 1948).

Metz, Robert. *CBS: Reflections in a Bloodshot Eye* (Chicago: Playboy Press, 1975).

Miller, Nathan. *FDR: An Intimate History* (Latham, NY: Madison Books, 1983).

Mooney, Booth. *Roosevelt and Rayburn* (Philadelphia: J. B. Lippincott Company, 1971).

Morgan, Arthur E. *The Making of the TVA* (Buffalo, NY: Prometheus Books, 1974).

Morgan, Joy Elmer. *The American Citizens Handbook* (Washington D.C.: National Education Association, 1941).

Mosco, Vincent. *Broadcasting in the United States* (Norwood, NJ: Ablex, 1979).

National Association of Broadcasters. *The Post War Future of Broadcasting* (Washington D.C.: National Association of Broadcasters, 1944).

Newell, Barbara Warne. *Chicago and the Labor Movement: Metropolitan Unionism in the 1930s* (Urbana: University of Illinois Press, 1961).

Noble, David F. *America By Design: Science, Technology and the Rise of Corporate Capitalism* (New York: Oxford University Press, 1979).

Paglin, Max D., ed. *A Legislative History of the Communications Act of 1934* (New York: Oxford University Press, 1989).

Paine, Thomas. *The Thomas Paine Reader* (New York: Penguin Books, 1987).

Paletz, David L., and Entman, Robert M. *Media Power Politics* (New York: Free Press, 1981).

Paley, William S. *As It Happened* (Garden City, NY: Doubleday & Company, Inc., 1979).

Peers, Frank W. *The Politics of Canadian Broadcasting, 1920–1951* (Toronto: University of Toronto Press, 1969).

Pool, Ithiel de Sola. *Technologies of Freedom* (Cambridge: Belknap Press, 1983).

Powe, Lucas A., Jr. *American Broadcasting and the First Amendment* (Berkeley: University of California Press, 1987).

——. *The Fourth Estate and the Constitution* (Berkeley: University of California Press, 1991).

Pusateri, C. Joseph. *Enterprise in Radio* (Washington D.C.: University Press of America, 1980).

Raboy, Marc. *Missed Opportunities: The Story of Canada's Broadcasting Policy* (Montreal: McGill-Queen's University Press, 1990).

Ray, William B. *FCC: The Ups and Downs of Radio–TV Regulation* (Ames: Iowa State University Press, 1990).

Rayburn, Sam. *"Speak, Mr. Speaker"* (Bonham, TX: Sam Rayburn Foundation, 1978).

Reck, Franklin M. *Radio From Start to Finish* (New York: Thomas Y. Crowell Company, 1942).

Robinson, Thomas Porter. *Radio Networks and the Federal Government* (New York: Columbia University Press, 1943).

Rollins, Jr., Alfred B. *Roosevelt and Howe* (New York: Alfred A. Knopf, 1962).

Rosen, Philip T. *The Modern Stentors; Radio Broadcasting and the Federal Government 1920–1934* (Westport, CT: Greenwood Press, 1980).

Rothafel, Samuel L., and Yates, Raymond Francis. *Broadcasting Its New Day* (New York: Arno Press, 1971).

Rundell, Hugh A., and Heuterman, Thomas H., eds. *The First Amendment and Broadcasting: Press Freedoms and Broadcast Journalism.* Pullman, Wash.: Washington State University, 1978.

Ryan, Charlotte. *Prime Time Activism: Media Strategies for Grassroots Organizing* (Boston: South End Press, 1991).

Sayre, Jeanette. *An Analysis of Radiobroadcasting Activities of Federal Agencies* (Cambridge, MA.: Radiobroadcasting Research Project, 1941).

Scannell, Paddy, and Cardiff, David. *A Social History of British Broadcasting, Volume One, 1922–1939* (Cambridge, MA: Basil Blackwell, 1991).

Schiller, Herbert I. *Culture, Inc.* (New York: Oxford University Press, 1989).

Schramm, Wilbur, ed. *Mass Communications* (Urbana: University of Illinois Press, 1960).

Schwoch, James. *The American Radio Industry and Its Latin American Activities, 1900–1939* (Urbana and Chicago: University of Illinois Press, 1990).

Shooshan, Harry M., III, ed. *Disconnecting Bell: The Impact of the AT&T Divestiture* (New York: Permagon Press, 1984).

Shurick, E.P.J., *The First Quarter-Century of American Broadcasting* (Kansas City: Midland Publishing Company, 1946).

Sklar, Martin J. *The Corporate Reconstruction of American Capitalism, 1890–1916* (New York: Cambridge University Press, 1988).

Skornia, Harry J., and Kitson, Jack William, eds. *Problems and Controversies in Television and Radio* (Palo Alto, CA: Pacific Books, 1968).

Slater, Robert. *This . . . is CBS: A Chronicle of 60 Years* (Englewood Cliffs, NJ: Prentice Hall, 1988).

Smith, Craig R. *Freedom of Expression and Partisan Politics* (Columbia, SC: University of South Carolina Press, 1989).

Smith, Sally Bedell. *In All His Glory: The Life and Times of William S. Paley* (New York: Simon & Schuster, 1990).

Smith, Stephen A., ed. *Free Speech Yearbook, Volume 26, 1987* (Carbondale and Edwardsville: Southern Illinois University Press, 1988).

Sobol, Robert. *RCA* (New York: Stein and Day, 1986).

Soley, Lawrence C., and Nichols, John S. *Clandestine Radio Broadcasting* (New York: Preager, 1987).

Sperber, A. M. *Murrow: His Life and Times* (New York: Freundlich Books, 1986).

Sterling, Christopher H. *Electronic Media, A Guide to Trends in Broadcasting and Newer Technologies 1920–1983* (New York: Praeger, 1984).

Sterling, Christopher, and Kittross, John M. *Stay Tuned: A Concise History of American Broadcasting* (Belmont, CA: Wadsworth, 1978).

Stone, Alan. *Public Service Liberalism: Telecommunications and Transitions in Public Policy* (Princeton: Princeton University Press, 1991).

Temin, Peter. *The Fall of the Bell System: A Study in Prices and Politics* (New York: Cambridge University Press, 1987).

The Commission on Freedom of the Press. *A Free and Responsible Press* (Chicago: University of Chicago Press, 1947).

Tuchman, Gaye. *Making News* (New York: Basic Books, 1978).

Villard, Oswald Garrison. *The Disappearing Daily* (New York: Alfred A. Knopf, 1944).

Waldrop, Frank C. *McCormick of Chicago* (Englewood Cliffs: Prentice-Hall, 1966).

Walker, Samuel. *In Defense of Civil Liberties: A History of the ACLU* (New York: Oxford University Press, 1990).

Wallace, James M. *Liberal Journalism and American Education, 1914–1941* (New Brunswick, NJ: Rutgers University Press, 1991).

Waller, Judith C. *Broadcasting in the Public Service* (Chicago: John S. Swift, 1943).

———. *Radio The Fifth Estate* (Boston: Houghton Mifflin Company, 1946).

Weinstein, James. *Ambiguous Legacy: The Left in American Politics* (New York: New Viewpoints, 1975).

———. *The Corporate Ideal in the Liberal State, 1900–1918* (Boston: Beacon Press, 1968).

———. *The Decline of Socialism in America, 1912–1925* (New York: Monthly Review Press, 1967).

Westbrook, Robert B. *John Dewey and American Democracy* (Ithaca and London: Cornell University Press, 1991).

Whale, John. *The Politics of the Media* (Atlantic Highlands, N.J.: Humanities Press, 1977).

White, Graham. *FDR and the Press* (Chicago: University of Chicago Press, 1979).

White, Llewellyn. *The American Radio* (Chicago: University of Chicago Press, 1947).

Williams, William Appleman. *The Great Evasion.* (Chicago: Quadrangle Books, 1964).

Wilson, H. H. *Pressure Group: The Campaign for Commercial Television.* (London: Secker & Warburg, 1961).

Winfield, Betty Houchin. *FDR and the News Media* (Urbana and Chicago: University of Illinois Press, 1990).

Wolfskill, George. *Happy Days Are Here Again! A Short Interpretive History of the New Deal* (Hinsdale, IL: The Dryden Press, 1974).

Books and Monographs (Prior to 1940)

Alexander, Gross W. *Ownership of Facilities—The Determinative Factor in the Control of Broadcasting* (Pasadena, CA: Pacific-Western Broadcasting Federation, 1930).

Aly, Bower, and Shively, Gerald D., eds. *A Debate Handbook on Radio Control and Operation* (Columbia, MO.: Staples Publishing Co., 1933).

American Civil Liberties Union. *Announcing the National Council on Freedom from Censorship* (New York: American Civil Liberties Union, 1931).

———. *Bills in Congress for Freedom of the Air* (New York: American Civil Liberties Union, 1936).

———. *How Goes the Bill of Rights?* (New York: ACLU Reports, 1936).

———. *Radio Censorship: Proposal for a Federal Investigation* (New York: American Civil Liberties Union, 1934).

———. *Scott Radio Bills and Supporting Memoranda* (New York: American Civil Liberties Union, 1935).

Archer, Gleason L. *Big Business and Radio* (New York: American Historical Company, Inc., 1939. Reprinted by Arno Press, 1971).

Arnold, Frank A. *Broadcast Advertising* (New York: John Willey & Sons, 1933).

Arnold, Thurman. *The Folklore of Capitalism* (New Haven and London: Yale University Press, 1937).

Atkinson, Carroll. *Development of Radio Education Policies in American Public School Systems* (Edinboro, PA: Edinboro Educational Press, 1939).

———. *Education by Radio in American Schools.* (Nashville, TN: George Peabody College for Teachers, 1938).

Aylesworth, Merlin H. *The Modern Stentor; Radio Broadcasting in the United States* (New York: National Broadcasting Company, 1928).

Bent, Silas, *Ballyhoo* (New York: Boni and Liveright, 1927).

———. *Strange Bedfellows* (New York: Horace Liveright, 1928).

Bickel, Karl A. *New Empires; The Newspaper and the Radio* (Philadelphia: J. B. Lippincott Company, 1930).

Bird, Win. W. *The Educational Aims and Practices of the National and Columbia Broadcasting Systems* (Seattle: University of Washington, 1939).

British Broadcasting Corporation. *The B.B.C. Year-Book 1930* (London: British Broadcasting Corporation, 1930).

———. *The B.B.C. Year-Book 1931* (London: British Broadcasting Corporation, 1931).

———. *The B.B.C. Year-Book 1932* (London: British Broadcasting Corporation, 1932).

———. *The B.B.C. Year-Book 1933* (London: British Broadcasting Corporation, 1933).

———. *The B.B.C. Year-Book 1934* (London: British Broadcasting Corporation, 1934).

Brockington. L. W. *Canadian Broadcasting: An Account of Stewardship* (Ottawa: Canadian Broadcasting Corporation, 1939).

Brown, Thad H. *The Federal Communications Law* (Cleveland: Western Reserve University, 1937).

Buehler, E. C., comp. *American Vs. British System of Radio Control: The Reference Shelf Volume 8, Number 10* (New York: The H. W. Wilson Company, 1933).

Chase, Stuart. *An Inquiry into Radio* (Pasadena, CA: Pacific-Western Broadcasting Federation, 1929).

Codel, Martin, ed. *Radio and Its Future* (New York: Harper and Bros., 1930).

———. *Senator Dill is Interviewed* (Washington, D.C.: National Association of Broadcasters, 1931).

Columbia Broadcasting System. *New Policies* (New York: Columbia Broadcasting System, 1935).

———. *Political Broadcasts* (New York: Columbia Broadcasting System, 1936).

———. *The Third Study of Radio Network Popularity Based on a Nation-Wide Audit Conducted by Price, Waterhouse and Company, Public Accountants* (New York: Columbia Broadcasting System, 1932).

Committee on Civic Education by Radio of the National Advisory Council on Radio in Education and the American Political Science Association. *Four Years of Network Broadcasting* (Chicago: University of Chicago Press, 1937).

Crane, Arthur G. *A Plan for an American Broadcasting Service and Proposals for the Immediate Establishment of Two Regional Units* (Laramie, WY: National Committee on Education by Radio, 1937).

Danielian, N. R. *A.T.&T.: The Story of Industrial Conquest* (New York: Vanguard Press, 1939).

Daniels, Josephus. *Tar Heel Editor* (Chapel Hill: University of North Carolina Press, 1939).

Darrow, Ben H. *Radio, The Assistant Teacher* (Columbus: R. G. Adams & Company, 1932).

Davis, H. O. *The Empire of the Air* (Ventura, CA: Ventura Free Press, 1932).

Davis, Jerome. *Capitalism and Its Culture* (New York: Farrar & Rinehart, 1935).

Davis, Stephen. *The Law of Radio Communication* (New York: McGraw-Hill, 1927).

Davis, W. Jefferson. *Radio Law* (Los Angeles: Parker, Stone and Baird Co., 1929).

de Haas, Anton, ed. *The Radio Industry: The Story of its Development* (Chicago: A. W. Shaw Company, 1928).

Debate: Resolved: That the United States Should Adopt the Essential Features of the British System of Radio Control and Operation (Chicago: University of Chicago Press, 1933).

Dill, Clarence C. *Radio Law* (Washington, D.C.: National Law Book Company, 1938).

Dunlap, Orrin E., Jr. *Advertising by Radio* (New York: The Ronald Press, 1929).

———. *Radio in Advertising* (New York: Harper and Bros., 1931).

———. *The Story of Radio* (New York: The Dial Press, 1935).

Evans, S. Howard. *Public Opinion and the Radio* (New York: National Committee on Education by Radio, 1937).

———. *Report on Radio Broadcasting Prepared for Senator Burton K. Wheeler* (Garden City, NY: 1935).

Ewbank, Henry. *Conservation of Radio Resources* (Madison, WI: WHA, 1934).

Farrell, Francis D. *Brief History of the Advisory Council of the National Broadcasting Company With Digest of its Important Actions* (New York: National Broadcasting Company, 1939).

Federal Council of Churches of Christ in America. *Broadcasting and the Public* (New York: The Abingdon Press, 1938).

Floherty, John J. *On the Air: The Story of Radio* (Garden City, NY: Doubleday, Doran, & Company, 1937).

Frost, S. E., Jr. *Education's Own Stations* (Chicago: University of Chicago Press, 1937).

———. *Is American Radio Democratic?* (Chicago: University of Chicago Press, 1937).

Goldsmith, Alfred N., and Lescarbours, Austin C. *This Thing Called Broadcasting* (New York: Henry Holt & Company, 1930).

Hall, T. H., ed. *Current Conflicting Views on American Vs. British Broadcasting* (Chicago: National Research Bureau, 1933).

Harney, Rev. John B. *The Catholic Faith* (New York: The Paulist Press, 1912).

———. *Education and Religion vs. Commercial Radio* (New York: Paulist Fathers, 1934).

————. *In the Matter of Section 307(c) of the Federal Communications Act of 1934; Brief on Behalf of Radio Station WLWL* (New York: Paulist Fathers, 1934).

Harris, E. H. *Radio, The Newspapers and the Public* (Nashville: Southern School of Printing, 1933).

Herring, E. Pendleton. *Public Administration and the Public Interest* (New York: McGraw-Hill, 1936).

Hettinger, Herman S. *A Decade of Radio Advertising* (Chicago: University of Chicago Press, 1933).

————, ed. *Radio—The Fifth Estate* (Philadelphia: The Annals of the American Academy of Political and Social Science, Volume 117, January 1935).

Hettinger, Herman S., and Neff, Walter J. *Practical Radio Advertising* (New York: Prentice-Hall, 1938).

Hill, Frank Ernest. *Listen and Learn* (New York: American Association for Adult Education, 1937).

House of Commons, Special Committee on Radio Broadcasting. *Minutes of Proceedings and Evidence* (Ottawa: F. A. Acland, 1932).

Kaltenborn, H. V. *Radio Bows to the Press* (New York: 1933).

————. *Radio in Educational Work* (Pasadena, CA: Pacific-Western Broadcasting Federation, 1929).

Kassner, Minna F., and Zacharoff, Lucien. *Radio is Censored!* (New York: American Civil Liberties Union, 1936).

Kerwin, Jerome. *The Control of Radio* (Chicago: University of Chicago Press, 1934).

Kirkpatrick, Clifford. *Report of a Research into the Attitudes and Habits of Radio Listeners* (St. Paul: Webb Book Publishing Company, 1933).

Koon, Cline M. *The Growth of British Broadcasting* (Columbus: Ohio State University, 1930).

————. *Some Public Service Broadcasting* (Chicago: University of Chicago Press, 1934).

Lee, Alfred McClung. *The Daily Newspaper in America* (New York. The Macmillan Company, 1937).

Lingel, Robert, ed. *Educational Broadcasting: A Bibliography* (Chicago: University of Chicago Press, 1932).

Lippmann, Walter. *Interpretations 1932–1935.* (New York: The Macmillan Company, 1936).

Metropolitan Life Insurance Company. *Radio As An Advertising Medium* (New York: Metropolitan Life Insurance Company, 1929).

Morgan, Joy Elmer, and Bullock, E. D., eds. *Selected Articles on Municipal Ownership* (Minneapolis: Wilson, 1911).

Muller, Helen M., comp. *Education by Radio; The Reference Shelf, Volume 8, Number 1* (New York: H. W. Wilson Company, 1932).

National Advisory Council on Radio in Education. *The National Advisory Council on Radio in Education* (New York: National Advisory Council on Radio in Education, 1930).

National Association of Broadcasters. *Broadcasting in the United States* (Washington, D.C.: National Association of Broadcasters, 1933).

————. *In the Matter of Section 307(c) of the Federal Communications Act of 1934 and Order No. 1 of the Broadcast Division* (Washington D.C.: National Association of Broadcasters, 1934).

National Broadcasting Company. *Analysis of History-Making NBC Contributions to the Art of Radio in 1932 Pointing to Even Greater Achievements in 1933* (New York: National Broadcasting Company, 1933).

———. *The Blue Network* (New York: National Broadcasting Company, 1927).

———. *Broadcast Advertising* (New York: National Broadcasting Company, 1929).

———. *Broadcasting. Volumes I–IV* (New York: National Broadcasting Company, 1935).

———. *Let's Look at Radio Together* (New York: National Broadcasting Company, 1935).

———. *NBC Markets* (New York: National Broadcasting Company, 1931).

———. *Survey of Courses in Radio Offered by American Colleges and Universities* (New York: National Broadcasting Company, 1935).

Nockels, Edward N. *Labor's Experience in Radio* (Washington D. C.: 1936).

———. *Public Interest, Convenience and Necessity, and the Last of the Public Domain* (Washington D.C.: 1936).

Orton, William A. *America in Search of Culture* (Boston: Little, Brown, and Company, 1933).

———. *Memorandum on Radio Policy* (Northampton, MA: 1934).

Pacific-Western Broadcasting Federation. *For a Genuine Radio University* (Los Angeles: Pacific-Western Broadcasting Federation, 1930).

———. *In The Public Interest* (Los Angeles: Pacific-Western Broadcasting Federation, 1929).

———. *"A Race Between Education and Catastrophe"* (Los Angeles: Pacific-Western Broadcasting Federation, 1931).

Paley, William S. *The American System of Broadcasting* (New York: Columbia Broadcasting System, 1937).

———. *The Direction of Progress in Radio Broadcasting* (New York: Columbia Broadcasting System, 1936).

———. *Radio as a Cultural Force* (New York, Columbia Broadcasting System, 1935).

Payne, George Henry. *The Fourth Estate and Radio and Other Addresses* (Boston: The Microphone Press, 1936).

———. *History of Journalism in the United States* (New York: D. Appleton and Company, 1920).

———. *Standards in Radio Will Cure Low Grade Programs* (Ithaca, NY: American Association of Agricultural College Editors, 1935).

Perry, Armstrong. *Radio in Education: The Ohio School of the Air and Other Experiments* (New York: The Payne Fund, 1929).

Phelps, Edith M., ed. *The University Debaters' Annual, 1932–33* (New York: The H. W. Wilson Company, 1933).

———. *The University Debaters' Annual, 1933–34* (New York: The H. W. Wilson Company, 1934).

President's Research Committee on Social Trends. *Recent Social Trends in the United States* (New York: Whittlesey House, 1934).

Randall, Harris K. *A Plan for the Establishment of Healthier Conditions of Competition Between the Publishing and Radio Broadcasting Industries* (Chicago: American Radio Audience League, 1932).

Rankin, E. R., ed. *Radio Control and Operation* (Chapel Hill: The University of North Carolina Extension Bulletin, 1933).

Reith, J. C. W. *Broadcasting Over Britain* (London: Hodder and Stoughton, 1924).

Riegel, O. W. *Mobilizing for Chaos: The Story of the New Propaganda* (New Haven: Yale University Press, 1934).

Rorty, James. *Order on the Air!* (New York: The John Day Company, 1934).

———. *Our Master's Voice: Advertising* (New York: The John Day Company, 1934).

Rothafel, Samuel L., and Yates, Raymond Francis, eds. *Broadcasting Its New Day* (New York: Arno Press, 1971. Originally published in 1926).

Royal Commission on Radio Broadcasting. *Report* (Ottawa: F. A. Aclund, 1929).

Sarnoff, David. *Network Broadcasting* (New York: National Broadcasting Company, 1938).

Schmeckebier, Lawrence F. *The Federal Radio Commission* (Washington D.C.: The Brookings Institution, 1932).

Seldes, George. *Freedom of the Press* (New York: Bobbs-Merrill, 1935).

———. *Lords of the Press.* (New York: Julian Messner, Inc., 1938).

Socolow, Walter. *The Law of Radio Broadcasting* (New York: Baker, Voorhis & Co., 1939).

Summers, H. B., comp. *Radio Censorship* (New York: H. W. Wilson Company, 1939).

Tyler, Tracy F. *Can Clubwomen Aid in Solving the Radio Problem?* (Washington D. C.: National Committee on Education by Radio, 1935).

———. *Some Interpretations and Conclusions of the Land-Grant Radio Survey* (Washington D.C.: National Committee on Education by Radio, 1933).

Tyson, Levering. *Education Tunes In* (New York: American Association for Adult Education, 1930).

Ventura Free Press. *American Broadcasting: An Analytical Study of One Day's Output of 206 Commercial Radio Stations Including Program Contents and Advertising Interruptions* (Ventura, CA: Ventura Free Press, 1933).

Waldrop, Frank, and Borkin, Joseph. *Television—A Struggle for Power* (New York: William Morrow & Company, 1939).

Webster, Bethuel, M., Jr. *Memorandum Re: An Executive Investigation of the Allocation and Use of Radio Broadcasting Facilities* (New York: American Civil Liberties Union, 1934).

———. *A Proposal to Promote Public Discussion Over the Radio* (New York: American Civil Liberties Union, 1934).

Wilbur, Ray Lyman, and Hyde, Arthur Mastick. *The Hoover Policies* (New York: Scribner's Sons, 1937).

Willey, Malcolm, and Rice, S. A. *Communication Agencies and Social Life* (New York: President's Research Committee on Social Trends in the United States: Monograph, 1933).

Woelful, Norman. *Molders of the American Mind* (New York: Columbia University Press, 1933).

Selected Journal Articles (Since 1940)

Allen, Michael Patrick. "Capitalist Response to State Intervention: Theories of the State and Political Finance in the New Deal." *American Sociological Review* 56 (October 1991):679–89.

Avery, Robert K. "Access and Ascertainment in Broadcasting: An Overview." *Western Journal of Speech Communication* 41 (1977):132–46.

Avery, Robert K., and Pepper, Robert. "An Institutional History of Public Broadcasting." *Journal of Communication* (Summer 1980):126–38.

Bagdikian, Ben H. "The Lords of the Global Village." *The Nation* (12 June 1989):805–20.

———. "Missing from the News." *The Progressive* 53 (August 1989):32–34.

Barron, Jerome A. "Access to the Press—A New First Amendment Right." *Harvard Law Review* 80 (1967):1641–78.

Benn, Tony, and Heffer, Eric. "A Strategy for Labour: Four Documents." *New Left Review* (July–August 1986):60–75.

Bensman, Marvin R. "The Zenith–WJAZ Case and the Chaos of 1926–27." *Journal of Broadcasting* 14 (Fall 1970):423–440.

Brown, James A. "Struggle Against Commercialism: The 1934 'Harney Lobby' for Nonprofit Frequency Allocations." *Journal of Broadcasting and Electronic Media* 33 (Summer 1989):273–91.

Brown, Stanley M., and Reed, John Wesley. "Regulation of Radio Broadcasting: Competitive Enterprise or Public Utility." *Cornell Law Quarterly* 27 (February 1942):249–66.

Buhle, Paul. "Between Bad Times and Better." *New Left Review* (May/June 1989):95–110.

Carey, James W. "A Plea for the University Tradition." *Journalism Quarterly* 55 (Winter 1978):846–55.

Clark, David G. "H. V. Kaltenborn's First Year on the Air." *Journalism Quarterly* 42 (Summer 1965):373–81.

———. "H. V. Kaltenborn and his Sponsors: Controversial Broadcasting and the Sponsor's Role." *Journal of Broadcasting* 12 (Fall 1968):309–21.

Carter, Stephen L. "Technology, Democracy, and the Manipulation of Consent." *Yale Law Journal* 93 (1984):581–607.

Cochran, Thomas C. "Media as Business: A Brief History." *Journal of Communication* 25 (Autumn 1975):155–65.

Cooney, Stuart. "An Annotated Bibliography of Articles on Broadcasting Law and Regulation in Law Periodicals, 1920–1955." *Journal of Broadcasting* 14 (Winter 1970):133–46.

Du Boff, Richard B. "The Rise of Communications Regulation: The Telegraph Industry, 1844–1880." *Journal of Communication* (Summer 1984):52–66.

Emery, Walter B. "Broadcasting Rights and Responsibilities in Democratic Society." *The Centennial Review* 8 (1964):306–22.

Ericson, C. George. "Swedish Radio Services in Chicago." *Swedish Pioneer Historical Quarterly* 24 (1973):157–62.

Ernst, Morris L. "Freedom to Read, See, and Hear." *Harper's Monthly* 191 (July 1945):51–53.

Ernst, Morris, and Lindley, Alexander. "Freedom of the Air." *Saturday Review of Literature* (4 January 1940):3–4, 14–15.

Ferguson, Thomas. "Industrial Structure and Party Competition in the New Deal: A Reply to Webber." *Sociological Perspectives* 34 (1991):493–526.

Ford, Frederick W. "The Meaning of Public Interest, Convenience, or Necessity." *Journal of Broadcasting* 8 (Winter 1964):205–18.

Friedrich, Carl J., and Sternberg, Evelyn. "Congress and the Control of Radio-Broadcasting I." *The American Political Science Review* 37 (October 1943):797–818.

Garvey, Daniel E. "Secretary Hoover and the Quest for Broadcast Regulation." *Journalism History* 3 (Autumn 1976):66–70,85.

Godfrey, Donald G. "Senator Dill and the 1927 Radio Act." *Journal of Broadcasting* 23 (1978):477–89.

———. "The 1927 Radio Act: People and Politics." *Journalism History* 4 (Autumn 1977):74–78.

Godfried, Nathan. "The Origins of Labor Radio: WCFL, the 'Voice of Labor', 1925–1928." *Historical Journal of Film, Radio and Television* 7 (1987):143–59.

Greene, Stephen L. W. "Who Said Lee de Forest Was the 'Father of Radio'." *Mass Comm Review* 18 (1991):49–59.

Hall, William M. "Radio Broadcasting Comes to Vermont: WLAX, The University of Vermont Radio Station." *Vermont History* 49 (1981):92–96.

Heinz, Catharine. "Women Radio Pioneers." *Journal of Popular Culture.* 12 (1978):305–14.

Herman, Edward. "Democratic Media." *Z Papers* 1 (1992):23–30.

Herring, James M. "Broadcasting and the Public Interest." *Harvard Business Review* 18 (1940):344–56.

Huberman, Leo. "Monopoly Control of Radio." *U.S. Week* (31 May 1941):16.

Kielbowicz, Richard B. "Modernization, Communications Policy, and the Geopolitics of News, 1820–1860." *Critical Studies in Mass Communication* 3 (1986):21–35.

———. "The Press, Post Office, and Flow of News in the Early Republic." *Journal of the Early Republic* 3 (Fall 1983):255–79.

Koppes, Clayton R. "The Social Destiny of Radio: Hope and Disillusionment in the 1920s." *South Atlantic Quarterly* 68 (Summer 1969):363–76.

LeDuc, Don R., and McCain, Thomas A. "The Federal Radio Commission in Federal Court." *Journal of Broadcasting* 14 (Fall 1970):423–40.

Lenehan, Mike. "Avoid the Dread Tune-out," *The Chicagoan* (February 1974):82–87.

Lichty, Lawrence W. "The Impact of FRC and FCC Commissioners' Backgrounds on the Regulation of Broadcasting.'' *Journal of Broadcasting* 6 (Winter 1962):97–110.

Loft, George E. "The Press–Radio Wars of the 1930s.'' *Journal of Broadcasting* 14 (Summer 1970):275–80.

Mander, Mary S. "The Public Debate About Broadcasting in the Twenties: An Interpretive History.'' *Journal of Broadcasting* 25 (Spring 1984):167–85.

Marquis, Alice Goldfarb. "Radio Grows Up.'' *American Heritage* 34 (1983):65–80.

———. "Written on the Wind: The Impact of Radio during the 1930s.'' *Journal of Contemporary History* 19 (1984):385–415.

McChesney, Robert W. "An Almost Incredible Absurdity for a Democracy.'' *Journal of Communication Inquiry* 15 (Winter 1991):89–114.

———. "Crusade Against Mammon: Father Harney, WLWL and the Debate Over Radio in the 1930s.'' *Journalism History* 14 (Winter 1987):118–30.

———. "Franklin Roosevelt, His Administration, and the Communications Act of 1934.'' *American Journalism* 5 (1988):204–30.

———. "Free Speech and Democracy! Louis G. Caldwell, the American Bar Association, and the Debate Over the Free Speech Implications of Broadcast Regulation, 1928–1938.'' *The American Journal of Legal History* 35 (October 1991):351–392.

———. "Labor and the Marketplace of Ideas: WCFL and the Battle for Labor Radio Broadcasting, 1927–1934.'' *Journalism Monographs*, No. 134, August 1992.

———. "Off Limits: An Inquiry Into the Lack of Debate over the Ownership, Structure and Control of the Mass Media in U.S. Political Life.'' *Communication* 13 (1992):1–19.

———. "Press–Radio Relations and the Emergence of Network, Commercial Broadcasting in the United States, 1930–1935.'' *Historical Journal of Film, Radio and Television* 11 (1991):41–57.

McKerns, Joseph P. "Industry Skeptics and the Radio Act of 1927.'' *Journalism History* 3 (Winter 1976–1977):128–131, 136.

Meek, Edwin E. "Eugene Octave Sykes, Member and Chairman of Federal Communications Commission and Federal Radio Commission, 1927–1939.'' *Journal of Mississippi History* 36 (1974):377–86.

Minasian, Jora R. "The Political Economy of Broadcasting in the 1920s.'' *Journal of Law and Economics* 12 (1969):391–403.

Moore, Herbert. "The News War in the Air.'' *Journalism Quarterly* 44 (Autumn 1967):43–52.

Nord, David Paul. "The FCC, Educational Broadcasting, and Political Interest Group Activity.'' *Journal of Broadcasting* 22 (Summer 1978):321–38.

Ostroff, David H. "Equal Time: Origins of Section 18 of the Radio Act of 1927.'' *Journal of Broadcasting* 24 (Summer 1980):367–80.

Rodnitzky, Jerome L. "Getting the Ear of the State: A Pioneer Radio Station in the 1920s.'' *History of Education Quarterly* 8 (1968):505–9.

Rorty, Richard. "The Intellectuals at the End of Socialism.'' *The Yale Review* 80 (April 1992):1–17.

Rosen, Philip T. "Broadcasting: The Politics of Innovation." *Continuity* (1981):51–61

———. "Marvel of Radio." *American Quarterly* 31 (1979):572–81.

Rowland, Willard D. "Continuing Crisis in Public Broadcasting: A History of Disenfranchisement." *Journal of Broadcasting and Electronic Media* 30 (Summer 1986):251–274.

Sanders, Keith P. "The Collapse of the Press–Radio News Bureau." *Journal of Broadcasting* 12 (Fall 1968):549–52.

Sarno, Edward F. "The National Radio Conferences." *Journal of Broadcasting* 13 (Spring 1969):189–202.

Severin, Werner J. "Commercial Vs. Non-commercial Radio During Broadcasting's Early Years." *Journal of Broadcasting* 20 (Fall 1978):491–504.

Schmidt, Benno C., Jr. "Access to Broadcast Media: The Legislative Precedents." *Journal of Communication* 28 (1978):60–68.

Smith, Robert R. "The Origins of Radio Network News Commentary." *Journal of Broadcasting* 9 (Spring 1965):113–22.

Soloski, John. "News reporting and professionalism: some constraints on the reporting of news." *Media, Culture and Society* 11 (1989):207–28.

Spalding, John W. "1928: Radio Becomes a Mass Advertising Medium." *Journal of Broadcasting* 8 (Winter 1963–64):31–44.

Stern, Robert H. "Regulatory Influences Upon Television's Development: Early Years Under the Federal Radio Commission." *American Journal of Economics and Sociology* 22 (1963):347–62.

Umhey, Frederick F. "Radio Stations Run by Labor." *American Federationist* 52 (December 1945):10–12.

Wagner, Paul H. "The Evolution of Newspaper Interest in Radio." *Journalism Quarterly* 23 (June 1946):182–88.

Williamson, Mary E. "Judith Cary Waller: Chicago Broadcasting Pioneer." *Journalism History* 3 (Winter 1976–1977):111–15.

Wilson, Howard Lee. " 'Top of the World' Broadcasts: Wyoming's Early Radio." *Annals of Wyoming* 43 (1971):5–52.

Journals, Magazines, Newsletters, Newspapers
(Prior to 1940)

Advertising Age.
Advertising and Selling.
Air Law Review.
American Bar Association Journal.
American Federationist.
American Newspaper Publishers Association Bulletin.
American Teacher.
American Mercury.
Atlantic Monthly.

Boston University Law Review.
Broadcasters' News Bulletin.
Broadcasting.
Buffalo Evening News.
Business Week.
California Broadcaster.
Capital Times, The.
Catholic Educational Review, The.
Century.
Chicago Tribune.
Christian Century, The.
Christian Science Monitor.
Common Sense.
Commonwealth.
Congressional Digest.
Corporate Practice Review.
Current History.
Des Moines Register.
Detroit News.
Dun's Review.
Editor & Publisher.
Educational Record.
Education by Radio.
Education News Bulletin.
Electronics.
Eventually News, The.
Federation News.
Forum, The.
Galveston Daily News.
Georgetown Law Review.
George Washington Law Review.
Harper's Monthly.
Harvard Business Review.
Harvard Law Review.
Heinl Radio Business Letter.
Journalism Quarterly.
Journal of Adult Education.
Journal of Business of the University of Chicago, The.
Journal of Education.
Journal of Home Economics.
Journal of Radio Law.
Journal of the American Association of University Women.
Journal of the National Education Association.
Kentucky Law Journal.
Labor News.
Listener, The.

Literary Digest, The.
Los Angeles Times.
Marquette Law Review.
Memphis Commercial Appeal.
Microphone.
Milwaukee Journal.
Modern Millwheel, The.
NAB Reports.
Nation, The.
National Catholic Education Association Bulletin.
National Lawyers Guild Quarterly.
Nation's Business.
New Republic, The.
New York Daily Worker.
New York Times, The.
Nineteenth Century.
North Carolina Teacher.
Ohio Wesleyan Magazine.
Philadelphia Public Ledger.
Portland Oregonian.
Printers' Ink.
Printers' Ink Monthly.
Public Opinion Quarterly.
Public Utilities Fortnightly.
Queen's Quarterly.
Radio Art.
Radio Broadcast.
Radio Digest.
Radio Engineering.
Radio Guide.
Radio News.
Radio Retailing.
Radio Stars.
Radio Today.
Roanoke Times.
Sacramento Bee.
San Francisco Chronicle.
Saturday Review of Literature.
School and Society.
Seattle Post-Intelligencer.
Standard Rate and Data Service.
Survey Graphic.
Torch, The.
Tulsa Tribune.
University of Pennsylvania Law Review.
U.S. Daily.

U.S. Week.
Variety.
Ventura Free Press.
Virginia Law Review.
Washington Post.
WCFL Radio Magazine.
Wichita Daily Eagle.
Wisconsin State Journal.

Proceedings

American Bar Association.
American Civil Liberties Union.
American Federation of Labor.
American Society of Newspaper Editors.
Congress of Industrial Organizations.
Department of Superintendence of the National Education Association.
Illinois State Federation of Labor.
Institute for Education by Radio.
Institute of Radio Engineers.
National Advisory Council on Radio in Education.
National Association of Broadcasters.
National Association of Deans of Women.
National Association of State Universities.
National Broadcasting Company Advisory Council.
National Catholic Educational Association.
National Committee on Education by Radio.
National Conference on Educational Broadcasting.
National Congress of Parents and Teachers.
National Education Association.
National University Extension Association.
Public Ownership Conference.

Government Publications

Advisory Committee on Education by Radio. *Report of the Advisory Committee on Education by Radio Appointed by the Secretary of the Interior* (Columbus: The F. J. Heer Printing Co., 1930).
Biennial Survey of Education 1928–1930 (Washington, D.C.: United States Government Printing Office, 1932).
Federal Communications Commission. *Digest of Hearings, Federal Communications Commission Broadcast Division, under Sec. 307(C) of the "Communications*

Act of 1934'' October 1–20, November 7–12, 1934 (Washington, D.C.: Federal Communications Commission, 1935).

———. *Public Service Responsibilities of Broadcast Licensees.* Washington, D.C.: Federal Communications Commission, 1946.

———. *Report on Chain Broadcasting* (Washington D.C.: United States Government Printing Office, 1941).

Federal Radio Commission. *Annual Report of the Federal Radio Commission to the Congress of the United States for the Fiscal Year Ended June 30, 1927* (Washington D.C.: Government Printing Office, 1927).

———. *Commercial Radio Advertising* (Washington, D.C.: United States Government Printing Office, 1932).

———. *Third Annual Report of the Federal Radio Commission to the Congress of the United States Covering the Period from October 1, 1928 to November 1, 1929* (Washington, D.C.: United States Government Printing Office, 1929).

Good References on Education by Radio. Compiled by Cline M. Koon and Martha R. McCabe. (Washington D.C.: United States Government Printing Office, 1932).

Proceedings of the Fourth National Radio Conference and Recommendations for Regulation of Radio (Washington D.C.: Government Printing Office, 1926).

Study of Communications by an Interdepartmental Committee, Letter from the President of the United States to the Chairman of the Committee on Interstate Commerce Transmitting a Memorandum from the Secretary of Commerce Relative to a Study of Communications by an Interdepartmental Committee (Washington, D.C.: United States Government Printing Office, 1934).

U.S. Congress. *Congressional Record.* Volumes 75–78.

U.S. Department of Commerce. *Recommendations for Regulation of Radio Adopted by the Third National Radio Conference* (Washington D.C.: Government Printing Office, 1924).

U.S. House of Representatives. 73rd Cong. 2nd sess. *Federal Communications Commission, Hearings Before the Committee on Interstate and Foreign Commerce on H.R. 8301* (Washington D.C.: United States Government Printing Office, 1934).

———. 70th Cong. 2nd sess. *Federal Radio Commission, Hearings Before the Committee on the Merchant Marine and Fisheries on H.R. 15430* (Washington D.C.: United States Government Printing Office, 1929).

———. 70th Cong. 2nd sess. *Hearings Before the Committee on the Merchant Marine and Fisheries on H.R. 8825* (Washington, D.C.: United States Government Printing Office, 1928).

———. 70th Cong. 1st sess. *Jurisdiction of Radio Commission, Hearings Before the Committee on the Merchant Marine and Fisheries on H.R. 8825* (Washington D.C.: United States Government Printing Office, 1928).

———. 73rd Cong. 2nd sess. *Radio Broadcasting, Hearings Before the Committee on Merchant Marine, Radio and Fisheries on H.R. 7968* (Washington D.C.: United States Government Printing Office, 1934).

———. 69th Cong. 1st sess. *To Regulate Radio Communication, Hearings Before the Committee on the Merchant Marine and Fisheries on H.R. 5589* (Washington D.C.: Government Printing Office, 1926).

U.S. Office of Education. *Problems Encountered by Radio Stations in Working with Schools* (Washington D.C.: United States Office of Education, 1935).

U.S. Senate. 70th Cong. 2nd sess. *Continuing Federal Radio Legislation to March 16, 1930, Hearings Before Committee on Interstate Commerce on S. 4937* (Washington, D.C.: United States Government Printing Office, 1929).

————. 70th Cong. 2nd sess. *Federal Radio Commissioners. Hearings Before Committee on Interstate Commerce on the Confirmation of Federal Radio Commissioners* (Washington, D.C.: United States Government Printing Office, 1928).

————. 72nd Cong. 2nd sess. *Fees for Radio Licenses, Hearing Before a Subcommittee of the Committee on Interstate Commerce on S. 5201* (Washington: United States Government Printing Office, 1933).

————. 73rd Cong., 2nd sess. *Hearings Before the Committee on Interstate Commerce on S. 2910* (Washington D.C.: United States Government Printing Office, 1934).

————. 70th Cong., 2nd sess. *Nomination of C. M. Jansky. Jr., and Arthur Batcheller. Hearings Before the Committee on Interstate Commerce* (Washington D.C.: United States Government Printing Office, 1929).

————. 69th Cong., 1st sess. *Radio Control. Hearings Before the Committee on Interstate Commerce on S. 1 and S. 1754* (Washington: Government Printing Office, 1926).

————. 72nd Cong. 1st sess. *To Amend the Radio Act of 1927. Hearings Before the Committee on Interstate Commerce on H.R. 7716* (Washington D.C.: United States Government Printing Office, 1932).

————. 72nd Cong. 2nd sess. *To Amend the Radio Act of 1927, Hearings Before the Committee on Interstate Commerce on H.R. 7716* (Washington D.C.: United States Government Printing Office, 1932).

Theses and Dissertations

Benjamin, Louis Margaret. "Radio Regulation in the 1920s: Free Speech Issues in the Development of Radio and the Radio Act of 1927." Ph.D. dissertation. University of Iowa, 1985.

Brown, James Anthony. "A History of Roman Catholic Church Policies Regarding Commercial Radio and Television Broadcasting in the United States, 1920 Through 1961." Ph.D. dissertation, University of Southern California, 1970.

Chamberlin, William Fay. "A History of Public Issues Programming Regulation by the Federal Communications Commission: More Rhetoric than Action." Ph.D. dissertation, University of Washington, 1977.

Crane, Jon Stephen. "Supreme Court Interpretations of 'Public Interest' in Broadcast Decisions: 1927–1979." Ph.D. dissertation, University of Massachusetts, 1980.

Feldman, Andrew. "Selling the 'Electrical Idea' in the 1920s: A Case Study in the

Manipulation of Consciousness.'' M.A. thesis, University of Wisconsin-Madison, 1989.

Godfrey, Donald G. ''A Rhetorical Analysis of the Congressional Debates on Broadcast Regulation in the United States, 1927.'' Ph.D. dissertation, University of Washington, 1975.

Jackaway, Gwenyth. ''The Press–Radio War, 1924–1937: The Battle to Defend the Professional, Institutional, and Political Power of the Press.'' Ph.D. dissertation, University of Pennsylvania, 1992.

Jorgenson, Erling S. ''Radio Station WCFL: A Study in Labor Union Broadcasting.'' M.A. thesis, University of Wisconsin, 1949.

Kelly, Francis Lawrence. ''The Institute for Education by Radio–Television—A History.'' Ph.D. dissertation. Ohio State University, 1972.

Long, Robert E. ''Thomas Amlie: A Political Biography.'' Ph.D. dissertation. University of Wisconsin, 1969.

Mackey, David R. ''The National Association of Broadcasters—Its First Twenty Years.'' Ph.D. dissertation, Northwestern University, 1956.

McChesney, Robert W. ''The Battle for America's Ears and Minds: The Debate Over the Control and Structure of American Radio Broadcasting, 1930–1935.'' Ph.D. dissertation, University of Washington, 1989.

McMahon, Robert Sears. ''Federal Regulation of the Radio and Television Broadcast Industry in the United States, 1927–1959, With Special Reference to the Establishment and Operation of Workable Administrative Standards.'' Ph.D. dissertation, Ohio State University, 1979.

Penn, John Stanley. ''The Origin and Development of Radio Broadcasting at the University of Wisconsin.'' Ph.D. dissertation, University of Wisconsin, 1959.

Prostak, Elaine J. '' 'Up in the Air': The Debate Over Radio Use During the 1920s.'' Ph.D. dissertation, University of Kansas, 1983.

Ruskaup, Calvin Frederick. ''The Other Side of Broadcasting: A History of Challengers to the Use of the Airwaves.'' Ph.D. dissertation, Ohio State University, 1979.

Smulyan, Susan Renee. '' 'And Now a Word From our Sponsors': Commercialization of American Broadcast Radio, 1920–1934.'' Ph.D. dissertation, Yale University, 1985.

Townsend, James Edward. ''A History of a Right of Access to Broadcasting.'' Ph.D. dissertation, University of Minnesota, 1981.

Manuscript Collections

American Civil Liberties Union Papers. Princeton University, Princeton, NJ.

American Federation of Labor Papers. State Historical Society of Wisconsin, Madison, WI.

American Telephone and Telegraph Corporate Papers. American Telephone and Telegraph Archives, Warren, NJ.

Thomas Amlie Papers. State Historical Society of Wisconsin, Madison, WI.

Edwin H. Armstrong Papers. Columbia University, New York, NY.

Harold D. Arnold Papers. American Telephone and Telegraph Papers, Warren, NJ.

Roger Baldwin Papers. Princeton University, Princeton, NJ.

Erik Barnouw Papers. Columbia University, New York, NY.

Bruce Barton Papers. State Historical Society of Wisconsin, Madison, WI.

Edward Bennett Papers. University of Wisconsin Archives, Madison, WI.

Orestes H. Caldwell Papers. State Historical Society of Wisconsin, Madison, WI.

Carnegie Corporation of New York Papers. Columbia University, New York, NY.

John J. Carty Papers. American Telephone and Telegraph Archives, Warren, NJ.

Martin Codel Papers. State Historical Society of Wisconsin, Madison, WI.

Edwin H. Colpitts Papers. American Telephone and Telegraph Archives, Warren, NJ.

Columbia Broadcasting System Records. Columbia Broadcasting System Corporate Press Services, New York, N.Y.

Commission on Freedom of the Press Papers. Columbia University, New York, NY.

James Couzens Papers. Library of Congress, Washington, D.C.

Edward H. Craft Papers. American Telephone and Telegraph Archives, Warren, NJ.

Josephus Daniels Papers. Library of Congress, Washington, D.C.

Lee DeForest Papers. Library of Congress, Washington, D.C.

Department of Agriculture Papers. National Archives, Washington, D.C.

Department of Commerce Papers. National Archives, Washington, D.C.

Clarence C. Dill Papers. Eastern Washington State Historical Society, Spokane, WA.

Stephen Early Papers. Franklin D. Roosevelt L!ibrary, Hyde Park, NY.

Harold Engel Papers. State Historical Society of Wisconsin, Madison, WI.

Lloyd Espenschied Papers. American Telephone and Telegraph Archives, Warren, NJ.

Henry Ewbank Papers. University of Wisconsin Archives. Madison, WI.

Federal Communications Commission Papers. National Archives, Suitland, MD.

John Fitzpatrick Papers. Chicago Historical Society, Chicago, IL.

William S. Hedges Papers. State Historical Society of Wisconsin, Madison, WI.

Stanford C. Hooper Papers. Library of Congress, Washington, D.C.

Herbert Hoover Papers. Herbert Hoover Library, West Branch, IA.

Roy W. Howard Papers. Indiana University, Bloomington, IN.

Roy W. Howard Papers. Library of Congress, Washington, D.C.

Louis McHenry Howe Papers. Franklin D. Roosevelt Library, Hyde Park, NY.

Leo Huberman Papers. University of Oregon, Eugene, OR.

Robert M. Hutchins Papers. University of Chicago, Chicago, IL.

Institute for Education by Radio and Television Papers. Ohio State University, Columbus, OH.

E.P.H. James Papers. State Historical Society of Wisconsin, Madison, WI.

C. M. Jansky Papers. State Historical Society of Wisconsin, Madison, WI.

Frank B. Jewett Papers. American Telephone and Telegraph Archives, Warren, NJ.

H. V. Kaltenborn Papers. State Historical Society of Wisconsin, Madison, WI.

Alice Keith Papers. State Historical Society of Wisconsin, Madison, WI.

Frederick J. Keppel Papers. Columbia University, New York, NY.

Alexander Meiklejohn Papers. State Historical Society of Wisconsin, Madison, WI.

Allen Miller Papers. State Historical Society of Wisconsin, Madison, WI.

Robert A. Millikan Papers. California Institute of Technology, Pasadena, CA.

Joy Elmer Morgan Papers. National Education Association, Washington, D.C.

National Association for the Advancement of Colored People Papers. Library of Congress, Washington, D.C.

National Association of Educational Broadcasters Papers. State Historical Society of Wisconsin, Madison, WI.

National Broadcasting Company Papers. State Historical Society of Wisconsin, Madison, WI.

National Bureau of Standards Papers. National Archives, Washington, D.C.

Office of Education Papers. National Archives, Washington, D.C.

Payne Fund, Inc., Papers. Western Reserve Historical Society, Cleveland, OH.

Public Affairs Director's Papers, University of Illinois, Urbana, IL.

Franklin D. Roosevelt Papers. Franklin D. Roosevelt Library, Hyde Park, NY.

James Rorty Papers. University of Oregon, Eugene, OR.

David Sarnoff Papers. David Sarnoff Research Center, Princeton, NJ.

Walter Dill Scott Papers. Northwestern University, Evanston, IL.

Society of St. Paul Papers. Catholic University, Washington, D.C.

Norman Thomas Papers. New York Public Library, New York, NY.

Tracy F. Tyler Papers. University of Minnesota, Minneapolis, MN.

U.S. Senate Committee on Interstate Commerce Papers. National Archives, Washington, D.C.

Robert F. Wagner Papers. Georgetown University, Washington, D.C.

Judith Waller Papers. State Historical Society of Wisconsin, Madison, WI.

WHA Papers. University of Wisconsin Archives. Madison, WI.

Ray Lyman Wilbur Papers. Hoover Institution on War, Revolution and Peace, Stanford, CA.

Owen D. Young Papers. St. Lawrence University, Canton, NY.

Oral Histories

Frank A. Arnold. Radio Pioneers Project, Columbia Oral History Collection, Columbia University, New York, NY.

Howard Barlow. Radio Pioneers Project, Columbia Oral History Collection, Columbia University, New York, NY.

Gus Bosler. Radio Pioneers Project, Columbia Oral History Collection, Columbia University, New York, NY.

Lyman Bryson. Radio Pioneers Project, Columbia Oral History Collection, Columbia University, New York, NY.

Orestes H. Caldwell. Radio Pioneers Project, Columbia Oral History Collection, Columbia University, New York, NY.

Phillips Carlin. Radio Pioneers Project, Columbia Oral History Collection, Columbia University, New York, NY.

Thomas H. Cowan. Radio Pioneers Project, Columbia Oral History Collection, Columbia University, New York, NY.

Lloyd Espenschied. Radio Pioneers Project, Columbia Oral History Collection, Columbia University, New York, NY.

Walter Evans. Radio Pioneers Project, Columbia Oral History Collection, Columbia University, New York, NY.

Raymond F. Guy. Radio Pioneers Project, Columbia Oral History Collection, Columbia University, New York, NY.

William Harkness. Radio Pioneers Project, Columbia Oral History Collection, Columbia University, New York, NY.

William S. Hedges. Radio Pioneers Project, Columbia Oral History Collection, Columbia University, New York, NY.

Herbert C. Hoover. Radio Pioneers Project, Columbia Oral History Collection, Columbia University, New York, NY.

Hans V. Kaltenborn. Radio Pioneers Project, Columbia Oral History Collection, Columbia University, New York, NY.

Donald G. Little. Radio Pioneers Project, Columbia Oral History Collection, Columbia University, New York, NY.

Lord John Reith. Radio Pioneers Project, Columbia Oral History Collection, Columbia University, New York, NY.

Bruce Robertson. Radio Pioneers Project, Columbia Oral History Collection, Columbia University, New York, NY.

Mark Woods. Radio Pioneers Project, Columbia Oral History Collection, Columbia University, New York, NY.

Unpublished Papers

Bagdikian, Ben H. "American Mass Media and the Future," paper presented to 1990 annual meeting, Association for Education in Journalism and Mass Communication.

D'Acci, Julie. "Early Radio and the Industrialization of Culture: WEAF 1922–1929," 1991.

Rowland, Jr., Willard D. "The Meaning of 'The Public Interest' in Communications Policy—Part I: Its Origins in State and Federal Regulation," paper presented to 1989 annual meeting, International Communication Association.

Personal Interviews

Nicholas Garnham, May 1989.

Ward L. Quaal, April 17, 1992.

Bethuel M. Webster, Jr., February 18, 1987.

INDEX